BASICS OF ELECTRONICS ENGINEERING

for

Diploma Engineers

DRDO, BHEL, DMRC, SSC, RRB &
Other Engineering (Diploma) Competitive Examinations

 **G K Publications (P) Ltd**

CL MEDIA (P) LTD.

Edition : 2019

ISBN : **978-93-89573-32-9**

Typeset by : *CL Media DTP Unit*

Administrative and Production Offices

Published by : **CL Media (P) Ltd.**
A-45, Mohan Cooperative Industrial Area,
Near Mohan Estate Metro Station,
New Delhi - 110044

Marketed by : **G.K. Publications (P) Ltd.**
A-45, Mohan Cooperative Industrial Area,
Near Mohan Estate Metro Station,
New Delhi - 110044

For product information :

Visit ***www.gkpublications.com*** or email to ***gkp@gkpublications.com***

Preface

In the recent years PSUs like BHEL, BEL, GAIL, IOCL, HPCL, ONGC and other Government sectors like DMRC, DRDO, RRB, Staff Selection Commission are preferring to hire Junior Engineers and Technicians which has resulted in a large job opportunities for diploma holders. As these PSUs also offer job security and decent perks, many candidates are attracted towards it, gradually increasing the competition level.

Unlike other competitive examinations, preparing for vacancy based exams of these PSUs is not an easy task as each exam has its own pattern, syllabus and trend. Most of these exams like to throw surprises based on the vacancies, leaving students amazed during their exam preparation with very less time for preparation. However, you can certainly guarantee yourself a smooth journey if you start early and plan it well. As the technical section of these exams hold the maximum scoring scope; it is very important to pay enough attention to this section.

This series focuses on the technical section of various exams conducted by PSUs such as DRDO, BHEL and other Government Sectors like DMRC and Railways for the Diploma Engineers. These books help to prepare for all the exams at a single go which saves time instead of preparing separately for each PSU's exam. Every chapter contains a brief theory followed by large number of practice questions. There is another section that includes questions asked in previous PSU exams. As a suggestion, please make sure that you spend enough time in understanding the fundamentals and concepts before going to practice exercise and previous years' solved questions.

GKP has also launched an Android App to provide you an update on all upcoming vacancies in the technical segment and it also has a lot of added content to aid your preparation.

We hope this little effort of ours will be helpful in achieving your dreams. If you have any suggestions on improvement of this book, you can write to us at gkp@gkpublications.com.

All the Best!

Team GKP

Contents

Instrumentation and Measurements

MEASUREMENT

It is defined as the process of estimating a quantity or variable (measurand).

Instrument

Instrument is a device to measure value or magnitude of a quantity or a variable.

Instrumentation

It provides the physical means to estimate the quantity.

Sensitivity

It is the ratio of output signal or response of the instrument to a change of input or measured variable.

OR

Sensitivity of an instrument is the ratio of the magnitude of the output signal to the magnitude of the input signal.

Efficiency

The efficiency of an instrument is the ratio of the measured quantity at full scale to the input power taken by the instrument.

Resolution or Discrimination

This is the smallest change in the measured value to which the instrument will respond.

Error

Difference between *measured value* and *true value* of a quantity is called error.

i.e., $$\delta A = A_m - A_t$$

where δA = error

A_m = measured value

A_t = true value

Accuracy

It is defined as closeness with which an instrument reading approaches the true value of the variable being measured.

Precision

It is a measure of the reproducibility of the measurements means precision is a measure of the degree to which successive measurements differ from one other.

Expected value

It is the most probable value that calculations indicate one should expect to measure.

MEASUREMENT SYSTEM

The treatment of instrument and measurement system characteristic can be divided into two distinct categories

1. **STATIC CHARACTERISTICS.**

   Static characteristic of a measurement system are in general, those that must be considered when the system or instrument is used to a condition not varying with time.

   Main static characteristics.

   (*i*) **Reproducibility**

   (*ii*) **Drift**

   (*iii*) **Dead zone**

   (*iv*) **Accuracy :** It is the closeness with which an instrument reading approaches the true value of the quantity being measured. It is specified in terms of limits of errors and is expressed as either percentage of scale or range of percentage of true value.

   (*v*) **Precision :** It is a measure of the reproducibility of the measurements, *i.e.* for a fixed value of a quantity, precision is a measure of the degree of agreement within a group of measurements. An indication of the precision of the measurement is obtained from the number of significant figures in which it is expressed. The more the significant figures, the greater the precision of measurement.

   (*vi*) **Sensitivity:**

   Galvanometer sensitivity. The sensitivity of galvanometer can be specified in terms of current sensitivity. Voltage sensitivity and megohm sensitivity.

   (*a*) **Current sensitivity :** It may be defined as the ratio of the deflection of the galvanometer to the current producing this deflection i.e.,

   $$S_I = \frac{d}{I}\ \frac{mm}{\mu A}$$

   where, d = deflection of the galvanometer in scale division in mm

   I = galvanometer current in μA.

(b) Voltage sensitivity : It may be defined as the ratio of the galvanometer deflection to the voltage producing this deflection. Therefore

$$S_V = \frac{d}{V} \frac{mm}{mV}$$

where, d = deflction of the galvanometer in scale divisions in mm

V= voltage applied to the galvanometer in mV.

(c) Megohm sensitivity : It may be defined as the number of megohms required in series with the (CRDX shunted) galvanometer to produce one scale division deflection when 1V is applied to the circuit. Numerically, it is equal to current sensitivity.

(vii) Static error.

It is the numerical difference between true value of a quantity and its value as obtained by measurement. *These are sub-divided into three types*

(a) Gross errors : These errors are due to human mistakes in reading or in using instruments or errors in recording observations.

(b) Systematic errors : These errors occur due to shortcomings of the instrument such as defective or worn parts or ageing or effects of the environment on the instrument.

- **Instrumental errors :** These are inherent in measuring instruments, because of their mechanical structure. These can be avoided by selecting a suitable instrument for the particular measurement application or by applying correction factors after determining the amount of instrumental error of calibrating the instrument against a standard.

- **Environment errors :** These are due to conditions external to the measuring device including conditions in the area surrounding the instrument such as effects of changes in temperature, humidity, barometric pressure or effect of magnetic or electrostatic fields.

- **Observational errors :** These are errors introduced by the observer. The most common is the parallax error introduced in reading a meter scale and the error of estimation.

(c) Random errors : These are due to unknown causes and are normally small and follow the low of probability. These are treated mathematically.

2. DYNAMIC CHARACTERISTICS.

Many measurements are concerned with rapidly varying quantities and therefore for such cases we must examine the dynamic relation which exist between output and the input. Performance criteria based upon dynamic relations constitute dynamic characteristics.

Q-METER

It is used to measure Q-factor of the coil and some electrical properties of coil and capacitors. The principle of the Q meter is based on series resonance.

ELECTRONIC MULTIMETER

This instrument can be used for measuring

(i)   DC and AC voltage

(ii) DC and AC currents

(iii) resistance values upto 50 MΩ

ELECTRICAL PRINCIPLES OF OPERATION

All electrical measuring instruments depend for their action on any of physical effect of electric current or potential.

Following are the effects generally used in the manufacture:

(i)   **Magnetic effect.** Voltmeters, ammeters, wattmeters, power etc.

(ii) **Thermal effect.** Ammeters, voltmeters, etc

(iii) **Chemical effect.** D.C. ampere hour meters (integrating meters).

(iv) **Electrostatic effect.** Voltmeters which can indirectly be used as ammeters and wattmeters.

(v)   **Electro-magnetic induction effect.** Voltmeters, ammeters, wattmeters and integrating meters used in A.C only.

ELECTRICAL INDICATING INSTRUMENTS

An indicating instrument is fitted with a pointer which indicates on scale the value of the quantity being measured. The moving system of such an instrument is usually carried by a spindle of hardened steel, having its ends tapered and highly polished to form pivots which rest is hollow-ground bearings, usually of saphire, set in steel screws. This arrangement eliminates pivot friction and the instrument is less susceptible to damage by shock or vibration.

Essential features. *Indicating instruments has three essential features :*

1. **Deflecting torque.** Whereby mechanical force is produced by the electric current voltage or power.

2. **Controlling torque.** Whereby the value of deflection is dependent upon the magnitude of the quantity being measured.

3. **Damping torque.** To prevent oscillation of the moving system and enable the latter to reach its final position quickly.

Deflecting device.

A deflecting device produces a deflecting torque which is caused by any one of the previously mentioned effects (i.e. thermal effect, chemical effect, electrostatic effect etc). With help of this deflecting torque needle or the pointer move from zero position to total final position.

Controlling devices.

There are two types of controlling devices :

(*i*) Spring control (*ii*) Gravity control

Damping device.

Owing to the inertia of the moving system, when subjected to the deflecting and restoring torques, a number of vibrations will be produced before coming finally to rest. To avoid this, a damping torque is required which opposes the motion and ceases when the pointer comes to rest. The degree of damping should be adjusted to a value which is sufficient to enable the pointer to rise quickly to its deflected position without overshooting. In that case, instruments is called *dead-beat*. If instruments is over-damped the movement is very slow.

Methods of Damping :

1. Air damping

2. Eddy current damping

3. Fluid friction damping

Principle types of electrical indicating instruments, and methods of control and damping :

S.No	Type of instrument	Suitable for measuring	Method of control	Method of damping
1.	Moving iron	Current and voltage, D.C. and A.C.	Hair springs	Air
2.	Permanent magnet moving coil	Current and voltage, D.C. only	Hair springs	Eddy current
3.	Thermocouple	Current and voltage, D.C and A.C.	As for moving coil	As for moving coil
4.	Electrodynamic or dynamometer	Current, voltage and power, D.C. and A.C	Hair springs	Air
5.	Electrostatic	Voltage only, D.C. and A.C	Hair springs	Air or eddy current
6.	Rectifier	Current and voltage, A.C. only	As for moving coil	As for moving coil

Note. Apart from the electrostatic type of voltmeter, all voltmeters are in effect milliammeter connected in series with non-reactive resistor having a high resistance.

DIFFERENCE BETWEEN AN AMMETER AND VOLTMETER

Ammeter and voltmeter work on the same principle. Ammeter has a low resistance so that when it is connected in series with any circuit, it does not change the current. Voltmeter has a high resistance and it is so designed that when connected in parallel to the circuit for measuring voltages it does not take appreciable current.

Ammeter of low range can be used as a voltmeter by connecting an external resistance in series with it.

ERRORS IN MEASUREMENT

The degree to which a measurement nears the true value is expressed in terms of the error of measurement. Error is defined as the deviation of true value from the desired value. It is expressed either *as absolute* or as a *percentage of error.*

Absolute error is defined as the difference between true value of the variable and the measured value of the variable, *i.e.*

$$\varepsilon_o = Y_n - X_n$$

where ε_0 = absolute error

Y_n = true value

X_n = measured value

Hence % Error $= \dfrac{\text{Absolute value}}{\text{True value}} \times 100$

$$= \dfrac{\varepsilon_o}{Y_n} \times 100$$

$$\text{\% Error} = \left(\dfrac{Y_n - X_n}{Y_n} \right) \times 100$$

Sources of Errors.

(*i*) Insufficient knowledge of process parameters and design conditions.

(*ii*) Poor maintenance.

(*iii*) Change in process parameters irregularities, upsets etc.

(*iv*) Poor design.

(*v*) Design limitations.

(*vi*) Due to person operating the instrument.

MEASUREMENT OF ELECTRIC VOLTAGE AND CURRENT

Moving iron instruments are used as ameters and voltmeters only. They work on both a.c. and d.c. systems.

1. Ammeter.

An instrument which is used to measure electric current in a circuit is called *ammeter*. An ammeter is always connected in series with the circuit and carries the current to be measured or fraction of it. This current flowing through the operating coil produced the desired deflecting torque. Since an ammeter is to be connected in series, therefore, it should have a low resistance. Hence, when a moving iron instrument is used as ammeter, the operating coil is provided with a few turns of thick wire so that it has low resistance.

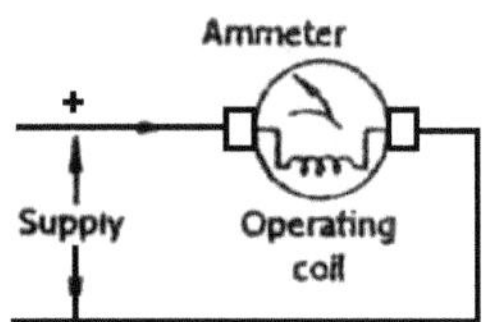

2. Voltmeter.

An instrument which is used to measure voltage between two points in a circuit is called *voltmeter*. A voltmeter is always connected in parallel with the portion whose voltage is to be measured. This current flowing through the operating coil of the meter produces the deflecting torque. Since voltmeter is connected in parallel and in order that its connection does not disturb the circuit conditions, therefore, the resistance of the voltmeter should be very high. To do so, a high resistance (of the order of kilo ohms) is connected in series with the coil of the instrument as shown.

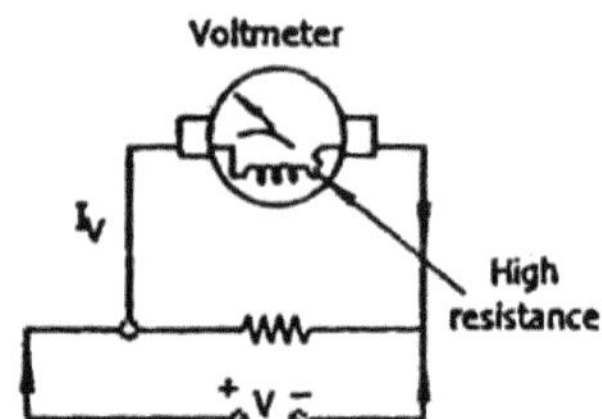

SHUNTS AND MULTIPLIERS.

Shunts and multipliers are the resistances connected in shunt or series with ammeter and voltmeters to enhance their measuring capacity.

Shunts

A resistance placed in parallel with an instrument (or galvanometer) to control the current passing through it, when placed in a circuit carrying a fairly large current is called *shunt*.

The shunt resistance used with a basic instrument may consists of a length of constant temperature resistance wire within the box of the instrument. Alternatively, there may be an external (manganin or constantan) shunt having very low resistance.

MULTIPLIERS.

A high resistance in series with a galvanometer is connected, to limit the current flowing through the meters so that it does not exceed the value for full scale deflection and thus prevents the instrument from being damaged. Such a resistance is called *multiplier*.

MEASUREMENT OF POWER

In D.C. circuits.

The power taken from a d.c. supply is given by the product of readings of an ammeter and voltameter

Power in d.c. circuit, P = VI.

$\therefore$ Power indicated by instruments

= Power consumed in load + Power loss in voltmeter

Thus in both the cases, power indicated by the instruments is equal to the power consumed by the load plus the power consumed by the instrument nearer to the load terminals. In order to obtain true power, corrections must be applied for power loss in instruments.

In A.C. circuits.

In a.c. circuits, power, $P = VI \cos \phi$

where V and I = voltage across the load and current through the load respectively

$\cos \phi$ = power factor of the load.

So Voltmeter-Ammeter method is not applicable in A.C. circuits, because of involvement of power factor.

WATTMETER

Wattmeters are used to take into account the power factor.

There are two types of wattmeters

(1) Induction type wattmeter

(2) Electrodynamometer type wattmeter.

MEASUREMENT OF RESISTANCE

Classification of Resistances.

(*i*) **Low resistance.** All resistances of the order of 1 ohm and under may be classified as low resistance.

(*ii*) **Medium resistance.** This class includes resistance from 1 upward to about 10,000 ohms.

(*iii*)**High resistance.** Resistance of the order of 100,000 ohms and above are classified as high resistance.

MEASUREMENT OF LOW RESISTANCES.

Methods used for measurement of low resistances are following.

(*i*) **Ammeter-Voltmeter method.**

Voltmeter can be connected in two ways as shown by dotted lines.

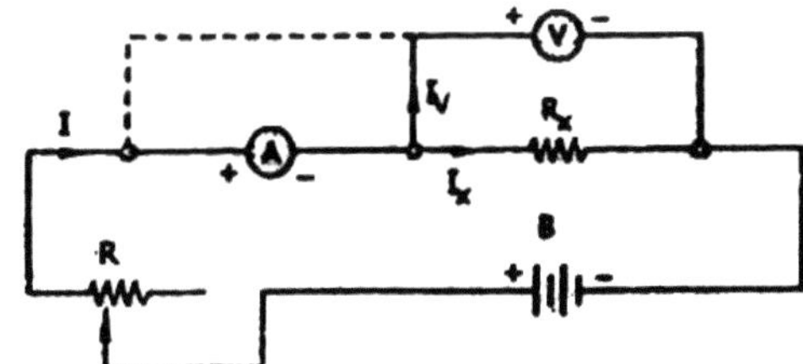

Current through ammeter = Current through unknown resistance + Current through voltmeter

$\therefore$ True value of unknown resistance,

$$R_x = \frac{R'}{\left(1 - \dfrac{R'}{R_v}\right)}$$

where, V = voltage reading

R_v = resistance of voltmeter

I = current read by ammeter

R' = circuit resistance = $\dfrac{V}{I}$

Accuracy of this method is limited by the accuracies of voltmeter and ammeter.

(ii) Kelvin's double bridge method.

It is modification of the Wheatstone bridge and provides increased accuracy. It incorporates the idea of second set of ratio arms, hence the name double bridge and the use of four terminal resistances for the low resistance arms.

P, Q and p, q are two pairs of known non-inductive resistances and one pair P, p or Q, q is variable.

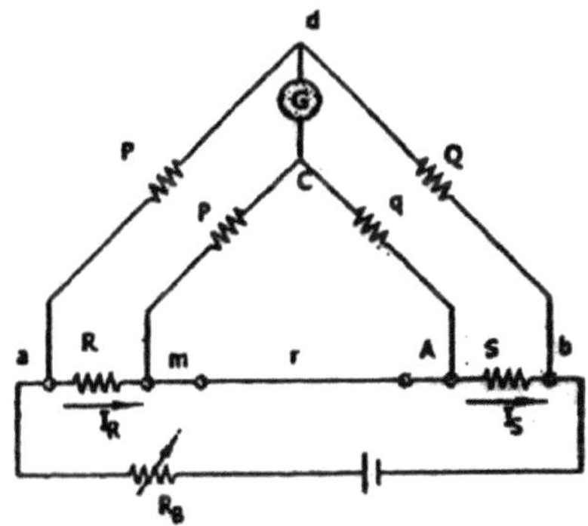

The ratio p/q is made equal to P/Q.

then $\qquad R = \dfrac{P}{Q} S.$

where R = Unknown resistance

S = Standard resistance of the order of magnitude as R

r = connecting link of low resistance

(iii) Potentiometer method.

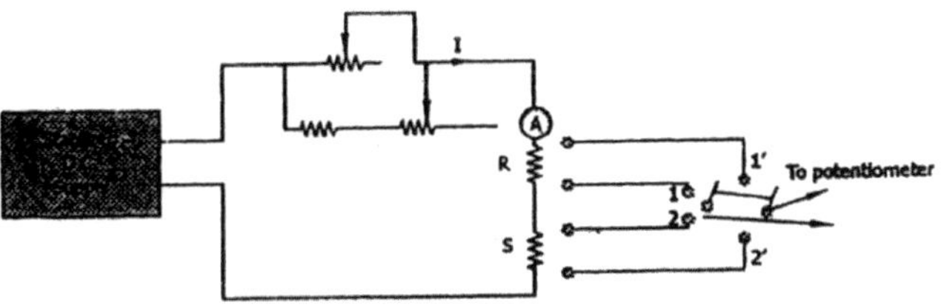

It is based on comparison of one resistance against another. The unknown resistance R, an ammeter A and a variable resistance for limiting current and a standard resistance S are connected in series with a low voltage, high current supply. The current flowing through the circuit is adjusted so that the potential difference across each of the resistor is about 1V. The voltage drop across both the unknown resistor R and standard resistor S are measured by a d.c. potentiometer.

$$\frac{R}{S} = \frac{\text{Potentiometer reading across R}}{\text{Potentiometer reading across S}} = \frac{V_R}{V_S}$$

MEASUREMENT OF MEDIUM RESISTANCE

(i) Ammeter-Voltmeter method.

This method is similar to that described for measurement of low resistance.

(ii) Substitution method.

R is the unknown resistance, S is standard variable resistance and r is regulating resistance. The switch is put at position 1 and resistance R is connected in the circuit, r is adjusted till the ammeter points to the chosen reading. Now the switch is thrown to position 2 putting the standard variable resistance S in the circuit. The value of S is varied till the same deflection as that for R is obtained in the ammeter. For same value of current, the value of unknown resistance R is equal to the dial settings of resistance S.

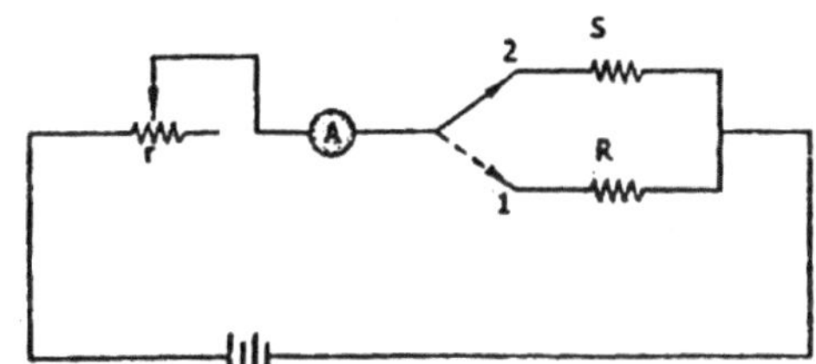

(iii) Wheatstone bridge method.

This method is one of the most widely used methods for measurement of medium resistance. It consists of known adjustable resistance P, Q, and S. The unknown resistance is R. The resistances are arranged to form two parallel circuits. A sensitive galvanometer is bridged across the two circuits between B and D.

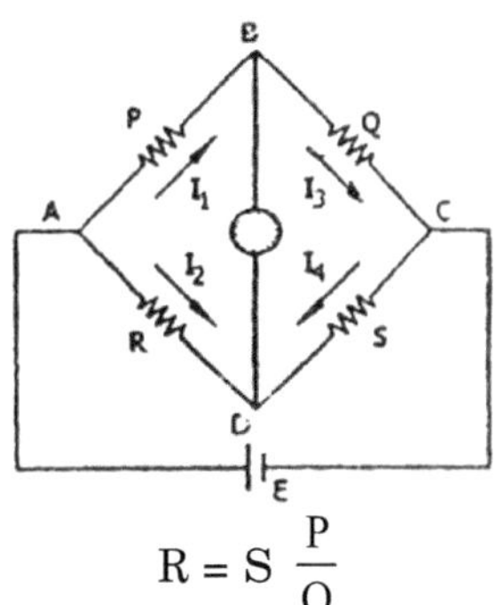

or $\qquad R = S \dfrac{P}{Q}$

The value of unknown resistance R is determined in terms of known resistances.

(*iv*) Carey-Foster bridge method.

This bridge is specially suited for the comparison of two nearly equal resistances.

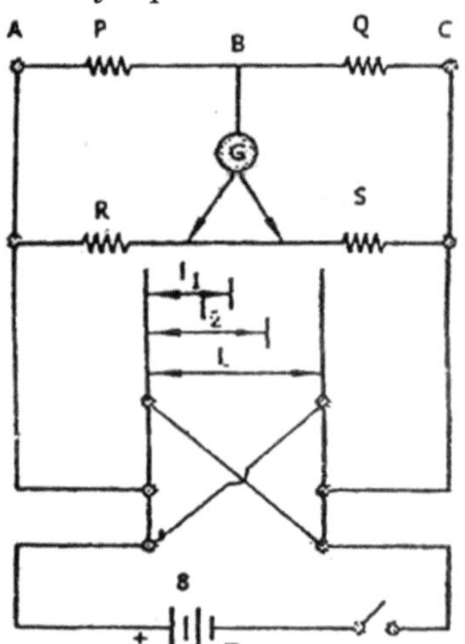

MEASUREMENT OF HIGH RESISTANCE

(*i*) Direct deflection method.

A guard terminal surrounding resistance terminal is connected to the battery side os a micro-ammeter. The guard terminal and resistance terminal are almost at the same potential and hence there is no flow of current between them. The leakage current I_L which would otherwise flow through the μ-ammeter, bypasses the μ-ammeter. The μ-ammeter indicates the current I_R only. The resistance value is determined by the readings of voltmeter and ammeter as,

$$R = \frac{V}{I_R}\,\Omega$$

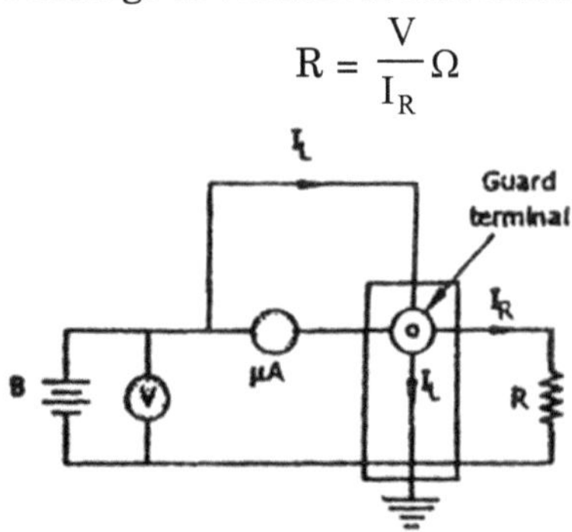

(*ii*) Megger method.

This the most commonly used method for measurement of high resistance.

INSTRUMENT TRANSFORMERS

These are used in a.c. systems for the measurement of current, voltage, power and energy. These also have a wide application in protection circuits of power system for the operation of various relays.

Advantages.

(*i*) These enable single range instruments to cover a large current or voltage range.

(*ii*) Power loss is small.

(*iii*) Measuring instruments can be located far from the high voltage circuit by using long loads connecting the instrument transformer to the instrument. Hence the instruments is isolated from high voltages and stray fields providing safety in use to both instrument and the observer.

(*iv*) By using current transformer with a suitably split and hinged core, upon which the secondary windings is wound, the current in a heavy current bus bar is measured without breaking the circuit.

(*v*) Due to inductance of instrument winding being in parallel with the non-inductive shunt, shunt on a.c. does not give a straight line relation between instrument current and by-passed current. In case of C.T., whole current passes through the primary, a proportional voltage is induced in the secondary which sends a current in direction proportion around the secondary circuit.

Disadvantage.

These transformers cannot be used for dc measurements.

TRANSDUCERS

These are the devices which convert energy from one form to another. Most of the quantities to be measured are non-electrical, e.g. temperature, pressure displacement etc. Since these quantities can not be measured directly, these are required to be sensed and changed into some other form.

Another name for a transducer is *pickup*. The transducer may be thought of consisting of following two important and closely related parts

(*i*) Sensing Element.

A detector or a sensing element is that part of a transducer which responds to a physical phenomenon.

(*ii*) Transduction Element.

A transduction element transform the output of a sensing element to an electrical output.

Classification of Transducer.

Transducer may be defined on the basis of

(*i*)   Transduction form used

(*ii*) Primary and secondary transducers

(*iii*) Passive and active transducers

(*iv*) Analog and digital transducers

(*v*)   As transducers and inverse transducers

Primary transducers sensed the mechanical quantities and secondary transducers converts the output signal from the primary transducer to electrical quantities.

Inverse transducer is defined as a device which converts an electrical quantity into a non-electrical quantity.

e.g. a piezoelectric crystal acts as an inverse transducer because when a voltage is applied across its surface, it changes its dimensions causing a mechanical displacement.

MEASUREMENT OF DISPLACEMENT

Here an inductive transducer is used for translating the linear motion into an electrical signal is used. A plate is placed at right angles to the axis of the coil. The displacement of plate causes a change in the inductance of the coil.

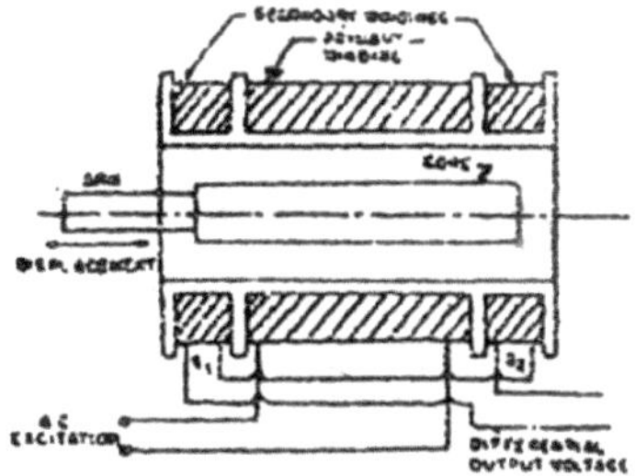

Linear Variable Differential Transformer (LVDT).

It is most widely used inductive transducer. It consists of single primary winding P and two secondary winding S_1 and S_2 wound on a cylindrical former. Primary winding is connected to an a.c. source. A movable soft iron core is placed inside former. The displacement to be measured is applied to an arm attached to the soft iron core. When the core is in null position, equal voltages are in the two secondary winding. When the core is moved to right of left, difference of the two voltages is produced.

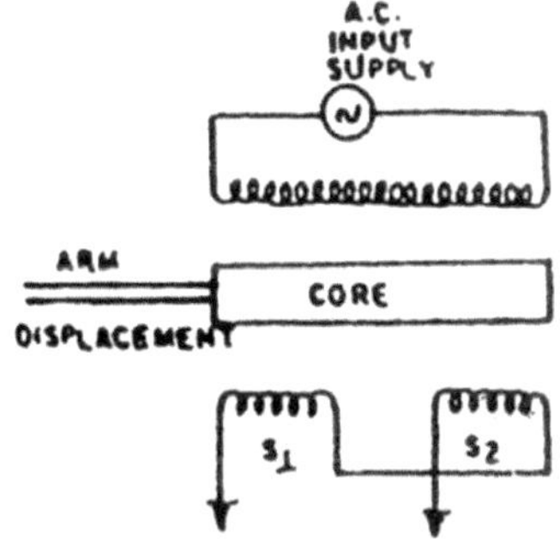

Difference of outputvoltages of secondary windings gives the amount of displacement.

Advantages.

(*i*)   Almost linear characteristics

(*ii*)   Infinite resolution

(*iii*)   Low power consumption

(*iv*)   Output impedance is constant

Disadvantages.

(*i*)   Affected by vibrations

(*ii*)   Sensitive to stray magnetic fields

(*iii*)   Performance affected by temperature

(*iv*)   Larger displacements necessary for appreciable differential output.

CATHODE RAY OSCILLOSCOPE (CRO)

It is a very useful and versatile laboratory instrument used for display, measurement analysis of waveforms and other phenomena in electrical and electronic circuits. It displays an input signal versus another signal or time.

An oscilloscope is one of the most important type of test equipment for checking electronic circuits because it can show the waveform of an applied voltage. The fluorescent screen of the cathode ray tube, displays a graph of voltage amplitude variations with respect to time. The vertical axis represents voltage while the horizontal axis is linear time base for the vertical signal.

Lissajous patterns

These are the traces on a oscilloscope screen which are used to find the phase angle between two sine wave voltages of the same frequency or for comparing sine wave voltages of the same frequency or for comparing sine waves of different frequencies. The purpose of the frequency comparison is to check an unknown frequency against a reference value. The patterns are only for sine wave signals. One is applied to the oscilloscope vertical input and the other to the horizontal input. Both horizontal and vertical deflections should have equal amplitude.

Parts of a CRO shown in the block diagram.

1. Cathode Ray Tube (CRT)   2. Vertical amplifier

3. Time base   4. Horizontal amplifier

5. Trigger circuit   6. Power supplies

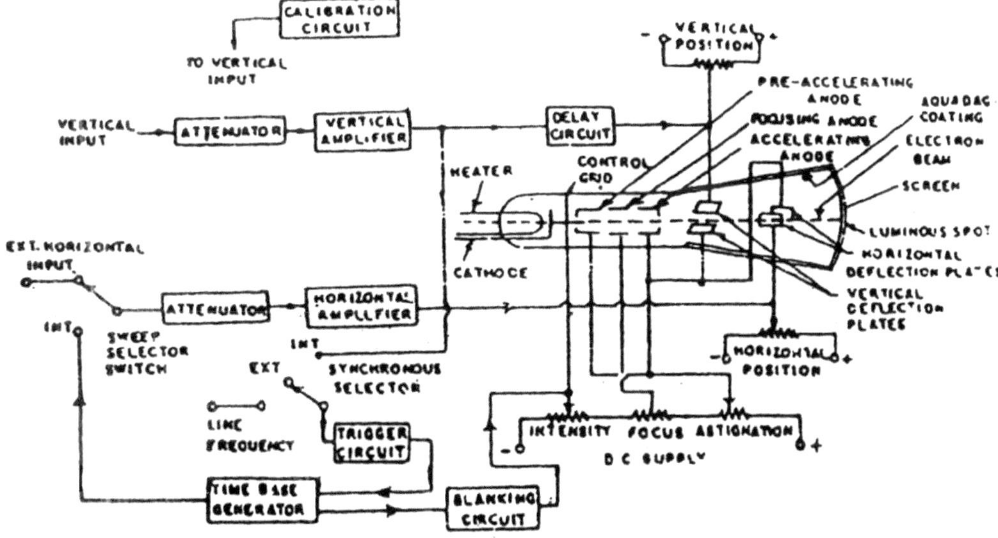

Fig. Block diagram of CRO

In an oscilloscope, a CRT generates the electron beam, accelerates it to a high velocity, deflects the beam to create the image and the electron beam finally becomes visible on the phosphor screen. The oscilloscope has a time base which generates the correct voltage to supply the CRT to deflect the spot at a constant time dependent rate. The signal to be viewed is fed to a vertical amplifier which increases the potential of the input signal to a level that will provide a usable deflection of the electron beam. To synchronize horizontal deflection with the vertical input such that the horizontal deflection starts at the same point of the input vertical signal each time it sweeps, a synchronizing or triggering circuit is used.

Vertical deflection system.

It provides an amplified signal of the proper level to drive the vertical deflection plates without introducing any appreciable distortion into the system. The attenuater sets the sensitivity of the oscilloscope.

Horizontal deflection system.

It consists of a time base generator, a trigger circuit and a horizontal amplifier. The time base generator controls the rate at which the beam is scanned across the face of the CRT and is adjusted from the front panel. The trigger circuit ensures that the horizontal sweep starts at the same point of the vertical input signal. The horizontal amplifier is similar to the vertical amplifier to increase the amplitude to the signal generated in the sweep generator to the level required by the horizontal deflection plates of the CRT.

Vertical delay line.

All electronic circuitry in the oscilloscope (attenuators, amplifiers, pulse shapers, generators etc.) causes a certain amount of time delay in the transmission of signal voltages to the deflection plates. The horizontal signal is initiated by the portion of the output signal applied to the vertical CRT plates. Signal processing in the horizontal channel consists of generating and shaping a trigger pulse that starts the sweep generator, whose output is fed to horizontal amplifier and then to the horizontal deflection plates. This whole process takes time of the order of 80 ns or so. Hence to allow the operator to observe the leading edge of the signal wave form, the signal drive for the vertical CRT plates must be delayed by atleast the same amount of time. The signal voltage to the CRT plates is delayed by some time and horizontal sweep is started prior to the vertical deflection.

CONTROLS OF CRO

In order to facilitate the proper functioning of CRO, various controls are provided on the front panel of CRO.

(*i*) Intensity control.

It regulates the bias on the control grid and affects the electron beam intensity. If the negative bias on the grid is increased, the intensity of electron beam is decreased thus reducing the brightness of the spot.

(*ii*) Focus control.

It regulates the positive potential on the focusing anode. If the positive potential on this anode is increased, the electron beam becomes quite narrow and the spot on the screen is a pin point.

(*iii*)Horizontal position control :

It regulates amplitude of d.c. potential which is applied to the horizontal deflection plates, in addition to the usual saw tooth wave. By adjusting this control, the spot can be moved to right or left as required.

(*iv*) Vertical position control.

It regulates the amplitude of d.c. potential which is applied to the vertical deflection plates addition to the signal. By adjusting this control, the image can be moved up or down as required.

APPLICATIONS OF CRO.

1. Examination of Waveforms.

    (*i*) Spot deflection for sinusoidal voltage signal applied to horizontal deflection plates.

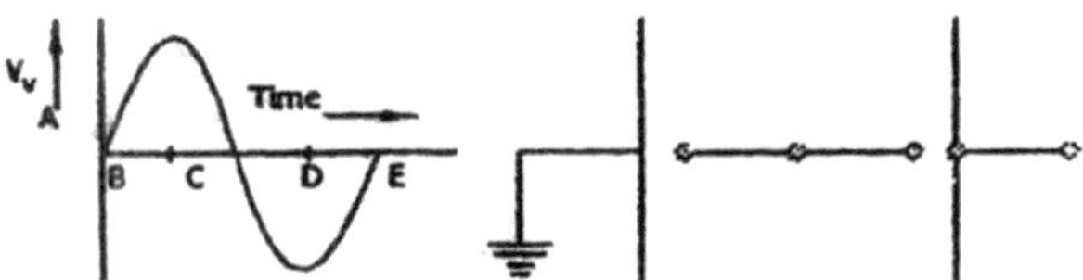

    (*ii*) Spot deflection for sinusoidal voltage signal applied to vertical deflection plates.

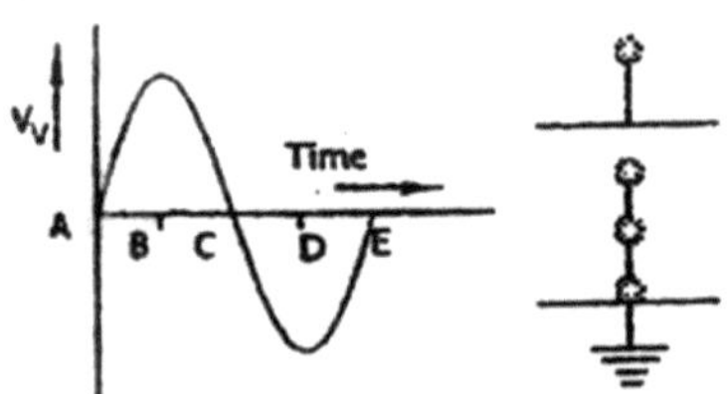

    (*iii*) Deflection for two sinusoidal voltage signals equal in magnitude and frequency and in phase applied to both horizontal and vertical deflection plates.

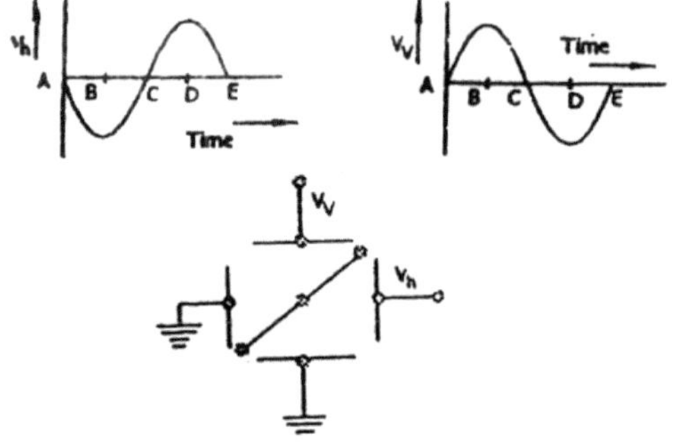

(*iv*) Deflection for two sinusoidal signals equal in magnitude and frequency but opposite in phase applied to both horizontal and vertical deflection plates.

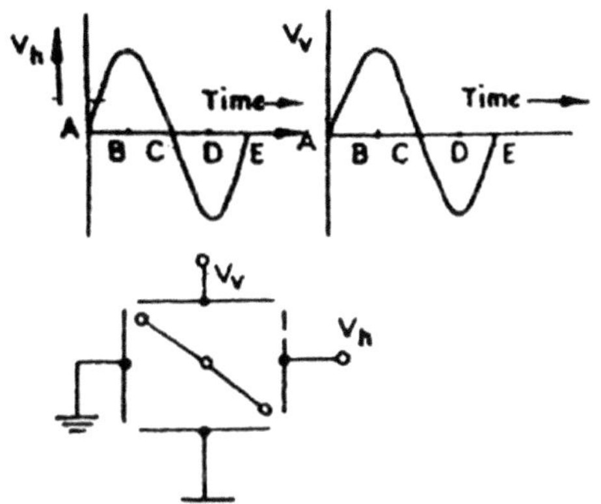

(*v*) Deflection for two sinusoidal signals of equal amplitude and frequency but 90° out of phase are applied to both horizontal and vertical deflection plates.

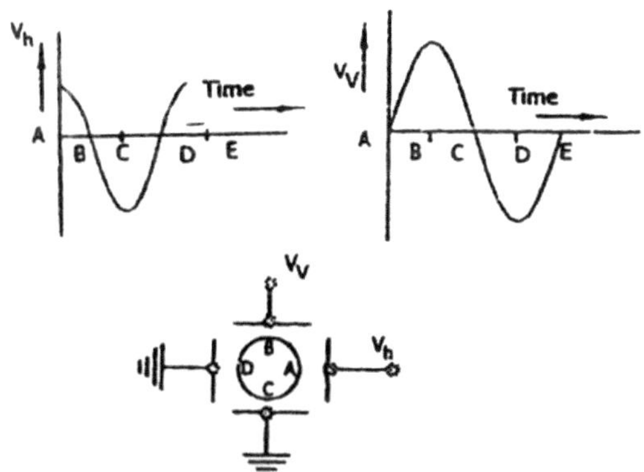

2. Measurement of Phase difference.

When two sinusoidal voltage signals are applied to deflection plates of CRO, the phase difference (ϕ) is determined as follows.

$$V_h = V_h \sin \omega t; \quad V_v = V_v \sin (\omega t + \phi)$$

Since deflection is directly proportional to amplitude of voltage, we have

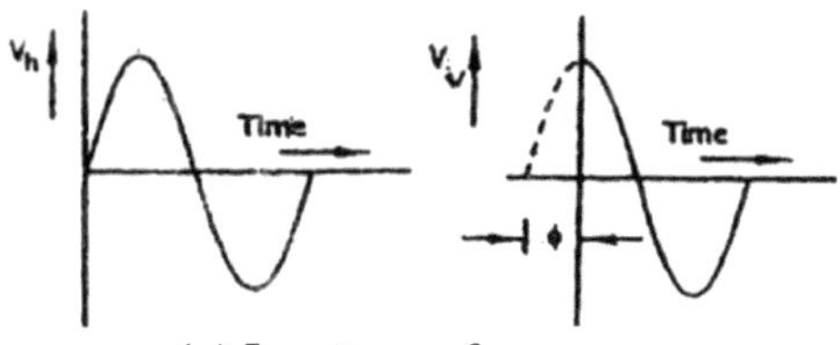

(a) Input waveforms

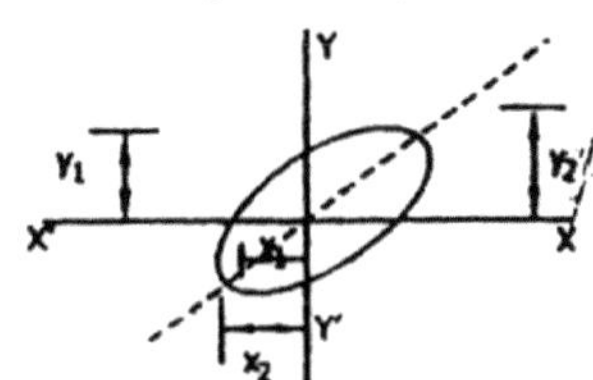

(b) Output on CRO (Lissajous pattern)

$$\sin \phi = \frac{Y_1}{Y_2} = \frac{X_1}{X_2}$$

3. Measurement of frequency.

Frequency of a signal can be accurately measured by Lissajous patterns. The signal of unknown frequency is applied to Y-plates. The signal of known frequency is applied to X-plates. Depending on the frequency ratio, patterns (circle or ellipses) are obtained.

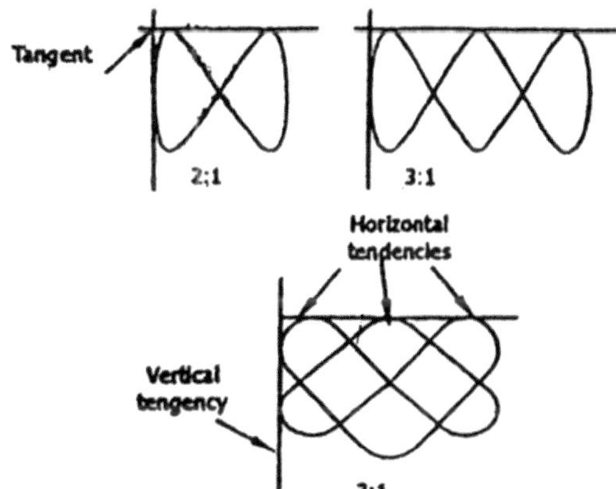

Fig. Some Lissajous patterns

For all the cases of patterns obtained, the ratios of the two frequencies is

$$\frac{f_y}{f_x} = \frac{\text{Number of horizontal tangencies}}{\text{Number of vertical tangencies}}$$

where, f_y = frequency of signal applied to Y-plates

and f_x = frequency of signal applied to X-plates

For open Lissajous patterns, free end is treated as 1/2 tangency.

4. Measurement of Voltage/Current of any electrical signal.

Measurement of voltage/current of any electrical signal is done, since the electrostatic beam is directly proportional to the deflection plate voltage. The spot is centred on the screen without applying any voltage signal to the deflection plates. The voltage is applied between a pair of deflection plates and deflection of the spot is observed on the screen. The magnitude of the deflection multiplied by the deflection factor gives the value of voltage applied. In case of an alternating voltage of sinusoidal waveform, the length of straight line is measured. Knowing the deflection sensitivity, peak to peak value of applied a.c. voltage can he found. The rms value of a.c. voltage applied will be equal to this peak to peak divided by $2\sqrt{2}$ for sinusoidal waveform.

The current is measured by passing through a non-inductive resistance and the voltage drop is measured by CRO.

MEASUREMENT OF SELF-INDUCTANCE (AC BRIDGES)

Self inductance is measured by

(*i*) **Maxwell's inductance Bridge.**

This bridge circuit measures an inductance by comparison with a variable standard self inductance.

(*ii*) **Maxwell's Inductance-Capacitance bridge.**

(*iii*) **Hay's bridge.**

Hay's bridge is suitable for coils having Q > 10, *i.e.* of high Q.

(*iv*) **Anderson's bridge.**

(*v*) **Owen's bridge.**

MEASUREMENTS OF CAPACITANCE.

Capacitance is measured by

(*i*) **DeSauty's bridge.**

(*ii*) **Scherring bridge.**

MEASUREMENT OF FREQUENCY (WEIN'S BRIDGE)

This bridge is suitable for measurement of frequency from 100 Hz to 100 kHz. Because of its frequency sensitivity, the Wein's bridge may be difficult to balance unless the waveform of the applied voltage is sinusoidal. The Wein's bridge is primarily known as a *frequency determining* bridge and its application in various useful circuits.

KEY POINTS

Time period (T)

Time taken by a cycle for its completion is *time period*. It is denoted by letter T and its unit is second.

$$T = \frac{1}{f}$$

where, f = frequency, (Hz)

Amplitude

Maximum value of an alternating quantity positive or negative direction with respect to its mean value is called *amplitude*.

Wavelength (λ)

The distance covered by a wave in one cycle time-period is called its *wavelength*. It is denoted by Greek letter λ. (lamhda) and its unit is metre.

Velocity of a wave (V)

The distance travelled by a wave in one second time is called its *velocity* It is denoted by letter V and its unit is metre per second (m/s).

$$V = f \cdot \lambda$$

where, V = velocity, m/s

f = frequency, Hz

λ = wavelength, m.

Phase

Comparative representation of two vectors of alternating quantities is called *phase*.

Three phase AC

An alternating current supply having 3 phases (120° apart from each other) is called *3-phase AC supply*.

It requires 3 phase-wires, one neutral wire and one earth wire for its transmission and distribution.

Peak value of AC

Maximum value of voltage or current in the positive or negative direction is called *peak value of AC*. It is also called '*amplitude*'.

Average value of AC

Average value of AC of a sine-wave form is always zero. Therefore, average of instantaneous values of voltage or current in half cycle of AC is called its *average value*.

$$I_{ave} = 0.637\, I_{max}$$

and $$E_{av} = 0.637\, E_{max}$$

R.M.S. value of AC

The root mean square of 'effective value' of AC is called R.M.S. value of AC.

$$E_{rms} = 0.707\, E_{max}$$

and $$I_{rms} = 0.707\, I_{max}$$

Instantaneous value of AC

The magnitude of an alternating quantity at any instance is called its *instantaneous value*.

Form factor

$$\text{Form factor} = \frac{\text{RMS value}}{\text{average value}} = \frac{0.707}{0.637} = 1.11$$

Peak factor

$$\text{Peak factor} = \frac{\text{Peak value}}{\text{RMS value}} = \frac{1}{0.707} = 1.414$$

AC values Indicated by common volt and ampere meters

RMS values

Electromagnetic induction

If a conductor is placed in a magnetic field and the magnetic flux passing through the conductor is made to change, an e.m.f. is induced in the conductor. This phenomenon is called *electromagnetic induction*.

Dynamically induced e.m.f.

When a conductor is moved in a magnetic field such that its movement produces a change in the magnetic filed, an e.m.f. is induced in it which is called *dynamically induced e.m.f.*

$$e = B\,l\,v\,\sin\theta$$

where e = induced e.m.f.; volts

       B = magnetic flux density; Wb/m^2

       l = length of the conductor; metres

       v = velocity of the conductor; m/s

       θ = angle between direction of magnetic flux and motion of the conductor.

Statically induced e.m.f.

When a conductor is placed in an alternating magnetic field and the presence of conductor produces a hindrance in the change in magnetic flux, an e.m.f. is induced in it called *statically induced e.m.f.*

$$e = \frac{-N\left(\theta_2 - \theta_1\right)}{t \times 10^8}$$

where,   N = number of turns of the conductor

     $\theta - \theta_i$ = change in magnetic flux, Wb

      t = time taken by the flux in changing from θ_1, to θ_2 seconds

Faraday's laws of electromagnetic induction

First law : The existence of induced e.m.f. lasts so long as the magnetic flux is changing.

Second law: The magnitude of induced e.m.f. is directly proportional to the rate of the change of magnetic flux.

where,   N = number of turns of the conductor.

     $d\phi$ = change in magnetic flux; Wb

     dt = time interval for a change; seconds.

(-) sign indicates that the direction of induced e.m.f. is opposite to the direction of change in magnetic flux.

Fleming's Right hand rule

If first and second fingers and the thumb of right hand are stretched in such a way that they remain mutually perpendicular, and the first linger points the direction of magnetic field and the thumb points the direction of motion then the second finger will point the direction of induced e.m.f. This rule is used for the determination of direction of the induced e.m.f. in alternators and generators.

Lenz's law

The direction of induced e.m.f. and current is such that it always opposes the cause producing them. Hence, direction of induced current is opposite to the direction of applied current.

ALTERNATOR

It is a machine which converts mechanical energy into AC electrical energy. It is also called an *'AC generator'*.

Working principle.

An alternator works on the principle of electromagnetic induction; whenever a conductor cuts the magnetic lines of force, and e.m.f. is induced in it.

Determination of power dissipation of a DC circuit

$$P = V.I.$$

$$P = \frac{V^2}{R}$$

$$P = I^2R$$

where,   V = potential difference, volts (r.m.s.) .

     I = current, amperes (r.m.s.)

Note : *Power dissipation of a pure inductive or capacitive circuit is zero.*

Power dissipation of an AC circuit

$$P = V.I \cos\phi$$

where, $\cos\phi$ = power factor

and ϕ = angle between voltage and current.

Power factor

The ratio R/Z is called *power factor* for an AC circuit.

$$P.\ E = \frac{\text{Real power}}{\text{Apparent power}}$$

$$RZ = \cos\phi$$

Note : *Power factor of a pure resistive circuit is one.*

Impedance formula

Series R-L circuit :

$$Z = \sqrt{R^2 + X_L^2}$$

where, Z = impedance, ohms

     R = resistance of the circuit, ohms

     X_L = inductive reactance, ohms

Series R-C circuit :

$$Z = \sqrt{R^2 + X_L^2}$$

where, X_C = capacitive reactance, ohms.

Series R-L-C circuit :

$$Z = \sqrt{R^2 + \left(X_L \sim X_C\right)^2}$$

Current of a circuit containing resistance, capacitance and inductance

$$I = \frac{E}{Z}\ \text{amps}$$

where, E = circuit E.M.F., volts.

Suceptance (B)

It is the reciprocal of reactance. Its unit is mho (Ω omega inverted).

$$B = \frac{1}{X}\ \text{mhos}$$

It may be inductive or capacitive.

Admittance (Y)

It is the reciprocal of impedance. Its unit is mho (Ω).

$$Y = \frac{1}{Z}\ \text{mhos.}$$

Resonance

In AC circuits, a condition in which inductive reactance becomes exactly equal capacitive reactance called *resonance*.

$$X_L = X_C$$

or $\qquad 2\pi \cdot f \cdot L = \dfrac{1}{2\pi\sqrt{L \cdot C}}$

Hence $\qquad Z = \sqrt{R^2 + (X_L - X_C)^2}$

Resonance frequency

For a L-C circuit, the frequency on which the resonance occurs is called" *resonance frequency.*

$$f_r = \dfrac{1}{2\pi\sqrt{L \cdot C}}$$

where $\qquad f_r$ = resonant frequency, hertz

$\qquad\qquad$ L = inductance, henrys

$\qquad\qquad$ C = capacitance, farads

Series resonant circuit

A series L-C circuit in which magnitudes of inductive and capacitive reactances are exactly

equal is called *series resonant circuit, 'acceptor circuit' or 'tuned circuit'.*

Characteristics :

A series resonant circuit has following characteristics :

(*i*) Minimum impedance.

(*ii*) Maximum circuit current.

(*iii*)$\cos \phi = 1$, hence voltage and current becomes in-phase.

(*iv*)Circuit current becomes proportional to the circuit resistance

$$\left(I \propto \dfrac{1}{R}\right)$$

Uses :

(*i*) For frequency selection in radio and TV receivers.

(*ii*) For I.E. tuning in radio and TV receivers,

(*iii*) For a band pass filter circuit.

Series resonance curve

It shows variations of circuit current within a narrow band of frequencies above and below the resonance frequency.

Selectivity of a resonant circuit

The ability of a resonant circuit of selecting desired frequency from a band of frequencies is called its *selectivity*.

Circuit-Q

The ratio of inductive reactance to the resistance is called *circuit-Q*. It is also called '*magnification factor*'.

$$Q = \dfrac{X_L}{R}$$

where, Q = circuit-Q (no unit)

$\qquad\quad X_L$ = inductive reactance, ohms

$\qquad\quad$ R = circuit resistance, ohms

Also, selectivity $\propto$ Q.

Bandwidth of a resonance curve

$$f_2 - f_1 = \dfrac{R}{2\pi \cdot L}$$

where $f_2 - f_1$ = upper and lower frequency limits of the band width; hertz

$\qquad\qquad$ R= circuit resistance; ohms

$\qquad\qquad$ L= inductance; henrys.

Parallel resonant circuit

A parallel L-C circuit in which magnitudes of inductive and capacitive reactances are exactly equal is called *parallel resonance circuit* or '*rejector circuit*'.

Characteristics :

(*i*) Maximum impedance

(*ii*) Minimum circuit current

(*iii*) $\cos \phi = 1$. hence voltage and current becomes in phase

(*iv*) Circuit current depends on the circuit impedance.

$$Z = L/C \text{ or } 1 \propto 1/R$$

Uses :

(*i*) As an I.F. trap' in the aerial circuit of radio and TV receivers.

(*ii*) As a plate load in I.F. and R.F. amplifiers.

(*iii*) As a band stop filter.

(*iv*) As a tank circuit in oscillators.

I.F. trap :

Parallel resonance curve shows variations of circuit impedance within a narrow band of frequencies above and below the resonance frequency.

ALTERNATING

Electric and magnetic quantities, such as current, voltage, flux, etc., are called *alternating* (as opposed to "*direct*") when their magnitude successively increase to a maximum in one direction, decrease to zero, increase in the opposite direction to maximum of equal value and decrease to zero again, following the same cycle over and over again in a regular manner.

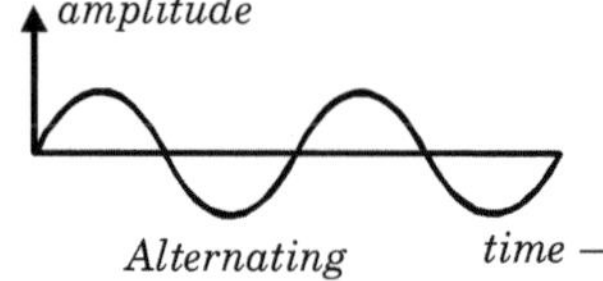

Alternator

One simple form of

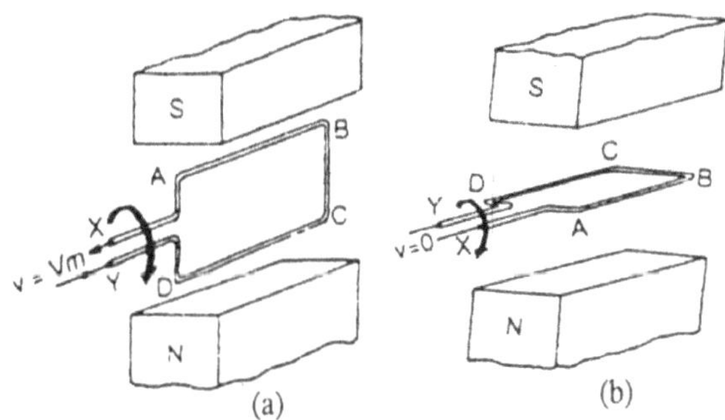

(*a*) A single loop alternator; the conductors AB and CD cut the magnetic field between the North and South magnetic pole pieces tit right angles, so the maximum or peak voltage is induced in [he coil.

(*b*) When the wire loop has rotated through one quarter turn both conductors are moving parallel to the magnetic field and so are not cutting the flux and there is zero induced voltage.

Alternating voltage generator. This is a loop of wire rotated in a magnetic field. The voltage induced in a conductor moving in a magnetic field is proportional to the rate at which the moving wire cuts the magnetic flux.

Electricity

It is a sort of energy which can be experienced in its applications like bulb, heater, motor, radio set etc.

Conductor

It is the substance, which readily allows a current to flow across.

Conductivity of substance

The number of free electrons present in the substance decides its conductivity.

Characteristics of a Good conductor

(*i*) Low specific resistance

(*ii*) Ductile

(*iii*) Rigid

(*iv*) Cheap.

Insulator

It is a substance, which hardly allows a current to flow across it. Most of the insulators have 4 or 8 electrons in their outermost shell.

Characteristics of a Good insulator

(*i*) High dielectric constant.

(*ii*) High breakdown voltage

(*iii*) Permanent, rigid

(*iv*) Least electric absorbent.

Semiconductor

It is a substance, which is neither a good conductor nor a good insulator. e.g. Germanium, Silicon etc.

ELECTRIC CURRENT OR CURRENT

It is the movement of electrons/charge carries across a conductor.

Types of Electric current

1. Direct Current (D.C)

It is the current whose direction and magnitude remain fixed.

2. Alternating Current (A.C)

It is the current whose direction and magnitude remain alternating at a definite rate.

Advantages of A.C. over D.C.

(*i*) A.C. can be transformed from low to high and high to low voltages easily.

(*ii*) It can be economically transmitted over long distances.

Advantages of D.C. over A.C

D.C. is essential for many electronic and industrial applications.

Flow of Electric current

There are three ways of flow of electric current :

1. Conduction current.

In this method, electrons transfer themselves from atom to atom in one direction, e.g. flow of current across a metallic conductor.

2. Displacement current.

When an insulator current is connected to a battery, the electrons tends to move in the direction of positive terminal. This momentary displacement of electrons is called *displacement current.*

3. Convection current.

It is the flow of electrons or ions from one electrode to another across vacuum or gas etc.

Current (I)

Unit of current is ampere.

One ampere

It is the magnitude of current, when one coulomb (charge of $1.6 \equiv 10$ electrons) of charge is passed through the point of a circuit in one second.

E.M.F. (Electro Motive Force)

It is the force which sets up a flow of current in a circuit.

Its unit is volt and symbol is E.

P.D (Potential Difference)

When a current is passed across a resistor, it causes a potential difference to be developed across that resistor which is called P.D. or potential difference.

Its unit is volt and symbol is V.

Potential

Electrical status of a body which decides direction of flow of electric current.

Work done in moving a unit charge from infinity to that point is called *potential.*

Difference between E.M.F. and P.D.

If magnitude of current flow in a circuit is zero, then P.D. will also be zero, whereas, e.m.f. will not be zero.

Resistance (R)

It is defined as natural property of every substance of producing hindrance to the flow of current across it.

One ohm

When a current of one ampere flowing through a conductor produces a p.d. of one volt, then resistance of that conductor is called *one ohm*.

Its unit is ohm and symbol is Ω(omega).

Conductivity

It is defined as natural property of a conductor of producing relaxation to the flow of current across it.

Its unit is mho and symbol is Ω (omega reversed).

One volt

If work done in transferring charge of one coulomb from one point to another in a circuit is one joule, then P.D. between two points is called *one volt*.

Power

It is the rate of doing work.

Its unit is joule/second.

Horse power

It is the commercial unit of mechanical power, .

1 H.P. = 746 watts.

M.H.P. (Metric Horse Power)

It is the inter nationally agreed unit of mechanical power.

1.M.H.P. = 735 watts.

MECHANICAL ENERGY.

There are two types of mechanical energy :

1. **Kinetic energy (KE)**

    A moving object is said to possess kinetic energy.

    $$KE = \frac{1}{2} m \cdot v^2 \ (\frac{1}{2} \times mass \times velocity^2)$$

2. **Potential energy**

    An object raised above the earth's surface is said to possess potential energy,

    P.E. = m.g.h. (mass × g × height).

Principal Effects of electric current

(*i*) **Magnetic effect.**

   A current carrying conductor is surrounded by a magnetic field.

(*ii*) **Heating effect**

   A current carrying conductor becomes hot

   $H = I^2.R.t$ (current^2 × resistance × time).

(*iii*)**Chemical effect**

   A flow of electric current through an inorganic solution decomposes the same into ions

   m = Z.I.t (E.C.E × current × time).

Ohm's Law

In a closed d.c. circuit, p.d. (*V*) developed across a conductor is directly proportional to the current (*I*) flowing through it.

If temperature and other physical conditions of the conductor have been kept constant,

$$V \propto I$$

or $\quad \dfrac{V}{I}$ = constant or V/I = R,

where, R = resistance of the conductor.

Resistance law

Resistance (R) of a conductor is directly proportional to length (*l*) and inversely proportional to cross-sectional area (A) of the conductor.

$$R \propto \frac{l}{A}$$

Resistivity (ρ)

Resistance of a piece of a material having length of one cm and a cross-sectional area of one square cm is called its *resistivity* or '*specific resistance*'.

$$\rho = \frac{R \times A}{I}$$

Temperature coefficient

The change in resistance of a resistor by increasing its temperature by 1°C.

$$R_t = R_0(1 + \alpha \cdot t)$$

where, R_t = resistance at t°C

$\quad$ R_t = resistance at 0°C

$\quad$ α = temperature coefficient/°C

$\quad$ t = temperature °C

Battery

A group of cells is called *a battery*.

Cell

Cell is a device meant for generating e.m.f. on account of chemical actions.

Primary and Secondary cells

(*i*) **Primary cell.**

   It is the cell, in which an e.m.f. is generated on account of chemical reactions.

   It can't be recharged.

(*ii*) **Secondary cell.**

   It is the cell in which electrical energy is stored in the form of chemical changes.

   It can be recharged again and again.

Anode.

It is the electrode through which current leaves an electrolyte.

Cathode.

It is the electrode through which the current enters an electrolyte.

Voltaic cell

The very first cell made by the famous scientist Mr. Volta is known as voltaic cell.

It consists of

(*i*) a glass container called *voltameter.*

(*ii*) dilute sulphuric acid as an electrolyte

(*iii*) copper rod as an anode

(*iv*) zinc rod as a cathode.

Chemical reactions :

(*i*) Dilute sulphuric acid decomposes into hydrogen and sulphate ions

$$H_2SO_4 \rightarrow 2H^+ + SO^-_4$$

(*ii*) Sulphate ions reach at zinc rod and make it negative

$$Zn^{++} + SO_4 \rightarrow ZnSO_4$$

(*iii*) Hydrogen ions reach at copper rod and make it positive

$$2H^+ + 2e \rightarrow H_2$$

Electrolyte

It is the chemical solution which undergoes chemical changes on account of conduction of current.

Defects of a voltaic cell

1. **Local action.**

   It is the loss of electrical energy due to formation of number of tiny cells within the zinc rod (due to impurity of zinc).

2. **Polarization.**

   It is the phenomenon in which hydrogen ions liberated at the copper anode make ii nonconducting alter some lime.

   It is minimized by amalgamating zinc rod (coating zinc rod with mercury). The mercury covering doesn't allow zinc's impurities to take part into chemical actions.

   It is minimize by employing granules of manganese dioxide (MnO_2) around the copper anode which converts hydrogen ions into water:

   $$2MnO_2 + 2H \rightarrow Mn_2O_3 + H_2O$$

Daniel cell

Mr. Daniel employed copper sulphate solution as a depolariser in place of manganese dioxide (MnO_2) and rest of the construction of his cell was similar to that of a voltaic cell. Daniel cell is no longer in use.

Leclanche cell

It is an improved type of Voltaic cell in which ammonium chloride (NH_4Cl) is filled in a zinc container which acts as a cathode. The carbon anode is placed in a porous pot filled with manganese dioxide (MnO_2) granules.

Chemical actions :

(*i*) Aqueous solution of NH_4Cl has NH^+_4 and Cl ions

$$NH_4Cl \rightarrow NH_4 + Cl^-$$

(*ii*) On connecting a load between anode and cathode:

At cathode: $\quad Zn \rightarrow Zn^{++} + 2e$

$$Zn^{++} + 2Cl \rightarrow ZuCl_2$$

At anode : $\quad 2NH_4 + 2e \rightarrow 2NH_3 + H_2$

In MnO : $\quad H_2 + 2MnO_2 \rightarrow Mn_2O_3 + H_2O$

$$2Mn_2O_3 + O_2 \rightarrow 4MnO_2 \text{ (from air)}$$

Note : Per cell e.m.f. of a Lechlanche 1.5 volts

Dry cell

It is a compact form of Lechlanche cell. It employs a paste consisting of ammonium chloride, zinc chloride and plaster of paris as an electrolyte.

Lead-acid cell

It is a secondary cell which is commonly referred as an accumulator. It consists of positive plates of lead peroxide (PbO_2), negative plates of spongy lead (Pb), dilute sulphuric acid (H_2SO_4) and a hard rubber container.

Chemical actions : *During charging*

$$H_2SO_4 \rightarrow 2H^+ + SO^-_4$$

At cathode : $\quad PbSO_4 + 2H^+ \rightarrow Pb + H_2SO_4$

At anode : $\quad PbSO_4 + SO^-_4 + 2H2O \rightarrow PbO_2 + 2H_2SO_4$

During discharging

$$H_2SO_4 \rightarrow 2H^+ + SO^-_4$$

At cathode : $\quad Pb + SO_4 \rightarrow PbSO_4$

At anode : $\quad PhO_2 + 2H^+ + H_2SO_4 \rightarrow PbSO_4 + 2H_2O$

Forming

Originally, the positive and negative plates of a lead-acid cell are made of a red lead (Pb_3O_4) and discharges (PbO) respectively. On filling dilute sulphuric acid (H_2SO_4) in the cell, chemical actions are started and positive plates get turned into PbO_2 while negative plates get turned into Pb. This process is called *forming.*

Note :

1. Specific gravity of electrolyte of *charged* lead-acid cell rises upto $1.25 - 1.28$ and e.m.f. becomes 2.1 to 2.2 volts.

2. Specific gravity of the electrolyte of *discharged lead-acid* cell drops upto 1.15-1.18 and the e.m.f. drops to 1.8 volts.

Specific gravity (S.G.)

Ratio of the density of a liquid to [he density of 4°C water referred as S.G. or specific density.

S.G. is measured by a hydrometer.

Hydrometer

Hydrometer is an instrument meant for the measurement of S.G. of a solution. It is based on the principle of Archimedes.

AHC (Ampere Hour Capacity)

AHC of a cell is equal the product of amperes and the hours for which the cell/battery is capable to work.

Lead-Acid Battery

Principal Defects

(*i*) **Corrosion :** Formation of an insulating layer onthe battery terminals called *corrosion*. It is a routine detect and it can be reduced by periodically cleaning and greasing the battery terminals.

(*ii*) **Sedimentation :** Formation of a pile of sediment at the bottom of a battery is called *sedimentation*. It can he minimized by using distilled water as and when required to be poured in the battery.

(*iii*) **Sulphation :** Deposition of a hard layer of lead sulphate on the plates of battery is called *sulphation*. Battery should not be left idle in order to avoid this defect.

(*iv*) **Buckling :** Bending of cell plates is called *buckling*. Battery should not be charged or discharged at a high current rate (above 25 A) in order to avoid this defect.

Preserving a lead-acid battery

To pressure a lead-acid battery for a long time in unused state, remove battery's electrolyte, wash it with distilled water and dry up battery's inner portion and then store it.

Alkaline Cell

Cell employing alkali electrolyte is called an *alkaline cell*.

Merits of Alkaline cell over Lead-acid cell

(*i*) Alkaline cell can withstand heavy current rate discharging.

(*ii*) It is light in weight and mechanically rigid.

(*iii*) It has no sulphation defect.

(*iv*) It is most suitable for electric operated vehicles.

Edison cell (or nickel-iron cell)

It consists of nickel plates steel tubes which arc perforated and are filled with paste of nickel-hydroxide $[Ni(OH)_2]$ to act as positive plates. Pockets of the negative plates are filled with ferrous hydroxide $[Fe(OH)_2]$. Caustic-potash and lithium hydroxide $[Li(OH)_2]$ mixture is used as an electrolyte.

Chemical actions in an Edison cell

1. *During charging* :

$$KOH \rightarrow K^+ + OH^-$$

At anode :

$$Ni(OH)_2 + 2OH \rightarrow Ni(OH)^4$$

At cathode :

$$Fe(OH)_2 + 2K^+ \rightarrow Fe + 2KOH$$

2. *During discharging* :

$$KOH \rightarrow K^+ + OH^-$$

At anode :

$$Ni(OH)_4 + 2K \rightarrow Ni(OH)_2 + 2KOH$$

At cathode :

$$Fe^+ + 2OH \rightarrow Fe(OH)_2$$

E.m.f.

In charged state : 1.4 volts

In discharged state : 1.1 volts

Nickel-cadmium cell or Junger cell

It is an alkaline cell in which active materials are nickel-hydroxide and cadmium.

Difference between Source and Load e.m.f. of a cell/battery

Open circuit voltage of a cell/battery is called *source e.m.f.* while voltage across the cell/battery is a closed circuit is called *load voltage* or *load e.m.f.*

Relation between Source and Load

$$E_s = I.r + V$$

where, E_s = source e.m.f. (volts)

     I = circuit current (amps)

     r = internal resistance (ohms)

     V = load voltage (I.R) (volts)

Cells joined in Series

In order to obtain a large e.m.f.

$$E_r = n.E$$

where, E_r = total e.m.f (volts)

     n = number of cells

     E = E.M.F. of one cell (volts)

Cells joined in Parallel

In order to obtain in a high current rate or current for more time than that with one cell.

$$I = \frac{n \cdot E}{R + n \cdot r}$$

where, I = circuit current (amps)

     n = number of cells

     E = e.m.f. of one cell (volts)

     R = load resistance (ohms)

     r = internal resistance of one cell (ohms)

Internal resistance of a cell

It is the resistance offered by a cell to the flow of electric currents through the cell itself.

Cells connected in Mixed group

For obtaining more e.m.f. and more current than that with one cell. Terminals are identified with the help of a D.C. voltmeter or galvanometer.

Constant Voltage charging method

In this method, charging voltage is maintained at a constant value. Hence, rate of initial charging current rests higher than the final changing current.

Constant Current charging method

In this method, charging current rate is maintained at a constant value by changing number of bulbs (loads).7

Ionization

It is the process in which atoms are changed into ions.

Ion

A charged atom is called an ion.

Cation

A positively charged ion is called a cation.

Anion.

A negatively charged ion is called an anion.

Electrolysis

The process of changing composition of a chemical solution by passing an electric current through the same is called *electrolysis.*

Applications of electrolysis

(*i*)   In electroplating purification of metals

(*ii*)   Extraction of metals

(*iii*) Electrotyping etc.

Bifilar Winding

It is a method of winding consisting of two contiguous insulated conductors connected so that they carry the same current in opposite directions. This results in a negligible magnetic field being produced. The technique is commonly used to wind noninductive resistors.

Bridge

An assembly of at least four circuit elements, such as resistors, capacitors, etc., together with a current source and a null point detecting device. Each of the circuit elements is arranged in one arm of the bridge. When bridge is balanced, i.e. zero response is obtained from the null detector, there is a calculable relationship between values of elements in the arms given by

$$\frac{ZA}{ZC} = \frac{ZB}{ZD}$$

A measuring equipment on a similar principle to the original. Wheatstone's Bridge in the measurement of D.C. resistance, which in later forms has been adapted to A.C. working up to the highest frequencies and to the measurement of capacitance, inductance.

Capacitance

The property of AC circuits which opposes any change in the amount of voltage is called capacitance or 'capacity'.

Practical unit of capacitance is the farad (F) but it is usually more convenient to make use of Microfarad (one million of farad).

One farad.

If a voltage of one volt causes one coulomb of charge to be accumulated in a capacitor, its capacity will be one farad.

$$C = Q/V$$

or   1 farad = 1 coulomb/ 1 volt

Sub-multiples of farad

(*i*)   Micro farad, $1\ \mu F = 10^{-6}F$.

(*ii*)   Pico farad, $1\ pF = 10^{-12}F = 10^{-6}\ \mu F$.

Capacitor

Any system possessing appreciable capacitance, i.e. in which an appreciable charge is produced by application of an e.m.f. If the e.m.f. is continuous, only a momentary rush of current will be produced (except for such small permanent current that the there may be due to leakage), but if the e.m.f. is alternating, a current will surge in and out of the capacitor which will be in advance of the e.m.f. in phase.

Capacitor or Condenser

A system of conductors capable of storing electric charge is called *capacitor*.

Effects of a Capacitance

(*i*)   It opposes any change in the amount of voltage.

(*ii*)   Voltage is lag behind the current by a quarter cycle (90°).

(*iii*) Electric charge is stored in the capacitor in the form of electrostatic field.

Electric energy stored by a capacitor

$$E = \frac{1}{2}C \cdot V_2$$

where,   E = energy stored (joules)

C = capacitance (farads)

V = voltage (volts)

Capacitive circuit

Voltage lag behind the current

Initially a capacitor has no charge, therefore, flow of current starts at its maximum value. When capacitor attains its full charge, the current reaches at zero and potential difference reaches its maximum.

Consequently, voltage is lagged behind the current by $90°$ in a pure capacitive circuit. But due to resistance of circuit, the angle of lag is found to be less than $90°$.

$$\cos\theta = \frac{R}{Z_c}$$

where, θ = angle of lag

$\quad$ R = circuit resistance (ohms)

$\quad$ Z_c = capacitive impedance (ohms)

Power dissipation. Power dissipation of a pure capacitive circuit is zero.

Time constant :

Time taken by a capacitor in attaining 63.3% of its full charge is called *time constant of capacitive circuit*

$$t = CR$$

where, $\quad t$ = time constant (seconds)

$\quad$ C = capacitance (farads)

$\quad$ R = resistance (ohms)

Total capacitance of two or more capacitors

1. Connected in series :

$$\frac{1}{C_T} = \frac{1}{C_1} + \frac{1}{C_2} + \frac{1}{C_3} + \text{\_\_\_\_\_\_\_}.$$

For identical capacitors $C_T = \dfrac{C}{n}$.

Connected in parallel :

$$C_T = C_1 + C_2 + C_3 + \text{\_\_\_\_\_\_\_}.$$

For identical capacitors

$$C_T = \frac{C}{n}$$

Factors effecting capacitance of a capacitor

It depends on

(*i*) area and number of plates

(*ii*) distance between plates

(*iii*) dielectric constant.

$$C = \frac{8.85\,K.A(N-1)}{t \times 10^8}\,\mu F$$

where, $\quad$ A = area of plates, cm^2

$\quad$ N = number of plates

$\quad$ t = thickness of dielectric (cm)

$\quad$ K = dielectric constant.

Capacitive reactance

It is the opposition offered by a capacitor to the flow of AC through it is called capacitive reactance. It is denoted by Xc and its unit is ohm.

$$EC = \frac{1}{2\pi \cdot f \cdot C}\,\text{ohms}$$

where, $\quad f$ = frequency (hertz)

$\quad$ C = capacitance (farads)

Stray capacitance

Generally, undesired capacitance is found between two conductors and between two turns of a coil which is called *stray capacitance* or *distributed capacitance*.

Dielectric constant

It is the ratio of capacitance of a capacitor with the substance used as dielectric to the capacitance with air used as dielectric.

It is expressed as a number.

Classification of Capacitors

1. Based on their working $\quad$ 2. Fixed

3. Adjustable $\qquad\qquad$ 4. Variable capacitor.

2. Based type of dielectric used in the capacitor

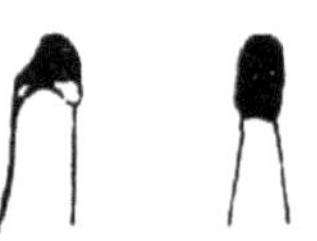

Mica capacitors $\qquad\qquad$ *Ceramic capacitors*

1. **Paper capacitor.**

   It consists of two long aluminium foils duly separated by wax paper strips and rolled together to take a cylindrical shape.

Tabular Paper capacitors

2. **Mica capacitor**

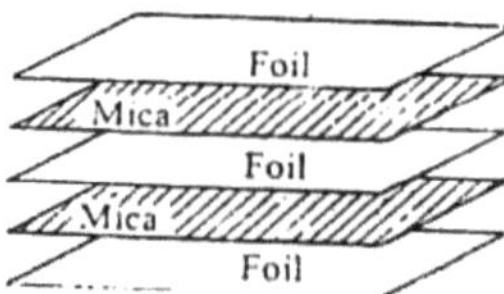

Its capacitance remains stable and unaffected from dampness.

3. **Polyester or Styroflex capacitor**

   It utilises a very fine polythene sheet as dielectric so as to reduce its size as compared to a paper capacitor. These capacitor are suitable for H.F. and transistorised circuits.

4. **Ceramic capacitor**

   It has a long life, small size and it can be made to have positive, negative or zero temperature coefficient.

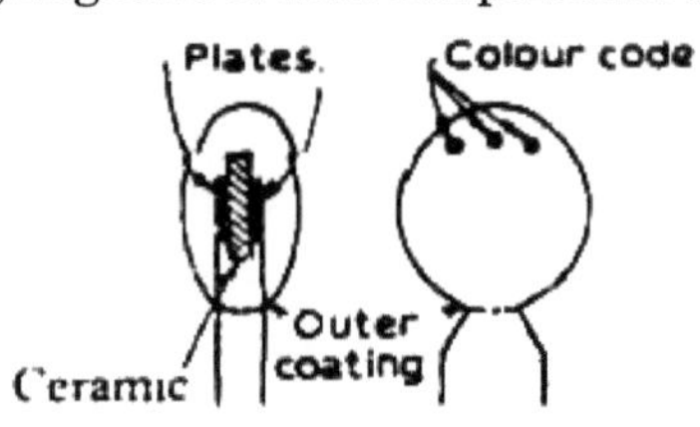

5. Electrolytic capacitor

It consists of an electrolyte between two sets of plates. The electrolyte forms an insulation layer on positive plates when capacitor is connected across a DC source. The insulation so formed acts as dielectric.

It has a high capacitance value in a small size.

There are two types of electrolytic capacitors—

(i) Wet electrolyte capacitor

(ii) Dry electrolytic capacitor.

6. Oil dielectric capacitor

There capacitors have a lung working file and highest working voltage upto 25000 volts.

7. Air dielectric capacitor.

Trimmer and padder are adjustable air or mica dielectric capacitors.

Capacitance value of a *trimmer* is kept between 3 to 30 pF or 4 to 70 pF. It is made in parallel plate, cup, wire type and disc shapes.

Capacitance value of a *padder* is kept between 400 to 600 pF. It is made in parallel plate shape.

Gang capacitor

It is a variable capacitor which has two or more sections. Each section consists of two sets of plates

(*i*) **Rotor :** Rotor place groups of all the sections are operated by a single shaft. Its capacitance value is kept between 135 to 500 pF, 90 to 210 pF etc.

(*ii*) **Starter**

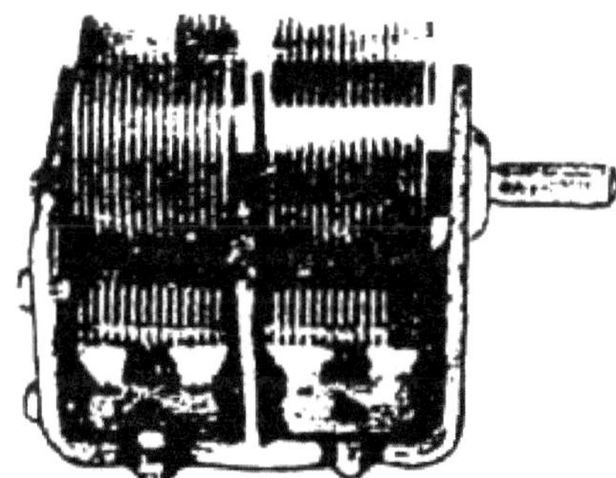

Capacitor Losses

If a charged capacitor is kept isolated, even then, after some time its charge gets reduced or lost. This effect is called *capacitor losses*.

Capacitor losses are of these types :

(i) Resistance loss

(ii) Leakage loss

(iii) Dielectric loss

Selection of capacitor

It depends on following factor :

(i) Working voltage (ii) Capacitance

(iii) Type of dielectric (iv) Circuit's requirement

(v) Price of capacitor

Effect of Temperature on Capacitance of a capacitor

Capacitance of a capacitor increases with a rise in temperature due to increase in the area of conductor plates. Ceramic capacitors may be designed to have positive, zero or negative temperature coefficient as per requirement.

Expressing Capacitance of a capacitor

Colour coding method :

The popular method of indexing capacitors is called '5-band method'.

In this method,

first band indicates temperature coefficient.

second third and fourth bands indicate capacitance value like carbon resistors.

Last and fifth band indicates tolerance.

The capacitance value is read in picofarads.

Tolerance of a capacitor

The permissible change in the capacitance value of a capacitor is called its *tolerance*.

It is expressed in terms of percentage.

Cascade Voltage Switch Logic (CVSL)

Basic form of this type of gate is a fully differential network which consists of two complementary NMOS networks connected to a pair of cross coupled PMOS pull up transistors.

Cathautograph

It is a system of transmission of visual writing in which a receiver similar to a Cathode Ray Oscillograph is used with a Fluorescent Screen on which writing caused by the moving "spot" remains visible for short time. The transmitter contains a stylus regulating two resistances as in the Telautograph and thus controls deflecting fields of the receiver.

Cathetron

It is a Grid-Controlled Mercury-Vapour rectifier with control electrode external to the tube.

Cathode ray

These rays consisting of a stream of negatively charged particles or Electrons given off from the cathode in a. highly exhausted tube, i.e. when gas pressure is reduced below 1/100,000 of an atmosphere.

Cathode ray Direction Finder

It is a radio-receiving apparatus with two aerials at right angles to each other, connected through amplifiers to the four plates of a Cathode Ray Oscillograph, the beam of which is so deflected as to show direction of the received signal.

Cathode ray Instruments

These are measuring instrument, in which indication is made by the movement of a beam of cathode rays falling on a fluorescent screen or photographic film.

e.g. Cathode ray oscillograph.

Cathode Ray Oscillograph

It is a cathode ray tube arranged with a fluorescent screen at one end upon which a narrow beam of cathode rays falls, and makes a visible spot of fluorescence. The beam is either in the field of two electromagnets, at right angles to one another and excited proportionally to the voltage and current in the circuit under investigation, or more usually, passes two similarly crossed electrostatic fields. Owing to the deflection of the beam by these fields, the spot is caused to execute energy curves corresponding to the circuit. The instrument can be used radio-frequencies as a wattmeter, or for the study of waveforms or phase differences. It can also be arranged for photographic recording.

Cathode ray Television tube

It is a cathode ray tube used in a television receiver with a large fluorescent screen opposite heated cathode upon which falls the sharply focussed electron beam modulated by the sampled incoming signals and deflected by a special set of electrodes in synchronism with the scanning beam in the transmitter.

Cathode Ray Tube

It is a Gas Discharge tube suitable for the production of cathode rays.

Circuit

It is a combination of electrical and/or electronic components connected together in a specific configuration to perform a specified function.

Circulator Junction

Y-junction circulator can be constructed in either rectangular waveguide or stripline. The waveguide tape, shown used at high microwave

frequencies. It consists of three H-plane junctions although E-plane circulators can also be made.

The stripline version shown in figure is principally applicable to the VHP and low microwave frequencies.

A multi port device, in which the incident wave to any port is transmitted to the next port, according to an order of sequence determined by the sense of a static magnetic biased field.

Colour Code

A method of marking electronic parts, such as resistors, with information for the user. The value, tolerance, voltage rating, and any special characteristic of the component may be indicated using coloured bands or dots painted on.

Colour Coding of Resistors

In order to give values of resistance on various resistors, a system of colour codes is used. Normally there are four colour bands on fixed moulded resistor as shown in the figure.

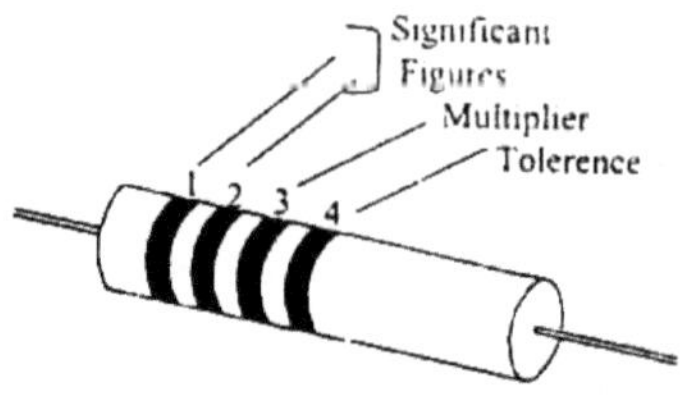

Bands are read from left to the right from the end that is nearest to the bands.

First and second bands represent first and second significant digits of the resistance value.

Third band represents number of zeros that follow the second digit

Fourth band represents tolerance in the value of the resistance.

However, if third band is gold or silver, it means a multiplying factor of 0.1 or 0.01 and if there is no fourth band the standard tolerance of ± 20% should be assumed.

Various colour codes :

Colour	Digit	Multiplying tolerance factor	
Black	0	$1 = 10^{0}$	
Brown	1	$10 = 10^{1}$	
Red	2	$100 = 10^{2}$	
Orange	3	10^{3}	
Yellow	4	10^{4}	
Green	5	10^{5}	
Blue	6	10^{6}	
Violet	7	10^{7}	
Gray	8	10_{8}	
White	9	10	
Gold	–	$0.1 - 10^{-1}$	± 5%
Silver	–	$0.01 = 10^{-2}$	± 10%
No colour	–	–	± 20%

Cyclogram

A record obtained from a cyclograph. Also, it is an instrument with an optical or electron-jet *"pointer"* moving in two dimensions under control respectively of different variables (to distinguish it from a true Oscillograph in which pointer moves in only one dimension under control of a single variable while time element is taken into account by movement of the screen or otherwise). In case of regular periodic functions, a closed figure or *cyclogram* similar to one of Lissajou's figures is produced.

D'Arsonoval Galvanometer

It is a direct-current galvanometer in which the current to be measured passes through a small rectangular coil suspended between poles of a permanent horseshoe magnet. Magnetic field produced in the coil reacts with the field of the magnet producing a torque and causing the coil to rotate about the vertical axis in the field. D'Arsonoval movement is used in most forms of galvanometer since it combines a high degree of sensitivity with low resistance and high damping.

Dielectric Fatigue

Resistance to breakdown decreases after prolonged application of high voltage stress across the dielectric.

Dielectric Heating

It is the heating of an insulating material by an ac field. The principle is used in Microwave ovens.

Dielectric Hysteresis

The electric flux in a dielectric not only depends upon present value of the electric force but also on the previous state of the material.

Doppler Effect

It is change in the apparent frequency of a source of electromagnetic radiation when there is relative motion between source and the observer.

$$f_0 = \frac{C - V_0}{C - V_s}$$

where f_a = observer frequency

V_0 = observer velocity

V_s = source velocity

C = speed of light

f = radar frequency

Doppler Frequency

It is the frequency shift between direct and reflected waves due to velocity of target obtained during moving target measurement in a radar system.

Photodiode or Photo conductive cell

It is a solid state equivalent of photo tube. It is made of cadmium sulphide.

Photo voltaic cell

It is an electronic device which converts light energy into electrical energy. It consists of a fine silicon water which emits electrons when subjected to light rays. A silver wafer collects the emitted electrons. The device is used in flashlights, calculators, spacecrafts etc.

VTVM (Vacuum Tube Voltmeter)

It is a highly sensitive voltmeter based on the application of vacuum tubes. It can measure voltages of the order of milli and micro volts level.

DVM (Digital Voltmeter)

It is a solid state equivalent of VTVM. In this meter, measure of AC/DC volts is displayed in digits by means of LCD.

Impedance bridge or LCR bridge' or 'AC bridge

It is a modified form of Wheatstone bridge which is used to measure resistance, capacitance, inductance and impedance of a circuit.

Pattern generator

It is an electronic equipment which produces horizontal bars, veritcal bars and cross-hatch required for TV receiver' alignment.

Frequency modulator

It is used in association with a signal generator for producing frequency modulated signals which are utilized in TV receiver alignment.

Distortion analyzer

It is an electronic equipment designed to measure the amount of distortion present in the AF stage of a receiver etc.

P_H meter

It is an electronic equipment made to measure that pH value of a solution.

Transistor tester

It is a simple instrument meant for transistor testing.

Electron Telescope

It is an apparatus for seeing through haze etc. by infrared rays in which an infrared ray image is formed by optical lenses on the cathode of an Electron Image Tube by which it is rendered visible.

Electron tube And Electron Valve

It is a discharge tube such as a Thermionic valve or "X" ray tube, in which there is a sufficiently high vacuum for the effect to be due to stream of electrons and not of gaseous ions.

e.g. a Kenotron or Coolidge Tube, often used indiscriminately for any Thermionic valve, Cathode ray tube etc.

Electrostatic Adhesion

It is adhesion between two substances or surfaces due to presence of opposite charges, which attract each other.

Electrostatic Focussing

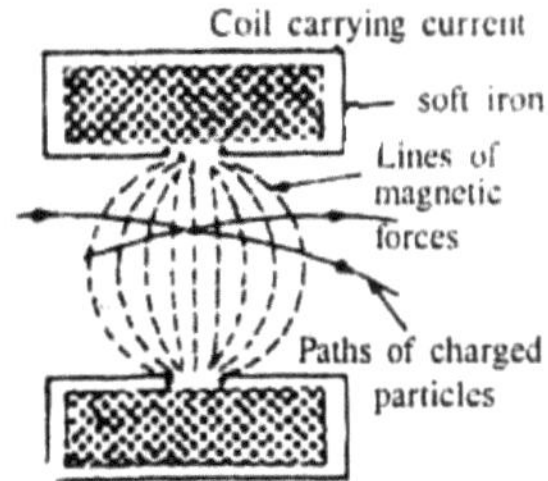

It is focussing of an electron beam by other action of electric field.

Feedback Capacitive

When feedback circuit employs a self capacitance to correct the phase of feedback signal, it is called *feedback capacitive.*

Half-wave Transmission

It is the long distance alternating current transmission in which line losses and pressure drops are less-ended by arranging the natural period of oscillation of line to be equal to four times the frequency so that resonance is produced.

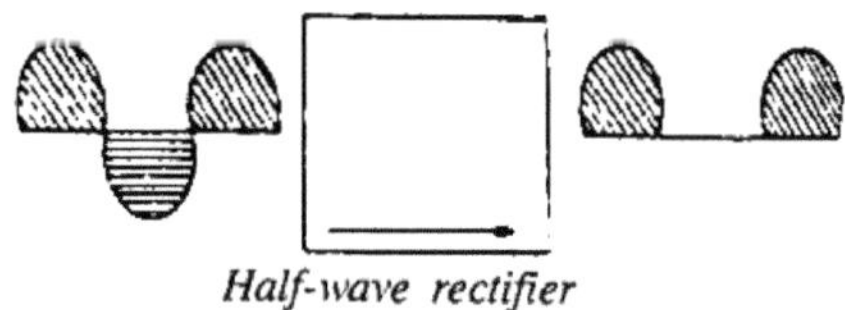

Half-wave rectifier

Impact Diode

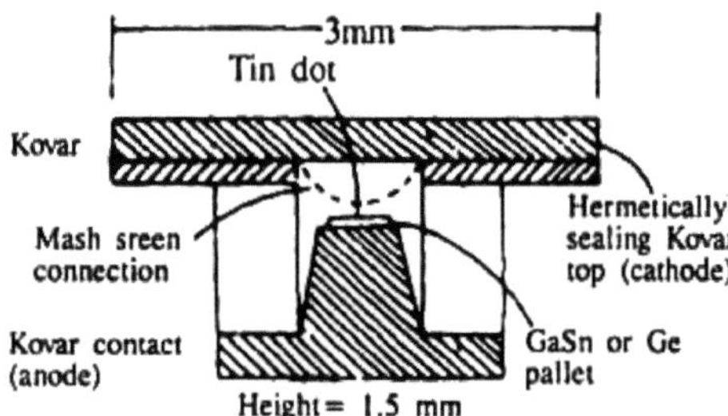

It is a acronym for Impact ionization Avalanche Transit Time. It is combination of delay involved in generating current multiplication, together with delay due to transit time through a drift space, provides necessary 180° phase difference between applied voltage and the resulting current in an IMPACT diode. It is used as microwave source.

Impatt (Double Drift)

DDR structure is superior in power generating capability over the original SDR structure by a factor of about 2.7 due to existence of two drift zones and because for a given impedance level the junction area can be made larger in a DDR device than an SDR. However DDR IMPATT is more difficult to be fabricated and is hence costlier than the SDR IMPATT.

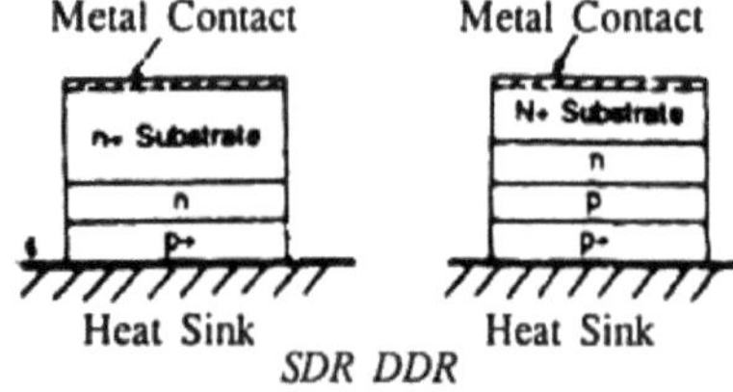

Lissa jou's Figures

It is any closed figures traversed by a point moving with the resultant of two periodic oscillatory motions at right angles. Originally applied Lissa jou's figures to certain experiments in connection with pendulums and sound. Now, it is used instruments as Cathode Ray Oscillograph.

Logic Analyzers

It is basically a multichannel oscilloscope with the ability to detect and display logic levels in several forms.

Maxwell Bridge

It is a four arms bridge for measurement of inductance in terms of capacitance and resistance.

METERS

It is an electronic device used for measuring current, voltage, flow to determine energy consumption.

ELECTRIC INSTRUMENTS

These are classified as follows :

I. Absolute Instrument

It can indicate only presence of an electrical quantity,

e.g. tangent galvanometer.

II. Secondary Instrument

It actually measures an electrical quantity on its pre-graduated scale,

e.g. voltmeter, ammeter etc.

Types of Secondary instruments

1. Indicating instrument

It displays the instantaneous value of an electrical quantity on a pre-graduated scale,

e.g. voltmeter, ammeter, ohmmeter etc.

2. Recording instrument

It records instantaneous value of an electrical quantity on a graph paper with respect to times axis.

3. Integrating instrument

It shows total quantity till the moment of measurement,

e.g. watt-hour meter.

Torque in indicating Instrument

There are three types of torque in an indicating instrument:

(i) Deflecting torque

It is the torque developed in the moving part of an instrument by the electrical quantity applied to the instrument.

(ii) Controlling torque

Controls deflection of the pointer of an instrument and brings the pointer back to zero.

Types Of Controlling Torques

(a) Spring control Controlling torque

In this method, a hair-spring is attached to the spindle of the moving part of the instrument to stop pointer's oscillations.

(b) Gravity control controlling torque

If a pointer is made to move in a vertical plane and a weight is attached to the pointer, then weight tries to attain such a position where it has a least distance from the ground.

(c) Magnetic control controlling torque

Damping torque

It stops oscillations of the pointer of an instrument is.

Methods of Developing Damping torque

(a) Air friction method

In this method, an aluminium piston or vane is attached to the pointer which moves in an air filled chamber and develops damping torque.

(b) Fluid friction method

In this method an aluminium vane is attached to the moving part of the instrument which moves in an oil filled chamber and develops damping torque.

(c) Eddy currents method :

In this method an aluminium disc is attached to the moving part of the instrument and the eddy currents induced in the disc produce the damping torque.

MOVING COIL (M.I.) INSTRUMENT

It is an electrical measuring instrument in which moving part is a coil

Main parts

It consists of following parts :

1. Coil
2. Permanent magnet
3. Two iron pole pieces
4. Axle
5. two hair springs
6. Bobbin, Balancing weights
7. Pointer and scale.

Working principle

A current carrying small, light and rectangular coil is suspended in the magnetic field of a permanent magnet. Magnetic field produced by the current produces a deflecting torque which moves the coil. The pointer attached to the coil indicates the magnitude of current on a p/e-graduated linear scale. _

Conversion of Moving coil meter into

1. Ammeter.

It can be done by connecting a 'shunt' across the coil.

$$R_{sh} = R_m / N - 1$$

where, R_{sh}, = shunt resistance, ohms

R_m = meter coil's resistance, ohms

N = meter multiplier ($\dfrac{I}{I_m}$)

I = circuit current, amperes

I_m = meter current, amperes.

2. Voltmeter.

It can be by connecting a high resistance in series with the coil.

$$R_t = Rm \ (N-1)$$

where, R_{si} = Series resistance, ohms

R_m = Meter coil's resistance, ohms

N = Voltmeter multiplier (V/V_m)

V = Circuit voltage, volts

V_m = Meter voltage, volts.

Merits :

(i) It is a highly sensitive instrument,

(ii) It has a low internal resistance,

(iii) It has a linear scale and a high efficiency.

Demerits :

(i) It can't be used for the measurement of alternating current.

(ii) It can't be used for the measurement of heavy currents (usually above 25 A).

MOVING IRON (M.I.) INSTRUMENT

It is an electrical measuring instrument in which moving part is an iron disc or a vane.

Types of Moving iron Instruments

There are two types of M.I. instruments:

1. Attraction type M.I. Instrument

In this instrument, an eccentric disc is suspended in the electromagnetic field of a fixed coil. When current to be measured is passed through the coil, an electromagnetic field is produced which attracts major portion of the disc. The pointer attached to the disk indicates magnitude of current passed through the coil on a pre graduated scale.

2. Repulsion type M.I. Instrument

In this instrument, a repulsive torque is developed between two iron vanes attached to the axle and body of the meter by the electromagnet of the coil. The pointer attached to the axle indicates magnitude of current passed through the fixed coil on a pre-graduated scale.

Merits :

(i) High amount of current can be measured easily.

(ii) It can measure both DC and AC.

Demerits :

(i) It is not suitable for converting it into a voltmeter.

(ii) Its scale has no uniformity.

OHM-METER

It is the instrument designed to measure resistance of a conductor directly in ohms.

Working principle :

It consists of a DC milliammeter, potentiometer, battery and a fixed resistor. All the components are connected in series. Pointer of the meter shows zero resistance on meeting its two probes. Actually, values of the fixed resistor and potentiometer are adjusted in such a way that pointer shows f.s.d. current which is marked as zero ohm. Therefore zero of an ohm-meter is found to be on right hand side instead of on left-hand side as in case of ammeters and voltmeters.

AVO METER OR MULTIMETER

It is combination of Ammeter, Voltmeter and Ohm-meter.

It is a general purpose meter for a radio-TV or electronic mechanic. It can he used for measuring direct current, AC/DC voltage and ohms. It is also used for testing various electronic components and for fault-tracing in electrical and electronic equipments.

ELECTROSTATIC VOLTMETER

It is a high voltage (kilovolts) measuring instruments. It is designed to work on the electrostatic attraction between two charged plates.

Merits.

(*i*) It is purely a voltmeter having infinite impedance.

(*ii*) The power consumption of the instrument is zero.

(*iii*)It is most suitable for AC voltage measurement.

HOT-WIRE METER

It is a AC/DC current measuring instrument which is based on the heating effect of electric current.

THERMO-COUPLE INSTRUMENT

It is an AC/DC current measuring instrument. It works on the principle that a DC e.m.f. is developed between a pair of rods of different metals when a temperature difference is maintained between the two rods. DC e.m.f. produced by a thermo-couple is used to measure amount of current which may be DC or AC.

A hot-wire meter is suitable to measure 100 MHz current.

Watt-Hour Meter or Energy meter

It is the instrument used to measure electrical power consumption of an equipment or a circuit. It is usually designed to measure kWh (kilo watt hours).

Measure DC Voltage Megger

It is the instrument used for the measurement of resistance of the order of kilo and mega ohms. It is a combination of a hand driven DC generator and an ohm-meter.

Wave Meter

It is the instrument meant for the measurement instrument.

Accuracy of Measuring Instrument

It is the measuring ability of an instrument of measuring accurately an electrical quantity

Clamp tester

It is an AC voltage and current measuring instrument employing induction principle.

Mosaic

In a camera tube, it is an assembly of mutually insulated electron emissive particles which serves to convert the optical image into an electron.

Oscilloscope

It is an instrument using cathode-ray tube to display signal's variation with time. It is also called *scope*. It is an apparatus for rendering visible the waveform of electrical oscillations or alternating currents; consisting of a tube containing nitrogen at a low pressure, with two aluminium electrodes nearly touching, between which a visible discharge takes place extending a distance up the electrodes proportional to the voltage. The waveform is seen by viewing this a rotating mirror. The name is also used for an instrument for indicating by the length of the negative glow in an auxiliary discharge tube, the amount of current passing in an "X" Ray Tube.

Owen Bridge

It is a four-arm bridge used for measurement of inductance in terms of known resistance and capacitance.

Plasma Accelerator

It is an accelerator that forms a high-velocity jet of plasma by using a magnetic field, an electric arc, a travelling wave, or other similar means.

Plasma Anodization

It is method of making passive thin-film circuits by using a low-pressure gas plasma of oxygen ions as the electrolyte to anodize evaporated aluminum films on a glass substrate in a vacuum. The result is an aluminum oxide film, to which aluminum electrodes can be applied.

Qualification tests

Electronics components and subassemblies have to go through severe tests for use in ruggedness equipments in abnormal conditions such as high altitude, hot climate, space applications etc. Qualification tests are performed on sample lots.

These are classified into two

(*i*) Group-I

(*ii*) Group-II

Test methods and conditions are given in referred standards quoted.

ELECTRIC SHOCK

Safety precautions observed by Electronic mechanic

1. Use rubber gloves, shoes, matting etc. to keep himself isolated from the earth contact.

2. Not putting a main-switch ON unless he is sure that no one else is working on the main line.

3. Collect all theoretical details regarding the job to be done by him.

Effects on Human body

It may cause suppression in breathing, reduction in pulse count, blisters on the body and even heart failure.

First aid provided to a victim

1. Release the victim from electric contact by putting the main switch to OFF or by pulling him while keeping yourself isolated from the earthy contact.
2. Loose victim's shoes, clothes etc. and protect him from cold.
3. Give *artificial respiration* if lie is unable to continue normal breathing.

   Simplest method of artificial respiration is

   Mouth to mouth resuscitation.

RECORD PLAYER

It is an equipment which reproduces recorded sound of a phone-records.

Main parts of Record player:

1. Electric motor

2. Turn table

3. Tone arm

4. Pickups

It is a device which produces AF output when its needle moves over a phone-record.

Type of pick-ups.

There are two types of pick-ups:

(i) *Magnetic pick-ups (obsolete now)*

(ii) *Cartridge pick-up*

It consists of a rocshell salt or ceramic crystal pick up associated with an osmium, sapphire or diamond needle. The device works on the principle of piezo electric effect.

Characteristics of a Good quality pick-up

(i) Uniform frequency response over 30 Hz to 12 kHz

(ii) Low mass.

(iii) Low pressure on the record and it should not be more than 20-25 grams.

(iv) High fidelity.

5. Drive Mechanism

Main parts of **drive mechanism of a record** player

(i) **Motor pulley:**

(ii) **Idler or Turn table pulley:**

(iii) **Trippling Device:**

The mechanism employed for switching-off a record players' motor and amplifier etc. after complete play of record is called tripping device.

Tripping mechanism:

(a) **Velocity trip:**

As the tone arm moves lastly in the turn-out groove of the record, the motor and the amplifier get switched-off.

(b) **Ratchet trip:**

In this method, tone arm runs towards the other side of the turn table pivot after complete play of a record and causes the motor etc. to be switched-off.

(iv) **Speed control assembly:**

Motor pulley drives an idle pulley and entire pulley drives the turn table. The different speeds, i.e., 78, 45, $33\frac{1}{3}$ and $16\frac{2}{3}$ rpm are obtained by rotting a speed control knob which turns the idler pulley to various steps of the motor pulley.

Faults commonly arising in record players

(i) Motor does not run

(ii) Motor speed is incurred

(iii) No AF output and

(iv) Defective amplification.

Record changer

It is a sort of record player which automatically changes to the next record after completing the play of its previous record. It contains additional mechanism to work out the stated function.

Phone-record

A phone-record is a shellac or hard plastic disc on which the vibrations of sound signals are stored in the form of up and down or side cuts on its long circuits groove.

Types of phone-records

(i) 78 RPM or NP, normal play record.

(ii) 45 RPM or EP, extended play record.

(iii) $33\frac{1}{3}$ RPM or LP, long play record.

(iv) $16\frac{2}{3}$ RPM or TP, transcription play record.

Stylus pressure gauge

It is a small instrument which is used for measuring stylus pressure acting on the record.

Wheatstone Bridge

It is an arrangement of 4 resistors designed by Mr. Wheat Stone.

Formula

$$\frac{P}{Q} = \frac{R}{S}$$

where, $\dfrac{P}{Q}$ = radio of arm resistances, ohms

R = resistance whose value is so adjusted that no current flows through the galvanometer, ohms

Q = unknown resistance, ohms

Strain Gauge

It is a device that measures strain at the surface of a solid body means of changes in the electrical properties of associated circuits.

Deflection system

It is meant for deflecting the electron beam prepared by electron gun in the horizontal and vertical directions. The system may be electrostatic or electromagnetic type. The later system is more popular because of its more sensitivity.

Sizes of picture Tubes

Picture tubes or CRT are manufactured in 2.5 cm. to 61 cm. size which is measured along the

diagonal of its screen.

Deflection intensity

It is the deflection per volt of an electron beam produced by deflection coils or plates. It is expressed in cm/volts.

Camera Tube

It is a thermonic valve used in TV cameras for converting light and shade picture elements into a video signal.

1. **Main parts**

    (*i*)   Camera, Electron gun

    (*ii*) Photo-sensitive screen.

2. *Electron gun*

    It is a sort of tetrode valve which consists of cathode, filament, accelerating anode, focussing anode and deflection yoke. A 'collector ' mounted along the periphery of screen acts is final anode of the tube. The gun generates a narrow beam of fast moving electrons.

3. *Photo-sensitive screen*

    It is made by sticking a number of silver cesium oxide particles in 625 lines (in general) on a mica sheet. Each particle acts as a tiny capacitor, and it stores electric charge in accordance to the intensity of light falling on it through the camera lens in association with a graphite plate.

Types of camera tubes

1. Iconoscope,
2. Image orthicon
3. Vidicon

TV System

(*i*) TV transmitter and

(*ii*) It consists of -TV: camera and scanning plus sync circuits, video amplifier., AM video transmitter, mike, audio amplifier., FM sound transmitter and antenna.

(*iii*) TV receiver: it consists of dipole antenna, common video and sound section, sound section, video section, sync. and EHT section.

Scanning

It is process of producing video signal by reading the picture elements by an electron beam.

Progressive scanning

In this system, each picture frame is divided in 625 lines (in general). Each lines is composed of thousands of picture elements. The electron beam 'reads' a line from left to right, then it is moved quickly from right to left for the scanning of next line.

Interlaced scanning

In this system, each picture frame is scanned twice. 312.5 lines are scanned in first turn and rest 312.5 lines in the second turn.

Frame frequency

It is the number of picture frames scanned per second. In CSIR (Council for Scientific and Industrial Research) system, it is kept 25 fps for progressive scanning and 50 fps for interlaced scanning.

Line scanning frequency

It is the number of horizontal lines scanned per second. In CSIR system, it is kept 15,625 cps for both types of scanning systems.

Trace and Retrace periods

Time taken by an electron beam in scanning one horizontal line is called *trace period* and the time taken by same in returning back is called *retrace period*.

Synchronization

It is the process of maintaining correct timing of the vertical and horizontal sweep motion and keep the receiver and transmitter locked in step.

Composite video signal

A video signal containing horizontal and vertical sync pulses, horizontal and vertical blanking pulses and equalizing pulses.

Aspect ratio

It is the ratio of width to the height of a TV picture. Its universal value is 4: 3.

Resolution

It is the degree of discrimination of a television image.

Flickering

It is the sensation due to periodic fluctuation in the light intensity of a TV screen.

Horizontal and Vertical Sync Pulses

These two types of pulses are mixed with video signal in order to synchronize TV transmitter and receiver. Frequency of horizontal. Pulses is kept 15,625 cps and that of vert pulses is kept 50 cps.

Voltage level of the two pulses is kept above 75% of the overall signal level.

Blanking pulses

These pulses are also mixed in the video signal for removing electron beam out of CRT screen during *'retrace period'* of scanning or picture building. Their voltage level is kept between 50% to 75% of the overall signal level.

Sync separator

It is a RC network associated to the sync separator stage. Its output is horizontal sync, pulses which is obtained across a resistor.

Integrating circuit

It is also a RC network associated to the sync separator stag. Its output is vert. sync, pulses which is obtained across a capacitor.

AGC stage of a TV receiver

A TV receiver employs a keyed typed AGC circuit which works only for strong signals and not for weak signals. The stage employs a NPN transistor, usually BC 158. A negative AGC bias is derived from the collector terminal to the transistor and the same is applied to RF tuner. AGC bias reduces RF amplification of strong signals and thus overall video and audio output levels are maintained at pre-decided voltage levels.

Raster

It is a basic picture frame prepared by synchronizing and deflection circuits on TV picture tube's screen.

Horizontal Oscillator

It generates a frequency of 15,625 Hz which is used to deflect electron beam of a picture tube in horizontal direction. Its frequency is controlled exactly to 15,625 Hz by applying horizontal sync, pulses.

AFC Circuit

Automatic Frequency Control It necessarily employed for keeping frequency of horizontal sync, pulses exactly to 15,625 Hz. In solid state TV receivers, IC 920 or IC 720 is used for AFC and horizontal oscillator stages.

Horizontal Output amplifier

Horizontal pulses of 15,625 Hz are applied to horizontal deflection coils after amplifying them by a horizontal Output amplifier or a *'line output amplifier'*.

Circuit employs two transistors

(*i*) BD 115 as hor driver

(*ii*) BU 205 as hor output amplifier.

Horizontal hold control

The linearity coil is connected in series with the hor. deflection coils and it helps in maintaining sequence of hor. deflection.

It is a potentiometer which is incorporated in the hor. oscillator stage to control *'rolling'* of picture in horizontal direction.

Vert oscillator

It produces a frequency of 50 Hz which is used to deflect electron beam of a picture tube in vertical direction. Its frequency is controlled exactly to 50 Hz by applying vert. sync. pulses.

Top and Bottom linearity controls

These are two potentiometers of *'pre-set'* type are provided in the vertical section for the alignment of picture display in top -Mid bottom sides respectively.

Height control

It is also a pre-set which is incorporated in vertical section for increasing or decreasing overall height of the picture.

Vert. amplifier

It is a 50 Hz amplifier. It amplifies output of vert oscillator so that same may drive vert deflection coils, in solid state TV receivers. IC-TDA 1044 is used for vert oscillator and vrt amplifier.

Booster capacitor

It is a high working voltage paper capacitor which helps in building up one kilovolts supply required for focussing anode of a picture tube.

Aquadag

Collector ring or *Final anode* of a picture tube is also called *aquadag*.

TV receiver

It is a Hybrid TV receiver based on the use of valves and solid state devices.

- The power supply section of a hybrid TV receiver has to prepare LT-AC for valve filaments and DC ranging from 20 volts to 300 volts. The power supply of a solid state TV receiver has to prepare DC supply only ranging from 10 to 110 volts.

- A zener diode is used to stabilize 27 volts DC applied to the RF tuner.

- VDR is used in vertical section for neutralising the effect of abrupt-voltage variations in the vertical signals.

Probable faults

(*i*) **if only hor./vert. line is present on the TV screen :**

    (*a*) Hor./vert. deflection coil is open.

    (*b*) Hor./vert. section is faulty.

(*ii*) **If the picture is tilted to one side :**

    Either yoke is disturbed or sync coil's alignment is disturbed.

(*iii*) **If the raster is short :**

    Either main supply is low or EHT is low.

(*iv*) If the raster is short

(*a*) Height control is disturbed.

(*b*) Vert. IC-TDA 1044 is defective.

(*c*) Booster capacitor is leaky.

(*v*) If sound is O.K. but picture is absent

(*a*) Video amplifier stage is detective.

(*b*) EHT is absent.

(*c*) PT filament is open.

(*d*) LOT or HUT diode is defective.

(*vi*) If picture is O.K. but sound is absent

(*a*) Sound take-off transformer is detective.

(*b*) Sound section is detective.

(*c*) Loudspeaker is defective.

(*vii*) Ghosting

Either TV's RF tuning is disturbed or antenna's direction is disturbed.

(*viii*) Snow effect :

Either feeder is loose or its connection with antenna has become rusty.

(*ix*) Vert rolling defect :

(*a*) Feeder connections are loose.

(*b*) Vert hold alignment is disturbed.

(*c*) AGC bias is more.

(*d*) VIF section is detective.

(*x*) Poor brightness

Either EHT line or video amplifier is detective.

Colour Television

There are three basic colours.

(*i*) Red

(*ii*) green

(*iii*) blue.

A three electron gun type picture tube is used in colour TV.

Every colour has a specific wavelength. Wavelengths of VIBGYOR (violet, indigo, blue, green yellow orange and red) colours ranges from 38 to 78 angstroms (one angstrom = 10^{-10} metre).

Wavelength of a colour is called its *hue*. Intensity of light (in terms of brightness) of a picture is called its *luminance*.

Percentage of white light present in a colour is called its *saturation*.

If there is not white light mixed to a colour, the same is called *fully saturated.*

Encoding and Decoding in TV system

Mixing of colour information of the simple luminous signals is called *encoding*. It is done at a TV transmitter. Separating process of colour information from a colour composite video signal (CCVS) is called decoding.

Chrominance

It is the video signal containing colour information.

Chroma processor

It is a decoder stage, followed by a triple stage video amplifier.

Television Principles

Pictures appear to move smoothly across the cinema screen because a number of *still pictures* are presented on the screen to the human eye in rapid succession, each *still picture* being slightly different from the proceeding one. Human eye has a characteristics called *persistence of vision*, by which signal to the brain caused by a light-source reaching eye survives for a very short time after the light source is removed. If *still pictures* are presented one after another to the human eye at a rate of more than 16 per second, an illusion of a moving scene is created but in some circumstances there can be significant flicker unless the rate is increased. Therefore, a television system must be designed to present pictures to the human eye from TV receiver at a high enough rate to minimize or eliminate flicker. Within a certain distance from the TV transmitting aerial, according to the amount of radio-frequency power radiated, a TV receiving aerial can pick up the combined vision-and sound-modulated wave to pass it to a TV receiver.

Thermionic Amplifier

Thermionic valve used as an amplifier or magnifier of the scale of the modulations of a telephone current, or trains of oscillations in radio-communication, by taking advantage of the fact that, under suitable conditions, small variations of e.m.f. applied between cathode and grid produce large variations in the current in the anode circuit. Several such valves may be used in cascade, i.e. with the *anode circuit* of one coupled to the Grid circuit of the next, so that several successive stages of amplification are produced.

Methods of Keying

Following methods are used in valve type transmitters

(*i*) Cathode

(*ii*) Blocked grid

(*iii*) Screen grid

(*iv*) Plate keying.

Trapezium Distortion

It is distortion of a trapezoidal pattern on the screen of a cathode ray tube instead of a square one and occurs when the deflecting voltage applied to plates is unbalanced with respect to the anode.

Wien Bridge

It is an A.C. bridge method of measuring dielectric losses in which capacitance to be tested and standard condenser form two arms, and variable resistances the other two.

Wire Wound Resistor

In this, the resistance wire such as nichrome wire is wound on a round hollow porcelain core. This assembly is coated with an enamel containing powdered glass. Commonly such resistors come in the range of upto 100 kΩ resistance.

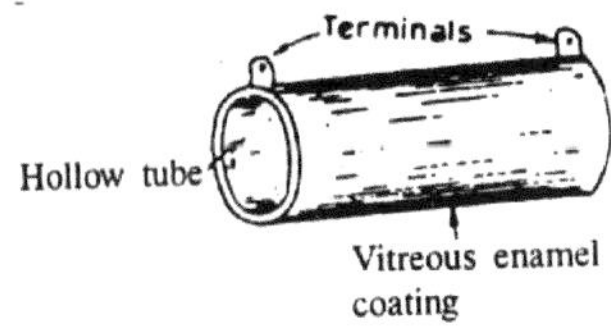

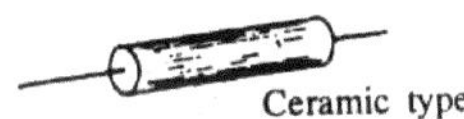

Xerography

It is a photographic technique of making copies of documents that uses electrical effects to form an image.

It is done by an intensity-modulated beam of ultraviolet radiation to leave a charge pattern corresponding to the brightness information of the original document.

DECIMAL MULTIPLE FACTORS

Prefix	Symbol	Factor
Deca	da	10^1
hecto	h	10^2
kilo	K	10^3
mega	M	10^6
giga	G	10^9
tera	T	10^{12}
peta	P	10^{15}
exa	E	10^{18}

SUBMULTIPLE FACTORS

deci	d	10^{-1}
centi	c	10^{-2}
milli	m	10^{-3}
micro	μ	10^{-6}
nano	n	10^{-9}
pico	p	10^{-12}
fcmto	f	10^{-15}
atto	a	10^{-18}

EXERCISE – I

1. Which one of the following statement is not correct ?

    (a) It is not possible to have precise measurement which are not accurate

    (b) Correctness in measure ment requires both accuracy and precision

    (c) Reproducibility and consistency are expressions that best describe precision in measurements

    (d) An instrument with 2% accuracy is better than another with 5% accuracy

2. The voltage of a circuit is measured by a voltmeter having an input impedence comparable with the output impedance of the circuit thereby causing error in voltage measurement. This error may be called

    (a) Gross error

    (b) Random error

    (c) Error caused by misue of instrument

    (d) Error caused by loading effect

3. The units whose sizes cannot be choosen independently are called

    (a) Derived units

    (b) Fundamental units

    (c) Absolute units

    (d) Auxiliary fundamental units

4. Thermocouples are

    (a) passive transducers (b) active transducers

    (c) both (a) and (b)   (d) output transducers

5. Three types of temperature transducers are compared as regards their sensitivity. The order in which they exhibit their sensitivities (highest to lowest) is

    (a) Thermistors, RTDs, thermocouples

    (b) Thermocouples, RTDs, thermistors

    (c) RTDs, thermistors, thermocouples

    (d) RTDs, thermocouples, thermistors

6. The temperature transducers exhibit no–linear behaviour. The order in which they exhibit no linearity (highest to lowest) is

    (a) Thermocouples, RTD, thermistors

    (b) Thermistors, thermocouples, RTDs

    (c) RTDs, thermocouples, thermistors

    (d) Thermistors, RTDs, thermocouples

7. Some wire-wound resistors have bifilar winding. This type of winding is used to

    (a) increase the thermal stability

    (b) reduce the tolerance

    (c) reduce the inductance of winding

    (d) double the power rating of the resistance

8. If practical units of voltage and current wave each made 20 times as large as they are at present, what would be the consequent alteration in the size of the unit of capacitance?

(a) 200 times   (b) 60 times

(c) 20 times   (d) Nil

9. What will happen if a voltmeter is connected like an ammeter in series to the load ?

(a) Meter will burn out

(b) Measurment will be too high

(c) Inadmissably high current will flow

(d) Almost no current in the circuit

10. If 1000 ohms/V meter is used to measure a resistance on 150 V scale, then meter resistance is

(a) 150 kΩ (b) 1 kΩ

(c) 6.67 ohms   (d) 0.001 ohm

11. Platinum is the commonly used metal for RTDs because

(a) platinum has a constant value of resistance temperature co-efficient of 0.0004/°C for a temperature range between 0 to 100° C.

(b) resistivity of platinum tends to increase less rapidly at higher temperatures

(c) platinum is available in pure form for commercial applications and has stability over higher ranges of temperature

(d) all of these

12. RTDs use the principle of change of resistance with temperature. The properties of a conductor material to be used as an element of an RTD should possess which of the following properties ?

(a) Change in resistance per unit change in temperature should be as small as possible

(b) Resistance of the materials should not have a continuous ad stable relationship with temperature

(c) Change of resistance with temperature should not be a linear function

(d) All of these

13. A vertical amplifier for a CRO can be designed for

(a) only a high gain

(b) only a broad bandwidth

(c) a constant gain times bandwidth product

(d) all of these

14. Effective reactance of an inductive coil

(a) increases because of stray capacitance as the frequency increases

(b) decreases because of stray capacitances as the frequency increases

(c) remain the same irrespective of the increase in frequency even if stray series capacitances are present

(d) none of these

15. DC voltage of the order of a few mV can be measured accurately using a / an

(a) moving coil voltmeter

(b) null-balancing potentiometer.

(c) moving iron voltmeter

(d) electrostatic voltmeter

16. *Accuracy* of a measuring instrument is determined by

(a) closeness of the value indicated by it to the correct value of the measurand

(b) repeatablity of the measured value

(c) speed with which the instruments's reading approaches the final value.

(d) least change in the value of the measurand that could be detected by the instrument.

17. Sensitivity of an instrument is the

(a) smallest increment in the input that can be detected with certainty

(b) largest input change to which the instrument fails to respond

(c) ratio of the change in the magnitude of the output to the corresponding change in the magnitude of the input

(d) closeness of the output values for repeated applications of a constant input.

18. Measurement of a quantity is a/an is an act of comparison of an unknown quantity with

(a) another quantity.

(b) a known quantity whose accuracy may be known or may not be known.

(c) a predefined acceptable standard which is accurately known.

(d) none of these

19. Voltage of a circuit is measured by a voltmeter having an input impendence comparable with the output impedance of the circuit thereby causing error in voltage measurement. This error may be called

(a) Gross error

(b) Random error

(c) Error caused by misuse of instrument

(d) Error caused by loading effect

20. In a.c. circuits, connection of measuring instruments cause loading errors which may affect

(*a*) only magnitude of quantity being measured

(*b*) only phase of the quantity being measured

(*c*) both magnitude and phase of the quantity being measured

(*d*) magnitude, phase and also waveform of the quantity being measured.

21. High torque to weight ratio in an analog indicating instrument indicates

(*a*) high friction loss

(*b*) low friction less

(*c*) nothing as regards friction loss

(*d*) none of these

22. In order to reduce errors on account of temperature, instruments are provided with shunts use series connected swamping resistance. In order that errors on account temperature changes be low, the swamping resistance should

(*a*) be made of a material giving a high resistance temperature co-efficient

(*b*) be made of a material having a low resistance temperature co-efficient with the value of swamping resistance equal to meter resistance

(*c*) be made of a material having low resistance temperature co-efficient and should have a value of about 20 30times that of meter resistance

(*d*) have an infinite value

23. Disadvantages of shunts for use at high currents is/are

(*a*) Difficult to achieve good accuracy with shunts

(*b*) Power consumption of the shunts is large

(*c*) Metering circuit is not electrically isolated from the power circuit

(*d*) all of these

24. At high frequency, accuracy of all the measuring meters

(*a*) increases

(*b*) decreases

(*c*) remains same

(*d*) depends upon type of meter

25. There will be serious errors, if power factor of non-sinusoidal waveforms is measured by electrodynamometer power factor meters. This is true of

(*a*) only single phase meters

(*b*) only 3 phase meters

(*c*) both single and three phase meters

(*d*) none of these

26. Power consumption of a d.c. voltmeter using a direct coupled amplifier when measuring a voltage 0.5 V is of the order of a few

(*a*) watt   (*b*) milliwatt

(*c*) microwatt   (*d*) nanowatt

27. A true rms reading voltmeter uses two thermocouples in order

(*a*) to increase sensitivity

(*b*) that second thermocouple cancels out the nolinear effects of the first thermocouple

(*c*) to prevent drift in the d.c. amplifier

(*d*) all of these

28. Advantages of instrument transformers is/are

(*a*) readings of instruments used in conjunction with them do not depend upon their resistance, inductance etc.

(*b*) readings of instruments transformers have been standardized and the rating of instruments used in conjunction used with them also get standardized. Therefore, there is reduction of cost and ease in replacements.

(*c*) metering circuit is electrically isolated from the power circuit thereby providing safety to operating personnel.

(*d*) all of these.

29. Errors in current transformers can be reduced by designing them with

(*a*) high permeability and low loss core materials, avoiding any joints in the core and also keeping the flux density to a low value.

(*b*) using primary and secondary windings as close to each other as possible

(*c*) using large cross-sections for both primary and secondary winding conductors

(*d*) all of these

30. Turns compensation is used in current transformers primarily for reduction of

(*a*) phase angle error

(*b*) both ratio and phase angle errors

(*c*) ratio error reduction in phase error is incidental

(*d*) none of these

31. A certain oscilloscope with 4 cm by 4 cm screen has its own speed output fed to its input at the x and y sensitivities are same. The oscilloscope will display a

(*a*) triangular wave   (*b*) diagonal line

(*c*) sine wave   (*d*) circle

32. In CRT aquadag carries

(*a*) aqueous solution of araphite

(*b*) sweep voltage

(*c*) secondary emission electrons

(*d*) none of these

33. If transients during switching of a power supply are to be studied, the which of the following oscilloscope will be preferred?

(a) An ordinary oscilloscope with high frequency sweep generator

(b) Dual beam oscilloscope

(c) Dual trace oscilloscope

(d) Storage oscilloscope

34. A signal of 10 mV at 75 MHz can be measured with which of the following instruments ?

(a) VTVM

(b) Cathod ray oscilloscope

(c) Moving iron voltmeter

(d) Digital multimeter

35. In measurements made using a Q-meter, high impedance elements should preferably be connected in

(a) star   (b) delta

(c) series   (d) parallel

36. Which meter is suitable for the measurement of 10 m V at 50 MHz ?

(a) Moving-iron voltmeter

(b) VTVM

(c) Electrostatic voltmeter

(d) C.R.O.

37. To minimize loading of the circuit under test, input impedance of a CRO

(a) be low

(b) be high

(c) be capacitive

(d) match with the output impedance of the circuit

38. Function of measurement systems is/are

(a) indicating function (b) recording function

(c) controlling function (d) all of these

39. Microprocessor based systems which are increasingly being used for dedicated applications in process instrumentation are

(a) inteligent instrumentation systems

(b) dumb instrumentation systems

(c) control instrumentation systems

(d) both (a) and (b)

40. Terms *Information* and *Signals* are usually considered as synonymous because

(a) information is the data or details relating to an object or event

(b) signals carry information about magnitude or time relating to an object or event i.e., a physical quantity

(c) both (a) and (b)

(d) none of these

41. Repeatability describes the closeness of output readings for the same input

(a) when same input is applied repetitively over a short period under same conditions of environments

(b) when there are changes in method of measurement under same conditions of environments

(c) both (a) and (b)

(d) none of these

42. In drift

(a) when calibration gradually shifts due to slippage, permanent set, zero drift sets in

(b) when there is proportional change in the indication all along the upward scale, the drift is called span drift or sensitivity drift

(c) when the drift occurs over a portion of span of an instrument, it is zonal drift

(d) all of these

43. Which of the following is true for accuracy?

(a) Accuracy is the closeness with which an instrument reading approaches the true value of the quantity being measured

(b) Point accuracy is the accuracy of the instrument only at one point on its scale

(c) When an instrument has uniform scale, its accuracy may be expressed in terms of scale range

(d) All of these

44. Largest deviation from the mean is

(a) range of doubt   (b) possible error

(c) either (a) or (b)   (d) standard deviation

45. Match list I with list II and select the correct answer from the codes given below the lists.

List -I	List-II
A. A device whose output is enlarged version of output	1. Calibration
B. The act or process of making adjustments or makings on scale so that the instruments readings conform to accepted standards	2. Signal
C. Measures and generates an opposing effect to maintain zero deflection	3. Amplifier
D. An action to convey information detector.	4. Null type

Codes :

	A	B	C	D
(a)	3	1	4	2
(b)	2	1	4	3
(c)	3	4	1	2
(d)	3	2	4	1

46. In modern measurement systems, undesirable static characteristics are

(a) dead zone

(b) drift

(c) static error and non-linearity

(d) all of these

47. In AC circuits, the connection of measuring instruments causes loading errors which may affect the measurand's

(a) magnitude   (b) phase

(c) waveform   (d) all of these

48. Backlash is

(a) unwanted signal tending to obscure the transducer signal

(b) maximum angle or distance through which any part of mechanical system may be moved in one direction without causing motion of the next part

(c) departure of instrument output from its calibrated value

(d) all of these

49. Uncertainty distribution is used to analyse

(a) single sample data   (b) multi sample data

(c) both (a) and (b)   (d) none of these

50. Active transducer is

(a) Photo emissive cell (b) Photo voltaic cell

(c) Selsyn   (d) All of these

51. Lower limit of useful working range of a transducer is determined by its

(a) error   (b) noise

(c) both (a) and (b)   (d) none of these

52. Resistance potentiometer is a zero order instrument with increase of load to potentiometer resistance, its non-linearity

(a) decreases

(b) increases

(c) increase as square root of the resistance

(d) remains constant

53. A capacitive transducer is working on the principle of change of capacitance with dis-placement. It exhibits non-linear characteristics. To make it linear, which of the following is used?

(a) Differential connection

(b) Measure very small displacement

(c) OPAMP

(d) All of these

54. Piezoelectric transducers are active transducers and they use Quartz and Rochelle salt, because they

(a) are polycrystalline in nature

(b) are basically made of barium titanate

(c) do not have piezo electric properties in their original state but these properties are created by special polarization on them

(d) all of these

55. Measurement of a quantity or a variable is an act of comparison of an unknown quantity

(a) or a variable with a predefined acceptable standard which is accurately known

(b) or a variable with another quantity or variable

(c) with a known quantity whose accuracy may be known or may not be known

(d) none of these

56. Measurement finds application in

(a) automatic control of processes and operations

(b) engineering experimental analysis

(c) monitoring of processes and operations

(d) all of these

57. Desirable static characteristics in the measurement systems is/are

(a) sensitivity   (b) reproducibility

(c) accuracy   (d) all of these

58. Multimeters are provided with separate scale for low a.c. voltages to

(a) have high accuracy

(b) improve readability of the scale

(c) both (a) and (b)

(d) none of these

59. A voltmeter with a broadband width has

(a) high noise level and high sensitivity

(b) low noise level and low sensitivity

(c) low noise level and high sensitivity

(d) high noise level and low sensitivity

60. A very accurate voltmeter gives an accurate reading when used for measuring voltage across a low resistance because

(a) meter sensitivity is too low

(b) meter senitivity is too high

(c) voltmeter is taking too low current

(d) higher scale has been selected

61. The maching interpretable outputs for an analog transducer can be had from

(a) teletypewriter

(b) punched cards and tapes

(c) magnetic tapes

(d) all of these

62. If an information is required to be stored over a short interval of time, which of the following is used ?

(a) CRO with photographic equipment

(b) Storage type oscilloscope

(c) Single number devices

(d) Direct writing recorder or a magnetic tape recorder

63. When measuring strain, ballast circuits use a capacitor to act as high pass filter. This is done when

(a) both static and dynamic strains are being measured

(b) dynamic strains are being measured

(c) static strains are being measured

(d) none of these

64. A signal gate in an electronic counter is to

(a) integrate the numerical display

(b) display the count

(c) control the duration of actual count

(d) to supply precise increments of time for frequency.

65. A flip-flop that produces one output pulse after receiving two input pulses is called

(a) binary circut   (b) negative pulse

(c) reset terminal   (d) stable state

66. Output of an and gate assume the 1-state only if all the

(a) inputs assume negative state

(b) inputs assume 1-state

(c) output assumes negative state

(d) none of these

67. INVERTER circuit has a

(a) single input and single output

(b) single input and multiple output

(c) multiple input and single output

(d) multiple input and multiple output.

68. Passive transducers are

(a) resistance and inductance

(b) resistance and capacitance

(c) capacitance and inductance

(d) any of these

69. Self generating transducers are

(a) externally powered

(b) not externally powered

(c) any of them

(d) none of them

70. Which of the following does not require auxiliary circuitry if used as transducer ?

(a) capacitance   (b) photocell

(c) resistance   (d) inductance

71. Plantiunum resistance thermometer can be used to measure the temperature upto

(u) 0–500°C   (b) 0–1000°C

(c) 0–5000°C   (d) 0–15000°C

72. Basic elements of an oscillation transducer are

(a) resistance and capacitance

(b) resistance and inductance

(c) inductance and capacitance

(d) any of the above

73. Smallest input signal to the instrument which produces detectable output of instrument is called

(a) resolution

(b) threshold sensitivity

(c) (a) or (b)

(d) sensitivity

74. Load cell cannot be used to measure

(a) pressure   (b) level

(c) weight   (d) volume

75. Most common method in thermocouple temperature measurement involves using a

(a) stroboscope   (b) strain gauge

(c) computer   (d) potentiometer

76. Thermisters are ideally suited to measure

(a) temperature over short spans

(b) temperature over long span

(c) temperature of bearing of motors

(d) temperature of motor winding

77. Sensing element of Resistance Temperature Detector may consist of

(a) coil

(b) foil

(c) thin film deposited material

(d) either (a) or (b) or (c)

78. Third wire in 3-wire RTD is used for

(a) dropping the voltage across RTD

(b) increasing the life of RTD

(c) providing better connection to the process

(d) compensation of lead wire resistance

79. Four leads in the RTD are used with

(a) single element RTD

(b) dual element RTD

(c) three element RTD

(d) four element RTD

80. Fluxmeter is used to determine
  (*a*) magnetic field strength
  (*b*) pressure
  (*c*) temperature
  (*d*) current

81. Magnetic tapes are used for
  (*a*) displaying the results
  (*b*) amplifying the signal
  (*c*) preserving the data and reproducing at later stage
  (*d*) none of these

82. Rotameter is uses to measure
  (*a*) rotary motion   (*b*) flow
  (*c*) linear motion   (*d*) level

83. Differential pressure transmitter with square root extractor used for flow measurement will have
  (*a*) non-linear scale   (*b*) linear scale
  (*c*) mass flow   (*d*) flow rate scale

84. Which of the following parameter can not be measured by ring-balance meter ?
  (*a*) Differential pressure
  (*b*) Pressure
  (*c*) Mass-flow rate
  (*d*) Flow

85. Variation in ambient temperature will affect the accuracy of
  (*a*) RTD   (*b*) thermocouples
  (*c*) thermisters   (*d*) thermometers

86. A thermister can be used to control
  (*a*) level of water tank (*b*) altitude
  (*c*) temperature   (*d*) all of these

87. Potentiometric instruments are normally
  (*a*) high frequency devices
  (*b*) low frequency devices
  (*c*) low frequency devices with frequency limit to 10 Hz
  (*d*) high frequency devices with frequency limit to 100 kHz

88. Hartley oscillator uses
  (*a*) coil with tap to ground
  (*b*) R-F circuit
  (*c*) L-C circuit
  (*d*) none of these

89. Wien bridge oscillator is used to generate
  (*a*) square wave
  (*b*) saw tooth wave
  (*c*) sine wave in audio frequency range
  (*d*) none of these

90. LVDT is a
  (*a*) capacitive tranducer
  (*b*) resistive transducer
  (*c*) inductive transducer
  (*d*) none of these

91. Which of the following is used for generation of pulses?
  (*a*) Diode   (*b*) CRO
  (*c*) Transformer   (*d*) Table multivibrator

92. Calibration of electronic voltmeter is done by
  (*a*) CRO   (*b*) Hay's bridge
  (*c*) multimeter   (*d*) 10 k potentiometer

93. Form factor of a sinusoidal wave is
  (*a*) 1   (*b*) 1.11
  (*c*) 1.2   (*d*) 1.3

94. Input impedance of an analog voltmeter should be
  (*a*) higher than impedance of circuit
  (*b*) zero
  (*c*) 1Ω
  (*d*) none of these

95. Digital voltmeter eliminates
  (*a*) interpolation errors (*b*) parallel error
  (*c*) slow speed   (*d*) all of these

96. Q meter measures
  (*a*) electrical properties of coils and capacitor
  (*b*) magnetic properties of coils and capacitors
  (*c*) either (*a*) or (*b*)
  (*d*) none of these

97. Active differentiators can be used in
  (*a*) compensating networks
  (*b*) electronic controller
  (*c*) phase compensation
  (*d*) all of these

98. Active differentiators can be used in
  (*a*) compensating networks
  (*b*) electronic controller
  (*c*) phase compensation
  (*d*) all of these

99. Piezoelectric transducer is used to measure
  (*a*) voltage   (*b*) force
  (*c*) frequency   (*d*) velocity

100. Potentiometer can be used on
  (*a*) a.c. only   (*b*) d.c. only
  (*c*) both (*a*) and (*b*)   (*d*) none of these

101. In velocity transducers, damping is obtained
  (*a*) mechanically   (*b*) electrically
  (*c*) magnetically   (*d*) all of these

102. Resistance thermometer uses

(a) platinum   (b) copper

(c) nickel   (d) all of these

103. In a thermocouple, thermal emf–depends upon

(a) temperature between junctions

(b) temperature of cold junction

(c) temperature of hot junction

(d) none of these

104. Automatic potentiometers are used for

(a) automatic recording by temperature on chart

(b) automatic process control

(c) both (a) and (b)

(d) none of these

105. Lissajous pattern obtained on CRO is used to determine

(a) amplitude of applied signal

(b) current in a circuit

(c) phase shift and frequency

(d) distortion in a system

106. Major application of constantan is in

(a) precision resistances

(b) thermocouples

(c) transistors

(d) heater elements for valves

107. Measurement finds application in

(a) automatic control of processes and operations

(b) engineering experimental analysis

(c) substituting dynamic parts

(d) both (a) and (b)

108. A null type of instrument as compared to a deflection type instrument has

(a) lower sensitivity   (b) faster response

(c) higher accuracy   (d) all of these

109. Accuracy is

(a) deviation from the true value

(b) closeness to true value

(c) measure of responsibility

(d) none of these

110. Error is defined as

(a) deviation from the true value

(b) smallest measurable value

(c) ratio of output signal response to the change in input signal

(d) none of these

111. Purely mechanical instruments cannot be used for dynamic measurements because they have

(a) higher response time

(b) high inertia

(c) large time constant

(d) all of these

112. Undesirable static characteristic in measurement systems,

(a) drift, static error and dead zone

(b) sensitivity and accuracy

(c) reproducibility and non-linearity

(d) drift, static error, dead zone and non-linearity

113. Desirable static characteristics are in the measurement systems is

(a) sensitivity   (b) reproducibility

(c) accuracy   (d) all of these

114. Purpose of CRO probe is to

(a) improve CMRR of input stage of CRO

(b) Do impedance matching

(c) compensate for cable and CRO input capacitance

(d) measure high voltage by potential division

115. A CRO has an electron gun having

(a) grid   (b) cathode

(c) focussing   (d) all of these

116. In a CRO spot deflections related to its applied voltage V and deflection sensitivity S as

(a) $V \times S^2$ (b) S/V

(c) V/S (d) $V \times S$

117. A CRO can be used to measure

(a) waveform   (b) frequency

(c) voltage   (d) all of these

118. When phase shift between same frequency signals applied to both horizontal and vertical plates is 90°, then figure on the screen is

(a) circle   (b) parabola

(c) straight line   (d) hyperbola

119. An aquadag is used in a CRO to collect

(a) secondary emission electrons

(b) primary emission electrons

(c) both (a) and (b)

(d) none of these

120. Source of emission of electrons in a CRT is

(a) acceleration anodes

(b) barium and strontium oxide coated cathode

(c) PN junction diode

(d) none of these

121. A vertical amplifier for a CRO can be designed for
  (*a*) constant gain times bandwidth product
  (*b*) only a high gain
  (*c*) only a broad bandwidth
  (*d*) none of these

122. Main controls in CRO are
  (*a*) intensity   (*b*) focus
  (*c*) position   (*d*) all of these

123. Pulse rise time is defined as the time taken by the pulse to go from
  (*a*) 0% to 90% of its amplitude
  (*b*) 10% to 90% of its amplitude
  (*c*) 10% to 100% of its amplitude
  (*d*) 0% to 100% of its amplitude

124. Sensitivity of an instrument is independent of
  (*a*) amplitude distortion
  (*b*) frequency response
  (*c*) both (*a*) and (*b*)
  (*d*) none of these

125. Accuracy is
  (*a*) measure of the consistency or reproducibility of the measurement
  (*b*) closeness with which an instrument reading approaches the true value of the quantity being measured
  (*c*) smallest measurable input change
  (*d*) ratio of the change in output signal of an instrument to a change in the input

126. In electrical measuring instruments, electrical energy is converted into
  (*a*) mechanical energy (*b*) heat energy
  (*c*) chemical energy   (*d*) sound energy

127. Voltmeter should be of very high resistance so that
  (*a*) its range is high
  (*b*) its accuracy is high
  (*c*) it may draw current to minimum possible extent
  (*d*) its sensitivity is high

128. If a voltmeter is connected like an ammeter in series with the load
  (*a*) measurement reading will be too high
  (*b*) almost no current will flow in the circuit
  (*c*) meter will burnout
  (*d*) an admissibly high current will flow

129. If an ammeter is connected like a voltmeter across the load circuit, then
  (*a*) reading will be too low
  (*b*) almost no current will flow through the meter
  (*c*) in-admissible high current will flow and meter may burn out
  (*d*) loading effect will be low

130. A moving iron ammeter coil has few turns of thick wire in order to have
  (*a*) high sensitivity
  (*b*) effective damping
  (*c*) low resistance and large current carrying capacity
  (*d*) large scale

131. A moving iron voltmeter coil has large number of turns of their wire in order to have
  (*a*) high resistance and draw a current as small as possible
  (*b*) high sensitivity
  (*c*) effective damping
  (*d*) large scale

132. A moving iron ammeter, when used on a.c. circuits, indicates
  (*a*) mean value of current
  (*b*) r.m.s. value of current
  (*c*) peak value of current
  (*d*) equivalent dc value of current

133. If connections of a moving iron voltmeter connected in a circuit are interchanged, then the voltmeter
  (*a*) will not give any deflection
  (*b*) will deflect in opposite direction
  (*c*) reading will remain unaffected
  (*d*) will burn off

134. Moving iron instruments normally have
  (*a*) spring control and pneumatic damping
  (*b*) spring control and eddy current damping
  (*c*) gravity control and pneumatic damping
  (*d*) gravity control and eddy current damping

135. Moving iron instrument can be used as
  (*a*) ammeter for measuring direct as well as alternating current
  (*b*) voltmeter for measuring direct as well as alternating voltage
  (*c*) for measuring direct currents and voltages
  (*d*) both (*a*) and (*b*)

136. Advantage of moving iron instrument is that
  (*a*) its sensitivity is high
  (*b*) it has linear scale
  (*c*) it can be used at high frequencies
  (*d*) it can be used under severe load conditions

137. Dynamometer type moving coil instruments are provided with
  (*a*) eddy current damping
  (*b*) pneumatic damping
  (*c*) fluid friction damping
  (*d*) electrostatic damping

138. Electro-dynamometer type moving coil instruments are mainly used as
 (a) indicator type instruments
 (b) standard instruments for calibration of other instruments
 (c) transfer instruments
 (d) both (a) and (b)

139. Electro-dynamometer type instrument reads actually
 (a) average value   (b) peak value
 (c) r.m.s. value   (d) instantaneous value

140. Gassing is the phenomenon which occurs in
 (a) cells
 (b) oil transformers
 (c) mercury arc rectifiers
 (d) both (a) and (b)

141. Measure of reproductibility of measurement is called
 (a) Resolution   (b) Precision
 (c) Fidelity   (d) Accuracy

142. Ratio of the measured quantity at full scale to the power taken by the instrument is
 (a) Instrument efficiency
 (b) Instrument sensitivity
 (c) Instrument resolution
 (d) Instrument fidelity

143. Difference between indicated value and true value of a quantity is called
 (a) relative error   (b) absolute error
 (c) gross error   (d) dynamic error

144. Varactor is a diode used as a
 (a) variable capacitor   (b) variable inductor
 (c) variable resistor   (d) high speed switch

145. Frequency errors in capacitors
 (a) decrease with frequency
 (b) increase with frequency
 (c) decrease with square of frequency
 (d) have no relation with frequency

146. Which of the following cannot measure current?
 (a) Electrostatic ammeter
 (b) Thermocouple wattmeter
 (c) Moving iron voltmeter
 (d) Electrodynamometer wattmeter

147. For instrument with very weak magnetic field which of the following is used ?
 (a) Air friction damping
 (b) Oil friction damping
 (c) Eddy current damping
 (d) None of these

148. All meters used for measuring currents, voltages and resistance etc. are basically
 (a) voltmeters   (b) ohm meters
 (c) multimeters   (d) current-meters

149. Mutual inductance can be determined by
 (a) Kuriyama method
 (b) Felici method
 (c) Heaviside-campbell bridge
 (d) Butterworth's method

150. In measurent with bridge method, common errors developed are
 (a) leakage errors   (b) eddy current errors
 (c) residual errors   (d) all of these

151. Most accurate method for measument of medium resistance is
 (a) Kelvin's Method
 (b) Substitution method
 (c) Wheat-stone bridge
 (d) Ammeter-voltmeter method

152. A resistance of 75 kΩ lies in the range of
 (a) low resistance   (b) high resistance
 (c) medium resistance (d) none of these

153. Which of the following is used to measure low impedance components ?
 (a) Series connection Q meter
 (b) Parallel connection Q meter
 (c) Both (a) and (b)
 (d) None of these

154. Which of the following is used to measure high impedance components ?
 (a) Series connection Q meter
 (b) Parallel connection Q meter
 (c) Both (a) or (b)
 (d) None of these

155. Which of the following is used for measurement of low resistance ?
 (a) Wein bridge   (b) Schering bridge
 (c) Maxwell's bridge   (d) Anderson bridge

156. Method used for measurement of medium resistance is
 (a) Kelvin Double bridge method
 (b) Wein bridge
 (c) Potentiometer
 (d) Substitution method

157. Insulating materials are used to
 (a) store very high currents
 (b) prevent short circuit between conducting wires
 (c) conduct very large current
 (d) prevent open circuit between voltage source and the load

158. Self balancing potentiometer is used for
  (a) industrial measurements
  (b) vibration measurements
  (c) experimental measurements
  (d) recorders

159. In slide wire potentiometer, frequency and waveform of supply should be
  (a) different as that of the voltage to be measured
  (b) same as that of the voltage to be measured
  (c) both (a) or (b)
  (d) none of these

160. Magnetometers are used for the measurement of
  (a) magnetic field   (b) electric field
  (c) electrostatic field   (d) none of these

161. Sensitive magnetometers require
  (a) lower permeability of alloy
  (b) higher permeability of alloy
  (c) higher susceptability of alloy
  (d) lower susceptability of alloy

162. Inaccurancy in balancing the bridge circuit is attributed to
  (a) thermo e.m.f.
  (b) resistance of the bridge
  (c) battery of the circuit
  (d) temperature

163. For a B.H curve, the ratio of ΔB to ΔH is called
  (a) flux density
  (b) incremental magnetization force
  (c) incremental permeability
  (d) M.M.F.

164. Grosset fluxmeter in a special type of ballastic galvanometer in which
  (a) controlling torque is small and damping is heavy
  (b) controlling torque is large and damping is heavy
  (c) controlling torque is large and damping is small
  (d) controlling torque is small and damping is small

165. Damping of ballastic galvanometer is kept very small
  (a) to make the system critically damped
  (b) in order to get first deflection is small
  (c) in order to get first deflection is large
  (d) to make system oscillating

166. To measure high Q inductors, bridge preferred is
  (a) Sohering bridge   (b) Hay's Bridge
  (c) Wien bridge   (d) Maxwell bridge

167. Damping in a ballastic galvanometer follows
  (a) exponential decay   (b) exponential rise
  (c) hyperbolic decay   (d) logarithmic decay

168. Hall effect is used for the measurement of
  (a) flux density of the field
  (b) charge
  (c) voltage
  (d) power

169. No picture, No sound, No raster, the trouble is in
  (a) Vertical oscillator   (b) R.F amplifier
  (c) Horizontal amplifier (d) None of these

170. Curie balance is used for the measurement of
  (a) flow   (b) pressure
  (c) susceptability   (d) permeability

171. Interlacing is used in T.V. because
  (a) it ensures scanning all lines on the screen
  (b) it vertical sync signals are not needed
  (c) it reduces flicker
  (d) it gives feeling of picture movement

172. In cables, induction testing method is used to find
  (a) short circuit fault   (b) earth fault
  (c) open circuit fault   (d) (b) or (c)

173. Breakdown of the insulation of the cable is called
  (a) earth fault   (b) short circuit fault
  (c) open circuit fault   (d) both (b) or (c)

174. Loop tests are applied to find
  (a) ground fault of the cable
  (b) open circuit fault
  (c) short circuit fault
  (d) both (a) or (c)

175. When insulation of the cable becomes faulty, the fault is
  (a) open circuit   (b) earth fault
  (c) short circuit fault   (d) none of these

176. Voltage drop test of cables is done
  (a) on single cable
  (b) when a second cable runs parallel to faulty one
  (c) with Llyod Fischer square
  (d) both (a) and (b)

177. Thermocouple meter can be used to measure
  (a) A.C. only
  (b) D.C. only
  (c) both A.C. and D.C.
  (d) none of these

178. Thermocouple meters are generally used for the measurement of

(a) A.C.

(b) D.C.

(c) high frequency A.C.

(d) low frequency A.C.

179. A band pass filter is usually designed as

(a) low pass filter followed by a high pass filter

(b) high pass filter followed by a low pass filter

(c) have a parallel tuned circuit.

(d) have a series tuned circuit

180. In the design of composite filler, the end half m derived sections are included to

(a) Realize required pass band characteristics

(b) Realize required stop band characteristics

(c) Achieve equal phase characteristics

(d) Realize constant value of characteristic impedance over operating frequency.

181. All the components in a parallel resonant circuit are ideal. The value of Q is

(a) R/WL   (b) WL/R

(c) R/WC   (d) W/RC

182. Which of the following instruments will be used to measure the temperature above 1400°C ?

(a) Thermometer

(b) Resistance pyrometer

(c) Thermo-electric pyrometer

(d) none of these

183. Standard method for measurement of temperature is

(a) mercury thermometer

(b) gas thermometer

(c) potentiometer

(d) none of these

184. Tangent galvanometer is

(a) absolute instrument

(b) primary instrument

(c) secondary instrument

(d) none of these

185. A voltmeter should have

(a) zero resistance   (b) low resistance

(c) high resistance   (d) infinite resistance

186. Which of the following instruments can be used to measure only a.c. currents ?

(a) Moving iron   (b) Induction type

(c) Hot wire   (d) Electrodynamic

187. Electrostatic instruments rely for their operation upon

(a) current

(b) voltage

(c) power

(d) force that exists between two oppositely charged plates

188. Which of the instruments are free from hysteresis and eddy current loss ?

(a) Moving iron

(b) Moving coil

(c) Electrodynamometer

(d) Electrostatic

189. In the moving coil instruments, torque is proportional to

(a) inductance of instruments

(b) first derivative of inductance with time

(c) first derivative of inductance with deflection angle

(d) none of these

190. Which of the following instruments have self balancing property ?

(a) Ammeters   (b) Galvanometric type

(c) Potentiometric type (d) Digital type

191. Internal resistance of the voltmeter is

(a) zero   (b) very small

(c) infinite   (d) very high

192. Internal resistance of an ammeter will be

(a) zero   (b) large

(c) infinite   (d) very small

193. Movement of the moving element of an electrical indicator dependent on

(a) restoring torque

(b) number of turns of the coil

(c) resistance of the indicator circuit

(d) all of these

194. Eddy current error does not exist in

(a) a.c. moving iron instruments

(b) d.c. moving iron instruments

(c) both (a) and (b)

(d) none of these

195. Moving iron instrument can read upto frequency of

(a) 5 kHz   (b) 1500 Hz

(c) 1 Hz   (d) 2500 Hz

196. Motor meters can be used to measure

(a) d.c. energy   (b) a.c. energy

(c) a.c. or d.c. energy (d) none of these

197. Induction wattmeters can be used to measure

(a) a.c. power

(b) d.c. power

(c) a.c. or d.c. power

(d) none of these

198. Pointer deflection of watt meter is proportional to

(a) torque produced

(b) current

(c) voltage

(d) either (a) or (c)

199. Principle type of current meter being employed is

(a) D' Arsonel Galvanometer

(b) electromagnetic

(c) thermal

(d) electrostatic

200. Most of the multimeters are of

(a) analog type

(b) digital type

(c) logical type

(d) graphical type

201. When it is required to measure an a.c. voltage with a d.c. component, then

(a) use output function of the multimeter

(b) use d.c. scale and subtract

(c) subtract D.C. reading from the a.c.

(d) none of these

202. When d.c. voltmeter is connected with polarities reversed, then

(a) pointer deflects down scale

(b) pointer remains stationary

(c) meter gets damaged

(d) pointer goes as usual

203. In a moving coil meter pole pieces are used to

(a) overcome damping

(b) provide damping

(c) yield accurate results

(d) none of these

204. Which of the following is commonest method of measuring 3-phase balanced or unbalanced power?

(a) One wattmeter method

(b) Two wattmeter method

(c) Three wattmeter method

(d) Four wattmeter method

205. Which of the following errors may arise in the wattmeter if it is not compensated for the errors?

(a) Voltage coil inductance

(b) Voltage coil capacitance

(c) Eddy currents

(d) All of these

206. Wattmeter

(a) has potential and current coils to measure the real power

(b) can measure d.c. power but not of 100 Hz frequency

(c) has 3 connections but two of them used

(d) none of these

207. In moving coil meters, scale used is

(a) linear

(b) non-linear

(c) square law

(d) none of these

208. Meter which measures d.c. only is

(a) moving coil

(b) moving iron

(c) thermo couple

(d) none of these

209. In moving coil meters, damping is provided by

(a) separate pair of magnets called damping magnets

(b) coil wound on a frame

(c) aluminium frame on which main coil is wound

(d) none of these

210. In moving iron meters, scale used is

(a) linear

(b) non-linear

(c) square law

(d) none of these

211. Instruments used to measure a very high in order to have

(a) high voltage range

(b) minimum current through the meter

(c) maximum loading effect

(d) more current supplied by the voltage source

212. Internal resistance of the milliameter must be very low for

(a) high accuracy

(b) high sensitivity

(c) maximum voltage drop across the meter

(d) minimum effect of the current in the circuit

213. When voltage is measured by a multimeter, the multiplier for voltage is

(a) a high resistance in series with the meter movement

(b) a high resistance in parallel with the meter movement

(c) less than one ohm in series with the meter movement

(d) less than one ohm in parallel with the meter movement

214. When ohmmete is used, the applied voltage to the circuit being checked is disconnected because

(a) voltage source will increase the resistance

(b) current will decrease the resistance

(c) ohmmeter has its own battery

(d) none of these

215. A shunt in a current meter is a resistance

(a) connected in series to increase its range

(b) connected across the metre to reduce its range

(c) connected across the meter to increase its range

(d) none of these

216. Shunts have

(a) very high resistance

(b) high resistance

(c) low resistance

(d) zero resistance

217. Range of voltmeter can be increased by connecting a

(a) low resistance in parallel

(b) low resistance in series

(c) resistance of high value in series with the meter movement

(d) none of these

218. In shunt Ohmmeter, maximum deflection signifies

(a) maximum resistance

(b) minimum resistance

(c) fault in the meter

(d) none of these

219. To connect ammeter in series

(a) open the circuit at one point and use the meter to the circuit

(b) open the circuit at +ve and –ve terminals of voltage source

(c) the short the resistance to be checked and connect the meter across it

(d) none of these

220. Voltage source can be converted into constant current source by adding

(a) high resistance in series with the voltage source

(b) low resistance in series with the voltage source

(c) low resistance in parallel with the voltage source

(d) high resistance in parallel with the voltage source

221. Moving coil instrument is used to measure

(a) direct current   (b) d.c. and a.c.

(c) low frequency a.c.   (d) high frequency a.c.

222. d.c. probes are generally used with a voltmeter to

(a) decrease its range

(b) increase its range

(c) filter a.c. signal

(d) none of these

223. Decibal scale is used to measure the level of

(a) dc signal   (b) a.c. signal

(c) a.c. current   (d) none of these

224. Purpose of rectifier in a multimeter is to

(a) filter d.c. voltage

(b) protect meter movement

(c) change from ac to dc

(d) change from d.c. to a.c.

225. An oscilloscope indicates

(a) peak to peak value of voltage

(b) d.c. voltage value

(c) rms value of a.c. voltage

(d) –ve peak value

226. Lissajous patterns can be used to determine

(a) phase shift

(b) voltage amplitude

(c) amplitude distortion

(d) frequency distortion

227. Which of the following instruments will be used to measure 500 k.V. a.c. voltage ?

(a) Moving coil voltmeter

(b) Moving iron voltmeter

(c) Hot wire instrument

(d) Electrostatic voltmeter

228. Deflection of hot wire instruments depends on

(a) voltage

(b) average value of current

(c) r.m.s. value of a.c.

(d) instantaneous value of a.c.

310. A RC circuit consists of a capacitor of $1\ \mu F$ in series with a resistor of $5\ k\Omega$. A d.c. voltage of 50 V is suddenly applied across the circuit. The value of voltage after 5 milliseconds will be

(a) 10.5V   (b) 25.3V

(c) 31.6V   (d) 44.6 V

230. Instrument used to measure a.c. is

(a) attraction type moving iron

(b) parmanent magnet

(c) induction type

(d) none of these

231. Torque produced in a wattmeter is proportional to
(*a*) average value of supply voltage
(*b*) r.m.s. value of currents in the two coils
(*c*) average value of currents in the two coils
(*d*) r.m.s. value of voltage

232. Higher the ohm/volt, rating of a voltmeter
(*a*) higher the sensitivity
(*b*) lower the sensitivity
(*c*) greater the accuracy
(*d*) none of these

233. Megger is used for measuring
(*a*) high voltages   (*b*) high currents
(*c*) high resistances   (*d*) high capacitances

234. In an oscilloscope, signal to be measured is applied to
(*a*) X–X input
(*b*) Y–Y input
(*c*) either X–x or Y–Y input
(*d*) none of these

235. Voltmeter used for very high frequency range is
(*a*) electrostatic voltmeter
(*b*) moving iron voltmeter
(*c*) moving coil
(*d*) thermionic voltmeter

236. Length of the sweep in a CRT is controlled by
(*a*) sync. control   (*b*) horizontal gain
(*c*) vertical gain   (*d*) none of these

237. Three-phase, four-wire energymeter is used to measure
(*a*) two phase energy
(*b*) single phase energy
(*c*) three phase balanced energy
(*d*) three phase unbalanced energy

238. Energymeter universally accepted to measure AC energy is
(*a*) motor meter
(*b*) induction type
(*c*) mercury motor meter
(*d*) electrostatic

239. Induction type single phase energymeter is
(*a*) ampere hour   (*b*) watt-hour meter
(*c*) wattmeter   (*d*) VAR meter

240. Creeping occurs in
(*a*) voltmeter   (*b*) wattmeter
(*c*) energymeter   (*d*) ammeter

241. Steady speed of the disc in the energymeter is achieved when
(*a*) braking torque is zero
(*b*) operating torque is equal to braking torque
(*c*) operating torque is half of braking torque
(*d*) operating torque is twice the braking torque

242. Fundamental frequency or standard frequency is that of
(*a*) rotation of earth   (*b*) rotation of moon
(*c*) rotation of sun   (*d*) none of these

243. Radio frequency is measured by
(*a*) weston frequency meter
(*b*) resonance frequency meter
(*c*) hetrodyne frequency meter
(*d*) none of these

244. Power factor meters have
(*a*) current coil   (*b*) voltage coil
(*c*) both (*a*) and (*b*)   (*d*) none of these

245. For paralleling of two alternators, which of the following meter is used ?
(*a*) power factor meter (*b*) frequency meter
(*c*) voltmeter   (*d*) synchroscopes

246. Secondary of the current transformer is always short circuited through low resistance ammeter or low resistance
(*a*) to get accurate measurement
(*b*) to avoid excessive current in the primary
(*c*) because current in the primary is not determined by load in primary
(*d*) none of these

247. Ratio error in the current transformer is attributed to
(*a*) power factor of the primary
(*b*) leakage flux
(*c*) exciting current
(*d*) wattless component of the current in primary

248. Material used for the core of current transformer should have
(*a*) high reluctance and low iron loss
(*b*) high reluctance and high iron loss
(*c*) low reluctance and high iron loss
(*d*) low reluctance and low iron loss

249. When secondary winding of current transformer is opened, then AT of primary will
(*a*) decrease   (*b*) increase
(*c*) remain same   (*d*) none of these

250. Primary of CT has

(a) thicker wire than secondary

(b) thinner wire than secondary

(c) same thick wire as secondary

(d) none of these

251. Transformer having secondary current of same order as magnetising current is

(a) CT

(b) PT

(c) power transformer

(d) distribution transformer

252. Percentage harmonic distortion is accurately measured with

(a) VTVM (b) oscilloscope

(c) vertical gain (d) none of these

253. Electrostatic voltmeter measures voltage

(a) directly

(b) by effect of current

(c) by effect of thermo emf

(d) none of these

254. A low Q factor has

(a) Flat response

(b) Peaked response

(c) Lower losses

(d) Higher losses and flat response.

255. Turns compensation in CT is used to

(a) eliminate ratio error

(b) eliminate phase angle error

(c) get transformation ratio equal to nominal ratio of transformer

(d) none of these

256. Carrier signal produced in a signal generator may be

(a) square (b) sinusoidal

(c) pulsed (d) all of these

257. Purpose of square wave output from an audio-oscillator is to

(a) test for phase distortion

(b) test for amplitude distortion

(c) test wide band amplifiers

(d) calibrate an oscilloscope

258. A CRO

(a) is a CRT plus additional accessories

(b) is same as CRT

(c) does not contain CRT

(d) none of these

259. Which of the following instrument is basically a charge meter ?

(a) D' Arsonval galvanometer

(b) Vibration galvanometer

(c) Duddel's oscillograph

(d) Ballistic galvanometer

260. Most of the instruments used in the power system's work are based on the principle of

(a) moving iron

(b) moving coil

(c) rectifier type

(d) electrodynamometer type

261. Deflection of hot wire instrument depends on

(a) average value of current

(b) r.m.s. value of a.c.

(c) instantaneous value of a.c.

(d) none of these

262. Multirange instruments generally have

(a) multicoil arrangement inside the meter

(b) multiple series or shunt resistance inside the meter

(c) dimension setting feature with the coil

(d) none of these

263. Which of the following is most sensitive ?

(a) Spot galvanometer

(b) Vibration galvanometer

(c) D' Arsonval galvanometer

(d) Pointer galvanometer

264. Which of the following can't be measured on ballistic galvanometer ?

(a) Capactitance (b) Inductance

(c) Charge (d) Current

265. Instrument transformers are usually used to extend the range of

(a) moving coil (b) moving iron

(c) induction type (d) electrostatic type

266. Common specification for secondary of CT are

(a) 1 A and 2 A (b) 2 A and 1 A

(c) 1.5 A and 3 A (d) 1 A and 5 A

267. Burden is associated with

(a) CT

(b) PT

(c) both (a) and (b)

(d) any electrical measuring instrument

268. Which of the following principle can not be used for designing a wattmeter ?

(*a*) Moving ironz

(*b*) Thermocouple type

(*c*) Electrodynamometer

(*d*) Electrostatic type

269. Angle between true load voltage and the instrument voltage for a VAR meter is

(*a*) 30° (*b*) 45°

(*c*) 60° (*d*) 90°

270. LVDT are preferred to pressure transducers because they have

(*a*) high sensitivity and ruggedness

(*b*) infinite resolution and low hysteresis

(*c*) linear characteristic for displacement upto 5 mm

(*d*) all of these

271. Four resistors are connected in series. Their values are 28.4Ω, 4.25Ω, 56.605Ω and 0.75Ω with an uncertainty of one unit in the last digit in each. Total series resistance (significant figures only) will be equal to

(*a*) 90Ω (*b*) 79Ω

(*c*) 78.5Ω (*d*) 79.225Ω

272. Change in capacitance in a transducer is measured with

(*a*) a.c. bridge

(*b*) oscillator circuit

(*c*) loss of charge method

(*d*) none of these

273. Disadvantage of capacitive transducer is

(*a*) sensitivity to pressure variations

(*b*) telemetery problems

(*c*) possibility of distorted signals due to long lead length

(*d*) none of these

274. Vector voltmeter is used for measuring

(*a*) filter transfer function

(*b*) complex insersion loss

(*c*) amplifier gain and phase shift

(*d*) all of these

275. Which meters have best accuracy ?

(*a*) Moving iron

(*b*) Moving coil

(*c*) Hot wire

(*d*) Thermocouple

276. A VTVM is more reliable as compared to multimeter for measuring voltage across low impedance because

(*a*) its sensitivity is very high

(*b*) it offers high input impedance

(*c*) it does not alter the measured voltage

(*d*) all of these

277. Duty cycle of a pulse of width 2 microsec and repetition frequency 4 kHz is

(*a*) 0.55 (*b*) 0.055

(*c*) 0.008 (*d*) 0.0006

278. Bridge used for measurement of inductance is

(*a*) Wheatstone Bridge (*b*) Kelvin Double Bridge

(*c*) Anderson Bridge (*d*) Schering Bridge

279. Bridge used for measurement of capacitance is

(*a*) Wheatstone Bridge (*b*) Kelvin Double Bridge

(*c*) Anderson Bridge (*d*) Scheong Bridge

280. A three and half digit voltmeter could measure a maximum voltage of

(*a*) 100 volts (*b*) 1000 volts

(*d*) 2000 volts (*d*) 10,000 volts

281. Lissajou's figures are used in a CRO while measuring

(*a*) Voltage magnitude (*b*) Voltage gain

(*c*) Frequency (*d*) Wave form

282. Which of the following is not used as an R.F. oscillator?

(*a*) Wien Bridge (*b*) Hartly

(*c*) Colpitts (*d*) Clapp

283. A decade counter needs

(*a*) 10 flip-flops (*b*) 4 flip-flops

(*c*) 5 flip-flops (*d*) 2 flip-flops

284. In crystal oscillators, valuable properties of a crystal are

(*a*) High Q and low L/C ratio

(*b*) High Q and L/C ratio

(*c*) Low Q and high L/C ratio

(*d*) Low Q and low L/C ratio

285. A series capacitance used in a filter circuit represents

(*a*) Low-pass (*b*) Band-pass

(*c*) High-pass (*d*) None

286. Linearity of time base waveforms can be improved by using

(*a*) Larger time constant

(*b*) High gain

(*c*) Larger value components

(*d*) Larger power supply voltages

287. The resistance of a circuit is measured by measuring current and power flow through the circuit. If limiting errors in the measurement of power and current are respectively $\pm 1.5\%$ and $\pm 1.0\%$, then limiting error in the measurement of resistance will be

(a) $\pm 1.5\%$
(b) $+ 2.5\%$
(c) $\pm 3.5\%$
(d) $\pm 5.5\%$

288. Nominal value of a resistor is $\pm 0.1\%$. A voltage is applied across the resistor and power consumed is estimated by the relation

$$P = E^2/R$$

The measured values of E and I are

$$E = 100V \pm 1\%$$
$$I = 10A \pm 1\%$$

The uncertainty in the power determination will be nearly

(a) 0.5%
(b) 0.23%
(c) 3.2%
(d) 23%

289. A set of ten independent measurements is given below : 1.570, 1.597, 1.591, 1.562, 1.577, 1.580, 1.564, 1.586, 1.550, and 1.575. The arithmetic mean is equal to?

(a) 1.501
(b) 1.5156
(c) 1.5704
(d) 1.5752

290. Which of me following magnetic material has least value of (B.H.)?

(a) Carbon Steel
(b) Cobalt steel
(c) Alnico
(d) Alcomax

291. Manganin is an alloy of

(a) copper, manganese and nickel
(b) copper, zinc and lead
(c) copper, aluminium and chromium
(d) copper, chromium and cadmium

292. Which is a Major application of constantan?

(a) Precision resistances
(b) Thermocouples
(c) Transistors
(d) Heater elements for valves.

293. Ryall crest voltmeter is used to measure

(a) peak voltage
(b) d.c. voltage
(c) all of the above
(d) r.m.s. voltage

294. Helipots are

(a) multi-turn potentiometers
(b) deects in metallic tranducers
(c) primary transducers for X-ray measurements
(d) none of these

295. Gauge factor for doped crystals is in the range

(a) 0.5 to 1
(b) 1 to 2
(c) 2 to 20
(d) 100 to 5000.

296. A nixie tube is a

(a) is a display device
(b) a.c. to d.c. converter
(c) d.c. to a.c. converter
(d) device for reducing distortion

297. In case of strain gauges, gauge factor 'k' is related to poissons ratio 'μ' by the relation

(a) $\mu = k + \frac{1}{2}$
(b) $\mu = k - \frac{1}{2}$
(c) $k = 1 - \mu$
(d) $k = 1 - 2\mu$

298. A three digit 0-1 V digital voltmeter will have a resolution of

(a) 0.15 V
(b) 1/3V
(c) 0.1 V
(d) 1 mV

299. The principle of working of thermocouple vacuum gauge is Variation of

(a) pressure of gases with temperature.
(b) thermal conductivity of gases with pressure
(c) kinetic energy of gases with pressure
(d) none of the above.

300. An accelerometer has a seismic mass of 0.05 kg and a spring constant of 3×10^3 N/m. Maximum mass displacement of + 0.02 m before the mass hits the stop. Maximum measurable acceleration will be equal to

(a) 400 m/s^2
(b) 600 m/s^2
(c) 800 m/s^2
(d) 1200 m/s^2

301. The dead zone in a certain pyrometer is 0.125 per cent of span. The calibration is 4000°C to 10000°C. What temperature change might occur before it is delected?

(a) 0.075°C
(b) 0.75°C
(c) 4.5°C
(d) 5°C

302. The transducers that convert input physical phenomenon into an electrical output in the form of pulses are called

(a) Secondary transducers
(b) Tuned transducers
(c) Analogue transducers
(d) Digital transducers

303. A digital voltmeter has a read-out range from 0 to 9999 counts. Resolution of the instrument in volts when full scale reading is 9.999 V will be equal to

(a) 1 μA
(b) 0.1 μV
(c) 1m μV
(d) 10 m μV

EXERCISE – II

1. DC voltage of the order of a few mV can be measured accurately using a / an **DMRC 2013**
   (a) moving coil voltmeter
   (b) null-balancing potentiometer.
   (c) moving iron voltmeter
   (d) electrostatic voltmeter

2. In measurements made using a Q-meter, high impedance elements should preferably be connected in **DMRC 2013**
   (a) star　　　　(b) delta
   (c) series　　　(d) parallel

3. Lissajous pattern obtained on CRO is used to determine **DMRC 2013**
   (a) amplitude of applied signal
   (b) current in a circuit
   (c) phase shift and frequency
   (d) distortion in a system

4. A CRO has an electron gun having **DMRC 2013**
   (a) grid　　　　(b) cathode
   (c) focussing　(d) all of these

5. If an ammeter is connected like a voltmeter across the load circuit, then **DMRC 2013**
   (a) reading will be too low
   (b) almost no current will flow through the meter
   (c) in-admissible high current will flow and meter may burn out
   (d) loading effect will be low

6. Megger is used for measuring **DMRC 2013**
   (a) high voltages　　(b) high currents
   (c) high resistances　(d) high capacitances

7. Loading effect is primarily caused by instruments having **DMRC 2014**
   (a) high resistance　(b) high sensitivity
   (c) low sensitivity　(d) high range

8. Measurement of an unknown voltage with a dc potentiometer loses its advantage of open-circuit measurement when **DMRC 2014**
   (a) the primary circuit battery is changed
   (b) standardization has to be done again to compensate for drifts
   (c) voltage is larger than the range of the potentiometer
   (d) range reduction by a factor of 10 is employed

9. The difference between the measured value and the true value is called **DMRC 2014**
   (a) gross error　　(b) relative error
   (c) probable error　(d) absolute error

10. A dual-trace CRO has **DMRC 2014**
   (a) one electron gun
   (b) two electron guns
   (c) one electron gun and one two-pole switch
   (d) two electron guns and one two-pole switch

11. A $3\frac{1}{2}$ digit voltmeter having a resolution of 100 mV can be used to measure maximum voltage of **DMRC 2014**
   (a) 100 V　　　(b) 200 V
   (c) 1000 V　　(d) 5000 V

12. A 300 V full-scale deflection voltmeter has an accuracy of ±2%, when it reads 222 V. The actual voltage **DMRC 2014**
   (a) lies between 217.56 V and 226.44 V
   (b) lies between 217.4 V and 226.6 V
   (c) lies between 216 V and 228 V
   (d) is exactly 222 V

13. The sensitivity of a voltmeter using 0 to 5 mA meter movement is **DMRC**
   (a) 50 ohm/volt　　(b) 100 ohm/volt
   (c) 200 ohm/volt　(d) 500 ohm/volt

14. An LVDT is used to measure displacement. The output of the LVDT is connected to a voltmeter of range 0 to 5 V through an amplifier having a gain of 250. For a displacement of 0.5 mm, the output of the LVDT is 2 mV. The sensitivity of the instrument would be **DMRC**
   (a) 0.1 V/mm　　(b) 0.5 V/mm
   (c) 1 V/mm　　　(d) 5 V/mm

15. It is required to measure temperature in the range of 1300°C to 1500°C. The most suitable thermocouple to be used as a transducer would be
   (a) Chromel-constantan **DMRC**
   (b) Iron-constantan
   (c) Chromel-alumel
   (d) Platinum-rhodium

16. A certain oscilloscope with 4 cm by 4 cm screen has its own speed output fed to its input at the x and y sensitivities are same. The oscilloscope will display a **DRDO**
   (a) triangular wave
   (b) diagonal line
   (c) sine wave
   (d) circle

17. When ohmmete is used, the applied voltage to the circuit being checked is disconnected because

(a) voltage source will increase the resistance

(b) current will decrease the resistance

(c) ohmmeter has its own battery

(d) none of these **DRDO**

18. Which of the following instruments will be used to measure 500 k.V. a.c. voltage ? **DRDO**

(a) Moving coil voltmeter

(b) Moving iron voltmeter

(c) Hot wire instrument

(d) Electrostatic voltmeter

19. A VTVM is more reliable as compared to multimeter for measuring voltage across low impedance because **DRDO**

(a) its sensitivity is very high

(b) it offers high input impedance

(c) it does not alter the measured voltage

(d) all of these

20. Thermocouples are **DRDO**

(a) passive transducers (b) active transducers

(c) both (a) and (b) (d) output transducers

21. Effective reactance of an inductive coil **DRDO**

(a) increases because of stray capacitance as the frequency increases

(b) decreases because of stray capacitances as the frequency increases

(c) remain the same irrespective of the increase in frequency even if stray series capacitances are present

(d) none of these

22. If transients during switching of a power supply are to be studied, the which of the following oscilloscope will be preferred? **DRDO**

(a) An ordinary oscilloscope with high frequency sweep generator

(b) Dual beam oscilloscope

(c) Dual trace oscilloscope

(d) Storage oscilloscope

23. Which of the instruments are free from hysteresis and eddy current loss ? **DRDO**

(a) Moving iron

(b) Moving coil

(c) Electrodynamometer

(d) Electrostatic

24. Some wire-wound resistors have bifilar winding. This type of winding is used to **RRB**

(a) increase the thermal stability

(b) reduce the tolerance

(c) reduce the inductance of winding

(d) double the power rating of the resistance

25. A dynamometer type wattmeter with a single scale marked for the smallest power range, has two current ranges, namely, 0-5 A and 0-10 A as well as two voltage ranges, namely, 0-150 V and 0-300 V. To carry out a load test on a 230 V/115 V, 1kVA, single phase transformer, the wattmeter is used on the high voltage side. The voltage and current ranges are chosen for maximum utilization of the scale. The multiplying factor to be used in this case is **RRB**

(a) 0.5 (b) 1.0

(c) 2.0 (d) 4.0

26. During intravascular measurement of arterial blood pressure, catheters may be introduced in different configurations, as shown in the figures below :

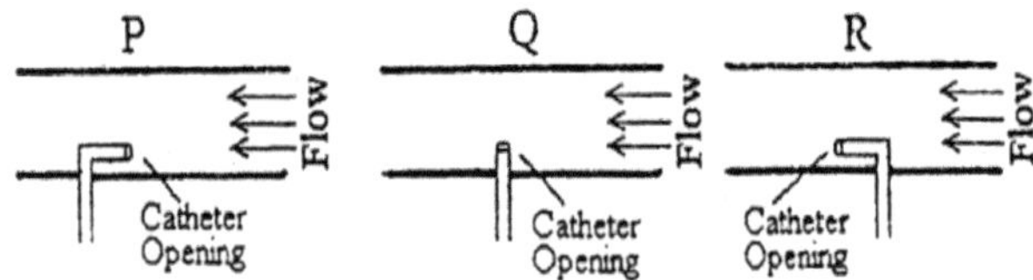

The static pressure will be measured correctly in the configuration (s) **RRB**

(a) P and Q but not in R

(b) R only

(c) Q only

(d) P and R but not in Q

27. Two sensors have measurement errors that are Gaussian distributed with zero means and variances σ_1^2 and σ_2^2, respectively. The two sensor measurements x_1 and x_2 are combined to form the weighted average $x = \alpha x_1 + (1-\alpha)x_2, 0 \leq \alpha \leq 1$. Assuming that the measurement errors of the two sensors are uncorrelated, the weighting factor α that yields the smallest error variance of x is

(a) $\dfrac{\sigma_2^2}{\sigma_1^2 + \sigma_2^2}$ (b) $\dfrac{\sigma_1^2}{\sigma_1^2 + \sigma_2^2}$ **RRB**

(c) $\dfrac{\sigma_2}{\sigma_1 + \sigma_2}$ (d) 0.5

28. A thermometer with time constant τ, initially at the ambient temperature, is used to measure the temperature of a liquid in a bath. The excess temperature of the thermometer and the liquid over the ambient are $\theta(t)$ and $\theta l(t)$, respectively, where t denotes the time. If $\theta l(t) = kt$, where k is a constant, the steady state error, defined as $\lim\limits_{t\to\infty} [\theta(t) - \theta l(t)]$, is **RRB**

(a) ∞ (b) 0

(c) $-k$ (d) $-k\tau$

29. In a laminar flow experiment, Fluid A is pumped through a straigth tube and the volumetric flow rate and pressure drop per unit length are recorded. In a second straight tube having twice the internal diameter of teh first one, Fluid B records the same pressure drop per unit length at the same volumetric flow rate. Assuming fully developed flow conditions in the tubes, the ratio of the dynamic viscosity of Fluid B to that of Fluid A is **RRB**

(a) 16   (b) 32

(c) 64   (d) 128

30. A measurement system for the rotational speed of a motor is shown in the ehfigure below. The system consists of an opaque disk attached to the motor shaft with a hole as shown. A light source and a photodetector are placed on two sides of the disk so that whenever the hole cross the light path, the photodetector receives light through the hole. THe photodetector circuit is also shown below. Assume sufficient light intensity and TTL logic levels for the inverter.

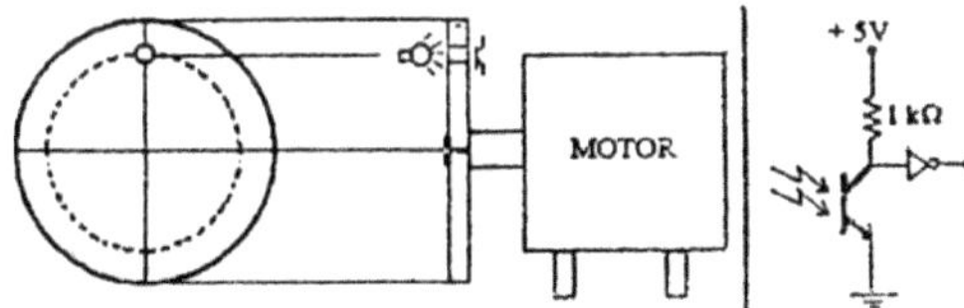

The output the photodetector is a   **RRB**

(a) triangular wave

(b) square wave with 50% duty cycle

(c) rectangular wave with duty cycle close to unity

(d) rectangular wave with duty cycle close to zero

31. A pH electrode, being used at $25°C$, has a source resistance of $10^{10}\Omega$. The electrode obeys the Nernst equation perfectly. The electronic voltmener, with which the potential is being measured, has an input impedance of $10^{11}\Omega$ and a gain of 100. If the pH of the analyte changes from 6.5 to 7.8, the change in voltage observed on the voltmeter is   **RRB**

(a) less than 6.8 V

(b) between 6.8 V and 7.19 V

(c) between 7.2 V and 7.49 V

(d) greater than 7.49 V

32. The linear sweep for the time base in an oscilloscope has deviation from its nominal waveform. The nominal (dashed line) and actual (solid line) sweep waveforms are shown in the following figure.   **RRB**

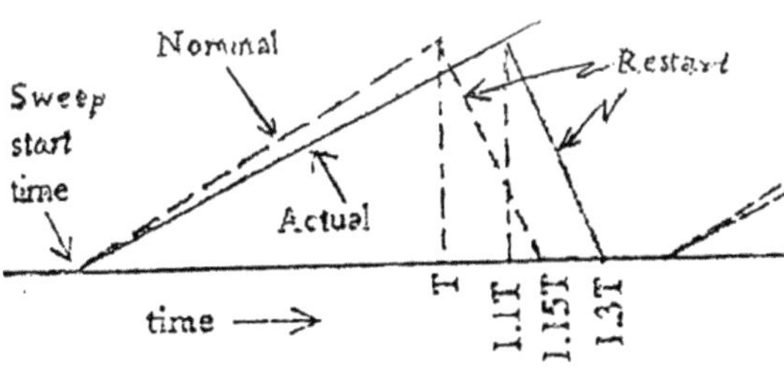

A 5V p-p sine wave with a frequency of 1 kHz will be measured on the oscilloscope as a sine wave with

(a) 4.45 V p-p and 1 kHz frequency

(b) 5 V p-p and 1 kHz frequency

(c) 5 V p-p and 1.1 kHz frequency

(d) 5 V p-p and 1.15 kHz frequncy

33. The figure shows a potentiometer of total resistance RT with a sliding contact.   **RRB**

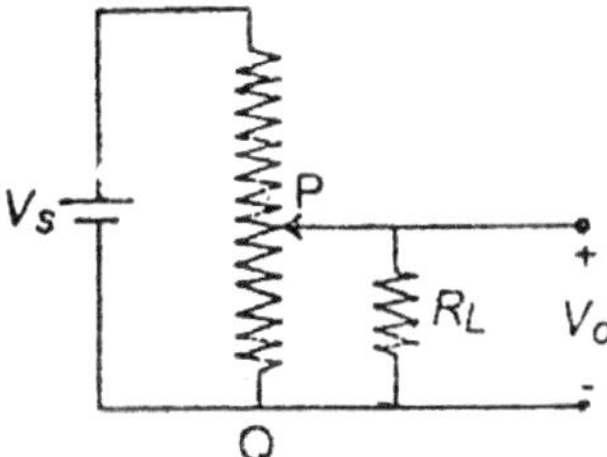

The resistance between the points P and Q of the potentiometer at the position of the contact shown is R_C and the voltage ratio $\dfrac{V_O}{V_S}$ at this point is 0.5. If the ratio $\dfrac{R_L}{R_T} = 1$, the ratio $\dfrac{R_c}{R_T}$ is

(a) $\dfrac{-1+\sqrt{5}}{2}$ (b) $\dfrac{1+\sqrt{5}}{2}$

(c) $-1+\sqrt{5}$ (d) $1+\sqrt{5}$

34. The speed of a gear having 60 teeth is measured using a proximity sensor. The output of the proximity sensor is fed to a counter with a gating time of 1s. The counter indicates a value of 120. The speed at which the gear is rotating is **RRB**

(a) 60 rpm

(b) 120 rpm

(c) 600 rpm

(d) 1200 rpm

35. A piezoelectric type accelerometer has a sensitivity of 100 mV/g. The transducer is subjected to a constant acceleration of 5 g. The steady state output of the transducer will be   **RRB**

(a) 0V   (b) 100 mV

(c) 0.5 V   (d) 5 V

36. A strain gauge has a nominal resistance of 600 Ω and a gauge factor of 2.5. The strain gauge is connected in a dc bridge with three other resistances of 600 Ω each. The bridge is excited by a 4 V battery. If the strain gauge is subjected to a strain of 100μm/m, the magnitude of the bridge output will be **RRB**

(a) 0V   (b) 250 μ V

(c) 500 μ V   (d) 750 μ V

37. To reduce the effect of fringing in a capacitive type transducer, **RRB**

(a) the transducer is shielded and the shield is kept at ground potential

(b) a guard ring is provided and it is kept at ground potential

(c) the transducer is shielded and the shield is kept at the same potential as the moving plate

(d) a guard ring is provided and it is kept at the same potential as the moving plate

38. A 2 A full-scale PMMC type dc ammeter has a voltage drop of 100 mV at 2 A. The meter can be converted into a 10 A full-scale dc ammeter by connecting a **RRB**

(a) 12.5 mΩ resistor in parallel with the meter

(b) 12.5 mΩ resistor in series with the meter

(c) 50.0 mΩ resistor in parallel with the meter

(d) 50.0 mΩ resistor in series with the meter

39. A $3\frac{1}{2}$ digit, 200 mV full scale DVM has an accuracy specification of ± 0.5 % of reading plus counts. When the meter reads 100mV, the voltage being measured is **RRB**

(a) any value between 99.5 mV and 100.5 mV

(b) any value between 99.0 mV and 101.0 mV

(c) exactly 99.5 mV

(d) exactly 100 mV

40. The two-wattmeter method is used to measure power in a 3-phase, 3-wire balanced inductive circuit. The line voltage and line current are 400 V and 10 A respectively. If the load power factor is 0.866 lagging, then readings of the two wattmeters are **RRB**

(a) 6000 W and 0 W

(b) 5000 W and 1000 W

(c) 4500 W and 1500 W

(d) 4000 W and 2000 W

41. Consider the AC bridge shown in the figure below, with A, L and C having positive finite values.

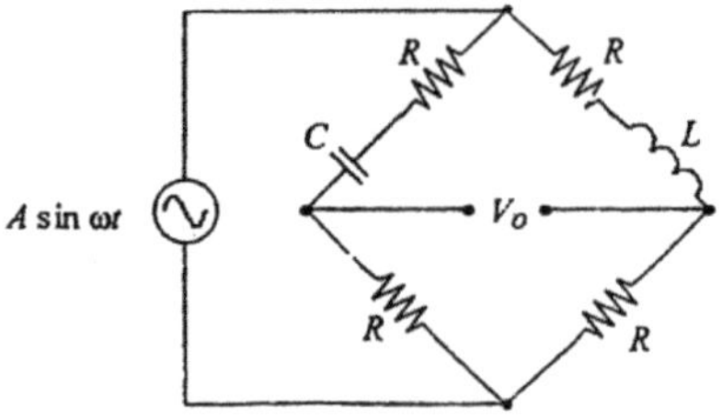

Then

(a) $V_0 = 0$ if $\omega L = \dfrac{1}{\omega C}$ **RRB 2012**

(b) $V_0 = 0$ if $L = C$

(c) $V_0 = 0$ if $R = \dfrac{1}{\omega\sqrt{LC}}$

(d) V_0 cannot be made zero

42. Consider a non-ideal voltage source whose output voltage is measured by a non-ideal voltmeter as shown below. **RRB 2012**

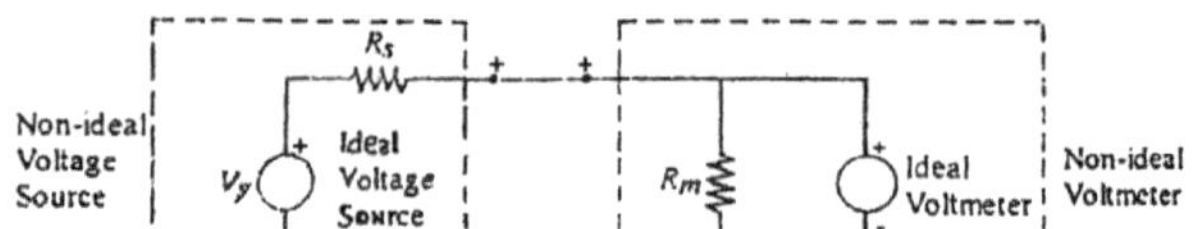

Let V_e be the difference between V_s and the measured voltage.

The $\dfrac{V_e}{V_s}$ is a function of

(a) R_m only   (b) R_s only

(c) $\dfrac{R_s}{R_m}$ (d) $R_m - R_s$

43. A thermistor has a resistance of 10 kΩ at 25°C and 1 kΩ at 100°C. The range of operation is 0°C – 150°C. The excitation voltage is 5V and a series resistor of 1 kΩ is connected to the thermistor. **RRB 2012**

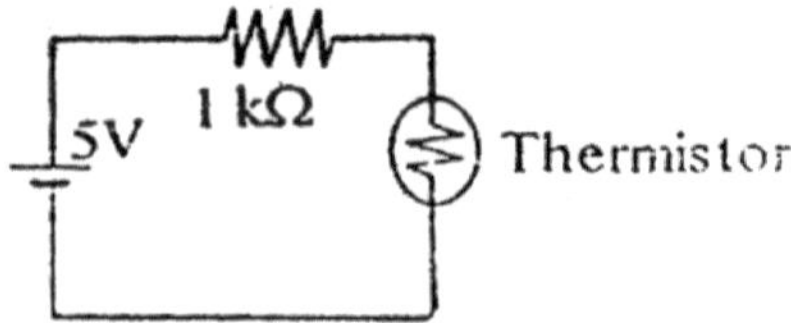

The power dissipated in the thermistor at 150°C is

(a) 4.0 mW   (b) 4.7 mW

(c) 5.4 mW   (d) 6.1 mW

ANSWERS

EXERCISE – I

1. (a)	**2.** (d)	**3.** (a)	**4.** (b)	**5.** (a)	**6.** (b)	**7.** (c)	**8.** (d)	**9.** (d)	**10.** (c)
11. (d)	**12.** (d)	**13.** (c)	**14.** (b)	**15.** (b)	**16.** (a)	**17.** (c)	**18.** (c)	**19.** (b)	**20.** (d)
21. (b)	**22.** (c)	**23.** (d)	**24.** (b)	**25.** (a)	**26.** (d)	**27.** (b)	**28.** (d)	**29.** (a)	**30.** (c)
31. (b)	**32.** (a)	**33.** (d)	**34.** (b)	**35.** (d)	**36.** (d)	**37.** (a)	**38.** (d)	**39.** (d)	**40.** (c)
41. (a)	**42.** (d)	**43.** (d)	**44.** (c)	**45.** (a)	**46.** (d)	**47.** (a)	**48.** (b)	**49.** (c)	**50.** (b)
51. (c)	**52.** (a)	**53.** (a)	**54.** (d)	**55.** (a)	**56.** (d)	**57.** (d)	**58.** (d)	**59.** (d)	**60.** (a)
61. (d)	**62.** (b)	**63.** (b)	**64.** (c)	**65.** (a)	**66.** (b)	**67.** (a)	**68.** (b)	**69.** (b)	**70.** (a)
71. (a)	**72.** (c)	**73.** (d)	**74.** (d)	**75.** (d)	**76.** (a)	**77.** (d)	**78.** (d)	**79.** (b)	**80.** (a)
81. (c)	**82.** (b)	**83.** (b)	**84.** (c)	**85.** (b)	**86.** (d)	**87.** (c)	**88.** (a)	**89.** (c)	**90.** (c)
91. (d)	**92.** (d)	**93.** (b)	**94.** (a)	**95.** (d)	**96.** (a)	**97.** (c)	**98.** (d)	**99.** (b)	**100.** (c)
101. (b)	**102.** (d)	**103.** (a)	**104.** (d)	**105.** (c)	**106.** (b)	**107.** (d)	**108.** (c)	**109.** (b)	**110.** (a)
111. (d)	**112.** (d)	**113.** (d)	**114.** (b)	**115.** (d)	**116.** (d)	**117.** (d)	**118.** (d)	**119.** (a)	**120.** (b)
121. (a)	**122.** (d)	**123.** (b)	**124.** (c)	**125.** (b)	**126.** (a)	**127.** (c)	**128.** (b)	**129.** (c)	**130.** (c)
131. (a)	**132.** (b)	**133.** (c)	**134.** (a)	**135.** (d)	**136.** (d)	**137.** (b)	**138.** (d)	**139.** (c)	**140.** (a)
141. (b)	**142.** (a)	**143.** (d)	**144.** (a)	**145.** (b)	**146.** (a)	**147.** (a)	**148.** (d)	**149.** (b)	**150.** (d)
151. (c)	**152.** (c)	**153.** (a)	**154.** (b)	**155.** (c)	**156.** (d)	**157.** (b)	**158.** (a)	**159.** (b)	**160.** (a)
161. (b)	**162.** (a)	**163.** (c)	**164.** (a)	**165.** (c)	**166.** (b)	**167.** (d)	**168.** (a)	**169.** (d)	**170.** (c)
171. (c)	**172.** (b)	**173.** (a)	**174.** (d)	**175.** (c)	**176.** (b)	**177.** (c)	**178.** (c)	**179.** (d)	**180.** (d)
181. (b)	**182.** (c)	**183.** (b)	**184.** (a)	**185.** (c)	**186.** (b)	**187.** (d)	**188.** (d)	**189.** (c)	**190.** (c)
191. (d)	**192.** (d)	**193.** (d)	**194.** (c)	**195.** (b)	**196.** (c)	**197.** (a)	**198.** (d)	**199.** (b)	**200.** (a)
201. (a)	**202.** (a)	**203.** (c)	**204.** (b)	**205.** (d)	**206.** (a)	**207.** (a)	**208.** (a)	**209.** (c)	**210.** (c)
211. (b)	**212.** (d)	**213.** (b)	**214.** (c)	**215.** (d)	**216.** (b)	**217.** (c)	**218.** (a)	**219.** (a)	**220.** (a)
221. (a)	**222.** (b)	**223.** (b)	**224.** (c)	**225.** (a)	**226.** (a)	**227.** (d)	**228.** (c)	**229.** (c)	**230.** (a)
231. (b)	**232.** (a)	**233.** (c)	**234.** (b)	**235.** (d)	**236.** (b)	**237.** (d)	**238.** (b)	**239.** (b)	**240.** (c)
241. (b)	**242.** (a)	**243.** (c)	**244.** (a)	**245.** (d)	**246.** (b)	**247.** (c)	**248.** (d)	**249.** (c)	**250.** (a)

251. (b) **251.** (d) **253.** (a) **254.** (d) **255.** (c) **256.** (d) **257.** (c) **258.** (a) **259.** (d) **260.** (c)

261. (b) **262.** (b) **263.** (a) **264.** (b) **265.** (c) **266.** (d) **267.** (d) **268.** (a) **269.** (d) **270.** (d)

271. (a b) **272.** (d) **273.** (c) **274.** (d) **275.** (b) **276.** (d) **277.** (c) **278.** (c) **279.** (d) **280.** (b)

281. (c) **282.** (a) **283.** (b) **284.** (b) **285.** (c) **286.** (a) **287.** (c) **288.** (b) **289.** (d) **290.** (a)

291. (a) **292.** (b) **293.** (a) **294.** (a) **295.** (d) **296.** (a) **297.** (b) **298.** (d) **299.** (b) **300.** (d)

301. (b) **302.** (d) **303.** (c)

EXERCISE – II

1. (b) **2.** (d) **3.** (c) **4.** (d) **5.** (c) **6.** (c) **7.** (c) **8.** (c) **9.** (d) **10.** (c)

11. (c) **12.** (c) **13.** (c) **14.** (c) **15.** (d) **16.** (b) **17.** (c) **18.** (d) **19.** (d) **20.** (b)

21. (b) **22.** (d) **23.** (d) **24.** (c) **25.** (c) **26.** (b) **27.** (b) **28.** (d) **29.** (*) **30.** (*)

31. (d) **32.** (d) **33.** (a) **34.** (b) **35.** (c) **36.** (c) **37.** (b) **38.** (a) **39.** (a) **40.** (d)

41. (c) **42.** (c) **43.** (c)

*** It indicate none of the given options is right.**

Electronic Devices

INTRINSIC SEMICONDUCTORS

In a pure semiconductor, an atom behaves as if there are 8 electrons in its valence shell (because of formation of covalent bonds) and the entire material behaves as an insulator at low temperature. A semiconductor atom needs energy of order of 1.1 eV which is easily available at room temperature. Due to thermal agitation of crystal structure, electrons from a few covalent bonds come out and the bond form which an electron comes out has a vacancy called **Hole** (of positive nature). This hole can be filled by some other electron from some other covalent bond. As the electrons from some other covalent bond moves to fill this vacancy a hole is created at its place. In other words we can say that hole has shifted its position from one covalent bond to another as an electron does this in an attempt to fill the hole. *Since, a hole moves in a direction opposite to that of an electron so a hole is treated as a positive charged carrier.*

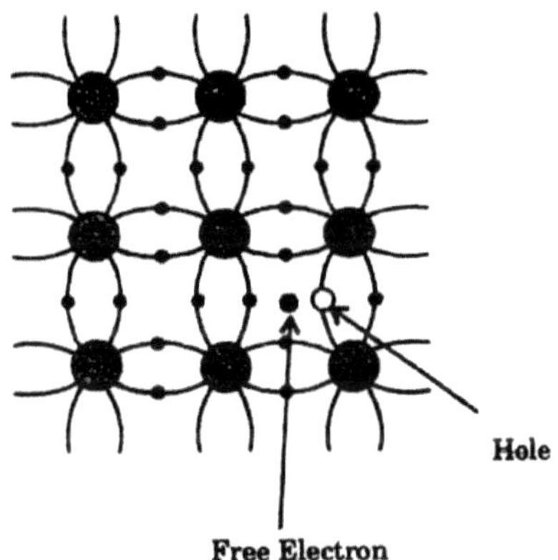

So, at room temperature a pure semiconductor will have electrons and holes wandering in random directions. These electrons and holes are called **intrinsic carriers** and such a semiconductor is called **intrinsic type semiconductor.**

EXTRINSIC SEMICONDUCTOR

P-type semiconductors

Consider a silicon crystal to which a trivalent impurity say Indium is added. The four silicon atoms surrounding the In atom, can share one electron each with the In atom which has got three valence electrons. In an attempt to have 8 electrons in valence shell, In atom borrows one of the nearly covalent bonds of electron. Thus, valence shell of the In atom possesses 8 electrons but a borrowed. Thus, for every trivalent impurity atom added, an extra hole will be created. As the trivalent impurity atoms accept electrons from the silicon crystal, it is called **acceptor impurity.**

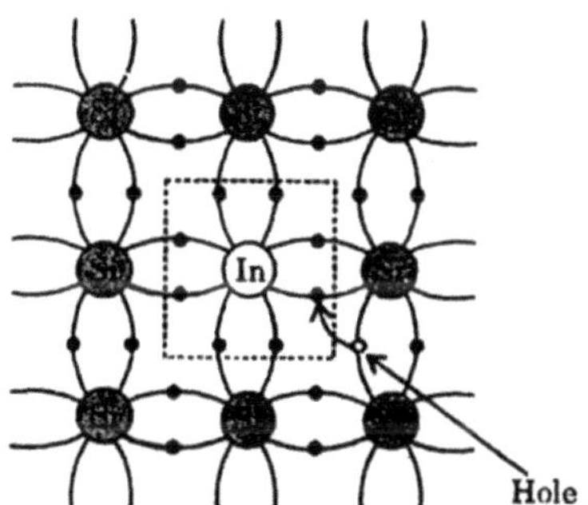

Si-crystal so obtained is called *p-type* as it contains excess free holes. Each hole is equivalent to positive charge. The holes so created are extrinsic carriers and the p-type Si-crystal obtained is called p-type extrinsic semiconductor.

n-Type Semiconductors

When the arsenic impurity atoms are added to the silicon crystal in a small ratio $(1 : 10^6)$, its atoms replace the silicon atoms here and there. The four electrons out of the five valence electrons of As atom take part in covalent bonding with four silicon atoms surrounding it. The fifth electron is set free. Obviously, the extra free electrons created in the crystal will be as many as the number of the pentavalent impurity atoms added. Since the pentavalent impurity increases the number of free electrons, it is called **donor impurity.** The silicon crystal so obtained is termed as n-type Si crystal. The electrons so set free in the silicon crystal are called **extrinsic carriers** and the n-type Si crystal is called n-type

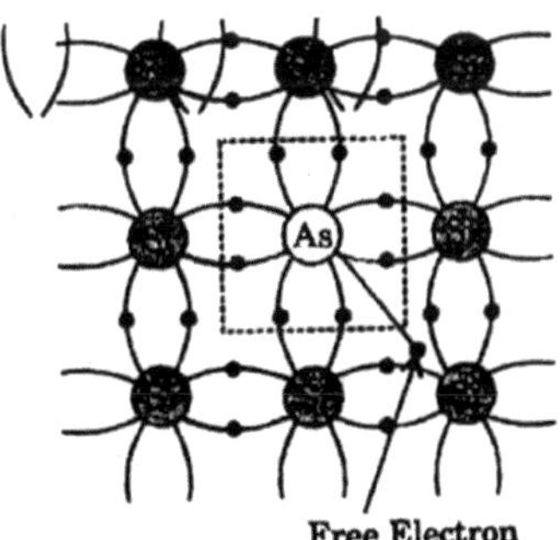

Due to thermal agitation, the pure Si crystal possesses a new electrons and holes. So, n-type Si crystal will have a large number of free electrons (majority charge carriers) and a small number of hole (minority charge carriers).

pn JUNCTION DIODE or Crystal Diode or Diode

It is formed when a p type semiconductor is joined with an n type semiconductor . The surface of contact of p and n is called **junction.** Due to combination a diffusion of electrons from n type to p type semiconductor and so on is expected as a result of which a depletion region (free from any type of charge carries) is formed. because of diffusion of holes and electrons the two section of diode no longer remain neutral, i.e. p section becomes slightly negative and n section becomes slightly positive. As a result of this it appears to us as if some fictitious battery is applied across the junction with its negative terminal connected to p region and positive terminal to n region.

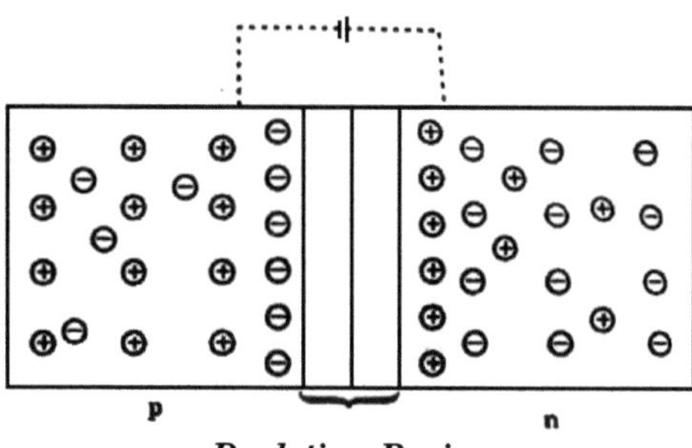

Depletion Region

Potential difference developed across the junction due to migration of majority charge carriers is called *potential barrier.* The potential barrier is of 0.7 V for Silicon and 0.3 for Germanium.

FORWARD BIAS

When an external DC source is connected such that p is conneced to positive terminal and n to the negative terminal, then diode is said to be **forward biased.**

In this case the majority charge carriers cross the junction thus making the depletion region thin and diode conducts and offers low resistance path to the flow of current.

SEMICONDUCTOR-DIODE

The semiconductor diode is formed by simply bringing n and p-type materials together (constructed from same base Ge or Si).

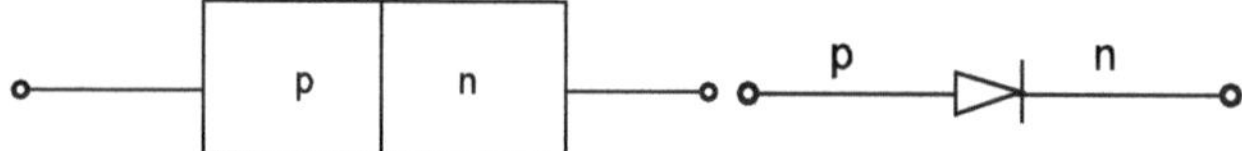

At the instant two materials are *joined,* the electron and holes in the region of junction will combine resulting in a lack of carriers in the region near the junction.

This region of uncovered positive and negative ions is called *depletion region* due to the depletion of carriers in this region.

BIASING OF DIODES.

(*i*) **No bias (V_D = 0).**

In the absence of an applied bias voltage, the net flow of charge in any one direction for a semiconductor is zero.

(*ii*) **Reverse bias condition ($V_D < 0$ V).**

If an external voltage V is applied across the p-n-junction such that positive terminal to n-type and negative terminal to p-type material, then depletion layer will be increased. This widening of depletion layer will establish too great a barrier for the majority carrier to overcome

However the number of minority carrier that find themselves entering the depletion region will not change.

(*iii*) **Forward-bias condition**

A forward bias condition is established by applying +ve terminal to p-type material and -ve terminal to the n-type.

The application of a forward bias potential will pressure electrons in the n-type material and holes in the p-type material with the ions near the boundary and reduce width of the depletion region.

Zener Region

When reverse bias voltage is increased to a very high value, then a point is reached where the I_S will suddenly goes to a very high value. And this reverse bias potential is represented by symbol V_z. As V_D increase in reverse direction, velocity of the minority carriers responsible for the reverse saturation current will also increase the velocity and kinetic energy of minority carrier - with collision with other atoms. The ionisation process occur hence avalanche break down occur. The maximum reverse-bias potential that can be applied before entering the zener region is called *peak inverse voltage.*

TYPES OF DIODES

1. **Zener diodes**

   In zener region, the characteristic drops in an almost vertical manner at a reverse bias potential denoted V_z. For zener diode ,direction of conduction of current is reversed to that of simple diode. Si is preferred in manufacturing of zener diode due to higher temperature and current capability.

2. **Light emitting diode (L.E.D) :** When a junction diode is forward biased, energy is released at junction in the form of light due to recombination of electrons and holes. In case of Si or Ge diodes, the energy ereleased in the infra-red region.

   In the junction diode made of GaAs, InP etc energy is released in visible region suchn a junction diode is called **light emitting diode (LED).** Its symbol .

   Solar cell : Solar cell is a device for converting solar energy into electrical energy. A junction diode in which one of the P or N sections is made very thin (so that the light energy falling on diode is not greatly asorbed before reaching the junction) can be used to convert light energy into electric energy; such diode is called as sola cell. Its symbol is [symbol].

3. Tunnel diode.

An *pn* junction diode has an impurity concentration of about 1 part in 10^8. With this amount of doping the width of the depletion region which constitutes a potential barrier at the junction, is of the order of a micron. This potential barrier restrains the flow of carriers from the side of the function where they constitute majority carriers to the side where they constitute minority carriers. If the concentration of impurity atoms is greatly increased say to 1 part in 10^3 the device characteristicsare completely changed.

SOME SPECIAL DIODES

Photodiode : A kimctopm diode made from "light or photo sensitive semiconductor" is called *photo diode*.

Its sysmbol is [symbol] When light of energy "hv" falls on the photodiode (here hv > energy gap) more electrons move from valence band to conduction band, and due to this current in circuit of photodiode in reverse bias, increases. As light intensity is increased, the current goes on increasing so photo diode is used, to detect light intensity.

JUNCTION DIODE AS A RECTIFIER

A rectifier is used for converting A.C. to D.C.

A diode conducts in Forward Bias and a diode does not conduct in Reverse Bias.

Half Wave Rectifier

It rectifies only one half of AC input.

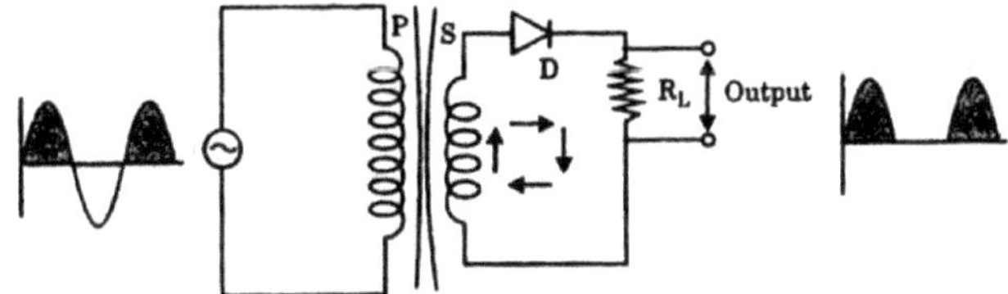

Full wave rectifier.

It has got 2 diodes, D_1 and D_2. When D_2 conducts, D_1 does not conduct. When D_1 conducts, D_2 does not conduct. It rectifies both halves of AC input and this output is also called a **pulsating D.C.**

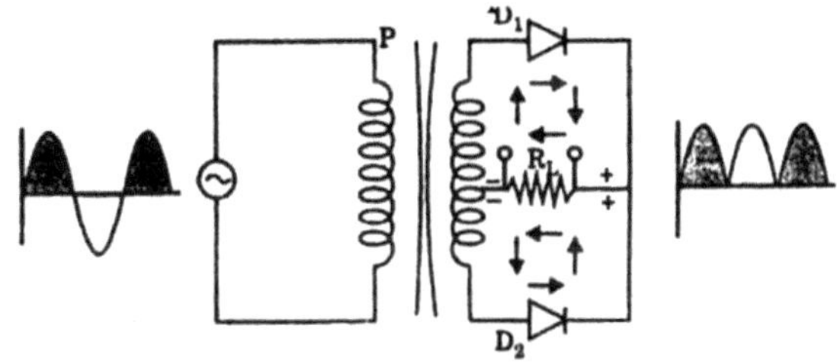

<u>KEY POINTS</u>

Arc Rectifier

It is a rectifier in which an arc struck between electrodes is so controlled as to be during the current wave direction in one only,

e.g. Metal rectifier.

A style of rectifier similar in principle to (thermionic rectifier except that the cathode is heated by the current itself and not by an external source.

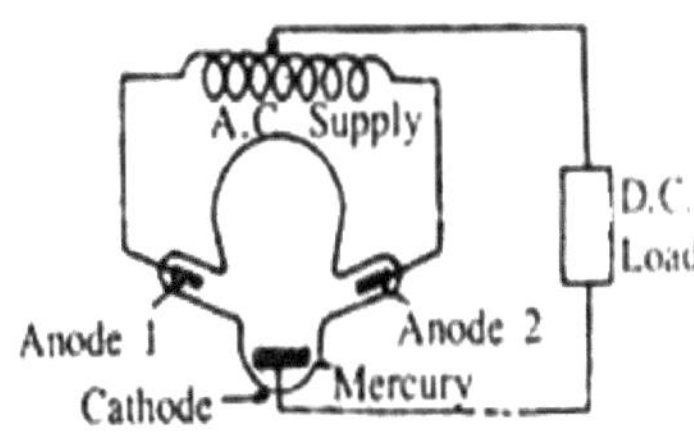

ARC Rectifier

CCD Filter

It is a circuit in which ability of a charge-coupled device to provide a precise predetermined delay time to an analog signal is utilized in order to produce a desired signal--processing function.

CCD Sensor

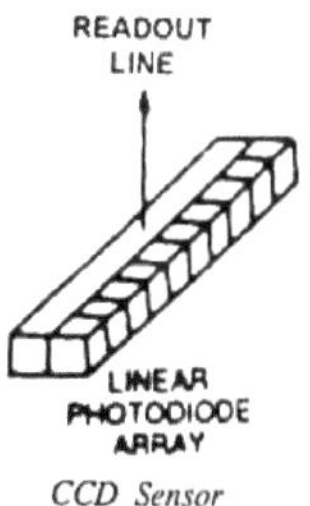

CCD Sensor

CCD as a linear image sensor uses silicon sensor (1,728 of them for group 3). While light is incident on the silicon charges accumulates proportion to incident light flux. In transverse direction accumulation is proportional to incident light flux. Transverse gates below the sensor transverse the accumulated charge to a CCD analog shift resister for the even number sensored and transverse gates above the sensor transverse charge to another CCD analog shift register for the odd number sensor. Clocking signals cause these charges to move down their respective analogue shift register where they emerge alternatively into preamplifier the output of which is a discrete time series of analog pulses corresponding to the diffused reflectance. On a row of elemental areas on the subject copy reported left to the right in turn.

CMOS (Complementary metal oxide Semiconductor)

It is an insulated gate field effect digital logic unit using both P and N MOS devices.

It is a complementary MOS; a MOST or IC involving both P-channel and N-Channel MOS-FETs.

Code

It is a combination of binary digits that represents information such as letters, numbers or symbols.

Code Converter

It is an electronic digital circuit which converts one type of coded information into another coded form.

CTL (Complementary Transistor Logic)

It is a logic system using emitter coupled circuits with a combination of PNP and NPN transistors.

Filtration after Rectification in the detection

After rectifying an modulated carrier wave, the output contains AF and RF components. AF component is the useful component while RF component becomes useless. So, useless RF component is by-passed to ground by filtration and the useful AF component is led to the following amplifier stage.

Solid state diode

It rectify a modulated RF signal. A solid stale diode is the simplest type of detector, which rectifies positive or negative half cycles of a modulated carrier wave as per circuit requirements. A capacitor connected across the load resistor is used to by-pass RF component of the rectifier output.

Simple crystal receiver

During early stage of electronic development, carborundum or galena crystals were used for detection. The radio receiver employing a crystal detector was called *crystal receiver*.

Diode

It is an electronic device that has only two electrodes. There are various types of diodes, their voltage characteristics determining their application. Diodes are most commonly used as rectifiers.

Diode Forward Voltage

The voltage across the electrodes of a diode when current flows. The current increases exponentially with voltage and therefore voltage is substantially constant over the range of currents in common use. A typical value is about 0-7 volts at 10 milliamps, making diodes very useful. The diode may also function as a voltage reference diode when it is used to provide a reference voltage, equal to the diode forward voltage, across its terminals.

Diode Transistor Logic (DTL)

It is a class of integrated logic circuits comprising of each input coming from a diode and the output taken from the collector of an inverting transistor.

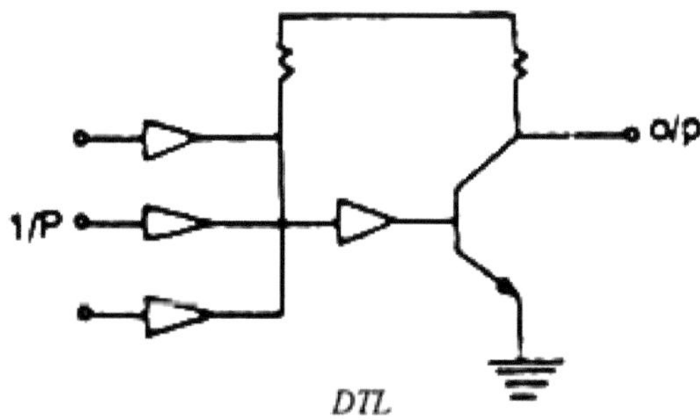

It is a family of integrated logic circuits in which each input signal comes through a diode and the output is taken from the collector of an inverting transistor. The basic circuit is NAND gate.

Dot Generator

It is a test generator used with a television receiver to adjust convergence of the picture tube. A pattern of evenly spaced dots or small squares is produced on a dark background and dynamic focussing is adjusted until a satisfactory image is formed on the screen.

Dot Interlace Scanning

It is a method of scanning, in which picture elements are explored in a regular but non sequential order.

Drift

It is deviation of the operating frequency of a crystal oscillator from its nominal value, generally owing to temperature variations. Drift often occurs during warm up or when device is nearing end of its useful life.

Dual-in-line package

It is a type of integrated circuit package.

Duplex

It is a process for bidirectional transmission of data along transmission line.

Electronic Device

A device which utilizes properties of electrons for ions moving in a vacuum, gas, or semiconductor. Timer is basically an oscillator generating very low frequency output. It is used for time control purposes in electric motors, photographic enlargers, electric heaters, radar etc.

Photo tube

It is a special type of vacuum diode which consists of a photo sensitive cathode and an anode. In this tube, a beam of light causes electrons emission from photo sensitive cathode. It is used in light operated counters and relays.

Photo resistor LDR (Light Dependent Resistor)

It is made of selenium and it is used in electronic counters.

Servo control

In this of control system, rotational portion of a motor is controlled by the *'feedback'* derived from its own output.

Transducer or Sensor

It is a device which is capable to convert one form of energy into another form or which is capable to produce equivalent variations in one form of energy by energy variations in the other form.

e.g., microphone, loudspeaker, pickup, LDR, fuel gauge etc.

Alarm

It is a warning device. An alarm employs a sensor and an electric alarm (bell). There are various types of alarms, e.g., fire alarm burglar alarm, water level alarm, flood alarm etc.

UJT Unijunction transistor

It consists of a single PN junction with two leads connected to the N region and one to the P region. Resistance between the two bases is kept 5 to 10k ohms. It is used in low frequency oscillators and timers.

SCR (Silicon Controlled Rectifier)

It is a three electrode diode. It has a cathode, anode and gate. It can conduct 30 to 100 amperes of current when its anode is made positive with respect its cathode as well as an energizing positive pulse is applied to its gate. It is used in switching circuits, regulated power supplies etc.

DIAC

It is a two electrode three layer bi-directional diode. It is used as trigger, dipper, speed controller for universal motors and in thermos controlled devices.

TRIAC

It is an equivalent to two SCRs joined together in parallel. It is used in time relays etc.

MOSFET or (Metal oxide semiconductor field effect transistor)

It is an improved type of FET in which gate voltage doesn't affect very much conduction of current through the transistor. It is used in digital circuits.

LASER

It is an electromagnetic wave having a frequency of the range of 5×10^5 MHz.

These waves are used in surgery, radar, welding, long distance communications etc.

ELECTRONIC TEST INSTRUMENTS

These are equipments and devices that use electronics to perform various test and checks for reliability and maintainability.

CRO (Cathode Ray Oscilloscope)

It is an electronic equipment designed for visual display of various electrical wave forms.

General purpose oscilloscope

Specifications:

Band width – DC to 50 MHz

Sensitivity – 5 m V/Div. to 0.1 mV/Div.

Time base – 0.5 sec/Div. to 0.1 u sec/Div.

Trigger – Auto normal TV line and frame

CRT – 8×10 cm rectangular

Emission

It is liberation of electrons or electromagnetic radiation from the surface of a metal solid or liquid. It has many types depending on cause which makes the electrons to leave the surface like-high potential or heat (called *thermionic emission*).

Emitter

Short for emitter region. It is that part of a bipolar junction transistor from which carriers flow, through the emitter junction into the base. The electrode attached to this is emitter electrode.

Emitter Coupled Logic or current mode logic

It is a group of integrated logic circuits coupled but their emitters. High Speed non saturating logic family.

Emitter Follower

It is a transistor amplifier using common collector mode of operation. The output is derived from the emitter. The transistor is biased such that it is non saturated and conducting mode. Then it has a constant value relative to base at all times and emitter follows the signal applied to the base. Voltage gain is nearly unity, but the current gain is high. It is used as buffer with high input impedance and low output impedance.

Encoder

It is a digital circuit which converts the information/ data into coded form.

End-around Carry

It is the final carry that is added to the result in 1's or 9's complement addition.

Energy Levels

It is the possible values of energy of an atom or molecule. Quantum theory dictates that only certain fixed values are possible and these may only change by an integral multiple of some fixed amount. An electron orbiting the nucleus of the hydrogen atom may only occupy certain orbits of different energy. These allowed states of energy of the atom are called *electronic energy level*. The *ground state* is the lowest possible energy level and higher states being called *excited states*. Total energy of an atom is composed of kinetic energy, as it translates kinetic energy through space.

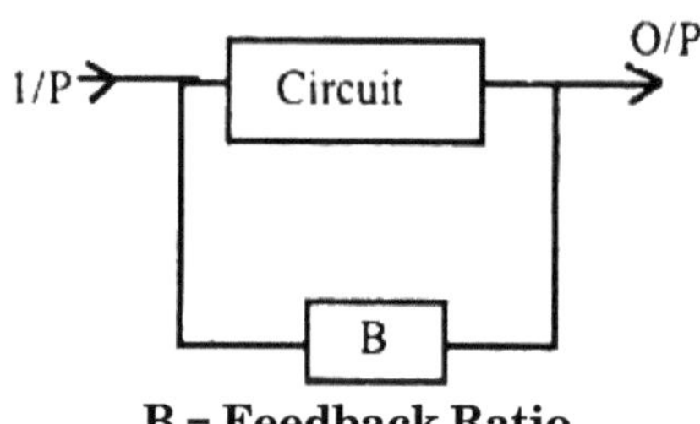

Energy Levels

Feedback

It is the process of feeding back a fraction of output energy of an energy changing device to input. The circuit that sends back the fractional energy is beta circuit and the circuit that generates output signal is 'mu circuit.'

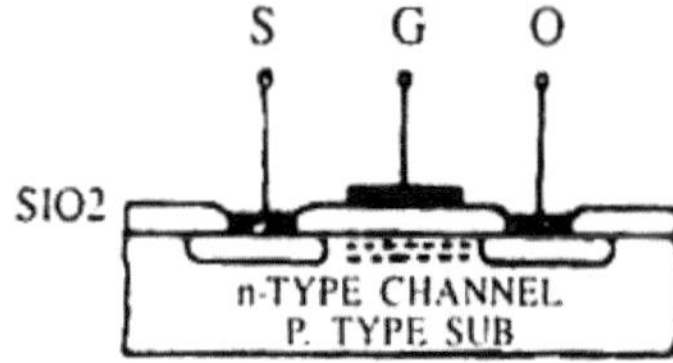

B = Feedback Ratio

Feedback Current

This is a form of feedback in which a fraction of current of the output load is fed back to the input.

Fermi Dirac

It is a system of quantum statics that is used to describe the behaviour of solids in terms of a free electron model. In this model, the most weakly bound electrons of the constituent atoms are considered to behave as a gas subject to certain conditions. The maximum electronic energy level that is occupied by an electron is a solid at a temperature of absolute zero. At higher temperatures, some electrons are excited into higher energy states. Then fermi level corresponds to the value of energy at which the Fermi-Dirac distribution function has a value given by Fermi Dirac function.

Fermi-dirac Function

It is a function expressing probability P(e) of finding occupying an energy level (E) by an electron.

This is given by :

$$P(E) = 1 + \exp (E - E_t)/kT \text{ joules}$$

where, E_t = fermi level

K = Boltzman constant

T = absolute temperature.

Field Effect Transistor (FET)

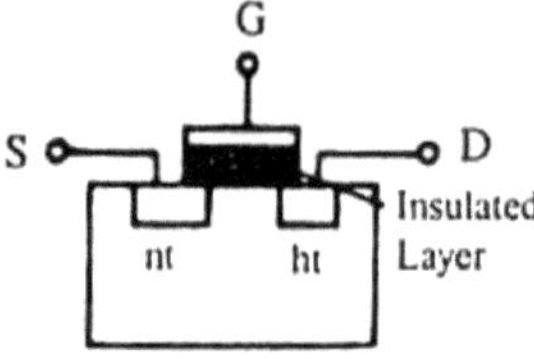

It is a majority carrier multi-electrode semiconductor device in which current flows through a narrow conducting channel between two electrodes and conduction through channel is modulated by an electric field applied through third electrode. *Three electrodes corresponding to three regions are*

(*i*) Source

(*ii*) Gate

(*iii*) Drain

Narrow channel connects source and drain while modulating signal is applied to gate.

Application of suitable bias to the device enables carriers to flow across the channel. FET is a unipolar device since charge carrier are majority device unlike a transistor which is a bipolar device. In both P channel and N channel, FETs are used.

FET Insulated Gate

This is a type of FET where channel is formed by the action of gate voltage. FET is formed by a wafer of semiconductor material that has two highly doped regions of opposite polarity diffused into it to form source and drain. Then insulating layer is formed on the surface between these regions and conductor deposited on top to form gate.

It is also called MISFET, MIST (Metal insulator silicon FET).

MOSFET, MOST (Metal oxide silicon FET).

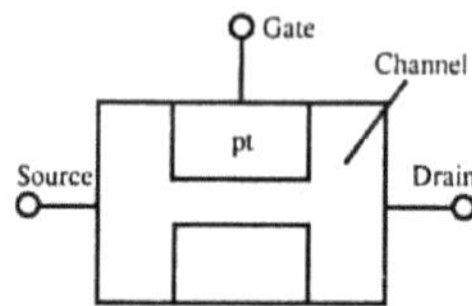

FET Junction

This FET employes conducting channel which is a part of the structure of device. It is also called JFET. It consists of a wafer of semiconductor flanked by two highly doped layers of opposite conductivity type *n* or *p*, forming source, drain and gate regions.

Pick's Law

The law is applied to achieve desired impurity profile in a particular specimen of semiconductor. The law states that *flows of atoms takes place from region of high concentration to low concentration if a concentration gradient of mobile impurity atoms exists in a semiconductor.*

At normal temperature impurity atoms are immobile until heated to a high temperature. A concentration gradient is formed by heating the semiconductor wafer in a gaseous atmosphere of impurity atoms, so that a high concentration exists at the surface. Under such conditions the impurity atoms diffuse into semiconductor according to Pick's law.

Film Resistor

It is a type of resistor, that uses a thin layer of resistive material deposited on an insulating core. For low power applications, film resistors are more stable than composition resistors and except for very high precision requirements, are smaller and less expensive than accurate wire-wound resistors.

Band Pass Filter (BPF)

It provides low attenuation to range of frequency signals having frequencies between lower cutoff frequency of filter and upper cutoff frequency of the filter. Frequencies rest outside this upper and lower limit are attenuated heavily.

Filter Butterworth :

This is a bandpass filter with output characteristics as shown where they have flat response in pass band.

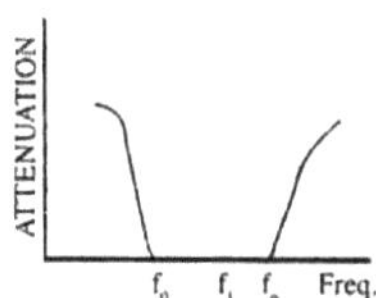

Filter Chebyshev (Tchebysheve).

This is bandpass filter with output characteristics as shown, where these have some variations sort of ripple in pass band but have more rapid increase of attenuation in unwanted bands, thus giving a sharper cutoff profile.

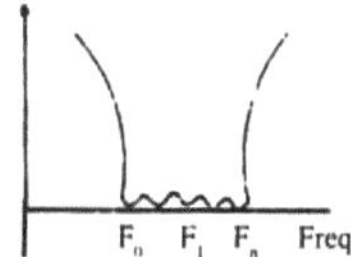

High Pass Filter (HPF)

It provides low attenuation to all frequency signals having frequency higher than the cut off frequency of filter. Frequencies below the cutoff are attenuated heavily.

Filter Passive

These filters employ impedance arranged in series and/or short (L.C networks).

Glitch

It is a current or voltage spike of short duration usually unwanted.

Grid

It is an electrode that has an open structure, such as a mesh or a plate with a hole in it, thus allowing an electron beam to pass through it.

The nationwide high voltage transmission line system that interconnects many electricity power stations. It transmits voltages of up to 400 kilovolts. Voltages as high as 735 kV are used in some countries anything made essentially of parallel wires or bars in one plane. Particularly a wire screen or auxiliary anode between hot cathode and the plate anode in a Thermionic valve.

Gunn diode

It is a negative-resistance microwave device that operates by means of Gunn effect. It is a diode formed from a sample of low resistivity n-type gallium arsenide that produces coherent microwave oscillations when a large electric field is applied across it.

Half - wave Rectification

It is the rectification, in which half-waves of the alternating current in one direction only are made use of while those in the reverse direction are suppressed. It is also called One Wave Rectification.

Integrated Circuit (I.C.)

It is a type of circuit in which all the parts are integrated on a single silicon chip of very small size.

Isolation Diode :

These diodes form by collector substrate junctions in bipolar integrated circuits to maintain isolation between parts of integrated circuit junctions by reverse biasing the junction.

Lapping

It is a method of reducing substrate/slice thickness for applications where accuracy of substrate thickness is critical like in case.

e.g., MMICs (Monolithic Microwave Integrated Circuits).

Liquid Crystal

It is an organic liquid consisting of long-chain molecules that line up under the influence of an applied electric field to give a quasi-crystalline structure of the liquid.

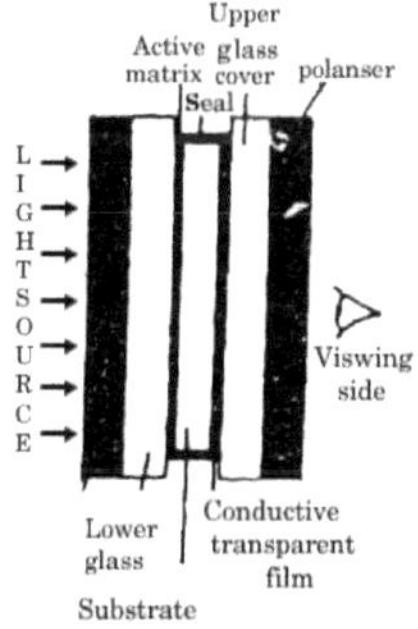

A change in the applied field causes a change in the reflectivity indices.

Liquid Crystal Display (LCD)

It is a type of passive display that uses liquid crystal display liquid crystals.

e.g., seven-segment numerical display of digital watches and pocket calculators.

LX

Liquid-crystal displays (LCD) are displays which consist of a very thin layer of liquid crystal fluid sealed between two glass plates. On inside of these plates, electrodes are etched in the form of characters. When in an electric field LX is applied, the molecular alignment of the fluid is disturbed. Due to difference in reflection, activated characters become visible.

Pin

It is connection point for logic integrated module.

PIN Diode

It consists of a layer of intrinsic semiconductor sandwiched between narrow layer of P and N semiconductor. Diode is used for microwave power switching, limiting and modulation. The intrinsic layer is lightly doped.

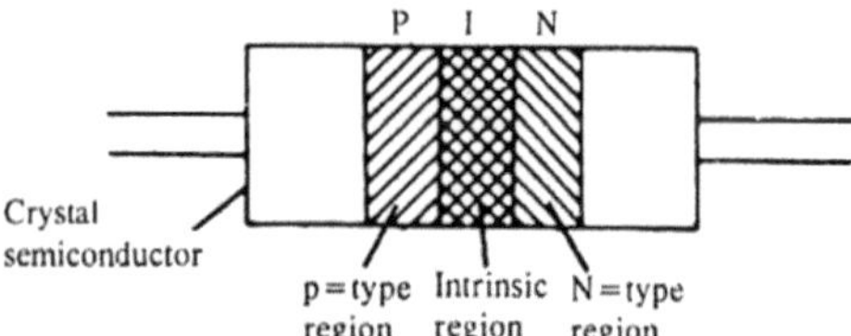

Planar process

It is method of fabricating semiconductor junction devices, in which a layer of silicon dioxide is grown on silicon substrate of required conductivity. Then photolithography is applied for etching oxide layer which then acts as mask. The junction between two semiconductors meet the substrate below oxide layer.

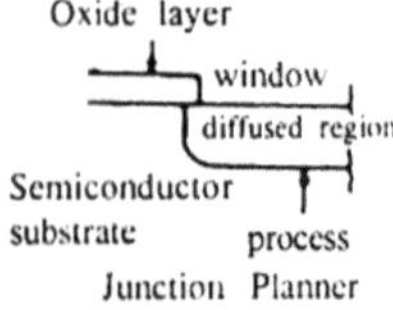

PN Junction

It is a two-terminal, solid state junction made from a semiconductor that has been treated to conduct current more readily in one direction than in the other. This treatment results in a p-type semiconductor at one end and an n-type semiconductor at the other end. PN junction forms the basis of most solid state devices, such as diodes, transistors, and silicon controlled rectifiers.

Pn pn Device

It is a three junction semiconductor device normally silicon with alternative p-type and n-type layers. The device has bistable current-voltage characteristic. It is used for power-switching purposes.

$$\boxed{p}\boxed{n}\boxed{p}\boxed{n}$$

pnp Transistor

It is a semiconductor device where collector and emitter are made from p-type semiconductor material while the base is made from n-type material. In normal operation, emitter is positive with respect to the base while collector is negative with respect to the base.

RECTIFICATION

It is conversion of an Alternating current into a Unidirectional current.

RECTIFIERS

Types of rectifiers are :

1. **Diode valve rectifier**

   Diode valve is a two electrode vacuum tube which consists of a cathode and an anode. When cathode is heated up by passing a current through its filament, it starts to emit electrons. Anode attracts emitted electrons if it is made positive with respect to cathode. If AC is applied to anode, then a current will flow for each positive half cycle only. In this way, AC will be converted into DC. Silicon diode is better tor the rectification of AC.

2. **Metal rectifier:**

   As, $\quad$ mechanical pressure $= \dfrac{\text{Force}}{\text{Area}}$,

   similarly $\quad$ electric pressure $= \dfrac{\text{Potential}}{\text{Area}}$.

   So, electric current can flow easily from a sharp edged point towards a flat surface even across a thin layer of an insulation.

   Type of Metal rectifiers:

   (*i*) Selenium rectifier

   (*ii*) Copper oxide rectifier

3. **Solid state Rectifiers:**

   Half-wave and Full-wave rectifier

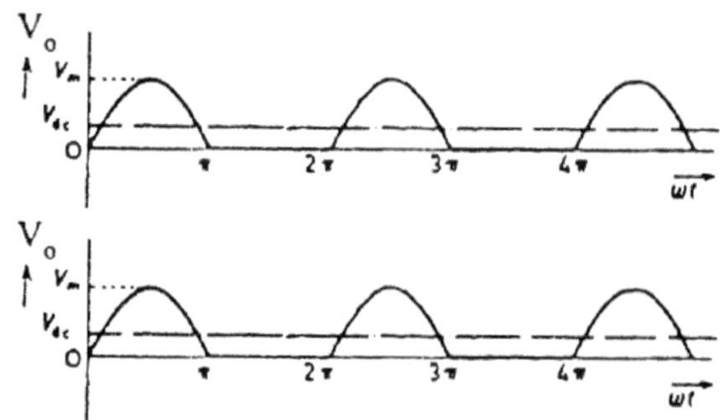

Output voltage from half wave rectifier

Half-wave rectifier circuit :

It provides DC output for positive half cycles only.

Maximum rectification efficiency of a half wave rectifier is 40.6%.

Ripple factor for a half wave rectifier is 1.21.

Full-wave rectifier:

It provides DC output for both half cycles of AC.

Advantages:

Advantages of full-wave rectifier circuit as compared to half-wave rectifier are follows:

(*i*) High efficiency.

(*ii*) Ordinary filter circuit is sufficient.

(*iii*) Provides more output current.

Bridge Rectifier

It is a transformer less full-wave rectifier. It requires 4 diodes.

Advantages:

Advantages of a bridge rectifier over full-wave rectifier are as follows:

Full-wave rectifier (two diodes type) requires a transformer with centre-tapped secondary, whereas, bridge rectifier does not require such transformer.

Battery Eliminator

It is an AC operated power supply unit which eliminates necessity of a battery for the operation of an electronic equipment.

Inverters

It is the device or circuit meant for the conversion of DC into AC. An inverter may both of dynamic or static type. Vibrator is a dynamic inverter while a solid state circuit meant for the purpose is called a static inverter.

Power supply unit

It is a sort of equipment which converts and modifies given input supply in accordance to the supply requirements of an electronic or electrical equipment.

Voltage Doubler

It is a rectifier circuit which doubles voltage supplied to it as well.

Types of Voltage doublers

1. **Half-wave voltage doubler**

2. **Full-wave voltage doubler**

3. **Voltage multiplier.**

    A rectifier circuit which can be made to multiply the given input voltage of three, four, five, six-times by employing the require number of diodes accordingly is called a voltage multiplier.

Ripple frequency

It is frequency of pulses present in the rectified output. It is equal to frequency of AC supplied as input to the rectifier circuit.

Ripple frequencies of full-wave wave rectifiers is 100 Hz.

Ripple frequency of half-wave rectifier is 50 Hz.

Pulsating DC

It is the DC in which output current of a rectifier varies between maximum and zero values in the positive direction.

Static Inverter

It is a low frequency (400 Hz) oscillator which is associated with amplifiers and other controlling circuits.

Plate AC voltage

It is the maximum AC voltage which can be applied safely across a diode.

Peak inverse voltage

It is the maximum AC voltage which can be applied safely across a diode in its non conducting state.

Peak plate current and Load current

Maximum amount of current which can flow through a rectifier is called its '*peak plate current*'.

Maximum amount of DC which can be supplied by a rectifier to the load is called *load current*.

FILTER CIRCUIT

It is a circuit which is capable of selecting desired type of current out of a mixture of two or more types of currents.

Elements of a Filter circuit

1. **Choke**

    It presents a high impedance to AC and a very low impedance to DC.

2. **Capacitor**

    DC can't pass through a capacitor, whereas impedance of a capacitor decreases by increasing frequency of AC supplied to it.

3. **Resistor**

    Basically, a resistor has no filtration property, but if it is used in series of a choke or capacitor, it increases circuit impedance.

4. **Crystal**

Classification of Filter circuits

1. **According to work.**

    (*i*) **Low-pass filter:**

    It is the circuit which allows low frequency currents (upto 100 Hz) and obstructs currents of all frequencies above a pre-decided valve. It consists of a choke connected in series or a capacitor connected in parallel to the given input.

    (*ii*) **High pass filter**

    It is the circuit which allows currents of higher frequencies above a predecided value and obstructs currents of all frequencies lesser than that value. It consists of a capacitor connected in series or a choke connected in parallel to the given input.

    (*iii*) **Band-pass filter**

    The circuit which allows currents of a narrow band of frequencies and obstructs currents of all other frequencies. It consists of a series resonant circuit connected in series or a parallel resonant circuit connected in parallel to the given input.

(*iv*) Band-stop filter

It is the circuit which obstructs currents of a narrow band of frequencies and allows currents of all other frequencies. It consists of a series resonant circuit connected in parallel or a parallel resonant circuit connected in series to the given input.

2. Classification filter circuits according to the input component

(*i*) Choke input filter:

It is the circuit in which input filter element is a choke. *Voltage regulation* of this type of circuit is better than any other type of circuit.

(*ii*) Capacitor input filter:

It is the circuit in which input filter element is a capacitor. *Voltage regulation* of the circuit is poor than that of a choke input filter.

(*iii*) Crystal input filter

It is the circuit in which a crystal (quartz etc.) is used as the input filter element. Crystal has a property of vibrating at an exact frequency for which same is designed hence it is used as a filter element also in communication receivers.

3. Classification filter as per circuit **design**

(*i*) Simple single element circuit

(*ii*) L-Type

(*iii*) T-type

(*iv*) H-type

(*v*) Multi section filters.

In these circuits, the filter elements are connected in L, T, II, 2x etc. pattern.

Cut-off Frequency of Filter

1. Alpha cut-off frequency of a filter

It is the frequency on which the circuit gain of a low-pass filter circuit begins to fall or circuit-gain of a high-pass filter circuit reaches to its maximum value.

2. Beta cut-off frequency of filter

It is the frequency on which circuit-gain of a low-pass filter circuit reaches to zero or circuit-gain of a high-pass filter circuit begins to rise.

Bleeder Resistor

It is a high value resistor connected across a diode's output is called bleeder resistor.

Advantages:

Advantages of employing a bleeder resistor in a filter circuit are as follows:

(*i*) It provides a discharging path to the filter capacitors in case no load is connected to the diode.

(*ii*) It improves voltage regulation.

(*iii*) It can be used as an output voltage divider.

Rectification Efficiency

It is be defined as the percentage of input ac power that is converted into useful dc output power *i.e,*

$$\eta = \frac{\text{d.c. power output}}{\text{a.c. power input}} \times 100$$

Ripple Factor

It is a measure of purity of DC output of a rectifier. It can be defined as

$$r = \frac{\text{rms value of the wave components}}{\text{average of DC value}}$$

Semiconductor

It is a small component having an electrical conductivity between high conductivity of metals and low conductivity of insulators. It has resistivity in the range of conductors and insulators and having a negative temperature coefficient of resistance. The conductivity increases not only with temperature but is also affected very considerably by the presence of impurities in the crystal lattice. Semiconductors are used in wide variety of solid-state devices including transistors, integrated circuits, diodes, photodiodes, and light emitting diodes.

Principal semiconductors

(*i*) Germanium diode.

It is a very sensitive diode and a forward bias of 0.1 volt is sufficient to conduct a forward current through out it.

(*ii*) Silicon diode.

It requires a minimum forward bias of 0.7 volts for the conduction of forward current through it.

Germanium and silicon are the principal semiconductors.

Characteristics of a semiconductor

(*i*) It has a crystalline structure.

(*ii*) Its conductivity is greatly affected by light rays of high intensity, ultra-violet rays and infra-red rays.

(*iii*) Its conductivity varies in accordance to the temperature variations.

Intrinsic and Extrinsic Semiconductors.

Intrinsic semiconductor

Semiconductor material in its pure form is called *intrinsic*

Extrinsic semiconductor : Semiconductor material added with other element is called *extrinsic* semiconductors, such as 'N type' and 'P type' materials.

(*a*) P-type material : When a trivalent element (such as indium, gallium) is added to tetravalent semiconductor (germanium or silicon) then a deficit of an electron is produced for each impurity atom; such type of material is called *'P-type' material.*

(*b*) **N-type material :** When a pentavalent element (such as arsenic, antimony) is added to tetravalent semiconductor, then a surplus electron is produced by each impurity atom; such type of material is called *'N-type' material*.

Acceptor atom

It is 'hole' producing impurity atom 'hole' is *empty space* for an electron.

Donor atom

It is *'free electron'* producing atom.

Doping

It is the act of adding up an element as an impurity to a semiconductor

P-N JUNCTION

Only P-type or N-type material acts as a common conductor, but when two small pieces of P and N-type materials are joined together by heat treatment, then junction so formed is called a *P-N junction*.

A P-N junction diode is capable to work as a rectifier, i.e. it can convert AC into DC.

Biasing

A P-N junction can be biased in forward and reverse states,

(*i*) **Forward biased :** When P terminal is connected to the positive and N terminal to the negative end of a battery, the junction is said to be forward biassed.

(*ii*) **Reverse biased :** P terminal is connected to the negative and N terminal to the positive end of a battery, the junction is said to be reverse biased.

Leakage current

Effective conduction of current lakes place in *'forward bias'* state, a small amount of current flows in reverse direction also. The conduction of leakage current is the result of recombination of free-electrons with holes.

Knee voltage

It is the minimum forward bias voltage required for conduction of current across a P-N junction.

Fabrication.

P-N junction diodes are fabricated in following two ways

(*i*) **Grown junction method**

In this method, say P-type material is melted and then allowed to cool slowly, so that molten material may take a crystalline shape. The crystals so developed are slightly lifted out and an impurity of N-type material is added to the molten material. In this way, lower portion of the crystal becomes of N-type while upper portion of the same remains of P-type.

(*ii*) **Fused junction method :**

In this method, few particles of indium are fused into a small and thin N-type crystal at 500-600°C. Thus a P-type dot is formed in the N-type material.

Effect of heat.

An increase in the temperature of a P-N diode gives a corresponding rise to the leakage current. Therefore, operating temperature of a P-N diode should be kept low for its long life.

Zener diode

It is a silicon diode having a lower value of inverse voltage (break down voltage) It has a property that its leakage current increases suddenly by increasing the reverse bias. It is used in voltage regulator circuits.

Break down voltage of a zener diode

Magnitude of inverse voltage ai which 'zener current' or 'avalanche current' starts to flow across a zener diode is called its *'break down voltage'* or *'safe inverse voltage'*.

Tunnel diode

P-N junction of a tunnel diode is designed in such a way that the electrons passing through the junction have to manage any how to cross the junction. It is used in amplifiers and oscillator circuits.

LED

It is a gallium-arsenide (Ga.As) diode which has a property of emitting light when its forward bias increases above a predecided voltage value.

Varactor diode

It is a P-N junction diode which is designed to work at high frequencies. Its internal capacitance varies in accordance to the signal applied, hence it is used for amplification, frequency multiplication and switching purposes.

Silicon Controlled Rectifier

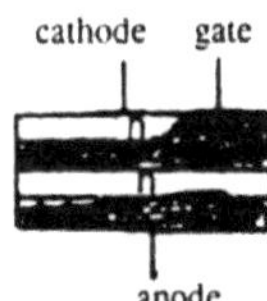

It is three junction three terminal semiconductor diode used for switching moderate power devices. It can be switched ON by a voltage pulse at gate at anode voltage less than the break over voltage. For turning OFF the device, a voltage pulse is applied to a second gate electrode.

Small Scale Integration (SSI)

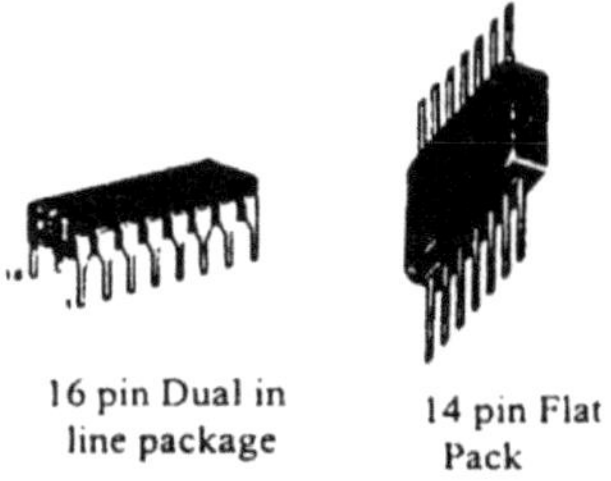

The least complex digital ICs are placed in small scale integration category. These are circuits with upto 12 equivalent gate circuits on a single chip.

Transistor

It is solid state equivalent of a triode valve. A solid state, current-gain device having a collector, base and emitter terminals. It is made by using both p-and n-type materials. It is are available in either PNP or NPN configurations. It is also called a *bipolar transistor*. It is a multielectrode semiconductor device in which current flowing between two specified electrodes is modulated by the voltage or current applied to one or more specified electrodes. The semiconductor material is usually silicon.

It transistor is called a solid state device because of its construction within a single crystal piece.

Valve

It is a unidirectional device. It is also *vacuum tube* because it is made in a perfectly evacuated glass tube.

Triode valve

It is a three electrode valve. Electrodes are

(*i*) Cathode,

(*ii*) Control grid

(*iii*) Anode (or plate).

Transistors over Vacuum tubes

(*i*) Transistor's have low working temperature (20-250°C)

(*ii*) Transistor's have limited power handling capability.

Thermal runway

If a transistor is subjected to a temperature of 800°C or above, it becomes nearly a conductor (in general). This phenomenon is called *thermal runway*.

Unipolar transistor

A transistor in which conduction of current is a result of movement or drift of only one type of charge carrier is called *unipolar transistor.*

Comparison of silicon transistors and Germanium transistors

(*i*) Silicon transistors are capable to work at a higher temperature with respect to germanium transistors,

(*ii*) Silicon transistors are capable to carry large current with respect to germanium transistors.

PNP and NPN Transistors

(*i*) **PNP transistor:** It consists of two P-regions and a thin N-region between them.

It transistor drifting of holes from emitter to collector is responsible for conduction of current in a PNP transistor.

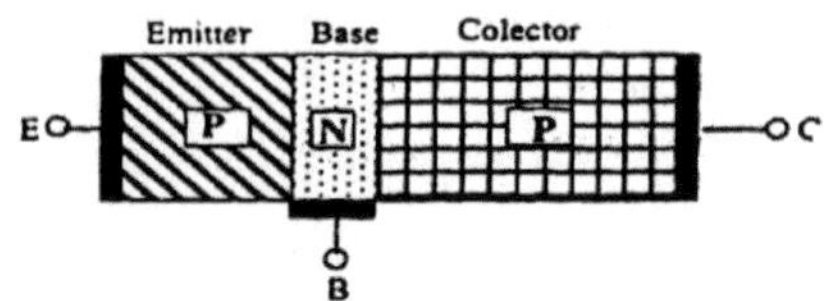

PNP-Type Junction Diode

(*ii*) **NPN:** Consequently, the flow of electrons from collector to emitter constitutes the current in PNP transistors consists of two N-regions and a thin P-region between them.

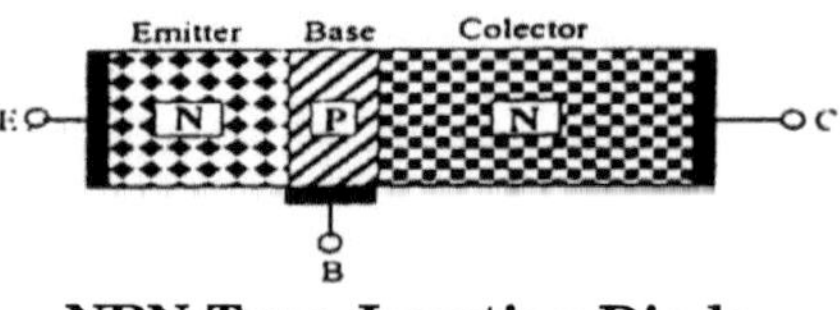

NPN-Type Junction Diode

The movement of free electrons from emitter to collector is responsible for the conduction of current in NPN transistor.

Effect of base bias variations

Magnitude of base bias voltage controls the number of charge carriers moving or drifting across the transistor. Therefore, a transistor is used for producing amplification, oscillations, modulation etc.

Methods of Manufacturing Transistors

There are three principal methods of fabricating transistors:

(*i*) **Junction of method :** In this method, small quantities of indium are doped into two opposite sides of a N-type wafer at about 500-6000°C temperature for making a PNP transistor. Similarly for making an NPN transistor, arsenic is doped into two opposite sides of a P-type water. This type of transistors are also called *alloy junction transistors.*

(*ii*) **Point contact method :** In this method, two sharply pointed indium-steel pins are fused in N-type pallet at about 500-6000°C temperature for making a PNP transistor. Similarly, for making an NPN transistor two arsenic steel pins are fused in a P-type pallet. A thin portion remained between two pins acts as 'base.'

(*iii*) **Diffused junction method:** In this method, small pits are made in P or N-type material by the pits by thermal action. This type of transistors are also called *epitaxial* or *homotaxial transistors.*

Point contact transistors have High value of current gain *'alpha'* (greater than one). These are capable to work at a frequency of 100 MHz above, and to carry more current.

These are capable to handle hundreds of watts of electrical power and can carry 10 or more amperes of current when installed with a suitable *'heat sink'*.

Heat sink is a metallic heat radiator mounted around a transistor (especially collector of the transistor).

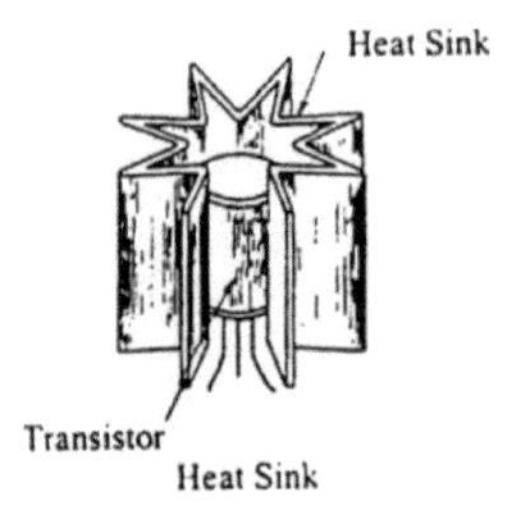

Transistor Characteristics

These are studied by plotting IE-VE and IC-VC curves.

(*i*) **IE-VE curves :** It show that emitter current depends on the emitter voltage and the collector voltage has a very little effect on the emitter current and hence transistor has a low input impedance.

(*ii*) **IC-VC curves :** It show that a transistor attains a high collector current at a low collector voltage and hence the transistor has a high output impedance.

Current gain Alpha (α)

It is ratio of the collector current variations to the emitter current variations on no-load and constant voltages

$$\alpha = \frac{I_C}{I_E}$$

where, IC = collector current variations

IC = emitter current variations

Note : Both current variations should be measured in the same units.

(*ii*) Beta (β)

It is ratio of the collector current variations to the base current variations on no load and constant voltages.

$$\beta = \frac{I_C}{I_B}$$

where, I_B = base current variations.

Relation between α and β

$$\beta = \frac{\alpha}{1-\alpha} \text{ or } \alpha = \frac{\beta}{1 + \beta}$$

Alpha cut-off frequency

The frequency at which gain of a transistor is reduced to *10.1%* of its gain at low frequency is called *alpha cut-off frequency of the transistor*.

Voltage gain of a transistor

It is ratio of the output voltage to the input voltage

$$V.G.= \frac{V_0}{V_i} = \frac{\text{Output voltage}}{\text{Input voltage}}$$

Power gain of a transistor

It is ratio of the output power to the input power

$$P.G.= \frac{\text{Output power}}{\text{Input power}} = \frac{P_0}{P_i}$$

Three Basic configurations of Transistors

There are three basic configurations of transistors:

1. Common base (CB) configuration

It is the transistor circuit in which base is kept common to the input and output circuits.

Characteristics

(*i*) Low input impedance (50 to 500 ohms).

(*ii*) High output impedance (1 to 10 mega ohms)

(*iii*) Current gain alpha = less than unity.

2. Common emitter (CE) configuration

It is the transistor circuit is which emitter is kept common to the input and output circuits.

Characteristics

(*i*) High input impedance (500 to 5000 ohms**)**

(*ii*) Low output impedance (50 to 500 kilo ohms)

(*iii*) Currem gain, β is = upto 98

(*iv*) Power gain uplo 5000 or 37 dB.

(*v*) 180° out of phase output.

3. Common collector circuits (CC) configuration

It is the transistor circuit in which collector is kept common to the input and output circuits.

It is also called emitter follower

Characteristics

(*i*) High input impedance (150 to 600 kilo ohms)

(*ii*) Low output impedance (100 to 1000 ohms)

(*iii*) Current gain, β = 99

(*iv*) Voltage and power gain is equal to or less than unity.

Tetrode Transistor

It has four terminals:

(*i*) Emitter   (*ii*) base-1

(*iii*)base-2   (*iv*) collector

Addition of fourth electrode base-2 enables it to work satisfactorily at high frequencies even.

FET (Field Effect Transistor)

It is a solid state device in which conduction of current is controlled by an electrostatic field. Its electrodes are called *source, drain and gate*.

Transistor Data

It is a reference book which contains following information regarding characteristics of transistors :

(*i*)   Maximum collector-emitter voltage

(*ii*)   Maximum collector current

(*iii*)   Leakage current

(*iv*)   Input output impedances

(*v*)   Current gain and power gain

(*vi*)   Alpha cut off frequency

(*vii*) Power dissipation

(*viii*) Working temperature

(*ix*)   Collector-base voltage and capacitance

(*x*)   Base current etc.

Transistor Manufacture

Many transistors or other elements, together with their interconnecting links, are made on a single chip to turn it into an IC, I usual method of manufacturer of monolithic ICs (mono= single, Iithos = stone, in this case silicon) has many similarities in technique with the making of a single silicon (planar) transistor.

Stages of manufacture are:

(*i*) A wafer of n-type silicon is oxidized to a depth of about 1 micron.

(*ii*) Then this oxide layer is partially etched off.

(*iii*) The wafer is exposed to a vapor of the acceptor element boron. This element diffused into the wafer to a predetermined depth (creating a p-type zone). The wafer surface is at the same time de-oxidized.

(*iv*) Then a part of the newly de-oxidized surface is etched away again.

(*v*) Then wafer is exposed to a vapor of the donor element phosphorus. This diffuses in (to create an n-type zone) the surface is again de-oxidized.

(*vi*) More etching away of the oxide surface follows, to separate what have become the base and emitter regions on the surface of the wafer.

(*vii*)Metal contacts are alloyed on to the etched areas,

TRF (Tuned Radio Frequency) receiver

It is a radio receiver in which detection is accomplished on a tuned radio frequency (without any frequency conversion).

Changing wave bands of a radio receiver

Wave bands of a radio receiver are changed by following means of:

(*i*) Rotary   (*ii*) Slide

(*iii*) Push button 3r   (*iv*)Piano type switch.

(*i*) **Rotary switch :** It consists of a long spindle on which a number of contractors of '*poles*' are mounted to establish contact with stator points or 'ways' type rotary switches. 4P-3W, 6P-3W, 6P-5W and 6P-8W b

(*ii*) **Slide switch :** A slide switch has 4 or 6 poles which can slide aver, 2, 3 or 5 ways.

(*iii*) **Push button or piano type switch :** It consists of '*contractor leaves*' and '*pins*'. '*Poles*' are made, by joining pole-pins and other pins act as '*ways*'.

IF amplifier

It is the amplifier which amplifiers at a definite radio frequency (with a narrow pass hand). A high gain pentode/transistor is used for the purpose.

Since an IF amplifier has to amplify at a definite frequency, therefore, circuit may designed to obtain maximum amplification and selectivity. The voltage gain of an IF amplifier may be of the order of 500 to 5000.

Ultradyne Reception

It is a system of radio reception, similar to the superheterodyne system, in which intermediate. Frequency is obtained from auxiliary oscillation superimposed upon anode circuit of the first valve.

UPS (Uninterrupted Power Supply)

It is a device used to supply in case of power failure. It comes in various VA ratings and stand by times.

Uranium (U)

It is a radioactive element. It's a atomic number is 92. Naturally occurring uranium is a mixture of $99.28\%^2{}''U$, 0.71%-*U, and 0.0058%-^{235}U. The nucleus of ^{235}U is capable of absorbing a neutron and thereupon undergoing fission into two highly radioactive fragments that fly apart with great energy, releasing neutrons. A chain reaction is possible because fission is induced by one neutron but release more than one neutron.

Vaccum Triode

It is the device which has ability to amplify small electrical signals (audio signals)

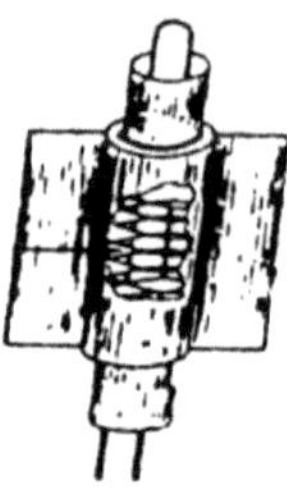

Variable speed Scanning

Beam in the transmitter owing to interconnect ion of the deflecting circuits and as apparent illumination of the screen depends upon the beam, the picture is reproduced. In method of scanning in cathode-ray television, speed of deflection of the scanning beam is governed by the optical density of the object (in this case a film). Beam in the receiver is of constant intensity and copies motion of the object.

Zener Breakdown

It is a type of breakdown observed in a reverse biased p-n junction that has very high doping concentration on both-sides of the junction. The build-in-field is high and the depletion layer narrow as a result of high level of doping.

Zener Diodes

These diodes are designed to operate in the break down region without damage. It is specified by its break down voltage and maximum power dissipation.

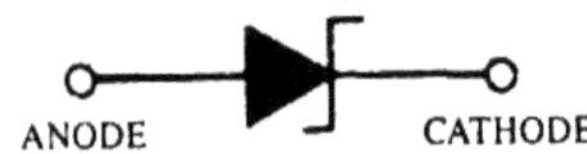

Circuit symbol of a zener diode

Z Modulation of CRT

Intensity of beam is modulated by an external signal.

Zone Levelling

It is method of *zone refining* in order to distribute impurities evenly throughout the bulk of the material. *Zone purification* is the application of zone refining in order to reduce concentration of an impurity in a material.

Standard Values of Commercially Available Resistors tolerance ± 10%

ohms (Ω)		kilo ohms $k\Omega$		Mega ohms $M\Omega$
1.0	33	1.0	33	1.0
1.2	39	1.2	39	1.2
1.5	47	1.5	47	1.5
1.8	56	1.8	56	1.3
2.2	68	2.2	68	2.2
2.7	82	2.7	82	2.7
3.3	100	3.3	100	3.3
3.9	120	3.9	120	3.9
4.7	150	4.7	150	4.7
5.6	180	5.6	180	5.6
6.8	220	6.8	220	6.8
8.2	270	8.2	270	8.2
10	330	10	330	10
12	390	12	390	12
15	470	15	470	15
18	560	18	560	18
22	680	22	680	22
27	820	27	820	—

Conductivity and Resistivity

Classification	Material	Conductivity (S/m)	Resistivity (Ohm)
Conductors	Silver	6.25×10^7	1.6×10^{-8}
	Copper	5.88×10^7	1.7×10^{-8}
	Aluminium	3.85×10^7	2.6×10^{-8}
Semi-conductors	Germanium	1.54	6.5×10^{-1}
	Silicon	5.0×10^{-4}	2.0×10^3
Insulators	Porcelain	3.33×10^{-10}	3.0×10^9
	Glass	5.88×10^{-12}	1.7×1011
	Hard rubber	1×10^{-16}	$1 - 10^{16}$

Some Derived Units

Physical	Quantity	Name of SI Unit	Symbol
Electric	Capacitance	Farad	F = A S/V
Electric	Charge	Coulomb	C = As
Electric	Conductance	Siemen (mho ℧)	S = A/V
Electric	resistance	ohm	Ω = V/A
Electric	potential	Volt	V=W/A
Force		Newton	$N = Kg\ m/s^2$
Frequency		hertz	Hz=cycles/s
Inductance		henry	H = V S/A
Magnetic	flux	Weber	Wb = Vs
Magnetic	flux density	Tesla	$T = Wb/m^2$
Power		Watt	W=J/s
Pressure		Pascal	Pa = N/m
Work,	energy, heat	Joule	J = Nm

EXERCISE – I

1. One electron volt equals
 (a) 1.6×10^{19} joule
 (b) 1.6×10^{16} joule
 (c) 9.1×10^{-31} joule
 (d) 91.1×10^{16} joule

2. At room temperature, resistivity of pure germanium expressed in ohm-cum is
 (a) 0.45
 (b) 4.5
 (c) 45
 (d) 450

3. At room temperature resistivity of pure silicon expressed in ohm-cm is
 (a) 2,300
 (b) 23,000
 (c) 230,000
 (d) 450

4. Resistivity range of semiconductors in ohm-meter is
 (a) 10^{-5} to 10^5
 (b) 10^{-5} to 10^{10}
 (c) 10^{-3} to 10^3
 (d) 10^{-1} to 10^6

5. Resistivity of a semiconductor depends on
 (a) the length of the semiconductor specimen
 (b) cross-sectional area of the semiconductor specimen
 (c) volume of the semiconductor specimen
 (d) the atomic nature of the semiconductor

6. Resistivity measurements are often used to determine
 (a) carrier mobility
 (b) carrier concentration in intrinsic semiconductor
 (c) carrier concentration in extrinsic semiconductor
 (d) life time of polycrystalline materials

7. An intrinsic semiconductor at absolute zero temperature
 (a) has only a few holes and a few electrons
 (b) has very large number of holes and electrons
 (c) behaves like a good conductor
 (d) behaves like a good insulator

8. A germanium atom contains
 (a) four valence electrons
 (b) six valence electrons
 (c) four protons
 (d) six protons

9. In Ge, an electron in the conduction band
   (a) is bound to its parent atom
   (b) has a higher energy than an electron in the valence band
   (c) has zero charge
   (d) is located near the top of the crystal

10. In Ge, when atoms are held together by the sharing of valence electrons
    (a) each shared atom leaves a hole
    (b) valence electrons are free to move away from the nucleus
    (c) velence electrons form irreversible covalent bands
    (d) valence electrons form reversible covalent bands

11. A hole is the vacancy created when
    (a) a free electron moves on application of electric field
    (b) an electron breaks its covalent band
    (c) an atomic core moves
    (d) an electron reverts from conduction band to valence band

12. When an electric field is applied to an intrinsic semiconductor at room temperature say from left to right
    (a) both electrons and holes drift to the right
    (b) both electrons and holes drift to the left
    (c) electrons drift to the right while the holes drift to the left
    (d) electrons drift to the left while holes drift to the right

13. Energy required to break a covalent in semiconductor is
    (a) always equal to 1.6 eV
    (b) greater in Ge than in Si
    (c) equal to the width of the forbidden energy gap
    (d) is the sae in Ge as in Si

14. At absolute zero, all the valence electrons in an intrinsic semiconductor are
    (a) in the conduction band
    (b) in the forbidden band
    (c) in the valence band
    (d) reduced to zero in number

15. Germanium
    (a) can not be purified by zone refining method
    (b) is usualy purified by the floating zone method
    (c) is more easily purified than silicon
    (d) has melting temperature higher than silicon

16. In a semiconductor, rate of diffusion of charge carriers
    (a) depends on the concentration gradient and the mobility
    (b) depends on the concentration gradient alone
    (c) depends on the mobility alone
    (d) is independent of concentration gradient and the mobility

17. Adjacent atoms in the crystalline structure of a semiconductor like germanium form
    (a) ionic bands   (b) metallic bands
    (c) molecular bands   (d) covalent bands

18. When a pure semiconductor is heated
    (a) its resistance increases
    (b) its resistance decreases
    (c) its atomic structure changes
    (d) it becomes metal

19. Valence electrons are
    (a) found in the nucleus
    (b) the inner core electrons of an atom
    (c) the outer orbit electrons
    (d) always free electrons

20. Pure semiconductors are poor conductor because
    (a) they have no valence electrons
    (b) all valence electrons are in electron-pairs
    (c) they have a number of holes
    (d) there are fewer electrons than protons

21. Hole in a lattice in defined as
    (a) free proton
    (b) free neutron
    (c) vacancy created by removal of electron from covalent band
    (d) acceptor ion

22. In a pure semiconductor, electric current is due to
    (a) holes alone
    (b) electrons alone
    (c) both holes and electrons
    (d) valence electrons alone

23. Forbidden energy gap between valence band and conduction band is least in the case of
    (a) mica   (b) pure silicon
    (c) pure germanium   (d) impure silicon

24. Temperature coefficient of resistance in a pure semiconductor is
    (a) zero
    (b) positive
    (c) negative
    (d) dependent on size of specimen

25. Forbidden energy gap in semiconductors is of the order of
(a) 7 eV
(b) 1 eV
(c) 0.1 eV
(d) 0.05 eV

26. At $0°K$, the forbidden energy gap in germanium is
(a) 0.785 eV
(b) 1.21eV
(c) 0.72 eV
(d) 1.1 eV

27. At $300°K$, the forbidden energy gap in germanium is
(a) 0.785 eV
(b) 1.21 eV
(c) 0.72 eV
(d) 1.1 eV

28. At $0°K$, the forbidden energy gap in silicon is
(a) 0.785 eV
(b) 1.21 eV
(c) 0.72 eV
(d) 1.1 eV

29. A $300°K$, the forbidden energy gap in silicon is
(a) 0.785 eV
(b) 1.21 eV
(c) 0.72 eV
(d) 1.1 eV

30. The diffusion length of a carrier depends on
(a) shape of the semiconductor
(b) life time of the carriers alone
(c) mobility and life time of the carriers
(d) mobility of the carriers alone

31. Donor impurity atom in a semiconductor result in new
(a) wide energy band
(b) narrow energy band
(c) discrete energy level just below conduction level
(d) discrete energy level just above valence level

32. Acceptor impurity atoms in a semiconductor result in new
(a) wide energy band
(b) narrow energy band
(c) discrete energy level just below conduction level
(d) discrete energy level just above valence level

33. If donor concentration N_D equals acceptor concentration N_A, resulting semiconductor is
(a) n-type
(b) p-type
(c) intrinsic
(d) may be p or n type depending on temperature

34. In n-type germanium with boron impurity, the ionisation energy is about
(a) 0.001 eV
(b) 0.01 eV
(c) 0.1 eV
(d) 1 eV

35. Mobility of free electrons in germanium at $300°k$ expressed in $cm^2/V\text{-}s$ is
(a) 1800
(b) 3800
(c) 1300
(d) 500

36. Mobility of free electrons in silicon at $300°k$ expressed in $cm^2/V\text{-}s$ is
(a) 500
(b) 1300
(c) 1800
(d) 3800

37. Mobility of holes in germanium of $300°k$ expressed in $cm^2/V\text{-}s$ is
(a) 500
(b) 1300
(c) 1800
(d) 3800

38. Mobility of holes in silicon at $300°k$ expressed in $cm^2/V\text{-}s$ is
(a) 500
(b) 1300
(c) 1800
(d) 3800

39. In n-type germanium with assenic impurity, the ionisaiton energy is about
(a) 0.001 eV
(b) 0.01 eV
(c) 0.1 eV
(d) 1 eV

40. In silicon at room temperature, concentration of thermally generated electrons/cm^3 is of the order of
(a) 10^8
(b) 10^{10}
(c) 10^{13}
(d) 10^{15}

41. In germanium at room temperature, concentration of thermally generated electrons/cm^3 is of the order of
(a) 10^{11}
(b) 10^{13}
(c) 10^{15}
(d) 10^7

42. In Ge or Si, light doping corresponds to impurity of following magnitude
(a) 1 in 10^8
(b) 1 in 10^6
(c) 1 in 10^5
(d) 1 in 10^4

43. In Ge or Si, medium doping corresponds to impurity of the following order
(a) 1 part in 10^8
(b) 1 part in 10^6
(c) 1 part in 10^5
(d) 1 part in 10^4

44. In Ge or Si, heavy doping approximately corresponds to impurity of magnitude
(a) 1 part in 10^8
(b) 1 part in 10^6
(c) 1 part in 10^5
(d) 1 part in 10^4

45. When germanium is doped with pentavalent impurity, the resulting material is
(a) p-type semiconductor
(b) n-type semiconductor
(c) intrinsic semiconductor
(d) no longer a semiconductor

46. When germanium is doped with trivalent impurity, the resulting material is
(a) p-type semiconductor
(b) n-type semiconductor
(c) intrinsic semiconductor
(d) no longer a semiconductor

47. A p-type semiconductor is
  (a) positively charged
  (b) negatively charged
  (c) electrically neutral
  (d) not used in semiconductor devices

48. An n-type semiconductor is
  (a) positively charged
  (b) negatively charged
  (c) electrically neutral
  (d) not used in semiconductor devices

49. In p-type semiconductor
  (a) $n = p$ (b) $p < n$
  (c) $p << n$ (d) $p >> n$

50. In n-type semiconductor
  (a) $n = p$ (b) $n < p$
  (c) $n >> p$ (d) $n << p$
  where n and p are densities of free electrons & holes respectively.

51. Through repeated zone refining, the residual impurity in a semiconductor is of the order of
  (a) 1 part in 10^3 (b) 1 part in 10^5
  (c) 1 part in 10^7 (d) 1 part in 10^{11}

52. Mobility of electron in a semiconductor
  (a) decreases as the temperature increases
  (b) increases as the temperature increases
  (c) has no effect on conductivity
  (d) is independent of temperature

53. Mobility of charge carrier in a semiconductor depends on
  (a) recombination rate
  (b) temperature of the semiconductor
  (c) resistivity of the semiconductor
  (d) charge per carrier

54. Movement of charge carriers from an area of high carrier concentration to an area of low carrier concentration is called
  (a) drift   (b) diffusion
  (c) recombination   (d) gradient

55. Change of carrier concentration along the length of a semiconductor is called
  (a) mobility
  (b) diffusion
  (c) concetration gradient
  (d) drift

56. When a free electron is recaptured by a hole, the process is called
  (a) recombination   (b) diffusion
  (c) drift   (d) restoration

57. In a semiconductor, movement of charge carriers under influence of an electric field is called
  (a) diffusion   (b) drift
  (c) mobility   (d) conductivity

58. Imperfections in the crystal structure result in
  (a) increased conductivity
  (b) decreased conductivity
  (c) increased mobility
  (d) decreased mobility

59. In pure silicon, major part of the drift current is due to free electrons because
  (a) there are more free electrons than holes
  (b) free electrons are in the valence band
  (c) mobility of electrons is greater than the mobility of holes
  (d) diffusion constant of electrons is greater than that of holes

60. At room temperature intrinsic carrier concentration is higher in germanium than in silicon because
  (a) carrier mobilities are higher Ge than in Si
  (b) energy gap in Ge is smaller than that in Si
  (c) Atomic number of Ge is larger than in Si
  (d) Atomic weight of Ge is larger than in Si

61. In preparing a semiconductor material for use in semiconductor devices the first step involved is
  (a) crystal growth   (b) chemical purification
  (c) crystal pulling   (d) zone refining

62. Final purification of germanium or silicon is generally accomplished by
  (a) chemical purification (b) crystal pulling
  (c) zone refining   (d) epitaxial growth

63. One reason why purification of silicon is difficult is that
  (a) its melting temperature is high
  (b) its surface tension is high
  (c) it does not form a single crystal
  (d) its resistivity is high

64. Seed crystal used in crystal growth is a
  (a) small crystal formed by epitaxial growth
  (b) single crystal with a specific orientation
  (c) single crystal containing donor impurity
  (d) single crystal containing acceptor impurity

65. Semiconductor may be made n-type by adding donor impurity
  (a) during zone refining
  (b) during chemical purification
  (c) during crystal pulling
  (d) before purification process

66. Epitaxial growth is best suited for growing
    (a) polycrystalline silicon
    (b) very thin single crystal layer on a substrate
    (c) single crystals several inches in size
    (d) single crystals several mm in size

67. Germanium epitaxial film may be doped by
    (a) using hydrogen as carrier
    (b) adding doping impurity in the melt
    (c) introducing the doping impurity in vapour form along with the germanium compound vapour
    (d) using chlorine to form the vapour compound

68. In the four point probe method of determining resistivity
    (a) one probe point must inject monority carriers
    (b) current flows in only a small area of the sample
    (c) curent source is connected to the two inner probes
    (d) the sample must be extrinsic

69. A requirement of four point probe method of determining resistivity is
    (a) curent must be low
    (b) current must be high
    (c) cross-section along the sample must be constant
    (d) currrent source is connected to two inner probes

70. Merit of four point probe method of determining resistivity is that
    (a) it needs very small current
    (b) it gives the average resistivity of the sample
    (c) it gives the resistivity at a localized region of the sample
    (d) it injects excess minority carriers

71. A normal atom is one which
    (a) has equal number of electrons and protons
    (b) always has four valence electrons
    (c) always has an atomic core with charge of $+ 4q$
    (d) always shares its electrons with other atoms

72. The n-types impurity
    (a) must have only three valence electrons
    (b) creates excess holes
    (c) creates excess electrons
    (d) can be added to Ge but not Si

73. The conduction band is
    (a) always located at the top of the crystal
    (b) the same as forbidden energy gap
    (c) a range of energies coresponding to the energies of free electrons
    (d) not an allowed energy band

74. If arsenic impurity is added to germanium
    (a) it creates more holes
    (b) it causes free-electron density to excess hole density
    (c) it causes increase in resistance of Ge sample
    (d) it results in new energy level just above valence level

75. If indium impurity is added to germanium
    (a) it creates excess electrons
    (b) it results in hole density to exceed free electron density
    (c) it causes increase in resistance of Ge sample
    (d) it results in a new energy level just below conduction level

76. A hole shifts its position basically due to
    (a) a valence electron from a neighbouring atom joinging the hole to fill the vacancy
    (b) breaking of covalent band
    (c) movement of atomic core
    (d) increase in temperature

77. In n-type semiconductor
    (a) holcs form thc mojority carrier
    (b) electrons form the mojority carriers
    (c) impurity is trivalent
    (d) free electron density equals the hole density

78. In p-type semiconductor
    (a) holes form the monority carrier
    (b) free electrons form the minority carriers
    (c) hole density equals free electron density
    (d) impurity is pentavalent

79. Drift current in germanium is caused by
    (a) thermal agitation of crystal lattice
    (b) concentration gradient of charge carriers
    (c) applied electric field
    (d) incidence of light

80. Donor impurity in germanium results in
    (a) increased forbidden energy gap
    (b) reduced forbidden energy gap
    (c) a narrow energy band slightly below conduction level
    (d) new discrete energy level slightly below cunduction level

81. Acceptor inpurity atoms in silicon result in
    (a) increased forbidden energy gap
    (b) reduced forbidden energy gap
    (c) new discrete energy level slightly below conduction band
    (d) new discrete energy level slightly above valence level

82. The transition region in an open circuited p-n junction contains
(a) free electrons only
(b) holes only
(c) both free electrons and holes
(d) uncovered immobile impurity ions

83. In a pn diode, hole diffuse from p-region to n-region because
(a) there is higher concentration of holes in the p-region
(b) holes are positively charged
(c) holes are urged to move by the barrier potential
(d) the free-electron in the n-region attract the holes

84. In an unbiased pn junction, the junction current at equilibrium is
(a) due to diffusion of majority carriers
(b) due to diffusion of minority carriers
(c) zero due to equal and opposite currents crossing the junction
(d) zero because no charges cross the junction

85. In an unbiased pn junction, zero current implies that
(a) the potential barier has disappeared
(b) number of holes diffusing from p-side to n-side equals the number of electrons diffusing fron n-side to p-side
(c) no carriers cross the junction
(d) total current crossing the junction from p-side to n-side equals the total current crossing the junction from n-side to p-side

86. In the energy band diagram of an open circuited pn junction, the energy band of n region has shifted relative to that of p-region
(a) downward by E_o
(b) upward by E_o
(c) downward by $E_o/2$
(d) upward by $E_o/2$
where E_o equals $q\,V_o$

87. In a pn diode, with the increase of reverse bias, the reverse current
(a) increases
(b) decreases
(c) remains constant
(d) may increase or decrease depending on the doping

88. A reverse based pn junction has
(a) net hole current
(b) net electron current
(c) extremely small constant reverse current
(d) very large current

89. In a Ge diode, reverse saturation current I_o is of the order of
(a) 1 pA
(b) 1 nA
(c) 1 A
(d) 1 mA

90. In a silicon diode, the reverse saturation current is of the order of
(a) 1pA
(b) 1nA
(c) 1 A
(d) 1mA

91. In Ge diode, the cutin voltage is about
(a) 0.2 volt
(b) 0.6 volt
(c) 1.1 volt
(d) 2 volt

92. In Si diode, the cutin voltage is about
(a) 0.2 volt
(b) 0.6 volt
(c) 1.1 volt
(d) 1.75 volt

93. In a pn diode, for constant value of current at room temperature dV/dT varies approximately at the rate of
(a) $- 2.5$ m V/deg C
(b) $- 25$ mV/deg C
(c) $+ 2.5$ mV/deg C
(d) $+ 25$ mV/deg C

94. Ge diode at room temperature for forward current of 26 mA has dynamic resistance of about
(a) $0.1\ \Omega$
(b) $1\ \Omega$
(c) $10\ \Omega$
(d) $1000\ \Omega$

95. The reverse bias on pn junction
(a) pushes the electrons and holes aways from the junction
(b) has no effect on the holes and electrons
(c) attracts holes and electrons towards the junction
(d) increases the reverse current

96. In a forward biased pn diode
(a) forward current is zero
(b) only holes cross the junction from p side to n side
(c) only electrons cross the junction from n-side to p-side
(d) both holes on the p-side and electron on the n-side cross the junction to the opposite sides.

97. In a pnp transistor operating in the active region, the concentraiton of minority carrier holes in the n-region at collector junction J_c is
(a) zero
(b) thermal equilibrium value p_{no} of emitter
(c) thermal equilibrium concentration of hole in collector region
(d) same as at J_E

98. As the magnitude of the collector junction reverse bias increases, the effective base width

(a) increases

(b) decreases

(c) remains unaltered

(d) first increases and later becomes constant

99. In an npn diffused junction transistor, the p-type base region is formed on the n-type collector region through process of

(a) alloying

(b) epitaxial

(c) change in the nature of doping during crystal growth

(d) diffusion of p-type impurity

100. In a pnp transistor operating in the active region; in the base region, the main stream of current is

(a) drift of holes

(b) diffusion of holes

(c) drfit of electrons

(d) diffusion of electrons

101. In a Ge BJT, for usual value of the collector current, the transistor α is of the order of

(a) 0.99   (b) 0.9

(c) 0.5   (d) 50

102. In a pnp Ge transistor, the cutin voltage is about

(a) –0.01 volt   (b) –0.1 volt

(c) –0.5 volt   (d) –5 volt

103. In a pnp Si transistor, the cutin voltage is about

(a) –0.01 volt   (b) –0.1 volt

(c) –0.5 volt   (d) –5 volt

104. In a BJT, as the conductivity of the base region increases, the punch through voltage

(a) remains unaltered

(b) increases

(c) decreases

(d) may increase or decrease depending on bias at J_E

105. The dynamic emitter resistance of a BJT operating in the active region is of the order of

(a) 0.01 Ω (b) 1 Ω

(c) 100 Ω (d) 10 kΩ

106. In active region operation of a transistor

(a) both junctions are reverse biased

(b) both junctions are forward biased

(c) Emitter junction is forward biased while collector junction is reverse biased

(d) Emitter junction is reverse biased while collector junction is forward biased

107. In cutoff region operation of a transistor

(a) both J_E and J_C are forward biased

(b) both J_E and J_C are reverse biased

(c) J_E is forward biased while J_C is reverse biased

(d) J_E is reverse biased while J_C is forward biased

where J_E and J_C are respectively the emitter and collector junctions

108. In saturation region operation of a transistor

(a) both J_E and J_C are forward biased

(b) both J_E and J_C are reverse biased

(c) J_E is forward biased while J_C is reverse biased

(d) J_E is reverse biased while J_C is forward biased

109. For active region operation of a pnp transistor

(a) Emitter is positive with respect to base

(b) Emitter is negative with respect to base

(c) Emitter is at the same voltage as base

(d) Base is at the same voltage as collector

110. For active region operation of npn transistor

(a) Emitter is positive with respect to base

(b) Emitter is negative with respect to base

(c) Emitter is at the same voltage as base

(d) Base is at the same voltage as collector

111. In a BJT, the base spreading resistance is of the order of

(a) 10Ω (b) 100Ω

(c) 1Ω (d) 1 kΩ

112. The value of voltage V_{BE}, cutoff in a pnp silicon transistor approximately equals

(a) 0   (b) 0.1 volt

(c) 0.2 volt   (d) 0.5 volt

113. The value of V_{BE}, cutoff in a pnp Ge transistor approximately equals

(a) 0   (b) 0.1 volt

(c) 0.2 volt   (d) 0.5 volt

114. MOS transistor

(a) has only one pn junction

(b) conducts when sufficient voltage is applied to the gate electrode

(c) has only two electrodes

(d) has gate electrode in direct contact with the silicon

115. In inverted operation of a transistor

(a) both junctions are reverse biased

(b) both junctions are forward biased

(c) emitter junction is reverse biased while collector junction is forward biased

(d) emitter junction is forward biased while collector junction is reverse biased

116. Most of the small signal transistors are
 (a) npn silicon transistor in plastic package
 (b) pnp silicon transistor in plastic package
 (c) npn germanium transistor in metallic case
 (d) pnp germanium gransistor in metallic case

117. Transistor is usually encapsuled in
 (a) graphite powder (b) enamel paint
 (c) epoxy resin (d) all the above

118. Encapsulation of transistor is done to
 (a) provide mechanical ruggedness
 (b) prevent photo-electric effects
 (c) prevent electrical interference
 (d) to case heat radiation

119. Power transistors are invariably provided with
 (a) heat sink (b) metallic casing
 (c) soldered connections (d) fan for heat removal

120. Heat sink removes heat from a power transistor mainly by
 (a) radiation 0(b) conduction
 (c) nature convection (d) forced convection

121. With both junctions reverse biased the transistor operates in
 (a) active region (b) cutoff region
 (c) saturation region (d) inverted region

122. In an npn transistor operating in the active region the main current crossing the collector junction from base side is
 (a) hole drift current
 (b) hole diffusion current
 (c) electron diffusion current
 (d) electron drift current

123. A transistor with emitter junction forward biased and collector junction reverse biased is said to operate in
 (a) active region (b) saturation region
 (c) cutoff region (d) inverted region

124. In a transistor, current I_{CBO}
 (a) increase with increase of temperature
 (b) decrease with increase of temperature
 (c) is normally greater for Si transistor than Ge transistor
 (d) mainly depends on the emitter base junction bias

125. In a transistor current I_{CBO} flow in
 (a) base and emitter leads
 (b) collector and emitter leads
 (c) base and collector leads
 (d) emitter, base and collector leads

126. In an npn transistor, the function of emitter is
 (a) to inject holes into base
 (b) to inject electrons into the base
 (c) to inject electrons into the collector
 (d) to inject holes into the collector

127. Pinch off voltage V_p for an FET is the drain voltage at which
 (a) significant drain current starts flowing
 (b) drain current becomes zero
 (c) all free charges get removed from the channel
 (d) avalanche break down takes place

128. In a JFET, beyond the pinch off voltage, as the drain voltage increases; the drain current
 (a) remains almost constant
 (b) decreases
 (c) increases
 (d) may increase or decrease

129. n-channel FETs are superior to p-channel FETs because
 (a) they have lower switching time
 (b) they have lower pinch off voltage
 (c) they have higher input impedance
 (d) mobility of charge carrier electron in n-channel FET is greater than the mobility of charge carrier hole in p-channel FET

130. The charge carriers in a p-channel FET are
 (a) electrons alone
 (b) holes alone
 (c) both electrons and holes
 (d) may be either electrons or holes

131. The charge carriers in an n-channel FET are
 (a) electrons alone
 (b) holes alone
 (c) both electrons and holes
 (d) may be either electrons or holes

132. When the gate-to-source voltage V_{GS} of an n-channel JET is made more and more negative, the drain current
 (a) increases
 (b) decreases
 (c) remains unchanged
 (d) may increase or decrease

133. When the gate to source voltage V_{GS} of a p-channel JFET is made more positive, the drain current
 (a) increases
 (b) decreases
 (c) remains constant
 (d) may increase or decrease

134. The input resistance of a JFET is of the order of
    (*a*) 1 kΩ (*b*) 10 kΩ
    (*c*) 10 MΩ (*d*) 100 MΩ

135. The main drawback of a JFET is its
    (*a*) high input impedance
    (*b*) low input impedance
    (*c*) higher noise
    (*d*) lower gain

136. Inter electrode capacitances in an FET are of the order of
    (*a*) 1 pF   (*b*) 100 pF
    (*c*) 0.1 F   (*d*) 1 F

137. The dynamic drain resistance of a JFET is of the order of
    (*a*) 1 kΩ (*b*) 10 kΩ
    (*c*) 500 MΩ (*d*) 100 MΩ

138. The dynamic drain resistance of MOSFET is of the order of
    (*a*) 10 kΩ (*b*) 500 kΩ
    (*c*) 5 MΩ (*d*) 100 MΩ

139. The magnitude of the threshold voltage V_T for enhancement MOSFET is of the order of
    (*a*) 4 volts   (*b*) 10 volts
    (*c*) 40 volts   (*d*) 100 volts

140. Out of the four devices mentioned below, the fastest switching device is
    (*a*) JFET   (*b*) BJT
    (*c*) MOSFET   (*d*) Triode

141. The JFET can operate in
    (*a*) depletion mode only
    (*b*) enhancement mode only
    (*c*) either depletion or enhancement mode at a time
    (*d*) both depletion and enhancement modes simultaneously

142. The input gate current of FET is
    (*a*) a few amperes
    (*b*) a few milli-amperes
    (*c*) a few micro-amperes
    (*d*) negligibly small

143. Which of the following transistor is affected by static electricity
    (*a*) npn transistor   (*b*) JFET
    (*c*) UJT   (*d*) MOSFET

144. Which of the following device has the highest input impedance
    (*a*) CE BJT   (*b*) CC BJT
    (*c*) JFET   (*d*) MOSFET

145. A field-effect transistor (FET)
    (*a*) has three pn junctions
    (*b*) uses a forward biased junction
    (*c*) depends on the variation of a magnetic field for its operation
    (*d*) depends on the variation of a reverse voltage its operation

146. The operation of a JFET involves
    (*a*) flow of minority carriers alone
    (*b*) flow of majority carriers alone
    (*c*) flow of both minority and majority carriers
    (*d*) use of a magnetic field

147. FET
    (*a*) has a very high input impedance
    (*b*) depends on minority carrier flow
    (*c*) uses a forward biased junction
    (*d*) uses a high concentration emitter junction

148. A pnpn device having no gate is called
    (*a*) UJT   (*b*) Triac
    (*c*) Schockley diode   (*d*) SCR

149. A pnpn diode is
    (*a*) a negative resistance device
    (*b*) a voltage controllable device
    (*c*) a controlled rectifier
    (*d*) a current controlled negative resistance device

150. In a pnpn diode, breakover condition is marked by
    (*a*) a sudden decrease in current
    (*b*) a sudden increase in current
    (*c*) diode getting burnt off
    (*d*) a sudden glow taking place

151. Holding current in a pnpn diode is the
    (*a*) maximum operating current
    (*b*) normal operating current
    (*c*) current corresponding to breakover voltage
    (*d*) minimum current to keep the device ON.

152. A pnpn diode
    (*a*) is always made of silicon
    (*b*) is always made of germanium
    (*c*) may be made of either silicon or germanium
    (*d*) may be made of any semiconductor

153. The pnpn diode
    (*a*) is unilateral device
    (*b*) is a bilateral device
    (*c*) may function either as a unilateral or as a bilateral device
    (*d*) functions as a bilateral device depending on the ambient temp.

154. In a pnpn diode, breakover takes place when
(a) $(\alpha_1 + \alpha_2) = 0.5$
(b) $(\alpha_1 + \alpha_2) = 0.9$
(c) $(\alpha_1 + \alpha_2) = 1.0$
(d) $\alpha_1 = \alpha_2$, where α_1 and α_2 refer to the constituent transistors

155. In a pnpn diode, the phenomenon of rate effect depends on
(a) rate of change of temperature
(b) rate of change of applied voltage
(c) avalanche breakdown
(d) negative resistance in the forward voltage condition

156. A bilateral pnpn diode switch
(a) consists of two pnpn diodes in parallel but in opposite order
(b) is a 3 layer semiconductor device
(c) is a unilateral device
(d) is a bilateral device

157. Over temperature range of $-60°$ to $+150°$C, sensitor has temperature coefficient of resistance of about
(a) -0.5% per deg C
(b) -0.2% per deg C
(c) $+0.7\%$ per deg C
(d) $+2.0\%$ per deg C

158. For Ge at room temperature, critical wavelength for photoconduction is
(a) 1.13 micron
(b) 1.73 micron
(c) 11.3 micron
(d) 17.3 micron

159. For Si at room temperature, critical wavelength for photoconduction is
(a) 1.13 micron
(b) 1.73 micron
(c) 11.3 micron
(d) 17.3 micron

160. Photoconductive cell most popularly used for visible light spectrum uses
(a) Ge
(b) Si
(c) G_A As
(d) Cadmium sulphide

161. In a photodiode, light is focussed to fall on
(a) p region only
(b) n-region only
(c) full p and n regions
(d) junction region only

162. Response time of PIN photodiode is of the order of
(a) 0.1 ns
(b) 1 ns
(c) 10 ns
(d) 1 milli-sec

163. In phototransistor, light is focussed to fall on
(a) emitter-to-base junction
(b) collector-to-base junction
(c) base region only
(d) all the three regions of the transistor

164. An npn phototransistor has typical sensitivity of the order of
(a) 25 A/mW/cm^2
(b) 250 A/mW/cm^2
(c) 2.5 mA/mW/cm^2
(d) 250 mA/mW/cm^2

165. Photovoltaic emf of a Ge photovoltaic cell is of the order of
(a) 0.1 volt
(b) 0.5 volt
(c) 1.1 volt
(d) 1.72 volt

166. Photovoltaic emf of a Si photovoltaic cell is of the order of
(a) 0.1 volt
(b) 0.5 volt
(c) 1.1 volt
(d) 1.72 volt

167. Conversion efficiency of a silicon solar cell is about
(a) 5%
(b) 10%
(c) 14%
(d) 25%

168. A semiconductor photo-diode uses
(a) photo-emissive effect
(b) photovoltaic effect
(c) photoconductive effect
(d) none of these

169. LED gives off visible light from
(a) region of depletion layer
(b) p region alone
(c) n region alone
(d) both p and n regions

170. LEDs have response time of the order of
(a) 0.1 ns
(b) 1 ns
(c) 100 ns
(d) 1 s

171. In LED, when excited electrons revert from conduction band to valence band, the phenomenon utilized is
(a) radioative recombination
(b) formation of photons
(c) energy transfer from one electron to other
(d) none of these

172. LEDs fabricated from Ga As emit radiation in
(a) ultraviolet region
(b) infrared region
(c) visible range
(d) none of these

173. LEDs fabricated from Ga As P emit radiation in
(a) ultraviolet region
(b) infrared region
(c) visible region
(d) none of these

174. In a tunnel diode, impurity concentration is of the order of
(a) 1 in 10^3
(b) 1 in 10^5
(c) 1 in 10^7
(d) 1 in 10^9

175. In a tunnel diode, depletion layer width is of the order of
(a) 100 Å
(b) 0.1 micron
(c) 1 micron
(d) 5 micron

176. Tunnel diode
(a) uses very heavy doping resulting in extremely small depletion layer width
(b) is a point contact diode with a very high value of reverse resistance

(*c*) has a small hole in its centre permitting tunnelling

(*d*) none of these

177. Tunnel diode is a pn diode with

(*a*) very high doping in p region

(*b*) very high doping in n region

(*c*) very high doping in both p and n regions

(*d*) low doping in both p and n region

178. Most important application of tunnel diode is

(*a*) as rectifier

(*b*) as switching device in digital circuits

(*c*) as voltage controllable device

(*d*) as oscillator

179. Avalanche break down results basically due to

(*a*) impact ionization

(*b*) strong electric field across the junction

(*c*) emission of electrons

(*d*) rise in temperature

180. Avalanche breakdown results at applied

(*a*) forward bias exceeding about 6 volt

(*b*) forward bias below 6 volts

(*c*) reverse bias exceeding about 6 volt

(*d*) reverse bias below 6 volts

181. Zener breakdwon results basically due to

(*a*) impact ionization

(*b*) strong electric field across the junction

(*c*) emission of electrons

(*d*) high thermal energy of the electrons

182. Zener breakdown results at applied

(*a*) forward bias exceeding about 6 volt

(*b*) forward bias below 6 volts

(*c*) reverse bias exceeding about 6 volt

(*d*) reverse bias below 6 volts

183. In a breakdown diode, the temperature coefficient of breakdown voltage Vz

(*a*) is always positive

(*b*) is always negative

(*c*) is always zero

(*d*) may be positive or negative

184. On increasing the current through the zener diode by a factor of 2, the voltage across the diode

(*a*) gets doubled

(*b*) becomes half

(*c*) remains almost unchanged

(*d*) becomes 4 times as large

185. The dynamic resistance of a zener diode

(*a*) increases with increase of its current

(*b*) decreases with increase of its current

(*c*) is almost independent of current

(*d*) may increase or decrease with increase of current

186. Two identical breakdown diodes on being connected in series have breakdown voltage of

(*a*) 20 volts   (*b*) 10 volts

(*c*) 40 volts   (*d*) 6 volts

187. Two breakdown diodes A and B have breakdown voltage ratings of 5.8 volts and 24 volts respectively. Then

(*a*) A is zener diode and B is avalanche diode

(*b*) A is avalanche diode and B is zener diode

(*c*) both are zener diodes

(*d*) both are avalanche diodes

188. The temperature coefficient of breakdown diode is defined as

(*a*) rate of change of breakdown voltage with temperature

(*b*) rate of change of dynamic resistance with temperature

(*c*) rate of change of power handling capacity with temperature

(*d*) rate of change of diode current with temperature

189. Zener breakdown diodes have breakdown voltage which

(*a*) has positive temperature coefficient

(*b*) has negative temperature coefficient

(*c*) is independent of temperature

(*d*) none of these

190. Avalanche breakdown diodes have breakdown voltage

(*a*) having positive temperature coefficient

(*b*) having negative temperature coefficient

(*c*) independent of temperature

(*d*) none of these

191. At $25°C$, a zener diode is rated at 2 watts. Its 8 power rating at $50°C$ will be

(*a*) 2 watts

(*b*) 1 watt

(*c*) greater than 2 watts

(*d*) much greater than 2 watts

192. In Schottky barrier diode, conduction is

(*a*) entirely by electrons

(*b*) entirely by holes

(*c*) mainly by holes but partly by electrons

(*d*) mainly by electrons but partly by holes

193. Maximum value of temperature coefficient of Vz in a breakdown diode is
(*a*) ±0.1 per cent/deg C (*b*) ±0.5 per cent/deg C
(*c*) +0.2 per cent/deg C (*d*) – 0.2 per cent/deg C

194. Unijunction transistor
(*a*) has only one pn junction
(*b*) has two pn junctions
(*c*) is a unipolar device
(*d*) is a bulk semiconductor device

195. In a UJT, instrinsic stand off ratio η is typically
(*a*) 0.2 (*b*) 0.4
(*c*) 0.7 (*d*) 0.99

196. A diode which utilizes cumulative multiplication of carriers through field induced impact ionization
(*a*) tunnel diode (*b*) varactor diode
(*c*) avalanche diode (*d*) zener breakdown diode

197. LCD consumes power of the order of
(*a*) a few microwatts
(*b*) a few milliwatts
(*c*) hundreds of milliwatts
(*d*) a few watts

198. LCDs have response time of the order of
(*a*) a few ns
(*b*) tens of ns
(*c*) a few milliseconds
(*d*) hundred of milliseconds

199. Transferred electron mechanism involved in Gunn diode consists in transfer of electrons
(*a*) from valence band to conduction band
(*b*) from valence band to satellite valley
(*c*) from central valley to satellite valley
(*d*) from satellite valleys to central valley

200. Performance of the following diode is not based on its negative resistance characteristic
(*a*) Gunn diode (*b*) IMPATT diode
(*c*) Tunnel diode (*d*) LSA diode

201. Transferred-electron bulk effect occurs in
(*a*) germanium (*b*) silicon
(*c*) gallium assenide (*d*) antimony

202. The main advantage of TRAPATT diode over IMPATT diode is its
(*a*) higher output
(*b*) higher efficiency
(*c*) lower noise
(*d*) capability to operate at higher frequencies

203. A zener diode is used for
(*a*) Voltage regulation (*b*) Rectification
(*c*) Noise suppression (*d*) Blocking a.c.

204. An SCR is a device having
(*a*) three layers with four junctions.
(*b*) three layers with two junctions.
(*c*) four layers with three junctions.
(*d*) two layers with three junctions.

205. Semi-conductor diode time constant is equal to
(*a*) value of majority carrier life time
(*b*) life time of minority carrier
(*c*) difussion capacitance time constant
(*d*) zero

206. To prepare a 'P' type semiconducting material the impurities to be added to silicon are
(*a*) Boron, Gallium
(*b*) Arsenic, Antimony
(*c*) Gallium, Phosphorous
(*d*) Gallium, Arsenic

207. FET is a good signal chopper because it
(*a*) exhibits no offset voltage at zero drain current
(*b*) occupies less space in integrated form
(*c*) has got high input impedance.
(*d*) is less noisy

208. In Bipolar Junction transistors, type of configuration which will give both voltage gain and current gain is
(*a*) CC (*b*) CB
(*c*) CE (*d*) None of these

209. $V^D - I^D$ characteristics of an FET are similar to that of
(*a*) Triode (*b*) Pentode
(*c*) Tertode (*d*) None of these

210. Transformer utilization factor for a Bridge Rectifier is given as
(*a*) 0.287 (*b*) 0.50
(*c*) 0.693 (*d*) 0.812

211. In every practical oscillatorm loop gain is
(*a*) slightly larger than unity
(*b*) slightly larger than ten
(*c*) infinity
(*d*) zero

212. Photoemission multipliers make use of
(*a*) Secondary emission
(*b*) Thermionic emission
(*c*) High emission
(*d*) Photoemission

213. By passing a triangular wave through a differentiating circuit the output wave shape is
(*a*) Spikes (*b*) Squarewave
(*c*) Sawtooth (*d*) Sinewave

214. Clipper circuits are used to obtain which one of the following waveforms?

   (*a*) Sharper   (*b*) Rectified

   (*c*) Fast rising   (*d*) Smaller amplitude

215. Zener diodes semiconductors are

   (*a*) Lightly doped   (*b*) Heavily doped

   (*c*) Medium doped   (*d*) Not at all doped

216. When a junction is formed between a metal and a semiconductor, the depletion layer is

   (*a*) more on the side of the metal

   (*b*) equal on both sides

   (*c*) less on the side of the metal

   (*d*) less on semiconductor side

217. Zener diodes are used in

   (*a*) Rectifiers   (*b*) Inverters

   (*c*) Demodulator   (*d*) Voltage regulators

218. A silicon transistor at a temperature of 25°C has leakage current ^{ICBO} of 10 microamps. If temperature rises to 55°C leakage current would be

   (*a*) 300 microamps   (*b*) 80 microamps

   (*c*) 22 microamps   (*d*) 10 microamps

Fill in the blanks

219. In a full wave rectifier operating from a 50 Hz main, ripple frequency is .....

220. Relationship between current through a semiconductor diode and voltage across it is......

221. The transconductance of a bipolar transistor operating at 1 m A emitter current is ....

222. Temperature co-efficient of the voltage across a forward biased diode operating at a constant current is .....

223. A vacuum triode has three electrodes called anode, cathode and ......

224. Most commonly use 'N' type impurity doping materials is ___

225. Flow of current in the semiconductor bulk of an FET involves the motion of ___ type of charge.

226. The cut in our turn on voltage for a silicon pn diode is ___ volt.

227. FETs are potentially good high frequency devices as they do not involve diffusion of ___ charge carriers.

228. Zener breakdown voltage decreases with

229. In saturation region, collector junction is ___ biased by atleast certain voltage.

230. Class-A amplifier operates essentially over ___ portion of its characteristics.

231. In comparison BJT generates ___ noise than an FET.

232. Voltage in a ___ cannot change suddenly if current is continuous in that element.

233. Two resonant tank circuits are frequently used to couple output of one state of a ___ amplifier to the input of the following stage.

234. Need for centre-tapped power transformer is eliminated by the ___ rectifier circuit.

235. Maximum theoretical efficiency achievable in a half-wave rectifier circuit is ___.

236. A Zener diode BJT regulator is better than a simple Zener diode regulator because it gives ___.

237. In a good differentiating circuit RC time constant must be ____ than the time period of the input wave.

238. A bistable multivibrator is also called ___.

239. Tetrode can be used as an oscillator due to its ___ characteristic.

240. When diode clipper is used in fast waveforms, then the stray ___ associated with the circuit may not be neglected.

241. It is not possible to use ___ clamping with a signal of arbitrary wave-form.

242. Silicon controlled rectifier is a ___ device.

243. Plate current in a diode under temperature controlled conditions is given by ___ law.

244. Maximum voltage that can be applied to a diode without destroying it is called ___.

245. Semiconductor used for fabricating an LED is

246. Frequency difference between image and its signal frequency is ____ the intermediate frequency.

247. Moving ____ meter is capable of measuring DC quantities only.

248. A circuit that can give square wave at the output for a sinusoidal input is the ____.

EXERCISE – II

1. Resistivity of a semiconductor depends on **DMRC 2013**
   - (a) the length of the semiconductor specimen
   - (b) cross-sectional area of the semiconductor specimen
   - (c) volume of the semiconductor specimen
   - (d) the atomic nature of the semiconductor

2. At $0°K$, the forbidden energy gap in silicon is
   - (a) 0.785 eV
   - (b) 1.21 eV
   - (c) 0.72 eV
   - (d) 1.1 eV **DMRC 2013**

3. When germanium is doped with trivalent impurity, the resulting material is **DMRC 2013**
   - (a) p-type semiconductor
   - (b) n-type semiconductor
   - (c) intrinsic semiconductor
   - (d) no longer a semiconductor

4. In a pnpn diode, the phenomenon of rate effect depends on **DMRC 2013**
   - (a) rate of change of temperature
   - (b) rate of change of applied voltage
   - (c) avalanche breakdown
   - (d) negative resistance in the forward voltage condition

5. Avalanche break down results basically due to
   - (a) impact ionization **DMRC 2013**
   - (b) strong electric field across the junction
   - (c) emission of electrons
   - (d) rise in temperature

6. Transferred electron mechanism involved in Gunn diode consists in transfer of electrons **DMRC 2013**
   - (a) from valence band to conduction band
   - (b) from valence band to satellite valley
   - (c) from central valley to satellite valley
   - (d) from satellite valleys to central valley

7. Halfwave rectifier has theoretical maximum efficiency of **DMRC 2013**
   - (a) 40.6%
   - (b) 81.2%
   - (c) 78.5%
   - (d) 50%

8. A capacitor filter at the output of a rectifier results in ripple which **DMRC 2013**
   - (a) increases with load resistance
   - (b) descreases with load resistance
   - (c) remain unattered with increase of load resistance
   - (d) none of these

9. Two resistors R_1 = 36 ohms and R_2 = 75 ohms, each having tolerance of $\pm$ 5% are connected in series. The value of the resultant resistance will be **DMRC**
   - (a) 111 ± 0 ohm
   - (b) 111 ± 2.778 ohm
   - (c) 111 ± 5.55 ohm
   - (d) 111 ± 7.23 ohm

10. The carrier mobility in a semiconductor is $0.4 \ m^2/Vs$. Its diffusion constant at 300 K will be (in m^3/s) **DMRC**
    - (a) 0.43
    - (b) 0.16
    - (c) 0.04
    - (d) 0.01

11. At very high temperatures, the extrinsic semiconductors become intrinsic because
    - (a) of drive-in diffusion of dopants and carries
    - (b) band to band transition dominates over impurity ionization
    - (c) impurity ionization dominates over band to band transition
    - (d) band to band transition is balanced by impurity ionization **DMRC**

12. Turns compensation in CT is used to **DRDO**
    - (a) eliminate ratio error
    - (b) eliminate phase angle error
    - (c) get transformation ratio equal to nominal ratio of transformer
    - (d) none of these

13. Which of the following method of biasing provides the best operating point stability **DRDO**
    - (a) Two battery bias
    - (b) Collector-to-base bias
    - (c) Fixed bias
    - (d) Self bias

14. In n-type silicon, each donor atom contributes
    - (a) one free electron **DRDO**
    - (b) 2 free electrons
    - (c) 3 free electrons
    - (d) 4 free electrons

15. Which of the following will serve as a donor impurity in silicon ? **DRDO**
    - (a) Boron
    - (b) Indium
    - (c) Germanium
    - (d) Antimony

16. In Si diode, the cutin voltage is about **DRDO**
    - (a) 0.2 volt
    - (b) 0.6 volt
    - (c) 1.1 volt
    - (d) 1.75 volt

17. In a transistor current I_{CBO} flow in **DRDO**
    - (a) base and emitter leads
    - (b) collector and emitter leads
    - (c) base and collector leads
    - (d) emitter, base and collector leads

18. Base-to-emitter voltage V_{BE} is a forward biased transistor decreases with increase of temperature at the rate **DRDO**
    - (a) 25 mV/deg C
    - (b) 0.25mV/deg C
    - (c) 2.5 mV/deg C
    - (d) 0.6 mV/deg C

19. Parameter hoe of a typical transistor is of the order of **DRDO**
    - (a) 2.5 S
    - (b) 25 S
    - (c) 250 S
    - (d) 2.5 mS

20. The reference unit in a dc voltage regulator is generally in the form of   **DRDO**

(a) a silicon breakdown diode

(b) a transistor

(c) a battery

(d) a differential amplifier

21. SCR is a   **DRDO**

(a) 2 layer device

(b) 3 layer device

(c) 4 layer device with one gate

(d) 4 layer device with two gates

22. After firing an SCR, if the gate pulse is removed, the SCR current   **DRDO**

(a) remains the same

(b) reduces to zero

(c) rises up

(d) rises a little and then falls to zero

23. A device that does not exhibit negative resistance characteristics is   **DRDO**

(a) FET   (b) UJT

(c) tunnel diode   (d) SCR

24. A certain oscilloscope with 4 cm by 4 cm screen has its own speed output fed to its input at the x and y sensitivities are same. The oscilloscope will display a   **RRB**

(a) triangular wave   (b) diagonal line

(c) sine wave   (d) circle

25. In Ge, when atoms are held together by the sharing of valence electrons   **RRB**

(a) each shared atom leaves a hole

(b) valence electrons are free to move away from the nucleus

(c) velence electrons form irreversible covalent bands

(d) valence electrons form reversible covalent bands

26. The operation of a JFET involves   **RRB**

(a) flow of minority carriers alone

(b) flow of majority carriers alone

(c) flow of both minority and majority carriers

(d) use of a magnetic field

27. A cascade voltage doubler can be used to provide any degree of voltage multiplication by   **RRB**

(a) using diodes with large PIV rating

(b) adding a step up transformer

(c) cascading diodes and capacitors

(d) increasing the values of capacitors

28. Effective reactance of an inductive coil   **RRB**

(a) increases because of stray capacitance as the frequency increases

(b) decreases because of stray capacitances as the frequency increases

(c) remain the same irrespective of the increase in frequency even if stray series capacitances are present

(d) none of these

29. If transients during switching of a power supply are to be studied, the which of the following oscilloscope will be preferred?   **RRB**

(a) An ordinary oscilloscope with high frequency sweep generator

(b) Dual beam oscilloscope

(c) Dual trace oscilloscope

(d) Storage oscilloscope

30. In N_2-washout estimation of lung volume using spirometry, the lung volumes at the beginning and the end of the washout are the same. Let T, V, and F denote temperature, volume and molar fraction (of N_2) respectively; subscripts S and L denote the spirometer and the lung; and t_1 and t_2 the beginning time and the end time of the experiment, respectively. Then   **RRB**

(a) $V_L = \dfrac{T_L}{T_S} \left[\dfrac{F_S(t_2)\, V_S(t_2)}{F_L(t_1) - F_L(t_2)} \right]$

(b) $V_L = \dfrac{T_L}{T_S} \left[\dfrac{F_L(t_2)\, V_S(t_2)}{F_L(t_1) - F_L(t_2)} \right]$

(c) $V_L = F_L(t_1)\, V_L(t_2)$

(d) $V_L = T_S F_S(t_2)\, V_S(t_2)$

31. The ECG of a patient is being recorded using the three standard frontal plane leads. if the cardiac vector is oriented at an angle of 45 degrees to Lead I and has a magnitude of 3mV, the voltages seen on Leads I, II and III are   **RRB**

(a) 1.50, 2.27, and 0.77 mV

(b) 2.12, 0.77, and 2.89 mV

(c) 2.12, 3.15, and 1.03 mV

(d) 2.12, 2.89, and 0.77 mV

32. The transmittance of a sample solution is monitored using 500 nm wavelength. The transmittance is reduced from 100% to 10% due to addition of pollutants. As a result, the absorbance recorded by the spectrophotometer changes from   **RRB**

(a) $0 \to 1$ (b) $2 \to 1$

(c) $0 \to 2$ (d) $0 \to 10$

ANSWERS

EXERCISE – I

1. (b)	**2.** (c)	**3.** (c)	**4.** (c)	**5.** (d)	**6.** (c)	**7.** (d)	**8.** (a)	**9.** (b)	**10.** (d)
11. (b)	**12.** (d)	**13.** (c)	**14.** (c)	**15.** (c)	**16.** (a)	**17.** (c)	**18.** (b)	**19.** (c)	**20.** (b)
21. (c)	**22.** (c)	**23.** (b)	**24.** (c)	**25.** (b)	**26.** (a)	**27.** (c)	**28.** (b)	**29.** (d)	**30.** (c)
31. (c)	**32.** (d)	**33.** (c)	**34.** (b)	**35.** (b)	**36.** (b)	**37.** (c)	**38.** (a)	**39.** (b)	**40.** (b)
41. (b)	**42.** (a)	**43.** (c)	**44.** (c)	**45.** (b)	**46.** (a)	**47.** (c)	**48.** (c)	**49.** (d)	**50.** (c)
51. (c)	**52.** (a)	**53.** (b)	**54.** (b)	**55.** (c)	**56.** (a)	**57.** (b)	**58.** (d)	**59.** (c)	**60.** (b)
61. (b)	**62.** (c)	**63.** (a)	**64.** (b)	**65.** (c)	**66.** (b)	**67.** (c)	**68.** (c)	**69.** (a)	**70.** (c)
71. (a)	**72.** (c)	**73.** (c)	**74.** (b)	**75.** (b)	**76.** (a)	**77.** (b)	**78.** (b)	**79.** (c)	**80.** (d)
81. (d)	**82.** (a)	**83.** (c)	**84.** (d)	**85.** (b)	**86.** (c)	**87.** (c)	**88.** (c)	**89.** (b)	**90.** (b)
91. (b)	**92.** (a)	**93.** (b)	**94.** (a)	**95.** (d)	**96.** (a)	**97.** (b)	**98.** (d)	**99.** (b)	**100.** (a)
101. (b)	**102.** (c)	**103.** (c)	**104.** (b)	**105.** (b)	**106.** (b)	**107.** (a)	**108.** (a)	**109.** (b)	**110.** (d)
111. (a)	**112.** (b)	**113.** (c)	**114.** (c)	**115.** (a)	**116.** (c)	**117.** (a)	**118.** (a)	**119.** (c)	**120.** (b)
121. (c)	**122.** (a)	**123.** (a)	**124.** (c)	**125.** (b)	**126.** (c)	**127.** (c)	**128.** (d)	**129.** (b)	**130.** (a)
131. (b)	**132.** (a)	**133.** (d)	**134.** (d)	**135.** (c)	**136.** (c)	**137.** (a)	**138.** (a)	**139.** (c)	**140.** (a)
141. (d)	**142.** (d)	**143.** (d)	**144.** (d)	**145.** (b)	**146.** (a)	**147.** (c)	**148.** (d)	**149.** (b)	**150.** (d)
151. (a)	**152.** (a)	**153.** (c)	**154.** (b)	**155.** (a)	**156.** (c)	**157.** (b)	**158.** (a)	**159.** (d)	**160.** (d)
161. (b)	**162.** (b)	**163.** (c)	**164.** (b)	**165.** (a)	**166.** (c)	**167.** (c)	**168.** (a)	**169.** (b)	**170.** (a)
171. (c)	**172.** (c)	**173.** (c)	**174.** (a)	**175.** (b)	**176.** (c)	**177.** (b)	**178.** (a)	**179.** (c)	**180.** (b)
181. (d)	**182.** (d)	**183.** (c)	**184.** (c)	**185.** (b)	**186.** (a)	**187.** (a)	**188.** (a)	**189.** (b)	**190.** (c)
191. (a)	**192.** (a)	**193.** (a)	**194.** (c)	**195.** (c)	**196.** (a)	**197.** (d)	**198.** (c)	**199.** (d)	**200.** (c)
201. (b)	**202.** (b)	**203.** (a)	**204.** (c)	**205.** (a)	**206.** (a)	**207.** (a)	**208.** (c)	**209.** (b)	**210.** (d)
211. (a)	**212.** (a)	**213.** (a)	**214.** (d)	**215.** (b)	**216.** (c)	**217.** (d)	**218.** (b)		

219. 100   **220.** $i = KEb^{3/2}$ **221.** 1000

222. Positive   **223.** Control grid   **224.** Arsenic /Antimoney

225. One   **226.** 0.7   **227.** Electron/ hole

228. Increases the diping   **229.** Forward   **230.** Linear

231. More   **232.** Inductor   **233.** I.F.

234. Bridge   **235.** 40.6%

236. Reduced zener impledance/stabilized output is available

237. Smaller   **238.** Flip-flop   **239.** Negative resistance

240. Capacitance   **241.** Positive   **242.** 4 layers

243. Child's   **244.** PIV (peak inverse voltage)   **245.** Silicon

246. Twice   **247.** Coil   **248.** Schmitt trigger.

EXERCISE – II

1. (d)	**2.** (b)	**3.** (a)	**4.** (a)	**5.** (c)	**6.** (d)	**7.** (a)	**8.** (b)	**9.** (c)	**10.** (d)
11. (b)	**12.** (c)	**13.** (d)	**14.** (a)	**15.** (d)	**16.** (a)	**17.** (b)	**18.** (c)	**19.** (b)	**20.** (a)
21. (d)	**22.** (c)	**23.** (a)	**24.** (b)	**25.** (d)	**26.** (a)	**27.** (c)	**28.** (b)	**29.** (d)	**30.** (c)
31. (b)	**32.** (b)								

Electronic Analog Circuits

TRANSISTORS

Transistors have replaced vacuum tubes, in most of the circuits.

Advantages of transistors :

1. Smaller in size
2. Light in weight
3. No heater or filament needed
4. Usually operate on low voltages
5. Consume little power
6. Improved circuit efficiency
7. Long life
8. Shock proof

A transistor is a silicon or germanium crystal containing three separate regions. Transistors may be NPN or PNP type both having three regions. The middle region is called *base* and the two outer regions are called *emitter* and *collector*.

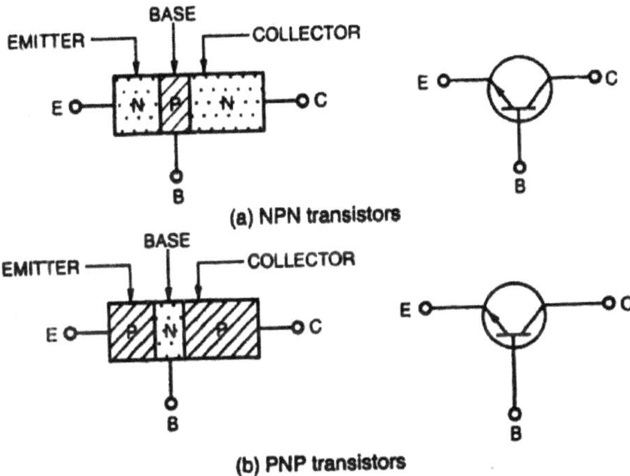

- collector region is made physically larger than the emitter region as it is required to dissipate more heat.
- emitter is heavily doped.
- base is lightly doped and is thin.
- emitter emits or injects electrons in case of PNP transistor (holes in case of PNP transistor) into the base.
- collector collects these electrons in NPN transistor (holes in PNP transistor).
- there are two PN- junctions in a transistor. The junction between emitter and base is called emitter junction. The junction between collectro and base is called the collector junction.
- PNP transistor is a complement of PNP transistor.

- NPN transistor is virtually a semi-conductor analogue of vacuum tube.
- junction of a transistor may be forward biased or reverse biased. Accordingly the region of operation of the transistor will be as shown below

Emitter junction	Collector junction	Region of operation
Forward biased	Reverse biased	Active
Forward biased	Forward biased	Saturation
Reverse biased	Reverse biased	Cut off
Reverse biased	Forward biased	Inverted

CLASSIFICATION

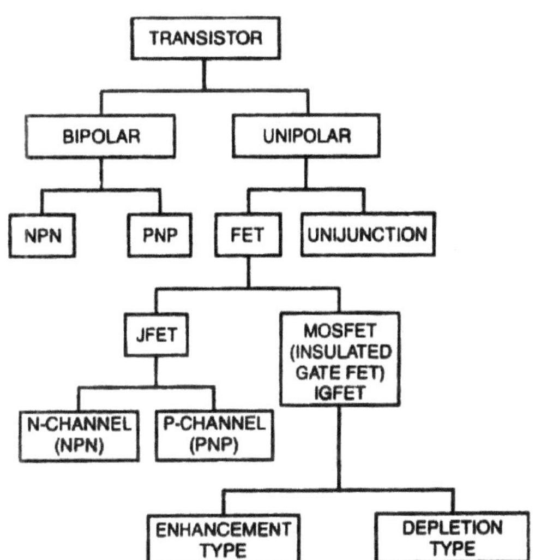

Bipolar : Bipolar uses both –ve and +ve charge carrier. Operation depends on 2 types of charge carriers holes and electrons. Current carriers have 2 polarities or poles since both holes and electrons make up the current flow through NPN or PNP devices.

Unipolar : Transistor having only one type of current carrier either (hole or electron).

Its operation depends on only one type of charge carries either hole or electron.

Transistor conducts through only one piece of semi-conductor material (P or N).

A bipolar transistor is like 2 pn-junction diodes connected back to back.

(*i*) Generally diffusion current is considered because drifts currents due to thermally generated minority carriers are usually very small and can be neglected.

(*ii*) The emitter is highly doped and base is lightly doped.

Reverse Leakage Current.

A leakage current in a transistor is due to flow of minority carriers. The concentration of these minority carriers is very much dependent on temperature. Hence leakage current is temperature dependent.

$I_{CEO} \rightarrow$ Between collector and emitter when base open.

$I_{CBO} \rightarrow$ Between collector and base when emitter is open.

BIOPOLAR JUNCTION TRANSISTORS

A diode cannot be used for amplifying purposes. For this purpose a transistor is used. A transistor is a three section semiconductor. It is of two types npn or pnp. It contains three parts,

(*a*) **Emitter :** It supplies majority charge carriers for current flow.

(*b*) **Base :** The base, which is always lightly doped, provides the junctions for proper interaction between Emitter and Collector.

(*c*) **Collector :** It collects majority charge carriers.

Diping level : emitter > base > collector

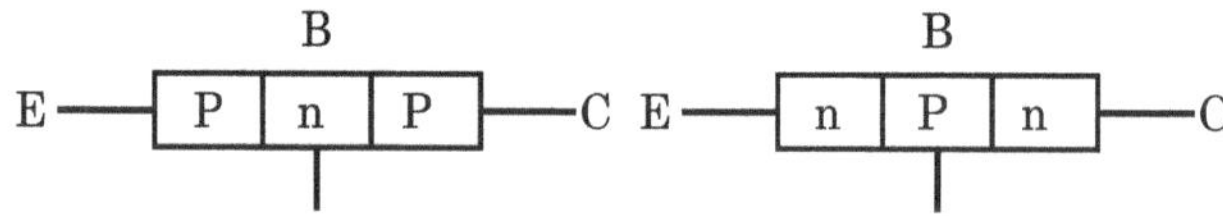

SYMBOL FOR TRANSISTOR

Cut off Region	Saturation Region	Active Region
BE: Reverse Bias	BE: Forward Biased	BE: Forward Biased
BC: Reverse Bias	BC: Forward Biased	BC: Reverse Bias

BE is forward biased and BC is reverse biased i.e. a transistor must be connected in the circuit in ACTIVE MODE.

Transistor working

$$I_e = I_b + I_c$$

The majority charge carriers (electrons in the case of emitter) are repelled towards base because of forward bias. Base contains holes as majority charge carriers and their number dinsity is small in comparison to number density of electrons in n region (or emitter or collector). As a result of this there is a very small probability of electron hole combination. In the base of transistor only 5% of electrons combine with holes and remaining 95% cross to collector and then swept by positive terminal of V_{cb} battery. Corresponding to each electron swept by positive terminal of V_{cb} battery the negative terminal of the V_{eb} battery leaves an electron which enters emitter of battery and hence current is carried inside as well as outside the transistor.

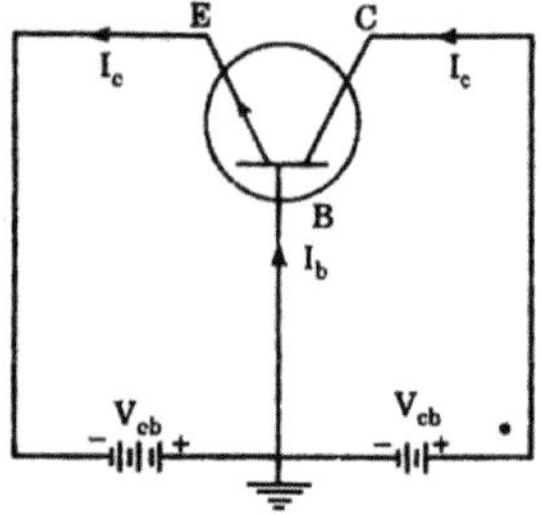

Note :

• All arrows point in the direction of conventional current. A similar explanation can also be provided in case of pnp transistor.

• For both the transistors

TRANSISTOR CONFIGURATIONS

In case of transistors any one of the three terminals can be chosen as reference or common terminal. Emitter is most frequently the common terminal. The voltage drops are positive going from the non-reference terminals to the reference terminal. NPN transistor connections are shown

Transistor connection	Positive voltages	Positive currents	Signal input
Common emitter CE	V_{BE} and V_{CE}	i_{BE} and i_{CE}	Base
Common base CB	V_{CB}	i_{CB}	Emitter
Common collector CC	V_{BC}	i_{BC}	Base

In case of PNP transistor all the acutal instantaneous voltages and currents have signs, which are opposite to the corresponding ones for NPN transistors.

TRANSISITOR BIASING

For proper operation of the amplifier circuit, biasing arrangement should ensure the following points :

1. The biasing arrrangement should fix the operating point Q so that equal amplification takes place during positive and negative half cycles of the input signal.

2. The operating point should be established so as not to allow the device to go into saturation or cut off regions during the peaks of the input signal.

3. The biasing arrangement should ensure stabilization of the operating point against shifts with temperature variations or with replacement of a transistor.

FIELD EFFECT TRANSISTORS (FET)

Field effect transistor. Operation depends on the flow of majority carriers only. So , it is a unipolar device.

No minority carrier current.

In N channel FET : Width of space between P regions is controlled by varying gate voltage (Controlled by gate-to- source potential).

Advantages :

1. Easy / Simpler to make

2. High input impedance (Mega Ω)

3. High power gain

4. Less noisy

5. No offset voltage at zero drain current

6. Occupies less space in IC form

FIELD EFFECT TRANSISTORS

Just as *npn* and *pnp* bipolar junction transistor, there are *n*-channel and *p*-channel field effect transistors.

FET is an unipolar device, *i.e.* either electron (*n*-channel) or holes (*p*-channel) conduction.

For the FET, an electric field is established by charge present that will control the conduction path of the output without the need for direct contact between the controlling and controlled quantities.

One of the most important characteristic of FET is its high input impedence ($1 - 1000$ MΩ). BJT outputs are more sensitive to change in input quantities while FET output is less sensitive to the change in input quantities or in other word FETs are more temperature stable than BJTs.

Types of field effect transistors.

1. JFET (Junction Field Effect Transistor).

Primarily difference between BJT and JFET is that BJT is a current controlled device where as JFET is a voltage-controlled device.

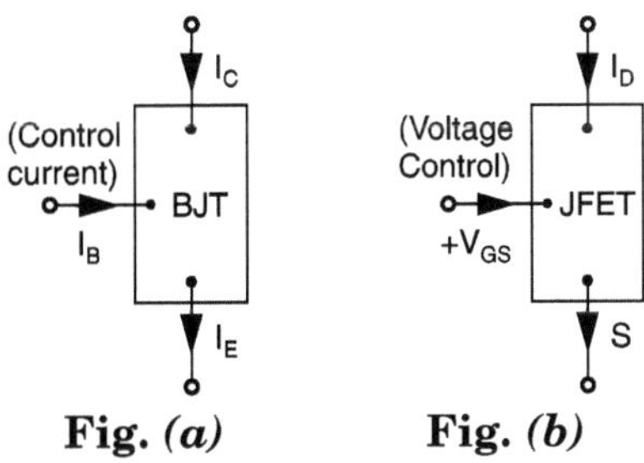

Fig. (a)   **Fig. (b)**

In Fig. *(a)* I_C is a direct function of level of I_B while in Fig. *(b)*, the current I_D will be a function of voltage V_{GS} applied to the input circuit.

In each case, current of output circuit is controlled by a parameter of the input circuit.

Construction : JFET is a three terminal device with one terminal capable of controlling the current between the other two. Basic construction of *n*-channel JFET is shown in the figure.

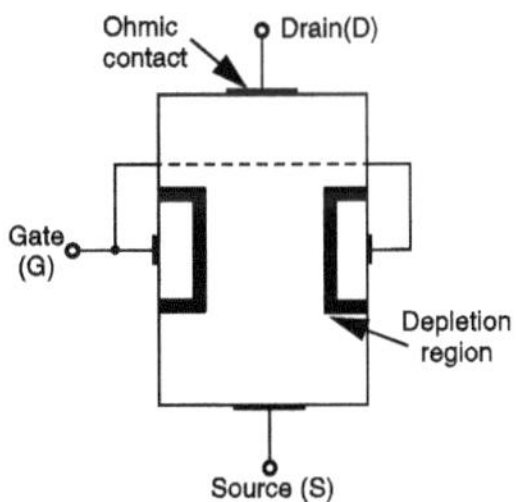

In absence of any applied potentials, JFET has two *pn* junctions under no bias conditions. Depletionlayer is void of free carriers and therefore unable to support conduction through the region.

Gate applied potential control the flow of charges from source to drain.

2. MOSFET (Metal Oxide Semiconductor Field Effect Transistor).

Construction of *n*-channel depletion type MOSFET :

A slab of *p*-type material is formed from a silicon base and is referred to as the substrate. It is the foundation upon which the device is constructed. The source and drain terminals are connected through metallic contact to *n*-doped regions linked by an *n*-channel. Gate is also connected to a metal contact surface but remains insulated from the *n*-channel by a very thin SiO_2 layer. SiO_2 is a particular type of insulator referred to as dielectric that sets up opposing electric field in the dielectric, when exposed to an externally applied field.

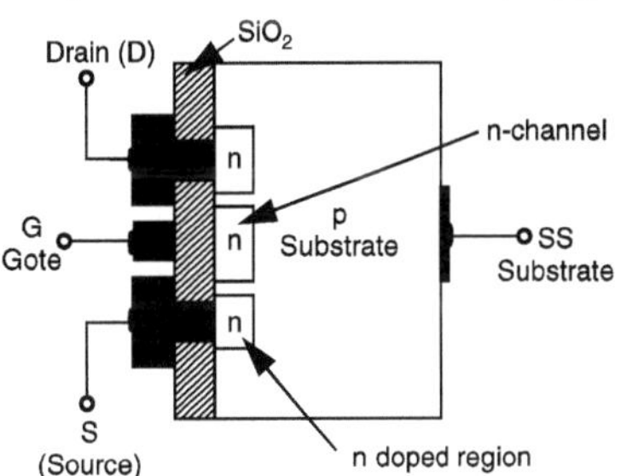

There is no electrical connection between gate terminal and the channel of a MOSFET. In addition to this, it is insulating layer of SiO_2 in the MOSFET construction that accounts for desirable very high impedance.

COMMON BASE AMPLIFIER

The base is common to emitter as well as collector.

(*a*) Here the voltages will be written with the base symbol (*b*) at second place. This indicates that base is common.

(*b*) The current in the common branch will be governed by the battery which is forward biased.

SINGLE STAGE TRANSISTOR AMPLIFIER

A single stage of amplifier can provide only a limited current gain or voltage gain. Most of the applications require much higher gain. Hence we usually use several amplifier stages connected in cascade i.e. connected such that output of one stage becomes input to the next stage. Thus a multistage amplifier or cascade amplifier may provide a higher voltage or current gain.

In most applications, an amplifier is required to provide large power output, generally at the cost of higher distortion. Such amplifiers are called *large signal amplifiers* or *power amplifiers*.

CLASSIFICATION OF AMPLIFIERS.

1. According to Frequency range.

(*i*) **DC (Direct coupled) amplifiers :** From zero frequency (dc) onwards.

(*ii*) **Audio frequency amplifiers :** 20 Hz to 20 kHz

(*iii*) **Video frequency amplifiers :** Upto a few MHz

(iv) Radio frequency (RF) amplifiers : From a few kHz to hundreds of MHz.

(v) Ultra high frequency (UHF) and Microwave amplifiers: Upto hundred or thousands of MHz.

2. According to Method of operation.

The position of the zero signal (quiescent) operating point and the extent of characteristic curves being used determine the category of operation. Thus amplifiers (using either BJT or FET) may be classified as class A, class AB, class B or class C amplifiers as per following definition.

(i) Class A amplifiers. In these operating point and the input signal magnitude are so selected that the output circuit current (collector current or drain current) flows all the time (for full cycle of the a.c. signal). A class A amplifier operates essentially over the linear portion of characteristic curves of the device.

(ii) Class B amplifier. In these operating point is placed at an extreme end of its characteristic curve with the result that zero signal current (or zero signal voltage) is almost zero. Hence zero signal output power is very small. With a sinusoidal input signal voltage, amplification takes place for only half the cycle. Thus if output circuit quiescent current is zero, on application of signal, the output current remains zero for half the cycle and flows for the remaining half cycle.

(iii) Class AB amplifier. In these operation lies in between class A and class B operations. Thus in a class AB amplifier, output current flows for more than half but less than the complete cycle of input sinusoidal signal.

(iv) Class C amplifier. In these operating point is so chosen that the output current flows for less than one-half of the input sinusoidal signal cycle.

3. According to Type of Load impedance.

Load impedance may be an untuned circuit or a tune circuit. Accordingly amplifiers may be classified as

(i) Untuned amplifiers. An untuned amplifier uses either a pure resistance or a complex impedance as the load impedance.

Untuned amplifiers may be further subdivided into two categories :

(a) Audio frequency amplifiers : These are used for amplifying frequencies in the audio frequency range i.e. upto 20 kHz. When we speak or play a sound instrument, sound frequencies so generated extend upto about 20 kc/s and corresponding electrical signal at the output of microphone also extends upto about 20 kHz. Amplifiers used for amplifying frequencies in audio frequency range (20 kHz) are, therefore, falled audio frequency amplifiers.

(b) Video frequency amplifiers : Vision signals such as produced at the output of a TV camera extend upto several MHz. Amplifiers designed for amplifying these signals of frequency extending upto several MHz are, therefore called video amplifiers or pulse amplifiers or wideband amplifiers.

(ii) Tuned amplifiers. A tuned amplifier uses one or more parallel tuned L-C circuits as the load impedance. Tuned amplifiers are used for amplification of signals consisting of either a single radio frequency (> 30 kHz) or a narrow band of requencies in the R.F. range. Tuned amplifiers are often referred to as radio frequency (R.F.) amplifiers.

4. According to number of stages and Method of coupling.

(i) Single stage amplifiers

(ii) Multistage amplifiers. *Multistage amplifiers may be further classified into following categories depending on the method of coupling.*

(a) Direct coupled (dc) amplifiers

(b) R.C. coupled amplifiers

(c) Transformer coupled amplifiers.

5. According to Primary function.

(i) Small signal amplifiers. These provide linear amplification with minimum distortion.

(ii) Large signal (Power) amplifiers. These are designed to provide large power output but at the same time permit somewhat higher distortion.

Note :

(i) Untuned small signal amplifiers use class A operation. Class AB, B or C operations can not be used because of large distortion.

(ii) Untuned large signal (power) amplifier may use class A operation but conversion efficiency is small. More commonly untuned power amplifiers use class AB or class B operations using pushpull circuit. Class AB or B operations provide higher conversion efficiency. But pushpull circuit is essential to keep distortion low. Single ended class AB or class B untuned amplifiers are never used. Further untuned amplifier can not use class C operation because the distortion is so large that even pushpull circuit can not handle it.

(iii) Class C operation is used only in tuned (radio frequency) amplifiers.

(iv) Several important waveshaping functions may be performed using AB or B overdriven amplifiers.

CASCADING OF AMPLIFIER STAGES

Cascading of amplifier stages is usually done to increase total gain of the amplifier. However, sometimes cascading is done to get the desired output and input impedance for specific applications.

Transistor amplifier may be connected in any of the three configurations.

(*i*)   Common emitter (CE)

(*ii*)   Common base (CB)

(*iii*)   Common collector (CC).

However, in cascade amplifiers meant for providing high gain, only CE amplifier stages are connected in cascade. CB and CC configurations can not be used for this purpose. The load impedance is a resistor while coupling is through a capacitor. Hence this cascade amplifier forms the so called *resistance - capacitance coupled* or *RC coupled amplifier*. R.C. coupled amplifier is most popularly used for audio frequency amplification.

AMPLIFIER CLASSES

One method generally employed to categorize amplifier is by class which basically represent the amount of output signal varies over one cycle of operation for a full cycle of input signal.

1. **Class A :** The amplifier circuits which falls into this category are linear as these operate in a small region in the middle of the load line.

2. **Class B :** This amplifier circuit provides an output signal varying over one-half the input signal cycle.

   Class B operation creates a very distorted output as reproduction of the input takes place for only 180° of the output signal swing. Power efficiency of class-B is more than that of Class-A.

3. **Class AB :** This amplifier is biased at a dc level above the zero base current level of class B and above one-half supply voltage level of class A. For class AB operation, the output signal during occurs between 180° to 360° and is neither class A nor class B operation as shown in the figure

4. **Class C :** 'ϕ' the output of class C amplifier is biased for operation atless than 180° of the cycle and will operate only with a tuned circuit which provides a full cycle of operation for the tuned frequency.

5. **Class D :** In this amplifier circuit, amplification is done with pulse signals which are ON for a short interval and OFF for a longer interval, which causes for its high efficiency.

LARGE SIGNAL AMPLIFIER (POWER AMPLIFIER)

In a multistage amplifier, first stage or the input stage and intermediate stages are usually small signal class A amplifier stages, while last stage (output stage) or sometimes last two stages are large signal amplifier (power amplifier) stages. Small signal amplifier stages serve to amplify the weak input signal to a sufficient large value to drive the final stage. The output stage generally feeds a transducer such as CR tube, loud speaker, servo-control motor etc. The large signal amplifier stage must be capable of handling large voltage or current swings and hence capable of delivering large power to the load.

Important features in the study of large signal amplifier are :

distortion, output power, conversion efficiency, bias stabilization and tendency of thermal runaway.

Large signal untuned amplifiers may be operated under class A, AB or B conditions but never under class C condition. A

Main features

(*i*) Circuits power efficiency,

(*ii*) Maximum amount of power that the circuit is capable of handling and

(*iii*) Impedance matching to the output device.

Power amplifier are classified on the basis of class. The amplifier classes represent the amount the output signal varies over one cycle of operation for a full cycle of input signal.

FEED BACK AMPLIFIER

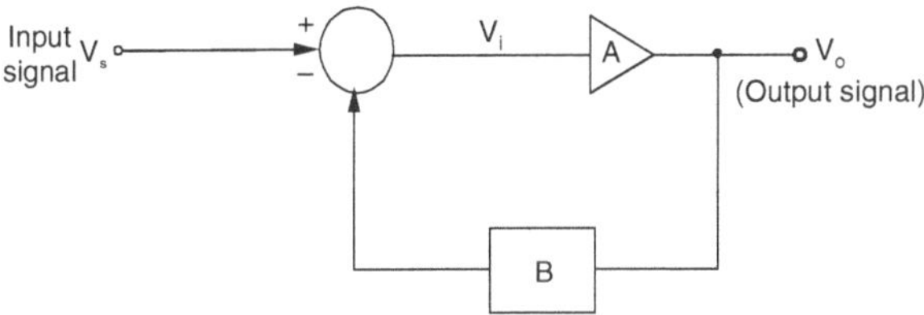

If the feedback signal is of opposite polarity to the input signal, then the negative feedback results. While negative feedback results in reduced overall voltage gain, following improvements are obtained, :

(*i*)   Higher input impedance

(*ii*)   Better stabilized voltage gain

(*iii*) Improved frequency response

(*iv*)   Lower output impedance

(*v*)   Reduced noise

(*vi*) More linear operation

Types of Feedback Connections.

(*i*)   Voltage -series feedback

(*ii*) Voltage - shunt feedback

(*iii*) Current - series feedback

(*iv*) Current - shunt feedback.

In the above feedback connections, the voltage refers to connecting the output voltage as input to the feedback network; current refers to tapping off some output current through the feedback network. Series refers to connecting the feedback signal in series with the input signal voltage, shunt refers to connecting the feedback signal in shunt (parallel) with input current source.

OSCILLATOR

It is divice which delivers a.c. output wave form of desired frequency from d.c. power even without input signal excitation.

The electric oscillations are produced by L-C circuit (i.e. tank circuit containing inductor and capacitor). These oscillations are damped one, i.e. their amplitude dercrease with the passage of time due to the small resistance of the inductor. In other words, the energy of the L-C oscillations decreases. If this loss of energy is compensated from outside, then undamped oscillations decreases. If this loss of energy is compensated from outside, then undamped oscillations decreases. If this loss of energy is compensated from outside, then undamped oscillations (of contant amplitude) can be obtained. This can be done buy using feed back arrangement and a transistor in the circuit.

L-C circuit producing L-C oscillations consists of an inductor of inductance L and capacitor of variable capacitance. Inductor of inductance L' is connected in the collector-emitter circuit through a battery and a tapping key (K). Inductors L and L' are inductively coupled

Types of Oscillator.

(i) Tuned Collector Oscillator

(ii) Hartley Oscillator : The radio frequency-choke (RFC) provides dc load to collector and keeps ac current out of the supply. Transistor and transformer provides $180°$ phase shift each, thus the resultant phase shift of $360°$ is provided between input and output signal.

(iii) Colpitt's Oscillator : The circuit of Colpitt oscillator is the same as that of Hartley oscillator except that the emitter tap is connected between the capacitances C_1 and C_2. L and C_1 and C_2 forms the tank circuit.

(iv) R - C Phase Shift Oscillator : To obtain a positive feedback essential for oscillations, the frequency determining circuit must introduce a phase shift of $180°$. This is obtained by 3-section of CR, CR, CR each providing a phase shift of $60°$. Another phase shift of $180°$ is provided by CE-transistor. Thus a total of $360°$ phase shift is provided by the circuit.

(v) Crystal Oscillator : It is seen that frequency of LC oscillator depends upon the values of tank circuit parameters. These values change with

time, temperature changes etc. Hence frequency of oscillation does not remain constant at desired value. For excellent stability of oscillation, piezoelectric quartz crystal is used in place of the tuned circuit in oscillator. Such an oscillator is called **crystal oscillator**.

(vi) Wien Bridge Oscillator : This oscillator is also called **audio frequnecy oscillator**. The main advantage of this oscillator is that the frequency may be varied over a frequency-range 1 : 10 whereas in RC oscillator, frequency cannot be varied it is fixed.

In this type of oscillator, both RC network and amplifier introduces a zero phase shift.

DIFFERENTIAL AMPLIFIER.

Differential amplifier is the first stage of op-amp. Differential amplifier consists of two transistors which are emitter coupled.

There are two type of signal to differential amplifier.

(i) Differential mode

(ii) Common mode.

OPERATIONAL AMPLIFIER (APPLICATION & CHARACTERISTICS)

An operational amplifier (OP amp) is basically a multistage high gain ($A_v > 10^5$), direct coupled amplifier with two differential inputs and a single ended output and uses feedback to control the overall response characteristics.

I stage : Difference amplifier

II stage : High gain linear amplifier

III stage : Emitter follower.

IV stage : DC level shifter and output amplifier.

IDEAL OP–AMPS.

An op-amp amplifies the difference between two input signals, exhibiting the open-loop voltage gain

Characteristics of Op–amp.

The ideal op-amp has three essential characteristics which serve as standards for assessing the goodness of a practical op-amp :

(i) Open-loop voltage gain A_{OL} is negatively infinite.

(ii) Input impedance R_d between terminals 1 and 2 is infinitely large; thus, the input current is zero.

(iii) Output impedance R_o is zero; consequently, the output voltage is independent of the load.

APPLICATIONS OF OP-AMP.

(i) Precision Rectifier

(ii) Band pass filter

(iii) Logarithmic amplifiers

(iv) Antilogarithmic amplifier.

KEY POINTS

AMPLIFIER

An apparatus capable of delivering a variablecurrent derived from an independent source of energy, in which scale of the variations is much greater than that of the variations in the e.m.f. supplied to it; and thus capable of being used to reinforce or *"amplify"* the effect of weak electrical oscillations; employed for this purpose extensively in radio-communication and the line telephony. It is also called a *magnifier.*

AF (Audio Frequency) amplifier

It is a working in the AF range, i.e. between 20 Hz to 20 kHz.

Amplifier

It is a triode or transistor based circuit which is capable to increase amplitude (or voltage) or power of an input signal.

Amplification

The output of a microphone, pickups, magnetic head etc. is found to be of the order of micro volts and the same is found incapable to drive a loudspeaker directly. Therefore, it becomes necessary to amplify the signal obtained from a sensing device before applying it to drive a unit or device or loudspeaker etc.

Amplifying a signal

The signal to be amplified is applied to the base of a transistor. The signal causes the base bias to vary in accordance to its own voltage variations which results in the corresponding variation of a collector current. The voltage developed across the collector load is many times greater than the input voltage and voltage of the applied input signal is said to be amplified.

Voltage and Power amplifier

Voltage amplifier is aimed to amplify voltage (or amplitude) of an input signal. Power amplifier amplifies the power of die input signal (P - V.I.)

Commonly used transistor circuit

CE (Common Emitter) circuit is a widely used type of circuit. Its input and output impedances are most suitable for matching two amplifier stages.

Coupling methods

Used for interstage coupling of two amplifier stages are:

1. **RC coupling method :** Coupling employing two resistors mid a capacitor as coupling elements is called *RC coupling.* One resistor acts as a load resistor of first stage and a capacitor feeds the signal to the following stage. Second resistor is used to provide u-discharging, path for the DC charge stored in the capacitor. This type of circuit remains Tree from '*direct pickups of radio waves*' defect.

2. **Impedance coupling method :** It is a modified form of RC coupling in which an inductive load is used in place of resistive load. The overall gain of an impedance coupled amplifier is higher than that of a RC coupled amplifier.

3. **Transformer coupling method :** It is a coupling employing a transformer as a coupling element. The primary of the transformer acts as an inductive load of the first stage and secondary acts as a signal source for the following stage. In this method, two amplifier stages remain isolated with each oilier to the DC source.

4. **Direct coupling method :** It is a coupling without using any coupling element. This method of coupling is distortionless and gives a uniform response over wide frequency range.

FEEDBACK

It is the phenomenon of feeding a portion of the output energy hack to the input circuit

It may be

(*i*) Positive or Regenerative

(*ii*) Negative or Degenerative.

Positive feedback.

If feedback voltage or current is inphase with the input signal, it is called *positive feedback.* Limited amount of positive feedback is useful, as it increases the overall amplification of an amplifier.

Negative feedback

If feedback voltage or current is out of phase to the input signal, it is called *negative feedback. Advantages of a negative feedback.*

(*i*) Stable gain.

(*ii*) High quality frequency response

(*iii*) Reduction in hum, noise and distortion

(*iv*) Reduction in output distortion

(*v*) Reduction in harmonic distortion.

These advantages are achieved at the cost of a small reduction in the amplification.

Types of Feedback amplifier circuits

1. **Voltage feedback circuit :** It is the method of deriving feedback in which its magnitude doesn't depend on the anode/collector current.

2. **Current feedback circuit :** The method of deriving feedback in which its magnitude depends on the anode/collector current.

Cathode /Emitter follower

An amplifier circuit which delivers output through the cathode emitter resistor is called *cathode/ emitter follower.* Phase of the output voltage follows phase of the input voltage.

Frequency response curve

The ability and quality of an amplifier circuit is studied by plotting a curve between input frequency and output AC voltage. Such a curve is called *frequency response curve* of an amplifier.

Bias stabilization

The process of applying stable bias voltage to the control gird/base of a triode/transistor is called *bias stabilization*. Magnitude of bias is kept stable in order to obtain distortionless amplification. A voltage divider is employed for supplying a stable bias to the base of a transistor. In some other circuits, a thermistor is used in the emitter circuit for the same purpose.

Impedance matching

It is the matching of impedances of two circuits for maximum transfer of energy from one circuit to the other. Best element for attaining a proper matching is a transformer.

Step-up transformer is used for matching a low input impedance to a high output impedance.

Step-down transformer is used for matching a high voltage impedance to a low voltage impedance.

Classification of Amplifiers

(according to their mode of operation)

1. **Class 'A' amplifier :** The amplifier circuit in which control-grid/base bias and signal voltages are adjusted in such a way that current in the output circuit flows for the entire duration of the input signal.

   This type of circuit has best fidelity, minimum distortion but low output power.

2. **'B' amplifier :** It is the amplifier circuit in which control-grid/base sias and signal voltages are adjusted in such a way that current in the output circuit flows for less than half time of the input signal.

   This type of circuit has, minimum fidelity, maximum distortion but maximum output power .

   These are used in push-pull audio stages .

3. **Class 'AB' amplifier :** It is the amplifier circuit in which control-grid/base bias and signal voltages are adjusted in such a way that current in the output circuit flows for less than full but more than half time of the input signal.

   This type of circuits are utilized in ordinary type of equipments. Their efficiency is 35-50%.

4. **Class 'C' amplifier :** It is the amplifier in which control-grid/base bias and signal voltages are adjusted in such a way that current in the output circuit remains for less than half time of the input signal.

   This type of circuit has, minimum fidelity, maximum distortion but maximum output power too.

   These are used for RF amplification in transmitters.

Push-pull Amplifier.

It is the power amplifier circuit in which two identical tubes/transistors are connected in such a manner that they are excited by equal but 180° out of phase input signals. Their outputs are combined in a center tapped transformer.

In this harmonic distortion is eliminated increases output power further.

Phase inverter.

It is an amplifier circuit which inverts the phase of the signal applied to it. The circuit eliminates necessity of an input push-pull transformer in a push-pull amplifier.

Complementary circuit

It is a sort of push-pull amplifier in which PNP and NPN transistors work together in push-pull mode. The circuit is completely RC coupled circuit.

Single end push-pull Amplifier

In a single end (SE) push-pull amplifier circuit, output push-pull transformer is replaced by a RC network.

DISTORTION

It is a change in the waveform of an output signal with respect to the input signal waveform during amplification.

Causes of Distortion

(*i*)   Leaky coupling or by-pass capacitors.

(*ii*) Weak transistors/tubes

(*iii*) Circuit is overloaded

(*iv*) Resistors have become defective

(*v*)   Improper matching of the circuit components

(*vi*) Low or high supply voltage

Types of Distortion

(***i***)   Amplitude or non-linear

(***ii***) Frequency

(***iii***) Phase and

(***iv***) **Cross-over distortion :** When current of one transistor affects current of the second transistor, then output wave from the signal gets distorted which is called *cross-over distortion*.

Optimum load

It is the value of cathode lee tor load of an amplifier on which circuit provides a maximum and distortionless amplification.

Volume and Tone controls

Volume control is a potentiometer which is usually connected in the input section of an AF driver stage.

Tone control is a potentiometer which is used to change tone of the reproduced AF signal. It is incorporated in the output AF stage.

P.A. (Public Address) Amplifier

It is an AF amplifier which incorporates 2-3 pre-amplifiers and a powerful AF amplifier. A number of pressure units or loudspeakers can be derived by a P.A. amplifier simultaneously.

Class 'AB 1' amplifier

It is a sort of class 'AB' amplifier in which there is no distortion in the positive half cycles of the output signal.

Class 'AB 2' amplifier

It is a sort of class 'AB' amplifier in which there is some distortion in the positive half cycle of the output signal but overall output rests higher than that of class 'AB2'.

Soft bias Device

It is a triode/transistor which attains cut-off state at a small control-grid/base voltage.

Amplitude

An expression usually employed for the peak value attained in either direction by a quantity executing periodic oscillations, such as an alternating current, and sometimes for the sum of the positive and negative values, especially when equal. The latter is preferable called *double Amplitude*.

Amplitude Modulation [COMM]

It is the process of varying amplitude of the sinusoidal carrier wave by amplitude of the modulating signal.

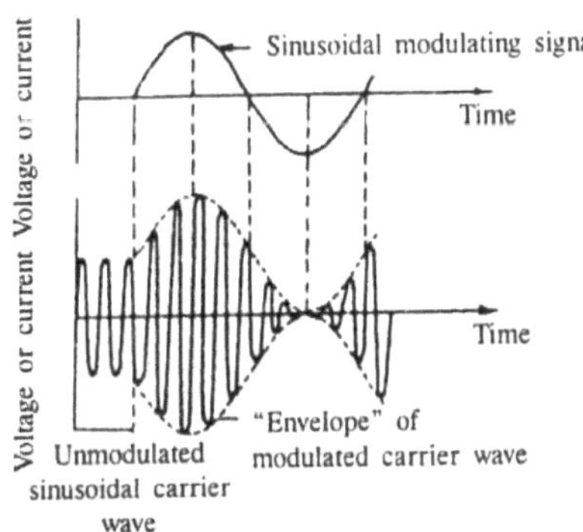

Amplitude modulated carrier wave

Amplitude Transmission Factor

It is the ratio of normalized complex wave amplitude of the transmitted wave at one port or transverse cross section to that of the incident wave at another port or transverse cross section of the transmission line.

Battery charger

It is an instrument used for battery charging purposes with AC supply.

Trickle charging method

In this method, sulphated battery can be revived by charging it at a very low current rate (1A) for a long time.

Maintenance of batteries :

Step :

1. Clean battery terminals periodically with a cloth piece soaked in warm water. Apply a small quantity of grease on the terminals after they get dry.

2. Keep the battery tight to the vehicle's body and keep the vent plugs tight.

3. Keep the battery plates well immersed in the electrolyte. Add distilled water as and when required.

4. Don't leave the battery idle.

5. Don't use a battery if its S.G has dropped to 1.15.

6. Don't charge or discharge a battery at a high current rate (above 25 A)

Battery charging

Precautions :

(*i*) Charge the battery in an airy room.

(*ii*) Remove the vents plugs during charging.

(*iii*) Keep flames etc. away from the battery.

(*iv*) Keep charging current rate not more than 3 to 6 amperes.

Merits of Secondary cells over Primary cells

(*i*) More terminal voltage.

(*ii*) Rechargeable.

(*iii*) Steady current.

High rate Discharge tester

It is meant for testing terminal voltage or charge condition of a lead-acid battery.

Solar battery

It is a device used to accumulate sun light energy in the form of electrical energy.

Bend E-plane

In this longitudinal axis of the waveguide remains in a plane parallel to the electric field vectors throughout the bend (corner).

Bend H-plane

In this, longitudinal axis of the waveguide remains in a plane parallel to the magnetic vectors throughout the bend.

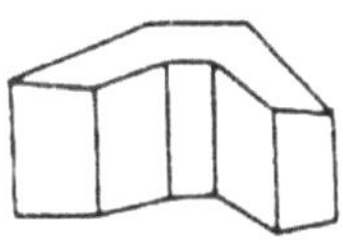

E-Bend

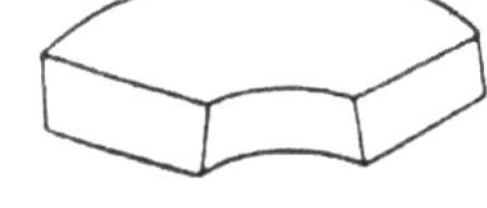

H-Bend

Cascade Amplifier

It is an Amplifier consisting of a number of Thermionic valves or transistors in Cascade Connection.

Chronotron

It is an electronic device that measures time intervals between events.

A pulse is initiated by each event and time interval is determined by position of the pulses along a transmission line.

Circuit Ringing

It is a low frequency oscillations setup in a radio receiver that are heard as a resonant tone during reception of a pulse of RF energy.

Class A Amplifier

It is a linear amplifier, in which output current flows for more than half but less than whole of the input cycle, i.e. angle of flow is between 1 and 21.

At low input-signal levels, class AB amplifiers tend to operate as class A amplifiers and at high input signal levels as class B amplifiers.

Class B Amplifier

It is a amplification by a valve, in which grid bias is sufficient to reduce the anode current to zero when no exciting grid voltage is present. It is particularly suitable in Push-Pull systems of amplification. A linear amplifier operated so that output current is cut off at zero input signal, i.e. angle of flow equals, and a half-wave rectified output is produced. Two transistors are required in order to duplicate input waveform successfully, each one conducting for half of the input cycle. Class B amplifiers are highly efficient but suffer from crossover distortion.

Class C Amplifier

It is a nonlinear amplifier in which output current flows for less than half the input cycle, i.e. angle of flow is less than 1. Although more efficient than other types of amplifier, class C amplifiers introduce more distortion.

Class D Amplifier:

It is an amplifier operating by means of pulse width modulation. Input signal produces a square wave modulated with respect to its mark space ratio. Then push-pull switches are operated by the modulated square wave, so that one switch operates with a high input level and the other with a low input level. Resultant output current is proportional to the mark space ratio and hence to the input current.

Collector

Short for collector region. The region in a bipolar junction transistor into which carriers flow from the base through the collector junction. The electrode attached to this region is the *collector electrode*.

Short for collector electrode.

Collector current Multiplication factor

The ratio of condensed current flow in the collector as the result of flow of holes or electrons respectively from an N type or P type base region into the collector to the current carried by these minority carriers, the collector voltage being held constant.

Collector efficiency

The term is used in transistors as ratio of useful power output to the dc power input.

Cut-off (Syn Black-out point).

It is the point at which current flowing through an electronic device is cutoff by the control electrode.

In a transistor, cutoff point is the minimum base current at which device conducts; in a valve it is the, minimum negative grid voltage (grid base) required to stop the current.

In a cathode-ray tube, cut-off bias is the bias voltage that just reduces electron-beam current to zero.

In all cases, the values are dependent on the conditions at the other electrodes, which must be specified.

Cut-off Frequency

It is the frequency at which attenuation of a passive network changes from a small value to a much higher value; the theoretical cut-off frequency.

Effective cut-off frequency is that frequency where insertion loss between two specified impedances has risen by a stated amount compared to the value at a reference frequency. An active network has the same cut-off frequency as a passive one with the same inductances and capacitances. The term is also applied to the limiting frequency of a filter. The frequency above or below which the attenuation of a circuit (e.g. a Loaded Cable or a piece of apparatus, such as a microphone) rises rapidly.

Also, it is the frequency that marks edge of the filter's passband and the beginning of the transition to the stopband. It is the frequency or frequencies at which relative attenuation measured, is 3dB.

Darlington pair

It is a compound connection of two transistors that operates as if it were a single transistor with an extremely high forward-current transfer ratio.

DC to DC Converter regulators

It has passed through various stages of evaluation with the development of different component technologies. The size was brought down drastically and increased performance in terms of regulation, efficiency, reliability, etc. have been achieved. Various building blocks of D/C converter regulator are shown in the figure:

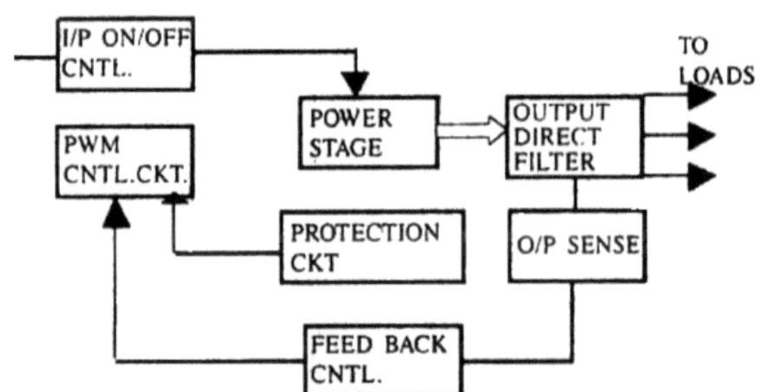

Electronic Circuits

It is a path or map with interconnecting and conducting lines forming an interface between various elements used in the field of electronic engineering.

AF oscillator

It is the used in the determination of frequency response of an AF amplifier.

Output meter

It is the instrument made to measure AF output of an amplifier.

Signal generator or Service oscillator

It is an instrument which generates modulated and unmodulated RF signals. It is used for alignment of various receivers.

Voltage stabilizer

It is the equipment which provides a stable voltage irrespective of supply voltage and load variations for satisfactory operation of sensitive electronic equipments.

Neutralising

Sometimes, unwanted oscillations are produced in RF amplifiers due to undesired regenerative feedback. This trouble is called *'whistling'*.

A neutralising circuit is incorporated in RF amplifiers for elimination of *whistling trouble*. The neutralising capacitors return the *'feedback energy'* back to the output circuit of the amplifier.

High frequency limitation of Transistor and Triodes

The amplification capability of a triode or transistor is found to be reduced at high frequencies. The major cause behind the trouble is *'interelectrode capacitance'*. Tetrode valves and transistors are used for RF amplification in which interelectrode capacitance is reduced to a minimum.

Cut-off frequency of a transistor

It is the frequency at which current gain alpha of a transistor falls to 0.707 times of a its maximum value. The cause behind the trouble is reduction in the number of charge carriers reaching at the collector.

Gain

It is increase in the variation of power voltage, or current contained in an amplifier or a repeater expressed in decibels.

Hall Effect

When a conductor carrying current, is placed in a magnetic field which is at right angles to the direction of current, an electromotive force is produced in direction that is perpendicular to both current and the magnetic field.

Hartley Oscillator

It is an oscillator that employs a transistor in common emitter configuration along with a parallel tuned circuit across collector and emitter.

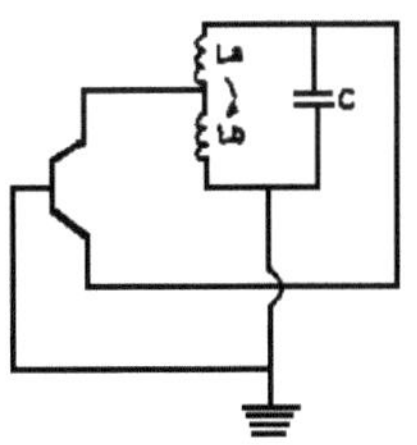

Hartley Bridge

It is an AC bridge that measures *mutual inductance.* As direct comparison with a standard known mutual inductance using impedance bridge measurements is not possible, due to self and mutual capacitance of coils, so in this bridge variable resistors common to both primary and secondary bridge circuits are used.

Hay Bridge

It is an AC bridge used for measurement of large inductance.

Hybrid circuit

It is a circuit made by a combination of different integration techniques.

Hybrid function

It is *sum of products* or *product-of-sums* expression that has been reduced by factoring; three or greater combinational levels of logic.

Hysteresis

It is quality of a logic device to recognize a 1 when it is in the 0 state at higher voltage than that necessary for recognizing a 0 when it is in the 1 state.

Impact Ionization

It is ionization of an atom or molecule due to loss of orbital electrons following a high energy collision.

Inverter

It is the digital circuit that performs inversion operation.

Local Oscillations

It is oscillations in a radio-receiving circuit due to action of the apparatus itself,

e.g. from a separate oscillator valve for heterodyne reception, or due to self oscillation.

Monostable

It means having only one stable state,

e.g., a multivibrator characterized by one stable state.

Negative Resistance Amplifier

It is a device which shows negative resistance due to which amplification of input signals takes place. It is used in microwave parametric amplifier.

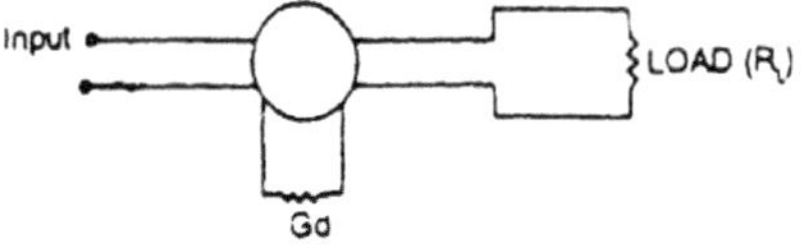

Neon tube Rectifier

It is a rectifier consisting of a tube containing neon at a low pressure with some cases provided with grid control.

Network

It is a system consisting of a number of impedances or sub assemblies connected together to perform specific function.

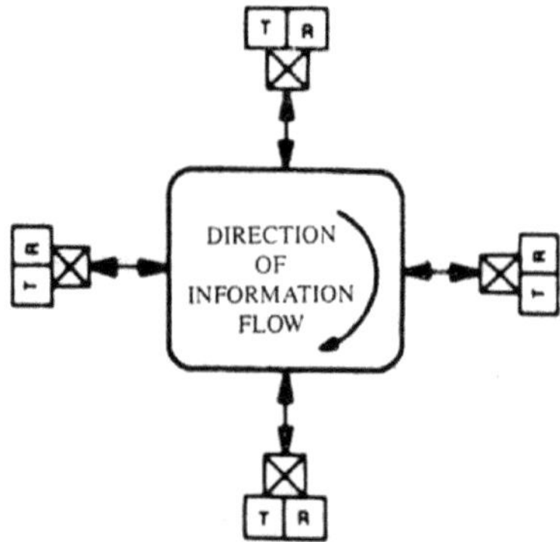

Operational Amplifier

It is an amplifier with an assumed infinite gain, infinite input impedance and zero output impedance.

Oscillator

It is the equipment which supplies ac voltage Frequency of the ac signal supplied by the instrument can be varied.

Parametric Amplifier

It is an amplifier used at microwave frequencies in which reactance of the device is varied in time by an alternating voltage called *pump voltage*. If suitable relation is maintained between pump voltage frequency and frequency of signal to be amplified, then energy from the pump frequency is transferred to the signal which gets amplified.

Paraphase Amplifier

It is an amplifier having two output signals which are 180 degrees out of phase with each other, It is often used to drive a push-pull amplifier stage.

Passive components

These components by themselves are not capable of amplifying or processing an electrical signal,

e.g. resistors, capacitors or inductors.

Pierce Oscillator

It is modification of a Colpitts oscillator, in which a piezoelectric crystal replaces inductor in the tank circuit betwen collector (plate) or emitter and base (grid) of the transistor (vacuum tube) circuit.

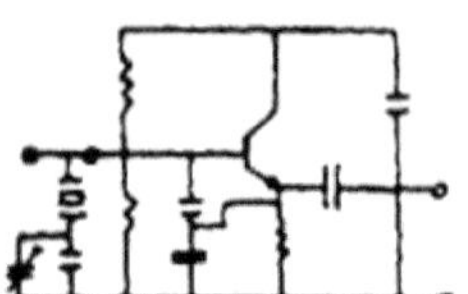

Piezo electric crystal

It is the crystal that exhibits piezoelectric effect. All ferroelectric crystals are piezoelectric as well as certain nonferrous electric crystals and some ceramics. The best known examples of piezo-electric crystals include quartz crystal, Rochelle salt, and barium titanate.

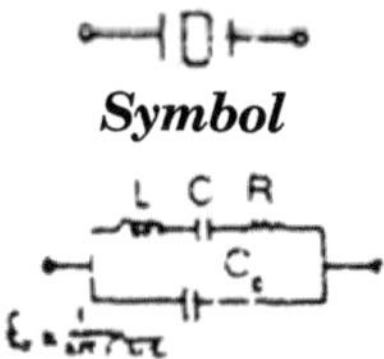

Piezo Electric Effect

It is effect that occurs when certain materials are subjected to mechanical stress. An electrical polarization is set up in crystal and faces of the crystal become electrically changed.

Power amplifier

It is an AF or RF amplifier that delivers maximum output power to a load rather than providing a maximum voltage gain. Sometimes an expression used in radio-reception for a low frequency amplifier for use as a final stage, particularly with a loud speaker of large size.

Push Pull Amplifier

It is an amplifier that uses two similar vacuum tubes or transistors with their grid or base leads connected in phase opposition while plate or collector leads are connected in parallel to a common load. It is used primarily as a frequency multiplier to emphasize even order harmonics.

Line transformer Matching system

Most of the electronic equipments manufactured by European countries are designed to work at 115 volts AC. In our country, such equipments essentially require a *'line matching transformer'*

(a 230 V to 115 V step down transformer).

Pre-amplifier

It is a voltage amplifier circuit which amplifies microvolts level AF signal produced by a pick-up, replay-head or a microphone.

Equalizer

It is a negative feedback type amplifier which acts as a low and high audio frequencies compensator in association with 1, 2, 3 or more tone controls during replay. Various tone controls produce different types of *'bass'* and *'treble'* tones.

Video amplifier

It is designed in such a way that it can amplify a wide band extending from 50 Hz to 6 MHz, i.e., it has to amplify AF range also in addition to RF range.

Low and High frequency compensation

In valve type video amplifier, *peaking coils* are used in the plate circuit in order to widen its frequency range, This phenomenon is called *low and high frequency compensation.*

Video pre-amplifier

In some TV circuits, a driver video amplifier stage is employed in addition to the main video amplifier, is called *pre-video amplifier.*

EHT (Extra High Tension) Voltage

It is a DC voltage of the order of 12 to 20 kilovolts which is applied to the *collector ring* or a *picture tube.* It is developed by stepping up 15,625 Hz horizontal output voltage during its flyback periods with the help of an EHT transformer and then by rectifying it by a EHT diode.

Electrodes of a Transistor

(*i*) Emitter,

(*ii*) Base

(*iii*) Collector.

Characteristics of Transistors

(*i*) Mechanically rugged construction

(*ii*) Small size

(*iii*) Low working voltage

(*iv*) Low power consumption

(*v*) Long working life

(*vi*) High efficiently.

OSCILLATOR

It is a electronic circuit which produces oscillations.

Essential requirements of an oscillator

A resonant circuit or a crystal which decides oscillatory frequency of an oscillator circuit is called *tank circuit.*

Damped oscillations

Oscillations whose amplitude goes on reducing continuously are called *damped oscillations.* This type of oscillations are produced by sparking.

Oscillatory frequency of a LC tank circuit

$$f = \frac{1}{2\pi LC}$$

where, f = frequency, Hz

L = inductance, henrys

C = capacitance, farads

Types of Oscillator Circuits

(*i*) Ticker feedback, oscillator oscillator

(*ii*) Hartley series fed and Hartley parallel fed oscillator

(*iii*) *Colpitts :* It is an oscillator, which employs a crystal in place of LC lank circuit. It is renowned as a stable frequency oscillator. Employs capacitive feedback oscillator

(*iv*) Tuned Plate Tuned Grid (TPTG) oscillator

(*v*) Electron coupled oscillator

(*vi*) Master oscillator power amplifier (MOPA) oscillator

(*vii*) Crystal oscillator

(*viii*) Multivibrator oscillator

(*ix*) Wein bridge oscillator

(*x*) Neon lamp oscillator

(*xi*) Thyratron sweep oscillator

(*xii*) Phase shift RC oscillator

(*xiii*) Beat frequency (BFO) oscillator

(*xiv*) Klystron oscillator

(*xv*) Magnetron oscillator.

Series fed and Parallel fed Hartley oscillators

In a series ted oscillator, both the AC and DC components of anode/collector current pass together through the feedback coil. On the other hand, in a parallel ted oscillator, only AC component of the anode/collector current passes through the feedback coil.

High voltage Power supply units

High power transmitters require high voltage power supply units. These units are designed to provide high current and high voltage both. These units incorporate air or water cooling system too.

MOPA (Master Oscillator Power Amplifier)

If a transmitter employs a single stage to act as RF oscillator and RF amplifier, the same is called MOPA.

BFO (Beat Frequency Oscillator)

It is an oscillator, in which a desired frequency is produced by 'beating' two radio frequencies. It is more useful for producing frequencies in the range of 20 *Hz* to 20 kHz in comparison to an ordinary AF oscillator.

Wafer

It is a large single crystal of semiconductor material, usually silicon, which is used as the substrate during manufacture of a number of chips. The number of viable chips that can be produced from a single wafer, typically up to 10 cm in diameter, depends on size and complexity of the circuits or components on the chips.

Yoke

It is a piece of ferromagnetic material that is used to connect permanently two or more magnetic cores and thus complete a magnetic circuit without surrounding it by a winding of any kind.

EXERCISE – I

1. Halfwave rectifier has theoretical maximum efficiency of
   - (a) 40.6%
   - (b) 81.2%
   - (c) 78.5%
   - (d) 50%

2. Fullwave rectifier has theoretical maximum efficiency of
   - (a) 40.6%
   - (b) 81.2%
   - (c) 78.5%
   - (d) 50%

3. The output voltage of halfwave rectifier using resistive load, no filter and sinusoidal input has ripple factor of
   - (a) 1.11
   - (b) 1.41
   - (c) 1.21
   - (d) 0.81

4. The output vlotage of a fullwave rectifier using resistive load, no filter and sinusoidal input has ripple factor of
   - (a) 1.11
   - (b) 1.41
   - (c) 1.21
   - (d) 0.81

5. In a rectifier using of capacitor filter, with increase of $\omega C R_L$, the dc output voltage V_{dc}
   - (a) increases
   - (b) decreases
   - (c) remains unaltered
   - (d) increases, reaches a maximum value and then decreases.

6. Bleeder resistor in power supplies is used to place
   - (a) an infinite load across the rectifier
   - (b) maximum load across the rectifier
   - (c) minimum load across the rectifier
   - (d) none of these

7. If the dc value of a rectified output is 300 volts and peak-to-peak ripple voltage is 10.4 volts, the ripple factor is
   - (a) 1.22%
   - (b) 3.47%
   - (c) 2.44%
   - (d) 6.94%

8. If the dc value of rectified output voltage of a rectifier is 300 volts and the rms ripple voltage is 6 volts, the ripple factor is
   - (a) 1%
   - (b) 2%
   - (c) 4%
   - (d) 0.5%

9. Capacitor filter is ideal for currents which are :
   - (a) small
   - (b) medium
   - (c) large
   - (d) very large

10. An inductor filter at the output of rectifier results in ripple which
    - (a) increases with load resistance
    - (b) descreases with load resistance
    - (c) remain unattered with increase of load resistance
    - (d) none of these

11. A capacitor filter at the output of a rectifier results in ripple which
    - (a) increases with load resistance
    - (b) descreases with load resistance
    - (c) remain unattered with increase of load resistance
    - (d) none of these

12. The function of a filter in a rectifier is to
    - (a) limit the total current in the rectifier
    - (b) limit the peak voltage of the rectifier
    - (c) limit the dc current
    - (d) reduce the ripple voltage in the output

13. The disadvantage of halfwave rectifier circuit is that the
    - (a) diode must have high PIV rating
    - (b) diode must have high power rating
    - (c) output voltage is difficult to filter
    - (d) diode must have high current rating

14. The function of centre tapping on the secondary in a fullwave rectifier is to
    - (a) step up the voltage
    - (b) step down the voltage
    - (c) isolate the load from ground
    - (d) cause the diodes to conduct alternately

15. A cascade voltage doubler can be used to provide any degree of voltage multiplication by
    - (a) using diodes with large PIV rating
    - (b) adding a step up transformer
    - (c) cascading diodes and capacitors
    - (d) increasing the values of capacitors

16. A fullwave voltage doubler output has ripple frequency
    - (a) half the supply frequency
    - (b) equal to the supply frequency
    - (c) double the supply frequency
    - (d) having no relation with the supply frequency

17. The circuit shown below is a

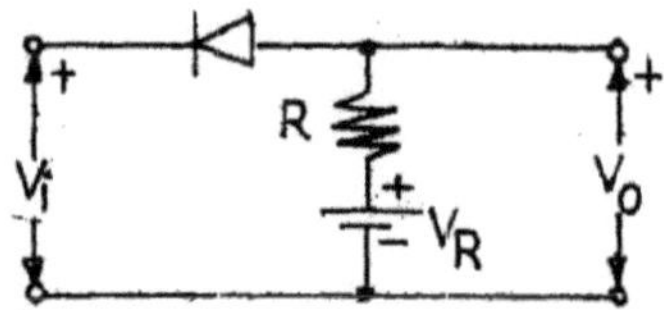

   - (a) cliper
   - (b) clamper
   - (c) differentiator
   - (d) integrator

18. The circuit shown below is a

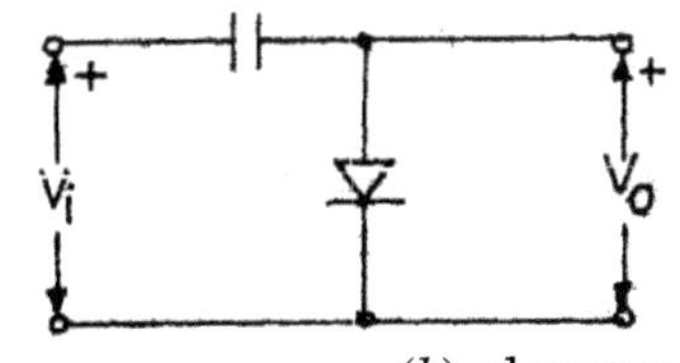

(a) cliper   (b) clamper

(c) differentiator   (d) integrator

19. Comparator circuits are used in

(a) address

(b) integrators

(c) converting sine to square wave

(d) differentiator

20. Bleeder resistor in a rectifier circuit is a fixed resistor connected across

(a) input of complete power supply

(b) output of complete power suppy

(c) midway

(d) none of these

21. An ideal power supply has

(a) zero internal resistance

(b) very large input resistance

(c) very large output resistance

(d) very low output resistance

22. With increase of load resistance, ripple voltage of rectifier with capacitor filter

(a) decreases

(b) increases

(c) remains constant

(d) gets multiplied

23. DC output drops from 50 volt with no load to 48 volt with full load. Percentage load regulation is

(a) 2%   (b) 4%

(c) 1%   (d) 8%

24. Excessive hum in a power supply is generally due to

(a) open filter choke   (b) capacitor

(c) defective rectifier   (d) any of these

25. Which of the following method of biasing provides the best operating point stability

(a) Two battery bias   (b) Collector-to-base bias

(c) Fixed bias   (d) Self bias

26. Stability factor S in fixed bias CE amplifier is given by

(a) β (b) $\beta + 1$

(c) $\dfrac{1}{\beta + 1}$ (d) $(\beta + 1)^2$

27. Base-to-emitter voltage V_{BE} is a forward biased transistor decreases with increase of temperature at the rate

(a) 25 mV/deg C   (b) 0.25mV/deg C

(c) 2.5 mV/deg C   (d) 0.6 mV/deg C

28. Typically Ge transistors are operated over temperature range extending from

(a) –25°C to +175°C   (b) –65°C to +75°C

(c) –65°C to +175°C   (d) –25°C to +75°C

29. To avoid permanent damage, the maximum temperature of collector junction JC in Ge transistor is generally restricted to

(a) +60°C   (b) +100°C

(c) +175°C   (d) +225°C

30. To avoid permanent damage, the maximum temperature of collector junction JC in Si transistor is generally restricted to

(a) +60°C   (b) +100°C

(c) +175°C   (d) +225°C

31. Parameter hfe of a typical transistor is of the order of

(a) 5   (b) 50

(c) 500   (d) 2000

32. Parameter hie of a typical transistor is of the order of

(a) 100Ω   (b) 1000Ω

(c) 10kΩ   (d) 100kΩ

33. Parameter hre of a typical transistor is of the order of

(a) 2.5×10^{-6} (b) 2.5×10^{-5}

(c) 2.5×10^{-4} (d) 2.5×10^{-3}

34. Parameter hoe of a typical transistor is of the order of

(a) 2.5 S   (b) 25 S

(c) 250 S   (d) 2.5 mS

35. With load impedance of 4 kΩ, the current gain of a typical CE amplifier stage has magnitude of the order of

(a) 0.98   (b) 5

(c) 50   (d) 400

36. With load impedance of 4 kΩ, voltage gain of a CE amplifier stage using a typical transistor has magnitude of the order of

(a) 0.98   (b) 5

(c) 50   (d) 400

37. With load impedance of 4 kΩ, the input resistance of a typical CE amplifier stage is of the order of

(a) 10Ω   (b) 100Ω

(c) 1000Ω   (d) 10kΩ

38. With source resistance Rs of 1000 Ω, the output impedance of a typical CE amplifier stage is of the order of
(a) 500Ω (b) 5kΩ
(c) 50kΩ (d) 500kΩ

39. With load resistance of 4 kΩ, the current gain of a typical CB amplifier stage is of the order of
(a) 0.98   (b) 5
(c) 50   (d) 500

40. With typical load resistance of 4 kΩ, voltage gain of a typical CC amplifier stage is of the order of
(a) 0.99   (b) 5
(c) 20   (d) 200

41. In a CE amplifier stage, on introducing a resistor Re in the emitter circuit, the input resistance Ri
(a) remain unlatered   (b) reduces
(c) increases nominally   (d) increases very much

42. Ignoring the biasing network, Darlington emitter follower has input resistance of the order of
(a) 20kΩ (b) 200kΩ
(c) 2MΩ (d) 20mΩ

43. The current gain of amplifier stage is lowest\in
(a) CB configuration
(b) CE configuration
(c) CC configuration
(d) same in all configurations

44. The voltage gain of amplifier stage is lowest in :
(a) CB configuration
(b) CE configuration
(c) CC configuration
(d) same in all configurations

45. Transistor amplifier stage has lowest input impedance in
(a) CB configuration
(b) CE configuration
(c) CC configuration
(d) same in all configurations

46. Transistor amplifier stage has highest input impedance in
(a) CB configuration
(b) CE configuration
(c) CC configuration
(d) same in all configurations

47. The input circuit of CB amplifier is
(a) emitter-base circuit
(b) emitter-collector circuit
(c) base-collector circuit
(d) collector-base-emitter circuit

48. In a multistage amplifier, the intermediate stages are always in
(a) CB configuration
(b) CE configuration
(c) CC configuration
(d) may have any configuration

49. Darlington circuit is obtained by connecting in cascade
(a) two emitter followers with input impedance of second transistor forming the load impedance of the first stage
(b) two CB stage
(c) two CE stage
(d) CE stage directly coupled to CB stage

50. Input resistances Ri of ideal voltage amplifier and ideal current amplifier are respectively
(a) ∞, 0   (b) 0, ∞
(c) ∞, ∞ (d) 0, 0

51. The current stability of an emitter follower may be improved by
(a) decreasing emitter circuit and base circuit resistances
(b) increasing emitter circuit and base circuit resistances
(c) decreasing emitter circuit resistance and increasing base resistance
(d) increasing emitter circuit resistance and decreasing base circuit resistance.

52. Which of the following transistor con-figurations gives useful current gain ?
(a) CE alone   (b) CB alone
(c) CC alone   (d) both CE and CC

53. The output resistance of an amplifier in the CC configuration
(a) is higher than that in CE and CB configurations
(b) depends strongly on the source resistance
(c) goes down as the source resistance
(d) is independent of the source resistance

54. Transistor ratings symbols using captical letter and with subscripts also in capital letters denote
(a) dc parameters
(b) ac parameters
(c) effective values
(d) instantaneous time varying values

55. An amplifier with a frequency response of 50 Hz to 8000 Hz
(a) can reproduce intelligence speech
(b) can be used as dc amplifier
(c) is considered a high fidelity amplifier
(d) constitutes inferior audio frequency amplifier

56. A carbon microphone having resistance of 100 ohms feeds a pre-amplifier. The best transistor configuration for pre-amplifier is
(a) CE
(b) CB
(c) CC
(d) any of three

57. In experimentally obtaining the frequency response curve of an amplifier
(a) generator output level is kept constant
(b) amplifier power supply is varied
(c) generator frequency is held constant
(d) amplifier output is kept constant

58. The input and output voltages of a CE amplifier are
(a) equal
(b) 180° out of phase
(c) always negative
(d) in phase

59. A transistor is said to be in quiescent state when
(a) it is unbiased
(b) no signal is applied to it
(c) no current is flowing in it
(d) emitter junction bias is equal to collector junction bias

60. When a positive voltage signal is applied at the base of a normally biased npn CE transistor
(a) emitter current decreases
(b) collector voltage goes less positive
(c) base current decreases
(d) collector current decreases

61. A CB amplifier is characterized by.
(a) low A_I, high A_V
(b) low A_I, low A_V
(c) high A_I, high A_V
(d) high A_I, low A_V

62. One characteristic of emitter follower is
(a) low input resistance
(b) low current gain
(c) low voltage gain
(d) high output resistance

63. The common collector amplifier is also called emitter follower because
(a) emitter current follows the collector current
(b) emitter voltage follows the collector voltage
(c) emitter voltage follows the base signal voltage
(d) emitter current follows the collector voltage

64. When a positive going signal is applied to the input of a normally biased common base npn transistor
(a) emitter current increases
(b) collector becomes more positive
(c) collector becomes more positive
(d) collector becomes more negative

65. CC amplifier has
(a) high R_i and high R_o
(b) low R_i and low R_o
(c) low R_i and high R_o
(d) high R_i and low R_o
where R_i is the input resistane and R_o is the output resistance.

66. In CC amplifier
(a) output is taken from the collector terminal
(b) input and output signals are in phase
(c) input resistance is low
(d) voltage gain is relatively high

67. Compared to CB amplifier, the CE amplifier has considerably
(a) higher current gain
(b) lower input resistance
(c) lower voltage gain
(d) lower current gain

68. CE amplifier has
(a) low R_i and low R_o
(b) high R_i and high R_o
(c) high R_i and low R_o
(d) high R_i and low R_o
where R_i is the input resistance and R_o is the output resistance.

69. A common base amplifier is so called because
(a) base region is located between emitter and collector regions
(b) base is common to the input and output circuits of the amplifier
(c) base is n-type in pnp transisor
(d) base is p-type in npn transistor

70. Common base amplifier has
(a) high R_i high R_o
(b) low R_i and low R_o
(c) high R_i and low R_o
(d) low R_i and high R_o
where R_i is input resistance and R_o is the output resistance.

71. In CB amplifier, current gain AI is the ratio of
(a) Change in I_C to change in I_E
(b) Change in I_B to change in I_E
(c) Change in I_E to change in I_B
(d) Change in I_C to change in I_B

72. In CE amplifier, current gain AI is the ratio of
(a) Change in I_C to change in I_E
(b) Change in I_B to change in I_E
(c) Change in I_E to change in I_B
(d) Change in I_C to change in I_B

73. In the high frequency hybrid-π model of a CE transistor, capacitance Ce accounts for
(a) excess minority carrier storage in the base region
(b) collector junction barrier capacitance
(c) emitter junction barrier capacitance
(d) collector junction diffusion capacitance

74. In the high frequency hybrid-π model of a CE transistor, conductance gbc accounts for

(*a*) bulk conductance of base region

(*b*) leakage conductance in the base region

(*c*) feed back action due to base width modulation

(*d*) none of these

75. In the high frequency hybrid-π model of a CE amplifier, capacitance Cc accounts for

(*a*) emitter junction barrier capacitance

(*b*) collector junction barrier capacitance

(*c*) collector junction diffusion capacitance

(*d*) emitter junction diffusion capacitance

76. Parameter fT of a transistor is the frequency at which the magnitude of CE short circuit current gain is

(*a*) half of the midband gain

(*b*) $1/\sqrt{2}$ of the midband gain

(*c*) one-tenth of midband gain

(*d*) unity

77. As the collector current IC increases, the value of fT

(*a*) remains constant

(*b*) decreases

(*c*) increases, reaches a maximum and then falls

(*d*) decreases, reaches a minimum and then rises

78. In a JFET, transconductance gm is of the order of

(*a*) 1 mS   (*b*) 100 mS

(*c*) 1 S   (*d*) 100 S

79. In a JFET, dynamic drain resistance rd is of the order of

(*a*) 1 kΩ (*b*) 10 kΩ

(*c*) 10 MΩ (*d*) 100 MΩ

80. In a MOSFET, dynamic drain resistance rd is of the order of

(*a*) 10 kΩ (*b*) 1 MΩ

(*c*) 10 MΩ (*d*) 100 MΩ

81. The input resistance rgs in small signal model of MOSFET is of the order of

(*a*) 100 KΩ (*b*) 1 MΩ

(*c*) 10 MΩ (*d*) 10^4 MΩ

82. The feed back resistance rgd in small signal model of MOSFET is of the order of

(*a*) 1 MΩ (*b*) 100 MΩ

(*c*) 10^4 MΩ (*d*) 10^6 MΩ

83. The feed back capacitance Cgd in small signal high frequency model of a JFET is of the order of

(*a*) 5 pF   (*b*) 50 pF

(*c*) 500 pF   (*d*) 1 F

84. The drain-to-source resistance Cds in high frequency model of a JFET is of the order of

(*a*) 1 pF   (*b*) 10 pF

(*c*) 100 pF   (*d*) 1000 pF

85. The gate-to-source capacitance Cgs in small signal high frequency model of a JFET is of the order of

(*a*) 5 pF   (*b*) 50 pF

(*c*) 500 pF   (*d*) 5000 pF

86. The input resistance of FET common source amplifier in its low frequency small signal operation is

(*a*) very small   (*b*) medium

(*c*) high   (*d*) almost infinite

87. In a class A amplifier with sinusoidal input signal, the output current flows for

(*a*) half the cycle   (*b*) full cycle

(*c*) less than half cycle   (*d*) more than half cycle

88. In a class AB amplifier with sinusoidal input signal, the output current flows for

(*a*) half the cycle   (*b*) full cycle

(*c*) less than half cycle   (*d*) more than half cycle

89. In a class B amplifier with sinusoidal input signal, the output current flows for

(*a*) half the cycle   (*b*) full cycle

(*c*) less than half cycle   (*d*) more than half cycle

90. In a class C amplifier with sinusoidal input ignal, the output current flows for

(*a*) half the cycle   (*b*) full cycle

(*c*) less than half cycle   (*d*) more than half cycle

91. Frequency distortion in an amplifier is caused by

(*a*) nonlinear dynamic characteristic of the active device

(*b*) reactive elements in the circuit

(*c*) ripple components in the circuit

(*d*) high temperature of operation

92. Nonlinear distortion in an amplifier is caused by

(*a*) nonlinear dynamic characteristic of the active device

(*b*) reactive elements in the circuit

(*c*) ripple components in the circuit

(*d*) high temperature of operation

93. In an RC coupled CE amplifier, reduction in voltage gain in the high frequency range results due to

(*a*) coupling capacitor C_b

(*b*) shunt capacitance in the input circuit

(*c*) shunt capacitance in the output circuit

(*d*) bypass capacitor in the self bias circuit

94. In an RC coupled CE amplifier, reduction in voltage gain in the low frequency range results due to

(a) coupling capacitor C_b

(b) shunt capacitance in the input circuit

(c) shunt capacitance in the output circuit

(d) potential divider biasing circuit from V_{CC} to ground

95. The 3-dB frequency of an amplifier is one at which gain reduces to

(a) unity

(b) zero

(c) $1/\sqrt{2}$ of its midband value

(d) half of its midband value

96. In an RC coupled CE amplifier, the lower 3dB frequency fL may be reduced by

(a) reducing the value of coupling capacitor C_b

(b) increasing the value of coupling capacitor C_b

(c) reducing the total effective shunt capacitance in the output circuit

(d) reducing the total effective shunt capacitanve in the input circuit of hybrid-π mode

97. In an RC coupled CE amplifier, the lower 3dB frequency fL may be increased by

(a) reducing the value of coupling capacitor C_b

(b) increasing the value of coupling capacitor C_b

(c) reducing the total effective shunt capacitance in the output circuit

(d) reducing the total effective shunt capacitance in the input circuit of hybrid-π mode

98. In a single statge RC coupled amplifier stage, phase shift in the true midband is

(a) zero   (b) 180°

(c) 270°   (d) 225°

99. In a single stage RC coupled CE amplifier, phase shift at lower 3-dB frequency is

(a) 0   (b) 135°

(c) 180°   (d) 225°

100. In a single stage RC coupled CE amplifier, phase shift at lower 3-dB frequency is

(a) 0   (b) 135°

(c) 180°   (d) 225°

101. Which of the following amplifiers produces the least distortion

(a) class A   (b) class AB

(c) class B   (d) class C

102. Class A amplifier is used when

(a) no phase inversion is required

(b) highest voltage gain is required

(c) dc voltages are to be amplified

(d) minimum distortion is desired

103. Effect of cascading several amplifier stages is to

(a) reduce the overall gain

(b) reduce the overall frequency response

(c) increase the overall gain and reduce the frequency response

(d) decrease the overall gain and increase the frequency response

104. Presence of emitter circuit bypass capacitor adversely affects the

(a) low frequency response

(b) midband response

(c) high frequency response

(d) response over the complete frequency range

105. In a cascade amplifier, the coupling method which is capable of providing highest gain is

(a) RC coupling   (b) direct coupling

(c) transformer coupling (d) impedance coupling

106. One advantage of transformer coupling in transistor amplifier is that

(a) it provides excellent response

(b) it is simple and less expensive than other coupling method

(c) low power supply may be used

(d) high efficiency and high power output is obtained

107. Low frequency response of an RC coupled amplifier can be improved by

(a) increasing the coupling capacitors only

(b) increasing the bypass capacitors only

(c) increasing both the coupling capacitor and bypass capacitor

(d) decreasing the bypass capacitor

108. In an amplifier, the output current flows for 200° of input cycle. The class of operation of the amplifier is

(a) A   (b) AB

(c) B   (d) C

109. When a transistor is cutoff

(a) maximum voltage appears across the load resistor

(b) maximum current flows

(c) base is heavily forward biased

(d) maximum voltage appears across the transistor

110. In an RC coupled amplifier, the coupling capacitor Cb must be large enough

(a) to disspate high power

(b) to pass dc current to the next stage

(c) not to attenuate the low frequencies

(d) to give good bias stability

111. An advantage of RC coupled amplifier is
(a) high efficiency
(b) economy
(c) excellent frequency response
(d) good impedance matching

112. In an RC coupled CE amplifier, typical value of coupling capacitor is
(a) 1000 pF
(b) 0.1 F
(c) 10 F
(d) 0.01 F

113. When a multistage transistor amplifier is required to amplify dc signals also, we must use
(a) RC coupling
(b) direct coupling
(c) transformer coupling
(d) double tuned circuits

114. Transformer coupling provides high efficiency because the
(a) collector voltage is stepped up
(b) dc resistance in the collector circuit is low
(c) collector voltage is stepped down
(d) flux linkages are incomplete

115. In RC coupled amplifier, the dc component is blocked by
(a) load resistor R_L
(b) coupling capacitor C_b
(c) the transistor
(d) the bypass capacitor C_z in the self bias circuit

116. In the output of a pushpull amplifier, the most disturbing harmomic distortion is the
(a) second harmonic
(b) third harmonic
(c) fourth harmonic
(d) fifth harmonic

117. Maximum theoretical collector circuit efficiency of class A series fed amplifier is
(a) 15%
(b) 25%
(c) 37.5%
(d) 50%

118. The maximum theoretical collector circuit efficiency of transformer coupled class A amplifier is
(a) 15%
(b) 25%
(c) 37.5%
(d) 50%

119. The maximum theoretical collector circuit efficiency of class B amplifier is
(a) 15%
(b) 25%
(c) 50%
(d) 78.5%

120. In a class B pushpull amplifier, ratio of the maximum collector dissipation to maximum ac power output is about
(a) 0.25
(b) 0.4
(c) 0.5
(d) 0.75

121. A transistor amplifier with collector circuit efficiency of 80% will certainly be
(a) class A
(b) class AB
(c) class B
(d) class C

122. A transistor amplifier with collector circuit efficiency of 15% is likely to be
(a) class A
(b) class AB
(c) class B
(d) class C

123. Which class of amplifier has the lowest collector circuit efficiency ?
(a) class A
(b) class AB
(c) class B
(d) class C

124. Harmonic distortion in amplifiers is due to
(a) positive feed back in the circuit
(b) power supply of the amplifier
(c) reactive circuit elements
(d) nonlinear characteristics of the active device

125. Higher power efficiency of a pushpull amplifier results from the fact that
(a) each transistor conducts on different half cycle of the input
(b) transistors are placed in CE configuration
(c) there is no collector current with zero input
(d) low forward biasing voltage is needed

126. The reason for cross-over distortion in a pushpull amplifier is that
(a) the transistors are overdriven at cross-over points
(b) switching of current from one transistor to the other
(c) the combined transfer characteristic of the two transistors is most nonlinear at zero base current
(d) the input signals rise fast at their zeros

127. Cross-over distortion in class B pushpull amplifier is eliminated by
(a) class C operation
(b) class AB operation
(c) elimination of output transformer
(d) reducing the transistor bias

128. A class B amplifier is biased
(a) at cutoff
(b) at nearly twice the cutoff bias
(c) at midpoint of load line
(d) such that I_B just equals I_C

129. The coupling method which produces minimum interference with frequency response is
(a) direct coupling
(b) impedance coupling
(c) RC coupling
(d) transformer coupling

130. Load impedance must match amplifier output impedance in order that
 (a) minimum power is transferred to the load
 (b) maximum power is transferred to the load
 (c) collector circuit efficiency is highest
 (d) signal-to-noise ratio is maximum

131. Which of the following types of amplifier operations causes maximum distortion ?
 (a) class A (b) class AB
 (c) class B (d) class C

132. The power gain of an amplifier is 60-dB. At half power frequencies, the gain has fallen to
 (a) 30 dB (b) 57 dB
 (c) $60\sqrt{2}$ dB (d) 20 dB

133. Compared to single ended amplifier, a pushpull amplifier offers
 (a) less distortion and less output power
 (b) less distrotion and more output power
 (c) more distortion and less output power
 (d) morc distortion and more output power

134. Class B pushpull amplifier suffers from
 (a) intermodulation distortion
 (b) intermodulation distortion
 (c) excessive harmonic distortion
 (d) phase distortion

135. In a class C amplifier, full cycle conduction of the current is achieved by employing
 (a) transformers (b) pushspull circuit
 (c) tunned circuit (d) complementary pair

136. Crossover distortion takes place in
 (a) tunned amplifier
 (b) power amplifiers
 (c) small signal amplifiers
 (d) video amplifiers

137. Class B amplifiers are characterized by
 (a) high conversion efficiency and high distortion
 (b) low conversion efficiency and low distortion
 (c) high conversion efficiency and low distortion
 (d) low conversion efficiency and high distortion

138. In a trans resistance amplifier
 (a) output voltage depends on input voltage
 (b) output voltage depends on input current
 (c) output current depends on input voltage
 (d) output current depends on input current

139. Emitter follower is characterized by
 (a) low output impedance and little distortion
 (b) low output impedance and significant distortion
 (c) significant output impedance and significant distortion
 (d) none of these

140. The input and output impedance in an ideal current amplificr are respectively
 (a) $0, \infty$ (b) $\infty, 0$
 (c) ∞, ∞ (d) $0, 0$

141. In a negative feed back amplifier, voltage sampling
 (a) tends to decrease the output resistance
 (b) tends to increase the output resistance
 (c) does not alter the output resistance
 (d) produces the same effect on output resistance as current sampling

142. In a negative feed back amplifier, current sampling
 (a) tends to decrease the output resistance
 (b) tends to increase the output resistance
 (c) does not alter the output resistance
 (d) produces the same effect on output resistance as voltage sampling

143. In a negative feed back amplifier, serires mixing
 (a) tends to increase the output resistance
 (b) tends to decrease the output resistance
 (c) does not alter the output resistance
 (d) produces the same effect on input resistance as the shunt mixing

144. In a negative feed back amplifier, voltage shunt mixing
 (a) tends to increase the output resistance
 (b) tends to decrease the output resistance
 (c) does not alter the output resistance
 (d) produces the same effect on intput resistance as the series mixing

145. Emitter follower is a negative feed back amplifier using
 (a) voltage series feed back
 (b) current series feed back
 (c) current shunt feed back
 (d) voltage shunt feed back

146. FET source follower is a negative feedback amplifier using
 (a) voltage series feed back
 (b) current series feed back
 (c) current shunt feed back
 (d) voltage shunt feed back

147. CE ammplifier with unbypassed resistor in emitter-to-ground circuit froms a case of negative feed back amplifier with

(a) voltage series feed back

(b) current series feed back

(c) current shunt feed back

(d) voltage shunt feed back

148. FET common source amplifier with unbypassed resistor in source-to-ground circuit forms a case of negative feedback amplifier using

(a) voltage series feed back

(b) current series feed back

(c) current shunt feed back

(d) voltage shunt feed back

149. A CE amplifier with a resistor connected between collector and base forms a case of negative feedback amplifier using

(a) voltage series feed back

(b) current series feed back

(c) current shunt feed back

(d) voltage shunt feed back

150. Feed back is said to be positive if

(a) the feed back signal gets subtracted from the input signal

(b) the feed back signal gets added to the input signal

(c) any increase in the output signal results in a feed back signal which on being mixed with the input signal causes further increase in the magnitude of the output signal

(d) none of these

151. Negative feed back in an amplifier results in

(a) more gain, more bandwidth

(b) more gain, less bandwidth

(c) less gain, more bandwidth

(d) less gain, less bandwidth

152. In a transconductance amplifier

(a) output voltage depends on input voltage

(b) output voltage depends on input current

(c) output current depends on input voltage

(d) output current depends on input current

153. In a single tuned capacitance coupled amplifier, the frequency respnse depnds on

(a) only the input circuit

(b) only the output circuit

(c) both input and output circuits

(d) neither input circuit nor the output circuit

154. In capacitance coupled single tuned amplifier, the effective Q of the output circuit, at resonance depends

(a) only on inductance L

(b) only on capacitance C

(c) only on effective shunt resistance R_t

(d) on susceptance of L (or C) and effective shunt resistance R_t

155. A single tuned tapped capacitance coupled amplifier, tapping on the coil is used to

(a) permit use of smaller coil

(b) permit use of smaller tuning capacitor

(c) permit maximum transfer of power

(d) permit adjustment of 3-dB bandwidth

156. In a double tuned amplifier, with coupling greater than critical, maximum transfer of power takes place

(a) only at the frequency of resonance f_o

(b) at one more frequency other than f_o

(c) at two more frequencies other than f_o

(d) at four more frequencies other than f_o

157. The bandwidth of a double tuned transformer coupled amplifier can be adjusted by varying

(a) value of the inductance

(b) the coefficient of coupling

(c) value of emitter circuit biasing resistor

(d) none of these

158. A double tuned circuit amplifier provides

(a) high gain for passband frequencies

(b) more flat response for all frequencies

(c) more flat response for all passband frequencies

(d) less harmonic distortion

159. A high -Q tuned circuit in a tuned amplifier permits it to have high

(a) selectivity   (b) fidelity

(c) sensitivity   (d) frequency range

160. An oscillator is basically an amplifier with

(a) zero gain   (b) very large gain

(c) infinite gain   (d) very low gain

161. In a feed back oscillator, constant amplitude oscillations are obtained when loop gain-Ab equals

(a) 0   (b) –1

(c) 1   (d) ∞

162. In a tuned collector oscillator, frequency ω of oscillation is

(a) equal to ω_o (b) less than ω_o

(c) more than ω_o (d) $\dfrac{\omega_o}{h_{fe}}$

where ω_o is the frequency of resonance.

163. RC phase shift oscillator using BJT employs
(a) voltage series feed back
(b) voltage shunt feed back
(c) current series feed back
(d) current shunt feed back

164. FET phase-shift oscillator uses
(a) voltage series feed back
(b) voltage shunt feed back
(c) current series feed back
(d) current shunt feed back

165. Crystal oscillator uses
(a) silicon crystal
(b) germanium crystal
(c) crystal diode
(d) piezo-electric quartz crystal

166. Effective Q of the equivalent electrical circuit of quartz crystal is of the order of
(a) 200
(b) 2000
(c) 20,000
(d) 10^5

167. Quartz crystal oscillators are popularly used because of
(a) high Q and high frequency stability
(b) low Q and high frequency stability
(c) low Q and large output power
(d) high Q and large output power

168. The crystal oscillator frequency is highly stable due to
(a) crystal structure
(b) high Q of the crystal
(c) vibration of the crystal
(d) rigidity of the crystal

169. Most likely application of a crystal oscillator is
(a) as an RF test oscillator
(b) as an electronic organ for home
(c) as a Hi-Fi test audio frequency sweep generator
(d) in commercial radio transmitter

170. A monostable multivibrator has
(a) two stable states
(b) one stable state
(c) no stable state
(d) two quasi-stablestates

171. An astable multibrator has
(a) two stable states
(b) one stable state
(c) no stable state
(d) none of these

172. A bistable multivibrator has
(a) two stable states
(b) one stable state
(c) no stable state
(d) two quasi-stable state

173. Shortest interval between pulses with which a binary can switch from one state to another is called
(a) rise time
(b) relaxation time
(c) resolving time
(d) delay time

174. Schmitt trigger is also known as
(a) squaring circuit
(b) blocking oscillator
(c) sweep circuit
(d) astable multivibrator

175. Monostable multivibrator may be used to generate
(a) sweep voltage
(b) pulses
(c) sinusoidal voltage
(d) sweep current

176. In a multivibrator, commutating capacitors reduce the
(a) transition time
(b) rise time
(c) settling time
(d) none of these

177. Astable multivibrator may be used as
(a) frequency to voltage converter
(b) voltage to frequency converter
(c) squaring circuit
(d) comparator circuit

178. Advantage of emitter coupled multivibrator over collector coupled multivibrator
(a) inherently self-starting
(b) output free of recovery transients
(c) possessing an isolated input
(d) all these

179. Which of the following circuits may be used for converting a sine wave into a square wave ?
(a) Schmitt trigger
(b) Bistable multivibrator
(c) Astable multivibrator
(d) Monostable multivibrator

180. Which of the following circuits is used for production of delays ?
(a) Astable multivibrator
(b) Bistable multivibrator
(c) Monostable multivibrator
(d) Schmitt tigger

181. Wideband amplifier usually employs RC coupling instead of transformer coupling because of its
(a) more flat frequency response in low frequency range
(b) more flat frequency response in high frequency range
(c) more flat frequency response over a wide frequency range
(d) less phase distortion

182. To make an RC coupled amplifier function as a wideband amplifier, it is necessary to compensate

    (*a*) for drop of gain in low frequency range

    (*b*) for drop of gain in high frequency range

    (*c*) for harmonic phase shifts that are not proportional to the frequency of the harmonics

    (*d*) all of these

183. For good transient response, the transfer function of the amplifier should not have

    (*a*) zeros in the left half of the s-plane

    (*b*) zeros in the right half of the s-plane

    (*c*) poles in the left half of the s-plane

    (*d*) poles in the right half of the s-plane

184. The following compensation method in amplifier leads to reduction in bandwidth

    (*a*) lead compensation

    (*b*) pole-zero compensation

    (*c*) Miller-effect compensation

    (*d*) dominant-pole compensation

185. In lag-compensation method for amplifiers, the zero introduced at fz is

    (*a*) higher than the pole introduced at f_p

    (*b*) lower than the pole introduced at f_p

    (*c*) equal to the pole introduced at f_p

    (*d*) double of the pole introduced at f_p

186. On the pole-zero diagram of an amplifier, the low cutoff frequency fL will be determined by

    (*a*) the pole farthest from the origin

    (*b*) the pole closest to the origin

    (*c*) the zero farthest from the origin

    (*d*) the zero closest to the origin

187. On the pole-zero diagram of an amplifier, the high cutoff frequency fh will be determined by

    (*a*) the pole farthest from the origin

    (*b*) the pole closest to the origin

    (*c*) the zero farthest from the origin

    (*d*) the zero closest to the origin

188. Bootstrap voltage sweep generator uses

    (*a*) negative feed back

    (*b*) positive feed back

    (*c*) both negative and positive feed backs simultaneously

    (*d*) no feed back

189. Miller integrator voltage sweep generator uses

    (*a*) negative feed back

    (*b*) positive feed back

    (*c*) both negative and positive feed backs simultaneously

    (*d*) no feed back

190. To increase the bandwidth, the distributed amplifier uses

    (*a*) transmission lines (*b*) tuned circuits

    (*c*) resonant cavities (*d*) cascode amplifier

191. The sampling unit in an automatic voltage regulator is generally in the form of

    (*a*) a zener diode   (*b*) a potentiometer

    (*c*) a transistor   (*d*) a silicon diode

192. The reference unit in a dc voltage regulator is generally in the form of

    (*a*) a silicon breakdown diode

    (*b*) a transistor

    (*c*) a battery

    (*d*) a differential amplifier

193. The comparison unit in a dc voltage regulator is generally in the form of

    (*a*) a silicon breakdown diode

    (*b*) CE amplifier

    (*c*) a potentiometer

    (*d*) a battery

194. The function of a pre-regulator in a voltage regulator is

    (*a*) to provide preliminary regulation

    (*b*) to amplify the unregulated input voltage

    (*c*) to provide a constant current to the collector of the dc amplifier

    (*d*) to amplify the differential signal

195. Tuned amplifiers are generally not used in

    (*a*) TV receivers

    (*b*) Radio receivers

    (*c*) Public address systems

    (*d*) Radar receivers

196. Darlington emitter follower has

    (*a*) high input resistance and unity voltage gain

    (*b*) low input resistance and unity voltage gain

    (*c*) high input resistance and voltage gain less than unity but close to unity

    (*d*) low input resistance and high voltage gain

197. The dynamic impedance of a Zener diode

    (*a*) increases with increase of current through it

    (*b*) decreases with increase of current through it

    (*c*) is independent of current through it

    (*d*) first increases, reaches a maximum and then decreases with increase of current through it

198. Stagger tuned amplifier generally employs

    (*a*) CE configuration (*b*) CB configuration

    (*c*) CC configuration (*d*) Darlington pairs

199. If an amplifier gain of 10,000 then gain is expressed in decibels is

(a) 10   (b) 40

(c) 80   (d) 100

200. If bandwidth of each R F amplifier is 800 kHz, then bandwidth of three such stages cascaded is

(a) 800 kHz   (b) 2400 kHz

(d) 400 kHz   (d) 200 kHz

201. Frequency of oscillations of an RC phase shift oscillator using three identical RC sections is

(a) $\dfrac{1}{RC}$ (b) $\dfrac{1}{\sqrt{6}}RC$

(c) $S\dfrac{\sqrt{6}}{RC}$ (d) $S\dfrac{\sqrt{3}}{RC}$

202. Amplifier in which current is proportional to the signal voltage, independent of source load resistance is called

(a) Current amplifier

(b) Voltage amplifier

(c) Transreesistance amplifier

(d) Transconductance amplifier.

203. An emitter follows has

(a) High input impedance and high output impedance

(b) High input impedance and low output impedance

(c) Low input impedance and high output impedance

(d) Low input impedance and low output impedance

204. To increase input resistance and decrease output resistance in negative feedback, the type used is

(a) Voltage shunt   (b) Current series

(c) Voltage series   (d) Current shunt

205. Coupling capacitance of a bipolar transistor amplifier must be

(a) 500 limes larger ilian than FHT amplifier

(b) 500 times lesser than the FET amplifier

(c) equal to that the FFT amplifier

(d) negligible to that of FET amplifier

206. Loop gain of an amplifier employing feedback (with feedback ratio B)is

(a) $\dfrac{1}{B}$ (b) B

(c) B^2 (d) $\dfrac{B}{P}$

207. For any uniform and symmetrical life, characteristic impedance is

(a) geometric mean of the open and short circuited impedances

(b) product of the open and short circuited impedances

(c) square of the product of open and short circuited impedances

(d) ratio of the above two impedances

208. Gain bandwidth product of the transistor amplifier is usually denoted as

(a) f^a (b) f^B

(c) f^y (d) None of these

209. A pulse amplifier is basically an amplifier with

(a) Wide band   (b) IF

(c) Narrow band   (d) Audio band

210. For harmonic generation, amplifier used is

(a) Audio amplifier

(b) Class-A amplifier

(c) RC amplifier

(d) Class-C turned amplifier

211. Choose the correct statement:

(a) $dB = 20 \log V_0/V_i$ (b) $dB = 20 \log I_0/I_i$

(c) $dB = 10 \log P_0/P_i$ (d) $dB = 20 \log P_0/P_i$

212. Response curve of an amplifier is a graph that shows

(a) output voltage with input voltage

(b) output current with input current

(c) output voltage with frequency

(d) output current with frequency.

213. If an amplifiers has a power gain of 3 B, then this signifies that

(a) $P_0 = 4P$ (b) $P_0 = 3P_i$

(c) $V_0/V_i = 2I_i/I_0$ (d) $2V_0/V_i = I_i/I_0$.

214. In FET amplifiers, input exciation is

(a) a current signal

(b) a voltage signal

(c) either a current or voltage signal

(d) none of these

215. Decibel is defined in terms of

(a) power ratio   (b) voltage level

(c) current level   (d) none of these.

216. "Power gain of a CB configuration is almost equal to its voltage gain." Is it true?

(a) Yes   (b) No

217. A source of 500 KΩ output impedance was to be connected to a load of 10Ω. The matching device or circuit could be of two types. One was by using a CC (common collector) stage in between and other to have a passive circuit having input and output impedances of 500 KΩ and 10Ω respectively. Finally, CC stage was preferred even though it demanded much more component count and circuit complexity. because

(a) it does not introduce any noise.

(b) its impedances are extremely stable and do not vary with various parameters.

(c) it does not alter circuit conditions because of its voltage gain being unity.

(d) none of these.

218. CB configuration having very small input impedance because

(a) of its inherent characteristics

(b) it has a very large resistance gain-(R_0/R_i)

(c) input is applied between emitter and base and emitter junction is always forward biased for operation.

(d) it is always fed from a low impedance source.

219. Power handling capability of a given transistor, is dependent upon.

(a) maximum junction temperature and expected ambient temperature.

(b) maximum temperature at which the junction of the device is permitted to operate.

(c) actual ambient temperature expected during operation

(d) none of these.

220. It is desired to design an amplifier with a voltage gain of 10,000. Output should be in phase with the input. Available CB stage has a gain of 100 per stage and CE has per stage gain of 25. The designed amplifier shall have

(a) two cascaded stages of CB configuration

(b) four cascaded stages of CE configuraiion

(c) two cascaded stages of CE configuration

(d) three cascaded stages of CF configuration followed by an emitter follower stage.

221. h-parameters of a transistor

(a) are constant

(b) vary with temperature

(c) are dependent upon collector current

(d) none of these.

222. High frequency response of a transformer coupled amplifier is generally limited by Transformer's

(a) leakage inductance and distributed capacitance.

(b) primary inductance.

(c) leakage inductance only.

(d) winding capacitance only.

223. Low frequency response of a transformer coupled amplifier is limited by

(a) transformer's leakage inductance

(b) transformer's primary inductance

(c) tesistance associated with transformer windings

(d) transformer interwinding capacitances.

224. In a voltage series feedback

(a) output resistance increases while input resistance decreases.

(b) output and input resistances are reduced.

(c) output and input resistances are increased

(d) output resistance decreases while input resistance increases.

225. An ideal power supply is characterized by

(a) very large output resistance

(b) very small output resistance

(c) zero internal resistance

(d) infinite internal resistance.

226. For an ideal noise free amplifier, noise figure is

(a) Zero   (b) Zero dB

(c) Infinity   (d) 1 dB

227. Wide bandwidth operation is offered by

(a) common emitter amplifier

(b) common base amplifier

(c) common collector amplifier

(d) none of these

228. In the negative feedback amplifier with gain A/K, noise generated in the amplifier is reduced by a factor of

(a) K   (b) $1 - K$

(c) 1/K   (d) $1/(1 - K)$

229. The type of negative feedback which results in the increase of both Z^{in} and Z^{out} of an amplifier is

(a) Voltage-shunt   (b) Voltage-series

(c) Current-shunt   (d) Current-series

230. An a saturated transistor

(a) B-E junction is forward biased while C-B junction is reverse biased.

(b) Both junctions are forward biased

(c) B-E junction is reverse biased while C-B junction is forward biased

(d) Both junctions are reverse biased

231. A good current amplifier has
(a) Low R_{in} and high R^{out}
(b) Low R_{in} and low R^{out}
(c) High R_{in} and low R^{out}
(d) High R_{in} and high R^{out}

232. The oscillator that has best frequency stability is
(a) Crystal oscillator
(b) Hartley oscillator
(c) Colpitt's
(d) Tuned collector oscillator

233. Bootstrap sweep circuit generally employs
(a) Emitter follower
(b) CH amplifier
(c) CB amplifier
(d) Tuned amplifier

234. Crystal oscillators are preferred to LC oscillators due to their.
(a) Compact size
(b) Temperature stability
(c) Frequency stability
(d) Simple circuitry

235. In Class B push pull amplifier, cross-over distortion is eliminated by
(a) Using matched transistors
(b) Adopting class AB operation
(c) Using complementary devices
(d) Combination of above.

236. In hybrid parameters representing two port network, the parameters represent
(a) Impedances only
(b) Admittances only
(c) Current and voltage gain only
(d) Combination of above

237. Pulse width of the output pulse of a monostable multivibrator with R = 10 ohms and C = 0.03 o μF is approximately
(a) 208 microsecond
(b) 503 microsecond
(c) 708 microsecond
(d) 908 microsecond

238. Voltage gain of an amplifier used with Bootstrap sweep theoretically shall be
(a) -1
(b) $+1$
(c) infinity
(d) no such consideration

239. A PNP transistor is generally made of
(a) Silicon
(b) Germanium
(c) Either silicon or germanium
(d) None of the above.

240. In a transistor the region that is very lightly doped and is very thin is
(a) Emitter
(b) Base
(c) Collector
(d) None of the above.

241. In a NPN transistor, when emitter junction is forward biased and collector junction is reverse biased, the transistor will operate in
(a) Active region
(b) Saturation region
(c) Cut of region
(d) Inverted region

242. A transistor will operate in inverted region if
(a) Emitter junction is forward biased and collector junction is reverse biased.
(b) Emitter junction is reverse biased and collector junction is forward biased.
(c) Emitter junction as well as collector junction are forward biased.
(d) Emitter junction as well collector junction are reverse biased.

243. Choose the correct statement:
(a) FET and junction transistor both are unipolar.
(b) FET and junction transistor both are bipolar.
(c) The FET is bipolar, while junction transistors are unipolar.
(d) The FET is unipolar, while junction transistors are bipolar.

244. The encapsulation of transistor is essential for
(a) Preventing ratio interference
(b) Preventing photo-emission effects
(c) Avoiding loss of free electrons
(d) Mechanical ruggedness.

245. A diac is a semiconductor device acts as a
(a) 2 terminal unidirectional switch.
(b) 2 terminal bidirectional switch.
(c) 3 terminal bidirectional switch.
(d) 4 terminal multidirectional switch.

246. Which of the following is essential for transistor action?
(a) The base region must be very wide.
(b) The base region must be very narrow.
(c) The base region must be made of some insulating material.
(d) The collector region must be heavily doped.

247. In a transistor, current ICBO flows when
(a) Some d.c. voltage is applied in the reverse direction to the emitter junction with the collector open circuited
(b) Some d.c. voltage is applied in the forward direction to the collector junction with the emitter open circuited.
(c) Some d.c. voltage is applied in the reverse direction to the collector junction with the emitter open circuited.
(d) Some d.c. voltage is applied in the forward direction to the emitter junction with the collector open-circuited.

248. The current I_{CBO}
  (a) Increases with increase in temperature.
  (b) Is normally greater for silicon transistors than germanium transistors.
  (c) Mainly depends on the emitter base junction bias.
  (d) Depends largely on the emitter doping.

249. Which of the following statement is false?
  (a) The zener diode is used as a constant voltage source.
  (b) The SCR is a silicon rectifier with a gate electrode to control when current flows from cathode to anode.
  (c) The gate electrode on the FET corresponds to the collector in bipolar transistor.
  (d) None of the above.

250. Thermal runaway of a transistor occurs when
  (a) Heat dissipation from transistor is excessive.
  (b) Transistor joints melt due to high temperature.
  (c) There is excessive leakage current due to temperature rise.
  (d) None of the above.

251. As compared to a CB amplifier, a CE amplifier has
  (a) Lower current amplification
  (b) Higher current amplification
  (c) Lower input resistance.
  (d) Higher input resistance

252. Which of me following is the fastest switching device?
  (a) JFET   (b) BJT
  (c) MOSFET   (d) Triode

253. Which of the following circuits does not require a coupling capacitor?
  (a) Resistance loaded   (b) Transformer coupled
  (c) Impedance coupled (d) Single tuned.

254. In an RC-coupled amplifier for improving the low frequency response.
  (a) Lower RL is provided
  (b) More bias is used
  (c) Less gain is provided
  (d) Higher Cc is used

255. Which of the following statement is correct?
  (a) The emitter injects holes into the base region of the PNP transistor and electrons into the base region of the NPN transistor.
  (b) The emitter injects electrons into the base region of the PNP transistor and holes into the base region of the NPN transistor.

  (c) The emitter junction is reverse biased in the NPN transistors and forward biased in PNP transistor.
  (d) None of the above.

256. Which of the following is not provided in a PNP transistor?
  (a) Base   (b) AB
  (c) B   (d) C

257. Which coupling produces the minimum interference with frequency response?
  (a) RC coupling   (b) Transformer coupling
  (c) Direct coupling   (d) Impedance coupling.

258. For an amplifier the power gain in decibels will be equal to voltage gain in decibles only when
  (a) $R_0 = 0$ (b) $R_0 = R_i = 0$
  (c) $R_0 = R$ (d) $R_0 = R_0$

Fill in the blanks

259. An amplifier has a gain bandwidth product of 10 MHz. If used as a feedback amplifier of gain 100, it lias a bandwidth of .....

260. Theoritical maximum efficiency of a class B power amplifier stage is ......

261. Difference amplifier is mainly used for its ___ property.

262. Gain of a voltage amplifier is 60 dB. It is numerically equal to ____.

263. Amplifiers are capacitively coupled to ensure____.

264. In a multistage amplifier system, stage with ___ frequency response will decide overall bandwidth.

265. Low frequency response of an R.C coupled amplifier is limited by ____.

266. Greater the frequency range of the amplifier (called bandwidth), smaller is the ___ of the pulse waveform.

267. Feedback means ___ a portion of the energy from the output of some device back to its input.

268. An amplifier circuit, containing inductance and capacitance which can be tuned to choose proper frequency is generally called ___ circuit.

269. Sweep circuits are used to generate ___ waveforms for use in the time base of CRO.

270. In an RC phase shift oscillator in FET can be used only if its amplification factor is ___ than 29.

271. The type of feedback present in a cathode follower is ___.

272. Main advantage of class-B mode over class-A mode of operation is ___.

273. In power amplifiers using transistors, thermal runways is a ___ process involving collector current and collector junction temperature.

274. _____ effect a quartz, crystal is utilized in a crystal oscillator.

275. To eliminate change in frequency of oscillation with load impedance, an isolating amplifier called ___ is often used.

276. Direct coupled amplifier are useful for amplifying ___ signals.

277. Less hum filtering of the power supply is required with a ___ amplifier than otherwise necessary.

278. Drain current in a JFET remains practically constant if it is operated ___.

279. A certain single stage amplifier has gain of $|A| = 90$ and lower half power frequency f^1 equal to 100 Hz. If 10% negative feedback is applied, then new value of f^1 would be ___.

280. Fall in the low frequency response of an R-C coupled amplifier is mainly due to presence of_____.

281. Oscillator circuit which uses a tapped coil is called ___.

282. Standard pulse generator usually employs ___ multivibrator.

283. Width of depletion layer in an unbiased function depends on ___ level on either side of the junction.

284. Realisation of large current across the ___ collector is transistor action.

285. Limitations of RC filter are overcome by replacing R by ___.

286. In an FET after _____ voltage, drain current remains saturated for a constant gate voltage.

287. Between ratings V^{CBO} of a transistor, higher of the two is ____.

288. In order to avoid cross over distrotion push full amplifier are operated in Class ___ mode.

289. Voltage gain of an emitter follower cannot be more than ___.

290. Monostable multivibrator is used as a _____ generator.

291. Voltage gain of a source follower is always ____ than unity.

292. An amplifier of pass band 450 kHz to 460 kHz is called ________.

293. Lower cut off frequency of a two stage RC-coupled amplifier is _____ than its value for the single stage amplifier.

294. Overall voltage gain of a multistage amplifier is obtained by ____ the gains of each stage expressed as voltage ratio.

295. Speech amplifiers are usually operated in class ____ operation.

EXERCISE – II

1. Darlington circuit is obtained by connecting in cascade **DMRC 2013**
(a) two emitter followers with input impedance of second transistor forming the load impedance of the first stage
(b) two CB stage
(c) two CE stage
(d) CE stage directly coupled to CB stage

2. Compared to CB amplifier, the CE amplifier has considerably **DMRC 2013**
(a) higher current gain
(b) lower input resistance
(c) lower voltage gain
(d) lower current gain

3. In the high frequency hybrid-π model of a CE transistor, conductance gbc accounts for **DMRC 2013**
(a) bulk conductance of base region
(b) leakage conductance in the base region
(c) feed back action due to base width modulation
(d) none of these

4. Presence of emitter circuit bypass capacitor adversely affects the **DMRC 2013**
(a) low frequency response
(b) midband response
(c) high frequency response
(d) response over the complete frequency range

5. A class B amplifier is biased **DMRC 2013**
(a) at cutoff
(b) at nearly twice the cutoff bias
(c) at midpoint of load line
(d) such that I_B just equals I_C

6. The feed back resistance rgd in small signal model of MOSFET is of the order of
(a) $1\ M\Omega$ (b) $100\ M\Omega$ **DMRC 2013**
(c) $10^4\ M\Omega$ (d) $10^6\ M\Omega$

7. The feed back capacitance Cgd in small signal high frequency model of a JFET is of the order of **DMRC 2013**
(a) 5 pF (b) 50 pF
(c) 500 pF (d) 1 F

8. The drain-to-source resistance Cds in high frequency model of a JFET is of the order of **DMRC 2013**

(a) 1 pF (b) 10 pF
(c) 100 pF (d) 1000 pF

9. The gate-to-source capacitance Cgs in small signal high frequency model of a JFET is of the order of **DMRC 2013**

(a) 5 pF (b) 50 pF
(c) 500 pF (d) 5000 pF

10. When a multistage transistor amplifier is required to amplify dc signals also, we must use

(a) RC coupling **DMRC 2013**
(b) direct coupling
(c) transformer coupling
(d) double tuned circuits

11. Transformer coupling provides high efficiency because the **DMRC 2013**

(a) collector voltage is stepped up
(b) dc resistance in the collector circuit is low
(c) collector voltage is stepped down
(d) flux linkages are incomplete

12. In RC coupled amplifier, the dc component is blocked by **DMRC 2013**

(a) load resistor R_L
(b) coupling capacitor C_b
(c) the transistor
(d) the bypass capacitor C_z in the self bias circuit

13. Which of the following types of amplifier operations causes maximum distortion ?

(a) class A (b) class AB **DMRC 2013**
(c) class B (d) class C

14. The power gain of an amplifier is 60-dB. At half power frequencies, the gain has fallen to

(a) 30 dB (b) 57 dB **DMRC 2013**
(c) $60\sqrt{2}$ dB (d) 20 dB

15. Compared to single ended amplifier, a pushpull amplifier offers **DMRC 2013**

(a) less distortion and less output power
(b) less distrotion and more output power
(c) more distortion and less output power
(d) more distortion and more output power

16. A transistor emitter base voltage (V_{EB}) of 20 mV has a collector current (I_C) of 5 mA. For V_{EB} of 30 mV, I_C is 30 mA. If V_{EB} is 40 mV, then the I_C will be **DMRC 2014**

(a) 55 mA (b) 160 mA
(c) 180 mA (d) 270 mA

17. An ideal constant voltage source is connected in series with an ideal constant current source. Considered together, the combination will be a

(a) constant voltage source **DMRC 2014**
(b) constant current source
(c) constant voltage and a constant current source or a constant power source
(d) resistance

18. In the circuit shown, it is required that $V_o = V_i$ the values of l, m, n are, respectively (x represents don't care condition) **DMRC**

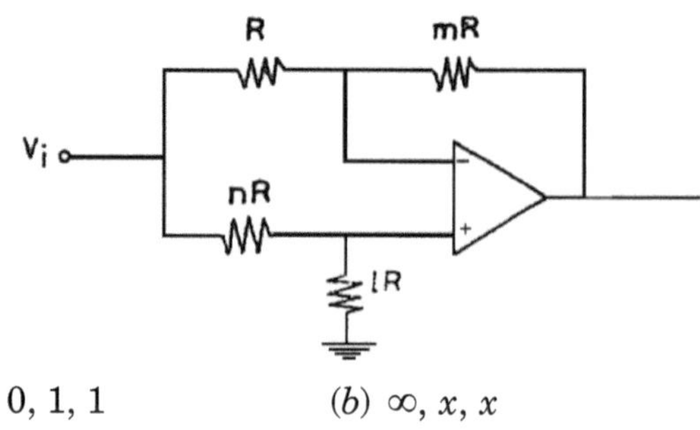

(a) 0, 1, 1 (b) ∞, x, x
(c) x, ∞, x (d) 0, x, ∞

19. The operation of a JFET involves **DRDO**

(a) flow of minority carriers alone
(b) flow of majority carriers alone
(c) flow of both minority and majority carriers
(d) use of a magnetic field

20. In a CE amplifier stage, on introducing a resistor Re in the emitter circuit, the input resistance Ri

(a) remain unlatered **DRDO**
(b) reduces
(c) increases nominally
(d) increases very much

21. In a class B amplifier with sinusoidal input signal, the output current flows for **DRDO**

(a) half the cycle (b) full cycle
(c) less than half cycle (d) more than half cycle

22. Class B amplifiers are characterized by **DRDO**

(a) high conversion efficiency and high distortion
(b) low conversion efficiency and low distortion
(c) high conversion efficiency and low distortion
(d) low conversion efficiency and high distortion

23. In a negative feed back amplifier, voltage shunt mixing **DRDO**

(a) tends to increase the output resistance
(b) tends to decrease the output resistance
(c) does not alter the output resistance
(d) produces the same effect on intput resistance as the series mixing

24. Astable multivibrator may be used as **DRDO**
  (a) frequency to voltage converter
  (b) voltage to frequency converter
  (c) squaring circuit
  (d) comparator circuit

25. The following compensation method in amplifier leads to reduction in bandwidth **DRDO**
  (a) lead compensation
  (b) pole-zero compensation
  (c) Miller-effect compensation
  (d) dominant-pole compensation

26. If feeback is introduced in the system the transient response **DRDO**
  (a) does not very
  (b) decays very fast
  (c) decays slowly
  (d) dies off

27. In the high frequency hybrid-π model of a CE transistor, capacitance Ce accounts for **DRDO**
  (a) excess minority carrier storage in the base region
  (b) collector junction barrier capacitance
  (c) emitter junction barrier capacitance
  (d) collector junction diffusion capacitance

28. In a class AB amplifier with sinusoidal input signal, the output current flows for **DRDO**
  (a) half the cycle
  (b) full cycle
  (c) less than half cycle
  (d) more than half cycle

29. In the output of a pushpull amplifier, the most disturbing harmomic distortion is the **DRDO**
  (a) second harmonic
  (b) third harmonic
  (c) fourth harmonic
  (d) fifth harmonic

30. As compared to oscillators, an inverter provides
  (a) low voltage output **DRDO**
  (b) low ferquency output
  (c) distortion less output
  (d) noiseless output

31. In a CE amplifier stage, on introducing a resistor Re in the emitter circuit, the input resistance Ri
  (a) remain unlatered **RRB**
  (b) reduces
  (c) increases nominally
  (d) increases very much

32. In a class B amplifier with sinusoidal input signal, the output current flows for **RRB**
  (a) half the cycle
  (b) full cycle
  (c) less than half cycle
  (d) more than half cycle

33. Class B amplifiers are characterized by **RRB**
  (a) high conversion efficiency and high distortion
  (b) low conversion efficiency and low distortion
  (c) high conversion efficiency and low distortion
  (d) low conversion efficiency and high distortion

34. In a negative feed back amplifier, voltage shunt mixing **RRB**
  (a) tends to increase the output resistance
  (b) tends to decrease the output resistance
  (c) does not alter the output resistance
  (d) produces the same effect on intput resistance as the series mixing

35. Astable multivibrator may be used as **RRB**
  (a) frequency to voltage converter
  (b) voltage to frequency converter
  (c) squaring circuit
  (d) comparator circuit

36. The following compensation method in amplifier leads to reduction in bandwidth **RRB**
  (a) lead compensation
  (b) pole-zero compensation
  (c) Miller-effect compensation
  (d) dominant-pole compensation

37. In a transistor current I_{CBO} flow in **RRB**
  (a) base and emiter leads
  (b) collector and emitter leads
  (c) base and collector leads
  (d) emitter, base and collector leads

38. Halfwave rectifier has theoretical maximum efficiency of **RRB**
  (a) 40.6%
  (b) 81.2%
  (c) 78.5%
  (d) 50%

39. Base-to-emitter voltage V_{BE} is a forward biased transistor decreases with increase of temperature at the rate **RRB**
  (a) 25 mV/deg C
  (b) 0.25mV/deg C
  (c) 2.5 mV/deg C
  (d) 0.6 mV/deg C

40. When light falls on the photodiode shown in the following circuit, the reverse saturation current of the photodiode changes from 100 μA to 200 μA. **RRB**

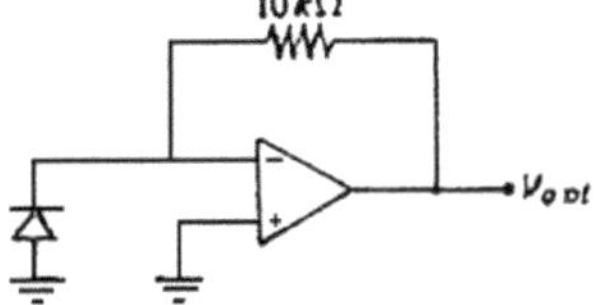

Assuming the op-amp to be ideal, the output voltage, V_{out}, of the circuit

(a) does not change

(b) changes from 1 V to 2 V

(c) changes from 2 V to 1 V

(d) changes from -1 V to -2 V

11. For common-collector amplifier, the current gain (A_I) is **RRB**

(a) $1 + h_{fe}$

(b) $\dfrac{1 + h_{fe}}{1 + h_{oe} R_L}$

(c) $\dfrac{1 + h_{fe}}{h_{oe} h_{ie}}$

(d) $\dfrac{1 + h_{fe}}{1 + h_{ie} R_L}$

42. A CMOS implementation of a logic gate is shown in the following figure : **RRB**

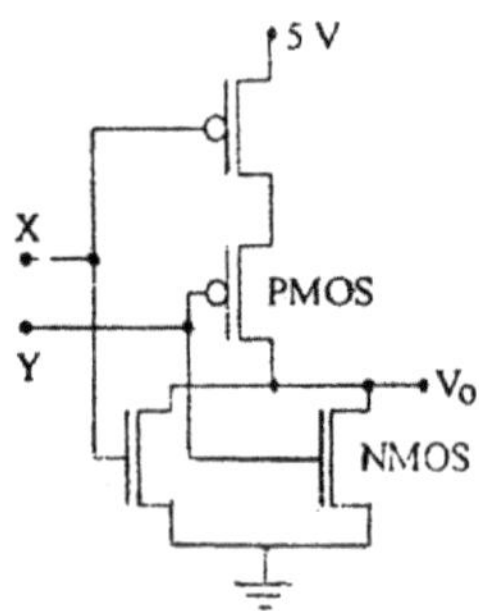

The boolean logic function realized by the circuit is

(a) AND

(b) NAND

(c) NOR

(d) OR

43. Consider the linear circuit with and ideal op-amp shown in the figure below. **RRB**

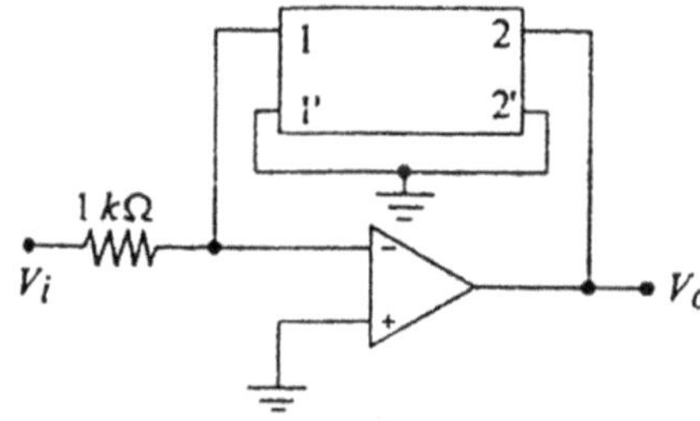

The Z-parameters of the two port feedback network are $Z_{11} = Z_{22} = 11$ kΩ and $Z_{12} = Z_{21} = 1$ kΩ. The gain of the amplifier is

(a) $+110$

(b) $+11$

(c) -1

(d) -120

44. A FET source follower is shown in the figure below: **RRB**

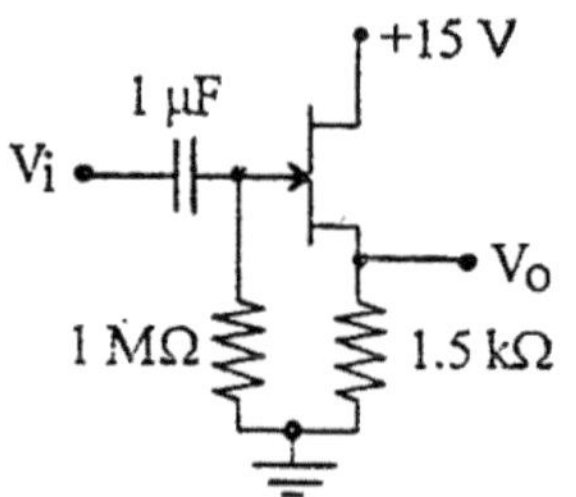

The nature of feedback in this circuit is

(a) positive current

(b) negative current

(c) positive voltage

(d) negative voltage

45. In the driven-right-leg system for reducing the common mode interference in ECG recording, the common mode voltage is sensed and connected to the right leg electrode. The desirable condition for the amplifier gain is

(a) a large positive gain

(b) a large negative gain

(c) a gain of 1

(d) a gain of -1 **RRB**

46. Find the V_0 **RRB 2012**

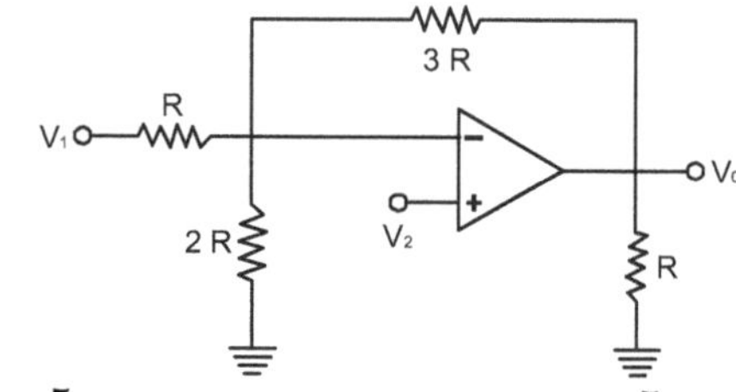

(a) $\dfrac{5}{2} V_1 - 3 V_2$

(b) $2V_1 - \dfrac{5}{2} V_2$

(c) $\dfrac{-3}{2} V_1 - \dfrac{7}{2} V_2$

(d) $-3V_1 + \dfrac{11}{2} V_2$

47. A FET source follower is shown in the figure below: **RRB 2012**

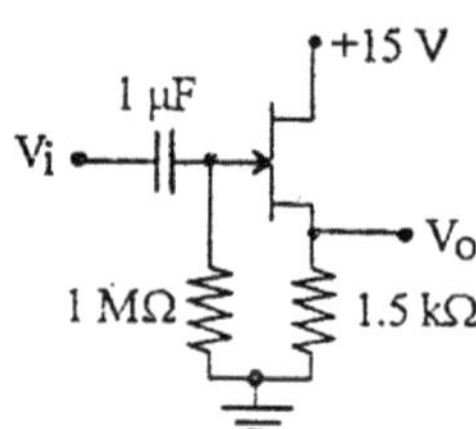

The nature of feedback in this circuit is

(a) positive current

(b) negative current

(c) positive voltage

(d) negative voltage

48. In the circuit shown below, for the MOS transistors, $\mu_c C_{ox} = 100$ mA/V^2 and the threshold voltage $V_T = 1$V. The voltage V_x at the source of the upper transistor is **RRB 2012**

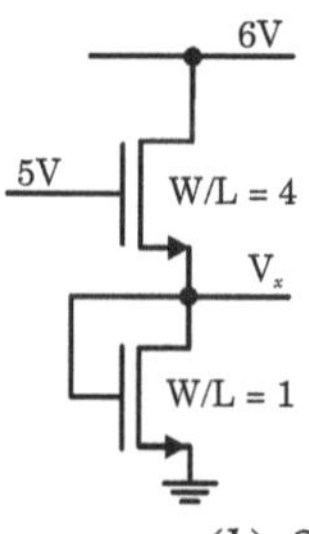

(a) 1 V

(b) 2 V

(c) 3 V

(d) 3.67 V

49. The figure shows a single op-amp differential amplifier circuit. **RRB 2012**

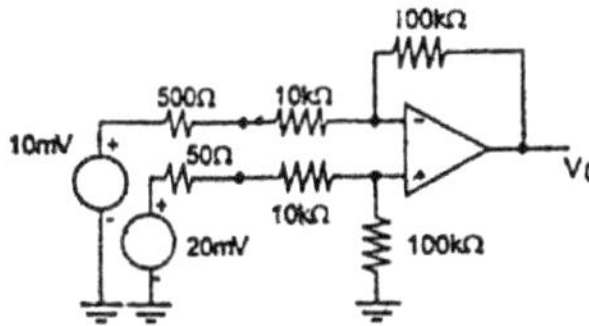

Which one of the following statements about the output is correct ? **RRB 2012**

(a) $V_0 \le 95$ mV

(b) 95 mV $< V_0 \le 98$ mV

(c) 98 mV $< V_0 \le 101$ mV

(d) $V_0 > 101$ mV

50. The three transistors in the circuit shown below are identical, with $V_{BE} = 0.7$ V and $\beta = 100$.

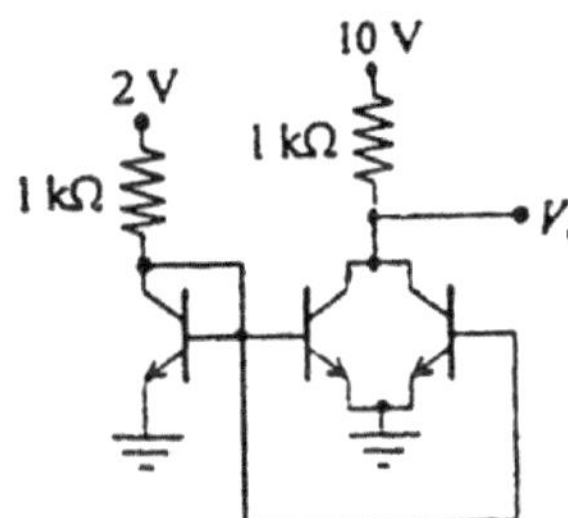

The voltage V_c is **RRB 2012**

(a) 0.2 V   (b) 2 V

(c) 7.4 V   (d) 10 V

51. The input signal shown in the figure below is fed to a Schmitt trigger. The signal has a square wave amplitude of 6 V p-p. It is corrupted by an additive high frequency noise of amplitude 8 V p-p.

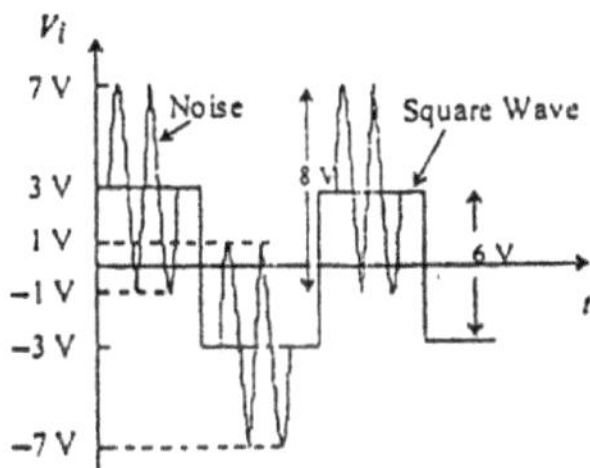

RRB 2012

Which one of the following is an appropriate choice for the upper and lower trip points of the Schmitt trigger to recover a square wave of the same frequency from the corrupted input signal Vi?

(a) ± 8.0 V   (b) ± 2.0 V

(c) ± 0.5 V   (d) 0 V

52. In the circuit shown below the switch (S) is closed whenever the input voltage (Vin) is positive and open otherwise. **RRB 2012**

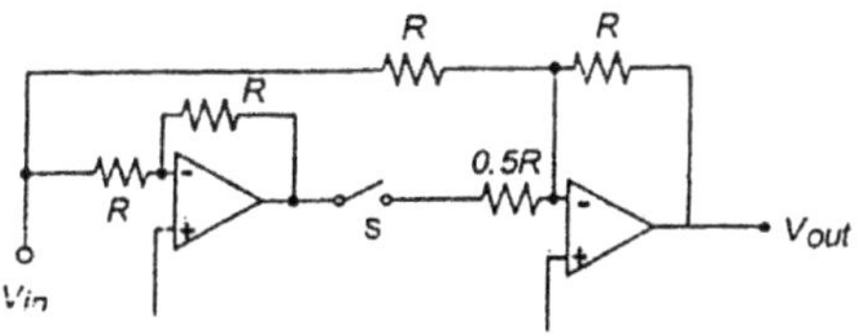

The circuit is a

(a) low pass filter   (b) level shifter

(c) modulator   (d) precision rectifier

53. For the BJT Q_1 in the circuit shown below, $\beta = \infty$, $V_{BEon} = 0.7$V. The switch is initially closed. At time $t = 0$, the switch is opened. The time t at which Q_1 leaves the active region is **RRB 2012**

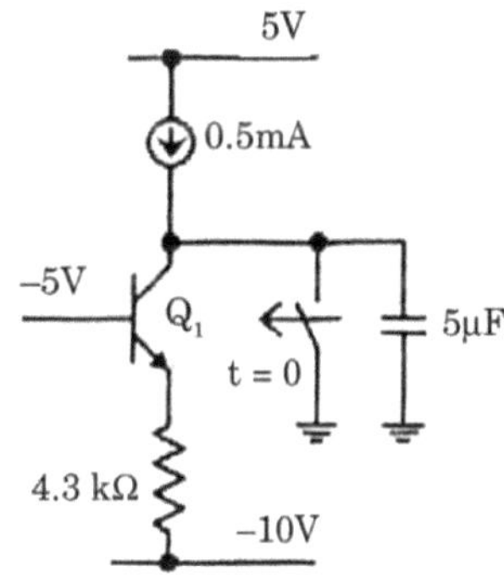

(a) 10 ms   (b) 25 ms

(c) 50 ms   (d) 100 ms

54. Consider the triangular wave generator shown below.

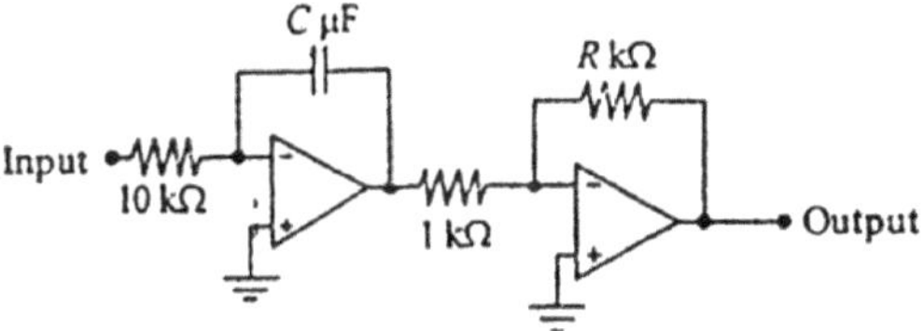

Assume that the op-amps are ideal and have ± 12 V power supply. If the input is a ± 5 V 50 Hz square wave of duty cycle 50 %, the condition that results in a triangular wave of peak to peak amplitude 5 V and frequency 50 Hz at the output is **RRB 2012**

(a) $RC = 1$ (b) $\dfrac{R}{C} = 1$

(c) $\dfrac{R}{C} = 5$ (d) $\dfrac{C}{R} = 5$

55. The potential difference between the input terminals of an op amp may be treated to be nearly zero, if **RRB 2012**

(a) the two supply voltages are balanced

(b) the output voltage is not saturated

(c) the op amp is used in a circuit having negative feedback

(d) there is a dc bias path between each of the input terminals and the circuit ground

ANSWERS

EXERCISE – I

1. (a)	**2.** (b)	**3.** (c)	**4.** (a)	**5.** (a)	**6.** (a)	**7.** (a)	**8.** (b)	**9.** (a)	**10.** (a)
11. (b)	**12.** (d)	**13.** (c)	**14.** (d)	**15.** (c)	**16.** (c)	**17.** (a)	**18.** (b)	**19.** (c)	**20.** (c)
21. (a)	**22.** (a)	**23.** (b)	**24.** (b)	**25.** (d)	**26.** (b)	**27.** (c)	**28.** (b)	**29.** (b)	**30.** (d)
31. (b)	**32.** (b)	**33.** (c)	**34.** (b)	**35.** (c)	**36.** (d)	**37.** (c)	**38.** (c)	**39.** (a)	**40.** (a)
41. (d)	**42.** (c)	**43.** (a)	**44.** (c)	**45.** (a)	**46.** (c)	**47.** (a)	**48.** (b)	**49.** (a)	**50.** (a)
51. (d)	**52.** (d)	**53.** (b)	**54.** (a)	**55.** (a)	**56.** (b)	**57.** (a)	**58.** (b)	**59.** (b)	**60.** (b)
61. (a)	**62.** (c)	**63.** (c)	**64.** (c)	**65.** (d)	**66.** (b)	**67.** (a)	**68.** (d)	**69.** (b)	**70.** (d)
71. (a)	**72.** (b)	**73.** (a)	**74.** (c)	**75.** (b)	**76.** (d)	**77.** (d)	**78.** (a)	**79.** (c)	**80.** (a)
81. (d)	**82.** (d)	**83.** (a)	**84.** (a)	**85.** (a)	**86.** (d)	**87.** (b)	**88.** (d)	**89.** (a)	**90.** (c)
91. (b)	**92.** (a)	**93.** (b)	**94.** (a)	**95.** (c)	**96.** (b)	**97.** (d)	**98.** (b)	**99.** (d)	**100.** (b)
101. (a)	**102.** (a)	**103.** (c)	**104.** (a)	**105.** (c)	**106.** (d)	**107.** (c)	**108.** (b)	**109.** (d)	**110.** (c)
111. (b)	**112.** (c)	**113.** (b)	**114.** (b)	**115.** (b)	**116.** (b)	**117.** (b)	**118.** (d)	**119.** (d)	**120.** (b)
121. (d)	**122.** (a)	**123.** (a)	**124.** (d)	**125.** (c)	**126.** (c)	**127.** (b)	**128.** (a)	**129.** (a)	**130.** (b)
131. (d)	**132.** (b)	**133.** (b)	**134.** (a)	**135.** (c)	**136.** (b)	**137.** (a)	**138.** (b)	**139.** (a)	**140.** (a)
141. (a)	**142.** (b)	**143.** (a)	**144.** (b)	**145.** (a)	**146.** (a)	**147.** (b)	**148.** (b)	**149.** (d)	**150.** (c)
151. (c)	**152.** (c)	**153.** (b)	**154.** (d)	**155.** (c)	**156.** (c)	**157.** (b)	**158.** (c)	**159.** (a)	**160.** (c)
161. (c)	**162.** (c)	**163.** (b)	**164.** (a)	**165.** (d)	**166.** (c)	**167.** (a)	**168.** (b)	**169.** (d)	**170.** (b)
171. (c)	**172.** (a)	**173.** (c)	**174.** (a)	**175.** (b)	**176.** (a)	**177.** (b)	**178.** (d)	**179.** (a)	**180.** (c)
181. (d)	**182.** (c)	**183.** (d)	**184.** (d)	**185.** (d)	**186.** (a)	**187.** (a)	**188.** (b)	**189.** (a)	**190.** (a)
191. (b)	**192.** (a)	**193.** (b)	**194.** (c)	**195.** (c)	**196.** (c)	**197.** (c)	**198.** (b)	**199.** (d)	**200.** (b)
201. (b)	**202.** (c)	**203.** (b)	**204.** (c)	**205.** (a)	**206.** (a)	**207.** (a)	**208.** (c)	**209.** (c)	**210.** (d)
211. (c)	**212.** (c)	**213.** (c)	**214.** (b)	**215.** (a)	**216.** (a)	**217.** (c)	**218.** (c)	**219.** (a)	**220.** (b)
221. (c)	**222.** (a)	**223.** (b)	**224.** (b)	**225.** (c)	**226.** (b)	**227.** (c)	**228.** (c)	**229.** (d)	**230.** (b)
231. (a)	**232.** (a)	**233.** (a)	**234.** (c)	**235.** (b)	**236.** (d)	**237.** (a)	**238.** (b)	**239.** (c)	**240.** (b)
241. (a)	**242.** (b)	**243.** (d)	**244.** (d)	**245.** (a)	**246.** (b)	**247.** (c)	**248.** (a)	**249.** (d)	**250.** (c)
251. (b)	**252.** (c)	**253.** (b)	**254.** (d)	**255.** (a)	**256.** (d)	**257.** (c)	**258.** (c)		

259. 100 kHz
260. 78.5%
261. Stable/zero drift.
262. 1000
263. More voltage gain.
264. Mid
265. Series coupling capacitance
266. Gain/amplitude
267. A small
268. Resonant/ Tuned
269. Sawtooth
270. Geater
271. Current series feedback
272. Efficiency
273. Self distruction
274. Piezo electric
275. Buffer
276. Low frequency.
277. Series
278. Beyond pinch off voltage
279. 1000 Hz/1 kHz.
280. Coupling capacitors (series)
281. Harley
282. Monostable
283. Doping
284. Base
285. Inductor
286. Pinch off
287. V 110
288. AB
289. Unity
290. Delay
291. Less
292. Tuned voltage amplifier.
293. Higher
294. Multiplying
295. A

EXERCISE – II

1. (a)	**2.** (a)	**3.** (c)	**4.** (a)	**5.** (a)	**6.** (d)	**7.** (a)	**8.** (a)	**9.** (a)	**10.** (b)
11. (b)	**12.** (b)	**13.** (d)	**14.** (b)	**15.** (b)	**16.** (a)	**17.** (b)	**18.** (b)	**19.** (a)	**20.** (d)
21. (a)	**22.** (a)	**23.** (b)	**24.** (b)	**25.** (d)	**26.** (b)	**27.** (a)	**28.** (d)	**29.** (b)	**30.** (b)
31. (d)	**32.** (a)	**33.** (a)	**34.** (b)	**35.** (b)	**36.** (d)	**37.** (b)	**38.** (a)	**39.** (c)	**40.** (b)
41. (b)	**42.** (c)	**43.** (d)	**44.** (c)	**45.** (b)	**46.** (d)	**47.** (d)	**48.** (c)	**49.** (b)	**50.** (c)
51. (b)	**52.** (b)	**53.** (c)	**54.** (c)	**55.** (a)					

Digital Techniques

NUMBER SYSTEM

NUMBER CONVERSION

1. Binary-to-Decimal Conversion.

To convert a binary number to its decimal equivalent, add the decimal equivalent of each position occupied by a 1.

$e.g.$ $(111001.01)_2 = 1 \times 2^5 + 1 \times 2^4 + 1 \times 2^3 + 0 \times 2^2$

$$+ 0 \times 2^1 + 1 \times 2^0 + 0 \times 2^{-1} + 1 \times 2^{-2}$$

$$= 2^5 + 2^4 + 2^3 + 0 + 0 + 1 + 0 + 0.25$$

$$= 32 + 16 + 8 + 1 + 0.25$$

$$= (57.25)_{10}$$

The subscript 2 and 10 respectively identify the base of binary and decimal number systems.

2. Decimal-to-Binary Conversion.

A decimal number can be converted to its equivalent binary form by *double dabble* method. It can be summarized as:

To convert a decimal number to its binary equivalent, progressively divide the decimal number by 2, noting the remainders; the remainders taken in reverse order form the binary equivalent.

To convert a decimal fraction to its binary equivalent, progressively multiply the fraction by 2, removing and noting the carries; the carries taken in forward order form the binary equivalent.

BINARY ARITHMETIC

1. Binary addition.

$$0 + 0 = 0$$
$$0 + 1 = 1$$
$$1 + 0 = 1$$
$$1 + 1 = 10$$
$$1 + 1 + 1 = 1 + 10 = 11$$

2. Binary subtraction.

The rules of binary subtraction are :

$$0 - 0 = 0$$
$$1 - 0 = 1$$
$$1 - 1 = 0$$
$$10 - 1 = 1$$

In subtraction, we subtract column by column, borrowing wherever necessary from higher position.

Signed numbers.

There are three binary signed number systems in decimal number system.

(*i*) Sign-magnitude representation :

In this representation, MSB is used to represent sign (0 for positive and 1 for negative) and the remaining bits are used to repersent magnitude of the number.

$e.g.$ binary 6–bit number 011010 represents a positive number and its value is 26, whereas 111010 represents a negative number written as – 26.

In general, maximum positive number that can be represented using sign-magnitude form is + $(2^{n-1} – 1)$ and maximum negative number that can be represented is – $(2^{n-1} – 1)$, where n is the number of bits.

(*ii*) One's complement notation.

In a binary number, if we replace each 0 by 1 and each 1 by 0, we obtain another binary number which is the one's complement of the first binary number.

$e.g.$ while $(0111)_2$ represents $(+7)_{10}$, $(1000)_2$ represents (-7).

In general maximum positive and negative number that can be represented are $(2^{n-1} – 1)$ and $– (2^{n-1} – 1)$ respectively.

(*iii*) Two's complement notation.

By adding a 1 to the one's complement of a binary number we get the two's complement of that binary number. This can also be used for representing negative numbers.

$e.g.$ 0101 represents + 5, whereas its 2's complement, 1011 (1's complement + 1) represents – 5. Here, for an n-bit number, maximum positive number that can be represented is + $(2^{n-1} – 1)$ and maximum negative number that can be represented is – (2^{n-1}).

Binary subtraction using two's complement.

Two's complement representation is usually preferred over other representations because of the ease in binary subtraction.

e.g., in evaluating (A – B) (A and B are binary numbers of course) we subtract B from A, adding the 2's complement of B to A. If a final carry is generated, it is discarded and the answer is given by the remaining bits which is positive (A is greater than B). If the final carry is 0, the answer is negative (B is greater than A) and is in the 2's complement form.

Rule used for finding 2's complement of a binary number.

Scan the number from LSB to MSB and write the bits as they are upto and including the occurrence of the first 1 and complement all other bits.

3. Binary Multiplication.

Binary multiplication is similar to decimal multiplication. In binary multiplication, say A × B, each partial product is either 0 or A itself (*i.e.* the multiplicand) as the multiplication is either by 0 or by 1 respectively.

4. Binary Division.

Binary division is again performed in a similar way to decimal division.

OCTAL NUMBER SYSTEM

It is one of the popular number system. There are $8(2^3)$ combinations of 3-bit binary numbers. Therefore, sets of 3-bit binary numbers can be conveniently represented by octal numbers with base 8.

These numbers are : 0, 1, 2, 3, 4, 5, 6 and 7.

Octal-to-Binary and Binary-to-Octal conversion.

Octal numbers can be converted to equivalent binary numbes by replacing each digit by its 3-bit binary equivalent.

e.g. $(642 . 71)_8 = (110100010 . 111001)_2$

Similarly, binary numbers can be converted into equivalent octal numbers by making groups of 3-bits starting from LSB and moving towards MSB for integer part.

e.g. $(101110011)_2 = 101110011 = (563)_8$

For fractional parts, we start grouping from the bit next to the binary point and move towards right.

e.g. $(0.10110110)_2 = 0.101010110 = (0.526)_8$

In forming the 3-bit groupings, sometimes we may have to add 0's to complete the MSD group in the integer part and the LSD group in the fractional part.

Table. Binary and Octal equivalents of decimal numbers 0–7

Decimal	Binary	Octal
0	000	0
1	001	1
2	010	2
3	011	3
4	100	4
5	101	5
6	110	6
7	111	7

HEXADECIMAL NUMBER SYSTEM

Hexadecimal numbers are extensively used in association with microprocessors. Hexadecimal means 16. There are 16 combinations of 4-bit binary numbers and sets of 4-bit binary numbers can be entered in the microprocessor in the form of hexadecimal digits. The base (or radix) of hexadecimal number is 16. This means that it uses 16 symbols to represent all numbers. These are

0, 1, 2, 3, 4, 5, 6, 7, 8, 9, A, B, C, D, E, F.

Since both numbers as well as alphabets are used to represent the digits in hexadecimal number system, it is also called as *alphanumeric number system.*

Table. Binary and hexadecimal equivalences of decimal numbers

Decimal	Binary	Hexadecimal
0	0000	0
1	0001	1
2	0010	2
3	0011	3
4	0100	4
5	0101	5
6	0110	6
7	0111	7
8	1000	8
9	1001	9
10	1010	A
11	1011	B
12	1100	C
13	1101	D
14	1110	E
15	1111	F

Since 16 digits are used, the weights are in powers of 16. The decimal equivalent of a hexadecimal string equals the sum of all hexadecimal digits multiplied by their weights.

$$e.g.\quad (F8E. 28)_{16} = F \times 16^2 + 8 \times 16^1 + E \times 16^0$$
$$+ 2 \times 16^{-1} + B \times 16^{-2}$$
$$= 15 \times 16^2 + 8 \times 16^1 + 14 \times 16^0$$
$$+ 2 \times 16^{-1} + 11 \times 16^{-2}$$
$$= 3840 + 128 + 14 + \frac{2}{16} + \frac{11}{256}$$
$$= (3982.167968775)_{10}$$

Conversion from decimal to hexadecimal is similar to the procedure used in binary and octal conversion except that here, 16 is used in dividing for integer part and multiplying for fractional part.

Hexadecimal-to-Binary and Binary-to-Hexadecimal conversions.

Hexadecimal numbers can be converted into equivalent binary by replacing each hexadecimal digit by its equivalent 4–bit binary number.

e.g. $(20E.CA)_{16} = (0010\ 0000\ 1110.1100\ 1010)_2$

$\qquad\qquad = (001000001110.11001010)_2$

Binary numbers can also be converted into hexadecimal numbers by making groups of four bits starting from LSB and moving towards MSB, for integers, and then replacing each group of four bits by its hexadecimal equivalents. Sometimes, in forming 4-bit groupings, 0's may be required to complete the most significant digit group in the integer part.

e.g. $(10100110111110)_2\ (0010\ 1001\ 1011\ 1110)_2$

$\qquad\qquad\qquad = (29BE)_{16.}$

For fractional part, the above procedure is repeated starting from the bit next to the hexadecimal point and moving towards the right. Here again, in forming 4-bit groupings 0's may be required to complete the least significant digit group.

e.g. $(0.00111110111101)_2\ = (0.0011\ 1110\ 1111\ 0100)_2$

$\qquad\qquad\qquad - (0.3EF4)_{16}$

BOOLEAN RELATIONS

Basic logic gate relations, operations.

(i) OR operation :

$A + 0 = A, \quad A + 1 = 1,$

$A + A = A, \quad A + \overline{A} = 1$

(ii) AND operation :

$A \cdot 0 = 0, \quad A \cdot 1 = A$

$A \cdot A = A, \quad A \cdot \overline{A} = 0$

(iii) NOT operation :

$A(\text{input}); \overline{A}\ (\text{output}) \qquad A \longrightarrow B = \overline{A}$

Some laws related to Logic gates.

(i) Commutative law : $A + B = B + A$

(ii) Associative law : $A + (B + C) = (A + B) + C$

(iii) Distributive law : $A \cdot (B + C) = A \cdot B + A \cdot C$

(iv) $A + (B \cdot C) = (A + B) \cdot (A + C)$

(v) $A = \overline{\overline{A}}$

De Morgan's theorem.

(i) $\overline{A + B} = \overline{A} \cdot \overline{B}$

(ii) $\overline{A \cdot B} = \overline{A} + \overline{B}$

SUM-OF-PRODUCTS/PRODUCT-OF-SUMS METHOD

Switching function (Boolean function) implied by a truth table may be stated as sum-or-products (SOP) or a product-of-sums (POS).

e.g. for an EXOR truth table.

$\qquad \text{Output} = \overline{A}\ B + A\ \overline{B} \qquad \text{(SOP form)}$

$\qquad \text{Output} = (A + B)\ (\overline{A} + \overline{B}) \qquad \text{(POS form)}$

Here each term contains all the inputs, *i.e.* individual Boolean variables in complemented or uncomplemented form called *literals*. This is the canonical or standard form. Each term in standard SOP form is called **minterm** and that each term in standard POS form is called **maxterm.** For n inputs there are 2^n –maxterms. Two logically different functions do not contain the same set of minterms (maxterms).

Table. Truth table

A	B	Y	Minterm	Maxterm
0	0	0	$\overline{A}\ \overline{B}$	$A + B$
0	1	1	$\overline{A}\ B$	$A + \overline{B}$
1	0	1	$A\overline{B}$	$\overline{A} + B$
1	1	1	AB	$\overline{A} + \overline{B}$

Output is given by the sum of minterm corresponding to 1 output.

$\qquad Y = \overline{A}\ B + A\overline{B} + AB \qquad \text{(SOP form)}$

Output can written as the product of those maxterms which correspond to 0 output, *i.e.*

$\qquad Y = A + B \qquad\qquad \text{(POS form)}$

The equivalence of these expression is established below :

$\qquad = \overline{A}\ B + A\overline{B} + AB$

$\qquad = \overline{A}\ B + A\ (\overline{B} + B)$

$\qquad = \overline{A}\ B + A = A + \overline{B}\ C$

$\qquad = (A + \overline{A})\ (A + B) \qquad \text{(Distributive law)}$

$\qquad = (A + B)$

CODES

1. Binary code.

This is obtained by converting decimal numbers to their binary equivalents. The CPUs of computers process only binary numbers.

2. BCD code.

This is a binary code in which decimal digits 0 to 9 are represented by their binary equivalents using four bits. As the weights in the BCD code are 8, 4, 2, 1, it is also called 8421 code.

e.g. decimal 257 converts to BCD as follows

$$\begin{array}{ccc} 2 & 5 & 7 \\ \downarrow & \downarrow & \downarrow \\ 0010 & 0101 & 0111 \end{array}$$

Therefore, 0010 0101 0111 is the BCD equivalent of $(257)_{10}$. The reverse conversion is similar. *e.g.,*

$$1001\ 1000\ 0110 = (986)_{10}$$

BCD numbers are very useful for input and output operations in digital circuits. It is used to represent decimal digits in systems like digital calculators, digital voltmeters, digital clocks, electronic counters etc.

3. Excess–3 code.

This code is derived from natural binary code by adding 3 to each number to be coded.

e.g. 7 in Excess-3 is represented as 1010.

It is quite useful because the nines complement of the decimal digit represented by this code can be easily obtained by simply complementing each bit.

e.g. 5 in excess-3 is 1000 and its 9's complement is 0111 in excess-3 code.

Therefore, it can be used for performing subtraction operation in digital computers.

4. Gray code.

In Gray code representation of successive numbers differs only by one bit and is therefore often used in digital systems.

e.g. 0100 represents 7 and 1100 represents 8 in Gray code.

A four-bit Gray code is obtained from the binary code in the following way :

$$G_3 = B_3$$
$$G_2 = B_3 \oplus B_2$$
$$G_1 = B_2 \oplus B_1$$
$$G_0 = B_1 \oplus B_0$$

e.g. the binary number 1101 in Gray code becomes 1011.

To generalize, the MSB of Gray code and binary code are the same. Subsequent Gray code bits are obtained by EX-Oring that bit of the binary code with its immediate higher bit.

Table. Some commonly used binary codes

Decimal Number	Binary	BCD	Excess-3	Gray
0	0000	0000	0011	0000
1	0001	0001	0100	0001
2	0010	0010	0101	0011
3	0011	0011	0110	0010
4	0100	0100	0111	0110
5	0101	0101	1000	0111
6	0110	0110	1001	0101
7	0111	0111	1010	0100
8	1000	1000	1011	1100
9	1001	1001	1100	1101
10	1010			1111
11	1011			1110
12	1100			1010
13	1101			1011
14	1110			1001
15	1111			1000

PARITY.

Odd and Even parity.

It is an arithmetic operation that is often used in a digital system for determining whether sum of the binary bits in a word is odd, which is called *odd parity*, or even which is called *even parity*.

e.g., 11000010 has odd parity while 01011100 has even parity.

Parity checker/Generator.

Exclusive OR gates are ideal for checking the parity of a binary number because output of this gate is 1, if and only if, one input is 1 and the other is 0. Alternatively stated, output is 1 if sum of the digits is 1, odd parity.

The concept can easily be extended to any number of inputs. Figure given below shows 4-input Exclusive-OR tree for checking parity of a 4-bit word. Input P' can be considered as a cascading input.

In this circuit Z = 1 or Y = 0, if the sum of the input bits A, B, C and D is odd.

Hence, if input P' is grounded (P' = 0), then P = 0 for odd parity and P = 1 for even parity.

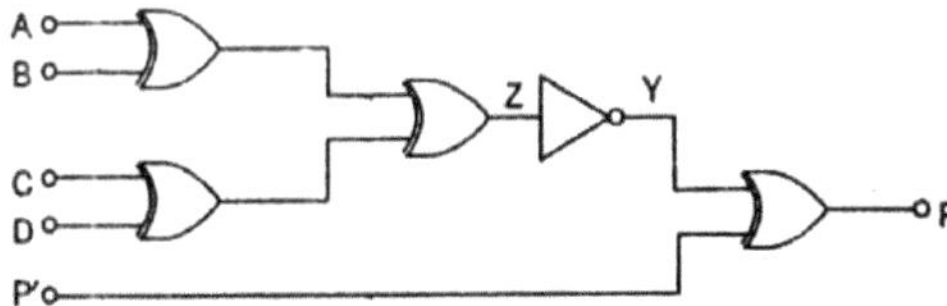

Fig. Odd parity checker/generator for a 4-bit word

The circuit of above figure may also be used to generate a parity bit P. Independently of the parity of the 4-bit input word, the parity of the 5-bit code A, B, C, D and P is odd. This statement follows from the fact that, if sum of A, B, C, and D is odd (even), then P is 0 (1) and therefore the sum of A, B, C, D and P is always odd. To get an even parity generator, delete the inverter in the circuit.

FLIP-FLOP.

SR FLIP FLOP

To serve the purpose of storing desired bits in the flip-flops, two-input NAND or NOR gates are used as shown in the figure below. The following observations are made from this figure and the truth-table.

Truth-table				
S	**R**	A_1	A_2	**State**
0	0	1	1	No change
0	1	1	0	Reset
1	0	0	1	Set
1	1	0	0	Race

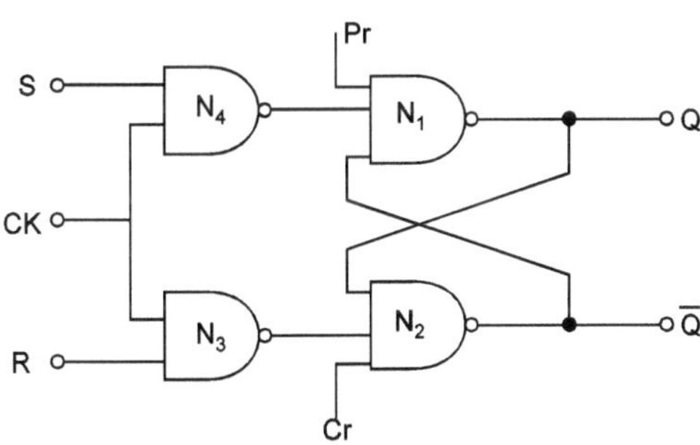

Set state : When S = 1 and R = 0, A_1 becomes 0, making Q = 1. So, $\overline{Q}$ = $\overline{1.1}$ = 0. This input condition sets the flip-flop (Q = 1, $\overline{Q}$ = 0) ; so it is called **set state.**

Reset state : When S = 0 and R = 1, A_2 becomes 0, making $\overline{Q}$ = 1 and Q = $\overline{1.1}$ = 0. This input condition resets the flip-flop (Q = 0, $\overline{Q}$ = 1); so it is called **reset state.**

No change : When S = R = 0, Q = $\overline{1.\overline{Q}}$ = Q and $\overline{Q}$ = $1.\overline{Q}$ = $\overline{Q}$. The flip-flop remains in whatever state it is in, the function is that of a basic memory cell.

Race : When S = R = 1, A_1 and A_2 both become 0. So Q = $\overline{Q}$ = 1. This is an undesired output state because if S and R now change to 0, A_1 and A_2 will be 1, both Q and $\overline{Q}$ will try to become 0. The actual state of the flip-flop depends on the relative delays of the two gates. If N_2 is faster, $\overline{Q}$ will become $\overline{1.1}$ = 0 first and will make Q = 1. Similarly, if N_1 is faster, Q will become 0 first and will make $\overline{Q}$ = 1. Similarly, if N_1 is faster, Q will become 0 first and will make $\overline{Q}$ = 1. This is called race condition. Here state of the flip-flop is uncertain, so this condition is not allowed.

This circuit is called an SR flip-flop. It is an asynchronous circuit because the output changes with changes as and when the S,R inputs change.

Clocked SR Flip-Flop

The SR flip-flop modified to include clock (CK) pulses is shown in the figure below.

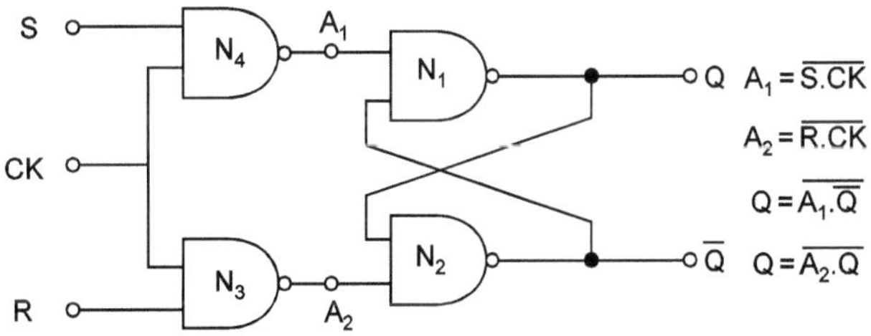

When CK = 1, A_1 = $\overline{S}$ and A_2 = $\overline{R}$, the circuit functions like the SR flip-flop. When CK = 0, A_1 = A_2 = 1, the circuit reduces to that of a basic memory cell and outputs remain unchanged (latched). Here N_1, and N_2 form the basic latch, whereas N_3 and N_4 control the state of the flip-flop.

The truth-table and logic-symbol of a SR flip-flop are as shown in figure below

Truth-table				
CK	**S**	**R**	Q_{n+1}	
1	0	0	Q_n	(SR enabled)
1	0	1	0	
1	1	0	1	
1	1	1	Not allowed	
0	×	×	Qn (SR disabled)	

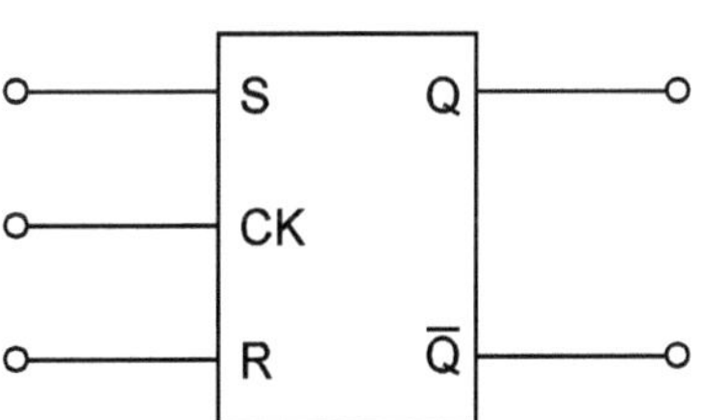

TRIGGERING

In level triggering, the output changes only when the clock is in HIGH or LOW level.

In the clocked SR flip-flop, output changes according to the input condition as long as clock is HIGH. This is called *positive level triggering*.

If clock pulse is inverted before applying it at the input, output will change only when the clock is LOW. This is called *negative level triggering*.

In *edge triggering*, output changes only when the clock pulse makes a transition (from LOW to HIGH or from HIGH to LOW).

PRESET AND CLEAR.

When power is turned on, flip-flop assumes a random state depending upon the time delay of the gates. It is often desirable to predefine the starting state (sets or reset) of the flip-flop. This is achieved by two inputs called preset. These inputs are applied in the interval between two clock pulses.

Assume CK = 0.

- When Pr = 0 and Cr = 1, Q is 1, so $\overline{Q} = \overline{1.1.1} = 0$; the flip-flop is **set**.

- When Pr = 1 and Cr = 0, $\overline{Q}$ is 1 and $Q = \overline{1.1.1} = 0$; the flip-flop is in **reset** state or cleared.

- When Pr and Cr are both 1, the circuit functions like normal clocked SR flip-flop.

- When Pr = Cr = 0, both Q and $\overline{Q}$ will become 1, which is not desired. So Pr = Cr = 0 is not allowed.

Pr and Cr inputs are applied direct, not in synchronism with the clock pulse. Thus, they are asynchronous inputs and are also called *direct set* and **direct reset** respectively. Since the desired function is performed when the corresponding input is Low (Pr = 0, Cr = 1 sets and Cr = 0, Pr = 1 clears the flip-flop); they are active low inputs (indicated by placing a bubble at these inputs). The symbol of a clocked SR flip-flop and its truth-table with active low preset.

Truth-table					
CK	*Pr*	*Cr*	*S*	*R*	Q_{n+1}
1	1	1	0	0	Q_n
			0	1	0
			1	0	1
			1	1	Not allowed
0	0	1	×	×	1 (Set)
0	1	0	×	×	0 (Reset)

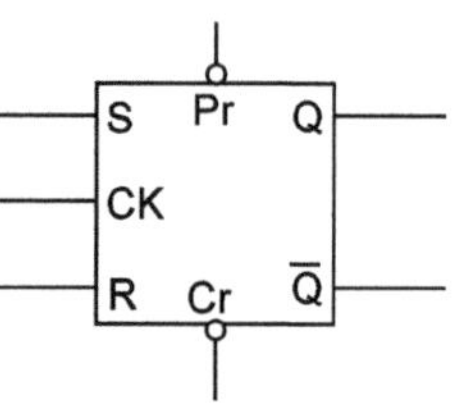

JK FLIP-FLOP.

In an SR flip-flop, the input combination S = R = 1 is not allowed because its output is uncertain.

Let us call this as JK flip-flop with inputs J and K.

Table : Truth-table SR/JK Flip-flops						
J	K	Q_n	Q_{n+1}	S	R	
0	0	0	0	0	0/1	Inactive
0	0	1	1	1/0	0	$Q_{n+1} = Q_n$
0	1	0	0	0	0/1	Reset state
0	1	1	0	0	1	$Q_{n+1} = 0$
1	0	0	1	1	0	Set state
1	0	1	1	1/0	0	$Q_{n+1} = 1$
1	1	0	1	1	0	Toggle state
1	1	1	0	0	1	$Q_{n+1} = \overline{Q}_n$

The K-maps with S and R as outputs, and taking J, K and Q_n as inputs, are shown in the figure below.

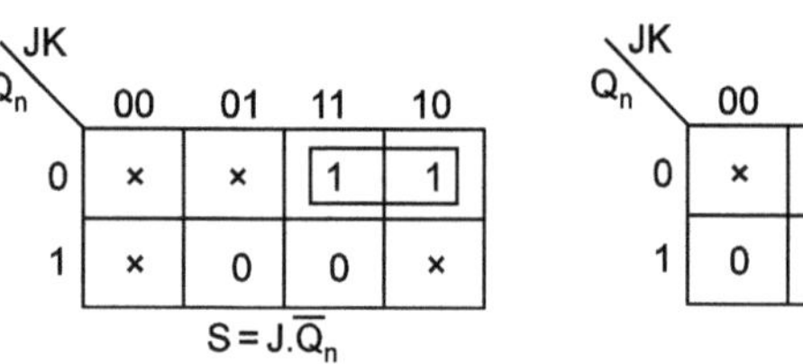

JK MASTER-SLAVE FLIP-FLOP.

This flip-flop is made of two SR flip-flops. The output of the first, called the *master flip-flop*, is given to the inputs of the second, called the *slave flip-flop*. The output of the slave is fedback to the inputs of the master. The master is triggered by a positive clock pulse and the slave is triggered by a negative clock pulse, obtained by inverting the clock pulse applied to the master. The circuit of a MS flip-flop is shown in the figure below.

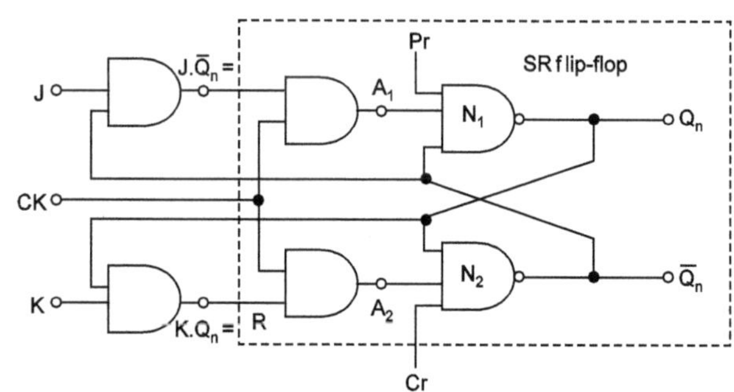

When the clock is high (CK = 1, Pr = 1, Cr = 1), the master is enabled, while the slave is disabled as $\overline{CK}$ = 0. So, the master functions like a JK flip-flop and its output appears at the input (S, R) of the slave. Since CK is low, the slave is inactive. Thus Q remains unchanged for the duration of the clock pulse t_p.

When the clock goes low, the slave functions like an SR flip-flop and its output changes to Q_M, which also appears at the input of the master. Since the clock is low, the master is inactive so that Q_M (and so S and R) remains unchanged as long as the clock remains low.

Thus, when the clock is high, Q_M changes according to JK flip-flop logic and it is transferred to Q when the clock goes low (negative edge transition). This eliminates the race-around condition as the output remains constant for the duration of one clock pulse. This flip-flop is called *master slave flip-flop* because the master decides the output, which is simply latched out by the slave.

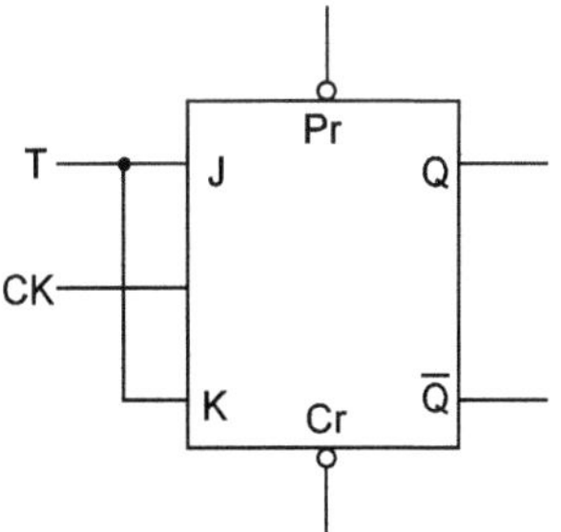

Table : Truth-table for JK master slave Flip-flop

Pr	Cr	CK	J	K	Q_{n+1}	States
0	0	×	×	×	?	Not desired
0	1	×	×	×	1	Preset
1	0	×	×	×	0	Clear
1	1	×	0	0	Q_n	Inactive
1	1	⎍	0	1	0	Zero
1	1	⎍	1	0	1	One
1	1	⎍	1	1	Q_n	Toggle

D FLIP-FLOP

In a D flip-flop the output follows the input whenever the flip-flop is triggered. This can be realized by means of a JK/SR flip-flop. The JK/SR inputs needs to achieve D logic are given in the truth table below.

Table : Truth-table JK/SR Flip-flop

D	Q_n	Q_{n+1}	J	K	S	R
0	0	0	0	0/1	0	0/1
0	1	0	0/1	1	0	1
1	0	1	1	0/1	1	0
1	1	1	0/1	0	0/1	0

T FLIP-FLOP

Two combinations of J and K inputs of a JK flip-flop are used to make a D flip-flop. These were J = 0, K = 1 and J = 1, K = 0. The remaining two combinations can be used to make a T flip-flop. These combinations are J = K = 0 and J = K = 1. As J = K for both the inputs, this is equivalent to a single input T (0/1) connected to both J and K as shown in the figure below along with its truth-table. This configuration is called **T flip-flop**.

LOGIC GATES

The logic gates are building blocks of digital electronics. They are used in digital electronics to change one voltage level (input voltage) into another (output voltage) according to some logical statement relating both. Thus, logic gate is a digital circuit, which works in accordance with some logical relationship between input and output voltages.

Truth Table. A logic gate may have one input or multiple inputs, but it has only one output. The relation between the possible values of input and output voltages are expressed in the form of a table called *truth table or table of combinations*.

Truth table of a logic gate is a table that shows all the input and output possibilities for the logic gate.

OR Gate

The OR gate is a two inputs and one output logic gate. It combines the inputs A and B with the output Y following the Boolean expression

$$Y = A + B$$

to be read as Y equals A OR B. The symbol of OR gate, its electrical analogue and its truth table are shown.

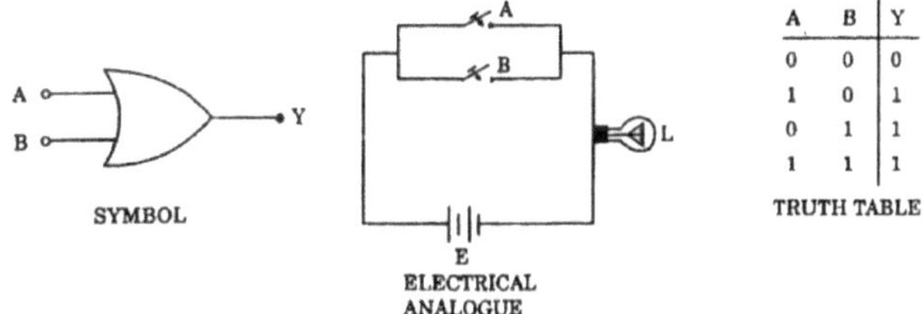

Realisation of OR Gate

The negative terminal of the battery is grounded and corresponds to the 0 state and the positive (i.e., voltage 5V in the present case) to the 1 state.

When both A and B are connected to 0, no current passes through the diode and therefore no voltage develops across R and the output is zero.

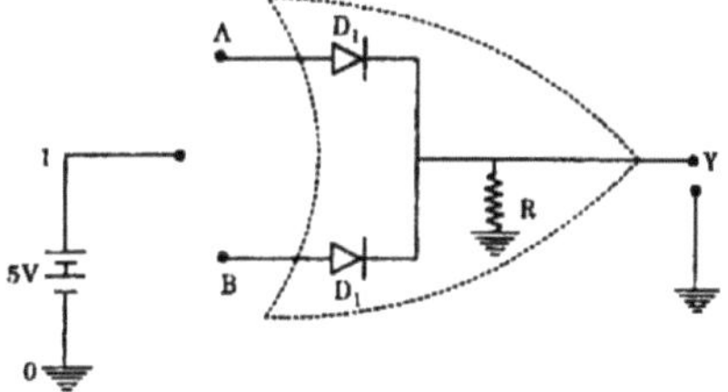

When input A is connected to zero and B to 1, the diode D_2 is forward biased and the current through it is limited by a current limiting resistance. This current causes a 5 V drop across the resistance assuming the diode to be ideal and this gives an output of 5 V or 1. Interchanging A and B to 1 and 0 will still give a 5 V drop across the resistance as D_1 will conduct.

When the terminals A and B are connected to 1, then both the diodes D_1 and D_2 conduct. However, the voltage drop across R cannot exceed 5 V or 1. Hence the truth table is satisfied.

AND Gate

The AND gate is also a two inputs and one output logic gate. It combines the inputs A and B with the output Y following the Boolean expression.

$$Y = A . B$$

to be read as Y equals A AND B. The symbol of AND gate its electrical analogue and its truth table are shown.

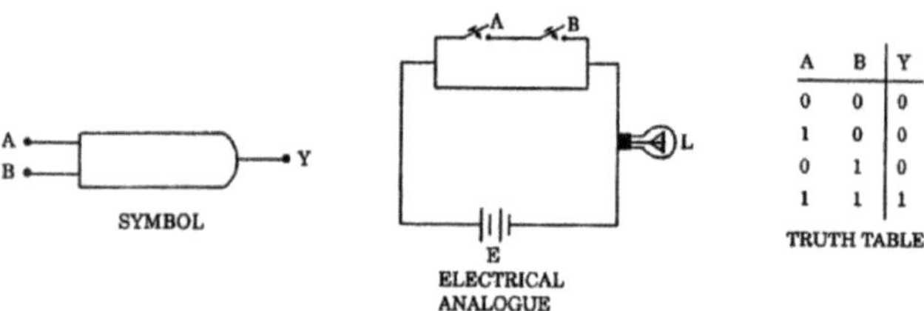

Realisation of AND Gate

The resistor R is connected permanently to the positive terminal of a 5 V battery.

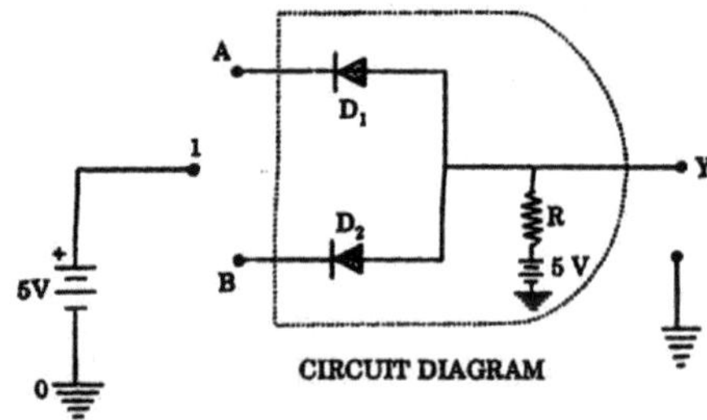

When both A and B are connected to zero, both the diodes conduct. The voltage output at Y will be the voltage across the diode which is 0 assuming the diodes to be ideal.

When A is connected to 0 and B to 1, the upper diode conducts while lower diode does not conduct as it is not forward biased. The voltage output of Y will then be the voltage across the upper diode which is 0.

When A is connected to 1 and B is connected to 0, the lower diode conducts and the outuput is 0.

When both A and B are connected to 1, none of the diodes conduct. Hence voltage at the output Y will be the battery voltage, i.e. Y will be 1.

Thus we see that the circuit in figure can perform the function of an AND gate. The output is 1 only when both the inputs are 1.

NOT Gate

It is a one input and one output logic gate. It combines the input A with the output Y following the Boolean expression.

$$Y = \overline{A}$$

to be read as Y equals NOT A. The way, the NOT gate gives the output, it is also called **Invertor or Negator**. It is represented by the symbol as shown in figure.

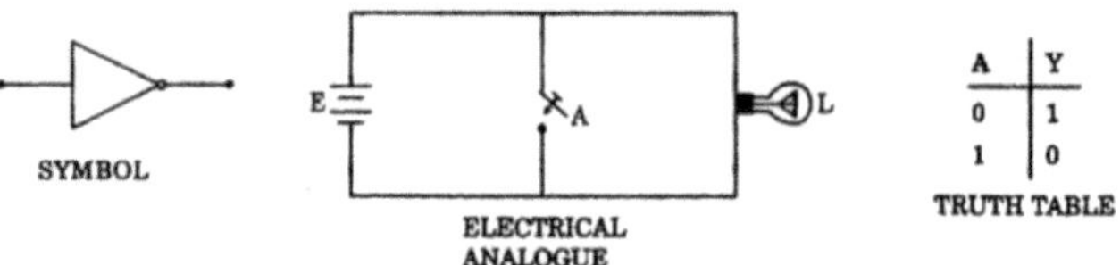

Realisation of NOT Gate

A NOT gate cannot be realised by diodes and we have to use a transistor.

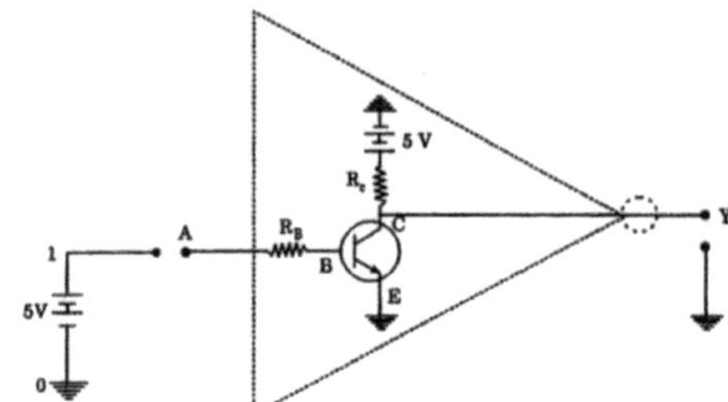

Choose R_B and R_C such that when 5 V (or voltage corresponding to 1 state) is applied at the base, a large collector current flows, the voltage at Y drops and the base-collector junction is forward-biased.

When A is connected to 0, the collector base is reverse biased and the base emitter junction is not forward biased. So the base current is zero and hence the collector current is zero. The transistor is then said to be in the cut-off mode and the voltage at Y is 5 V, which corresponds to the 1 state. When A is connected to 1, the transistor goes to saturation, the voltage drop across R_C is almost equal to 5 V and the output Y is very nearly 0 V corresponding to 0 of truth table.

COMBINATION OF GATES

Various combinations of three basic gates, i.e. OR, AND and NOT give rise to complicated digital circuits.

1. NAND GATE

It is a logic circuit in which AND gate is followed by a NOT gate.

If output (Y') of AND gate is connected to the input of NOT gate, the gate so obtained is called NAND gate. The logic symbol of the NAND gate is as shown in the figure.

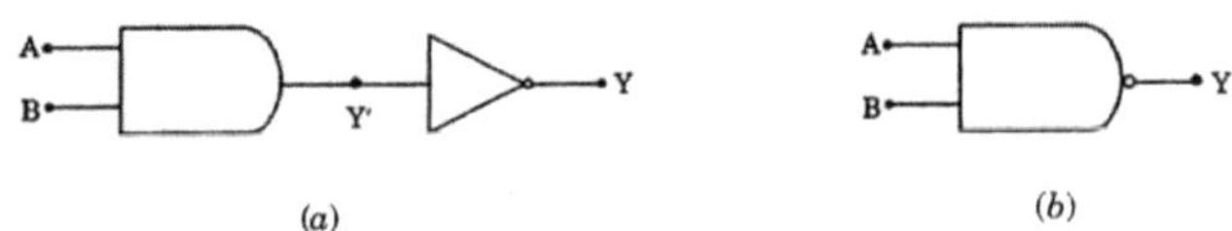

The truth table of NAND gate can be obtained by combining the truth tables of AND and NOT gates. It will be as given in the figure.

A	B	Y′	Y		A	B	Y
0	0	0	1		0	0	1
1	0	0	1		1	0	1
0	1	0	1		0	1	1
1	1	1	0		1	1	0

Boolean expression for the NAND gate is $Y = \overline{A.B}$

2. NOR GATE

It is logic circuit in which OR gate is followed by a NOT gate. If the output (Y′) of OR gate is connected to the input of a NOT gate, the gate so obtained is called the NOR gate. The logic symbol of the NOR gate is shown in the figure.

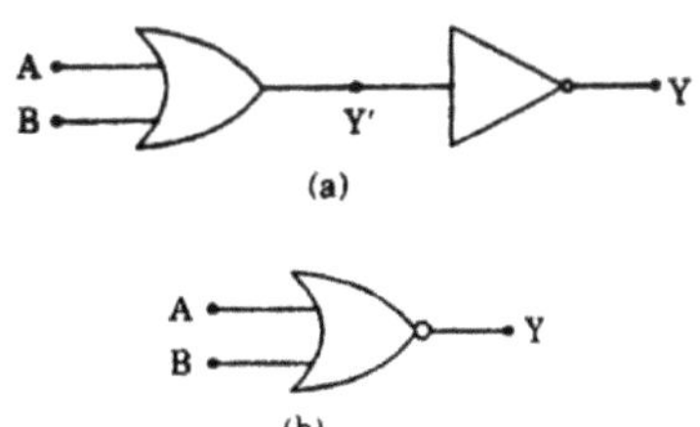

The truth table of NOR gate can be obtained by combining the truth tables of OR and NOT gates.

A	B	Y′	Y		A	B	Y
0	0	0	1		0	0	1
1	0	1	0		1	0	0
0	1	1	0		0	1	0
1	1	1	0		1	1	0

Boolean expression for the NOR gate is

$$Y = \overline{A + B}$$

KEY POINTS

A.C. CIRCUITS

A.C. circuit is an interconnection of electric elements. These elements can be electrical devices like motors and alternators and resistances/capacitors etc.

Active Electronics Components

These are components which are capable of amplifying or processing an electrical signal

e.g. diodes, triodes, transistors etc.

Accumulator

It is a register in a microprocessor in which result of a given operation is stored temporarily.

A/D Conversion

It is the process in which Analog signal is converted into Digital form.

Adder

It is a digital circuit which performs the addition of numbers.

Addend

In the addition operation, the number which is added 10 a second number called *augend*.

Impedance (Z)

It is the total opposition offered by an AC circuit to UK-flow of AC. Its unit is ohm.

Reactance (X)

It is the opposition offered by an inductor or a capacitor to the flow of AC through it. Its units is ohm.

And Gate

It perform logical multiplication, commonly called AND function. It is composed of two or more inputs and a single output.

Truth Table for a two point AND gate :

Inputs		Output
A	B	X
0	0	0
0	1	0
1	0	0
1	1	1

Possible logic level for a 2 pt. AND gate

Binary Numbers

Binary system is a base two system with two digits 0 and 1. The position of the 1 or 0 in a binary number indicate its weight or value within the number.

Some Decimal to Binary conversions :

Decimal Number	Binary Number
0	0
1	1
2	10
3	11
4	100
5	100
6	110
7	111
8	1000 etc

Value of a given binary number in terms of its decimal equivalent can be determined by adding product of each bit and its weight.

e.g. binary number 1101011 can be converted to decimal equivalent as

Binary number	1	1	0	1	1	1	1
Binary weight	2_6	2_5	2_4	2_3	2_2	2_1	2_0
Weight value	64	32	16	8	4	2	1

$$= 1 \times 64 + 1 \times 32 + 1 + 0 + 1 \times 8$$
$$+ 0 + 1 \times 2 + 1 \times 1$$
$$= 64 + 32 + 8 + 2 + 1$$
$$= 107$$

Binary Arithmetic

Basic arithmetic operations in binary numbers can be performed in the similar way as ordinary arithmetic

Addition :
```
   1001
+  1101
-------
  10110
```

Subtraction :
```
  101
- 011
-----
  010
```

Muliplication :
```
      111
×     101
---------
      111
     0000
   111000
---------
   100011
```

Division :
```
         11
    100)1100
        100
        ----
         100
         100
         ----
         000
```

For decimal values, weight values of the binary digits are taken as 2^{-1}, 2^{-2}, 2^{-3} etc.

Decimal to Binary Conversions

The simplest way of converting from decimal to binary is repeated division by 2 until the quotient is zero.
e.g. Binary equivalent of 15 can be obtained as.

```
2 | 15
2 | 7 – 1      Remainder
2 | 3 – 1      Remainder
2 | 1 – 1      Remainder
  | 0 – 1      Remainder
```

First remainder is called *least significant bit* and is written on extreme right.
Then the remainders are written from right to left. Extreme left digit is called *most significant* MSB.
Hence $(15)_{10} = (1111)_2$.

Binary Coded Decimal (BCD)

It means that each decimal digit is represented by a binary code of four bits.

Bipolar

It is used represent a junction type of semi conductor device.

e.g. PNP transistor or NPN transistor.

Bit

Binary digit 1 or o.

Bootstrap Amplifier

A single stage amplifier in which output load is connected between negative end of the . supply and the cathode, and signal voltage is applied between grid and cathode.

The name is meant to indicate that, a change in grid voltage *'pulls'*, potential of input source by an amount equal to output signal.

Comparator

It is a device which compares values of two digital quantities and produce an output depending on relationship of the two quantities.

Complement

It is the inverse function in Boolean Algebra.

e.g., complement of 1 is 0 and complement of 0 is 1.

Complementary Logic

It consists of two full blown network:

(*i*) P-net

(*ii*) N-net.

Each of the these networks can be obtained from K-map by first finding the functions $f(0)$ and $f(1)$ in a optimum manner.

Counter

It is a device used for counting electronic events such as pulses etc.

Decode

It is finding out the meaning of coded information.

Decoder

It is a digital circuit which converts the coded information into n familiar form.

Decrement

To reduce or decrease contents of a register or counter by one.

Delay

It is the time gap between occurrence of an event at one point in a circuit and the corresponding occurrence of a related event at same other point.

Morgan's Theorems

1. Complement of a product of terms is equal to sum of the complements of each term.

2. Complement of a sum of terms is equal to the product of the complements of each term.

Differential Non Linearity

It indicates the worst case difference between actual analogue voltage change and the ideal LSB (Least Significant Bit) voltage change, in A/D converter. Differential non-linearity occurs when one or few of the codes of A to D converter are not of the actual quantization step width varies from the ideal step width of LSB. Differential non linearity produces significant effect when low level signal is digitized.

Digital Electronics

It is a field of electronics wherein devices operate on basis of discrete numerical techniques in which the variables are represented by coded pulses or state.

Memory unit

It is the unit which stores informations fed to a computer.

GATE

It is a logic unit which is designed to operate with a particular type of signal only.

e.g. NOT, OR, AND, NOR, NAND, EX-OR and Flip-Flop.

NOT gate

It is an inverter logic. With input 1, its output becomes zero and with input 0, its output remains 1.

Difference between OR and AND logics

For input 1 applied to any one or more than one input terminals of OR logic, the output becomes 1. Logic AND requires 1 input on all of its input terminals so as to give an output 1

NOR and NAND logics

$$NOR = OR + NOT$$

In a NOR logic, output of its OR portion is inverted by its NOT portion.

$$NAND - AND + NOT.$$

In a NAND logic, the output of its AND portion is inverted by its NOT portion.

EX-OR logic

It is an exclusive (special) type of OR logic which gives an output 1 with an input 1 applied to any one input terminals but the output becomes zero for input 1 applied to its both input terminals.

Flip-flop logic

It has two operating states. There exists no certainty that in which way the device will start functioning on applying two identical inputs simultaneously at both of its input terminals.

Positive and Negative logic units

Positive logic unit:

It operates with positive input/inputs.

Negative logic unit :

It operates with negative input/inputs.

DTL, TTL, DTML and DCI'L

DTL = Diode-Transistor Logic.

TTL = Transistor-transistor Logic

DTML = Diode-Transistor Micro Logic

DCTL = Direct Coupled Transistor Logic.

BINARY SYSTEM

It is a system of counting based on two digits-0 and 1.

Bit and Byte

A binary digit (0 or 1) is abbreviated as *bit* and a group of 4 or 8 bits is called a *byte*.

Conversion of Decimal numbers into Binary numbers

Divide given decimal number with 2 till 0 is obtained and write balance of each division on the right side.

Now write balances commencing from left side in a bottom to top order. The number so obtained will be the requisite number.

Conversion of Binary number to Decimal number

Read the binary numbers commencing from right to left side and multiply each binary digit with 2^0, 2^1, 2^2, etc. Respectively and then add the products to obtain requisite decimal number

Binary Addition and Substraction

1. **Rules for Addition:**

   $$0 + 0 = 0$$
   $$0 + 1 = 1$$
   $$1 + 0 = 1$$
   $$1 + 1 = 0 \quad \text{and carry 1.}$$

2. **Rules for Substraction:**

   $$0 - 0 = 0$$
   $$1 - 0 = 1$$
   $$1 - 1 = 0$$
   $$0 - 1 = 1 \quad \text{here 1 is borrowed.}$$

Binary Multiplication and Division

1. **Rules for Multiplication:**

   $$0 \times 0 = 0$$
   $$0 \times 1 = 0$$
   $$1 \times 0 = 0$$
   $$1 \times 1 = 1$$

   The process of adding a number to the same number repeatedly is called multiplication,

2. **Rules for division:**

   The process of subtracting a number from another number repeatedly is called *division*.

Multivibrator

It is a relaxation oscillator meant for generating a non-sinusoidal wave in which :feedback for each stage is derived from output of the other in order to sustain in oscillations.

BCD encoder

It is the unit which converts decimal numbers' to binary numbers.

Binary to Decimal Decoder

It is the unit which converts binary numbers into decimal numbers.

LED display

Each decimal digit can be displayed by 7 LEDs. So. 8 digit display system employ a 65 LEDs display unit including decimal points (in fractional numbers, a number is followed by a decimal point).

Electronic counter

It is an electronic equipment based on logic units which is meant for counting RPM etc.

Operational amplifier

It is a high gain IC based direct coupled amplifier.

Differential amplifier

It is a special type of amplifier which gives an output only if a voltage difference exists between its two inputs.

Clock oscillator

It is a free running multi vibrator type circuit which is used for producing high frequencies.

LCD Liquid Crystal Display

Liquid crystal is a dense mixture of solids and liquids. Its enemy dissipation is much lesser than that of LED (1/10,000th part), that is why in some type of display purposes LCD is preferred over LED display.

Digital Paper

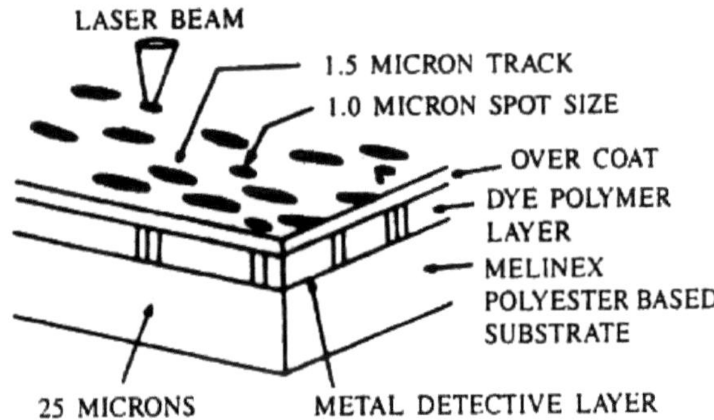

It is a flexible optical recording medium made from a sandwich of thin polymer films. It is similar to material used in computer tapes but data is written or read optically by a laser. Storage capacity on paper costs only one penny and takes less space than equivalent amount of information on a magnetic tape.

Digital To Analog Converter

It is the device which converts a binary input to an analogue output.

Digital VCR

It uses computer chip to store a digitized image of the frame in its RAM (Random Access Memory) Digital circuit ensure that, a complete video field is grabbed into memory. Digital video effect such as dazzling picture in picture, super still frame etc. are achieved by rotating analogue play back signal to an A/D converter. Then digital information processed and stored in dynamic RAM.

Digital Voltmeter (DVM)

It is a voltmeter that displays voltage in numeric form. Input is analog.

Digitize

It is Conversion of an image into a series of dots. It is often used to store images on disk for the computer.

Digitron Syn. Nixie Tube

Type of cold-cathode scaling tube that has several cathodes (usually ten) shaped into the form of characters (usually the digits 0 to 9). As voltage pulses are received, cathode required is selected by a switching connection to one side of the power supply and a glow discharge illuminates the character. These tubes are widely used for display purpose in calculators, counters, etc.

Induction heating

It is the process of melting various metals by employing the heating property of eddy currents. For this purpose, a heavy and 1 kHz to 5 kHz alternating current is passed through a coil placed around a crucible. The process is useful in preparing alloys.

Exclusive OR

It is a logic function that is true if one but not both of the variables are true.

Fan Out

It is the number of equivalent gate inputs that a logic gate can drive.

Flat Pack

It is a type of integrated circuit package.

F Layer

It is an ionized layer in the F-region of the ionosphere. It exists as a single layer. It is sometimes called F2 layer in the night hemisphere. Stratifies into F1 and F2 layer in the day hemisphere.

F1 layer.

It is one of the regular ionospheric layers at an average height of about 225 km, which occurs during the day light and follows the sun closely.

F2 layer.

It is the most useful ionospheric layer for radio wave propagation. It is the most highly ionised and highest of the layer, having an average night height of 225 km. and mid-day height of about 300 km. This layer is ionized throughout the day. This ionization is least just before dawn and maximum in the early afternoon.

FLIP-FLOP

It is a bistable device used for storing a bit of information.

Frequency Convertors

It is a part of a frequency counter (often made as plug-in) which converts the frequency to be measured down to a value measurable by the counter.

Necessity of Frequency conversion

Practically, no RF amplifier is capable to amplify equally all broadcasted radio frequencies. Therefore, signal frequency received by the aerial is converted into a *'definite and low frequency'* IF. A high order of selectivity, sensitivity and stability can he achieved by operating a radio receiver on the IF.

IF

A definite and low radio frequency produced by super hetrodyning is called *intermediate frequency* or IF.

Suitable values of IF for a domestic radio receiver 452 kHz, 455 kHz, 456 kHz, 465 kHz and 470 kHz.

Frequency changer

A RF amplifier stage which produces IF as a result of heterodyning of signal and local oscillator frequencies is called *frequency changer*, *converter* or *mixer* stage.

Working of a Converter stage

A converter stage consists of local oscillator and a *'mixer'*. Equal and simultaneous change in the signal and oscillator frequencies is achieved by means of a gang capacitor. Output of the converter is tuned to IF of the receiver.

Full Adder

It is a digital circuit that adds two binary digits and an input carry to produce a sum and an output carry.

Fuzzy logic

It is a logic circuit in a video camera, to evaluate focus and lighting condition.

Gate

It is a logic circuit which performs a specific logic operation such as AND or OR gate.

Half Adder

It is a logic device that adds two binary bits and provides a sum carry out.

Hexadecimal Numbers

These has a base of sixteen, i.e., it is composed of 16 digits and character :

0 to 9 and A, B, C D, E and F.

Weight of each digit or character is 16°, 16' etc. from right to left etc.

$$(E5)_{16} = 14 \times 16 - H\,5 \times 1 = (229)_{10}$$

Hold Time

It is the time interval required for the control levels to remain on the inputs to a flip-flop after triggering edge of the clock in order to reliably activate the device.

Index Register

It is a register used for indexed addressing in a microprocessor.

Indexing

It is modification of the address of the operand contained in the instruction of a microprocessor.

Inversion

It is a process of conversion of a HIGH level to a LOW level or from a LOW level to a HIGH level.

Jk Flip-flop

It is a flip-flop capable of operating as a type T or type D, depending on the J and K leads. Flip-flop will go to the 1 state on receipt of the clock pulse, when J is high and K is low, the flip-flop will switch to the 0 position at the clock pulse when J is low and K is high. When both J and K are high, the flip-flop will complement its initial state on receipt of the clock pulse. JK Flip-flop is a flip-flop whose inputs are designated J and K. When both J and K are low, the flip-flop remains except at its previous state. These devices are almost invariably clocked and their outputs are same as the R-S type accept when logical one appears together at the inputs. In these circumstances, the device complements its state.

Johnson Counter

It is a type of digital counter characterized by a unique sequence of stales.

Logic

It is any precisely defined formal reasoning system that includes well formed-formulae, axioms, and rules of inference that allow new theorems to be deduced from the axioms and other existing theorems. It is used explicitly as a representation and reasoning LOGIC tool by many, and implicitly in (he operation of host, AI systems. LOGIC is system of representing validity of an output by analyzing inputs.

In computer language, logic is a form of mathematics based upon two-state truth tables. Electronic logic uses two-state gates and flip-flops to perform decision-making functions.

Logic Chip

It is clipped to an integrated circuit where it makes contact with each pin on the I.C.

Logic Gate

These are devices which produce logical output depending upon logical input conditions.

Commonly used gates are :

"AND, OR, NAND, NOR, NOT and Exclusive-OR."

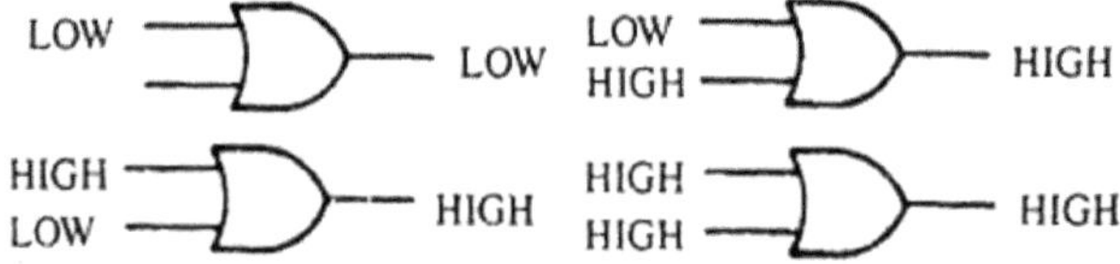

Logic Levels

In digital systems two voltage levels represent two binary digits 1 and 0.

Let there be 4-5V and 0V two logic level voltages.

Then +5V is called as *high level* and 0V as *low level*.

Microprocessor

It is an integrated circuit containing all necessary computational and control circuitry on a single silicon chip, and is brains of a microcomputer. It control washing machines, petrol pumps, word processors and electronic games and are often used in telephone exchanges to perform tasks which were at one time carried out only by hard-wired circuits. Microprocessors are available which operate with 8-bit (1 byte), 16-bit, 32 bit, 64-bit and more data unit, each 8-bit unit representing a character signal.

Modulus

It is maximum number of states in a counter sequence.

Multiplexing

It is an operation performed with digital logic circuits called multiplexers

Time-division Multiplexing.

The TDM is the procedure by which a number of different channels can be transmitted over a common circuit by allocating the common circuit to each channel in turn for a given period of time.

NAND (Not AND) Gate

It is an AND gate to which has been added an inverted output.

It is the A gate that is enabled when both its inputs, are present or high. When a NAND gate is enabled, its output is low. The term NAND is a contraction of the words, NOT and AND.

Negative Logic

It is system of logic in which a LOW represents a 1 and a HIGH represents 0.

NOR Gate

It is an OR gate to which has been added an inverter at its output. It is combination of a NOT and an OR circuit. It is the binary circuit having two or more inputs and a single output, in which output is OFF (0) if any one of the inputs is ON (1) only if all inputs are OFF together.

NOR Circuit

It is a binary circuit having a single input and a single output in which output is always opposite of the input. When input is ON (1) the output is OFF (0) and vice versa. This circuit is also called *inverter circuit*.

Octal Number system

It is composed of eight digits :

0, I, 2, 3, 4, 5, 6 and 7.

To count or write above seven we begin another column and start over 10, 11, 12, 13, 14 etc.

OR Gate

It performs logical addition, called OR function. It has two or more inputs and one output.

Possible logic levels for a 2 Input OR gate

Truth Table for Two point OR gate :

Inputs		Output
A	**B**	**X**
0	0	0
0	1	1
1	0	1
1	1	1

PAL

It is abbreviation for phase attenuation line. A colour TV system in which chrominance signal is resolved into the components in Quadrature Relative phase of Quadrature Components is reversed on alternate lines to minimize phase errors.

Positive Logic

It is system of logic in which a HIGH represents 1 and a LOW represents 0.

Power dissipation of a Logic circuit

It is the supply power when a logic circuit is operating with a 50% duty cycle (i.e., when it is in the 0 state half of the time and in the 1 state the other half of the time).

Priority Encoder

It is a digital logic circuit that produces a coded output corresponding to highest-valued input.

Propagation Delay

It is the time interval between occurrence of an input transition and corresponding output transition.

Race condition

It is a condition in the logic network in which the differences in propagation times through two or three more signal paths in the network can produce an erroneous output.

Radix

It is base of number system. The number of digits in a given number system.

Registers

these are digital circuits used for the temporary storage and shifting of information.

RS Flip Flop

It is a flip-flop whose inputs are designated R and S. A flip-flop with two inputs; a reset, which puts in the 0 state, and a set, which puts it in the 1 state. A flip-flop with two inputs a set input and a rest input. If set input is enabled (high), then flip-flop goes to 1 state. If reset input is enabled (high), flip-flop goes to 0 state.

Truth Table : RS FF

Input		Output	
R	S	X	X
0	0	—	—
1	0	1	0
0	1	0	1
1	0	—	—

RS-232

It is a standard communication interface between a modem and terminal devices that complies with EIA Standard. Another term for a serial port, a common standard for serial data communication between pieces of computer equipment.

Venn Diagram

It is a diagram that represents ANDs and ORs by intersecting circles.

CONVERSIONS FROM DECIMAL TO OTHER CODES

Decimal	Binary	Octal
0	0	0
1	1	1
2	10	2
3	11.	3
4	100	4
5	101	5
6	110	6
7	111	7
8	1000	10
9	1001	11
10	1010	12
11	1011	13
12	1100	14
13	1101	15
14	1110	16
15	1111	17
16	10000	20
17	10001	21
18	10010	22
19	10011	23
20	10100	24
21	10101	25
22	10110	26
23	10111	27
24	11000	30
25	11001	31
26	11010	32
27	11011	33
28	11100	34
29	11101	35
30	11110	36
31	11111	37
32	100000	40
33	100001	41
34	100010	42
35	100011	43
36	100100	44
37	100101	45
38	100110	46
39	100111	47
40	101000	50
41	101001	51
42	101010	52
43	101011	53
44	101100	54
45	101 101	55
46	101110	56
47	101 111	57
48	110000	60
49	110001	61
50	110010	62
51	110011	63
52	110100	64
53	110101	65
54	110110	66
55	110111	67
56	11 1000	70
57	111001	71
58	111010	72
59	111011	73
60	111100	74
61	111101	75
62	111110	76

63	111111	77		96	1100000	140
64	100000	100		97	1100001	141
65	1000001	101		98	1100010	142
66	1000010	102		99	1100011	143
67	1000011	103				
68	1000100	104				
69	1000101	105				
70	1000111	106				
71	1000111	107				
72	1001000	110				
73	1001001	111				
74	1001010	112				
75	1001011	113				
76	1001100	114				
77	1001101	115				
78	1001110	116				
79	1001111	117				
80	1010000	120				
81	1010000	121				
82	1010010	122				
83	1010011	123				
84	1010100	124				
85	1010101	125				
86	1010110	126				
87	1010111	127				
88	1011000	130				
89	1011001	131				
90	1011010	132				
91	1011011	133				
92	1011100	134				
93	1011101	135				
94	1011110	136				
95	1011111	137				

POWERS OF TWO

n	2^n	2^{-n}
0	1	1.0
1	2	0.5
2	4	0.25
3	8	0.125
4	16	0.0625
5	32	0.03125
6	64	0.015625
7	128	0.0078125
8	256	0.00390625
9	512	0.001953125
10	1024	0.0009765625
11	2048	0.00048828125
12	4096	0.000244140625
13	8192	0.000 1220703 L25
14	16384	0.00006103515625
15	32768	0.000030517578125
16	65536	0.0000152587890625
17	131072	0.00000762939453125
1 8	262144	0.0000038 1 4697265625
19	524288	0.0000019073486328125
20	1048576	0.00000095367431640625
21	2097152	0.000000476837158203125
22	4194304	0.00000023848579101 5625
23	8388608	0.0000001 1 920928955078125
24	16777216	0.00000005960464477 5390625
25	33554432	0.0000000298023223876953125

EXERCISE – I

1. Decimal number 15 may be written in binary system as

(*a*) 1110   (*b*) 1111

(*c*) 1100   (*d*) 1001

2. Decimal number 74 may be written in binary system as

(*a*) 1001010   (*b*) 1001001

(*c*) 1001011   (*d*) 100011

3. Decimal number 21.125 may be written in binary system as

(*a*) 10101.001   (*b*) 10100.001

(*c*) 10101.010   (*d*) 10100.100

4. Decimal equivalent of binary number 1111.01 is

(*a*) 14.25   (*b*) 15.25

(*c*) 15.01   (*d*) 7.25

5. Decimal equivalent binary number 0.1011 is

(*a*) 0.6875   (*b*) 6.875

(*c*) 0.4375   (*d*) –0.6875

6. Radix of octal number system is

(*a*) 2   (*b*) 4

(*c*) 8   (*d*) 10

7. Decimal equivalent of octal number 57 is

(*a*) 47   (*b*) 65

(*c*) 54   (*d*) 50

8. Octal equivalent of decimal number 49 is

(*a*) 61

(*b*) 59

(*c*) 47

(*d*) 53

9. Maximum number of binary bits required to represent a digit of octal number is

(a) 2   (b) 3

(c) 4   (d) 5

10. Octal equivalent of decimal $(51)_{10}$ is

(a) $(63)_8$ (b) $(41)_8$

(c) $(67)_8$ (d) $(27)_8$

11. BCD equivalent of decimal number $(85)_{10}$ is

(a) 1000–1100   (b) 1000–0101

(c) 1101–1010   (d) 1101–0101

12. BCD equivalent of decimal number $(43)_{10}$ is

(a) 101–011   (b) 1000–0011

(c) 0100–0011   (d) 0011–0100

13. Excess-3 code is also known as

(a) weighted code

(b) cyclic redundancy code

(c) self complementing code

(d) algebraic code

14. Which of the following codes is an unweighted code?

(a) 8421 code   (b) Excess-3 code

(c) 2421 code   (d) 63210 code

15. Which of the following codes is a weighted code?

(a) Excess-3 code   (b) Shift-counter code

(c) Gray code   (d) 5111 code

16. Excess-3 equivalent of decimal number $(8)_{10}$ is

(a) 1011   (b) 1101

(c) 1110   (d) 1001

17. The gray code equivalent of binary number $(1000001)_2$ is

(a) 1100001   (b) 1100011

(c) 1000011   (d) 110101

18. Decimal number $(85)_{10}$ is encoded as 11000101 in

(a) 8421 code   (b) 4421 code

(c) 2421 code   (d) 2221 code

19. Binary equivalent of gray code number 101 is

(a) 101   (b) 110

(c) 100   (d) 111

20. Number of binary bits required to represent a hexadecimal digit is

(a) 3   (b) 4

(c) 5   (d) 6

21. Hexadecimal equivalent of decimal number 1000 is

(a) 3 E 8   (b) 4 E 8

(c) 3 CF   (d) 3 E 7

22. Binary subtraction 1111-111 will yield

(a) 1100   (b) 1000

(c) 1001   (d) 1010

23. Binary addition 1001 + 1101 yields

(a) 11100   (b) 11010

(c) 10110   (d) 11000

24. One's compliment of 010001 is

(a) 101110   (b) 101111

(c) 01110   (d) 011110

25. The 2's compliment of binary number 0.01011 is

(a) 1.10101   (b) 0.10101

(c) 0.10100   (d) 1.10100

26. ASC-II code is used as

(a) an alphabatic code   (b) a cyclic code

(c) a weighted code   (d) an alphanumeric code

27. ASC-II code is

(a) a 4-bit code   (b) a 6-bit code

(c) a 7-bit code   (d) none of these

28. Binary division 1010.1011×11.01 yields

(a) 110.11   (b) 100.11

(c) 101.10   (d) 101.11

29. A six-bit alpha-numeric code is able to code

(a) 36 characters   (b) 48 characters

(c) 64 characters   (d) 128 characters

30. Number 17 in BCD representation is

(a) 10001   (b) 001 111

(c) 10 111   (d) 100 01

31. Cyclic codes are useful in

(a) arithmetic computation

(b) continuously varying digital signals representation

(c) randomly varying digital signals representation

(d) transferring the information

32. BCD equivalent of Gray code number 1001 is

(a) 1001   (b) 1110

(c) 1100   (d) 1101

33. Hexadecimal equivalent of decimal number 15 is

(a) 100 A   (b) OF

(c) 1111   (d) 0101

34. Decimal equivalent of hexadecimal number 11 A is

(a) 282   (b) 272

(c) 200   (d) 202

35. Octal equivalent of binary number 01000100111

(a) 4236   (b) 2117

(c) 1084   (d) 41.836

36. Hexadecimal equivalent of binary number 10001101011001 is

(a) 2359   (b) 9493

(c) 8D62   (d) 8DF2

37. Binary 1000 when multiplied by binary 1111 results in binary

(a) 1111111   (b) 1111100

(c) 1111000   (d) 1110000

38. Byte signifies

(a) an integrated circuit

(b) a string of 2 bits

(c) a string of 4 bits

(d) a string of 8 bits

39. 1k-byte is precisely equal to

(a) 1012 bits   (b) 1024 bits

(c) 1000 bits   (d) 1020 bits

40. Hexadecimal number system is

(a) an obsolete system no longer in use

(b) widely used in analysing and programming microprocessors

(c) used in calculators only

(d) none of these

41. Hexadecimal system uses digits from

(a) 1 to 16   (b) 1 to 9

(c) 1 to 6   (d) 0 to 9

42. Main advantage of hexadecimal number system is

(a) case of conversion from hexadecimal to decimal and vice-versa

(b) ease of conversion from hexadecimal to binary and vice-versa

(c) case of conversion from hexadecimal to gray code and vice-versa

(d) use of number and alphabets

43. Binary coded decimal (BCD) numbers express each decimal digit as a

(a) unit   (b) bit

(c) byte   (d) nibble

44. BCD numbers are useful whenever

(a) binary to BCD conversion is desired

(b) binary to hexadecimal conversion is desired

(c) decimal information is transferred into or out of digital system

(d) none of these

45. The equipment uses BCD numbers is

(a) pocket calculator   (b) electronic counter

(c) digital voltmeter   (d) all of the above

46. How many bytes are there in binary number 1011 1001 0110 1110?

(a) 1   (b) 2

(c) 3   (d) 4

47. What does 4-k represent?

(a) 4000   (b) 4048

(c) 4182   (d) 4069

48. Which of the following hexadecimal number just prior to F 52B?

(a) E 52 A   (b) F 51 B

(c) F 52 A   (d) F 52 B

49. Which of the following hexadecimal numbers represents an odd decimal number ?

(a) FF   (b) EG

(c) CC   (d) AA

50. Which of the following hexadecimal numbers represents an even decimal number?

(a) DB   (b) D5

(c) BF   (d) AC

51. $\overline{A} + \overline{B} + \overline{C}$ = D represents a

(a) NOR gate   (b) NAND gate

(c) EX-OR gate   (d) AND gate

52. $\overline{A} \cdot \overline{B} \cdot \overline{C}$ = D represents a

(a) NOR gate   (b) NAND gate

(c) EX-OR gate   (d) AND gate

53. Output of which of the following gates in 1 only if atleast one of its inputs is 0?

(a) NOR gate   (b) NAND gate

(c) EX-OR gate   (d) AND gate

54. Output of which of the following gates is 0 only if at least one of its inputs is 1?

(a) NOR gate   (b) NAND gate

(c) EX-OR gate   (d) AND gate

55. $\overline{AB}$ = Y is the Boolean expression for

(a) OR gate   (b) NOR gate

(c) NAND gate   (d) EX-OR gate

56. $\overline{A + B}$ = Y is the Boolean expression for

(a) AND gate   (b) NAND gate

(c) NOR gate   (d) EX-OR gate

57. Which gate has the output low only when both inputs are high?

(a) AND   (b) NAND

(c) OR   (d) NOR

58. NOR gate is logically equivalent to

(a) an OR gate followed by an AND gate

(b) an OR gate followed by a NAND gate

(c) an AND gate followed by OR gate

(d) an OR gate followed by an inverter

59. A NAND gate is equivalent to

(a) an AND gate followed by a OR gate

(b) an AND gate followed by an inverter

(c) an inverter following by OR gate

(d) an inverter followed by an AND gate

60. NAND gate is called a universal gate because

(a) it is most commonly used

(b) all logical functions can be realized by use of NAND gates alone

(c) all minimization techniques can be applied to it

(d) it can realize AND and NOT functions

61. $A\overline{B} + \overline{A}B$ = D represents

(a) an OR gate   (b) an EX-OR gate

(c) a NOR gate   (d) a NAND gate

62. Complementary function is represented by

(a) NOR gate   (b) NOT gate

(c) NAND   (d) EX-OR gate

63. Boolean expression for three input AND gate is

(a) A. B. C = D   (b) A + B + C = D

(c) $\overline{A} \cdot \overline{B} \cdot \overline{C}$ = D   (d) $\overline{A} + \overline{B} + \overline{C}$ = D

64. Boolean expression for three input OR gate is

(a) $\overline{A} + \overline{B} + \overline{C}$ = D   (b) A + B + C = D

(c) A. B. C= D   (d) $\overline{A} \cdot \overline{B} \cdot \overline{C}$ = D

65. Which of the following is used extensively where lowest power consumption is necessary ?

(a) CMOS

(b) NMOS

(c) PMOS

(d) all of these

66. The circuit given below is functionally equivalent to

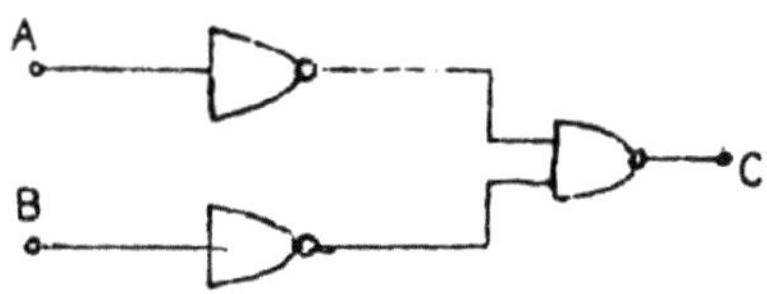

(a) OR gate   (b) NOR gate

(c) AND gate   (d) NAND gate

67. The circuit given below is functionally equivalent to

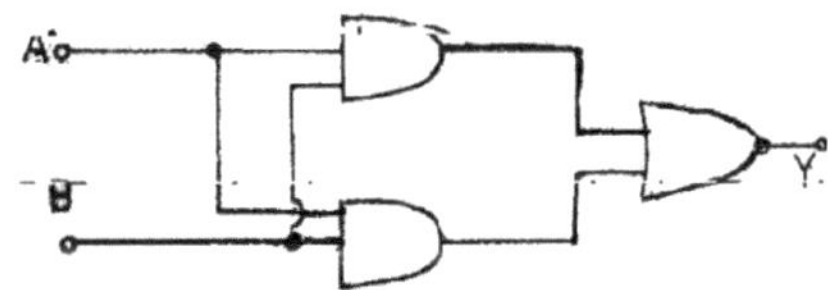

(a) EX-OR gate   (b) comparator

(c) inhibit gate   (d) NAND gate

68. The circuit given below is functionally equivalent to

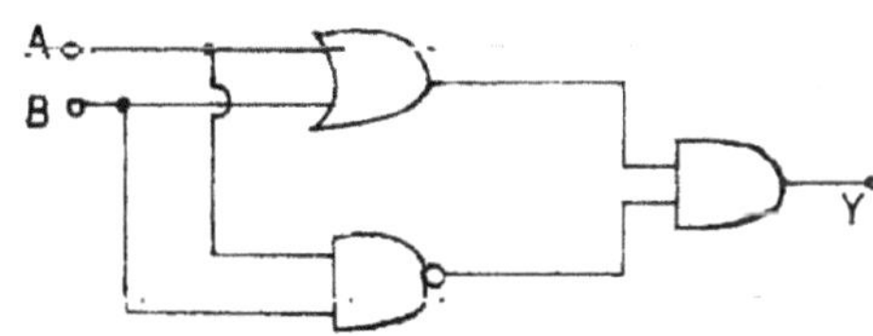

(a) EX-OR gate   (b) NOR gate

(c) AND gate   (d) NAND gate

69. Half-adder is also known as

(a) AND circuit   (b) NAND circuit

(c) NOR circuit   (d) EX-OR circuit

70. Which of the following is a universal gate ?

(a) AND

(b) OR

(c) EX-OR

(d) NAND

71. Logic 1 in positive logic system is represented by

(a) zero level

(b) lower voltage level

(c) higher voltage level

(d) negative voltage

72. Which of the following statements is true ?

(a) $A + \overline{A}B$ = A

(b) $A (\overline{A} + B)$ = AB

(c) $AB + A\overline{B}$ = A

(d) $CA + C\overline{A}B$ = CA + CB

73. An AND circuit

(a) is a memory circuit

(b) gives an output when all input signals are present simultaneously

(c) is a negative OR circuit

(d) is a linear circuit

74. The following symbol represents a

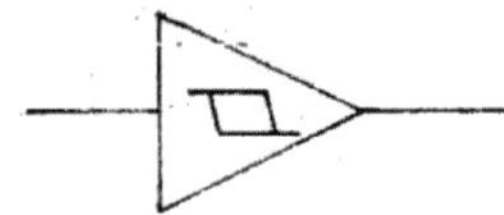

(a) inverter   (b) buffer

(c) schmitt trigger   (d) flip-flop

75. Which of the following symbols represents a buffer ?

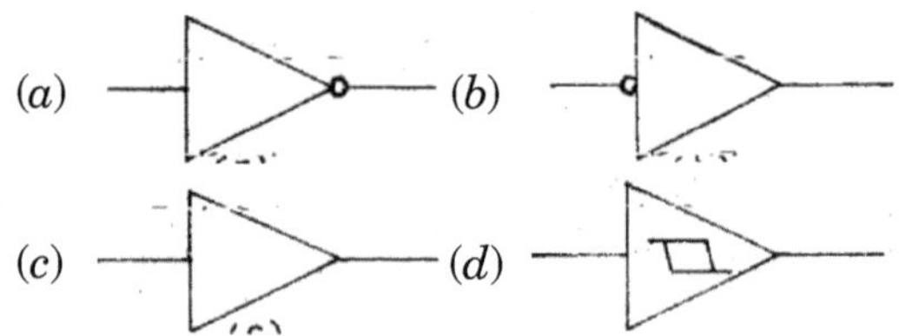

76. An alternative way of showing a two input NOR gate is

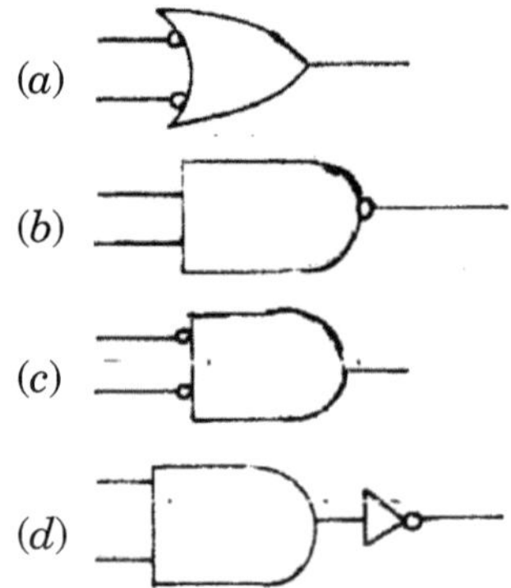

77. An alternative symbol for two input NAND gate is

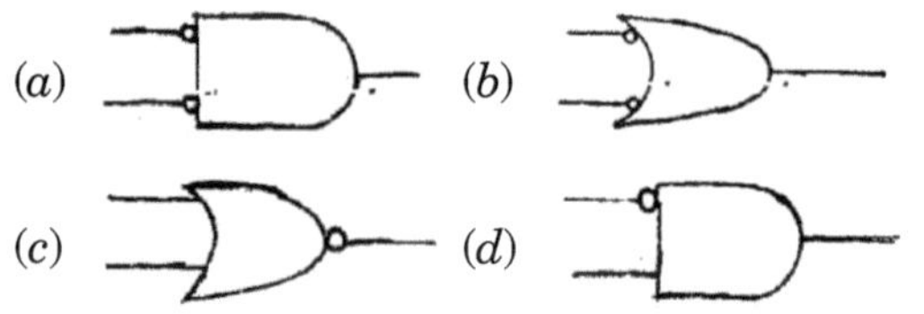

78. Which of the following is not functionally a complete set ?

(a) AND, OR   (b) NAND

(c) NOR   (d) AND, OR, NOT

79. In which of the following gates, the output is high if and only if all inputs are high ?

(a) NOT

(b) AND

(c) OR

(d) XOR

80. In which of the following gates the output is high if and only if at least one input is high ?

(a) NOT   (b) AND

(c) OR   (d) NAND

81. In which of the following gates the output is high if and only if at least one input is low ?

(a) NOT   (b) AND

(c) OR   (d) NAND

82. In which of the following gates the output is 0 if and only if at least one input is 1 ?

(a) NOT   (b) AND

(c) NOR   (d) NAND

83. For which of the following logic gates, the output is complement of the input ?

(a) NOT   (b) AND

(c) OR   (d) XOR

84. Let A and B be the inputs to a NAND gate. Then the output is equal to

(a) $A + B$ (b) $A . B$

(c) $\overline{A . B}$ (d) $\overline{A} . \overline{B}$

85. Let A and B be the inputs to a XOR gate. Then the output is given by

(a) $A + B$ (b) $A.B$

(c) $\overline{A.B}$ (d) $\overline{A}.B + A.\overline{B}$

86. The NAND gate can function as a NOT gate if

(a) inputs are connected together

(b) inputs are left open

(c) one input is set to 0

(d) one input is set to 1

87. What is the minimum number of two-input NAND gates used to perform the function of two-input OR gate ?

(a) one   (b) two

(c) three   (d) four

88. Which of the following gates are added to the inputs of the OR gate to convert it into NAND gate ?

(a) NOT   (b) AND

(c) OR   (d) XOR

89. Which logic function is produced by adding inverters to the inputs of an AND gates ?

(a) NAND   (b) NOR

(c) XOR   (d) OR

90. Which logic function is produced by adding an inverter to each input and the output of an AND gate ?
(a) NAND (b) NOR
(c) OR (d) XOR

91. Which of the following gates is known as "concidence detector" ?
(a) AND (b) OR
(c) NOT (d) NAND

92. An AND gate may be visualized as
(a) switches connected in series
(b) switches connected in parallel
(c) MOS transistor connected in series
(d) none of these

93. An OR gate may be imagined as
(a) switches connected in series
(b) switches connected in parallel
(c) MOS transistors connected in series
(d) none of the above

94. Which of the following gates would have output 1 when one input is 1 and the other input is 0 ?
(a) OR (b) AND
(c) NAND (d) both (a) and (c)

95. Which gate is formed by adding an inverter at the output of an OR gate ?
(a) NOR (b) XOR
(c) EQUIVALENCE (d) NAND

96. What is minimum number of NAND gates needed to perform the logic function A.B ?
(a) 1 (b) 2
(c) 3 (d) 4

97. Which of the following is functionally a complete set?
(a) AND, OR (b) AND, XOR
(c) NOT, OR (d) AND, OR, NOT

98. Which of the following is not true ?
(a) $0 + A = A$ (b) $1 + A = 1$
(c) $A + A = A$ (d) $1 . A = 1$

99. How many bits are required to encode all twenty six letters, ten symbols and ten numerals ?
(a) 5 (b) 6
(c) 7 (d) 46

100. Which table shows the electrical state of a digital circuits output for every possible combination of electrical states in the input ?
(a) function table (b) truth table
(c) routing table (d) ASC-II table

101. The circuit given below is a

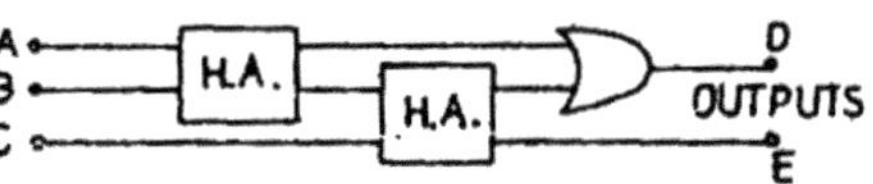

(a) full adder (b) full subtractor
(c) parity checker (d) none of these

102. How many truth table can be made from one function table ?
(a) one (b) two
(c) three (d) any number

103. A positive AND gate is also a negative
(a) NAND gate (b) NOR gate
(c) AND gate (d) OR gate

104. By placing an inverter between both input of an S.R. flip-flop, it becomes
(a) J – K flip-flop
(b) D – flip-flop
(c) T – flip-flop
(d) Master slave JK flip-flop

105. Most of the linear ICs are based on the two-transistor differential amplifier because of its
(a) input voltage dependent linear transfer characteristic
(b) high voltage gain
(c) high input resistance
(d) high CMRR

106. Among the following, the slowest ADC (Analog to digital converter) is
(a) parallel-comparator (i.e. flash) type
(b) successive approximation type
(c) integrating type
(d) counting type

107. The output of a logic gate is "1" when all its input are at logic "0", the gate is either
(a) a NAND or an EX-OR gate
(b) a NOR or an EX-OR gate
(c) an AND or an EX-NOR gate
(d) a NOR or an EX-NOR gate

108. The Q output of a J–K flip-flop is '1'. The output does not change when a clock-pulse is applied. The inputs J and K will be respectively (X-denotes don't care state)
(a) 0 and X
(b) X and 0
(c) 1 and 0
(d) 0 and 1

109. Data can be changed from spatial code to temporal code and vice-versa by using
  (a) ADCs and DACs
  (b) shift-registers
  (c) synchronous counters
  (d) timers.

110. The output of a logic gate is '1' when all its inputs are at logic '0'. The gate is either
  (a) a NAND or an EX-OR gate
  (b) a NOR or an EX-NOR gate
  (c) a OR or an EX-NOR gate
  (d) a AND or an EX-OR gate

111. A switch-tail ring counter is made by using a single D flip-flop. The resulting circuit is a
  (a) SR flip-flop (b) JK flip-flop
  (c) D flip-flop (d) T flop-flop

112. In the following question, match each of the items in list I with an approximate item on the list II and select the correct answer from the codes given below lists

List I	**List II**
A. Shift register can be used	1. for code conversion
B. A multiplexer can be used	2. to generate memory slip to select.
C. A decoder can be used	3. for parallel-to-serial conversion
	4. as a many-to-one switch
	5. for analog-to-digital conversion.

  Codes :

	A	B	C
(a)	1	2	3
(b)	3	4	1
(c)	5	4	2
(d)	1	3	5

113. Which one of the following is equivalent to AND-OR realization?
  (a) NAND-NOR realization
  (b) NOR-NOR realization
  (c) NOR-NAND realization
  (d) NAND-NAND realization.

114. Which logic gate is similar to the function of two parallel switches ?
  (a) AND (b) NAND
  (c) OR (d) NOR

115. Which logic function has the output low only when both inputs are high ?
  (a) OR (b) NOR
  (c) AND (d) NAND

116. Which of the following is an inverter ?
  (a) common base amplifier
  (b) common collector amplifier
  (c) common emitter amplifier
  (d) all of the above

117. A combination of AND function and NOT function results in
  (a) OR gate (b) inversion
  (c) NAND gate (d) NOR gate

118. Which gate is formed by inverting output of the AND gate ?
  (a) OR gate (b) NOR gate
  (c) NAND gate (d) none of the above

119. Which gate corresponds to the action of parallel switches ?
  (a) OR gate (b) NOR gate
  (c) NAND gate (d) AND gate

120. Number of full-adders in a 4-bit parallel adder will be
  (a) two (b) three
  (c) four (d) five

121. A half adder includes
  (a) a NAND gate with OR gate
  (b) a AND gate with XOR gate
  (c) only AND gate
  (d) neither OR nor XOR nor AND gate

122. A logic circuit corresponding '—' sign is
  (a) AND gate (b) NOR gate
  (c) NAND gate (d) OR gate

123. A NAND gate is called a universal logic element because
  (a) it is used by every body
  (b) any logic function can be realised by NAND gates alone
  (c) all the minimization techniques are applicable for optimum NAND gate realisation
  (d) many digital computers use NAND gates

124. The "bubble" or small circle, on the output of the NAND gate and NOR gate represents
  (a) addition (b) subtraction
  (c) product (d) complementation

125. How many inputs can be supplied to a logic gate with a fan in factor of four ?
    (a) two   (b) three
    (c) four   (d) eight

126. Circuit used for a clock generator is
    (a) a free running MV
    (b) JK flip-flop
    (c) either of (a) and (b)
    (d) none of these

127. How many flip-flop circuits are needed to divide by 16 ?
    (a) two   (b) four
    (c) eight   (d) sixteen

128. An index register in a digital computer is used for
    (a) address modification
    (b) for indirect address
    (c) storing one of the operands
    (d) pointing to the stack address

129. An index register in digital computer is register to be used for
    (a) performing arithmetic and logic operations
    (b) temporary storage of result
    (c) counting number of times a program is executed
    (d) address a modification purpose

130. A toggle operation is used
    (a) without a flip-flop
    (b) with a flip-flop
    (c) with a gate circuit
    (d) with a flip-flop and a gate circuit

131. Which of the following is used as a data selector ?
    (a) encoder   (b) decoder
    (c) multiplexer   (d) demultiplexer

132. The op.amp. is used in
    (a) A/D converters   (b) D/A converters
    (c) shift registers   (d) none of these

133. Which family of logic circuits uses filed effect transistors ?
    (a) TTL   (b) CMOS
    (c) both (a) and (b)   (d) none of these

134. Which mode is there in extracting information from storage ?
    (a) read mode
    (b) write mode
    (c) read and write mode
    (d) neither read nor write mode

135. Read and write capabilities are available in
    (a) RAM   (b) ROM
    (c) both (a) and (b)   (d) none of these

136. Which of the following is a temporary memory ?
    (a) RAM   (b) ROM
    (c) both   (d) none

137. Which of the following changes analog voltage to binary data ?
    (a) A/D converter   (b) D/A converter
    (c) both (a) and (b)   (d) schmitt trigger

138. Which converter has a binary input ?
    (a) A/D   (b) D/A
    (c) both (a) and (b)   (d) none of these

139. Out of LCD and LED which display consumes the least power ?
    (a) LCD
    (b) LED
    (c) both consume same power
    (d) uncertain

140. Which multi-vibrator can be used as a clock timer?
    (a) astable   (b) bistable
    (c) both (a) and (b)   (d) none of these

141. A half adder has
    (a) 2 inputs and 2 outputs
    (b) 2 inputs and 3 outputs
    (c) 3 inputs and 3 outputs
    (d) none of these

142. When the input to a seven segment decoder is 0100, the number on display will be
    (a) 0   (b) 2
    (c) 4   (d) 9

143. In register index addressing mode, effective address is given by
    (a) index register value
    (b) sum of the index register value and the operand
    (c) operand
    (d) difference of the index register value and the operand

144. The refreshing rate of dynamic RAM is in the range of
    (a) 2 micro-seconds   (b) 2 milli-seconds
    (c) 50 milli-seconds   (d) 500 milli-seconds

145. Which is ultraviolet light erasable and electrically programmable ?
    (a) ROM   (b) RAM
    (c) PROM   (d) EPROM

146. A J–K master slave flip-flop could be converted into a T flip-flop by making

(a) $J = \sqrt{k}$

(b) $K - \sqrt{J}$

(c) J = K

(d) CLK = 0

147. Octal number system has

(a) Two different digits only

(b) Seven different digits

(c) Eight different digits

(d) Ten different digits

148. Binary multiplication is done using

(a) Two's complement

(b) One's complement

(c) Shift and add

(d) Successive substraction

149. A wired AND gate uses

(a) Common emitter configuration

(b) Common collector configuration

(c) Open emitter configuration

(d) Open collector configuration

150. Which of the following is a universal gate?

(a) AND

(b) OR

(c) NOR

(d) XOR

151. To represent a decimal number 35 in binary, the minimum number of bits required are

(a) 6

(b) 5

(c) 4

(d) 10

152. Binary equivalent to the decimal fraction 0.68 is

(a) 0.1010111

(b) 0.101

(c) 0.10111

(d) 0.010001

153. To add binary number 1101 with 1111 which of the fllowing is needed

(a) Three full adders

(b) One full adder with one half adder

(c) Three full adders and one half adder

(d) Four half adders

EXERCISE – II

1. A flip-flop that produces one output pulse after receiving two input pulses is called **DMRC 2013**

(a) binary circut

(b) negative pulse

(c) reset terminal

(d) stable state

2. BCD equivalent of Gray code number 1001 is

(a) 1001

(b) 1110 **DMRC 2013**

(c) 1100

(d) 1101

3. Main advantage of hexadecimal number system is **DMRC 2013**

(a) case of conversion from hexadecimal to decimal and vice-versa

(b) ease of conversion from hexadecimal to binary and vice-versa

(c) case of conversion from hexadecimal to gray code and vice-versa

(d) use of number and alphabets

4. $\overline{A} \cdot \overline{B} \cdot \overline{C}$ = D represents a **DMRC 2013**

(a) NOR gate

(b) NAND gate

(c) EX-OR gate

(d) AND gate

5. NOR gate is logically equivalent to **DMRC 2013**

(a) an OR gate followed by an AND gate

(b) an OR gate followed by a NAND gate

(c) an AND gate followed by OR gate

(d) an OR gate followed by an inverter

6. The circuit given below is functionally equivalent to **DMRC 2013**

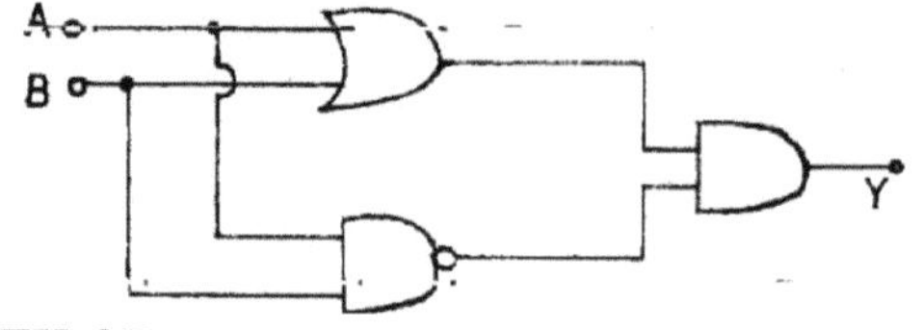

(a) EX-OR gate

(b) NOR gate

(c) AND gate

(d) NAND gate

7. Which of the following gates are added to the inputs of the OR gate to convert it into NAND gate ? **DMRC 2013**

(a) NOT

(b) AND

(c) OR

(d) XOR

8. How many bits are required to encode all twenty six letters, ten symbols and ten numerals ?

(a) 5

(b) 6 **DMRC 2013**

(c) 7

(d) 46

9. By placing an inverter between both input of an S.R. flip-flop, it becomes **DMRC 2013**

(a) J – K flip-flop

(b) D – flip-flop

(c) T – flip-flop

(d) Master slave JK flip-flop

10. Which family of logic circuits uses filed effect transistors ? **DMRC 2013**

  (a) TTL   (b) CMOS

  (c) both (a) and (b)   (d) none of these

11. Which of the following changes analog voltage to binary data ? **DMRC 2013**

  (a) A/D converter   (b) D/A converter

  (c) both (a) and (b)   (d) schmitt trigger

12. Radix of octal number system is **DRDO**

  (a) 2   (b) 4

  (c) 8   (d) 10

13. The 2's compliment of binary number 0.01011 is

  (a) 1.10101   (b) 0.10101 **DRDO**

  (c) 0.10100   (d) 1.10100

14. Which of the following hexadecimal numbers represents an odd decimal number ? **DRDO**

  (a) FF   (b) EG

  (c) CC   (d) AA

15. Which of the following is not functionally a complete set ? **DRDO**

  (a) AND, OR   (b) NAND

  (c) NOR   (d) AND, OR, NOT

16. An OR gate may be imagined as **DRDO**

  (a) switches connected in series

  (b) switches connected in parallel

  (c) MOS transistors connected in series

  (d) none of the above

17. When the input to a seven segment decoder is 0100, the number on display will be **DRDO**

  (a) 0   (b) 2

  (c) 4   (d) 9

18. An index register in digital computer is register to be used for **RRB**

  (a) performing arithmetic and logic operations

  (b) temporary storage of result

  (c) counting number of times a program is executed

  (d) address a modification purpose

19. Which of the following codes is an unweighted code? **RRB**

  (a) 8421 code   (b) Excess-3 code

  (c) 2421 code   (d) 63210 code

20. Boolean expression for three input OR gate is

  (a) $\overline{A} + \overline{B} + \overline{C} = D$ **RRB**

  (b) $A + B + C = D$

  (c) $A . B . C = D$

  (d) $\overline{A} . \overline{B} . \overline{C} = D$

21. Which logic function is produced by adding inverters to the inputs of an AND gates ? **RRB**

  (a) NAND   (b) NOR

  (c) XOR   (d) OR

22. Among the following, the slowest ADC Analog to digital converter) is **RRB**

  (a) parallel-comparator (i.e. flash) type

  (b) successive approximation type

  (c) integrating type

  (d) counting type

23. A logic circuit implements the boolean function $F = \overline{X} . Y + X . \overline{Y} . \overline{Z}$. It is found that the input combination $X = Y = 1$ can never occur. Taking this into account, a simplified expression for F is given by **RRB**

  (a) $\overline{X} + \overline{Y} . \overline{Z}$ (b) $X + Z$

  (c) $X + Y$ (d) $Y + X . \overline{Z}$

24. Let $X = X_1 X_0$ and $Y = Y_1 Y_0$ be unsigned 2-bit numbers. The function $F = 1$ if $X > Y$ and $F = 0$ otherwise. The minimized sum of products expression for F is **RRB**

  (a) $Y_1 . Y_0 + X_0 . Y_0 + \overline{X}_1 . \overline{X}_0 . \overline{Y}_1$

  (b) $X_0 . \overline{Y}_1 + Y_1 . \overline{Y}_0 + X_1 . \overline{X}_0$

  (c) $Y_1 . \overline{X}_1 + Y_0 . \overline{X}_1 . \overline{X}_0 . + Y_1 . Y_0 . \overline{X}_0$

  (d) $X_1 . \overline{Y}_1 + X_0 . \overline{Y}_0 . \overline{Y}_1 + X_0 . X_1 . \overline{Y}_0$

25. A MUX circuit shown in the figure below implements a logic function F_1. The correct expression for F_1 is **RRB**

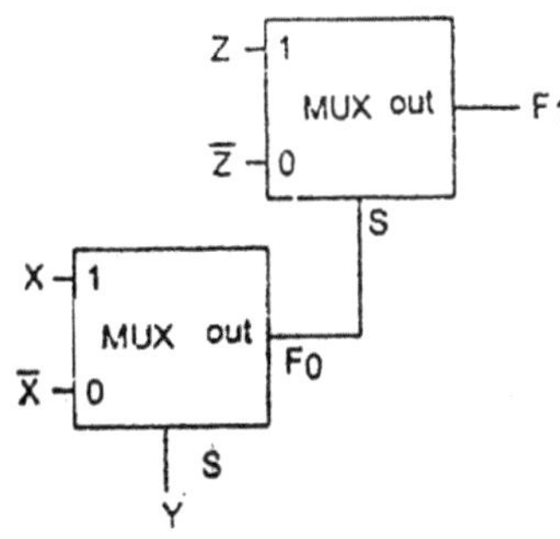

The correct expression

  (a) $\left(\overline{X \oplus Y}\right) \oplus Z$ (b) $\overline{\left(X \oplus Y\right) \oplus Z}$

  (c) $(X \oplus Y) \oplus \overline{Z}$ (d) $(X \oplus Y) + Z$

26. A sequential circuit is shown in the figure below. Let the state of the circuit be encoded as $Q_A Q_B$. The notation $X \to Y$ implies that state y is reachable from state X in a finite number of clock transitions.

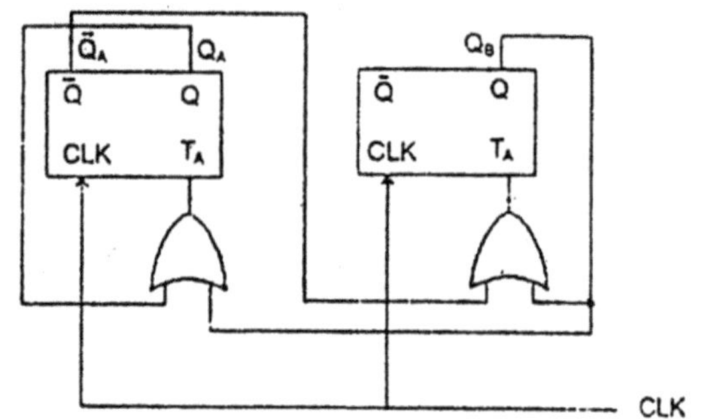

Identify the INCORRECT statement.   **RRB**

(a) $01 \to 00$ (b) $11 \to 01$

(c) $01 \to 11$ (d) $01 \to 10$

27. The circuit shown in the figure below works as a 2-bit analog to digital converter for $0 \le V_{in} \le 3$ V.

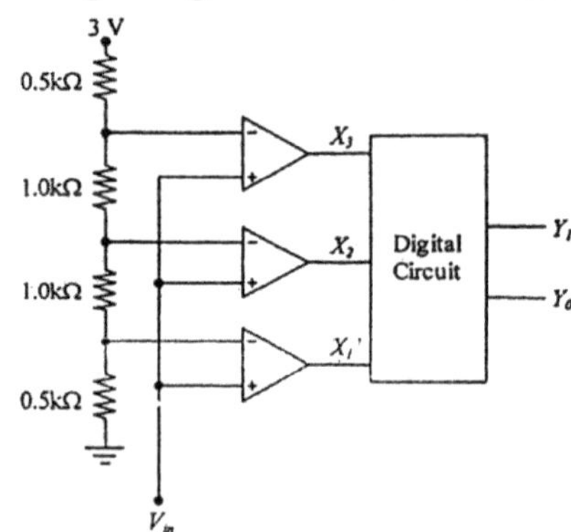

The MSB of the output Y_1, expressed as a boolean function of the inputs X_1, X_2, X_3 is given by   **RRB**

(a) X_1 (b) X_2

(c) X_3 (d) $X_1 + X_2$

28. 8-bit signed intergers in 2′s complement form are read into the accumulator of an 8085 microprocessor from an I/O port using the following assembly language program segment with symbolic addresses.   **RRB**

```
BEGIN :     IN PORT
            RAL
            JNCBEGIN
            RAR
END :       HLT
```

This program

(a) halts upon reading a negative number

(b) halts upon reading a positive number

(c) halts upon reading a zero

(d) never halts

29. The pulse width T of an asynchronous pulse is measured by a counter with an edge-triggered clock of known frequency fc as shown in the figure below :

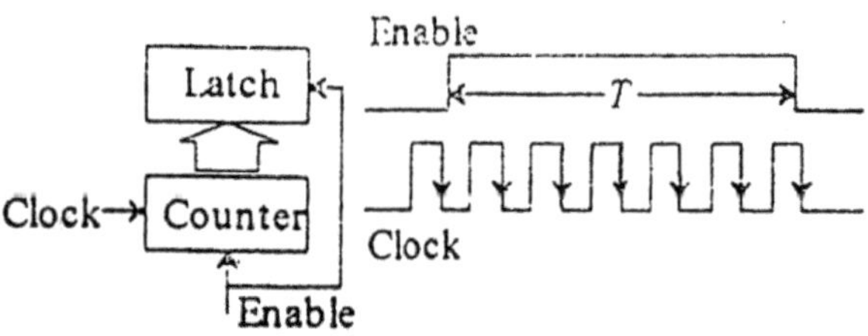

The pulse, whose width is to be measured, is applied to the Enable pin of the counter. The counter counts while the Enable is high and is held reset to zero otherwise. The counter output is latched by the negative edge of the Enable signal. The measured pulse width is taken to be N times the clock period, where N is the count reached at the end of a count cycle.

Assuming no overflow, the measurement error will be limited to x% of T if   **RRB**

(a) $T > \dfrac{100}{x\,f_c}$ (b) $T < \dfrac{100}{x\,f_c}$

(c) $T > \dfrac{200}{x\,f_c}$ (d) $T < \dfrac{200}{x\,f_c}$

30. Min-term (Sum of Products) expression for a Boolean function is given as follows.   **RRB**

$$f(A, B, C) = \Sigma m\,(0, 1, 2, 3, 5, 6)$$

where A is the MSB and C is the LSB. The minimized expression for the function is

(a) $A + (B \oplus C)$ (b) $(A \oplus B) + C$

(c) $\overline{A} + (B \oplus C)$ (d) $\overline{ABC}$

31. Given that the initial state $(Q_1 Q_0)$ is 00, the counting sequence of the counter shown in the following figure is, $Q_1 Q_0 =$ **RRB**

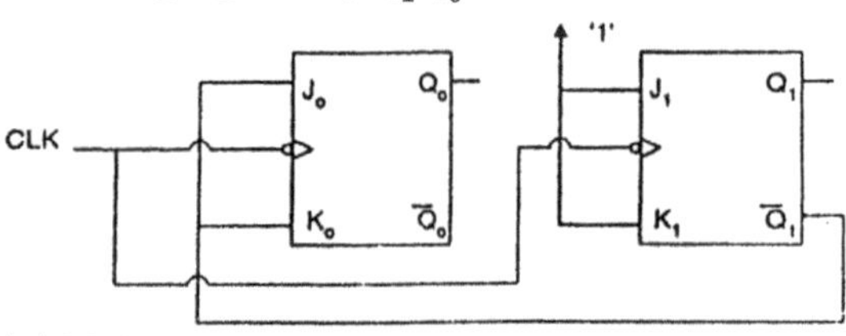

(a) 00-11-01-10-00   (b) 00-01-11-10-00

(c) 00-11-10-01-00   (d) 00-10-01-11-00

32. All the logic gates in the circuit shown below have finite propagation delay.   **RRB**

The circuit can be used as a clock generator, if

(a) X = 0

(b) X = 1

(c) X = 0 or 1

(d) X = Y

33. A CMOS implementation of a logic gate is shown in the following figure : **RRB 2012**

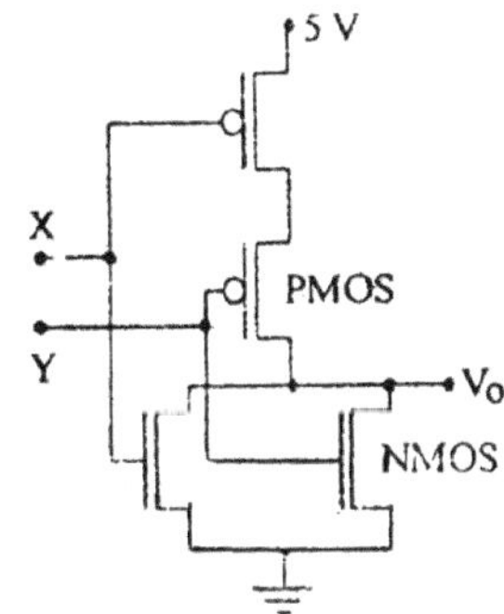

The boolean logic function realized by the circuit is

(a) AND   (b) NAND

(c) NOR   (d) OR

34.

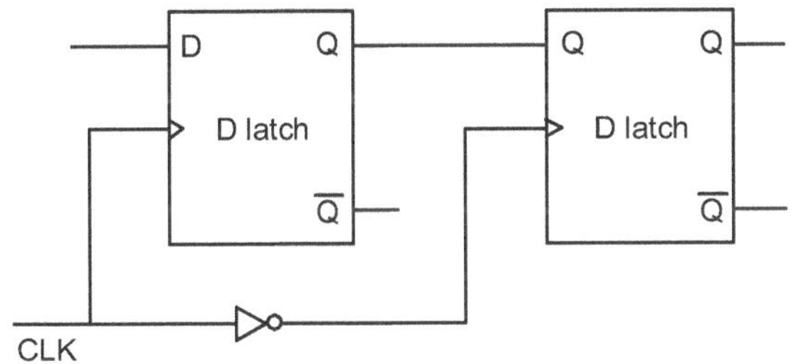

Current option is **RRB 2012**

(a) Jk flip-flop

(b) SR flip-flop

(c) Toggle flip flop

(d) Master-slave arrangement

35. The logic function implemented by the circuit below is (ground implies a logic "0"). **RRB 2012**

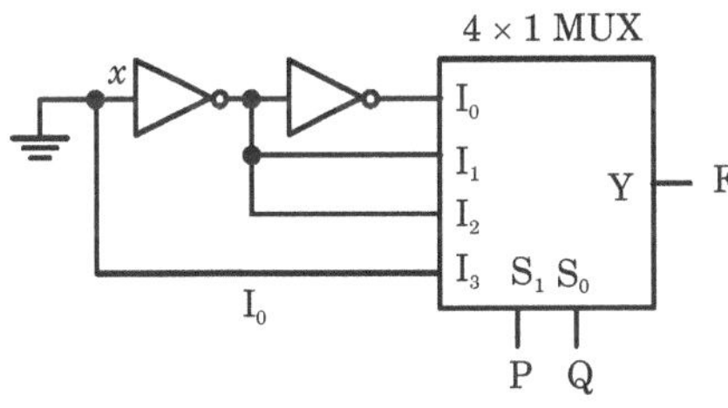

(a) F = AND (P, Q)   (b) F = OR (P, Q)

(c) F = XNOR (P, Q)   (d) F = XOR (P, Q)

36. Consider the given circuit. **RRB 2012**

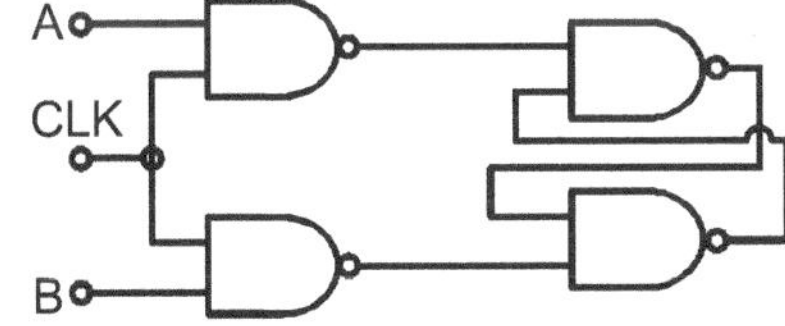

In this circuit, the race around

(a) does not occur

(b) occurs when CLK = 0

(c) occurs when CLK = 1 and A = B = 1

(d) occurs when CLK = 1 and A = B = 0

37. In the circuit shown **RRB 2012**

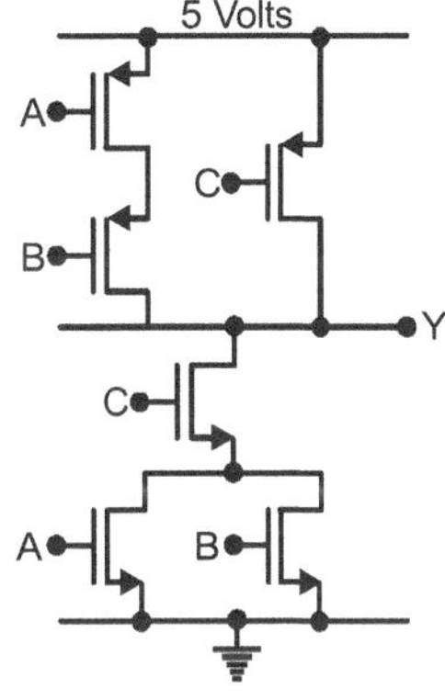

(a) $Y = \overline{A}\overline{B} + \overline{C}$ (b) $Y = (A+B)C$

(c) $Y = \left(\overline{A} + \overline{B}\right) + \overline{C}$ (d) $Y = AB+C$

38. In the sum of products functions **RRB 2012**

$f(X,Y,Z) = \Sigma(2, 3, 4, 5)$, the prime implicants are

(a) $\overline{X}Y, X\overline{Y}$

(b) $\overline{X}Y, X\overline{Y}\overline{Z}, X\overline{Y}Z$

(c) $\overline{X}Y\overline{Z}, \overline{X}YZ, X\overline{Y}$

(d) $\overline{X}Y\overline{Z}, \overline{X}YZ, X\overline{Y}\overline{Z}, X\overline{Y}Z$

39. A number N is stored in a 4-bit 2's complement representation as

$$a_3 \quad a_2 \quad a_1 \quad a_0$$

It is copied into a 6-bit register and after a few operations, the final bit pattern is

$$a_3 \quad a_3 \quad a_2 \quad a_1 \quad a_0 \quad 1$$

The value of this bit pattern in 2's complement representation is given in terms of the original number is N as **RRB 2012**

(a) $32\,a_3 + 2N + 1$ (b) $32\,a_3 - 2N - 1$

(c) $2N - 1$ (d) $2N + 1$

ANSWERS

EXERCISE – I

1. (b)	**2.** (a)	**3.** (a)	**4.** (b)	**5.** (a)	**6.** (c)	**7.** (a)	**8.** (a)	**9.** (b)	**10.** (a)
11. (b)	**12.** (c)	**13.** (c)	**14.** (b)	**15.** (d)	**16.** (a)	**17.** (a)	**18.** (b)	**19.** (b)	**20.** (b)
21. (a)	**22.** (b)	**23.** (c)	**24.** (a)	**25.** (a)	**26.** (d)	**27.** (c)	**28.** (d)	**29.** (c)	**30.** (b)
31. (b)	**32.** (b)	**33.** (b)	**34.** (a)	**35.** (b)	**36.** (a)	**37.** (c)	**38.** (d)	**39.** (b)	**40.** (a)
41. (d)	**42.** (b)	**43.** (d)	**44.** (c)	**45.** (d)	**46.** (b)	**47.** (d)	**48.** (c)	**49.** (a)	**50.** (d)
51. (b)	**52.** (a)	**53.** (b)	**54.** (a)	**55.** (c)	**56.** (c)	**57.** (b)	**58.** (d)	**59.** (b)	**60.** (b)
61. (b)	**62.** (b)	**63.** (a)	**64.** (b)	**65.** (a)	**66.** (a)	**67.** (b)	**68.** (a)	**69.** (d)	**70.** (d)
71. (c)	**72.** (a)	**73.** (b)	**74.** (c)	**75.** (c)	**76.** (c)	**77.** (b)	**78.** (a)	**79.** (b)	**80.** (c)
81. (d)	**82.** (c)	**83.** (a)	**84.** (b)	**85.** (d)	**86.** (a)	**87.** (c)	**88.** (a)	**89.** (b)	**90.** (c)
91. (a)	**92.** (a)	**93.** (b)	**94.** (d)	**95.** (a)	**96.** (b)	**97.** (a)	**98.** (d)	**99.** (b)	**100.** (a)
101. (a)	**102.** (b)	**103.** (d)	**104.** (b)	**105.** (d)	**106.** (b)	**107.** (d)	**108.** (b)	**109.** (a)	**110.** (b)
111. (d)	**112.** (b)	**113.** (d)	**114.** (c)	**115.** (d)	**116.** (c)	**117.** (c)	**118.** (c)	**119.** (a)	**120.** (c)
121. (b)	**122.** (b)	**123.** (b)	**124.** (d)	**125.** (c)	**126.** (a)	**127.** (b)	**128.** (a)	**129.** (d)	**130.** (b)
131. (c)	**132.** (c)	**133.** (b)	**134.** (a)	**135.** (a)	**136.** (a)	**137.** (a)	**138.** (b)	**139.** (a)	**140.** (a)
141. (a)	**142.** (c)	**143.** (b)	**144.** (a)	**145.** (d)	**146.** (c)	**147.** (b)	**148.** (c)	**149.** (a)	**150.** (c)
151. (a)	**152.** (a)	**153.** (c)							

EXERCISE – II

1. (a)	**2.** (b)	**3.** (b)	**4.** (a)	**5.** (d)	**6.** (a)	**7.** (a)	**8.** (b)	**9.** (b)	**10.** (b)
11. (a)	**12.** (c)	**13.** (a)	**14.** (a)	**15.** (a)	**16.** (b)	**17.** (c)	**18.** (d)	**19.** (b)	**20.** (b)
21. (b)	**22.** (b)	**23.** (a)	**24.** (d)	**25.** (b)	**26.** (d)	**27.** (c)	**28.** (b)	**29.** (b)	**30.** (c)
31. (a)	**32.** (b)	**33.** (c)	**34.** (d)	**35.** (d)	**36.** (a)	**37.** (a)	**38.** (a)	**39.** (b)	

CLASSIFICATION OF MATERIALS BASED ON ENERGY BAND THEORY

Based on the ability of various materials to conduct current, the materials are classified as conductors, insulators and the semiconductors.

A metal which is very good carrier of electricity is called *conductor*, e.g. copper and aluminium.

A very poor conductor of electricity is called *insulator*. e.g. glass, wolld mica diamond.

A metal having conductivity which is between conductor and an insulator is called *semiconductor*. e.g. silicon and germamium are the examples of a semiconductor does not conduct current at low temperatures but as temperature increases these materials behave and good conductors.

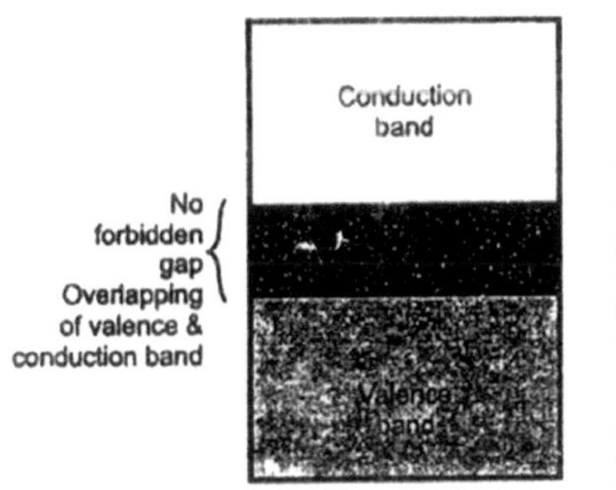

(a) Conductor

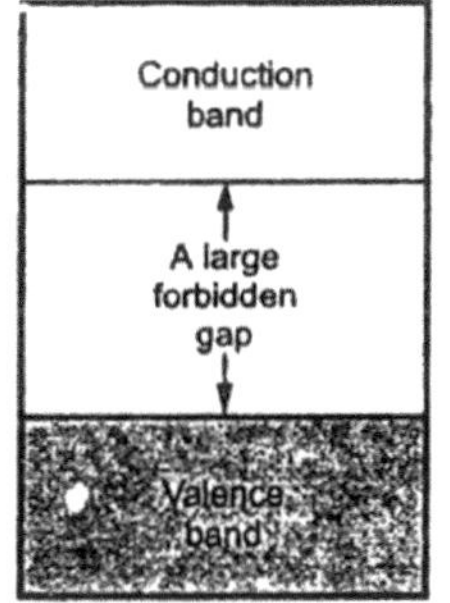

(b) Insulator

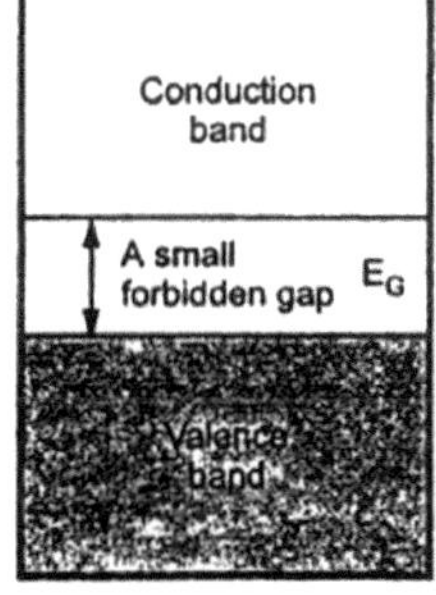

(c) Semiconductor

Fig. Energy band diagrams

1. CONDUCTORS.

A material having large number of free electrons can conduct very easily.

e.g. Copper has 8.5×10^{28} free electrons per cubic metre which is a very large number. Hence copper is called *good conductor*. In fact, in the metals like copper, aluminium there is no forbidden gap between valence band and conduction band. The two bands overlap. Hence even at room temperature, a large number of electrons are available for conduction. So without any additional energy, such metals contain a large number of free electrons and hence called *good conductors*.

2. INSULATORS.

In case of such insulating material, there exists a large forbidden gap in between conduction band and the valence band. Practically it is impossible for an electron to jump from the valence band to the conduction band. Hence such materials cannot conduct and called *insulators*. The forbidden gap is very wide, approximately of about 7 eV is present in insulators. For a diamond, which is an insulator, the forbidden gap is about 6 eV. Such materials may conduct only at very high temperatures or if they are subjected to high voltage. Such a conduction is rare and is called *breakdown of an insulator*. The other insulation materials are glass, wood, mica, paper etc.

The insulating materials used in electrical engineering may be gases, liquids, solids or vacuum.

Gases that serves as dielectrics are air, nitrogen, hydrogen, sulphur hexafluoride etc. Liquid dielectrics that are commonly used are mineral oils, synthetic hydrocarbons, etc. and they are used not only as insulating media but also to improve heat conduction property of apparatus.

Solid insulators are extremely diverse in origin and properties, they may be natural organic substances like paper, cloth, rubber etc. or inorganic materials like mica, glass and ceramic or synthetic materials like plastics.

Dielectric materials provide electrical insulation between conductors and also acts as stores of electrical charges.

When main function is that of insulation, the materials are called *insulants*.

When the charge storage is the main function they are called *dielectrics*.

The dielectric strength of an insulation is that value of voltage which causes electrical rupture of an insulating material, in practical use it is defined under the specific conditions and is measured in volts per unit thickness of the materials. Another important property is the dielectric constant, which determines the share of the electric stress which is absorbed by the material.

A good insulating material should be of low permittivity giving a high discharge stress, free from gaseous insulation to avoid local stress concentration, free from moisture and ionic contamination to limit loss tangent and electro-chemical deterioration, resistant to erosion by discharges and resistant to thermal and chemical deterioration.

3. SEMICONDUCTORS.

Now consider materials, which are neither insulators nor conductors. Such materials are called *semiconductors*. The forbidden gap is very narrow about 1 eV. In such materials, the energy provided by the heat at room temperature is sufficient to lift the electrons from the valence band to the conduction band. Therefore at room temperature, semiconductors are capable of conduction. But at 0°K or absolute zero (–273° C), all the electrons of semiconductor materials find themselves locked in the valence band. Hence at 0°K, the semiconductor materials behave as perfect insulators. In case of semiconductors, forbidden gap energy depends on the temperature.

For silicon and germanium, this energy is given by,

$E_G = 1.21 - 3.6 \times 10^{-4} \times T$ eV (for Silicon)

$E_G = 0.785 - 2.23 \times 10^{-4} \times T$ eV (for Germanium)

where, T = absolute temperature in °K

Assuming room temperature to be 27° C, i.e. 300 °K, the forbidden gap energy for Si and Ge can be calculated from the above equations. The forbidden gap for the germanium is 0.72 eV while for the silicon it is 1.12 eV at room temperature. The silicon and germanium are the two widely used semiconductor materials in electronic devices.

At room temperature, the materials classified as semiconductors have a resistivity between that of a typical metals and that of a typical insulators. However resistivity of semiconductors in general depends strongly on temperature. This classification is not satisfactory because at very low temperature, semiconductors may behave as insulators.

Another classification may be the temperature co-efficient of resistivity ($d\rho/dT$).

Metal = positive temperature co-efficient of resistivity $\left(+ \dfrac{\partial \rho}{\partial T} \right)$

Semiconductor = negative temperature co-efficient of resistivity $\left(- \dfrac{\partial \rho}{\partial T} \right)$

Insulator = negative temperature co-efficient of resistivity $\left(- \dfrac{\partial \rho}{\partial T} \right)$.

Semiconductor and insulator behaviour with respect to temperature is same but their resistivity is different only quantitavely. Various semiconductors are such as metal-oxide and sulphides *e.g.* Pb S - is used photo conductive devices. BaO - in oxide coated cathodes. Cesium antimonide - in photo multipliers etc.

Chemical Bond in Si and Ge.

In solid state Si and Ge both [Fourth Group] crystallize into what is called *diamond structure*. In this structure, a given atom is surrounded by four others occupying the corner of a regular tetrahedran.

The bonds between a given atom in this structure and its neighbours are called *electron - pairs bonds*, each partner contributing one electron to each bond. Since each atom has four valence electrons, it has just enough to provide for electron pair bonds with four atom (Homopolar bond).

O : O : O : O

O : O : O : O ← Electron

O : O : O : O

Electron pair bond

At absolute zero temperature, Si and Ge behaves like insulator. Let the temperature is raised, *i.e.* vibration carried out by the atoms in the lattice are made more voilent. Then some of the valence electrons may then absorb a sufficient amount of energy from the lattice vibrations to be released from the bonds and once set free they can move through the crystal and contribute to conductivity.

Thus as the temperature of material is raised from zero to some temperature T > 0, a number of bonds will be broken and conduction may be observed as a result of the motion of the electrons and holes under influence of an external field.

For pure Ge and Si the number of free electrons must be equal the number of mobile holes. Semiconductor of this kind are called as intrinsic semiconductor.

Intrinsic semiconductor are distinguished from extrinsic semiconductor in which the charge carriers (electron or holes) are present as a result of impurities built into the crystal. At a given temperature there are certain average number of electrons and an equal number of holes in the material. As the temperature is increased, average number of free charge carriers increases, *i.e.*

bond electrons $\rightleftarrows$ free election + holes.

Density of conduction electrons,

$n = 5 \times 10^{21} \, T^{3/2} \, e^{-wg/2\,kT}$ per m^3

where, W_g = energy gap between conduction level and valence level

Conductivity of a semiconductor depends strongly on the magnitude of the energy gap W_g, i.e. conductivity of a material is proportional to the density of charge carriers.

Types of semiconductors.

(*i*) **n-type semiconductors :** n-type semiconductors are formed by doping with elements from Vth group of periodic table P, As and Sb. Addition of a percent of such elements may increase the conductivity by several powers of ten. As the impurity increases the ionisation energy decreases.

(*ii*) **p-type semiconductor :** p-type semiconductors are formed by doping with element from the third group, *i.e.* B, Al, Ba, In. At absolute zero, the holes remains bound to the impurities, but as the temperature is increased, valence electrons may be excited into the bound holes with the result that holes are created in the valence band.

At low temperature conductivity results predominantly from holes produced by excitation of valence electrons into acceptor levels.

INTRINISIC SEMICONDUCTORS.

A sample of semiconductor in its purest form is called an *intrinsic semiconductor*. The impurity content in intrinsic semiconductor is very very small, of the order of one part in 100 million parts of semiconductor. For achieving such a pure form, the semiconductor materials are carefully refined.

Crystal structure of instrinsic semiconductor.

Consider an atomic structure of an instrinsic semiconductor material like silicon. An outermost shell of an atom is capable of holding eight electrons. It is said to be completely filled and stable, if it contains eight electrons. But the outermost shell of an intrinsic semiconductor like silicon has only four electrons. Each of these four electrons form a bond with another valence electron of the neighbouring atoms. This is nothing but sharing of electrons. Such bonds are called *covalent bonds*. The atoms align themselves to form a three dimensional uniform pattern called *cyrstal*.

The crystal structure of germanium and silicon materials consists of repetitive occurrence in three dimensions of a unit cell. This unit cell is in the form of a tetrahedron with an atom at each vertex. But such a three dimensional structure is very difficult to represent pictorially. Hence a symbolic two dimensional structure is used to represent a three dimensional crystal form, as shown below in the Fig. (*a*).

Fig. (*a*) shows two dimensional representation of a germanium crystal structure. Germanium has a total of 32 electrons. So its first orbit consists of 2 electrons, second consists of 8, third consists of 18 and the valence shell consists of 4 electrons. As there are 4 valence electrons, it is called *tetravalent atom*.

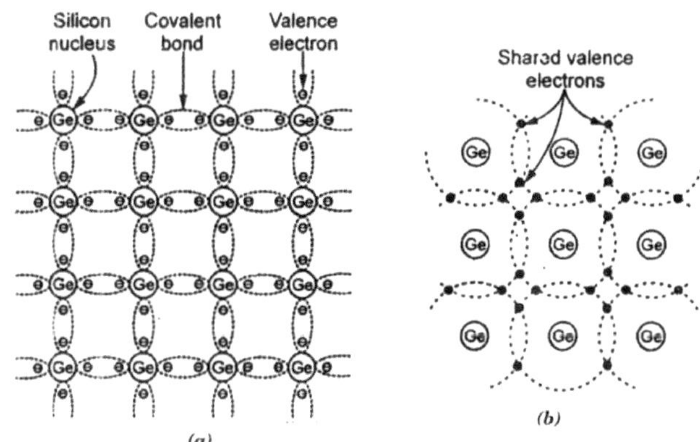

Fig. Two dimensional representation of germanium crystal

CONDUCTIVITY OF METALS

The most characteristic properties of the metals are their high electrical conductivity.

e.g. electrical conductivity of silver at room temperature is 0.6×10^8 ohm^{-1}m^{-1} as compared to 10^{-16} ohm^{-1} m-1 for a good insulator and 2×10^{-2} ohm^{-1} m^{-1} for semiconductor such as germanium.

High conductivity of metals is due to *free or conduction* electrons. These free electrons are able to move throughout the lattice and hence do not belong to particular atom. The only electrons which have this high degree of freedom are those corresponds to the valence electrons in the atoms.

The free electrons in a metal can accept a series of discrete energy levels. At absolute zero, all energy levels below a certain value w_F are filled and all those above w_F being empty. w_F is called *Fermi-level of electrons.*

SUPER CONDUCTIVITY.

The electrical resistivity of mercury disappeared completely at temperature below approximately 4.2°K. We define a transition temperature T_c at which transition from normal state to the super conducting states occurs.

Transition temperature of all elements having super conductivity lie below 10°K.

The elements which are at room temperature are good conductors Cu, Ag etc. are absent from the list of super conductive elements. In fact super conducting elements are relatively poor conductors at room temperature. Super conducting compounds and alloys do not necessarily have super conducting elements components.

Relative permeability for super conductor is zero, this is called *perfect diamagnetism.*

Ideal magnetic behavior of super conductors falls into two classes :

(*i*) **Soft super conductors :** These are completely diamagnetic, *i.e.* B = 0 inside the interior or M = –H. This behaviour is called *Meissner effect or perfect diamagnetism,* *i.e.* below the critical field H$_c$, specimen excludes all the magnetic lines of forces inside the specimen or it will become a diamagnetic material. These are called *soft super conductors.*

The value of H_c are always too low for these material, *e.g.* Al, Zn, Ga etc.

(*ii*)**Hard super conductors :** In these the magnetic flux starts to penetrate the specimen at a field H_{c1}, which is lower than critical field H_{c2}. The specimen is in the mixed state between H_{c1} and H_{c2} and it has super conducting properties upto H_{c2}. Above H_{c2} the specimen is a normal conductor. These conductors are called *hard super conductors* which have a large amount of hysteresis induced by mechanical treatment.

MAGNETIC MATERIALS

The classification of magnetic materials is done in terms of magnetic properties of the atomic dipoles and interaction between them. The first distinction we can make is that between materials whose atoms carry permanent magnetic dipoles and those in which permanent magnetic dipoles are absent; the permanent dipole may exists even in the absence of a field. Materials which lack permanent magnetic dipoles are called *diamagnetic.*

If there are permanent magnetic dipoles associated with the atoms in a material, such a material may be classified depending on the interaction between individual dipoles.

(*i*) **Paramagnetic materials :** If interaction between atomic permanent dipole moments is zero or negligible, the material will be *paramagnetic.*

(*ii*) **Ferromagnetic materials :** If dipole interact in such a manner that they tend to line up in parallel, the material will be *ferromagnetic.*

(*iii*) **Antiferromagnetic or ferromagnetic materials :** The neighbouring dipoles tend to line up so that they are antiparallel. The material is antiferromagnetic or ferrimagnetic depending on the magnitudes of dipoles on the two *sub-lattices* as indicated schematically for a one dimensional models shown.

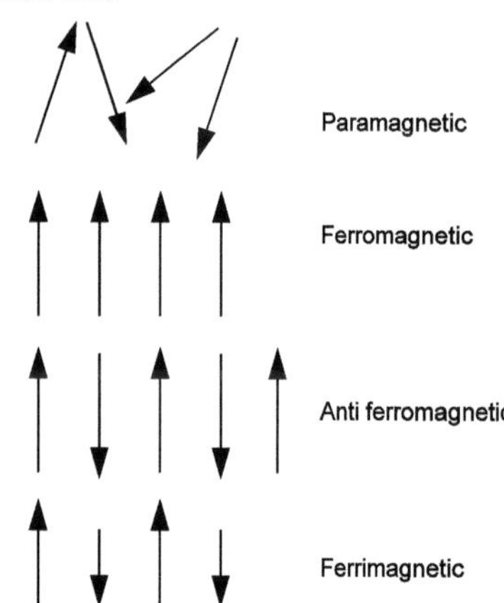

In the ferromagnetic case, there is a large resultant magnetization, whereas in an antiferromagnetic configuration, the magnetization vanishes. In the case of ferrimagnetic materials, there may be relatively large net magnetization resulting from the tendency of antiparallel alignment of neighbouring dipole moments of unequal magnitude. Ferrimagnetic materials are thus similar to ferromagnetic ones in the sense that both kinds may exhibit a large magnetization.

On the other hand ferrimagnetic materials resemble antiferromagnetic materials with respect to the tendency for antiparallel alignment of neighbouring dipole moments.

SEMICONDUCTOR MATERIALS

- Important properties of semiconductor materials Ge and Si is that they form a very definite pattern that is periodic in nature, *i.e.* they have single crystal structure.

- Both Ge and Si have four electrons in outer most orbit.

- Both Ge and Si are tetravalent atoms and they form covalent bonding as shown in the figure.

- An increase in temperature of a semiconductor can result in a substantial increase in the number of free electrons in the material. Semiconductor material such as Ge and Si show that a reduction in resistance with increase in temperature are said to have a negative temperature co-efficient.

Dopping process.

The characteristics of semiconductor materials can be altered significantly by the addition of certain impurity atoms into the relatively pure semiconductor material called *doping process.*

A semiconductor material that has been subjected to the doping process is called *extrinsic material.*

***n*-type material.**

n-type material is created by introducing those impurity elements that have five valence electron (penta valent) such as antimony, arsenic and phosphorous. These diffused impurities with five valence electrons are called *donar atoms.*

***p*-type materials.**

p-type material is formed by doping a pure germanium or Si crystal with impurity atoms having three valence electrons. These doping materials are Boron, Gallium and Indium.

The diffused impurities with three valence electrons are called *acceptor atoms.* The *p*-type materials are also electrically neutral.

If a valence electron acquires sufficient kinetic energy to break its covalent bond and fills the void created by a hole, then a vacancy or hole will be created in the covalent bond that released the electron.

- In *n*-type of material, the electron is called *majority carrier* and the hole is called *minority carrier.*

- In *p*-type material holes are *majority carriers* and electron are *minority carriers.*

KEY POINTS

Types of Generators
(*i*) Permanent magnet type
(*ii*) Self-excited
(*iii*) Separately excited.

MOTOR
It is a machine which converts electrical energy into mechanical energy.

Fleming's left hand rule
If first and second fingers and the thumb of left hand are stretched in such a way that they remain mutually perpendicular, and the first finger points the direction of magnetic field and the second finger points the direction of applied e.m.f., then the thumb will point the direction of motion of the conductor. This rule is used for the determination of direction of rotation of an armature of a motor.

Clear
To reset, as in case of a counter, flipflop or a register.

Clearance Hole
Area without conductive material in a conductive pattern around a plated through hole of a multilayer printed board in order to prevent any electrical connection to the plated through hole.

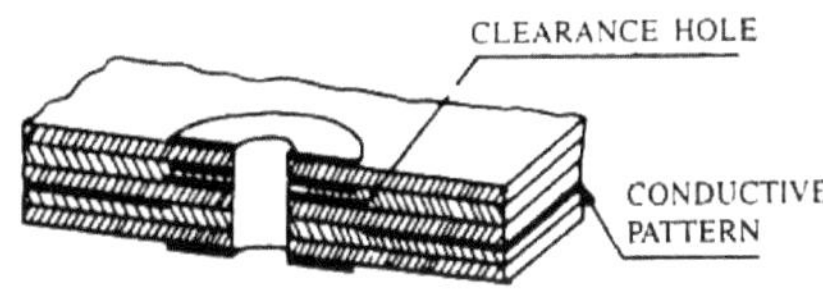

Demagnetization Curve
It is a portion of magnetic hysteresis loop which depicts peak value of residual magnetism and how the magnetization reduces to zero as the- demagnetization force is applied.

Fuse
It is a wire or strip of metal, mounted in suitable fittings, designed to melt and to interrupt the circuit when a predetermined maximum current is exceeded. Also, it is an apparatus for electrically firing explosives, consisting of a case containing necessary priming charge and a wire heated by the current which passes when the firing key is depressed.

Fused coating
It is a metallic coating (usually thin or solder alloy) which has been melted and solidified forming a metallurgical bond to base metal.

Gold Schmidt high Frequency alternator
It is an alternator for producing currents at Radio-frequencies, in which no attempt is made to provide a sufficiently high frequency. It is multiplied by introducing harmonics by means of oscillating circuits in connection with both field and the armature. Accumulative effect is produced by the interaction between stator and the rotor, and very high frequencies can be obtained.

Gyro Magnetic Resonance
When a ferrite is placed in a magnetic field, it has a resonance frequency, is a constant called the gyro magnetic ratio (approximately 2.8 me oersted, varying with material composition), and HI is a magnetic field inside the ferrite.

The phenomenon of ferromagnetic resonance is the principle of operation of many ferrite devices. Electrons spin about their own axis, and they also process about the stationary magnetic field HI at a frequency if damping losses are neglected. If microwave energy of this same frequency and polarization is incident upon the spins, the spins will interact with it and couple energy from it. The coupled energy is used to widen the angle between axis of the electron and internal magnetic field. To detect resonance, measure loss in decibels of the incident. Microwave energy loss versus magnetic field shows that resonance is not a sharp effect. There is a definite spreading out of the loss region. The points marked A and A′ are 3.0 dB higher than the minimum point and the distance between them is called *line width H.*

Normally line width is measured in *oersteds*, and smaller the linewidih, better the ferrite.

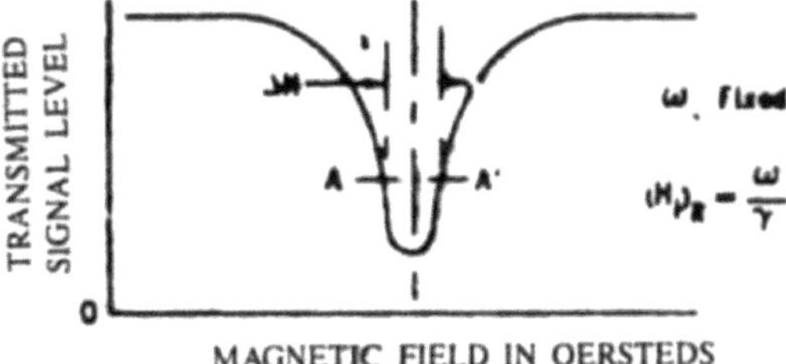

Listed Wire
It is wire of uniform resistance provided with a sliding contact that can make a connection at any desired point along the length. Slide wires are used to provide a variable resistance, as a potentiometer, or to provide a desired resistance ratio.

Magnetic Amplifier
It is any form of amplifier depending upon properties of ferromagnetic materials.

Magnetic Hysteresis
It is observed in ferromagnetic materials below the Curie point where magnetization of the material varies non linearly with the magnetic field strength and also lags behind it. A plot of magnetization M or magnetic flux density B against magnetic field

strength "H" shows a covered area called *hysteris loop*. The area enclosed depends upon nature of the material. Minimum area occurs with soft iron. Value of magnetization at zero field-Remanence Value of magnetic flux density corresponding to remanence-residual induction,

Magnetic Moment

It is a measure of strength of a magnet. When a magnet is placed in a magnetic field of density B, magnet experiences a torque

$$T = m \times B$$

where *m* = magnetic moment.
It is also called *magnetic dipole moment*.

Magnet

It is a piece of iron or other magnetic material which can attract small iron pieces towards it.

Properties of A Magnet

1. A freely suspended magnet always rests in north-south direction.
2. Like poles of two magnets repel and unlike poles attract each other.
3. Each magnet has two poles : North and South.

Magnetism

It is the property of certain materials of attracting small iron pieces towards them.

Molecular theory of Magnetism

Every molecule of a substance behaves like tiny magnet because of its spin motion. It has a North and a South pole. When these tiny magnets are set in a definite linear order, then substance then starts to behave as a magnet.

Types of magnets

Magnets are of two types:
(*i*) **Natural**
(*ii*) **Artificial.**
    These are of two types :
    (*i*) Permanent magnets
    (*ii*) Temporary magnets

Uses of Permanent magnets

Permanent magnets are used in small motors, magnetoes, loudspeakers, electrical measuring instruments etc.

Materials used for making permanent magnets

(*i*) Tungsten steel,
(*ii*) Cobalt steel,
ALNICO or ALCONEX alloy

Types of Magnetic materials

There are three types of magnetic materials:
1. **Ferro-magnetic-materials**
    It has a permeability of 200 to 1000,
    e.g. iron steel etc.

2. **Dia-magnetic-materials**
    It has a permeability of less than 1,
    e.g. antimony, bismuth etc.
3. **Para-magnetic-materials**
    It has a permeability of slightly greater than 1,
    e.g. copper, aluminium etc.

Magnetic Field

It is the space around a magnet in which influence of the magnet can be detected.

Magnetic line of Force

It is an imaginary closed curve which starts from North-pole and terminates at South-pole of the magnet. The curve completes its path through the magnet from South-pole to north-pole.

Direction of Line of Force

A tangent drawn at any point on a line force represents direction of magnetic field acting at that point.

Magnetic Flux

The bunch of magnetic lines of force is called *magnetic flux*. [Magnetic Flux] Its unit is weber.

Magnetic Flux Density

'Magnetic field strength' per unit area is called *magnetic flux density*

$$B = \frac{\phi}{A} \ \text{Wb/m}^3$$

where,   B = magnetic flux density, Wb/m^2
      ϕ = magnetic flux, Weber
      A = area perpendicular to plane, metre^2.

Electromagnet

A soft iron bar when placed inside a direct current carrying coil acts like a magnet and it is called an *electromagnet*.
It is a temporary magnet and its magnetism lasts so long as the current is flowing through its coil.

Characteristics of an Electromagnet

(*i*) It's magnetic field strength can he varied by changing magnitude of current.
(*ii*) Its polarity can be changed by changing direction of the current passed through its coil.
(*iii*) Its magnetic field strength can be made thousand times greater in comparison to a permanent magnet.
(*iv*) In many equipments and machines only electromagnetism is used as a call-bell in houses, offices hotels etc.

Pocketing

It is mass removal of material, within a predetermined boundary by means of NC machining. NC tool path is automatically generated on the system. Machining begins at an inner point of the pocket and continues to the outer boundary in ever-widening machining passes.

EXERCISE – I

1. Mass of an electron in kg equals
   - (a) 9.1×10^{-19}
   - (b) 9.1×10^{-31}
   - (c) 1.6×10^{-19}
   - (b) 1.6×10^{-31}

2. The radius of lowest stationary state in hydrogen atom is
   - (a) 0.529 m
   - (b) 0.529 m
   - (c) 0.529 Angstrom
   - (d) 13.6 Angstrom

3. The total energy of electron in stationary state in hydrogen atom is
   - (a) $\dfrac{13.6}{n} e\mathrm{V}$
   - (b) $\dfrac{-13.6}{n^2} e\mathrm{V}$
   - (c) $\dfrac{13.6}{n^2} e\mathrm{V}$
   - (d) $\dfrac{-13.6}{n^3} e\mathrm{V}$

4. The ground state in the energy level diagram of hydrogen atom is
   - (a) lowest state
   - (b) higher state
   - (c) $n = 2$ state
   - (d) $n = 4$ state

5. The ionization energy of hydrogen atom is
   - (a) $1.36\,e\mathrm{V}$
   - (b) $13.6\,e\mathrm{V}$
   - (c) $1.61\,e\mathrm{V}$
   - (d) $16.1\,e\mathrm{V}$

6. In an atom, an excited electron returns to the original stationary state
   - (a) always in one jump
   - (b) always in two jumps
   - (c) in one or more jumps
   - (d) two or more jumps

7. For photo-excitatio n to take place, the energy of the incident photon must
   - (a) always equal W
   - (b) be less than W
   - (c) always exceed W
   - (d) be twice W

   where W is energy difference between the two stationary states

8. For photo-ionization to take place, the energy of the incident photon must be
   - (a) less than E_i
   - (b) exactly equal to E_i
   - (c) equal to or greater than E_i
   - (d) several times E_i

   where E_i is the ionization energy

9. The relaxation time of an excited electron is of the order of
   - (a) nano-seconds
   - (b) microseconds
   - (c) multiseconds
   - (d) seconds

10. As the distance of an orbiting electron from the nucleus increases, the algebraic value of potential energy of the electron
    - (a) remain unaltered
    - (b) increases
    - (c) decreases
    - (d) may increase or decrease

11. The energy required to liberate an electron from an atom is called
    - (a) kinetic energy
    - (b) potential energy
    - (c) excitation energy
    - (d) ionization energy

12. Electron occupying the ground state is at its
    - (a) lowest energy level
    - (b) highest energy level
    - (c) Fermi level
    - (d) zero total energy level

13. Photon signifies
    - (a) vibration of atoms in the crystal at $0°\mathrm{K}\,°$
    - (b) vibration of atoms in the crystal at any temperature
    - (c) quantum of light energy
    - (d) one foot candle of light

14. As per wave mechanics theory of atom, the principal quantum number n can have
    - (a) one positive integer values
    - (b) only negative integer values
    - (c) both positive and negative integer values
    - (d) integer as well as fractional values

15. As per wave mechanics theory of atom, the angular momentum quantum number 1 can have
    - (a) only positive integer values
    - (b) only negative integer values
    - (c) both positive and negative integer values
    - (d) zero as well as positive integer value

16. As per wave mechanics theory of atom, the magnetic quantum number m_1 can have
    - (a) only positive integer values
    - (b) only negative integer values
    - (c) both positive and negative integer values
    - (d) zero as well as positive and negative integer value

17. The 1st subshell in a solid has per atom vacancy for
    - (a) 1 electron
    - (b) 2 electrons
    - (c) 4 electrons
    - (d) 6 electrons

18. The 2s subshell in a solid has per atom vacancy for
    - (a) 1 electron
    - (b) 2 electrons
    - (c) 4 electrons
    - (d) 6 electrons

19. The 2p subshell in a solid has per atom vacancy for
    - (a) 1 electron
    - (b) 2 electrons
    - (c) 4 electrons
    - (d) 6 electrons

20. The 3p subshell in a solid has per atom vacancy for
    - (a) 1 electron
    - (b) 2 electron
    - (c) 4 electrons
    - (d) 6 electrons

21. The 3d subshell in a solid has per atrom vacancy for
   (a) 2 electron   (b) 4 electrons
   (c) 10 electrons   (d) 14 electrons

22. The 4d subshell in a solid has per atom vacancy for
   (a) 2 electron   (b) 4 electrons
   (c) 10 electrons   (d) 14 electrons

23. The 4f subsell in a solid has per atom vacancy for
   (a) 4 electron   (b) 6 electrons
   (c) 10 electrons   (d) 14 electrons

24. Silicon has valency of
   (a) 2   (b) 3
   (c) 4   (d) 5

25. Germanium has valency of
   (a) 2   (b) 3
   (c) 4   (d) 5

26. For forming p–type germanium, the impurity atoms have valency of
   (a) 3   (b) 4
   (c) 5   (d) 6

27. For forming n-type germanium, the impurity atoms have valency of
   (a) 3   (b) 4
   (c) 5   (d) 6

28. A germanium atom contains
   (a) 2 orbiting electrons (b) two protons
   (c) four valence electrons(d) six valence electrons

29. A silicon atom contains
   (a) 2 valence electrons (b) 2 protons
   (c) 4 valence electrons (d) 6 valence electrons

30. Quantum states with the same energies are said to be
   (a) equal to energy states
   (b) degenerate states
   (c) complementary states
   (d) none of these

31. The valence electrons are
   (a) free electrons
   (b) outer orbit electrons
   (c) inner core electrons
   (d) located in the nucleus

32. In n-type germanium, each donor atom contributes
   (a) one free electron   (b) 2 free electrons
   (c) 3 free electrons   (d) 3 free electrons

33. In n-type silicon, each donor atom contributes
   (a) one free electron   (b) 2 free electrons
   (c) 3 free electrons   (d) 4 free electrons

34. In p-type silicon, each acceptor atom contributes
   (a) one hole   (b) 2 holes
   (c) 3 holes   (d) 4 holes

35. In p-type germanium, each acceptor atom contributes
   (a) one hole   (b) 2 holes
   (c) 3 holes   (d) 4 holes

36. Germanium has atomic numer equal to
   (a) 6   (b) 14
   (c) 32   (d) 44

37. Silicon has atomic number equl to
   (a) 6   (b) 14
   (c) 32   (d) 44

38. The structure of silicon crystal is
   (a) like that of diamond
   (b) like that of NaCl
   (c) like that of cesium chloride
   (d) body centred cubic

39. The structure of germanium crystal is
   (a) like that of diamond
   (b) like that of cesium chloride
   (c) like that of NaCl
   (d) body centred cubic

40. The type of chemical bond in germanium or silicon is
   (a) ionic   (b) valence
   (c) van der Waal   (d) none of these

41. In germanium, the strength of the crystal results from
   (a) forces between nuclei
   (b) forces between electrons and nuclei
   (c) forces between neutrons
   (d) electron pair bonds

42. Plastics and glasses are
   (a) crystalline   (b) liquid
   (c) solid solution   (d) amorphous

43. Crystal structure of most of the common metals is
   (a) hexagonal   (b) cubic
   (c) orthoromic   (d) none of these

44. The primary bonds are
   (a) ionic, metallic and Van der Waal bonds
   (b) ionic, covalent and Van der Waal bonds
   (c) ionic, covalent and metallic bonds
   (d) none of these

45. Molecules with identical composition but different structures are called
 (a) isobars
 (b) isotherms
 (c) isomers
 (d) free radicals

46. Forces responsible for weaker secondary bond arise from
 (a) internal dipoles
 (b) metallic bonds
 (c) activation energy
 (d) covalent bond

47. The Miller indices of the diagonal plane of a cube are
 (a) 1110
 (b) 110
 (c) 101
 (d) 011

48. Atomic packing factors in a crystal is given by
 (a) total volume/atom volume
 (b) atom volume/total volume
 (c) total volume/number of atoms
 (d) number of atoms/total volume

49. Bravais lattice are
 (a) chemical composition of metals
 (b) internal arrangement of atoms
 (c) metals with cavalent bonds
 (d) none of these

50. As the temperature increases, the vibrational frequency of the atoms in a solid
 (a) decreases
 (b) increases
 (c) may increase or decrease
 (d) remains constant

51. The nucleus of an atom consists of
 (a) electrons and protons
 (b) electrons and neutrons
 (c) only protons
 (d) protons and neutrons

52. The nature of crystal binding in germanium is
 (a) ionic
 (b) metallic
 (c) covalent
 (d) Van der Waal type

53. Which of the following will serve as a donor impurity in silicon ?
 (a) Boron
 (b) Indium
 (c) Germanium
 (d) Antimony

54. Which of the following statements is correct?
 (a) Copper has partially filled conduction band.
 (b) Diamond has completely filled conduction band but empty valence band
 (c) silicon has a partially filled conduction band and an empty valence band.
 (d) The energy gap between conduction and valence bands in diamond is smaller than in silicon.

55. Ultra violet radiation is emitted when electron jumps from an outer stationary orbit to
 (a) first stationary orbit
 (b) second stationary orbit
 (c) third stationary orbit
 (d) fourth stationary orbit

56. n-type semiconductors
 (a) are negatively charged
 (b) are produced when indium is added as an impurity to germanium
 (c) are produced when phosphorus is added as an impurity to silicon
 (d) none of these

57. The energy required to change the speed of one electron from rest to 0.6 c is nearly
 (a) 0.085 MeV
 (b) 0.13 MeV
 (c) 0.26 MeV
 (d) 0.37 MeV

58. X-rays are produced by
 1. bombarding metallic targets with high speed electrons
 2. decelerating fast moving electrons
 3. accelerating electrons to high speeds
 4. heating a filament to high temperature
 Codes :
 (a) 1 & 2 only
 (b) 3 and 4 only
 (c) 2 & 3 only
 (d) 1 & 4 only

59. Which of the following is not electromagnetic in nature ?
 1. alpha raya
 2. X-rays
 3. gamma rays
 4. cathode rays
 Codes :
 (a) 1 & 2 rays
 (b) 2 & 3 only
 (c) 3 & 4 only
 (d) 1 & 4 only

60. When a soap bubble is charged
 (a) it contracts
 (b) it expands
 (c) it does not undergo any change in size
 (d) none of these

61. Two close-packed crystal structures are
 (a) bcc and fcc
 (b) fcc and hcp
 (c) bac and hcp
 (d) fcc and sc

62. Electronic configuration of carbon is
 (a) $1s^2\,2s^2$
 (b) $1s^2\,2s^2 2p^6 3s^2$
 (c) $1s^2 2s^2 2p^6$
 (d) $1s^2 2s^2 2p^2$

63. In the Fermi Dirac statistics, the probability of electron occupation of an energy level equal to the fermi level is
 (a) 0
 (b) 0.25
 (c) 0.5
 (d) 1.0

64. The most important primary force of attraction in the formation of solids is

(a) electromagnetic (b) electrostatic

(c) quantum-electronics (d) quantum-magnetic

65. If a sample of germanium and a sample of silicon have the same impurity density and are kept at room temperature

(a) both will have equal value of resistivity

(b) both will have equal negative resistivity

(c) resistivity of germanium will be higher than that of silicon

(d) resistivity of silicon will be higher than that of germanium

66. Semiconductor A has a higher band gap than semiconductor B. If both A and B have the same dimensions, the same number of electrons at a given temperature and the same electron and hole mobilities, then

(a) A has the same number of holes as B

(b) A has larger number of holes than B

(c) A has lesser number of holes than B

(d) any of the above statements at (a), (b) or (c) could be true.

67. Which of the following crystallographic defects contributes to electronic defects ?

(1) Thermal vibration (2) Point defects

(3) Line defects   (4) surface defects

Select the correct answer using the codes given below

Codes

(a) 1, 2 and 3   (b) 2, 3, and 4

(c) 1, 3 and 4   (d) 1, 2 and 4

68. Some of the electrons are injected into the interior of a conductor surrounded by an insulator. The injected electrons will

(a) distribute themselves uniformly

(b) distribute themselves randomly

(c) be confined at the point of injection

(d) travel to the surface of the conductor

69. In a certain temperature range, the electrical conductivity of a semiconductor increases with increase in temperature. This is because

(a) both carrier concentration and mobility of carriers increase with increasing temperature

(b) both carrier concentration and mobility of carriers decrease with increasing temperature

(c) carrier concentration increases substantially but the mobility of carriers decreases with increase of temperature

(d) carrier concentration remains constant but the mobility of carriers increases with increase in temperature.

70. If temperature of an extrinsic semiconductor is increased so that the intrinsic carrier concentration is doubled, then

(a) the majority carrier density doubles

(b) the minority carrier density doubles

(c) the minority carier density becomes times the original value

(d) both majority and minority carrier densities doubles.

71. Kinetic energy of free electrons in a metal is (where K is de Broglie wave number of the electrons)

(a) inversely proportional to K

(b) inversely proportional to square of K

(c) proportional to K

(d) proportional to square of K.

72. At room temperature, the current in an intrinsic semiconductor is due to

(a) holes   (b) electrons

(c) ions   (d) holes and electrons

73. Current through the ionized gas in gas tube

(a) flucturatee   (b) remains constant

(c) assumes infinity (d) assumes zero value

74. *Consider the following statements*:

The energy band gap in Ga As

(1) is indirect

(2) is direct

(3) is 1.43 eV

(4) corresponds to wavelength of 0.89 m

(Given $h = 6.63 \times 10^{34}$ joule-sec.)

Of these statements

(a) 1 alone is correct

(b) 2, 3 and 4 are correct

(b) 2 and 3 are correct

(d) 1 and 4 are correct

75. Consider a singly crystal of an instrinsic semiconductor. The number of free carriers at the Fermi level at room temperature is

(a) half the total number of electrons in the crystal

(b) half the number of free electrons in the crystal.

(c) half the number of atoms in the cystal

(d) zero

76. The effect of doping intrinsic semiconductor is to

(a) move the Fermi level away from the centre of the forbidden band

(b) move the Fermi level twoards the centre of the forbidden band

(c) change the crystal structure of the semiconductor

(d) Keep the Fermi level at the middle of the forbidden band.

77. For a photoconductor with equal electron and hole mobilities and perfect ohmic contacts at the ends, and increase in the intensity of optical illumination results in

(*a*) a change in open circuit voltage

(*b*) a change in short circuit current

(*c*) a reduction of resistance

(*d*) an increase of resistance

78. Consider the following statements about conditions that make a metal-semiconductor rectifying :

(*a*) N-type semiconductor with its work function ϕ_s greater than the work function ϕ_m of the metal

(*b*) N-type semiconductor with its work function ϕ_s smaller than the work function ϕ_m of the metal

(*c*) P-type semiconductor with its work function ϕ_s greater than the work function ϕ_m of the metal

(*d*) P-type semiconductor with its work function ϕ_s smaller than the work function ϕ_m of the metal

Of these statements

(1) 1 and 3 are correct

(2) 2 and 3 are correct

(3) 1 and 4 are correct

(4) 2 and 4 are correct

79. Silicon is not suitable for fabrication of light emitting diodes because it is

(*a*) an indirect band gap semiconductor

(*b*) a direct band gap semiconductor

(*c*) a wide band gap semiconductor

(*d*) a narrow band gap semiconductor

80. *Consider the following statements:*

Compared to silicon, gallium arsenide (Ga As) has

(1) higher signal speed since electron mobility is higher

(2) poorer crystal quality since stoichiometric growth is difficult

(3) easier to grow crystals since vapour pressure of arsenic is high

(4) higher optoelectronic conversion efficiency

Of these statements

(*a*) 1, 2, 3 and 4 are correct

(*b*) 1, 2 and 3 are correct

(*c*) 3 and 4 are correct

(*d*) 1, 2 and 4 are correct.

81. When a solid crystal of sodium is formed, the 3s bond will have

(*a*) half as many states as the number of atoms

(*b*) same number of states as there are atoms

(*c*) twice as many states as there are atoms

(*d*) no states at all

82. The relaxation time (τ) in a perfect dielectric is

(*a*) 0   (*b*) 1

(*c*) $1 < \tau < \infty$ (*d*) ∞

83. Germanium and silicon photosensors have their maximum spectral response in the

(*a*) infra-red region   (*b*) ultraviolet region

(*c*) visible region   (*d*) X-ray region

84. The allowed encrgics for the electrosystem of an atom are determined using

(*a*) Einstein's theory of relativity

(*b*) Planck's theory

(*c*) Schrodinger's equation

(*d*) Pauli exclusion principle

85. Atual field seen by an atom in a dielectric is

(*a*) lower than the applied field

(*b*) higher than the applied field

(*c*) equal to the applied field

(*d*) higher or lower depending upon the particular solid

86. Which variety of copper has the best conductivity?

(*a*) Pure annealed copper

(*b*) Hard drawn copper

(*c*) Induction hardened copper

(*d*) Copper containing traces of silicon

87. Which variety of copper has the best mechanical strength ?

(*a*) Annealed copper   (*b*) Hard drawn copper

(*c*) Cast copper   (*d*) soft coppper.

88. Which of the following materials has negative resistance temperature coefficient ?

(*a*) Tungsten   (*b*) Steel

(*c*) Tin   (*d*) Carbon

89. Constantan contains

(*a*) copper and nickel

(*b*) copper and tungsten

(*c*) tungsten and silver

(*d*) silver and tin

90. Nichrome is an alloy of

(*a*) Silver, copper and nickel

(*b*) Aluminium, tin and copper

(*c*) Nickel, chromium and iron

(*d*) Chromium, manganese and copper

91. If a body having identical properties all over, is called

(*a*) Homogeneous   (*b*) Isotropic

(*c*) Elastic   (*d*) Isotropic

92. Materials which undergo recoverable deformation and exhibit rubber-like elasticity are called
(a) Rubber
(b) Elastomers
(c) Creep-elastic
(d) Elasto-plastic

93. Materials which exhibit the same elastic properties in all directions are called
(a) isentropic
(b) isotropic
(c) inelastic
(d) visco elastic

94. Which of the following is the heaviest?
(a) Molecule
(b) Atom
(c) Electrons
(d) Proton

95. Material whcih has zero temperature coefficient of resistance is
(a) manganin
(b) porcelain
(c) carbon
(d) aluminium

96. Dielectric constant for vacuum is
(a) infinity
(b) 100
(c) 1
(d) zero

97. Dielectric strength of which of the following material is the highest ?
(a) Porcelain
(b) Soft rubber
(c) Glass
(d) Polystyrene

98. Which material can be used at temperatures above 100°C ?
(a) Polythene
(b) Teflon
(c) Rubber
(d) Paraffin wax

99. Materials having a high dielectric constant, which is non-linear, are
(a) ferroelectric materials
(b) elastomers
(c) super-dielectrics
(d) hard dielectrics

100. Temperature beyond which substances lose their ferroelectric properties, is called
(a) critical temperature
(b) curie temperature
(c) inversion temperature
(d) conversion temperature

101. Which of the following is the ferroelectric material?
(a) Rochelle salt
(b) Postassium dihydrogen phosphate
(c) Barium titanate
(d) All of these

102. Curie point for Rohelle salt is about
(a) 1000°C
(b) 250°C
(c) 240°C
(d) absolute zero

103. Materials which lack permanent magnetic dipoles are called
(a) diamagnetic
(b) ferromagnetic
(c) semi-magnetic
(d) none of these

104. Germanium has
(a) ionic bond
(b) coralent band
(c) semi-magnetic
(d) none of these

105. Most commonly used materials as photo cathode tor the photoelectric commission are
(a) Barium and Calcium
(b) Cesium and Rubidium
(c) Arsenic and Boron
(d) Thorium and Tungston

EXERCISE – II

1. A Hall effect transducer can be used to measure
DMRC 2014
(a) displacement, temperature and magnetic flux
(b) displacement, position and velocity
(c) position, magnetic flux and pressure
(d) displacement, position and magnetic flux

2. Quantum effects have to be taken into account in determining the properties of materials if
DMRC 2014
(a) $E_F = \dfrac{3}{2}KT$
(b) $E_F < \dfrac{3}{2}KT$
(c) $E_F > \dfrac{3}{2}KT$
(d) $E_F >> \dfrac{3}{2}KT$

3. The Ohm's law for conduction in metals is
(a) $J = \sigma E$
(b) $J = \dfrac{E}{\sigma}$ **DMRC 2014**
(c) $J \propto \sigma E$
(d) $J \propto \dfrac{E}{\sigma}$

4. In Ge, when atoms are held together by the sharing of valence electrons **DRDO**
(a) each shared atom leaves a hole
(b) valence electrons are free to move away from the nucleus
(c) velence electrons form irreversible covalent bands
(d) valence electrons form reversible covalent bands

5. When a pure semiconductor is heated **DRDO**

(a) its resistance increases

(b) its resistance decreases

(c) its atomic structure changes

(d) it becomes metal

6. When germanium is doped with pentavalent impurity, the resulting material is **DRDO**

(a) p-type semiconductor

(b) n-type semiconductor

(c) intrinsic semiconductor

(d) no longer a semiconductor

7. Drift current in germanium is caused by **DRDO**

(a) thermal agitation of crystal lattice

(b) concentration gradient of charge carriers

(c) applied electric field

(d) incidence of light

8. Ge diode at room temperature for forward current of 26 mA has dynamic resistance of about

(a) $0.1\ \Omega$　　　　(b) $1\ \Omega$　　**DRDO**

(c) $10\ \Omega$　　　　(d) $1000\ \Omega$

9. In a BJT, as the conductivity of the base region increases, the punch through voltage **DRDO**

(a) remains unaltered

(b) increases

(c) decreases

(d) may increase or decrease depending on bias at J_E

10. In a transistor, current I_{CBO} **DRDO**

(a) increase with increase of temperature

(b) decrease with increase of temperature

(c) is normally greater for Si transistor than Ge transistor

(d) mainly depends on the emitter base junction bias

11. Some of the electrons are injected into the interior of a conductor surrounded by an insulator. The injected electrons will **DRDO**

(a) distribute themselves uniformly

(b) distribute themselves randomly

(c) be confined at the point of injection

(d) travel to the surface of the conductor

12. Materials which undergo recoverable deformation and exhibit rubber-like elasticity are called

(a) Rubber　　　　(b) Elastomers **DRDO**

(c) Creep-elastic　　(d) Elasto-plastic

13. Temperature beyond which substances lose their ferroelectric properties, is called **DRDO**

(a) critical temperature

(b) curie temperature

(c) inversion temperature

(d) conversion temperature

14. A hole is the vacancy created when **DRDO**

(a) a free electron moves on application of electric field

(b) an electron breaks its covalent band

(c) an atomic core moves

(d) an electron reverts from conduction band to valence band

15. In n-type silicon, each donor atom contributes

RRB

(a) one free electron　　(b) 2 free electrons

(c) 3 free electrons　　(d) 4 free electrons

16. Which of the following will serve as a donor impurity in silicon ? **RRB**

(a) Boron　　　　(b) Indium

(c) Germanium　　(d) Antimony

17. A 300°K, the forbidden energy gap in silicon is

(a) 0.785 eV　　　　(b) 1.21 eV　**RRB**

(c) 0.72 eV　　　　(d) 1.1 eV

18. Maximum value of temperature coefficient of Vz in a breakdown diode is **RRB**

(a) ±0.1 per cent/deg C

(b) ±0.5 per cent/deg C

(c) +0.2 per cent/deg C

(d) – 0.2 per cent/deg C

19. The energy required to liberate an electron from an atom is called **RRB**

(a) kinetic energy　　(b) potential energy

(c) excitation energy　(d) ionization energy

20. In n-type germanium, each donor atom contributes

RRB

(a) one free electron　　(b) 2 free electrons

(c) 3 free electrons　　(d) 4 free electrons

21. Bravais lattice are **RRB**

(a) chemical composition of metals

(b) internal arrangement of atoms

(c) metals with cavalent bonds

(d) none of these

22. Electronic configuration of carbon is **RRB**

(a) $1s^2\,2s^2$　　　　(b) $1s^2\,2s^2 2p^6 3s^2$

(c) $1s^2 2s^2 2p^6$　　(d) $1s^2 2s^2 2p^2$

23. Kinetic energy of free electrons in a metal is (where K is de Broglie wave number of the electrons) **RRB**

(a) inversely proportional to K

(b) inversely proportional to square of K

(c) proportional to K

(d) proportional to square of K.

24. Curie point for Rohelle salt is about **RRB**

(a) 1000°C

(b) 250°C

(c) 240°C

(d) absolute zero

ANSWERS

EXERCISE – I

1. (b)	**2.** (c)	**3.** (b)	**4.** (b)	**5.** (b)	**6.** (c)	**7.** (a)	**8.** (c)	**9.** (b)	**10.** (b)
11. (d)	**12.** (b)	**13.** (c)	**14.** (a)	**15.** (d)	**16.** (d)	**17.** (b)	**18.** (b)	**19.** (d)	**20.** (d)
21. (c)	**22.** (c)	**23.** (d)	**24.** (c)	**25.** (c)	**26.** (a)	**27.** (c)	**28.** (c)	**29.** (b)	**30.** (b)
31. (a)	**32.** (a)	**33.** (a)	**34.** (a)	**35.** (a)	**36.** (c)	**37.** (b)	**38.** (a)	**39.** (a)	**40.** (b)
41. (d)	**42.** (d)	**43.** (b)	**44.** (c)	**45.** (c)	**46.** (a)	**47.** (b)	**48.** (b)	**49.** (b)	**50.** (d)
51. (d)	**52.** (c)	**53.** (d)	**54.** (a)	**55.** (a)	**56.** (c)	**57.** (b)	**58.** (a)	**59.** (d)	**60.** (a)
61. (b)	**62.** (d)	**63.** (c)	**64.** (b)	**65.** (d)	**66.** (b)	**67.** (a)	**68.** (d)	**69.** (c)	**70.** (d)
71. (b)	**72.** (d)	**73.** (c)	**74.** (c)	**75.** (b)	**76.** (a)	**77.** (c)	**78.** (a)	**79.** (b)	**80.** (c)
81. (a)	**82.** (a)	**83.** (c)	**84.** (b)	**85.** (d)	**86.** (a)	**87.** (b)	**88.** (d)	**89.** (a)	**90.** (c)
91. (a)	**92.** (b)	**93.** (b)	**94.** (d)	**95.** (a)	**96.** (c)	**97.** (d)	**98.** (b)	**99.** (a)	**100.** (b)
101. (d)	**102.** (c)	**103.** (a)	**104.** (b)	**105.** (c)					

EXERCISE – II

1. (a)	**2.** (d)	**3.** (c)	**4.** (d)	**5.** (b)	**6.** (b)	**7.** (c)	**8.** (a)	**9.** (b)	**10.** (c)
11. (d)	**12.** (a)	**13.** (b)	**14.** (b)	**15.** (a)	**16.** (d)	**17.** (d)	**18.** (a)	**19.** (d)	**20.** (a)
21. (b)	**22.** (d)	**23.** (b)	**24.** (c)						

Control Systems

SYSTEM

A system is a combination or an arrangement of different physical components which act together as an entire unit to achieve certain objective.

Control system.

Control system is an interconnection of the physical components to provide a desired function, involving some kind of controlling action in it.

Controller.

The element of the system which controls the plant or the process is called **controller.**

TIME VARYING AND TIME-INVARIANT SYSTEM

(*i*) **Time varying control systems :** In this system parameters of the systems are varying with time. It is independent of whether input and output are functions of time or not.

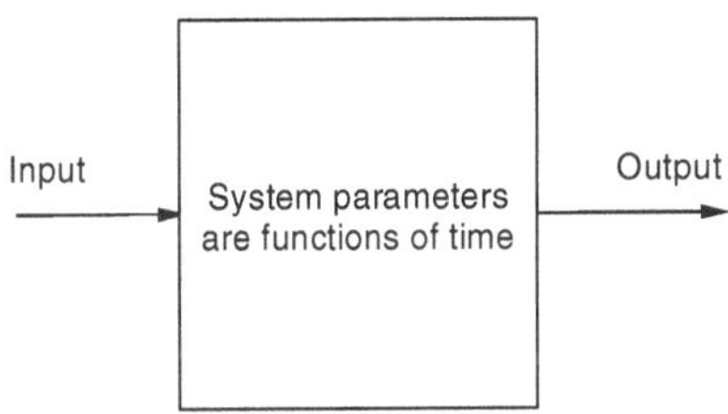

(*ii*) **Time invariant system :** In this system if even though the inputs and outputs are functions of time but the parameters of system are independent of time, which are not varying with time and are constants.

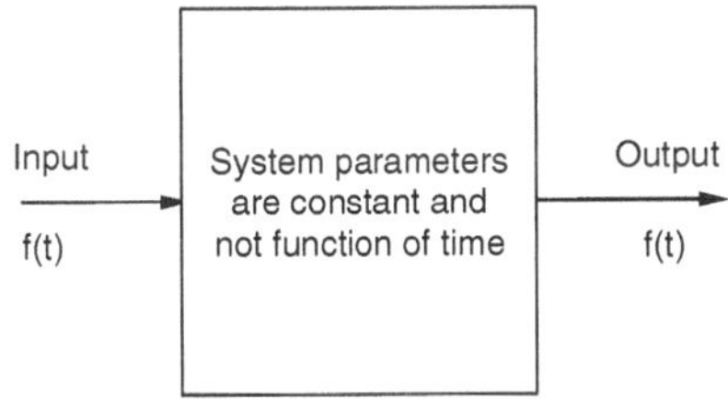

Linear systems.

A system is said to be linear, if superposition principle applies to it.

Linear system must satisfies following two properties:

(*i*) $f(x + y) = f(x) + f(y)$

(*ii*) $f(\alpha x) = \alpha \cdot f(x)$

Servomechanism.

It is a feedback control system in which the output is mechanical position, velocity or acceleration.

OPEN AND CLOSED LOOP SYSTEMS

1. **Open loop system :** A system in which output is dependent on input but controlling action or input is totally independent of the output or changes in output of the system, is called an *open loop system.*

   In these output has no effect upon the control action.

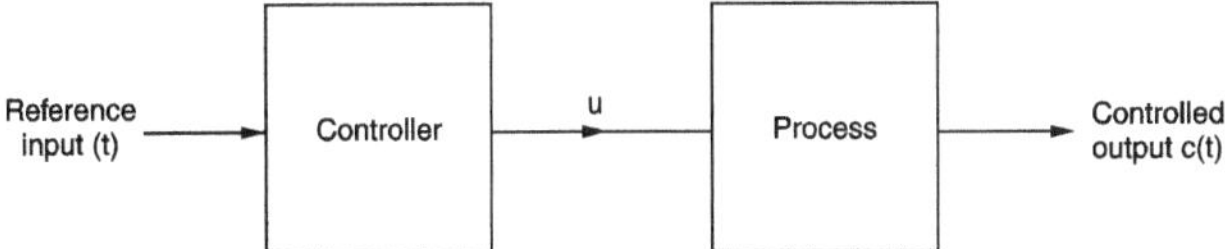

Advantages :

(**i**) Such systems are simple to design and hence economical.

(**ii**) Very much convenient when output is difficult to measure.

(**iii**) Easy from maintenance point of view.

(**iv**) Generally these are not troubled with the problems of stability.

Disadvantages :

(**i**) Inaccurate and unreliable.

(**ii**) Such system cannot sense environmental changes.

(**iii**) To maintain the quality and accuracy, recalibration of the controller is necessary time to time.

2. **Closed loop system :** A system in which controlling action or input is somehow dependent on the output or changes in output is called a *closed loop system.*

   In these output signal has direct effect upon the control action.

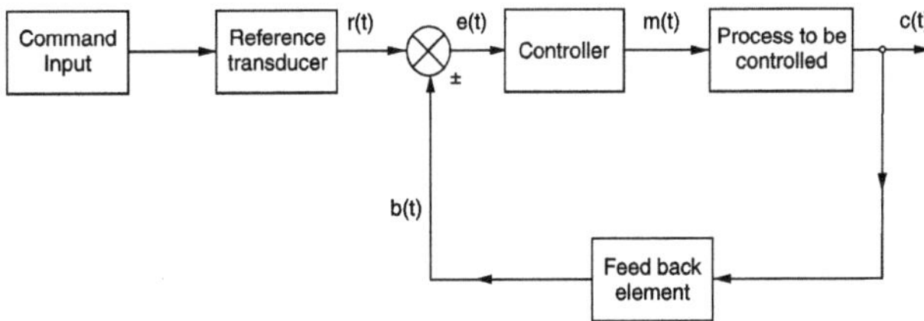

$r(t) \rightarrow$ Reference *input*,

$c(t) \rightarrow$ Controlled *output*,

$e(t) \rightarrow$ Error signal,

$m(t) \rightarrow$ Manipulated signal,

$b(t) \rightarrow$ Feedback signal

Advantages :

(*i*) Accuracy of such system is always very high.

(*ii*) In closed loop system, there is reduced effect of nonlinearities and distortions.

(*iii*) Such system senses environmental changes.

(*iv*) Band width of such system, i.e. operating frequency zone for such system is very high.

Disadvantages :

(*i*) Such systems are complicated and time consuming from design point of view and hence costlier.

(*ii*) Due to feedback, system tries to correct the error time to time. Tendency to overcorrect the error may cause oscillations without bound in the system.

Comparison of Open loop and Closed loop control systems.

Open loop systems		Closed loop systems	
(*i*)	Any change in output has no effect on the input	(*i*)	Changes in output, affects the input
(*ii*)	Output measurement is not required for operation of system	(*ii*)	Output measurement is necessary
(*iii*)	Feed back element is absent	(*iii*)	Feedback element is present
(*iv*)	Error detector is absent	(*iv*)	Error detector is necessary
(*v*)	It is inaccurate and unreliable	(*v*)	Highly accurate and reliable
(*vi*)	Highly sensitive to the disturbances	(*vi*)	Less sensitive to the disturbances
(*vii*)	Highly sensitive to the environmental changes	(*vii*)	Less sensitive to the environmantal changes
(*viii*)	Bandwidth is small	(*viii*)	Bandwidth is large
(*ix*)	Generally are stable in nature	(*ix*)	Stability is the major consideration while designing
(*x*)	Simple to construct and cheap	(*x*)	Complicated to design and hence costly
(*xi*)	Highly affected by non-linearities	(*xi*)	Reduced effect of non-linearities

FEEDBACK SYSTEM

Feedback is a property of closed loop system. Feedback permits the output to be compared with the input to the system, so that the appropriate control action may be formed as some function of the output and input.

Advantages and Disadvantages :

(*i*) Increased accuracy

(*ii*) Reduced sensitivity

(*iii*) Reduced effects of non-linearities and distortion

(*iv*) Increased bandwidth

(*v*) Tendency towards oscillation or instability.

Feedback characteristics.

One of the primary purpose of using feedback in control system is to reduce the sensitivity of the system to parameter variations.

The sensitivity of closed loop system with respect to variation in G is reduced by a factor $(1 + GH)$ as compared to that of open loop system.

TRANSFER FUNCTION

It is defined as the ratio of Laplace transform of output (reponse) of the system to Laplace transform of input (excitation or driving function), under the assumption that all initial conditions are zero.

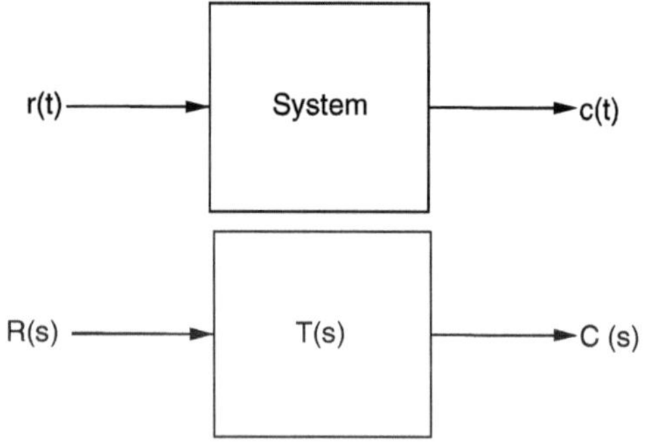

$C(s) \rightarrow$ Laplace of $c(t)$, $R(s) \rightarrow$ Laplace of $r(t)$

If $T(s)$ is the transfer function of the system, then

$$T(s) = \frac{\text{Laplace transform of output}}{\text{Laplace transform of input}} = \frac{C(s)}{R(s)}$$

Properties of transfer function

(*i*) Transfer function of a system is the Laplace transform of its impulse response, i.e. if input to a system with transfer function P(s) is an impulse and all initial values are zero, then transform of the output is P(s).

(*ii*) The system transfer function can be determined from the system differential equation by taking the Laplace transform and ignoring all terms, arising from initial values. The transfer function P(s) is then given by

$$P(s) = \frac{Y(s)}{X(s)}$$

(*iii*) The system differential equation can be obtained from the transfer function by replacing s variable with the differential operator D defined as

$$D = \frac{d}{dt}.$$

(*iv*) Stability of a time-invarient linear system can be determined from the characteristic equation. Denominator of the system transfer function set equal to zero is the characteristic equation. Consequently if all the roots of the denominator have negative real parts, the system is stable.

(*v*) Roots of the denominator are the system poles and roots of the numerator are the system zeros. The system transfer function can then be specified to within a constant by specifying the system poles and zeros. This constant usually denoted by 'K' is the **system gain factor.**

Poles of a Transfer function.

The values of 's' which make the transfer function infinite after substituting in the denominator of a transfer function are called *poles of that transfer function.*

So, values of s_1, s_2, s_3....s_n are called *poles of the transfer function.*

Zeros of a Transfer function.

The values of 's' which make the transfer function zero after substituting in the numerator are called *zeros of that transfer function.*

So, values of s_a, s_b ...s_m are called *zero of the transfer function.*

- Poles and zeros may be real or complex - conjugates or combination of both types.
- Poles and zeros may be located at the origin is s-plane.

BLOCK DIAGRAM REPRESENTATION

Block diagram is a pictorial representation of the given system. It is a very simple way of representing the given complicated practical system.

It explains the cause and effect relationship existing between input and output of the system, through the blocks.

To draw block diagram of a practical system, each element of practical system is represented by a block. Each block (which is called *functional block*) explains mathematical operation on the input by the element to produce the corresponding output. The actual mathematical function is indicated by inserting corresponding transfer function of the element inside the block.

For a closed loop systems, the function of comparing different signals is indicated by the summing point while a point from which signal is taken for the feedback purpose is indicated by take off point in block diagrams.

Steps to use block diagram reduction rule :

(*i*) Reduce series blocks

(*ii*) Reduce parallel blocks

(*iii*) Reduce minor feedback loops

(*iv*) Shift summing point to the left and take off point to the right as far as possible

(*v*) Repeat steps (*i*) to (*iv*) till canonical form is obtained

Block diagram reduction rules

1.	Associative Law	The two or more summing points directly connected can be interchanged.	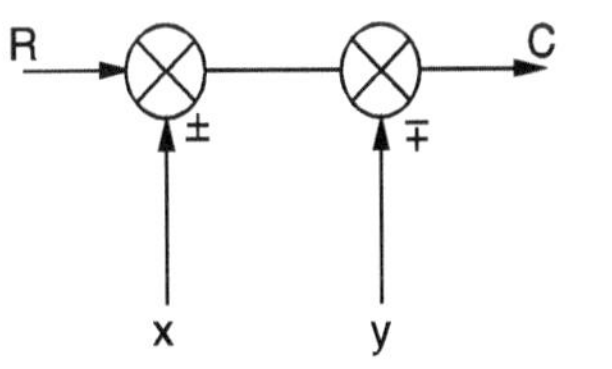 R ± ∓ C x y	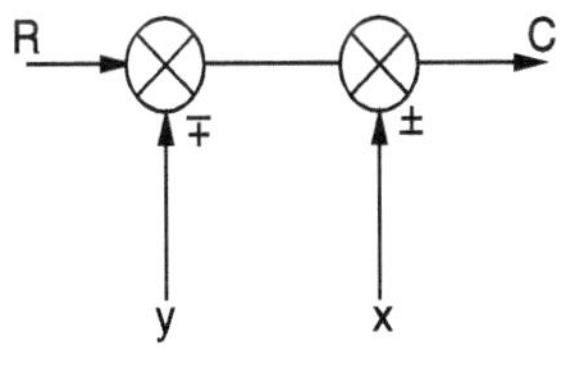 R ∓ ± C y x
2.	Blocks in Series	Transfer function of such blocks get multiplied.	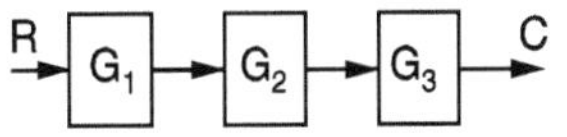 R G_1 → G_2 → G_3 C	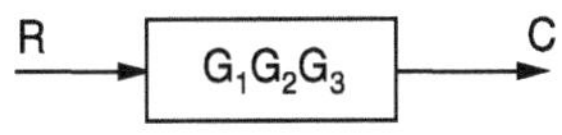 R $G_1 G_2 G_3$ C

3.	Blocks in Parallel	Transfer function of such blocks get added algebrically.	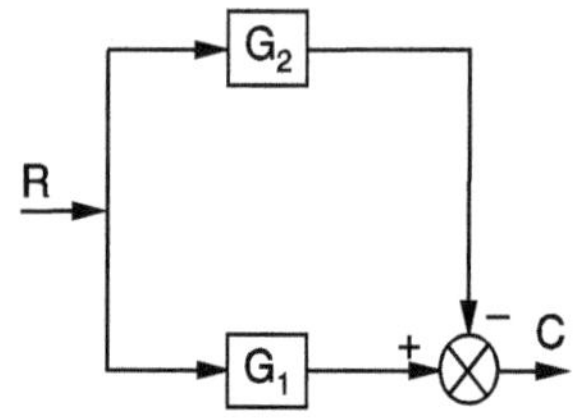	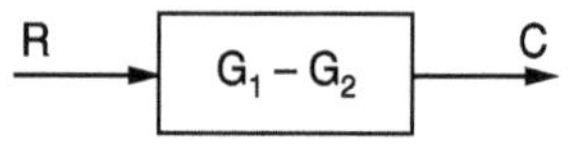
4.	Shifting summing point behind the block	Add a block of transfer function equal to recipro-cal of block behind which summing point is to be shifted in series with all signals at that summing	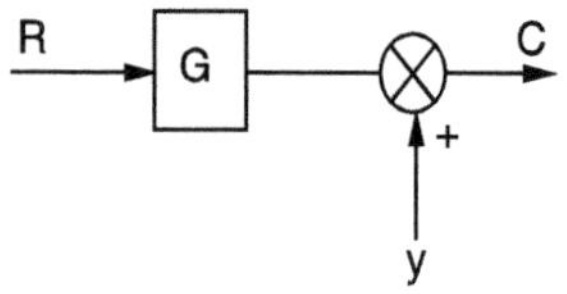	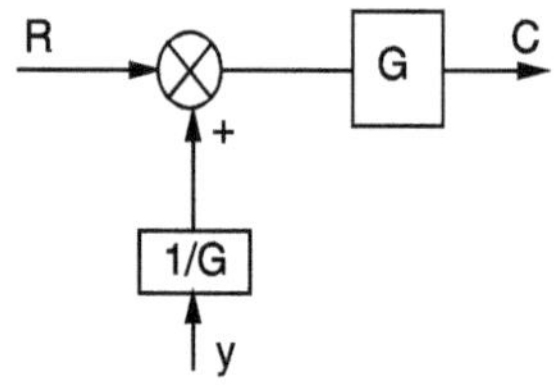
5.	Shifting summing beyond the block	Add a block of transfer function same as the block beyond which summing point is to be shifted in series with all signals at that summing point.	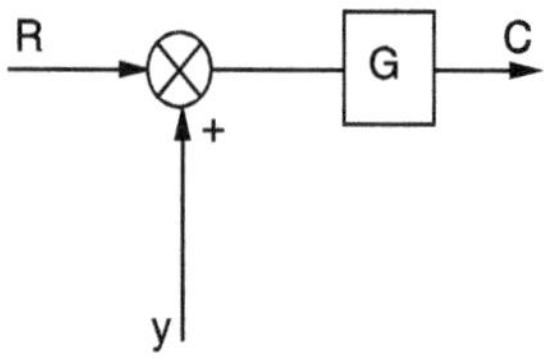	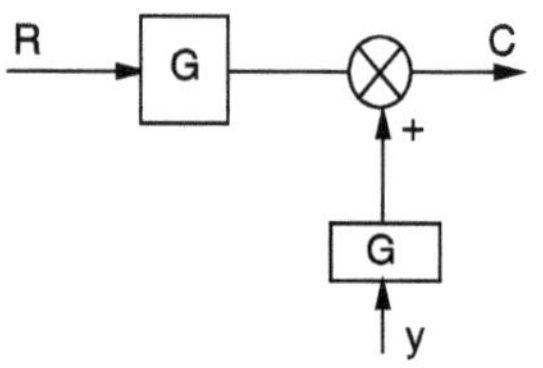
6.	Shifting a take off behind the block	Add a block of transfer function equal to the block behind which take off point is to be shifted in series will all the signals at that take off point.	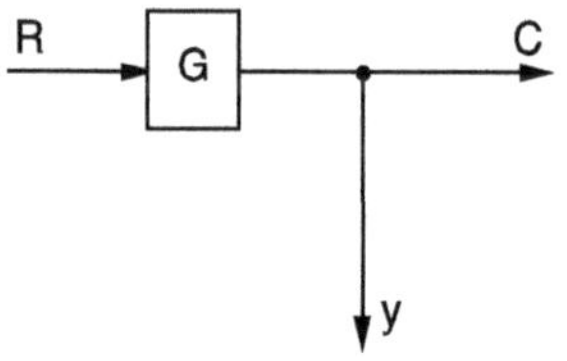	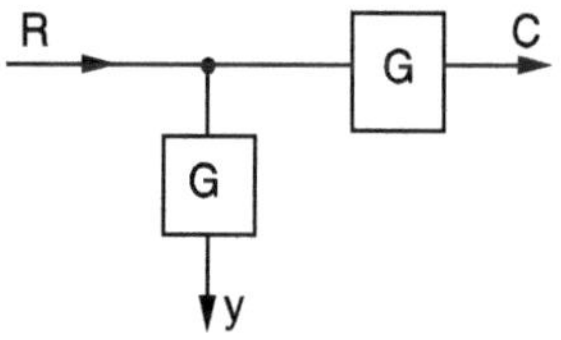
7.	Shifting a take off beyond the block	Add a block of transfer function equal to recipro-cal of block beyond which take off point is to be shifted in series with all signals at that take off point.	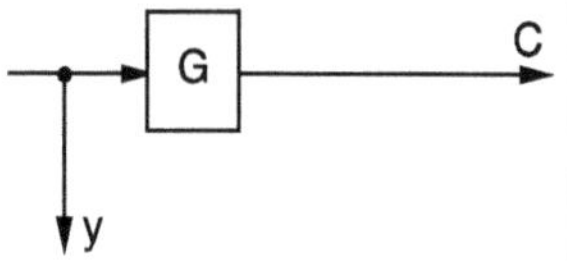	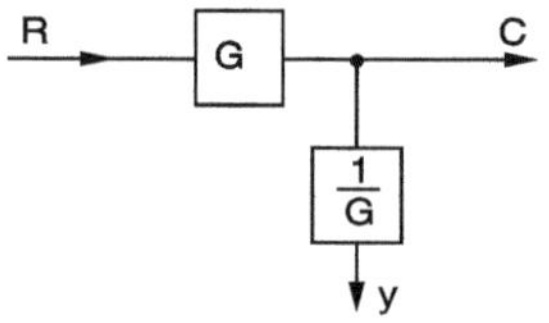
8.	Removing minor feedback loop	Use the standard transfer function of a simple closed loop system.	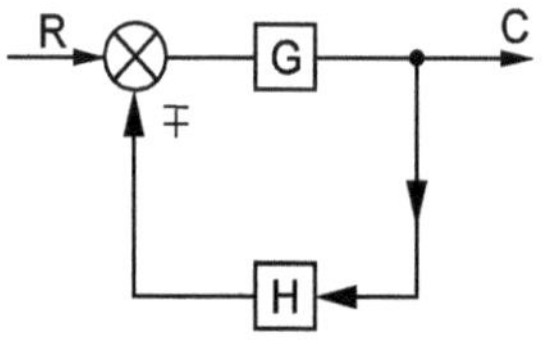	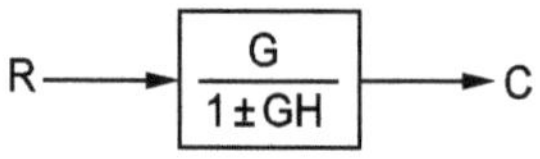
9.	Shifting take off point after summing point	Add a new summing point to compensate for the shift as shown	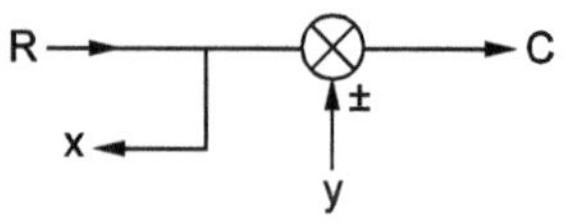	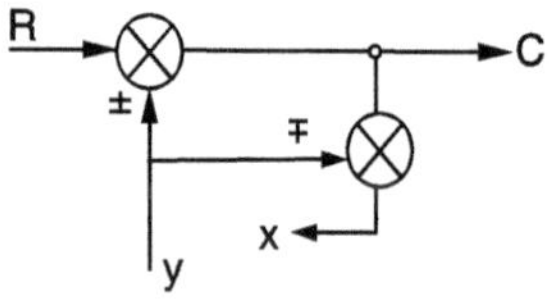
10.	Shifting a take off point before a summing point	Add a summing point to compensate for a shift of take off point.	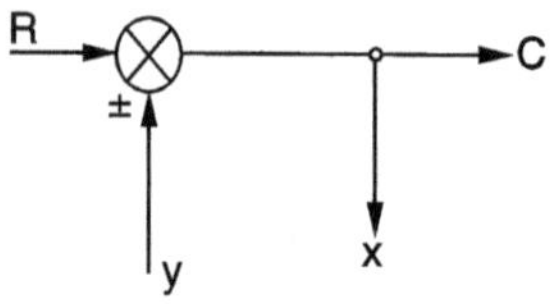	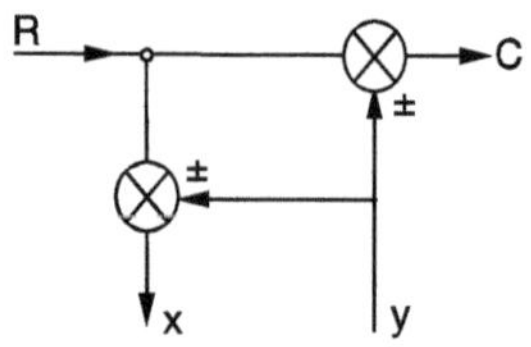

TIME RESPONSE ANALYSIS

First order system tracks the unit step input with zero steady state error.

Time response of second order system.

(*i*) As ξ increases, the response becomes progressively less oscillatory till it becomes critically damped ($\xi = 1$).

(*ii*) Critically damped means just non-oscillatory.

(*iii*) The response becomes over damped for $\xi > 1$.

In short, we can summarize above as

$$\xi = 0 \qquad \Rightarrow \text{ oscillatory system}$$
$$0 < \xi < 1 \quad \Rightarrow \text{ under damped system}$$
$$\xi = 1 \qquad \Rightarrow \text{ critically damped system}$$
$$\xi > 1 \qquad \Rightarrow \text{ over damped system}$$

Time response specification of second order system.

Delay time (t_d) : It is the time required for the response to reach the half the final value.

Rise time (t_r) : It is the time required for the response to rise from 10 to 90% of its final value.

Peak time (t_p) : It is the time required for the response to reach the first peak of the over shoot.

Maxmum overshoot (M_p) : It is the maximum value of the response curve measured from unity.

Overshoot : It is the maximum difference between the transient and steady state solutions for a unit-step function input. It is a measure of relative stability and is represented as percentage of final value of the output.

Settling time t_s : It is defined as the time required for the response to unit-step function input to reach and remain within, a specified percentage of its final value.

Steady state error : Steady state error for various type of inputs and for various type of system is shown in the following table :

Type of impact	Steady State errors		
	Type - 0	Type - 1	Type - 2
Unit step	$\dfrac{1}{1 + k_p}$	0	0
Unit - ramp	∞	$\dfrac{1}{k_v}$	0
Unit - parabolic	∞	∞	$\dfrac{1}{k_a}$

Here, k_p = position error constant = $\lim\limits_{S \to 0} G(s)$

k_v = velocity error constant = $\lim\limits_{S \to 0} sG(s)$

k_a = acceleration error constant = $\lim\limits_{S \to 0} s^2 G(s)$

STABILITY ANALYSIS

Stability of a system means that small changes in the system input, in initial conditions or in system parameters do not result in large change in system output.

For a linear time invariant system to be stable following two notions of system stability are to be satisfied.

(*i*) When the system is excited by a bounded input, the output is bounded.

(*ii*) In the absence of input , output tends towards zero (equilibrium state of the system), irrespective of initial conditions.

CONDITIONS FOR STABILITY.

Necessary but not sufficient system is that all the coefficient of its characteristic equation be real and have the same sign and none of the coefficient should be zero, *i.e.* for the system to be stable, all the roots should have negative real part *i.e.* all roots are in the left half of s-plane.

First step in analysing the stability of the system is to examine its characteristic equation. If some coefficient are negative or zero, then it can be concluded that the system is not stable.

Stable system.

A linear time invariant system is said to be stable if :

(*i*) system is excited by a bounded input output is also bounded and controllable.

(*ii*) in the absence of the input, output must tend to zero irrespective of the initial conditions.

Unstable system.

A linear time invariant system is said to be unstable if

(*i*) for a bounded input it produces undounded output.

(*ii*) in the absence of input, output may not be returning to zero.

Critically or Marginally stable system.

A linear time invariant system is said to be critically or marginally stable if for a bounded input its output oscillates with constant frequency and amplitude, such oscillations of output are called *undamped oscillations* or *sustained oscillations*.

STABILITY IN FREQUENCY DOMAIN

Nyquist Stability Criterion .

Nyquist plots. The Nyquist method handles systems with time delay without the necessity of approximations and hance yields exact results about both absolute and relative stability of the system.

Polar plot. It is the locus of tips of the phasors of various magnitudes plotted at the corresponding phase angles for different values of frequencies from 0 to ∞.

Nyquist Plot Analysis.

Pole – zero configuration :

Consider closed loop transfer function

$$\frac{C(s)}{R(s)} \text{ as } \frac{C(s)}{R(s)} = \frac{G(s)}{1 + G(s)H(s)}$$

- Poles of $1 + G(s)\,H(s)$ = Open loop poles of a system
- Zeros of $1 + G(s)\,H(s)$ = Closed loop poles of a system

From Nyquist point of view, the system is absolutely stable if all the zeros of $1 + G(s)\,H(s)$,

i.e. closed loop poles of the system are located in the left half of s plane.

Encirclement :

A point is said to be encircled by a closed path, if it is found to lie inside that closed path.

Analytic function and Singularities.

A function is said to be analytic at a point in a plane if its value and its derivative has finite existence at that point.

If at a point in a plane, the value of function or its derivative is infinite, the function is said to be non analytic at that point and such a point is called *singularity of the function*.

Mapping theorem.

For a closed - loop system to be stable, the Nyquist plot of $G(s)\,H(s)$ must encircle the point $-1 + j0$ as many times as the number of poles of $G(s)\,H(s)$ that are in the right half of s plane.

Equation generally used is, $\qquad N = P - Z$

where, $\quad N$ = number of encirclement of point $-1 + j0$

$\qquad P$ = number of poles of $G(s)\,H(s)$ that are on the right half of s-plane

$\qquad Z$ = number of zeros of $G(s)\,H(s)$

For stabiity of closed-loop, Z should be zero

i.e. $\qquad N = P$

HURWITZ CRITERION

The necessary and sufficient condition to have all roots of characteristic equation in left half of s-plane is that, the sub-determinants, D_K, $K = 1, 2 \dots n$ obtained from Hurwitz's determinant 'H' must all be positive.

ROUTH STABILITY CRITERION

This criterion is based on the ordering the coefficients of characteristic equation into an array, called *Routh array*.

In the process of generating the Routh array, missing terms are regarded as zero. Also all the elements of any row can be divided by a positive constant to simplify the computational work.

For the system to be stable each term in first column should be positive.

Number of sign change of first column corresponds to the number of roots of the characteristic equation in the right half of the s-plane.

ROUTH'S CRITERION

The necessary and sufficient condition for system to be stable is

"All the terms in the first column of Routh's array must have same sign. There should not be any sign change in first column of Routh's array."

If there are any sign changes existing, then

(**i**) system is unstable.

(**ii**) the numbers of sign changes equals the number of roots lying in the right half of the s-plane.

ROOT LOCUS

A plot of the points in the complex plane satisfying the angle criterion is the root locus.

(**i**) The root locus is symmetrical about the real axis (τ-axis).

(**ii**) As k increases from zero to infinity, each branch of the root locus originates from an open-loop pole with $k = 0$ and terminate either on an open loop zero or at an infinity with $k = \infty$.

(**iii**) A point on the real axis lies on the locus if the number of open loop poles plus zero on the real axis to the right of this point is odd.

(**iv**) $(n - m)$ branches (where n = number of poles and m = number of zeros) of root locus which tend to infinity do so along straight line asymptotes, whose angles are given by

$$\phi_A = \frac{(2q + 1)180°}{n - m}; q = 0, 1, 2 \ \dots (n - m - 1)$$

(**v**) The asymptote cross the real axis at a point known as centroid.

(**vi**) Break away points on the root locus are the solution of $\dfrac{dk}{ds} = 0$.

(*a*) If all the roots of the characteristic equation have negative real parts, the system is stable

(*b*) If any root of the characteristic equation has a positive real parts or if there is a repeated root on the $j\omega$-axis, the system is unstable

(*c*) If the condition (a) is satisfied except for the presence of one or more nonrepeated roots on the $j\omega$-axis, the system is marginally stable

Root locus method : In this roots of the characteristic equation are plotted for all values of a system parameter.

For frequency response, there are three commonly used repres sentations of sinusoidal transfer functions.

(*a*) Bode plot or logarithmic plot

(*b*) Polar plot

(*c*) Phase plot or log-magnitude plot

Relation between location of roots of the characteristic equation and open loop frequency response can be studied by Nyquist stability criterion.

The relation between constant M and N circles to log-magnitude and phase angle is called *Nicholas chart*.

FREQUENCY RESPONSE ANALYSIS

Consider a linear system with a sinusoidal input,

$$r(t) = A \text{ Sin } \omega t$$

Under steady state, the system output as well as the signals at all other points in the system are sinusoidal. The steady state output may be written as

$$C(t) = B \text{ Sin } (\omega t + \phi)$$

The magnitude and phase relationship between the sinusoidal input and the steady state % of a system is termed as the frequency response.

Cut-off Frequency.

The frequency at which M has a value of $\dfrac{1}{\sqrt{2}}$ is of special significance and is called *cutoff frequency*, ω_c.

Polar Plot.

The sinusoidal transfer function $G(j\omega)$ is a complex function and is given by

$$G(j\omega) = Re[G(j\omega)] + jI_m[G(j\omega)]$$

or

$$G(j\omega) = [G(j\omega)] < G(j\omega)$$

$$= M\angle\phi$$

Here ϕ is measured in counter clockwise direction. As ω is varied from 0 to ∞, the magnitude M and phase angle ϕ change and hence tip of the phasor $G(\tau w)$ traces a locus in complex plane. The locus thus obtained is called *polar plot*.

Bode Plot.

The transfer function can be represented on a logarithmic plot which consists of two graphs, one giving the logarithmic of $|G(j\omega)|$ and the other phase angle of $G(j\omega)$ both plotted against frequency in logarithmic scale.

$$G(j\omega) = |G(j\omega)| e^{j\phi\omega}$$

$$ln \ G(j\omega) = ln \ |G(j\omega)| + j\phi\omega$$

The real part is the natural logarithmic of magnitude and is measured in a basic unit called *neper*.

The standard procedure is to plot $z_0 log|G(j\omega)|$ and phase angle $\phi(\omega)$ vs. log ω, *i.e.* frequency on a logarithmic scale and unit is called *decibel (dB)*.

$$log_{10} \frac{\omega_2}{\omega_1} = 1 \text{ means } \omega_2 = 10 \ \omega, \ ;$$

this range of frequencies is called a *decade*.

Gain Margin.

It may be defined as reciprocal of the gain at the frequency at which the phase angle becomes 180°.

The frequency at which the phase angle is 180° is called *phase cross-over frequency*.

Phase Margin.

The frequency at which gain becomes equal to 1 is called *gain cross--over frequency*, *i.e.* at the frequency at which dB plot crosses the 0-dB line.

$$\therefore \ \text{Phase margin} = \angle G(j\omega)\big|_{\omega = \omega_c} + 180°$$

where ω_c = frequency where gain is 0-dB.

Phase margin is always +*ve* for stable feed back system.

EXERCISE – I

1. Effect of feedback on the plant is to
  (*a*) control system transient response
  (*b*) reduce the sensitivity to plant parameter variations
  (*c*) both (*a*) and (*b*)
  (*d*) none of these

2. Open loop system
  (*a*) output control the input signal
  (*b*) output has no control over input signal
  (*c*) some other variables control the input signal
  (*d*) neither output nor any other variable has any effect on input

3. Electrical resistance is analogous to
  (*a*) intertia   (*b*) dampers
  (*c*) spring   (*d*) fluid capacity

4. Output of feedback control system should be a function of
  (*a*) input
  (*b*) reference and output
  (*c*) feedback signal
  (*d*) none of these

5. Transient response in the system is basically due to
  (*a*) stored energy   (*b*) forces
  (*c*) friction   (*d*) coupling

6. Transfer function of a system is defined as the ratio of output to input in
  (*a*) Z-transform
  (*b*) Fourier transform
  (*c*) Laplace transform
  (*d*) all of these

7. transfer function of a system can be used to study its
   (a) steady state behaviour
   (b) transient behaviour
   (c) both (a) and (b)
   (d) none of these

8. Automatic control system in which output is a variable is called
   (a) closed loop system
   (b) servomechanism
   (c) automatic regulating system
   (d) process control system

9. With feedback system, sensitivity to parameter
   (a) decreases   (b) increases
   (c) becomes zero   (d) becomes infinite

10. With feedback system, tranient response
    (a) decays constantly (b) decays slowly
    (c) decays quickly   (d) rises fast

11. In control system non-linearity caused by gear trains is
    (a) Backlash   (b) Dead space
    (c) Coulomb friction   (d) Saturation

12. Time sharing of an expansive control system can be achieved by using a/an
    (a) a.c. control system
    (b) analog control system
    (c) sampled data control system
    (d) none of these

13. Laplace transform is not applicable to non-linear system because
    (a) non-linear systems are time varying
    (b) time domain analysis is easier than frequency domain analysis
    (c) initial conditions are not zero in non linear systems
    (d) superposition law is not applicable to non-linear system

14. Linear differential transformer is an
    (a) electromechanical device
    (b) electric device
    (c) electromagnetic device
    (d) electrostatic device

15. Which of the following is not a desirable feature of a modern control system ?
    (a) No oscillation   (b) Accuracy
    (c) Quick response   (d) Correct power level

16. Device used for conversion of coordinates is
    (a) Synchros
    (b) Microsyn
    (c) Synchro resolver
    (d) Synchro transformer

17. Most common use of the synchros is as
    (a) error detector
    (b) transmission of angular data
    (c) transmission of arithmetic data
    (d) for synchronisation

18. In a closed loop system, source power is modulated with
    (a) error signal   (b) reference signal
    (c) actuating signal   (d) feed back signal

19. Non-linearity in the servo system due to saturation is caused by
    (a) servo motor   (b) gear trains
    (c) relays   (d) none of these

20. Microsyn is the name given to
    (a) potentiometer
    (b) magnetic amplifier
    (c) resolver
    (d) rotary differntial transformer

21. Differential is used in synchro differential unit for generators only
    (a) indicating difference of rotation angle of two synchro generators only
    (b) indicating sum of rotation angle of the synchor genes rators only
    (c) both (a) and (b)
    (d) none of these

22. Value of $i(0^+)$ for the system whose transfer function is given by the equation

$$I(s) = \frac{2s + 3}{(s + 1)(s + 3)} \text{ is}$$

    (a) 0   (b) 1
    (c) 2   (d) 3

23. If transfer function of the system is $\dfrac{1}{Ts + 1}$, then steady state error to the unit step input is
    (a) 1
    (b) zero
    (c) T
    (d) infinite

24. Power amplification in a magnetic amplifier can be increased
    (a) by negative feed back
    (b) by positive feed back
    (c) with higher inductane of a.c. coil
    (d) none of these

25. Friction coefficient is usually kept low to
    (a) minimize velocity-lag error
    (b) maximize velocity-lag error
    (c) minimize time constant
    (d) maximize speed of response

26. If for second order system, damping factor is less than one, then system response will be
(a) under damped   (b) over damped
(c) critically damped   (d) none of these

27. In the derivative error compensation, damping
(a) decreases and settling time increases
(b) increases adn settling time increases
(c) decreases and settling time decreases
(d) increases and settling time decreases

28. Second-derivative input signal adjust
(a) time constant of the system
(b) time constant and supress the oscillations
(c) damping of the system
(d) gain of the system

29. For unity damping factor, the system will be
(a) under damped   (b) critically damped
(c) over damped   (d) oscillatory

30. System generally preferred is
(a) under damped   (b) critically damped
(c) over damped   (d) oscillatory

31. For second order linear system, settling time is
(a) $\dfrac{1}{4}$ of the time constant

(b) $\dfrac{1}{2}$ of the time constant

(c) 4 times the time constant
(d) 2 times the time constant

32. For a desirable transient response of a second order system damping ratio must be between
(a) 0.4 and 0.8   (b) 0.8 and 1.0
(c) 1.0 and 1.2   (d) 1.2 and 1.4

33. If overshoot is excessive, then damping ratio is
(a) equal to 0.4   (b) less than 0.4
(c) more than 0.4   (d) infinity

34. Physical meaning of zero initial condition is that the
(a) system is at rest and stores no energy
(b) system is at rest but stores energy
(c) reference input to working system is zero
(d) system is working but stores no energy

35. A low value of friction coefficient
(a) minimize velocity lag error
(b) maximize velocity lag error
(c) minimize time constant of the system
(d) maximize time constant of the system

36. If gain of the system is increased, then
(a) roots move away from the zeros
(b) roots move towards origin of the s-plot
(c) roots move away from the poles
(d) none of these

37. If gain of the critically damped system is increased, the system will behave as
(a) under damped   (b) over damped
(c) critically damped   (d) oscillatory

38. Settling time is inversely proportional to product of the damping ratio and
(a) time constant
(b) maximum overshoot
(c) peak time
(d) undamped natural frequency of the system

39. If gain of the system is zero, then the roots
(a) coincide with the poles
(b) move away from the zeros
(c) move away from the poles
(d) none of these

40. 0 type system has
(a) zero steady state error
(b) small steady state error
(c) high gain constant
(d) high error with high k

41. At resonance peak, ratio fo output to input is
(a) zero   (b) lowest
(c) highest   (d) none of these

42. Relation between Fourier integral and Laplace transform is through
(a) time domain   (b) frequency domain
(c) both (a) and (b)   (d) none of these

43. Steady state error is always zero in response to the displacement input for
(a) type 0 system
(b) type 1 system
(c) type 2 system
(d) type (N > 1) system for N = 0, 1, 2....N

44. If steady state state error for type 1 system for unit ramp input is kept constant, then constant output is
(a) distance   (b) velocity
(c) acceleration   (d) power

45. For type 2 system, position error arises at steady state when input is
(a) ramp
(b) step displacement
(c) constant acceleration
(d) none of these

46. To decrease the type number of system
(a) first integrator and then diffrentiator is inserted
(b) first diffentiator and then integrator is inserted
(c) only diffrentiator is inserted in the forward path
(d) only integrator is inserted in the forward path

47. If feeback is introduced in the system the transient response
(a) does not very   (b) decays very fast
(c) decays slowly   (d) dies off

48. The frequency range over which response of the system is within acceptable units is called
(a) system band width
(b) system modulation frequency
(c) system demodulation frequency
(d) system carrier frequency

49. Lead compensation in the system add
(a) zeros   (b) poles
(c) both (a) and (b)   (d) none of these

50. In type 1 system, steady state accleration error is
(a) 0   (b) 1
(c) infinity   (d) none of these

51. Lead lag compensation improve
(a) transient response of the system
(b) steady state response of the system
(c) both (a) and (b)
(d) none of these

52. If open loop transfer function of a system is

$$G(s)H(s) = \frac{K}{s(1 + T_1s)(1 + T_2s)}$$

then system will be
(a) unstable   (b) conditionally stable
(c) stable   (d) marginally stable

53. Transient response of system is basically because of
(a) coupling   (b) forces
(c) friction   (d) stored energy

54. The difference of the reference input and the actual output signal is called
(a) error signal   (b) controlling signal
(c) actuating signal (d) transfer function

55. In a second order system, if the damping factor ξ is less than unity, the system will be
(a) under damped   (b) over damped
(c) critically damped (d) freely oscillating

56. If value of ξ for a given control system is unity, the system response will be
(a) underdamped   (b) critically damped
(c) overdamped   (d) oscillatory

57. If a system is critically damped and the gain is increased, the system
(a) becomes overdamped
(b) becomes underdamped
(c) becomes oscillatory
(d) remains critically damped

58. If initial conditions in a system are zero, it means that the system is
(a) working with zero reference input
(b) working but does not store energy
(c) at rest and has no energy stored in any of its parts
(d) at rest but stores energy

59. For a type 1 system, the position error arises at steady state when there is a
(a) constant acceleration input
(b) step displacement input
(c) ramp or velocity input
(d) none of these

60. The acceleration lag error of type 2 system is
(a) independent of the gain constant
(b) inversely proportional to gain constant
(c) directly proportional to gain constant
(d) directly proportional to square of gain constant

61. The phase shift of the second order system with transfer function $1/s2$ is
(a) 180°   (b) –180°
(c) 0   (d) 90°

62. For type three system, the lowest frequency asymptote will have the slope of
(a) – 20 dB/octave   (b) – 6 dB/ocatave
(c) – 12 dB/octave   (d) – 18 dB/octave

63. Which of the following compensate is used to increase the damping of a heavily underdamped system ?
(a) Phase-lag   (b) Phase-lead
(c) Phase lag lead   (d) None of these

64. To decrease time constant of the servomechanism
(a) decrease torque of servomotor
(b) increase damping of the system
(c) increase intertia of the system
(d) decrease inertia of the system

65. Servomechanism is called proportional error device when output of the system is function of
(a) error
(b) error and its first derivative
(c) first derivative of error
(d) none of these

66. Which of the following motor is suitable for servomechanism ?
(a) a.c. series motor   (b) 1 ϕ induction motor
(c) 2 ϕ induction motor (d) 3 ϕ induction motor

67. Servomechanism with step-displacement input is
(a) Type 0 system   (b) Type 1 system
(c) Type 2 system   (d) Type 3 system

68. Main difference between servomotor and standard motor is that servomotor has
(a) low inertia and higher starting torque
(b) low inertia and low starting torque
(c) high inertia and high starting torque
(d) none of these

69. A servomechanism is a feedback control system required to control
(a) position
(b) a derivative of position
(c) either (a) or (b)
(d) none of these

70. A servo system must have
(a) feedback system
(b) power amplifier to amplify error
(c) capacity to control position or its derivative
(d) all of these

71. The servomechanism with unit step input will fall in the category of
(a) type 0 system   (b) type 1 system
(c) type 2 system   (d) type 3 system

72. If poles of the system are lying on the imaginary axis in s-plane, then system will be
(a) stable   (b) marginally stable
(c) conditionally stable (d) unstable

73. According to Hurwitz criterion, the characteristic equation
$$s^4 + 8\,s^3 + 18\,s^2 + 16\,s + 5 = 0 \text{ is}$$
(a) unstable   (b) marginally stable
(c) conditionally stable(d) unstable

74. A system is called absolutely stable if oscillations set up in the system are
(a) damped out
(b) self-sustaining and tend to last indefinitely
(c) negative peaked only
(d) none of these

75. Best method to determine stability and transient response of the system is
(a) Bode plot   (b) Signal flow graph
(c) Nyquist plot   (d) Root locus

76. If poles of system are lying on the imaginary axis in s-plane, then system will be
(a) unstable   (b) marginally stable
(c) conditionally stable (d) unstable

77. Number of pure integrations in the system transfer function determine
(a) degree of stability
(b) stability of the system
(c) transient performance of the system
(d) steady state performance

78. Which system conveniently see the impact of poles and zeros on phase and gain margin ?
(a) Root locus
(b) Nyquist plot
(c) Routh-Hurwitz criterion
(d) Bode plot

79. Factor which cannot be can cancelled from numerator and denominator of $G(s)\,E(s)$ in
(a) Bode plot   (b) Nyquist plot
(c) Root locus analysis (d) none of these

80. If value of gain is increased, then roots of the system will move to
(a) origin   (b) lower frequencies
(c) higher frequencies(d) none of these

81. Intersection of root locus branches with the imaginary axis can be determined by the use of
(a) Polar plot   (b) Routh's criterion
(c) Nyquist criterion   (d) None of these

82. If gain is zero, then
(a) roots move away from zeros
(b) roots coincide with poles
(c) roots move away from poles
(d) none of these

83. To increase damping of a pair of complex roots compensator used is
(a) phase lag   (b) phase lead
(c) phase lag lead   (d) one with 60° lead circuit

84. For type 3 system, lowest frequency asymptote will have the slope of
(a) 15 db/octave   (b) – 16 db/octave
(c) 17 db/octave   (d) – 18 db/octave

85. If a pole is added to a system, it causes
(a) lag compensation
(b) lead compensation
(c) lead-lag compensation
(d) none of these

86. For steady state transient inprovement, compensator used is
(a) lead copensator   (b) lag compensator
(c) lead-lag compensator(d) none of these

87. Information between number of poles and zeros of the closed loop transfer function is given by
(a) Routh Hurwitz criterion
(b) Bode diagram
(c) Root locus method
(d) Nyquist plot

88. To study time delay of the system which of the following is used ?
(a) Nyquist plot
(b) Bode plot
(c) Routh Hurwitz method
(d) Nicholas chart

89. Closed loop poles are
  (a) zeros of 1 + G(s). H(s)
  (b) zeros of G(s) H(s)
  (c) poles of G(s) H(s)
  (d) poles of 1 + G(s) H(s)

90. Maximum overshoot is function of
  (a) damping ratio
  (b) natural frequency of oscillation
  (c) both (a) and (b)
  (d) damped frequency of oscillation

91. Feedback control systems are basically
  (a) low pass filter   (b) high pass filter
  (c) band pass filter   (d) band stop filter

92. A linear system obeys the principle of
  (a) homogenity
  (b) reciprocity
  (c) superposition and homogenity
  (d) none of these

93. If a system has some poles lying on the imaginary axis, it is
  (a) unconditionally stable
  (b) conditionally stable
  (c) marginally stable
  (d) unstable

94. The most suitable method for determining the stability and transient response of a system is
  (a) Bode plot
  (b) Root locus
  (c) Nyquist criterion
  (d) Routh Hurwitz criterion

95. At the point where $180°$ locus crosses the j-axis, the system is
  (a) absolutely stable   (b) absolutely unstable
  (c) conditionally stable   (d) none of these

96. The steady state error of a control system may be minimized by
  (a) increasing the inertia of the system
  (b) decreasing the inertia of the system
  (c) decreasing the torque of servomotor
  (d) increasing the damping of the system

97. If poles are more than zeros in G(s) F(s), then number of root locus segment is equal to
  (a) number of poles
  (b) number of zeros
  (c) sum of poles and zeros
  (d) difference of poles and zeros

98. For $G(s) \, F(s) = \dfrac{k(s+z)}{s+p}$, $(z < p)$, the plot is
  (a) one pole on the imaginary axis
  (b) one zero on the right hand side of the plane

  (c) one pole and one zero on the left hand side of plane
  (d) 2 poles and 2 zeros on the left hand side of the plane

99. Number of root-locus segments which do not terminate on the zeros is equal to
  (a) number of poles
  (b) number of zeros
  (c) sum of poles and zeros
  (d) difference of poles and zeros

100. In a root locus plot, the increase in k damping ratio
  (a) increases   (b) decreases
  (c) remain same   (d) none of these

101. In a root locus plot, with increase in k,
  (a) increase overshoot of the response
  (b) derease overshoot of the response
  (c) not change overshoot of the response
  (d) none of these

102. In a root locus plot, increase in k
  (a) result in decrease in the damped and undamped natural frequencies
  (b) result in increase in the damped and undamped natural frequencies
  (c) not change the damped and undamped natural frequencies
  (d) none of these

103. In root plot if k is greater than critical value, then, with increase in k, value of the real part of the closed loop
  (a) increases   (b) decreases
  (c) remain same   (d) none of these

104. Algebraic sum of the angles of the vectors from all poles and zeros to the point on any root-locus segment is
  (a) $90°$
  (b) $180°$
  (c) $45°$
  (d) $110°$ and its odd multiples

105. Plot of the constant gain loci of the system is
  (a) asymptote
  (b) circle with centre at the origin
  (c) parabola
  (d) ellipse

106. In root locus technique, angle between adjacent asymptote is
  (a) $180°/(m + n)$ (b) $360°/(m + n)$
  (c) $360°/(m - n)$ (d) $180°/(m - n)$

107. Routh criterion tells us the number of roots lying
  (a) in the right half of s-phane
  (b) in the left half of s-plane
  (c) on the origin of s-plane
  (d) none of these

108. Intersection of root lucus branches with imaginary axis may be determined by the use of
  (a) Nyquist criterion
  (b) Routh criterion
  (c) Polar plot
  (d) none of these

109. When all the terms in a row of Routh array are zero, the characteristic equation has roots on
  (a) positive real axis (b) negative real axis
  (c) imaginary axis (d) none of these

110. The root locus plot is symmetrical about the real axis because there are
  (a) all roots occurring in pair
  (b) more real roots
  (c) more imaginary roots
  (d) complex roots occurring in conjugate pairs

111. The break away points of root loci are
  (a) open loop poles (b) closed loop poles
  (c) open loop zeros (d) closed loop zeros

112. The break away points of the root locus are
  (a) on the axis only
  (b) on the imaginary axis only
  (c) points where multiple roots of characteristic equation occur
  (d) solution of GH $(s) = 0$

113. The number of root loci branches which do not terminate at zeros are equal to number of
  (a) poles
  (b) zeros
  (c) sum of (a) and (b)
  (d) difference of (a) and (b)

114. For characteristic equation having more number of poles than zeros, the number of root locus branches will be equal to
  (a) number of zeros
  (b) number of poles
  (c) sum of (a) and (b)
  (d) difference of (b) and (a)

115. At breakaway point, several branches of root loci coalese because system characteristic equation has
  (a) single root
  (b) all root on right hand side of s-plane
  (c) serval roots
  (d) imaginary roots only

116. If the system gain K is increased, roots of the system move to
  (a) lower frequencies
  (b) higher frequencies
  (c) origin
  (d) none of these

117. The roots move away from the poles when the system gain is
  (a) increased
  (b) lowered
  (c) zero
  (d) none of these

118. When gain K of a system becomes zero, the roots of the loci
  (a) move away from the poles
  (b) move away from the zeros
  (c) coincide with the poles
  (d) coincide with the zeros

119. The number of root Loci which extends to infinity equals
  (a) excess of poles over zeros in G (s) H (s)
  (b) excess of zeros over poles in G (s) H (s)
  (c) number of poles in G (s) H (s)
  (d) number of zeros in G (s) H (s)

120. The algebraic sum of the angles of the vectors from all poles and zeros to the point on any root locus segment is
  (a) always 180°
  (b) 180° or odd multiple thereof
  (c) always 90°
  (d) 90° or odd multiple thereof

121. The root loci of a system has four separate loci. The system can have
  (a) four poles and four zeros
  (b) four poles or four zeros
  (c) two poles and two zeros
  (d) two poles and six zeros

122. The root loci of a system has three asymptotes. The system can have
  (a) three poles
  (b) four poles and one zero
  (c) five poles and two zero
  (d) all of these

123. In a root locus plot, increase in K will
  (a) decrease the natural frequency
  (b) increase the natural frequency
  (c) not alter the natural frequency
  (d) none of these

124. Frequency response mean
  (a) transient response of a system to a sinusoidal input
  (b) steady state response of a system to a sinusoidal input
  (c) oscillatory response of a system to a sinusoidal input
  (d) none of these

125. Bode plot approach is applied to
(a) minimum phase network
(b) non-minimum phase network
(c) any network
(d) none of these

126. Type of transfer function used in Bode plot is
(a) G(s)   (b) C(j)
(c) G(jw)   (d) G(js)

127. Bode analysis method can be applied if transfer function has no poles
(a) and zeros on R.H. of s-plane
(b) if transfer function has no poles on R.H. of s-plane
(c) if tranfer function has no zero on R.H. of s-plane
(d) to all transfer functions

128. A complex-conjugate pair of poles near the jw axis will produce a
(a) high oscillatory mode of transient response
(b) steady state mode of response
(c) sinusoidal mode of response
(d) none of these

129. Frequency range over which response of the system is within acceptable limits is called
(a) system modulation frequency
(b) system demodulation frequency
(c) system carrier frequency
(d) system band width

130. Polar plots for+ve and –ve frequencies
(a) are always symmetrical
(b) can never be symmetrical
(c) may be symmetrical
(d) none of these

131. Slope in Bode plot is expressed as
(a) $-6\,db$/decade   (b) $-6\,db$/octave
(c) $-8\,db$/octave   (d) $-7\,db$/octave

132. Transfer founction, when the Bode diagram is plotted should be of the form
(a) $(1+T)$ (b) $(1+s)$
(c) (Ts) (d) $(1+Ts)$

133. In Nyquist criterion roots of the characteristic equation are given by
(a) zeros of open loop transfer function
(b) zeros of closed loop transfer function
(c) poles of closed loop transfer function
(d) poles of open loop tsansfer function

134. Nyquist stability criterion requires polar plot of
(a) characteristic equation
(b) closed loop transfer function
(c) open loop transfer function
(d) none of these

135. Gain margin expressed in decibels is
(a) positive if Kg greater than 1 and negative for Kg less than 1
(b) negative if Kg is greater than 1 and positive for Kg less than 1
(c) always zero
(d) infinity for Kg equal to 1

136. By adding a pole at $s = 0$, Nyquist plot of the system will
(a) shift 90° clockwise
(b) shift 90° anticlockwise
(c) shift 180°
(d) not change at all

137. Gain margin of first or second order system is
(a) zero   (b) 1
(c) 100   (d) infinite

138. For relative stability of the system, which of the following is sufficient ?
(a) Gain margin   (b) Phase margin
(c) Both (a) and (b)   (d) None of these

139. For all frequencies, a unit circle in the Nyquist plot transforms into
(a) db line of amplitude plot in Bode diagram
(b) 1 db line of amplitude plot in Bode diagram
(c) either (a) and (b)
(d) none of these

140. Cut off frequency is the frequency at which magnitude of closed loop frequency responce is
(a) $1\,db$ below its zero frequency
(b) $2\,db$ below its zero frequency
(c) $3\,db$ below its zero frequency
(d) $4\,db$ below its zero frequency

141. Bandwidth gives an indication of
(a) characteristic equation of the system
(b) speed of response of a control system
(c) transfer function of the control system
(d) transients in the system

142. Cut off rate is the slope of log-magnitude curve
(a) at the start of curve
(b) at the end of of curve
(c) near the cut off frequency
(d) none of these

143. Polar plots for positive and negative frequencies
(a) are always symmetrical
(b) can never be symmetrical
(c) may or may not be symmetrical
(d) none of these

144. The gain margin is the reciprocal of gain at the frequency at which the phase becomes
(a) 0   (b) 90°
(c) 180°   (d) 270°

145. The Bode diagram method is applied to
(*a*) minimum phase network
(*b*) non-minimum phase network
(*c*) all pass network
(*d*) every network of the control system

146. In Nyquist criterion the roots of the characteristic equation are given by
(*a*) zeros of the closed loop transfer function
(*b*) poles of the closed loop transfer function
(*c*) zeros of the open loop transfer function
(*d*) poles of the open loop transfer function

147. For a close–loop system to be stable
(*a*) loop transfer function should have all poles in LHS of s–plane
(*b*) loop transfer function should have all zeros in RHS of s–plane
(*c*) there is no restriction on location of poles and zeros in the loop transfer function
(*d*) loop transfer function should have all zeros in LHS of s–plane

148. If the Nyquist criterion for a closed–loop system is known, then the stability of the system
(*a*) can not be found
(*b*) can be found by studying the system behaviour around point $(1, j0)$
(*c*) is the same as the stability of the loop transfer function
(*d*) can be found by studying the behaviour of the system about a point $(-1, j0)$

149. The $-180°$ phase line of Bode diagram is equal to
(*a*) positive imaginary axis in Nyquist plot
(*b*) negative imaginary axis in Nyquist plot
(*c*) positive real axis in Nyquist plot
(*d*) negative real axis in Nyquist plot

150. Which of the following system conveniently displays the impact of poles and zeros on phase margin and gain margin?
(*a*) Root locus
(*b*) Nyquist plot
(*c*) Bode plot
(*d*) Routh–Hwrwitz criterion

151. Laplace transform of an impulse function is
(*a*) 1
(*b*) $\dfrac{1}{s}$
(*c*) $\dfrac{1}{s^2}$
(*d*) 0

152. Under force-voltage analogy, velocity is analogous to
(*a*) Charge
(*b*) Capacitance
(*c*) Inductance
(*d*) Current.

153. In force-current analogy, capacitance is analogous to
(*a*) Mass
(*b*) Velocity
(*c*) Displacement
(*d*) Momentum

154. Laplace transform of e^{-2t} is given by
(*a*) 1/2s
(*b*) 2/s
(*c*) 2/s + 1
(*d*) 1/s + 2

155. Increased Laplace transform of $\dfrac{1}{s(s+2)}$ is given by
(*a*) $1/2\,[1 - 4^{2t}]$
(*b*) $1/2\,[1 + e^{-2t}]$
(*c*) $1/2\,[1 - e^{2t}]$
(*d*) $1/2\,[1 + e^{2t}]$

156. Laplace transform method of solution is applicable 10 equations containing
(*a*) Differential terms only
(*b*) Integral terms only
(*c*) Scalar terms only
(*d*) None of these

157. If a zero appears on the first column of the Routh table, the system is
(*a*) Necessarily stable
(*b*) Necessarily unstable
(*c*) Marginally stable
(*d*) None of these

158. Which of the following informations can be concluded about the transient behaviour of the system?
(*a*) 25% maximum overshoot to step command.
(*b*) 50% maximum overshoot to step command.
(*c*) 75% maximum overshoot to step command.
(*d*) None of the above.

159. d.c. gain of the system represented by the transfer Function $P(s) = \dfrac{1}{s+1}$ is equal to
(*a*) 1
(*b*) 2
(*c*) 5
(*d*) 10

160. Transfer function of a system is given by $P(s) = 2/s + 2$ for $\omega = 10$, the gain will be equal to
(*a*) 0.444
(*b*) 0.333
(*c*) 0.25
(*d*) 0.196

161. Which of the following methods can be used to determine relative stability of a control system?
(*a*) Routh stability criterion
(*b*) Hurwitz stability criterion
(*c*) Root-locus technique
(*d*) None of these.

162. Routh table was constructed from characteristic equation of a control system first column of the table contained following integers, 1, 4, 5, 6, 13. The system is
(*a*) stable
(*b*) unstable
(*c*) marginally stable
(*d*) none of these

163. A type system under parabolic input will have
  (a) actuating signal which will increase with time
  (b) actuating signal which will decrease with time
  (c) parabolic output
  (d) any of these

164. Which of the following best defines a transfer function?
  (a) Ratio of system response to system input function.
  (b) Ratio of system input function to system response.
  (c) Laplace transform of system response minus the Laplace transforms of the system input function.
  (d) Ratio of the Laplace transform response to the Laplace transform of the system input function.

165. Analysis of control systems by Laplace transform technique is NOT possible for which one of the following?
  (a) Linear systems
  (b) Time-invariant systems
  (c) Discrete-time systems
  (d) Unstable continuous-time systems

166. In order to have impulse response of a control system approaching zero with time tending to infinity
  (a) Poles of the system must have position real parts,
  (b) Poles of the system must lie on the L.H.S. of the S-plane,
  (c) Zero of the system must be on the L.H.S. of the S-plane,
  (d) None of these.

EXERCISE – II

1. Laplace transform of $\sin(\omega t + \alpha)$ is **DMRC 2014**

  (a) $\dfrac{\alpha}{s^2 + \alpha^2} \exp\left(\dfrac{s}{\alpha\omega}\right)$

  (b) $\dfrac{\omega}{s^2 + \omega^2} \exp\left(\dfrac{s}{\alpha\omega}\right)$

  (c) $\dfrac{s}{s^2 + \alpha^2} \exp\left(\dfrac{s}{\alpha\omega}\right)$

  (d) $\dfrac{\omega}{s^2 + \alpha^2} \exp\left(\dfrac{s}{\alpha\omega}\right)$

2. Inverse Laplace transform of the function $\dfrac{2s+5}{s^2 + 5s + 6}$ is **DMRC 2014**

  (a) $2 \exp(-2.5\,t) \cos h\, 0.5\,t$
  (b) $\exp(-2t) - \exp(-3t)$
  (c) $2 \exp(-2.5\,t) \sin h\, 0.5\,t$
  (d) $2 \exp(-2.5\,t) \cos 0.5t$

3. Consider a random sinusoidal signal $x(t) = \sin(\omega_o\, t + \phi)$ where a random variable 'ϕ' is uniformly distributed in the range $\pm \dfrac{\pi}{2}$. The mean value of $x(t)$ is **DMRC 2014**

  (a) zero (b) $\dfrac{2}{\pi} \sin(\omega_o t)$

  (c) $\dfrac{2}{\pi} \cos(\omega_o t)$ (d) $\dfrac{2}{\pi}$

4. An RC driving-point impedance function has zeros at $s = -2$ and $s = -5$. The admissible poles for the function would be **DMRC**
  (a) $s = 0;\ s = -6$
  (b) $s = -1;\ s = -3$
  (c) $s = 0;\ s = -1$
  (d) $s = -3;\ s = -4$

5. Which one of the following system is nonlinear? [$y(t)$ = output; $x(t)$ = input] **DMRC**
  (a) $y(t) = 2x\,(t-1) - 3x\,(t-2) + x(t-3)$
  (b) $y(t) = 5x(t)$
  (c) $y(t) = 2x\,(t-1) - x(t-2) - x(t-4)$
  (d) $y(t) = 2x(t) + 3.6$

6. Of the following transfer function of second order linear time-invariant systems, the underdamped system is represented by **DMRC**

  (a) $H(s) = \dfrac{1}{s^2 + 4s + 4}$

  (b) $H(s) = \dfrac{1}{s^2 + 5s + 4}$

  (c) $H(s) = \dfrac{1}{s^2 + 4.5s + 4}$

  (d) $H(s) = \dfrac{1}{s^2 + 3s + 4}$

7. The impulse response of a single-pole system would approach a non-zero constant as $t \to \infty$ if and only if the pole is located in the s-plane

(a) on the negative real axis **DMRC**

(b) at the origin

(c) on the positive real axis

(d) on the imaginary axis

8. For a desirable transient response of a second order system damping ratio must be between **DRDO**

(a) 0.4 and 0.8

(b) 0.8 and 1.0

(c) 1.0 and 1.2

(d) 1.2 and 1.4

9. For type 3 system, lowest frequency asymptote will have the slope of **DRDO**

(a) 15 db/octave

(b) $-$ 16 db/octave

(c) 17 db/octave

(d) $-$ 18 db/octave

10. Type of transfer function used in Bode plot is **DRDO**

(a) $G(s)$

(b) $G(j)$

(c) $G(jw)$

(d) $G(js)$

11. By adding a pole at $s = 0$, Nyquist plot of the system will **DRDO**

(a) shift 90° clockwise

(b) shift 90° anticlockwise

(c) shift 180°

(d) not change at all

12. Open loop system **RRB**

(a) output control the input signal

(b) output has no control over input signal

(c) some other variables control the input signal

(d) neither output nor any other variable has any effect on input

13. Settling time is inversely proportional to product of the damping ratio and **RRB**

(a) time constant

(b) maximum overshoot

(c) peak time

(d) undamped natural frequency of the system

14. If feeback is introduced in the system the transient response **RRB**

(a) does not very

(b) decays very fast

(c) decays slowly

(d) dies off

15. If poles of the system are lying on the imaginary axis in s-plane, then system will be **RRB**

(a) stable

(b) marginally stable

(c) conditionally stable

(d) unstable

16. Valuve of $i(0^+)$ for the system whose transfer function is given by the equation **RRB**

$$I(s) = \frac{2s+3}{(s+1)(s+3)} \text{ is}$$

(a) 0

(b) 1

(c) 2

(d) 3

17. To decrease time constant of the servomechanism

(a) decrease torque of servomotor **RRB**

(b) increase damping of the system

(c) increase intertia of the system

(d) decrease inertia of the system

18. Let $x(t)$ be a continuous-time, real-valued signal band-limited to F Hz. The Nyquist sampling rate, in Hz, for $y(t) = x\,(0.5t) + x(t) - x(2t)$ is **RRB**

(a) F

(b) 2F

(c) 4F

(d) 8F

19. Consider the following standard state-space description of a linear time-invariant single input single output system : $\dot{x} = Ax + Bu$, $y = Cx + Du$. Which one of the following statements about the transfer function CANNOT be true if $D \neq 0$?

(a) The system is unstable **RRB**

(b) The system is strictly proper

(c) The system is low pass

(d) The system is of type zero

20. A random variable is known to have a cumulative distribution function $F_x(x) = U(x)\left(1 - \dfrac{x^2}{b}\right)$ its density function is **RRB**

(a) $U(x)\dfrac{2x}{b}\left(1 - e^{-x^2/b}\right)$

(b) $U(x)\dfrac{2x}{b}e^{-x^2/b}$

(c) $U(x)\left(1 - \dfrac{x^2}{b}\right)\delta(x)$

(d) $\left(1 - \dfrac{x^2}{b}\right)\delta(x) + e^{-x^2/b}$

21. The Z-transform corresponding to the Laplace transform function $G(s) = \dfrac{10}{s(s+5)}$ is **RRB**

(a) $\dfrac{2Ze^{-5z}}{(Z-1)(Z-e^{-T})}$

(b) $\dfrac{2(1 - e^{-5z})Z}{(Z-1)(Z-e^{-5T})}$

(c) $\dfrac{e^{-5T}}{(Z-1)^2}$

(d) $\dfrac{e^{-T}}{Z(Z-e^{-3T})}$

22. $H(e^{j\omega})$ is the frequency response of a discrete time LTI system and $H_1(e^{j\omega})$ is the frequency response of its inverse function. Then **RRB**

(a) $H(e^{j\omega})H_1(e^{j\omega}) = 1$

(b) $H(e^{j\omega})H_1(e^{j\omega}) = \delta(\omega)$

(c) $H(e^{j\omega})*H_1(e^{j\omega}) = 1$

(d) $H(e^{j\omega})*H_1(e^{j\omega}) = \delta(\omega)$

23. In the circuit shown in the figure, the input signal is $v_i(t) = 5 + 3\cos\omega t$. **RRB**

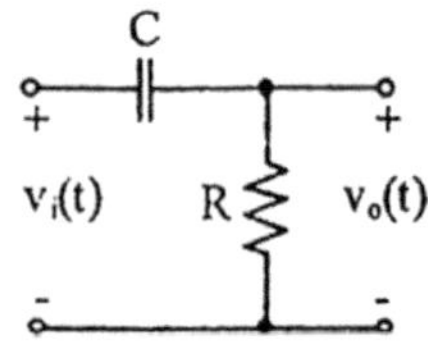

The steady state output is expressed as $v_0(t) = P + Q\cos(\omega t - \phi)$. If $\omega CR = 2$, the values of P and Q are

(a) $P = 0$ and $Q = 6 / \sqrt{5}$

(b) $P = 0$ and $Q = 3 / \sqrt{5}$

(c) $P = 5$ and $Q = 6 / \sqrt{5}$

(d) $P = 5$ and $Q = 3$

24. Consider the discrete-time signal $x(n) = \left(\dfrac{1}{3}\right)^n$ $u(n)$, where $u(n) = \begin{cases} 1, n \geq 0 \\ 0, n < 0 \end{cases}$. Define the signal $y(n)$ as $y(n) = x(-n)$, $-\infty < n < \infty$. Then $\displaystyle\sum_{n=-\infty}^{\infty} y(n)$ equals **RRB**

(a) $-\dfrac{2}{3}$

(b) $\dfrac{2}{3}$

(c) $\dfrac{3}{2}$

(d) 3

25. A cascade control system with proportional controllers is shown below.

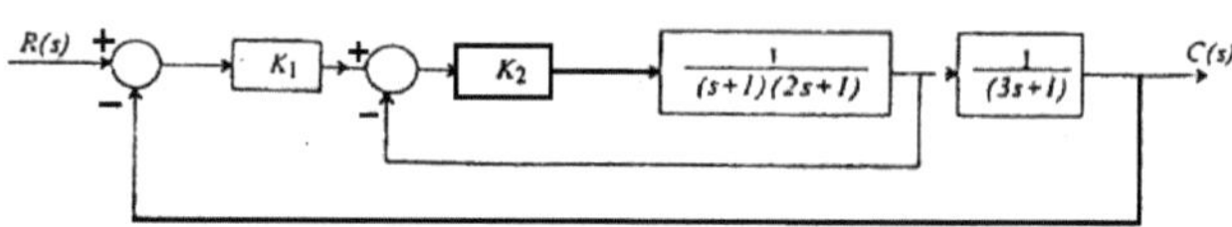

Theoretically, the largest values of the gains K_1 and K_2 that can be set without causing instability of the closed loop system are **RRB**

(a) 10 and 100

(b) 100 and 10

(c) 10 and 10

(d) ∞ and ∞

26. The open loop transfer function of a unity feedback system is $G(s) = \dfrac{K(s+2)}{(s+1+j1)(s+1-j1)}$. The root locus plot of the system has **RRB**

(a) two breakaway points located at $s = -0.59$ and $s = -3.41$

(b) one breakaway point located at $s = -0.59$

(c) one breakaway point located at $s = -3.41$

(d) one breakaway point located at $s = -1.41$

27. If a first order system and its time response to a unit step input are as shown below, the gain k is **RRB**

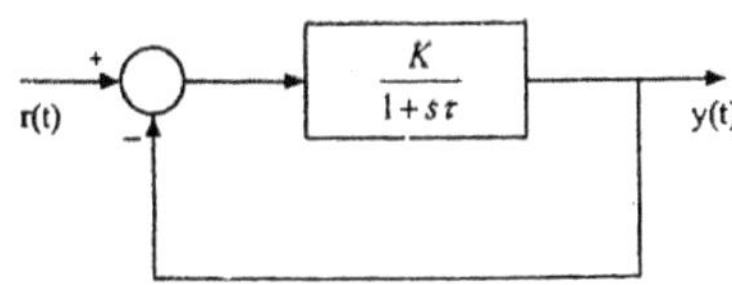

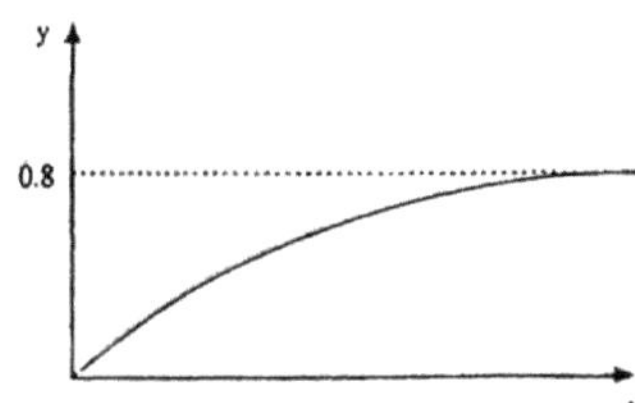

(a) 0.25   (b) 0.8

(c) 1   (d) 4

28. The state space representation of a system is

given by $x = \begin{bmatrix} 0 & 1 \\ 0 & -3 \end{bmatrix} x + \begin{bmatrix} 1 \\ 0 \end{bmatrix} u,\ y = [1\ 0]\ x$

The transfer function $\dfrac{Y(s)}{U(s)}$ of the system will be

(a) $\dfrac{1}{s}$ (b) $\dfrac{1}{s(s+3)}$ **RRB**

(c) $\dfrac{1}{s+3}$ (d) $\dfrac{1}{s^2}$

29. A closed loop control system is shown below. The range of the controller gain K_C which will make the real parts of all the closed loop poles more negative than –1 is **RRB**

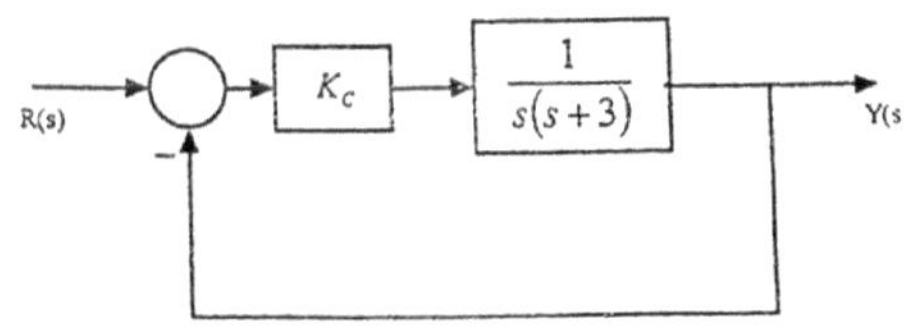

(a) $K_C > -4$ (b) $K_C > 0$

(c) $K_C > 2$ (d) $K_C < 2$

30. The value of the integral of the complex function

$f(s) = \dfrac{3s+4}{(s+1)(s+2)}$ along the path $|s| = 3$ is

(a) $2\pi j$ (b) $4\pi j$ **RRB**

(c) $6\pi j$ (d) $8\pi j$

31. For k = 0, 1, 2, ..., the steps of Newton-Raphson method for solving a non-linear equation is given as

$$x_{k+1} = \frac{2}{3}\,x_k + \frac{5}{3}x_k^{-2}.$$

Starting from a suitable initial choice as k tends to ∞, the iterate x_k tends to **RRB**

(a) 1.7099

(b) 2.2361

(c) 3.1251

(d) 5.0000

32. Which of the following integrals provides a measure of the rapidity of change in a random variable f(t) ? **RRB**

(a) $\displaystyle\lim_{T \to \infty} \frac{1}{2T} \int_{-T}^{+T} f\,(d)\,dt$

(b) $\displaystyle\lim_{T \to \infty} \frac{1}{2T} \int_{-T}^{+T} f^2\,(t)\,dt$

(c) $\left[\displaystyle\lim_{T \to \infty} \frac{1}{2T} \int_{-T}^{+T} f^2\,(t)\,dt\right]^{1/2}$

(d) $\displaystyle\lim_{T \to \infty} \frac{1}{2T} \int_{-T}^{+T} f\,(t)\,f(\,t + \tau)\,dt$

33. The fourier series for a periodic signal is given as $x\,(t) = \cos\,(1.2\,\pi t) + \cos\,(2\pi t) + \cos\,(2.8\pi t)$. **RRB** The fundamental frequency of the signal is

(a) 0.2 Hz

(b) 0.6 Hz

(c) 1.0 Hz

(d) 1.4 Hz

34. The Fourier transform of a function $g(t)$ is given as

$$G\,(\omega) = \frac{\omega^2 + 21}{\omega^2 + 9}$$

Then the function g(t) is given as **RRB**

(a) $\delta\,(t) + 2\exp\,(-3\,|\,t\,|\,)$

(b) $\cos 3\omega t + 21\exp\,(-3t)$

(c) $\sin 3\omega t + 7\cos \omega t$

(d) $\sin 3\omega t + 21\exp\,(3t)$

35. A digital filter has the transfer function **RRB**

$$H(z) = \frac{z^2 + 1}{z^2 + 0.81}$$

If this filter has to reject a 50 Hz interference from the input, then the sampling frequency for the input signal should be

(a) 50 Hz

(b) 100 Hz

(c) 150 Hz

(d) 200 Hz

36. The solution of the integral equation **RRB**

$$y(t) = t \exp(t) - 2 \exp(t) \int_0^t \exp(-\tau)\, y(\tau)\, d\tau \text{ is}$$

(a) $\dfrac{1}{2}(\exp(t) - \exp(-t))$

(b) $\dfrac{1}{2}(\exp(t) + \exp(-t))$

(c) $\dfrac{(\exp(t) - \exp(-t))}{(\exp(t) + \exp(-t))}$

(d) $\dfrac{(\exp(-t) + \exp(t))}{(\exp(-t) - \exp(t))}$

37. The transfer function of a position servo system is given as $G(s) = \dfrac{1}{s(s+1)}$. **RRB**

A first order compensator is designed in a unity feedback configuration so that the poles of the compensated system are placed at $-1 \pm j1$ and -4. The transfer function of the compensated system is **RRB**

(a) $\dfrac{s+3}{2(s+5)}$

(b) $\dfrac{2s+3}{s+5}$

(c) $\dfrac{5(s+1.6)}{s+5}$

(d) $\dfrac{3(2s+3)}{s+4}$

38. The signal flow graph representation of a control system is shown below. **RRB**

The transfer function $\dfrac{Y(s)}{R(s)}$ is computed as

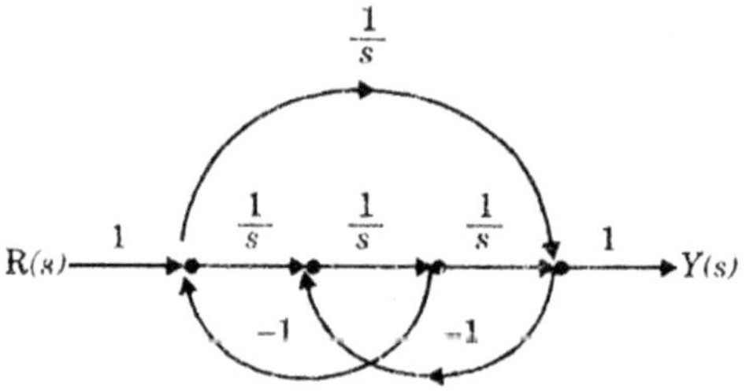

(a) $\dfrac{1}{s}$

(b) $\dfrac{s^2 + 1}{s(s^2 + 2)}$

(c) $\dfrac{s(s^2 + 1)}{s^2 + 2}$

(d) $1 - \dfrac{1}{s}$

39. A unity feedback system has the following open loop frequency response : **RRB**

ω (rad/sec)	2	3	4	5	6	8	10
$\lvert G(j\omega)\rvert$	7.5	4.8	3.15	2.25	1.70	1.00	0.64
$\angle G(j\omega)$	$-118°$	$-130°$	$140°$	$150°$	$157°$	$170°$	$-180°$

The gain and phase margin of the system are

(a) 0 dB, $-180°$

(b) 3.88 dB, $-170°$

(c) 0 dB, $10°$

(d) 3.88 dB, $10°$

40. The root locus of a plant is given in the following figure. The root locus crosses imaginary axis at $\omega = 4\sqrt{2}$ rad/s with gain K = 384. It is observed that the point $s = -1.5 + j1.5$ lies in the root locus. The gain K at $s = -1.5 + j\,1.5$ is computed as **RRB**

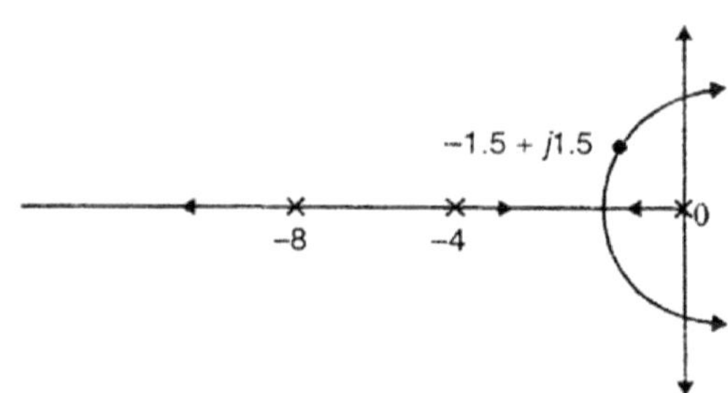

(a) 11.3

(b) 21.2

(c) 41.25

(d) 61.2

41. If the unilateral L.T. of signal $f(t)$ is given as $\dfrac{1}{S^2+S+1}$ then the Laplace transform of signal $t.f(t)$ will be _____ **RRB 2012**

(a) $\dfrac{1}{\left(S^2+S+1\right)^2}$

(b) $\dfrac{1}{S^2+S+1}$

(c) $\dfrac{-2S+1}{S^2+S+1}$

(d) $\dfrac{2S+1}{\left(S^2+S+1\right)^2}$

42. Let $x(t)$ be a continuous-time, real-valued signal band-limited to F Hz. The Nyquist sampling rate, in Hz, for $y(t) = x\,(0.5t) + x(t) - x(2t)$ is

(a) F   (b) 2F   **RRB 2012**

(c) 4F   (d) 8F

43. Consider the periodic signal $x(t)=(1+0.5\cos 40\,\pi t)$ $\cos 200\,\pi t$, where t is in seconds. Its fundamental frequency, in Hz, is **RRB 2012**

(a) 20   (b) 40

(c) 100   (d) 200

44. A feedback control system with high gain K, is shown in the figure below : **RRB 2012**

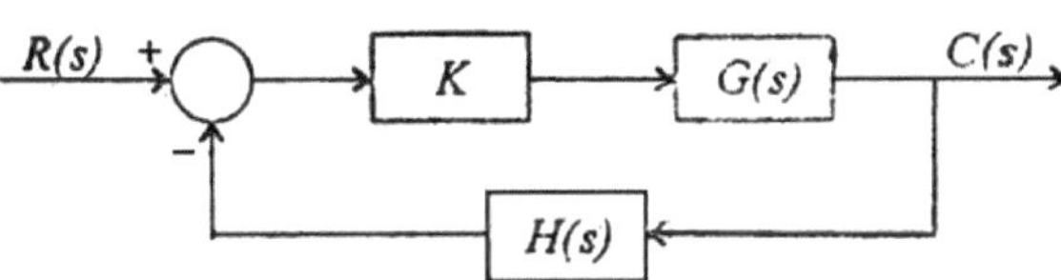

Then the closed loop transfer function is

(a) sensitive to perturbations in G(s) and H(s)

(b) sensitive to perturbations in G(s) but not to perturbations in H(s)

(c) sensitive to perturbations in H(s) but not to perturbations in G(s)

(d) insensitive to perturbations in G(s) and H(s)

45. Consider the following standard state-space description of a linear time-invariant single input single output system : $\dot{x} = Ax + Bu, y = Cx + Du.$ Which one of the following statements about the transfer function CANNOT be true if $D \neq 0$?

(a) The system is unstable **RRB 2012**

(b) The system is strictly proper

(c) The system is low pass

(d) The system is of type zero

46. A system having differential equation $y'(t)+5y(t)=u(t)$ and $y(0) = 1$. Then output response of the system is **RRB 2012**

(a) $0.2 + 0.8e^{-5t}$

(b) $0.8 - 0.2e^{-5t}$

(c) $0.2 - 0.8e^{-5t}$

(d) $0.8 + 0.8e^{-5t}$

47. The signals x(t) and h(t) shown in the figures are convolved to yield y(t). **RRB 2012**

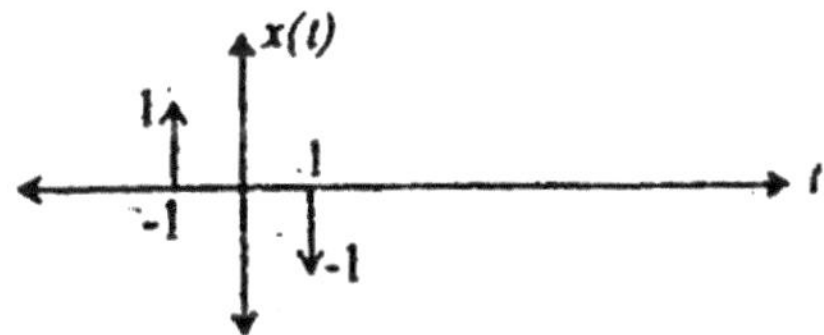

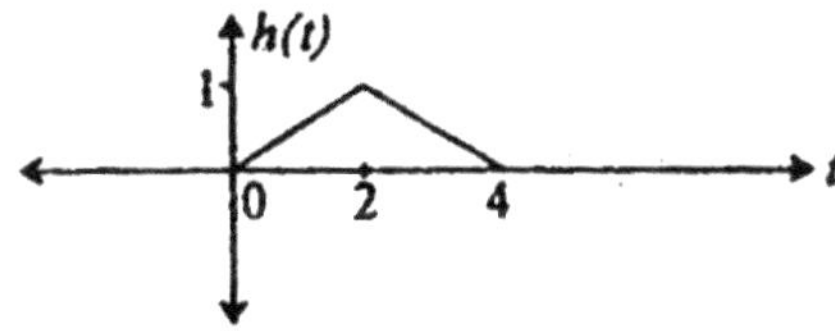

Which one of the following figures represents the output y(t) ?

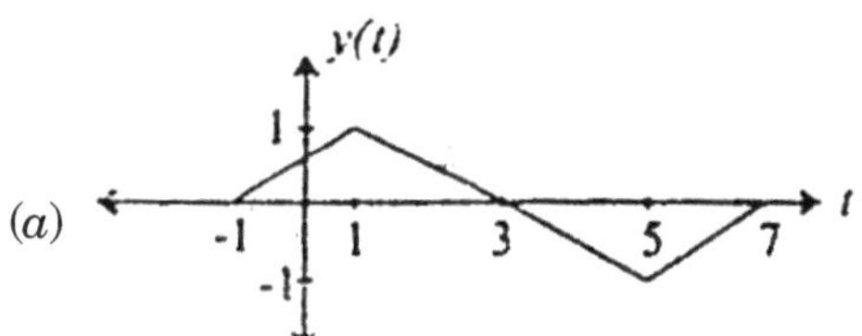

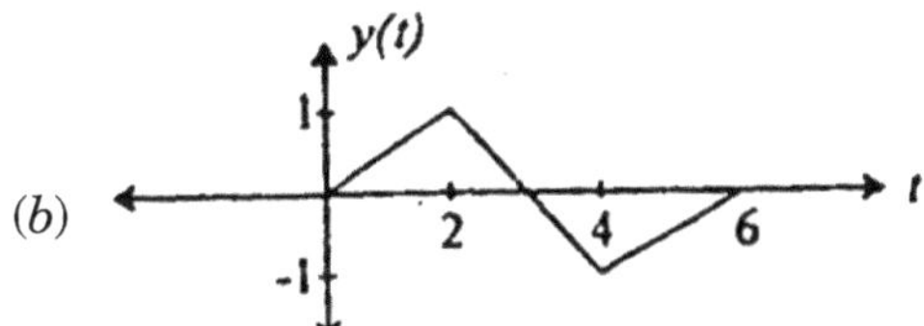

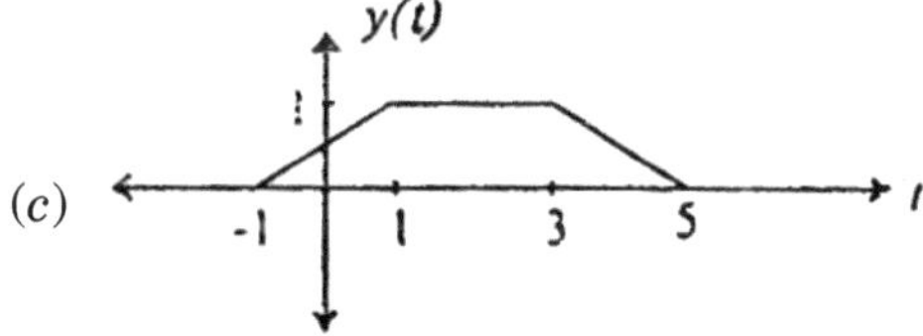

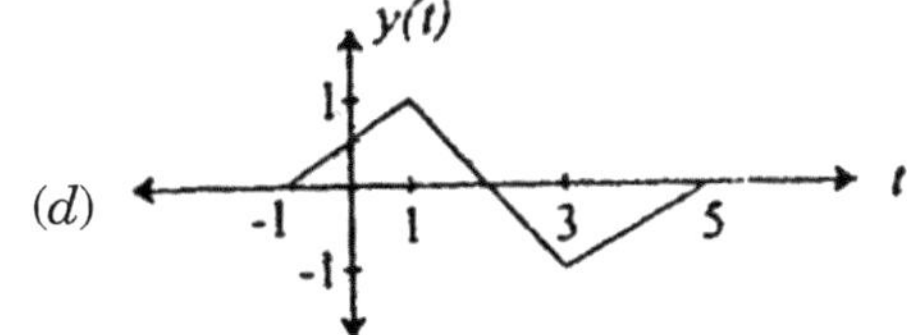

48. Consider the discrete-time signal x(n) = $\left(\dfrac{1}{3}\right)^n$ u(n), where u(n) = $\begin{cases} 1, n \geq 0 \\ 0, n < 0 \end{cases}$. Define the signal y(n) as y(n) = x(–n), $-\infty < n < \infty$. Then $\sum\limits_{n=-\infty}^{\infty} y(n)$ equals **RRB 2012**

(a) $-\dfrac{2}{3}$ (b) $\dfrac{2}{3}$

(c) $\dfrac{3}{2}$ (d) 3

49. Let the signal x(t) have the Fourier transform X(ω). Consider the signal y(t) = $\dfrac{d}{dt}$ $[x(t - t_d)]$ where t_d is an arbitrary delay. The magnitude of the Fourier transform of $y(t)$ is given by the expression. **RRB 2012**

(a) $|X(\omega)|.|\omega|$

(b) $|X(\omega)|.\omega$

(c) $\omega^2.|X(\omega)|$

(d) $|\omega|.|X(\omega)|.e^{-j\omega t_d}$

50. If x[n] = (1/3)$^{|n|}$ – (1/2)^n u[n], then the region of convergence (ROC) of its Z-transform in the Z-plane will be **RRB 2012**

(a) $\dfrac{1}{3} < |z| < 3$

(b) $\dfrac{1}{3} < |z| < \dfrac{1}{2}$

(c) $\dfrac{1}{2} < |z| < 3$

(d) $\dfrac{1}{3} < |z|$

51. A system with transfer function is excited by sin(ωt). The steady-state output of the system is zero at. **RRB 2012**

$$G(s) = \dfrac{\left(s^2 + 9\right)(s + 2)}{(s + 1)(s + 3)(s + 4)}$$

Find ω at which steady state output is zero

(a) ω = 1 rad/s   (b) ω = 2 rad/s

(c) ω = 3 rad/s   (d) ω = 4 rad/s

52. Given f(z) = $\dfrac{1}{z+1} - \dfrac{2}{z+3}$. If C is a counterclockwise path in the z-plane such that $|z+1| = 1$, the value of $\dfrac{1}{2\pi}\oint_c f(z)dz$ is **RRB 2012**

(a) –2

(b) –1

(c) 1

(d) 2

53. For the closed loop system shown below to be stable, the value of time delay TD (in seconds) should be less than **RRB 2012**

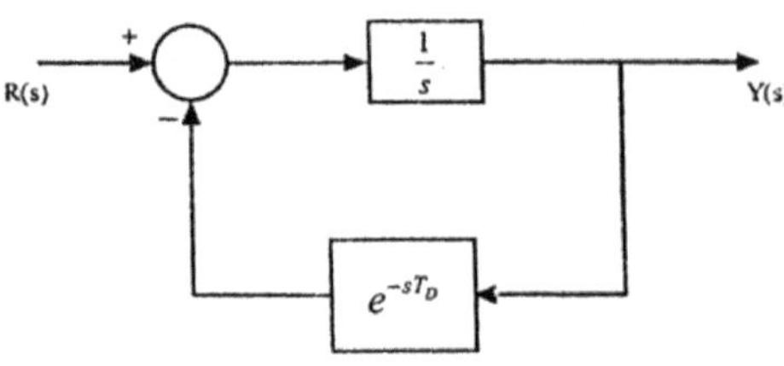

(a) $\dfrac{\pi}{4}$

(b) $\dfrac{\pi}{3}$

(c) $\dfrac{\pi}{2}$

(d) π

54. The value of the integral of the complex function

$$f(s) = \dfrac{3s + 4}{(s + 1)(s + 2)}$$ along the path $|s| = 3$ is

(a) $2\pi j$

(b) $4\pi j$ **RRB 2012**

(c) $6\pi j$

(d) $8\pi j$

55. For k = 0, 1, 2, ..., the steps of Newton-Raphson method for solving a non-linear equation is given as **RRB 2012**

$$x_{k+1} = \dfrac{2}{3}\, x_k + \dfrac{5}{3} x_k^{-2}.$$

Starting from a suitable initial choice as k tends to ∞, the iterate x_k tends to

(a) 1.7099

(b) 2.2361

(c) 3.1251

(d) 5.0000

56. The state variable description of an LTI system is given by **RRB 2012**

$$\begin{pmatrix} \dot{x}_1 \\ \dot{x}_2 \\ \dot{x}_3 \end{pmatrix} = \begin{pmatrix} 0 & a_1 & 0 \\ 0 & 0 & a_2 \\ a_3 & 0 & 0 \end{pmatrix} \begin{pmatrix} x_1 \\ x_2 \\ x_3 \end{pmatrix} + \begin{pmatrix} 0 \\ 0 \\ 1 \end{pmatrix} u$$

$$y = \begin{pmatrix} 1 & 0 & 0 \end{pmatrix} \begin{pmatrix} x_1 \\ x_2 \\ x_3 \end{pmatrix}$$

where y is the output and u is the input. The system is controllable for

(a) $a_1 \neq 0,\ a_2 = 0,\ a_3 \neq 0$

(b) $a_1 = 0,\ a_2 \neq 0,\ a_3 \neq 0$

(c) $a_1 = 0,\ a_2 \neq 0,\ a_3 = 0$

(d) $a_1 \neq 0,\ a_2 \neq 0,\ a_3 = 0$

57. Which of the following integrals provides a measure of the rapidity of change in a random variable f(t) ? **RRB 2012**

(a) $\lim\limits_{T \to \infty} \dfrac{1}{2T} \displaystyle\int_{-T}^{+T} f\,(d)\,dt$

(b) $\lim\limits_{T \to \infty} \dfrac{1}{2T} \displaystyle\int_{-T}^{+T} f^2\,(t)\,dt$

(c) $\left[\lim\limits_{T \to \infty} \dfrac{1}{2T} \displaystyle\int_{-T}^{+T} f^2\,(t)\,dt \right]^{1/2}$

(d) $\lim\limits_{T \to \infty} \dfrac{1}{2T} \displaystyle\int_{-T}^{+T} f\,(t)\,f(\,t + \tau)\,dt$

58. Given **RRB 2012**

$$x(t)*\,x(t) = t\,\exp\,(-\,2t)\,u(t),$$

the function $x\,(t)$ is

(a) $\exp\,(-\,2t)\,u(t)$ (b) $\exp\,(-t)\,u(t)$

(c) $t\,\exp\,(-t)\,u(t)$ (d) $0.5t\,\exp\,(-t)\,u(t)$

59. The fourier series for a periodic signal is given as

$x\,(t) = \cos\,(1.2\,\pi t) + \cos\,(2\pi t) + \cos\,(2.8\pi t)$.

The fundamental frequency of the signal is

(a) 0.2 Hz   (b) 0.6 Hz   **RRB 2012**

(c) 1.0 Hz   (d) 1.4 Hz

60. The Fourier transform of a function $g(t)$ is given as

$$G\,(\omega) = \dfrac{\omega^2 + 21}{\omega^2 + 9}$$

Then the function g(t) is given as   **RRB 2012**

(a) $\delta\,(t) + 2\,\exp\,(-3\,|t\,|)$

(b) $\cos\,3\omega t + 21\,\exp\,(-\,3t)$

(c) $\sin\,3\omega t + 7\,\cos\,\omega t$

(d) $\sin\,3\omega t + 21\,\exp\,(3t)$

61. A digital measuring instrument employs a sampling rate of 100 samples/second.

The sampled input $x(n)$ is averaged using the difference equation

$y\,(n) = [x(n) + x(n-1) + x\,(n-2) + x\,(n-3)]\,/4$

For a step input, the maximum time taken for the output to reach the final value after the input transition is **RRB 2012**

(a) 20 ms   (b) 40 ms

(c) 80 ms   (d) ∞

62. Let y[n] denote the convolution of h[n] and g[n], where h[n] = $(1/2)^n$ u[n] and g[n] is a causal sequence. If y[0] = 1 and y[1] = 1/2, then g[1] equals **RRB 2012**

(a) 0   (b) $\dfrac{1}{2}$

(c) 1   (d) $\dfrac{3}{2}$

63. The asymptotic Bode plot for the gain magnitude of a minimum phase system G (s) is shown in the figure given below. The transfer function is G (s) = **RRB 2012**

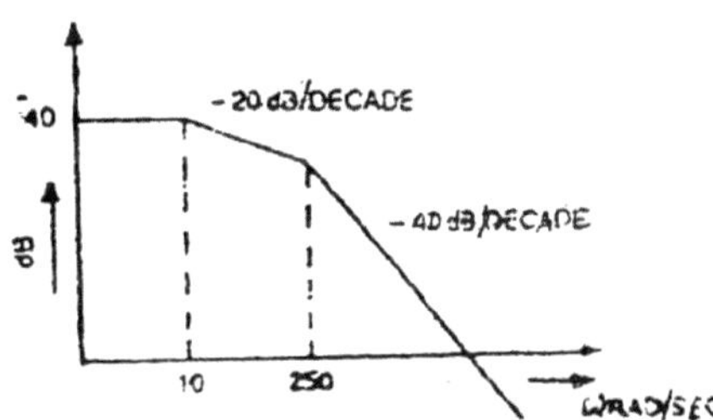

(a) $\dfrac{100}{(1 + s\,/\,10)(1 + s\,/\,250)}$

(b) $\dfrac{40}{s(s + 250)}$

(c) $\dfrac{100}{(s + 10)(s + 250)}$

(d) $\dfrac{100s}{(s + 10)(s + 250)}$

64. The maximum value of f(x) = $x^3 - 9x^2 + 24x + 5$ in the interval [1, 6] is **RRB 2012**

(a) 21   (b) 25

(c) 41   (d) 46

ANSWERS

EXERCISE – I

1. (c)	**2.** (d)	**3.** (b)	**4.** (b)	**5.** (a)	**6.** (c)	**7.** (c)	**8.** (d)	**9.** (a)	**10.** (c)
11. (a)	**12.** (c)	**13.** (d)	**14.** (a)	**15.** (a)	**16.** (c)	**17.** (b)	**18.** (a)	**19.** (a)	**20.** (d)
21. (a)	**22.** (c)	**23.** (b)	**24.** (d)	**25.** (a)	**26.** (a)	**27.** (d)	**28.** (b)	**29.** (b)	**30.** (a)
31. (c)	**32.** (u)	**33.** (b)	**34.** (a)	**35.** (a)	**36.** (c)	**37.** (a)	**38.** (d)	**39.** (a)	**40.** (b)
41. (c)	**42.** (c)	**43.** (d)	**44.** (b)	**45.** (c)	**46.** (c)	**47.** (b)	**48.** (a)	**49.** (b)	**50.** (c)
51. (c)	**52.** (c)	**53.** (d)	**54.** (a)	**55.** (a)	**56.** (b)	**57.** (b)	**58.** (c)	**59.** (c)	**60.** (b)
61. (b)	**62.** (d)	**63.** (b)	**64.** (d)	**65.** (a)	**66.** (c)	**67.** (b)	**68.** (b)	**69.** (c)	**70.** (d)
71. (b)	**72.** (b)	**73.** (a)	**74.** (a)	**75.** (d)	**76.** (b)	**77.** (d)	**78.** (d)	**79.** (c)	**80.** (c)
81. (b)	**82.** (b)	**83.** (b)	**84.** (d)	**85.** (b)	**86.** (c)	**87.** (d)	**88.** (a)	**89.** (a)	**90.** (b)
91. (a)	**92.** (c)	**93.** (c)	**94.** (b)	**95.** (b)	**96.** (a)	**97.** (a)	**98.** (c)	**99.** (d)	**100.** (b)
101. (a)	**102.** (b)	**103.** (c)	**104.** (d)	**105.** (b)	**106.** (c)	**107.** (a)	**108.** (b)	**109.** (c)	**110.** (d)
111. (c)	**112.** (c)	**113.** (d)	**114.** (b)	**115.** (c)	**116.** (b)	**117.** (a)	**118.** (c)	**119.** (a)	**120.** (b)
121. (b)	**122.** (d)	**123.** (b)	**124.** (b)	**125.** (a)	**126.** (a)	**127.** (a)	**128.** (a)	**129.** (d)	**130.** (a)
131. (b)	**132.** (d)	**133.** (c)	**134.** (c)	**135.** (a)	**136.** (a)	**137.** (d)	**138.** (c)	**139.** (c)	**140.** (c)
141. (b)	**142.** (c)	**143.** (a)	**144.** (c)	**145.** (a)	**146.** (b)	**147.** (c)	**148.** (d)	**149.** (d)	**150.** (b)
151. (a)	**152.** (d)	**153.** (a)	**154.** (d)	**155.** (a)	**156.** (d)	**157.** (b)	**158.** (a)	**159.** (a)	**160.** (c)
161. (a)	**162.** (d)	**163.** (a)	**164.** (d)	**165.** (c)	**166.** (b)				

EXERCISE – II

1. (b)	**2.** (a)	**3.** (d)	**4.** (b)	**5.** (d)	**6.** (d)	**7.** (b)	**8.** (a)	**9.** (d)	**10.** (a)
11. (a)	**12.** (d)	**13.** (d)	**14.** (b)	**15.** (b)	**16.** (c)	**17.** (d)	**18.** (c)	**19.** (a)	**20.** (c)
21. (b)	**22.** (a)	**23.** (c)	**24.** (d)	**25.** (d)	**26.** (c)	**27.** (d)	**28.** (a)	**29.** (b)	**30.** (c)
31. (a)	**32.** (d)	**33.** (a)	**34.** (a)	**35.** (b)	**36.** (c)	**37.** (c)	**38.** (b)	**39.** (d)	**40.** (d)
41. (d)	**42.** (c)	**43.** (b)	**44.** (c)	**45.** (a)	**46.** (a)	**47.** (d)	**48.** (d)	**49.** (d)	**50.** (c)
51. (c)	**52.** (c)	**53.** (c)	**54.** (c)	**55.** (a)	**56.** (d)	**57.** (d)	**58.** (a)	**59.** (a)	**60.** (a)
61. (b)	**62.** (a)	**63.** (a)	**64.** (c)						

7

CHAPTER

Communication

BASIC COMMUNICATION SYSTEM.

The function of a communication system is to communicate a message. The message comes from the information source, which originates it, in the sense of selection one message from a finite set.

Elements of communication system

It consists of the following elements :

1. Source of information.
2. Coder – for transforming information into a form suitable for transportation over a transmission system.
3. Transmission system.
4. Decoder, for transforming the signal into a form suitable for interpretation by the receiver.
5. Receiver of information.

Coding

Coding involves transformation of signal along with the modification of the signals from its associated source so that there is a distinct difference between several coded signals, but the coding must not destroy the identity of the information. This process is called *modulation*.

Decoder

It involves

(*i*) filtering out i.e., selecting the desired signal for addressee and rejecting all other signals

(*ii*) transforming the signal back into a form in which it can be handled by the normal decoding process. This is called *demodulation*.

Modulation.

In the process of modulation, the information is impressed on a high frequency sine wave.

Some characteristics of a high frequency sine wave is varied in accordance with the instantaneous value of the (modulating) signal.

A sine wave is represented by $\quad e = E \sin(\omega t + \phi)$

where e = instantaneous value of the sine wave called *carrier*

$\quad\quad$ E = its maximum amplitude

$\quad\quad \omega$ = angular frequency

$\quad\quad \phi$ = its phase relation with respect to some reference.

- Any of these three parameters (E, ω and ϕ) of the carrier may be varied by the modulating signal, giving rise to Amplitude Modulation (AM), Frequency Modulation (FM) or Phase Modulation (PM).

- The signal itself cannot be transmitted over long distance because of difficulties involved in the propagation of electromagnetic waves at frequencies corresponding to the audio spectrum i.e., below 20 kHz.

- Some of greatest difficulties for efficient radiation and recept are quarter wavelength of the frequency used.

- All sound in concentrated within the range from 20Hz to 20 kHz, so all signals from the different source will be hopelessly mixed up.

- In order to separate various signals it is necessary to translate them all to different portions of electromagnetic spectrum. This will also overcome difficulty of poor radiation at low frequencies. Once signal is translated, tuned circuit is employed in front of the receiver to ensure that desired section of the spectrum is admitted and all the unwanted ones are rejected. The tuning of such a circuit is made variable so that receiver can select any desired transmission within a predetermined range.

RADIO SPECTRUM

Frequency Band			Typical Uses
Very Low Frequency	VLF	(3 to 30 kHz)	Long distance point to point communication.
Low Frequency	LF	(30 - 300 kHz)	Radio navigation.
Medium Frequency	MF	(0.3 - 3 MHz)	Broadcasting, marine.
High Frequency	HF	(3 - 30 MHz)	Radio telephony.
Very High Frequency	VHF	(30 - 300 MHz)	FM broadcasting, Television, Mobile radio, Radio navigation.
Ultra High Frequency	UHF	(0.3 - 3 GHz)	Television. Mobile radio, Radio navigation, Radar.
Super High Frequency	SHF	(3 - 30 GHz)	Multi-channel telephony links Radar. Satellite communication.

AM Modulators

It is possible to make output current of a class C amplifier proportional to the modulating voltage by applying this voltage in series with any of the *dc* supply voltages for this amplifier. Thus cathode (or emitter), grid (or base) and anode (or collector) modulations of class C amplifier are all possible. Though the angle of conduction for this amplifier is less than 90°, the tuned circuit in the output makes the current nearly sinusoidal.

Class C amplifier is modulated by introduction of the modulating voltage in series with the grid-bias. Thus modulating voltage is superimposed on the fixed negative grid bias.

Hence amplifier of the total bias is proportional to amplitude of the modulating signal and varies at a rate equal to the modulating frequency.

AM Transmitter

Figure shows the block diagram of a standard high level broadcast transmitter. The oscillator being crystal-controlled, produces constant carrier frequency which is further amplified by *RF* amplifier. The audio input is amplified by audio amplifier. Both these signals are fed to modulator and the resulting modulated output is amplified and fed to the antenna.

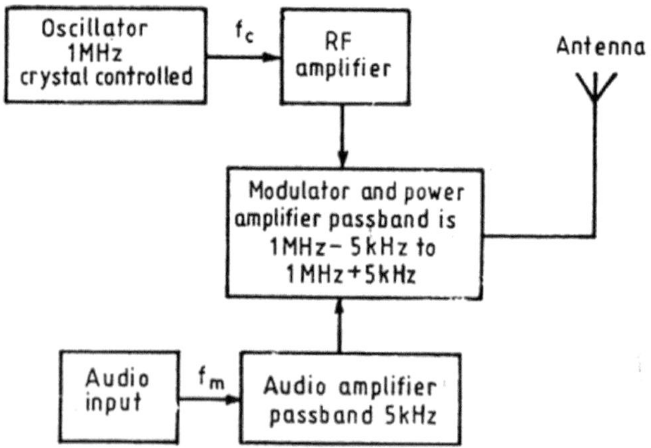

TYPES OF MODULATION

1. Double-Sideband Modulation (DSB)

In DSB modulation instantaneous amplitude is directly proportional to the message signal.

The spectral range covered by the message signal is called **baseband**, and therefore message signal is called *baseband signal*.

As seen from the spectrum, transmission bandwidth required for DSB modulation is 2ω. Since in this type of modulation, there is no identifiable carrier contains, therefore, it is also called *Double-sideband Suppressed Carrier (DSB-SC) modulation*.

Production of DSB

It can be shown that if two voltages are applied to the input of a non-linear device in an additive manner (here modulating signal and the carrier), output of the device may be a d.c. component, carrier, modulating signal and their harmonics, and more significantly sum and difference of carrier and modulating signal. Thus process of amplitude modulation takes place and becomes principle of balanced modulation for generating double side-bands. This is based on *Ven der Bijl* modulation system which shows that harmonics and inter-modulation distortion occur in audio and RF amplifiers.

Demodulation of DSB singals.

The baseband signal $m(t)$ can be recovered from a, DSB-SC wave by first multiplying it with a locally generated sinusoidal wave and then low-pass filtering the product. Here, it is being assumed that local signal is exactly in the phase and frequency synchronism with the incoming carrier. This type of modulation is called *synchronous detection or coherent detection*.

2. Single-Sideband Modulation (SSB)

In this type of modulation, modulated wave consists of either upper sideband or the lower sideband, since any of them contains complete information about the message signal. This modulation is well suited for the transmission of voice signals by virtue of the energy gap that exists in the spectrum of the voice signals between zero and few hundred hertzs. This modulation require reduced bandwith requirement and minimum transmitted power but cost and complexity of its implementation.

The carrier may be removed or attenuated and so can one of the two side-bands. The resulting signal will require less transmitted power and will occupy less band width and yet practically perfectly acceptable communication will be possible.

Single side-band modulation (SSB) has been quite possible the fast spreading form of modulation. Among its great advantages is the ability to transmit good communication quality signals using a very narrow band-width with relatively low power for the distances involved.

Production of SSB.

It can be produced by either of the following two methods :

1. **Filter Method.** In this method, from the output of balanced modulator, the unwanted side-band is removed (actually heavily attenuated) by a filter. The filter may be LC type crystal or mechanical. Basically such a filter must have a flat pass-band and extremely high attenuatioin outside the pass-band. Higher the attenuation, the better it is.

2. Phase-Shift Method. In the system shown in the figure, when both upper sidebands leads the input carrier voltage by 90°, while the other lags it by 90°, LSB are thus out of phase and when combined in the adder, they cancel each other. USB are in phase at the adder and will thus add giving SSB in which LSB has been cancelled.

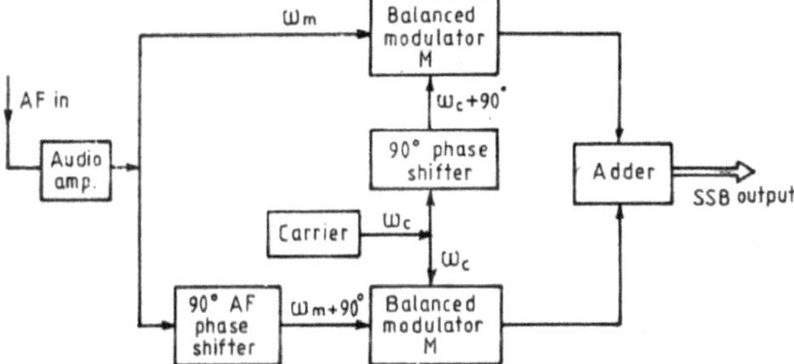

Demodulation of SSB signals.

Demodulation of SSB signal can be done by using the coherent detector. In the process involved, first single-sideband signal $x_{SSB}(t)$ is multiplied by a local carrier and passing the resulted signal through a low-pass filter.

3. Vestigial-Sideband (VSB) Modulation

In this type of modulation, one sideband is passed almost completely and just a trace of other sideband is retained. Hence, channel bandwidth required is in excess of the message bandwidth by an amount equal to width of the vestigial sideband.

This type of modulation is used in television signal transmission that contains significant components at extremely low frequencies.

The typical bandwidth required to transmit a VSB signal is 1.25 times to that of SSB.

A VSB signal can be generated by passing a DSB signal through a sideband shaping filter.

FREQUENCY–DIVISION MULTIPLEXING.

The technique incorporating the separation of signals in frequency, is called *frequency-division multiplexing* (FDM).

Spectra of the message signals and sum of the modulated carriers are shown in the figure

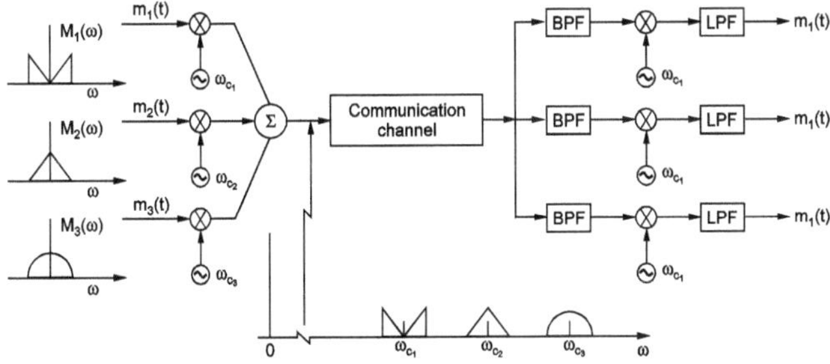

FDM is used in telephone system, telemetry, commercial broadcast, television, and communication networks.

ANGLE-MODULATION

In angle modulation, spectral components of the modulated waveform are not related in any simple fashion to the message spectrum. In addition, superposition does not apply to angle-modulated signal, *i.e.,* this modulation is non-linear modulation. Again, bandwidth of the angle-modulation signal is much greater than the message bandwidth.

Types of angle Modulation.

(*i*) Phase Modulation (PM)

Pulse Modulation. It is a system in which continuous waveforms are sampled at regular intervals. Information regarding the signal is transmitted only at the sampling times, together with any synchronising pulse that may be required. If samples are taken at sufficient frequency, the original signal may be reconstituted from the information contained by the samples.

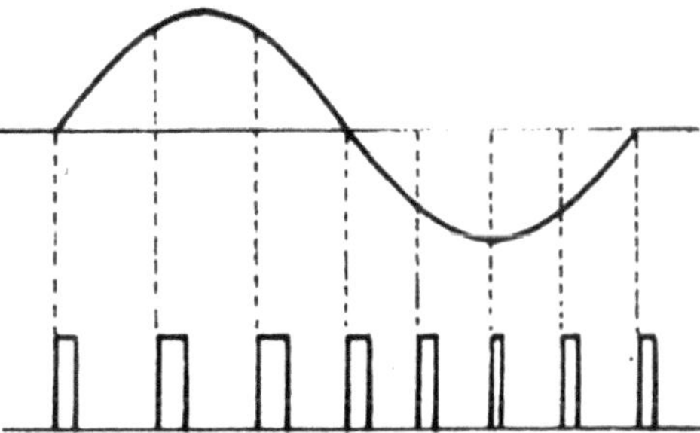

Pulse Amplitude Modulation. In this system, signal is sampled at regular intervals, and each sample made proportional to the amplitude of the signal at the instant of sampling as shown in Fig. To generate PAM, the signal to be converted into PAM is fed to one input of an *AND* gate.

Pulse-Time Modulation. In PTM, the signal is sampled, but the pulse indicating instantaneous sample amplitudes themselves have a constant amplitude. However, one of their timing characteristics is varied being made proportional to the sampled signal amplitude at that instant as shown in Fig. The variable characteristic may be the width, position or frequency of the pulse. But the third one is out of practical application. As in case of *FM*, amplitude limiters can be used to provide a good degree of noise immunity.

Sampling Theorem. This states that, if sampling rate in any pulse modulation system exceeds twice the maximum signal frequency, the original signal can be reconstructed in the receiver with small distortion. The sampling theorem is used in practice to determine minimum sampling speeds.

(*ii*) Frequency Modulation (FM)

If frequency of the carrier is made to-vary according to the modulating signal, frequency modulation waves are obtained. It is assumed that the phase relations of a complex modulating signal will be preserved. By the definition of frequency modulation., the amount by which the carrier frequency is varied from its unmodulated value, called the deviation, is made proportional to the instantaneous value of the modulating voltage. The rate at which this frequency variation or oscillation takes place is equal to the modulating frequency. The principle is shown in the figure

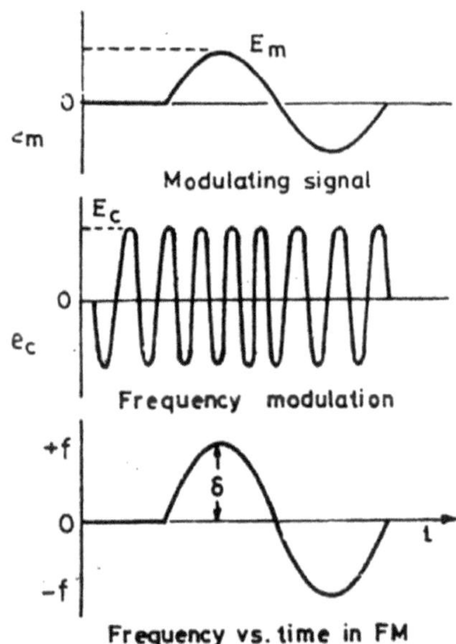

Advantages of FM.

1. Amplitude of the frequency modulated wave in FM is independent of the depth of modulation whereas in AM it is dependent on this parameter.

2. There is a large decrease in noise and hence an increase in the signal-to-noise ratio in FM. This is due to following reasons :

   (*i*) There happens to be less noise at frequencies at which FM is used

   (*ii*) FM receivers can be fitted with amplitude limiters to remove amplitude varriations caused by noise.

3. It is possible to reduce noise still further by increasing deviation. This is a feature that AM does not have.

4. FM transmitters operate in the upper VHF and UHF ranges, and at these frequencies, space wave is used for propagation, so that radius of reception is limited. It is thus possible to operate several independent transmitters on the same frequency with considerable less interference.

Disadvantages of FM

1. Much wider channel is required by FM.

2. *FM* transmitting and receiving equipment tends to be more complex and hence it is more expensive.

Phase Modulation.

If phase of the carrier is varied according to the instantaneous amplitude of the modulation signal, the process is called *phase modulation*. The expression of a PM wave is

$$e = \text{A} \sin (\omega_c\, t + \phi_m \sin \omega_m\, t)$$

Clearly, ϕ_m is maximum value of phase change introduced by the modulating signal. It is proportional to the maximum amplitude of the modulating signal, i.e.

$$\phi_m = KE_m = m_p$$

Therefore

$$\therefore \qquad e = \text{A} \sin (\omega_c\, t + m_p \sin \omega_m\, t)$$

FM receivers.

The superheterodyne *FM* receiver shown in the figure is similar to AM receiver, but basic differences are as follows :

1. Much higher operating frequency in *FM*.

2. Need for limiting and de-emphasis in *FM*.

3. Different method of demodulation.

4. Different method of obtaining *AGC*

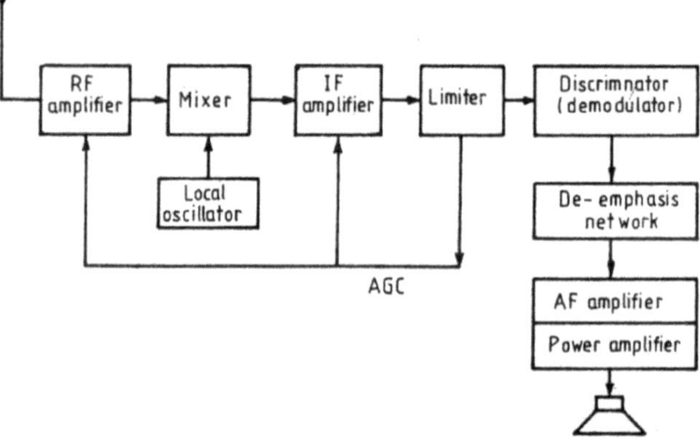

Typical receiver operating at 88 *MHz* may have an *IF* stage of 10.7 *MHz* and a band width of 200 *kHz*.

RF amplifier is always used in an *FM* receiver. The reason is to reduce the noise figure, which could otherwise be a problem because of the large bandwidths needed for *FM*. It is also required to match input impedance of the receiver to that of antenna. To meet the second requirement, grounded gate (or base) amplifiers are employed.

FM Demoduator. It is basically a frequency-to-amplitude converter which converts the frequency deviation of the incoming carrier into an *AF* (audio frequency) amplitude variation indentical to that of modulating signal.

DEMODULATION OF ANGLE-MODULATED SIGNALS.

Frequency demodulation is done by using a popular device called *frequency discriminator,* whose instantaneous amplitude is directly proportional to the instantaeous frequency of the input FM signal. Basically, frequency discriminator consists of a *slope circuit* followed by an *envelope detector.* An ideal slope circuit is characterized by a transfer function, that is purely imaginary, varying linearly with frequency inside a prescribed frequency interval.

DIGITAL COMMUNICATION SYSTEMS

Pulse-Code Modulation.

In common with the other forms of pulse modulation. The PCM uses the sampling technique, but it differs from the others in that it is a digital process. That is, instead of sending a pulse train capable of continuously varying one of the parameters, the PCM generator produces a series of numbers, or digits (hence the name digital process). Each one of these digits, almost always in binary code, represents approximate amplitude of the signal sample at that instant.

In PCM, the total amplitude range which the signal may occupy is divided into a number of standard levels. Since these levels are transmitted in a binary code, the actual number of levels is invariable a power of 2. By a process called *quantizing,* the level actually sent at any sampling time is the nearest standard level.

In pulse-code modulation (PCM) a message signal is represented by a sequence of coded pulses, which is accomplished by representing the signal in discrete form in both time and amplitude. The basic operations involved are sampling, quantizing and encoding. The low-pass filter prior to sampling is included to prevent aliasing of the message signal. The quantizing and encoding operations are usually performed in the same circuit, which is called *analog-to-digital converter.* The basic operations in the receiver are regeneration of unpaired signals, decoding and reconstruction of the train of quantized samples as shown in Fig. (c). Regeneration along the transmission path also occurs at the intermediate points as it being necessary.

If time-division-multiplexing is employed, then proper synchronization between receiver and transmitter is needed.

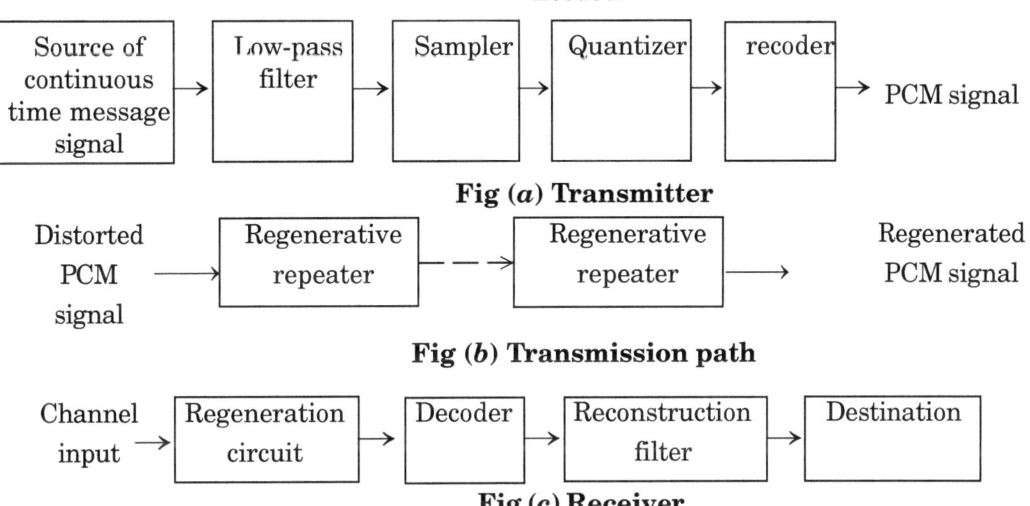

Fig (*a*) Transmitter

Fig (*b*) Transmission path

Fig (*c*) Receiver

Generation and of Demodulation PCM. The signal is sampled and converted to PAM, the PAM is quantities and encoded and supervisory signals are then added. The signal is then sent directly via cable, or modulated and transmitted. Because PCM is very immune to noise, amplitude modulation may be used, so that PCM-AM is quite common.

At the receiver, the signaling information is extracted and PCM is translated into corresponding PAM pulse which are there demodulated in the usual way. In fact the 'quantized wave' would be the output for that signal from an ideal receiver.

An integrating RC circuit is used for reconversion in the receiver. The applied pulse are fed to it and it is then sampled and discharged immediately after the arrival of the last pulse.

ANALOG PULSE MODULATION SYSTEMS

In the *pulse modulation* systems, the carrier is a train of discrete pulses rather than a sinewave. Any one characteristics of this pulse train, i.e. amplitude, width or position can be changed in proportion with the amplitude of modulating signal. This will yield PAM (pulse amplitude modulation), PWM (pulse width modulation) or PPM (pulse position modulation) signals, respectively.

PULSE AMPLITUDE MODULATION (PAM)
Naturally sampled PAM.

In the PAM system, the amplitude of the pulsed carrier is changed in proportion with the instantaneous amplitude of the modulating signal x (t). The carrier is in the form of train of narrow pulses .The PAM signal is then sent by either wire or cable or it is used to modulate another carrier.

Types of PAM

There are two types of PAM systems.

(*i*)   Double polarity PAM

(*ii*)   **Single polarity PAM** : In single polarity PAM, a fixed dc level is added to the continuous signal x (*t*). Due to this, modulated pulses are always positive.

Detection of PAM

The PAM signal can be detected (demodulated) by passing it through a low pass filter. The low pass filter cutoff frequency is adjusted to W so that all the high frequency components are removed and the original modulating signal is recovered back.

Advantages of PAM

Simplicity of generation and detection.

Disadvantages of PAM

(*i*)   The amplitude of PAM signal changes according to the amplitude of modulating signal x (t). Therefore like AM, PAM signal gets affected due to the additive noise. The added noise then cannot be removed easily.

(*ii*)   The transmission bandwidth is much larger than the maximum frequency content in x_s (t).

(*iii*) Due to changes in amplitudes of PAM pulses, the transmitted power does not remain constant.

PULSE WIDTH MODULATION (PWM)

Pulse-Width Modulation. This form of PTM is also often called PDM (Pulse duration modulation). In this system as shown in Fig, we have a fixed amplitude and starting time of each pulse, but the width of each pulse made proportional to the amplitude of the signal at that instant.

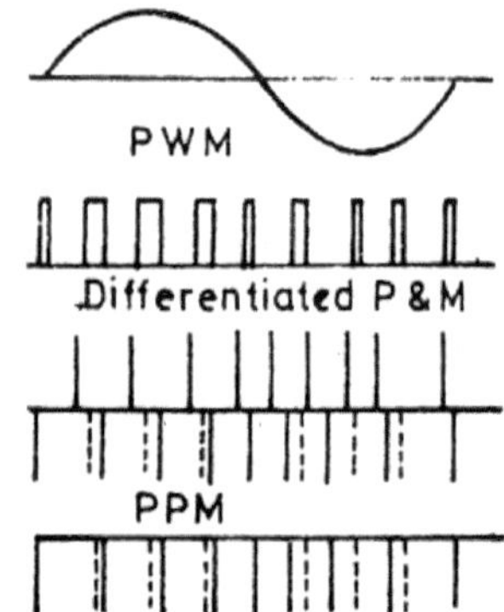

When pulse-width modulation has the disadvantage compared with pulse-position modulation *(PPM),* that its pulse are of varying width and therfore of varying power content. This means that the transmitter must be powerful enough to handle the maximum width pulse, although the average power transmitted is perhaps only half of the peak power. On the other hand, *PWM* will still work if synchronisation between transmitter and receiver fails whereas pulse-position modulation will not.

One of the methods of generating pulse-width modulation consists of applying trigger pulse (at the sampling rate) to control the starting time of pulse from a monostable multivibrator, and feeding in the signal to be sampled to control the duration of these pulses.

The demodulation of pulse-width modulation is quite a simple process. The *PWM* is fed to an integrating circuit from which a signal emerges whose amplitude at any time is proportional to the pulse width at that time.

Other type of a pulse analog modulation is the pulse width modulation (PWM). In PWM, width of the modulated pulses varies in proportion with the amplitude of modulating signal.

As seen from the waveforms, amplitude and frequency of the PWM wave remains constant. Only width changes. That is why *information* is contained in the width variation. This is similar to FM. As the noise is normally *additive* noise, it changes amplitude of the PWM signal. At the receiver, it is possible to remove these unwanted amplitude variation very easily by means of a limiter circuit. As the information is contained in the width variation, it is unaffected by the amplitude variations introduced by the noise. Thus PWM system is more immune to noise than the PAM signal.

Advantages of PWM

(*i*)   Less effect of noise, i.e. very good noise immunity.

(*ii*)   Synchronization between the transmitter and receiver is not essential (which is essential in PPM).

(*iii*) It is possible to reconstruct PWM signal from a noise contaminated PWM. Thus it is possible to separate out signal from noise (which is not possible in PAM).

Disadvantages of PWM

(*i*)   Due to variable pulse width, pulses have variable power contents. So transmitter must be powerful enough to handle maximum width pulse, though average power transmitted can be as low as 50% of this maximum power.

(*ii*)   In order to avoid any waveform distortion, bandwidth required for the PWM communication is large as compared to band width of PAM.

Pulse Position Modulation (PPM).

The amplitude and width of the pulse is kept constant in this system in which the position of each pulse, in relation to the position of are current reference pulse is varied by each instantaneous sampled value of the modulating wave. As mentioned in connection with *PWM,* pulse-position modulation has the advantage of requiring constant transmitter power output, but the disadvantages of depending on transmitter-receiver synchronisation.

Pulse-position modulation may be obtained very simply from *PWM*. Considering *PWM* and its generation again, it is seen that each such pulse has a leading edge and a trailing edge. However in this case the repetition rate of the leading edge is fixed whereas that of the trailing edges is not. Their position depends on pulse width, which is determined by the signal amplitude at that instant. Thus, it may be said that the trailing edges of *PWM* pulse are in fact, position modulated.

When *PPM* is demodulated in the receiver, it is again first converted into *PWM*, this is done with a flip-flop, or bistable multivibrator.

Advantages of PPM

(*i*) Due to constant amplitude of PPM pulses, information is not contained in the amplitude. Hence noise added to PPM signal does not distort the information. Thus it has good noise immunity.

(*ii*) It is possible to reconstruct PPM signal from the noise contaminated PPM signal. This is also possible in PWM but not possible in PAM.

(*iii*) Due to constant amplitude of pulses, transmitted power always remains constant. It does not change as it used to, in PWM.

Disadvantages of PPM

(*i*) As position of the PPM pulses is varied with respect to a reference pulse, a transmitter has to send synchronizing pulses to operate timing circuits in the receiver. Without them the demodulation won't be possible to achieve.

(*ii*) Large bandwidth is required to ensure transmission of undistorted pulses.

Quantizing Noise. The distortion produced by quantizing process is called quantizing noise, becasue errors are random in character. The randomness occur simply because the difference between the digit sent and the actual signal at that instant is completely unpredictable.

The obvious method of reducing quantizing noise is to increase the number of standard levels unitl the noise level becomes acceptable.

Multiplexing. To increase the traffic handling capacity of the line first automatic transmitters, receives and printers were developed to replace more keys, sounder and slow speed manual operations. The multiplex operation of the line was developed to utilise the line all the time. Multiplexing is the transmission of a number of separate signals together simultaneously without interference. In *Time-Division Multiplex* (TDM), interleaving in the time domain, of pulses belonging to different transmission is done. Use is made of the fact that pulses are generally narrow and separation between successive pulses is rather wide. That being the case it is possible, provided the two ends of a link are synchronised to use the wide spaces for pulses belonging to other transmissions.

TIME- DIVISION MULTIPLEXING (TDM)

This multiplexing is commonly used for the transmission of several different signals through a single channel.

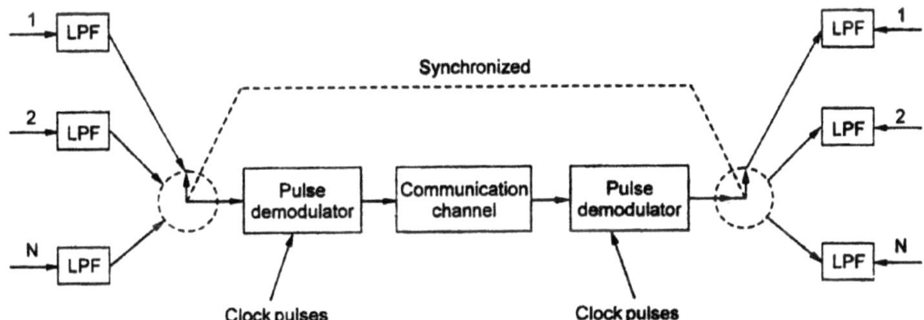

If all input signals have the same bandwidth f_m and are sampled equally, then

$$T = \frac{T_s}{n}$$

where n = number of input signals,

$$T_s = \frac{1}{f_s} \le \frac{1}{2f_m} \text{ is the sampling interval of each signal}$$

If the resultant time-multiplexed signal is low-pass signal of bandwidth f_{TDM}, then the minimum sampling rate is $2f_{\text{TDM}}$.

DELTA MODULATION

In delta modulation (DM), an incoming meassage signal is oversampled to increase the correlation between adjacent samples of the signal. This rate is much higher than the Nyquist rate.

KEY POINTS

Vibrator

It is an electromagnetic device which is used to convert DC into AC.

These are of two types :

(*i*) Synchronous : It gives a DC output directly.

(*ii*) Non-synchronous : It gives AC output and a rectifier is required for converting it into DC.

Access Holes

It is series of holes in successive layer each set having their centers on the same axis. These holes provide access to the surface of the land in one of the layer of a multiple layer printed board.

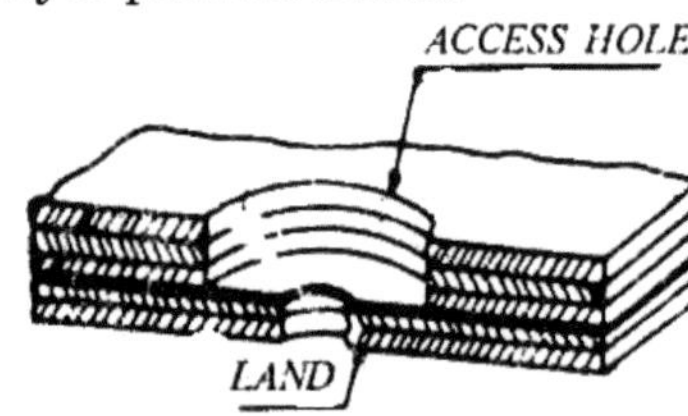

Access Holes in Successive Layers

ACOUSTICS

It is the science of sound including production, transmission and effects.

Sound

It is a form of energy which can be experienced by human ears

Velocity of sound : In dry air = 332 metres per second In water = 1435 metres per second.

Type of Sound waves

1. Audible waves
2. Infrasonic waves
3. Ultrasonic waves

Sound waves propagation

Sound waves are propagated in the form of vibration of the j-medium particles. Sound waves can't be propagated in the absence of a medium

Audible waves

Waves which can be heard by human ears are called *audible waves*. Their frequency range extends from 20 Hz to 20 kHz but it may vary from person to person in accordance to his age.

Infrasonic waves

Waves having a frequency of less than 20 Hz are called *infrasonic waves.*

These waves are inaudible.

Ultrasonic waves

Waves having a frequency of more than 20 kHz are called *ultrasonic waves.*

These waves are used for communications, determination of depth of sea, increasing agricultural yields, improving quality of seeds etc.

Hi-Fi sound

Sound available at the output of a loudspeaker or a headphone which contains all fundamental and harmonic frequencies (of the input signal applied to the receiver) is called *High-Fidelity* or *Hi-Fi sound.*

Hi-Qu sound

Sound available at the output of a loudspeaker or a headphone which is free from all sorts of distortion is called *High-Quality* or *Hi-Qu sound.*

Record sound

Sound cannot be stored in its original form because it exists in the shape of waves. But, the effect of sound can be stored by '*mechanical*' and '*magnetic*' systems.

Storing of Sound

Sound is stored on a gramophone record in me form of crests and troughs.

Sound is stored in the form of re-setting of magnetic panicles on celluloid tape.

Frequency range of sound waves produced by Man and Musical instruments

30 Hz to 12 kHz

Harmonic frequency

It is the frequency equal to a multiple or sub-multiple of a natural (fundamental) frequency of oscillation.

e.g. harmonic frequency of 2 kHz note will be 2, 4, 6, 8 kHz etc. and 1, 0.5 kHz etc.

Microphone

It is an instrument meant for the conversion of sound waves into equivalent electrical waves.

Types and klorking principles of microphones

1. **Carbon microphone.**

    In this, electrical AF waves are produced by applying a variable pressure developed by sound waves on a pair of surfaces of quartz or roshell salt crystal, i.e. Piezo electric effect.

    It is preferred in public address system and a crystal or ribbon microphone is preferred in sound recording system.

2. **Crystal microphone.**

    In this, the electrical AF waves are produced by applying a variable pressure developed by sound waves on a pair of surfaces of quartz or roshell salt crystal, i.e. Piezo electric effect.

3. **Dynamic microphone.**

    It works on Faraday's laws of electromagnetic induction. It is also called '*moving coil microphone*'.

    Because a carbon microphone acts like a variable resistor, therefore, a DC source of supply is essential to set up a current flow in the microphone's circuit.

4. **Ribbon microphone.**

   It works on Faraday's laws of electromagnetic induction.

5. **Capacitor microphone.**

   The charging and discharging currents of a capacitor are converted into AC signals by varying the capacity of a capacitor with the application of sound waves.

6. **Lips microphone.**

   It is a crystal microphone which can be used just in front of speaker's mouth.

7. **Cordiod microphone.**

   It is also a crystal microphone which can be used on speaker's neck or chest.

Types of Microphones

Accordance to pressure and velocity considerations

Pressure operated microphones are unidirectional microphones

e.g. such as carbon, crystal, dynamic and capacitor microphones.

Velocity operated microphone

e.g. Ribbon microphonebecause sound waves can enter it from either of its two sides..

Headphone

It is an electromagnetic device meant for the conversion of AF waves into sound waves which can be heard by a single person.

Earphone

It is the miniature form of a headphone or a loudspeaker.

LOUDSPEAKER

It is an electromagnetic device meant tor the conversion of AF waves into sound waves which can be heard by a number of persons at a time.

Types of Loudspeakers

There are two types of loudspeakers :

1. Magnetic loudspeakers : These are obsolete now.

2. Dynamic loudspeakers :

These consists of coil which moves to and fro in the magnetic field of a permanent or electro magnet when supplied with an AF signal. A diaphragm attached to the voice coil also vibrates to and from in the air and produces sound waves.

Unit loudspeaker

It is an electromagnetic device which converts AF signals into powerful sound waves with the help of a power amplifier. It consists of a *pressure unit* and a horn.

Column speaker

It is a wooden box containing 2-4 small and big loudspeakers employed for equal reproduction the entire AF range of 20 Hz to 20 kHz.

Coaxial or Triaxial speaker

It consists of two or three small and large size cones respectively fitted to a single axil (i.e. voice coil).

Microphone mirror

It is a high impedance microphone used for obtaining echoes of the fundamental notes.

Decibel

It is a logarithmic unit which is used to measure intensity of sound in comparison to another sound.

$$dB = 10 \log \left(\frac{P_2}{P_1} \right)$$

where, P_1 = intensity of first sound

P_2 = intensity of second sound

Woofer

It is a loudspeaker having a large dia meter (15 cm and above).

Tweeter

It is a loudspeaker having a small dia meter (less than 10 cm.)

All mains receiver

A radio-receiving set in which all the necessary supplies of voltage and current are drawn from the mains including high and low tension.

Amplitude Reflection Factor

It is the ratio of normalized complex wave amplitude of the reflected wave to that of the incident wave at a port or transverse cross section of the transmission line.

Antenna Pattern

It is a graph of the radial component of the poynting vector at a constant radius, as a function of some angle in the coordinate system used.

ANSI

It is acroynm for American National Standards Institute.

Antenna Log Periodic

These are wideband antennas. Radiation resistance and pattern band widths are independent of frequency over a wide band.

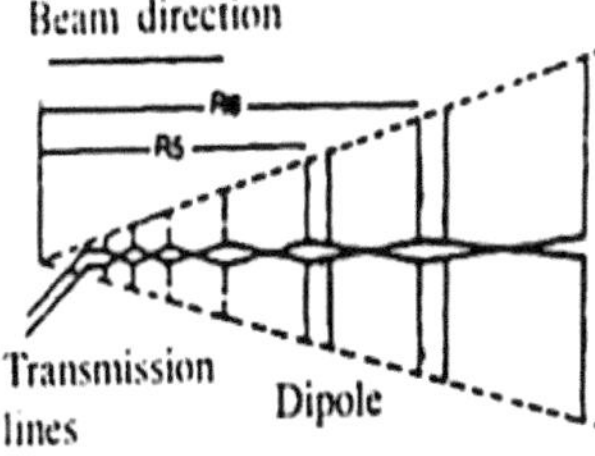

Antenna Discone

It consists of cone and disc in closed proximity. It is ground plane antenna and similar to vertical dipole antenna.

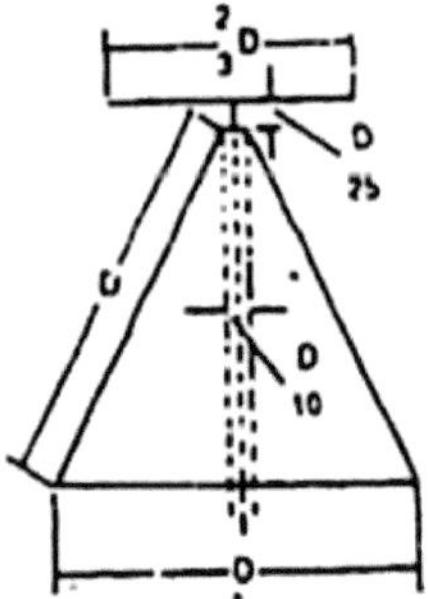

Antenna Folded Dipole

It is a simple compensating network for increasing bandwidth of a dipole antenna. LC circuit is parallel resonant where it offers increased impedance at resonant frequency.

Antenna Loop

It is formed by a single coil carrying RF energy. Since dimensions are usually much smaller than wavelength, the current out may be assumed to be in phase. Thus the loop is surrounded by a magnetic field every where perpendicular to loop.

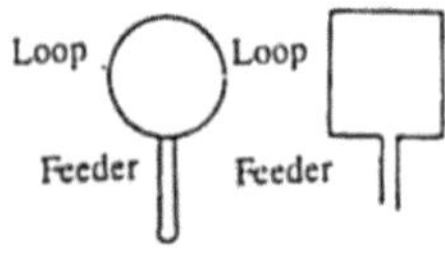

Antenna Loop

Aperture Jitter

It is the time taken by A to D converter to assign output code when trigger was applied. Error in time placement of the aperture jitter normally caused by noise or short term stability in time base, the jitter in aperture samples ihc voltage at point P_1 in time and reports it as having occurred at right point P_2. This type of error is particularly serious when the wave forms acquired during different acquisition are being compared. Aperture jitter differential non linearity and missing codes cause a converter to have less resolution than indicated by the number of its outputs bits.

Arc System Of Radio- Communication

A system in which Continuous waves are produced by connecting an Oscillating circuit to an arc of special character, so that advantage is taken of certain relations between current through the arc and voltage between its electrodes to produce an instability resulting in the continuance of oscillations.

Arithmetic Logic Unit (ALU)

It is the main part of the central processing unit in a computer.

Astable : It means having no stable value.

Asynchronous Communication

It is a way of transmitting data serially from one device to another, in which each transmitted character is preceded by a start bit and followed by a stop bit. This is also called *start / stop transmission.*

Asynchronous Transfer Mode (ATM)

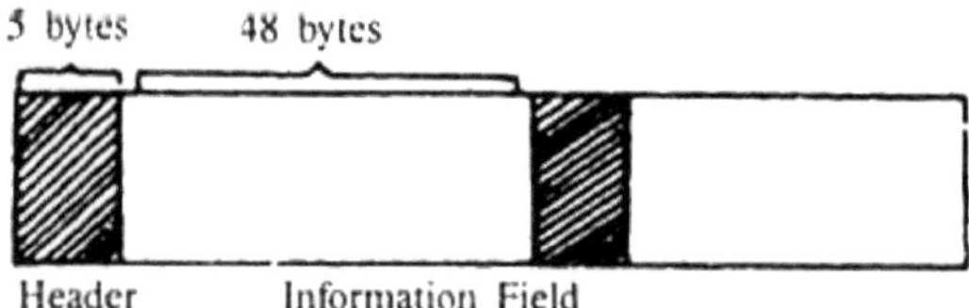

This is the technology selected by CCITT to deliver a broadband ISDN services for the world wide telecommunications services. Broadband services such as video telephony, LAN connectivity and multimedia are covered under this. It is based upon packet switched technology a fixed packet of 53 bytes (48 byte information and 5 byte header).

Atmospheric Duct

An almost horizontal layer in the troposphere extending from the level of a local minimum of the modified refractive index as a function of height, down to level where minimum value is again encountered or down to the earth surface if minimum value is not again encountered. Thus, radio waves are continuously refracted, so they are propagated around curvature of the earth of distances which sometimes reach 1000 km. It is also called *Super Refraction.*

Attenuation

The losses that occur and reduce progressively the amplitude and power in a line.

These losses are of two types :

1. Losses due to heat dissipation caused by the resistance of the conductors and insulation resistance between the conductors,

2. Dielectric losses which effect alternating current (ac) only and are dependent on the dimensions and type of insulant between conductors themselves and between conductors and earth.

Attenuation Compensator Or Equalizer

It is a combination of resistance, inductance and capacitance to compensate for the variation of attenuation with frequency in a line.

Attenuation Constant

It is natural logarithm of the ratio of the amplitudes of waves at unit distance apart along the line of propagation.

Attenuation constant of a telephone line is given by

$$\alpha = \log e \left| \frac{I_s}{I_1} \right|$$

where, I_s = current sent on line

I_1 = current received.

Attenuation constant can also be defined as reciprocal of the length of the line in which amplitude is reduced in the ratio of 2.71828 to one.

Augend

In the addition process, it is the number to which the adder is added.

Back Contact Spring (in Telephony)

It is a spring which makes contact with a Main Contact Spring in the normal position.

Backward wave Oscillator (BWOs) or Carcinolrons

These are TWT (Travelling Wave Tube) oscillators in which they interact with an electromagnetic wave supported by a periodic slow wave structure.

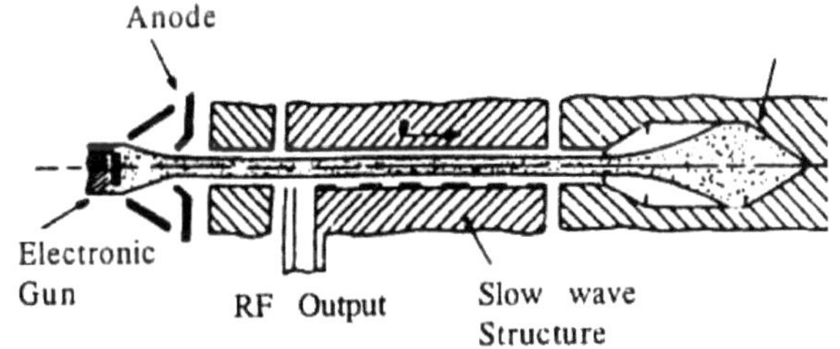

The essential difference between BWO and TWT is that, in the former electron beam and electromagnetic wave propagate in opposition directions and RF power is extracted at the output port located near the gun.

Main advantages of BWO are its electronic tuning range and its insensitivity to load variations, and these factors have driven development of the tube as a millimetre wave source. As present BWO is the most powerful and reliable wave generator reaching in frequency to 1300 GHz.

Balanced Mixer

It is a hybrid junction with crystal diode in one pair of uncoupled arms, arm of the remaining part being fed respectively from a signal source and a local oscillator, the resulting signals from the diode are added in such a manner that effect of noise issuing from the crystal mixers are minimized at the common output.

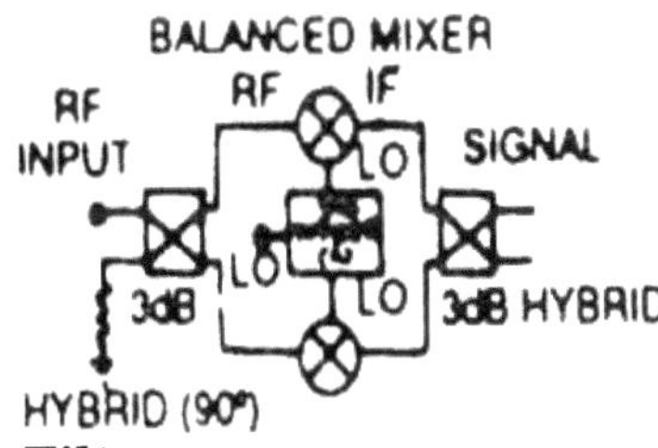

Band Pass Filter

It is a frequency filter which permits only passage of oscillations between certain limits of frequency. It is sometimes used to improve selectivity of radio-receivers.

Base

It is one of the three regions in a bipolar transistor.

Basic electricity

It is a fundamental characteristic of all matter, associated with electron and proton of the atom, whose movement, free or controlled, lead to the development of fields of force and generation of kinetic or potential energy.

Bridge Duplex Telegraph System

A Duplex telegraph system in which receiving instrument occupies position of a galvanometer in a Wheatstone's Bridge, so that outgoing current does not affect home instrument although part of the line current flows through the distant receiver.

Bridge Rectifier

It is a full-wave rectifier circuit in the form of a bridge, with a rectifier in each arm.

Bridging Condenser

It is a condenser of fixed value shunting Bridge rectifier piece of apparatus of divert oscillations of the higher frequencies.

Bridging Telephone

It is a telephone receiver placed in parallel with another, or with some other apparatus to divert oscillations of the higher frequencies.

Bright Emitter Valve

It is a thermionic valve with a filament which has to be raised to bright incandescence to give sufficient electronic emission.

Broadcasting Satellites [Comat]

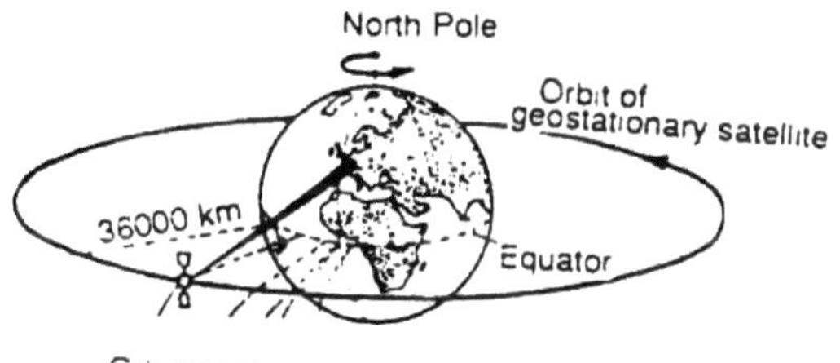

Boradcasting satellites on geostationary orbit

Use of this new generation of satellites (with higher Broadcasting satellites on geostationary orbit power, greater bandwidth and special directive antennae) has now made it possible for satellites to be used to broadcast programs direct to users.

Broad Side Array

Possibly the simplest array consists of a number of dipoles of equal size equally spaced along a straight line with all dipoles fed in the same base from the same source. Such an arrangement is called *broad side array*. It is shown in the figure below together with pattern.

Broad Side Arra

Bus Topology

The bus configuration use bidirectional T coupler to exert and insert signals to a single main transmission line, as shown in figure. The bus carries many multiplexed signals and information travel both downstream and upstream. A typical application for this topology, also called *multidrop network*, is in a computer center, with the LAN interconnecting a CPU and its peripheral-disks, printer etc.

Byte

A group of 8 bits.

Cable

It is a conductor for transmitting electric currents, composed of several wires of strands laid up together, with or without insulating and protective coverings.

Cable Television Tree And Branch

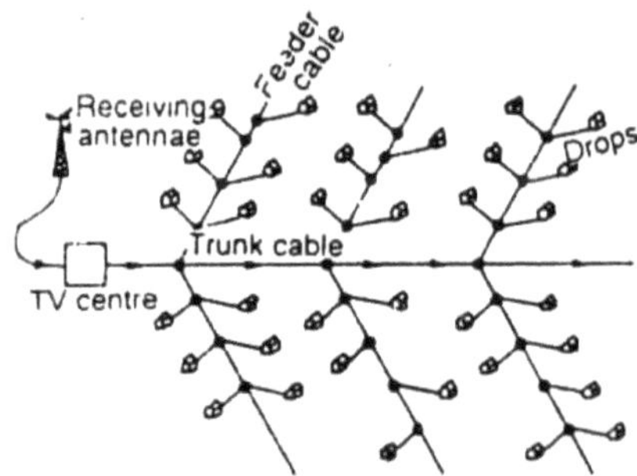

All programmes are initiated at or fed into the system from a single main center; all programmes are fed out into the network from this center. Wide-bandwidth cables are needed into every house. Selection of programmes to watch is carried out at the TV receiver itself since all the programmes are carried into every house.

Cable TV tree and branch network

Cable TV Star Network

All programmes are initiated at or fed into the system from a single main center; all programmes are fed from this center to a number of *intelligent* distribution centers. Wide-bandwidth cables are needed for these links. Star-type distribution system is more flexible than a tree-and branch system in its ability to provide for new features-particularly interactive features.

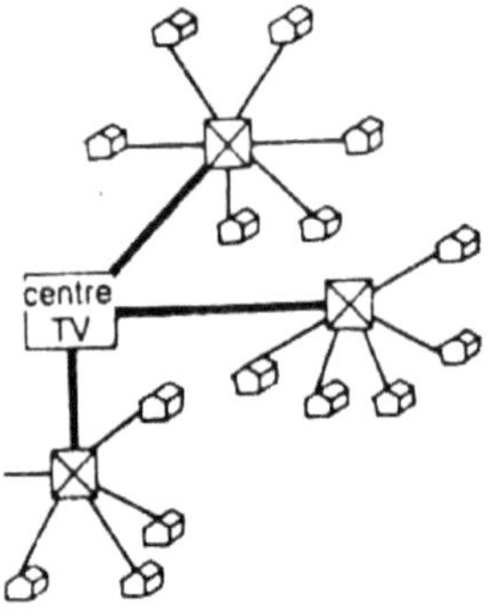

Calender Recording Bridge

It is a form of Wheatstone slide wire bridge used for resistance thermometers and pyrometers in which sliding contact is shifted automatically to the zero position by the current in the *Galvanometer circuit*, so that it can be used to move a recording pen on a resistance chart.

Callindicator

It is a apparatus used in manual telephone exchanges linked up to automatic exchanges which translates calling impulses from the latter into a visible signal.

It is a signalling device in an electric lift indicating from which floor a call has been made.

Calling Device

It is a device used in automatic telephone systems for sending impulses to make a call.

e.g. Calling dial.

Campbell Bridge

It is an a.c. bridge used to measure self inductance in terms of a mutual inductance, M.

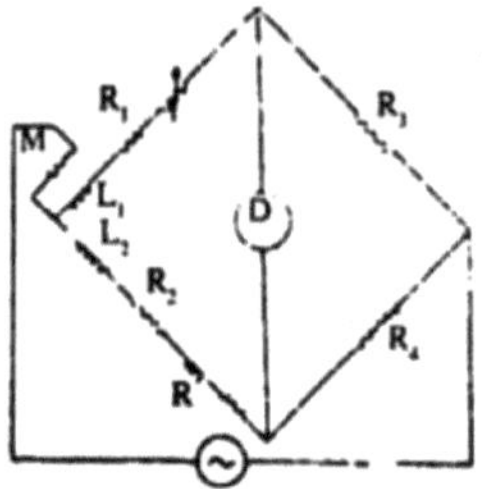

Permittivity

The dielectric constant of a capacitor is also called its *permittivity*.

Carrier Wave

It is a wave with properties to enable it to be transmitted through a selected physical medium after it has been modulated.

Carrier Wave Syn. Carrier

It is the wave that is intended to be modulated in modulation or, in a modulated wave, the carrier-frequency spectral component.

The process of modulation produces spectral components falling into frequency bands at either upper or lower side. Continuous high frequency waves propagated either in space or along a circuit, upon which audio-frequency modulations corresponding to the voice waves are superposed.

Carrier Wave Telephony

Simultaneous transmission of several messages each employing a different carrier current of different frequency superposed upon a circuit used for other purposes, and modulated according to the telephone (or telegraph) signals, employing separate receivers for each message tuned to resonate to the individual frequencies of the separate messages. Special arrangements are employed including wave filters, etc. to eliminate frequencies that are not within the ranges or *bands* actually required.

Carrier Working

By amplitude modulation, be changed in frequency from its original audio frequency (of 300-3400 Hz) up to a higher *carrier frequency.*

Most of the world's long-distance telephony systems utilize, 12-channel group.

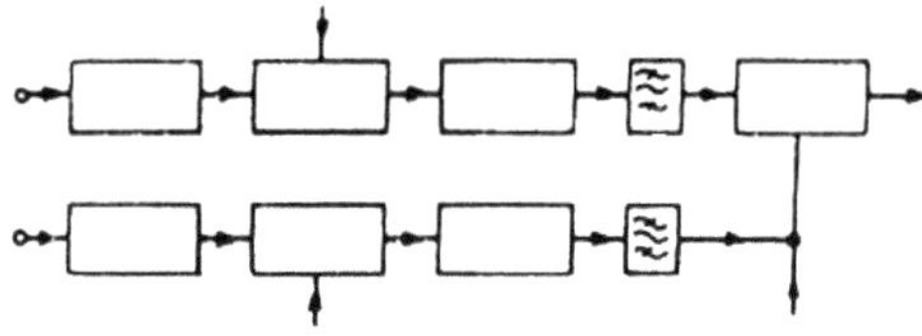

Schematic diagram of transmitting equipment for a carrier system

Cellular Automata

Advances in microelectronics have made possible design of a wide variety of innovative structure with Very Large Scale Integrated (VLSI) circuits. However, design of complex VLSI circuits within reasonable cost demands two essential prerequisites; 'regularity' and 'simplicity'. These two qualities are inherent to the Cellular Automate (CA) structure. A large variety of physical systems have been simulated using this structure.

Cellular phone

It provide an anolog RF link from a handset in a car, briefcase to a low power ratio transistor/receiver located in a cell. This cell represents a small of a city. The entire area in a city is divided into a number of cells to form a network. As the mobile vehicle moves from one cell to other, cell is automatically transferred on to the next cell.

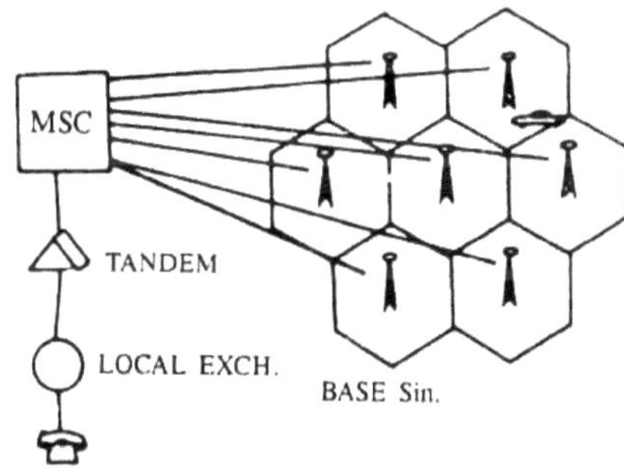

Cellular Mobile Network

Cellular Radio

Instead of covering whole area by high-power fixed radio stations, the area is divided up into small cells, only a few kilometers across. As subscriber density for mobile telephones increases, the cell pattern can be changed to accommodate it. First of all, more working channels are brought into service in the cell, then size of the cell is decreased, either by creation of new cells or by changing the boundaries with adjoining cells. A single multi-channel transmitter and receiver is located in each cell. The transmitters used such low power that the same radio frequency bands can be used again and again, in separated cells, permitting number of simultaneous users 10 jump up from only hundreds to many thousands.

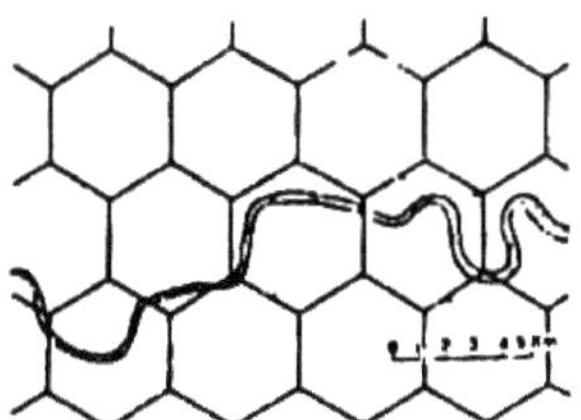

Charge-Coupled Device (CCD)

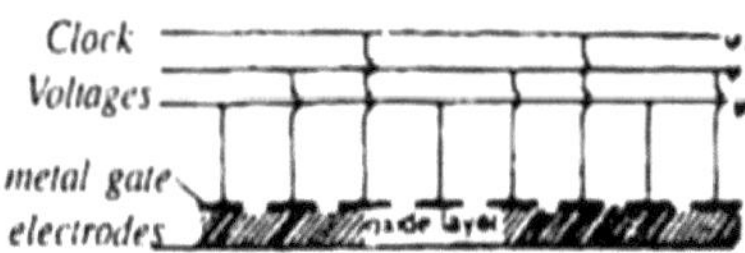

It is a charge-transfer device that consists of any array of MOS capacitors suitably designed, so that they are coupled and therefore charges can be moved through the semiconductor substrate in a controlled manner. CCD can perform a wide variety of electronic functions. The device is essentially an analogue shift register and can be used for signal processing. It can be used to form analogue or digital serial memories. The device may also be used for imaging, as in the solid-state camera. Choke Joint

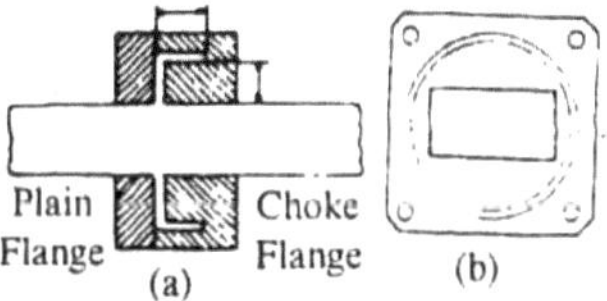

Choke Joint

It is a method of joining section of transmission line or waveguide for microwaves which prevents leakage and high ohmic losses by making joint in the form of a choke coupling. Length of slot is kept p/4 to have slot at waveguide joint discontinuity.

Circulating Memory

It is a memory which has means of delaying transmission of information and also means for regeneration and insertion of information into delay system.

Circuit level Power Combining

It is the techniques used to combine output of Impatt Oscillators at microwaves. Device level combining is generally limited due to number of devices dial can be combined on a small area. However circuit level combining has been more popular with the techniques used being basically an extension of those employed at lower frequency.

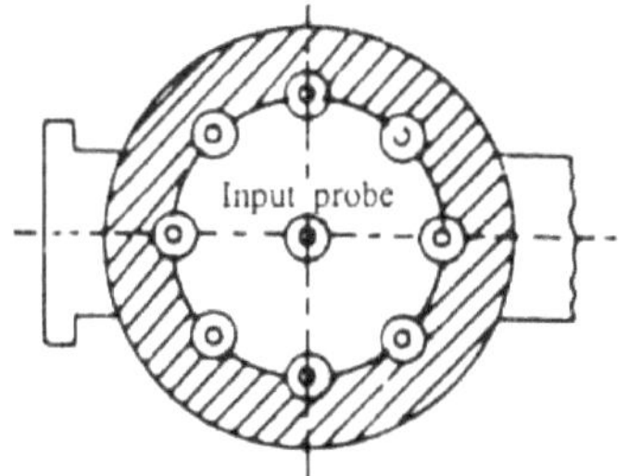

Power combiner IMPATT

There are two categories of combiners :

(*i*) Those that combine the out put of N devices in a single step (called *N-way combiners*)

(*ii*) Tree or chain combining structure.

Coaxial Cable

With increased frequency of an alternating current, the current lends to flow along the outer skin of a conductor, and ordinary twin and quad type cables become inefficient. A special type of cable suitable for use at high frequencies has one of its conductors completely surrounded by the second one, in the form of a tube. This type of cable is called *coaxial cable*.

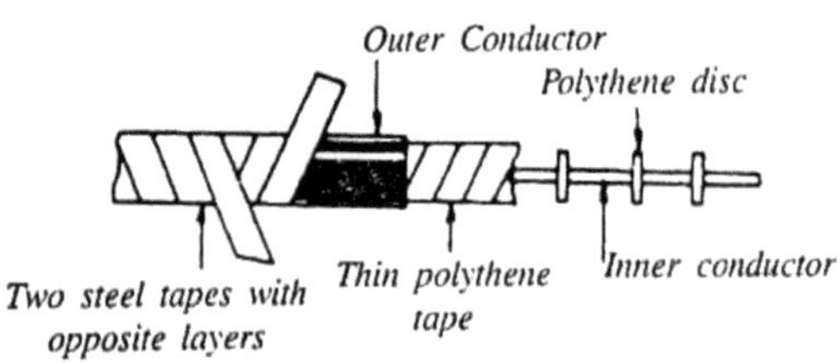

Air-dielectric coaxial cable

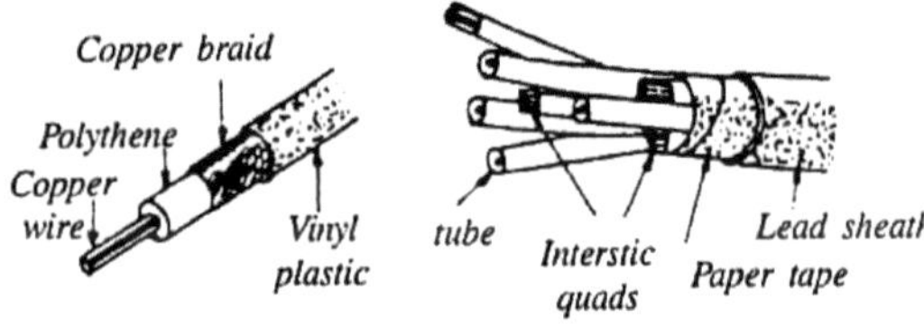

Solid dielectric flexible coaxial cable.   *four-tube coaxial cable*

Coaxial Cavity

It is a resonator for microwaves which consists of cylindrical conductor on the axis of a cylindrical cavity.

Colour Burst

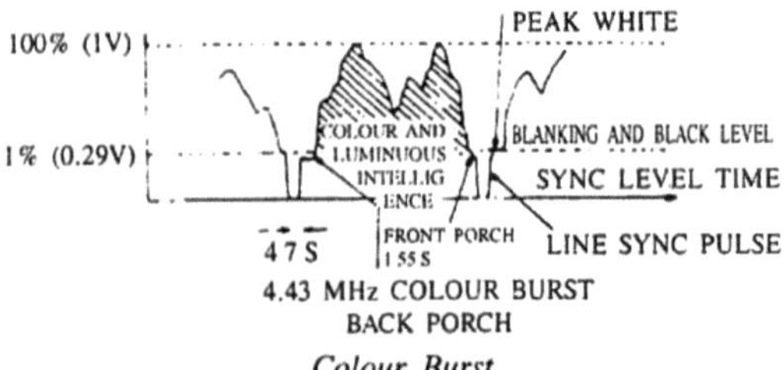

Colour Burst

It is part of the composite colour signal used to establish a reference for demodulating chrominance signal in a colour picture tube.

Color Separation Overlay (CSO)

It is a technique used in colour television for superimposing part cf one scene on another. When a particular colour, such as blue, occurs in one scene viewed by a camera, the output of another camera filming a different scene in automatically switched in to replace areas of the chosen colour in the original picture.

Color Television Principles

There are separate electron guns in the cathode ray tube of a color receiver, one for each of the three primary colours. These guns, although called *red gun, green* and *blue gun*, emit exactly the same sort of electrons. However, inside face of the tube is coaled with special phosphors in a carefully dimensioned pattern, so that electron beam from the red gun is always focussed to hit tiny dots of material which glows red when hit. Green electrons hit spots which glow green and the "blue electrons" hit spots which glow blue. Human eye adds these primary colors together so that if, for example, all three are present on adjacent spots in the area look white.

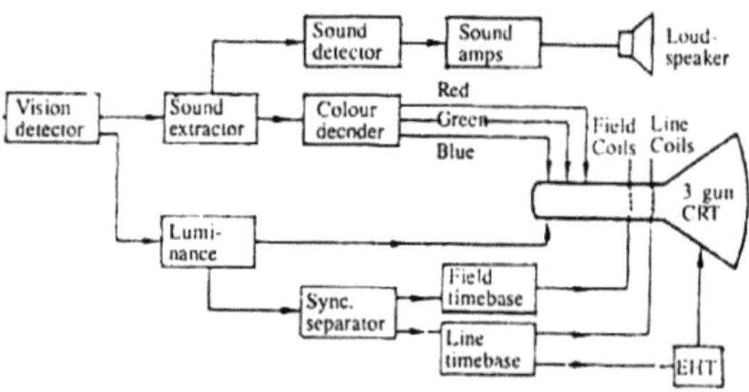

Principles of Color Television Receiver

Colpitts Oscillator

It is an oscillator with a tuned tank (resonant) circuit connected between grid and anode of a valve, or between base and collector of a transistor, and in which tank capacitance is made up of two capacitors in series with their common connection at cathode or emitter potential.

Combinational circuit (Combinatorial circuit)

It is a logic circuit whose outputs at a specified time are functions only of the inputs at that time. In practice, any physically realizable combinational circuit will have a finite transit time, or delay, between inputs changing and the outputs changing intention of the term combinational is to include algebraic elements (AND gates, OR gates, etc.) and preclude memory elements (flipflops, etc.). Analysis and synthesis of combinational circuits is facilitated by Boolean algebra and Karnaugh maps.

Combinatorial Explosion

It is fundamental problem in any search-based system that limits its practical usefulness with large problem spaces, in which number of alternatives to explore increases very fast as the search progresses.

e.g. for example, a search tree with branching factor 5 can only be explored one level deeper by a computer 5 times faster.

Command Guidance

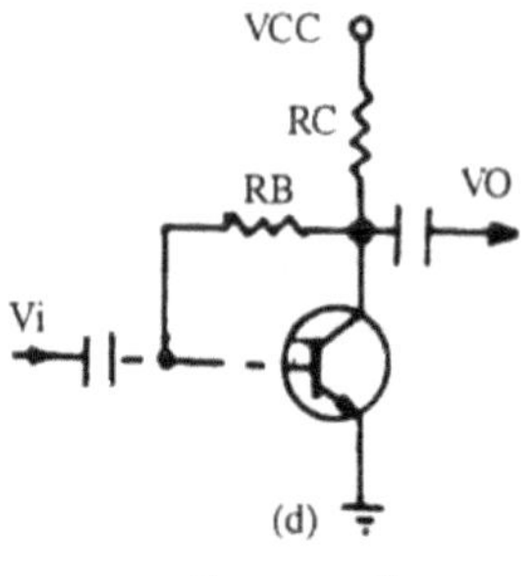

Common Base

It is electronics guidance of guided missiles or aircraft, in which missile receives its guidance from signals from an outside agency to follow a directed path in space.

Common-base Connection

This type Connection is commonly used as a voltage amplifier state. Syn. grounded-base connection. A method of operating transistor in which base is common to both the input and output circuits and is usually earthed. Emitter is used as the input terminal and collector as the output terminal.

Communication System

It is a system (computer) that acts as the interface between another computer or terminal and a network, or a computer controlling data flow in a network.

Telephony

It is a system of communication through wires in which messages are exchanged between two stations by conversation.

Telegraphy

It is a system of communication through wires in which message are exchanged between two stations by means of Morse-keys.

Radiotelephony

It is a system of communication through radio-waves in which messages are exchanged by conversation between a mobile station and a base station

Trans-receiver

It is a combined unit consisting of a transmitter and a receiver.

Walkie-Talkie

It is small and portable trans-receiver which is used by a person (while under movement) to establish radio communication with a base station.

Radar (Radio Angle Detection And Ranging).

It is the electronic equipment which is used to determine direction and distance of a *'target'* present at land, sea or in the space by employing phenomenon of reflection of radio waves by a conductor surface.

Principal parts of a Radar

(*i*)   Pulse modulator

(*ii*) Transmitter

(*iii*) Transmitter/Receiver switch

(*iv*) Receiver

(*v*)   Indicator

(*vi*) Tuner

Function of Transmitter/Receiver switch or Duplexer

It is a fast speed device which connects radar's antenna to the transmitter and then within no time it changes connection of the antenna from transmitter to receiver.

Use of satellite:

All electromagnetic waves (radio waves) above 30 MHz have a tendency to travel along line of sight, i.e. along straight line. Therefore, normal communication range employing such waves does not extend beyond 80 km radius around the transmitting antenna.

Satellite acts as a reflector and transponder to such waves and enables them to reach over the entire globe.

Transponder is an electronic equipment which retransmits the radio waves received by it.

Communication Satellite (COMSAT)

An artificial unmanned satellite in earth orbit that provides high capacity communication link between widely separated locations on earth. International telephone services and exchange of live television programmes and news are achieved by transmitting microwave signals, suitably modulated, from an IMM I I station to an orbiting satellite and back to another earth location. Earth satellites placed in different spots in the geostationary orbit 36000 km (22500 miles) above the equator that serve as relay stations for communications signals transmitted from Earth stations. These satellites orbit Earth once every 24 hours, giving the impression that they are *parked* in one spot over the equator. Once in this orbit, a satellite is capable of reaching 43 percent of Earth's surface with a single radio signal. Most communications satellites are launched by NASA, weigh several thousand pounds, and are powered by solar panels.

Some communications satellites are:

Comstar, Westar, Intelsat V, Satcom, Insat, and Marisat.

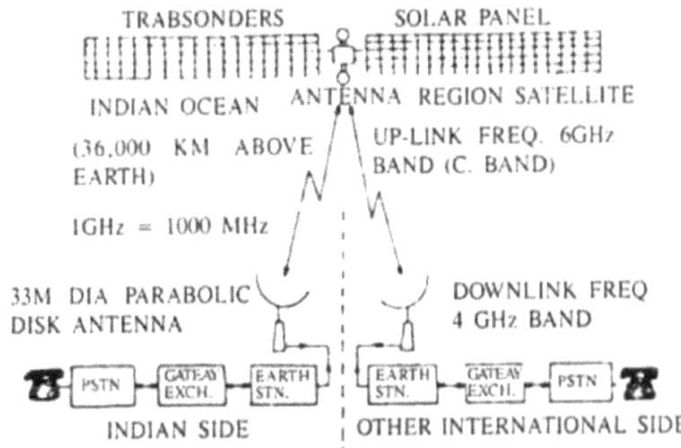

Communication Sattelite

Microwaves

The radio waves whose wavelength lies between 10 to 100 cm or even less are called *microwaves*. These waves are used in radio and TV communications, research, agriculture, physiology, industries etc.

Conical Scanning

Radar antennas are used Conical Scanning for search and scanning objects. Here a parabolic antenna is mounted slightly off in the center and rotated about axis of parabola. Radio or radar scanning in which direction of maximum responses forms a cone.

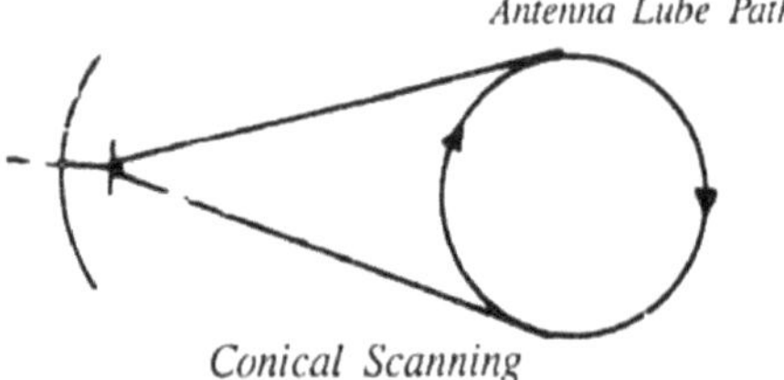

Conical Scanning

Control Grid

It is the particular Grid in a Thermionic valve with more than one grid, used as the control electrode.

Also, it is a grid to control the discharge in any form of vacuum, gas or vapour arc tube.

Coolidge (X Ray tube)

It is a form of powerful "X" ray tube with incandescent tungsten Cathode and water-cooled or air-cooled Anode working with a higher vacuum than earlier tubes, i.e. with gas pressures as low as about 0.003 millionth of an atmosphere, and having a self-rectifying effect which enables alternating current to be used without a rectifier.

Coplanar Waveguide (CPW)

It consist of a strip of thin metallic film deposited on the surface of a dielectric slab with two ground electrodes running adjacent and parallel to strip on the same surface as shown in the figure. There is no low frequency cut off because of the quasi-TEM mode of conducting strip and the ground elec-trodes is tangential, so air dielectric boundary produces a discontinuity in displacement current density at the interface giving rise to an axial as well as transverse component of RF magnetic field providing elliptical polarization.

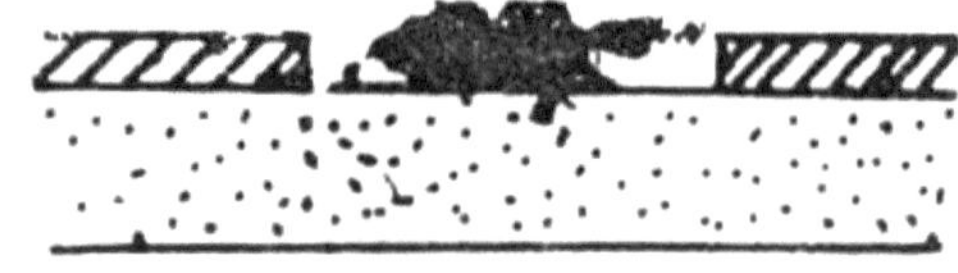

Cordless Telephone System

CT1

This is first generation cordless Telephone system, (also called CTO). Analog technology is used which often results in interference and poor quality of speech. Base units are often incompatible with PBX systems.

CT 2

This is second generation cordless Telephone system. CT2 is entirely different from Cellular and first generation cordless telephones. Here speech is digitized, giving a consistent quality over a wide range of signal strengths. CT2 consists of a network of public base stations that can be accessed in the same way as a personal base unit linked into PSN (Public Switched Network). Users will be able to make outgoing calls (but not receive them) if they are within 100-200 metres of base station. It uses FDMA (Frequency Division Multiple Access).

CT 3

This is third generation cordless telephone system offering two way telepoint service. It uses Time Division Multiple Access (TDMA) format, allowing more channels over same carrier.

Cosmic radiation or Cosmic rays

Radiation of even shorter wave length than Gamma rays and of great penetrating power, which can be detected particularly at high altitudes by the ionization which they all use, also called *Ultra Gamma* and *Penetrating radiation* or *rays*. Thought by some to originate in the upper atmosphere and by others to be extra terrestrial cosmic origin and variously explained as due to disintegration of atoms or to radiation due to shock of the recreation of matter from radiation.

Cross Bar Mixer

This is a type of microwave mixer using combination of stripline and waveguide. The LO signal is injected through a waveguide to a suspended substrate stripline transition and applied to the beam lead diodes with opposite polarity. RF signal is applied directly from the waveguide to the diode pair. IF signal is extracted via a microstrip line etched on the same substrate.

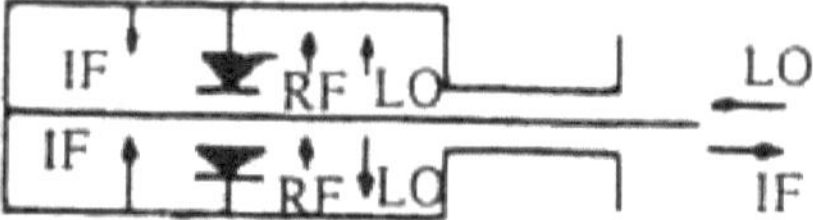

RF : Radio Frequency
IF : Intermediate Frequency
LO : Local Oscillator

Crossbar switches and Reed relays

Both used in telephone exchanges. Basic concept is quite different from that of step-by-step exchanges. Instead of each switch or selector having its own little distributed *brain*, there is a central *brain* which controls all switches. This *central brain* or *register/marker* is rather like a computer; it registers number dialled, it checks that the calling number is permitted to make the call, and tests to see if the called number is engaged.

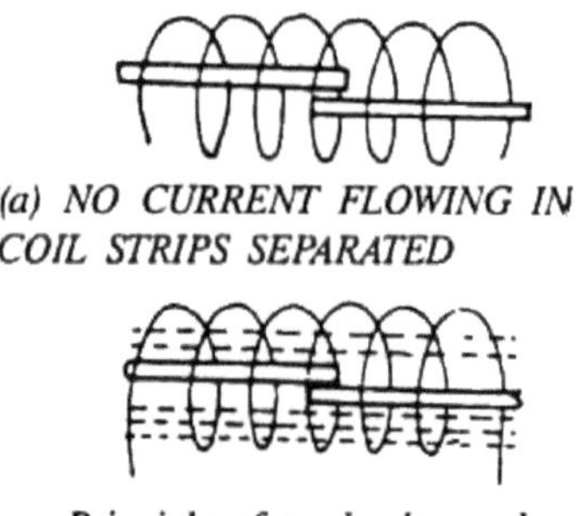

Principle of reed relay and crossbar exchange

Cryotron

It is a normally resistive element which can be maintained at the threshold of superconductivity by surrounding it with a strong magnetic field. It is used in memory and switching devices in computer networks.

Crystal Detector

It is a detector of electric waves used in radio-communication depending upon the unidirectional conductivity of a contact between a crystal and another substance. It is used in a suitably tuned circuit without a battery in series with a telephone receiver in which successive rectified oscillations produce a cumulative effect on the diaphgram and become audible.

CTE (Channel Translating Equipment)

It is an equipment which translates 12 voice channels into one group.

CW Impatt Oscillator

These are microwave solid state sources employing Impatt diodes, For frequencies above 10 GHz CW IMPATT Oscillator employs both the SDR (Single Drift Region) and DDR (Double Drift Region) diode with the emphasis being on the DDR structure. The maximum power output from the device and its negative conductance depends on the ratio of the width of the avalanche region to that of the total space charge width and should be as small as possible. Typically this is of the order of 1:3 the space charge region width varies with both temperature and bias current increasing about 10% due to each of its factor in a typical millimetre wave diode. This determines the transit time which in turn determines optimum operating frequency.

Magnetron

A magnetron designed to be updated with dc, ac or unfiltered rectified voltage supply.

Cyclotron

It is an accelerator travel with two semicircular hollow metal electrodes (known from their shape as dees). A unipolar magnetic field, H, at right angles to the plane of the dees, causes the particles to execute circular orbits within the dees, orbital radius, being proportional to particle velocity and magnetic field. Particles are accelerated by a radio frequency field as they pass between the dees and thus orbital radius increases.

Cyclic Redundancy Check (CRC)

It is an error-checking method for used transmitting data. It is often used when sending and receiving data using modems and communications programs.

Cystadyne Reception

It is a system of radio reception employing a crystal detector polarized by battery which gives it the property of negative resistance, enabling it to be used somewhat like a thermionic valve for amplification, reaction etc.

Data Communication

It is communication of data between two points. Computer system consists of translation, interface and modulation/ demodulation unit.

Decibel (One-tenth of a Bel)

It is abbreviated as dB.

It is the standard unit for expressing transmission gains or losses.

$$dB = 10 \log \left(\frac{P_0}{P_1} \right) \quad \text{or} \quad dB = 20 \log \left(\frac{V_0}{V_1} \right)$$

where, P_0 = output power

P_1 = input power

V_0 = output Voltage

V_1 = input Voltage.

Delta Modulation

It is a form of digital modulation in which 1 bit per sample is sent to indicate whether signal is larger or smaller than previous sample. It is used in conjunction with Differential PCM.

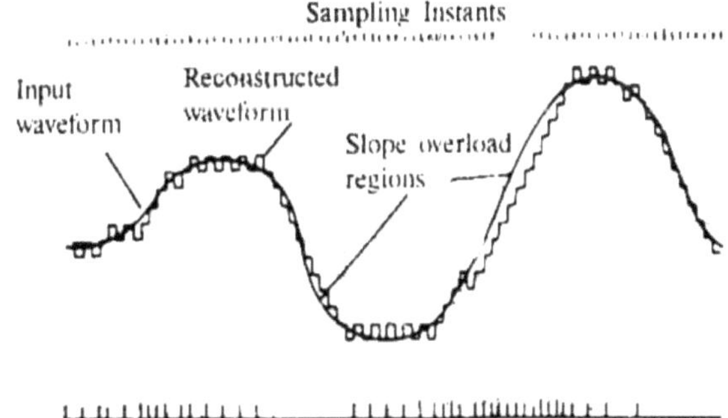

Delta Rays

It is a class of rays emitted by radioactive substances consisting of the projection of negatively charged corpuscles at a much slower speed than that in the case of Rays.

Delta Sigma Modulation

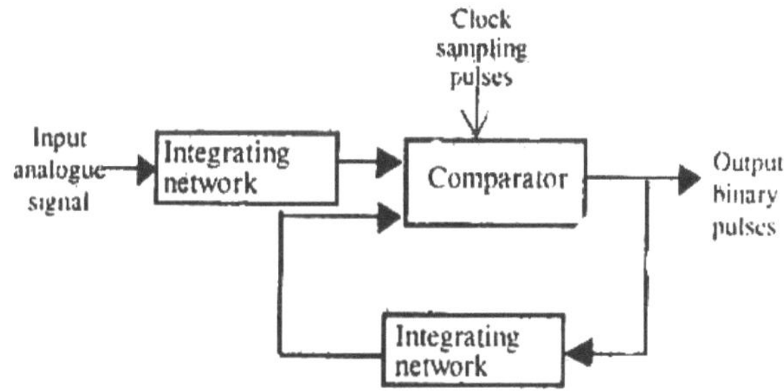

It is a variant of delta modulation, in which integral of the input signal is encoded rather signal itself. This may be achieved by processing normal dual modulation encoder by a integrating network.

DETECTION

The process of separating' the signal wave from a modulated carrier wave is called *detection* or *demodulation*.

Since, resultant AF voltage of a modulated carrier wave rests zero, therefore it is necessary to separate the useful signal from a modulated carrier wave.

Steps involved in detection:

1. Rectification
2. Filtration.

Rectification of modulated carrier wave

By rectification, the positive or negative half cycles of an modulated carrier wave are removed, so that resultant AF voltage of the wave may no longer remain zero.

Types of Detectors

1. Diode detector

It is a detector employing a valve or PN junction diode. Only PN junction diode detectors are used now a days.

2. Infinite impedance detector.

It is the detector which has an infinite input impedance. This type of circuit is operated in such a way that the output is available only for positive half cycles.

3. Regenerative detector

It is the detector employing positive feedback. Regeneration increases sensitivity of the circuit.

4. Power detector

It is the detector which incorporates an AF amplifier also in it. The circuit provides a higher AF output.

Order of Detectors (sensitivity)

1. Regenerative
2. Power
3. Infinite impedance
4. Diode detector.

Differential Microphone

It is a form of microphone in which extra sensitivity is obtained and effect of non-linear relation between pressure and resistance-of carbon is avoided by utilising two carbon elements, one subjected to increase of pressure on one side of the diaphragm and the second to decrease ,of pressure on the other side.

It is also called Push-Pull microphone and Double Button microphone.

Duplexers

It is a device which enables a transmitter and a receiver to be used with same antenna.

Dipole Antenna

An aerial commonly used low frequencies below 30 megahertz. It consists of a centre-fed open aerial excited in such a way that standing wave of current is symmetrical about midpoint of the aerial.

These are different types:

(*i*) Fed at the centre of one of the dipoles;

(*ii*) multiple folded dipole consists of more than two parallel halfwave dipoles.

Originally an aerial (used for short waves) consisting of two straight bars in line of a length equal to half the wave length to be received, but extended to include any single straight rod aerial about one-half wavelength long. A half wave dipole has a length equal to half the wavelength, a full-wave dipole has a length of one wavelength; a folded dipole consists of two parallel halfwave dipoles separated by a small fraction of the wave length, connected at their outer ends.

Direct Satellite Broadcasting

Mainly employs for video and audio transmission from studio to satellite, from where it is re-radiated, even entire globe can be covered. Using small dish antenna users can receive multi channel programms.

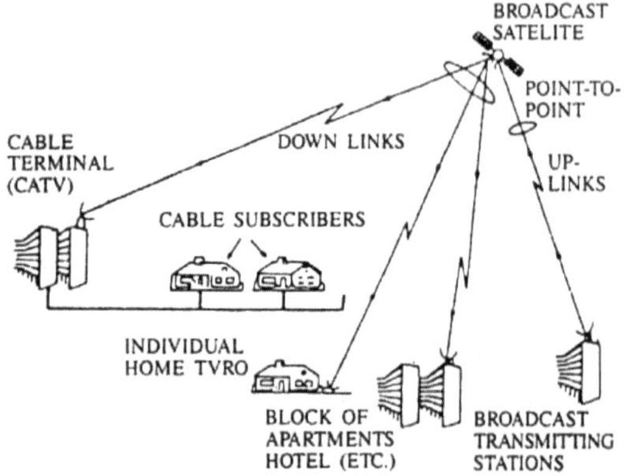

Direct To Line (DTL)

DTL multiplex is better alternative, which eliminates intermediate group and super group translating equipment. Individual VF channel are directly translated to the base band as shown in the figure. Basic channel unit is the main building block. Each can hold upto 12 channel units. Each modern unit has an internal frequency synthesizer.

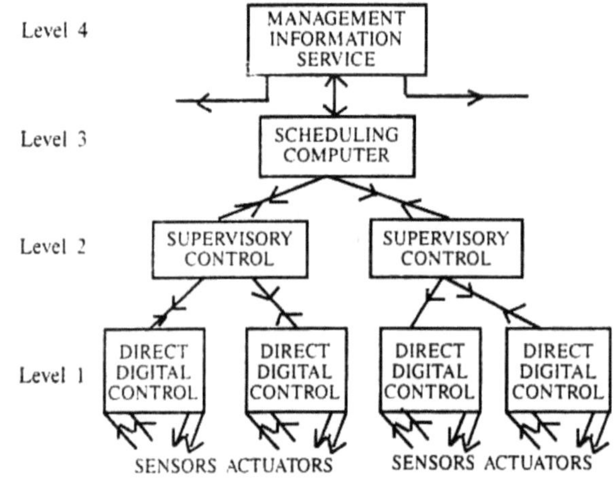

Direct to Line Concept

Directional Coupler

It is a transmission coupling device for sampling for measurement or exciting an incident or reflected wave in a waveguide or any transmission line such as micro strip, coaxial cable etc. A four port device consisting of two transmission line coupled in such a manner that a single travelling wave in any transmission line will induce a single travelling wave in the other, direction of the propagation of the later wave being dependent upon (that of the former).

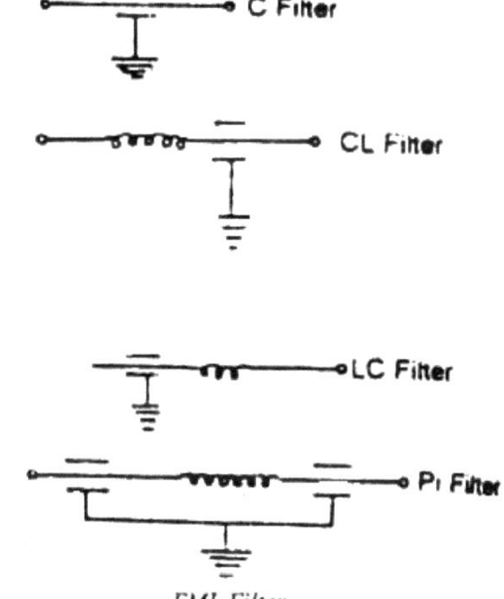

Directional Radio-communication

It is the radio communication, in which waves are confined as nearly as possible to the direction between transmitting and receiving stations.

Dissipation Factor

It is the relation between conductivity and permittivity of a dielectric at a given frequency. It is also called Q *factor*. It is governed by equation.

$$D = \frac{a}{We}$$

where, $\quad$ W = 2 pie times frequency

$\qquad\quad e$ = permittivity of material

Distribution Networks

Connection between a subscriber and the local telephone exchange consists of a pair of wires in a telephone cable. Since a large telephone exchange may have 11X000 or more subscribers, the local line is transformed into a network which can be quite complicated. To layout networks cable distribution is required. Many modern telephone switching systems incorporate concentration stages which can be either collected (i.e. in the same building as rest of the exchange) or remote (i.e. many kilometers away, fed by PCM systems back to main part of the exchange). Use of remote concentrators to serve telephone subscribers in small towns means that cable pairs to such subscribers will not be in future need of the heavy gauge which was in the past needed to feed them all the way back to the nearest city; comparatively fine gauge cables can now be used for distribution to these subscribers.

Earth Wire

A wire, connected to earth, running above the conductors in H.T transmission lines, to minimize the effects of lightning, to contact earth currents in case of leakage and in other ways to lessen interfere i.e., with neighbouring communication circuits.

Eddy current Transmitter

It is a telephone transmitter consisting of a disc of aluminium foil vibrating under the influence of the sound waves in a constant magnetic field produced by two slab coils. Suitable connections are made to render eddy currents induced in the disc available for reproduction.

Electronic Communication Technology

It is a field of study encompassing electrical, electronics, data communications areas.

Electromagnetic Interference (EMI) fillers

These absorb and eliminate high frequency which may produce electromagnetic interference in PC boards circuits. These are used in suppression of radiation noise in computers, peripheral equipment, and digital circuit application equipment to suppress noise in audio-visual equipment.

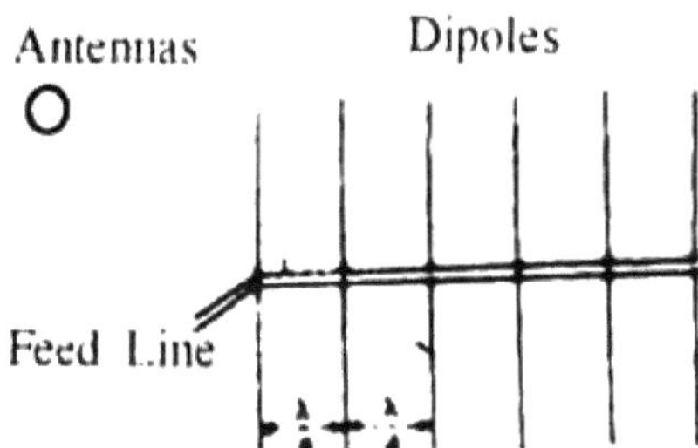

EMI Filter

End Fire Array

A number of elements are added to a structure of antenna, to make its gain higher in a particular direction. The physical arrangement the end fire array is the same as that of the broadside, array however although that magnitude in the current in each element is still the same as in every other element, there is now a phase difference between these current. This is progressive from left to right as there is a phase lag between succeeding elements equal in hertz to their spacing in wavelength. The pattern of the end fire array as shown is quite different from that of the broadside array. It is in the plane of the array not at right angles to it and is unidirectional rather than bidirectional. Any array with that pattern arrangement is said to have *end fire action*.

Extended Interaction

It is the interaction between an electron beam or stream and nearly synchronous travelling radio frequency signal over a physical distance comparatively to (or greater than) a wave length.

Extended Interaction Oscillator (EIO)

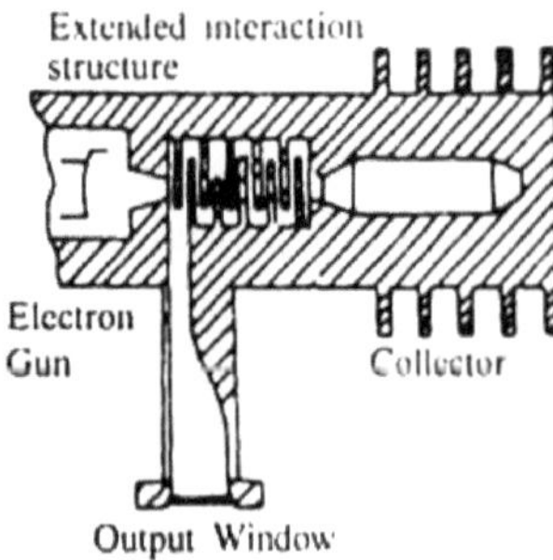

It is also called distributed interaction oscillator. It is a floating drift tube klystron with multiple gaps. It has potential as a millimeter wave source particularly due to its light weight efficiency and high power output characteristic. As with the klystron the device can be used either as an oscillator.

Facsimile Apparatus

It is an apparatus which enables documents to he transmitted from one place to other, over telephone lines.

Facsimile Bandwidth

It is the range of frequencies that is required for adequate transmission of the copy. A form carrier wave is often used for facsimile transmission, the derived electrical signals, the facsimile based band being used to modulate the carrier before transmission,

Facsimile PC

In this facsimile system is merged with a personal computer to send direct computer output from the screen to the receiver.

Facsimile Transmission

It is a method of transmitting any type of document (text or graphics) to produce a copy of the object at the receiver side. Subject copy is scanned under a scanner to produce electrical signals which are sent on telephone line by usual modulation and multiplexing techniques.

Figure Of Merit (C/T of an Earth station)

Capacity of an earth station to receive weakest signal from satellite is given by

$$C/T = C/N + 10 \log B + 10 \log k \mathrm{B}(db)$$

where,

g = gain of antenna at frequency (receive)
T = effective noise temperature of receiving system in deg. Kelvin.
C/T – carrier to thermal noise power.
k = Boltzman's constant.
C/N = ratio of carrier to noise power.
B = Band width

Fin Line

For frequency in the range 30 to 100 GHz, the integrated fin line offers a versatile media. It is a quasi-planar transmission line which well comes the disadvantage it is having to maintain tight dimensional tolerances as in a waveguide and incorporates advantages of a planner transmission line.

Fin line basically consists of a thin dielectric substrate which bridges broad walls of a rectangular waveguide metals fins and circuits elements are defined on one or both sides of the substrate using thin film technique.

Fin Line Mixer

This type of balanced mixer is used for ultra large RF and IF bandwidth. This is hybrid planar mixer with planer substrate containing diodes with two or three type of transmission lines. Fin fine suspended, microstrip line and shielded microstrip line are used. RF input ports uses a wave guide to fin line transmission centrally located with the waveguide to yield a balanced line transformer, terminated by a diode pair.

Frequency Band

It is a particular range of frequencies that forms part of larger continuous series of frequencies. The internationally agreed radio frequency bands are shown in the Table.

Microwave frequencies, ranging from VHP to EHF bands (i.e. from 0.225 to 100 gigahertz are usually subdivided into bands designated by letters. These are not internationally agreed but the commonly used subdivisions are shown. Limits for the bands may differ slightly from those shown. Entire electromagnetic spectrum is shown below.

Band	Frequency Range
L	1 – 2 Gc
S	2 – 4 Gc
C	4 – 8 Gc
X	8 – 12 Gc
Ku	12 – 18 Gc
K	18 – 26 Gc
Ka	26 – 40 Gc
V	40 – 60 Gc
W	75 – 110 Gc

Heterodyning

It is the process of producing a lower frequency by *'healing'* two high frequencies.

Superheterodyning

In this process, any frequency received by the aerial of receiver is converted into a *'definite and low frequency'*. A radio receiver based on the phenomenon of superheterodyning is called *superheat receiver*.

Tuning ratio

It is the ratio of the lowest and highest radio frequencies. A gang capacitor having a tuning ratio of 1:2 can be made easily and thus a low tuning ratio is preferred.

Image frequency

It is the frequency other than signal frequency which produces the same IF.

Since, OF – SF (I) – IF

But SF (2) – OF is also equal to IF.

So, SF (2) is called *image frequency* for SF (1).

The value of IF should be chosen high enough in order to reject the image frequency. If IF value is high enough, then image frequency will shift far enough from the signal frequency and it will not disturb reception of the signal frequency.

Decoupling

An unwanted coupling is found between any two stages of a receiver due to their operation by a single DC source. This unwanted coupling promotes frequency mixing1 defect. This defect is eliminated by a RC or LC network connected to the anode/ collector circuit. A *'decoupling circuit'* prevents AC portion of the output current of a stage to pass through the DC source.

Direct pick-up of Radio waves

The electromagnetic field of radio waves is so spread and so strong that it is capable to induce RF voltages in the components of an electronic equipment directly. The trouble is eliminated by employing RC coupled circuits and by using proper screens shields for the RF

Components oscillator tracking

Since, a single gang capacitor is employed for the tuning of a signal frequency over different wave bands, therefore, oscillator coils of different wave bands may require minor capacitance adjustment in order to maintain OF – SF = IF relation. *'Trimmers'* and *'padders'* are used for this purpose and the process of their setting is called *oscillator tracking*.

Band spreading

In order to facilitate tuning of a signal frequency in short wave band reception, a wave band is spread out over the entire dial length and this phenomenon is called *band spreading*. A short wave band such as 13 m, 16 m, 19 m, 25 m etc. can be spread with the help of a capacitor connected in series with the main tuning capacitor.

Conversion gain

The amount of voltage gain of a frequency converter stage is called its conversion gain.

$$\text{Conversion gain} = \frac{\text{IF voltage}}{\text{Signal voltage}}$$

Factors affecting Ability of a radio receiver

1. Sensitivity.

The ability of a radio receiver of producing sufficient AF output even for weak RF signals is called its *sensitivity*.

2. Selectivity.

The ability of a radio receiver of selecting a desired frequency out of the radio frequencies present at the aerial and to suppress all other frequencies is called its *selectivity*.

3. Stability
4. Fidelity
5. Signal to noise ratio.

Frequency Division Multiplexing (FDM)

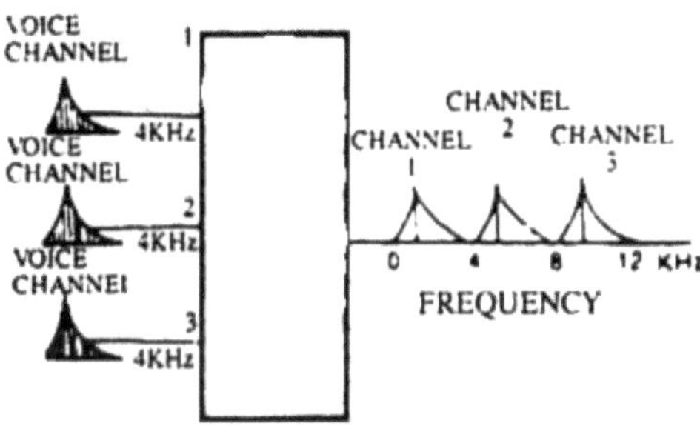

It is a form of multiplex operation in which each user of the system is assigned a different frequency band. Transmitted signals contain several carrier waves each of a different frequency and separately modulated with a different input signal. At the receiver, a number of tuned circuits are used to separate different carrier frequencies.

Frequency Modulation [COMM.]

It is a method of superimposing information signals on to a carrier signal in which modulating signal varies frequency of a carrier wave. This has a number of advantages over amplitude modulation.

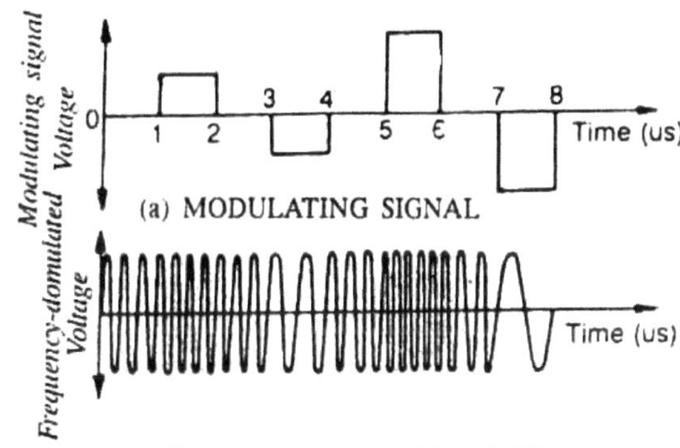

Fig. *Frequency Modulated Wave*

Uses of Frequency modulation

It is used for following purposes :

(*i*) Sound broadcasting in the VHP band

(*ii*) Sound signal of 625-line television broadcasting

(*iii*) Some mobile systems

(*iv*) Multichannel telephony systems operating in the UHF band.

The price which must be paid for some of the advantages of frequency modulation over double sideband amplitude modulation is a wider bandwidth requirement.

Frequency Spectrum

Sum of carrier and modulatk signal frequencies is called *upper side-frequency*. Difference between carrier and modulating signal frequencies is called *lower side-frequency*.

Together these form *frequency spectrum.*

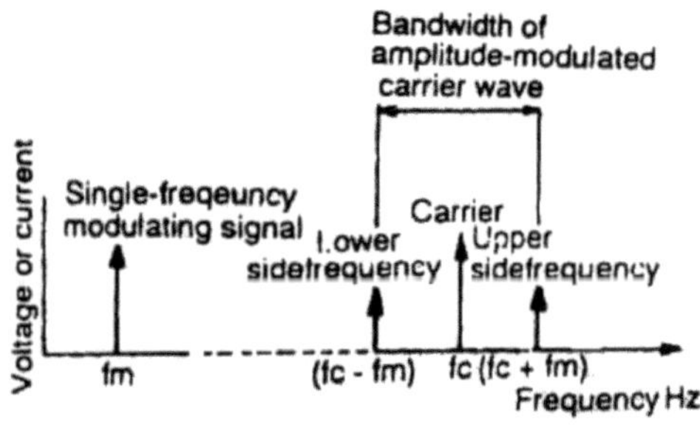

Full Duplex

Simultaneous bidirectional transmission of data on a transmission line.

Fundamental frequency

Frequency of the fundamental component is also called *baseband frequency.*

Fundamental wavelength

It is the wavelength corresponding to the fundamental frequency of the oscillations in a particular circuit, upon which harmonics may or may not be superposed.

Gateway

It connects earth station to a public switched communication system. It supports subscriber's database and performs subscriber verification and billing.

Geostationary Earth Orbit

It is the earth orbit at which motion of earth and of body in space are equal. It is at altitude of 36000 km above the earth surface.

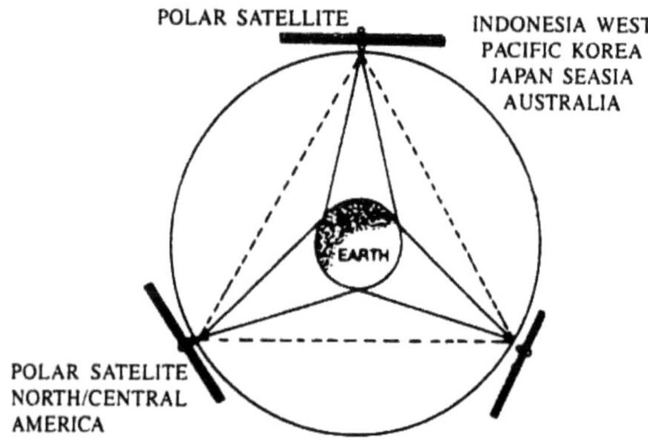

Gunn Effect

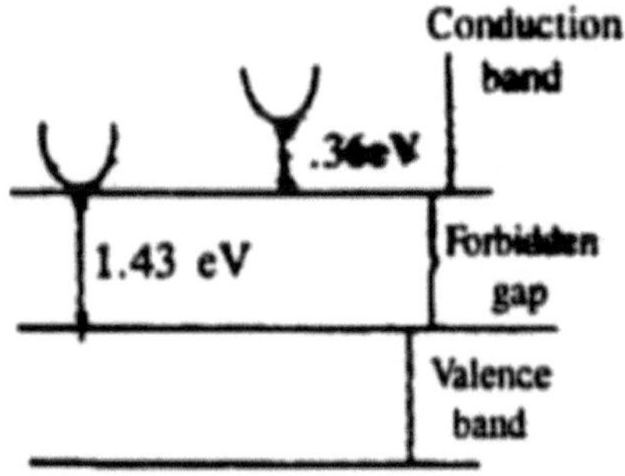

It is an effect that occurs when a large d.c. electric field is applied across a short sample of type gallium arsenide. At values above the threshold value, typically several thousand volts, per cm, coherent microwave oscillations are generated. In 1963 Gunn discovered transferred electron effect. This effect is instrumental in the generation of microwave oscillation in bulk semiconductor materials. The effect was found in gunn to be exhibited by gallium arsenide and indium arsenide and indium phosphide but telluride and indium arsenide have also subsequently been found to possess it. It marked the first instance of useful semiconductor device depending on the properties of an material. If a relatively small dc voltage is placed across a thin slice of gallium arsenide, such as the one shown in figure, then negative resistance will manifest itself under certain conditions. Basically these consist merely of ensuring that voltage gradient across the slice is in excess of about 3300 v/cm. Then oscillation will occur if slice is connected to a suitable tuned circuit. The original device oscillated without a tuned circuit because of the unevenness of impurity distribution in the original sample. Since voltage gradient across the slice of GaAs is very high, hence electron velocity is also high, so that oscillation occurs at microwave frequencies.

Halfwave-length Aerial

It is a transmitting aerial with an effective height equal to half the wavelength of the waves to be radiated.

H Bend

It is a waveguide passive component that brings a smooth change in the direction of axis maintained perpendicular to the plane of polarization.

Helical Antenna

This antenna consists of a loosely wound helical spring by a ground plane which is simply a screen made of chicken mesh.

There are two modes of radiation

(*i*) *Normal (meaning perpendicular)* : In this, radiation is in direction normal to the axis of the helix.

(*ii*)*Axial* : It produces a broadband fairly directional radiation in the axial direction.

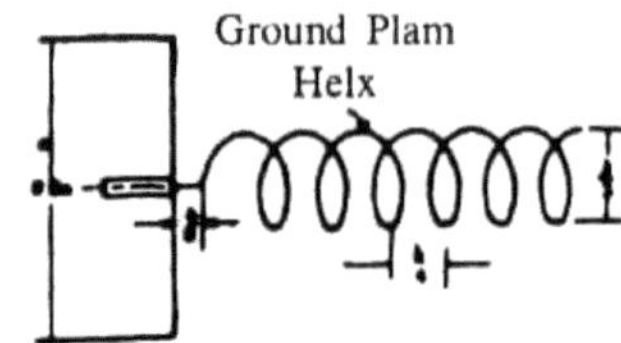

Howler

It is an oscillator that generates high pitched audio frequency tone in order to attract attention of an operator a sort of audible warning. This is also used as a null point detector in bridge measurements.

Howling

If a telephone receiver is placed face to face with transmitter, connected up in the usual way, a continuous sound or *howling* is produced by a cumulative effect setting up oscillations of electrical constants of the circuits and mechanical constants of the diaphgram.

The term is applied indiscriminately to accidental loud continuous noise in radio receivers, due to oscillations in radio-frequency or audio-frequency circuits.

Hum

It is a low pitched audio frequency noise in AF systems. Usually originates from mains supply at frequencies which are harmonics of supply frequency.

Hybrid mode

It is a waveguide mode such that both electric and magnetic fields have components in the direction of propagation.

Hybrid Junction

It is a four port device in which power fed into any port is equally divided between two other ports having matched termination; furthermore, power fed into the remaining port is equally divided between the same two ports.

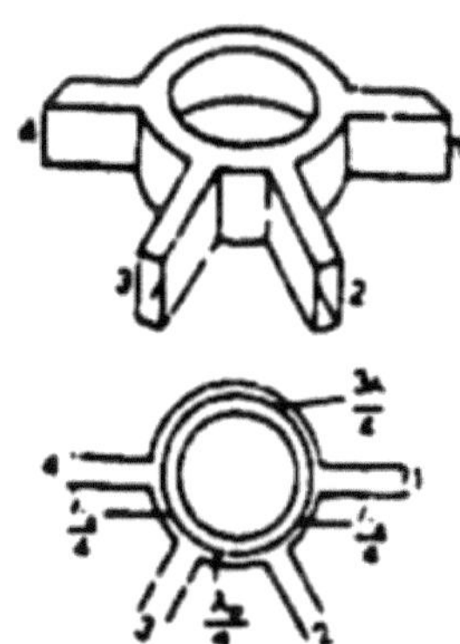

Magic tee :

If another arm is added to either of T junction then a *hybrid T junction* or *magic tee* is obtained. Such a junction is symmetrical about an imaginary plain bisecting arms three and four and has some very useful and interesting properties. The arm is connected to arm 1 and 2 but not to arm 3 and similarly arm 3 is also connected to arm 1 and 3 but not to arm 4. This applies to dominant mode only and occurs only if each arm is terminated in a correct load. If a signal is applied to arm 3 of the magic tee, it will be divided at the junciion with some entering arm 1 and some entering arm 2 but none will enter arm 4.

Hyperdyne Reception

It is a system of radio reception similar to the earlier forms of super heterodyne reception, but employing a higher intermediate frequency (about 200 kc.), with Screen Grid Amplifiers.

Ikonophone

It is an experimental apparatus combining television by line currents with telephony to render the distant speaker's face *visible*.

Iridium Communication System

It is iridium implements in space based global cellular system in a distributed architecture, in which each satellite is required to carry only 1/77 of the system capacity. Indium Satellite system is designed to provide global, digital portable personal communication services. Subscriber to indium system would use mobile radio units with small antenna to reach a galaxy of 77 satellites interconnected through digitally switched radio communication. Satellite are located approximately 780 kms above the earth.

Infrared Transmission

It is optical in nature carried by beam of light invisible to the naked eyes. It provides a compact and inexpensive means of line of sight narrow band transmission and among and between buildings within the same general area for it is limited distances of few hundred metre, though unaffected by most artificial light and weather conditions, very heavy snow or fog degrades its quality. Infrared is not side the broadcast portion the radio spectrum it is moderately secure.

Isolator (One way attenuator)

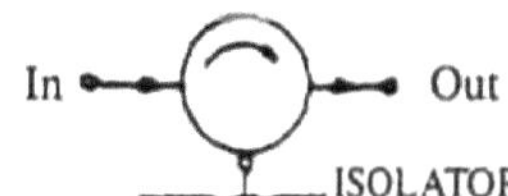

It is a two-port device having much greater attenuation in one direction of propagation than in the opposite direction.

Isolator Resonance :

It is an Isolator, whose operation depend upon absorption in a gyromagnetic resonance frequency.

Isolator Rotation :

It contains atleast one non reciprocal polarization rotator.

Jamming

It is sending of disturbing radio signals to interfere with the reception of another message.

e.g. as in the operations of war time.

It is interference due to any signals other than those it is desired to receive.

Jumper wire in Automatic telephony

It is a temporary connecting wire in a cross-connection field during repair or rearrangement of permanent connections.

Junction selector in Automatic telephony

It is a selector responding to the current impulses of the exchange code in a call dialled, the function of which is to make connection through a vacant junction line between a First selector and an appropriate thousands Selector in the wanted exchange.

Junction T or Tee Junction or Tee

It is a junction of waveguide in which longitudinal waveguide axes form a 'T'.

Junction 'Y'

It is a junction waveguide in which longitudinal axis forms a 'Y'.

Klystron amplifier

In this the electron beam interacts with additional cavities between input and output cavities in order to increase band or gain width or both. It is used at microwave frequencies.

Multicavity Klystron :

These are used where high power is needed. Here three or more cavities are coupled to the electrons beam to provide a high overall gain. Velocity modulated beam leaving first cavity interacts with the second and subsequent cavities in such a way that induced amplified voltage in each cavity demodulates the beam received the preceding cavity, so that beam becomes more strongly bunched and ultimately yields a highly amplified wave.

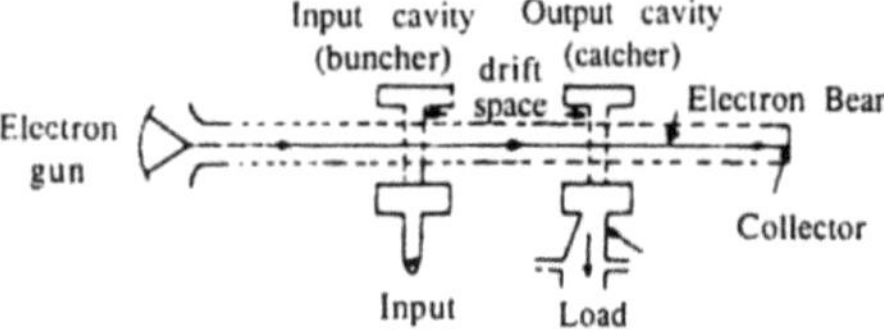

Laddertron

It is invented by Fujiwala. It is a multi gap Klystron using ladders. However instead of using many resonant cavities in the multicavity Klystron, a single larger cavity is used. An electron beam flows through a drift section between two parallel conducting plates with several slots cut on them.

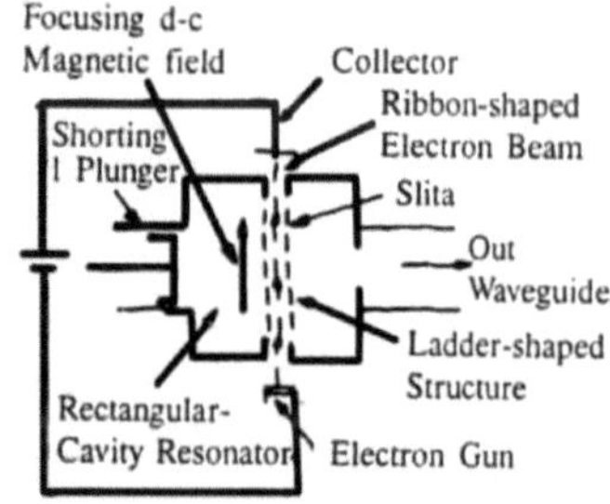

The latter, forms the ladder shaped standing wave structure from which tubes derives its names. Output from the many gaps is arranged to excite a specific mode in the single cavity resonator just as in the coaxial magnetron. Resonator is tuned by a shorting plunger attached to the cavity and power is coupled out at a window on the cavity wall.

Laryngaphone

It is a telephone transmitter in which voice vibrations are taken up by a pad pressed on to the exterior of the throat instead of from the sound issuing situations in that it does not pick up extraneous sounds.

Leased Line Modem

These are high speed modems connected to leased line. Normally, Dialling and answering features are not provided in these modems.

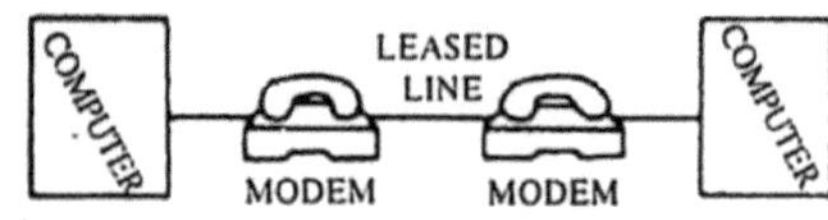

Lens Antenna

It is dielectric lens where a divergent beam is collimated. Refraction takes place more at edges than near the center. If a parallel beam is received, it will converge for reception at focal point.

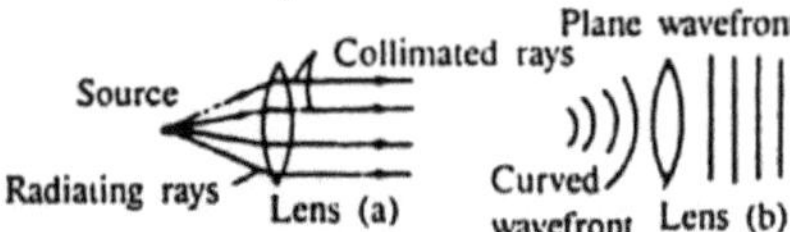

Line Communication System

Electronic signal is passed to the destination by a wire or cable link, with the energy travelling at a speed of upto 60% that of light (depending on type of line).

At the destination, a second transducer converts the electronic signal back into the original energy form. Other items are also used, as required, such as amplifiers, which do not change signal from one form of energy to another but inserted to increase power level of signals to compensate for losses encountered.

Log-periodic

These are much used for point-to-point services. These do not give quite so much directional gain as rhombics but these take up much less land area. These are able to operate efficiently over wide frequency bands; variants can be used for VHP or HF services.

A *fog-periodic antenna* is made up of a series of rod or wire dipoles with a common ratio both between lengths of adjoining rods or wires and spacings between them.

Look Angle

Elevation angle of a satellite is called look angle.

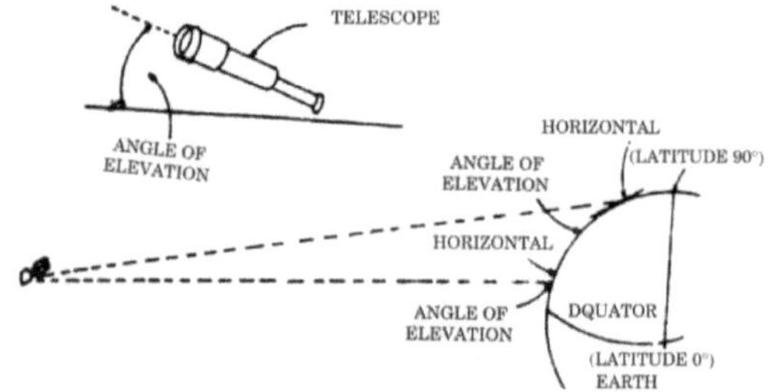

Loop

In a radio direction finder, one of the two aerial systems used at right angles to each other.

It is part of a computer program in which machine repeats a segment of the program over and over.

Luxemburg Effect

Transfer of the effect of modulations of the waves sent out from a powerful radio-transmitter to the carrier wave of another station, at different frequency passing through the same region of the atmosphere, causing signals of the former station is called Luxemburg Effect.

Magnetron

A trans crossed field microwave oscillator tube characterized by a reentrant slow-wave circuit of circular cylindrical geometry which also serves as the anode. The static-magnetic field is along the axis of the cylindrical anode.

Magic T

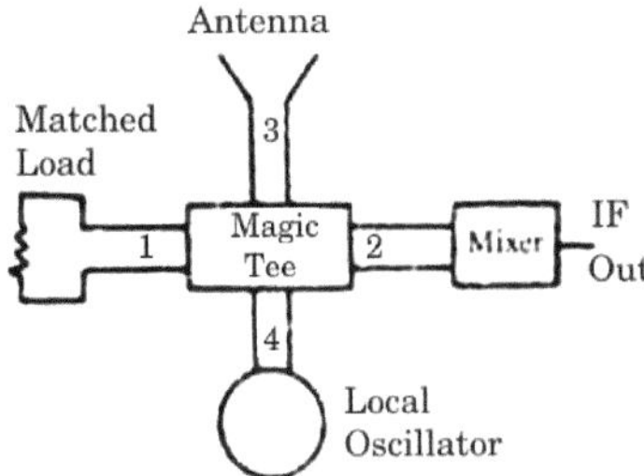

It is hybrid T provided with internal matching elements making it reflective for an incident wave at any port when remaining ports have matched termination.

Magnetic crossed field Modulator

A frequency doublet consists of an annular coil surrounded by hollow toroid magnetic material. The toroidal winding carries a direct voltage and alternating current is input to the annular winding. The output voltage at toroidal winding has a frequency that is double of the input signals and hence it works as a *frequency doubler*.

Magneto-ionic Wave component (radio waves)

At a given frequency, either of the two characteristic plane electromagnetic waves that can travel in a homogeneous magneto-ionic medium without change of polarization are called *ordinary and extraordinary wave components*.

Magneto Telephone System

It is the telephone system in which call signals are actuated by magneto generators at the subscriber's stations.

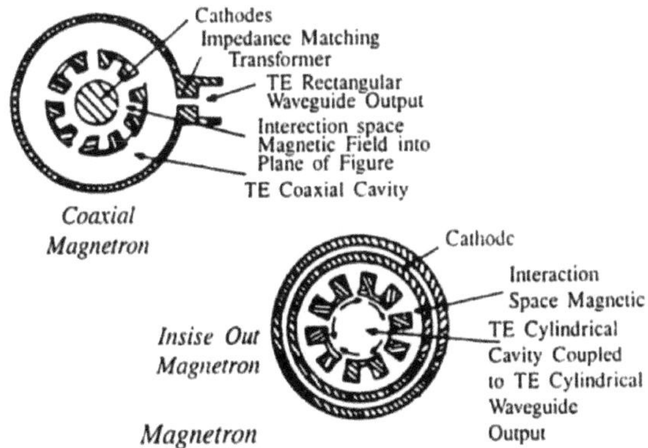

Magnetron Rectifier

It is a gas tube rectifier, in which electrodes are not heated and electron stream is controlled by a magnetic field.

Magnetron, Rising Sun

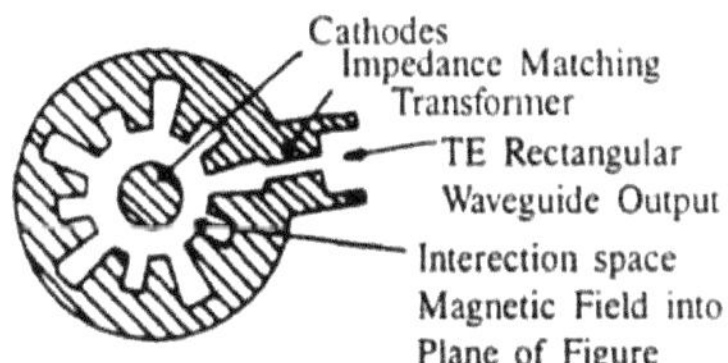

It contains alternate cavities of two different resonant frequencies, allowing different modes of operation to be selected at the output.

Magnetron Travelling Wave

It is a magnetron whose operation depends upon interaction of electron with a travelling radio frequency field having constant angular or linear velocity.

Magnetron Voltage Tunable (MVT)

It is magnetron in which output frequency can be varied linearly by varying the anode voltage. This is achieved by virtue of controlled electron injection and a heavily loaded radio frequency circuit.

Magnifier

It is an amplifier in radio telephony. A term used in cable telegraphy in preference to relay or amplifier, for an apparatus for amplifying signals received over a submarine cable by controlling a circuit otherwise than by opening and closing contacts.

Magnetization codes

Various magnetization codes are used. Some most common are shown below :

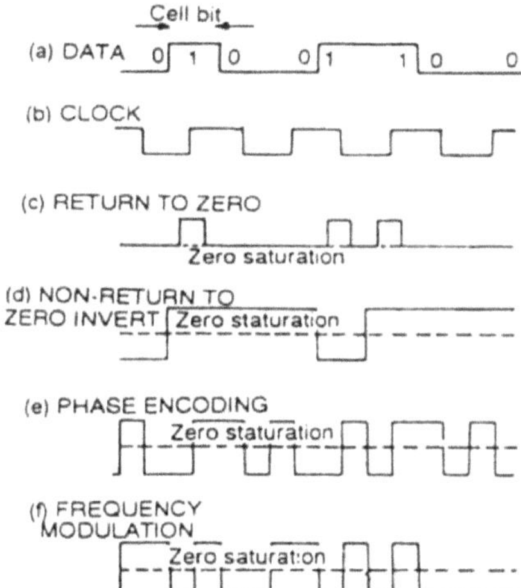

Marconi system of Radio communication

Originally employing an earthed aerial containing the spark gap and coherent in its own circuit, the system was later improved by the addition of coupled tuned circuits production and detection, leading up to the valve and other methods of transmission and reception and short wave (beam) system with highly-directive aerials.

Manchester

It is a format for recording digital data on a magnetic surface.

Maser

It is an acronym for microwave amplification by stimulated emission of radiation. It is a source of intense coherent monochromatic radiation in the microwave region of the electromagnetic spectrum. It can be used as a microwave amplifier or oscillator.

Types of masers :

1. Maser Gas :

This was the first type of Maser. It used ammonia. A gas has low density of atoms, so power available is low and bandwidth available is narrow. These are not suitable for microwave applications but being of high purity are used as frequency standards.

2. Maser Solid State :

It uses paramagnetic material such as ruby, which has multiple energy levels and transitions involving photons of microwave energy.

Masking

It is a special effect in which part of picture signals is suppressed electronically with a view to its substitution by another picture signals.

Mass Spectrum

It is a spectrum obtained by deflecting a beam of Positive Rays emitted from a tube, containing a residual gas to be investigated, by electric or magnetic fields. Extent of the deflection depends upon me (ratio of the mass of the projected positively charged particles of which rays are composed to the atomic charge); thus, every element has its characteristic spectrum lines like those of the light spectrum.

Microstrip

Microstrip

It is a transmission line consisting of a conducting strip and a parallel extending conducting surface bonded to opposite side of the thin electric substrate. Electromagnetic field propagates through dielectric guided by upper conductor. It is used at microwave frequencies components such as filters, couples, mixers, can be printed on dielectric.

Microphone

It is an instrument devised for magnifying small sounds. Now, it is used in a slightly different form as a telephone transmitter. The ordinary carbon microphone consists of a diaphragm set in vibrating are used to limited extent for radio-telephony and for experimental purposes. The term has come to be applied to any variety of sensitive telephone transmitter, whether dependent upon variation of resistance or not. It may also be defined as change in the resistance of a mass of loosely packed carbon granules and corresponding undulations in the current through the instrument faithfully copying form of the original sound waves

Microphone amplifier.

It is an amplifier, used in conjunction with a broadcasting microphone to amplify variations of current caused thereby before their transmission to Control or Modulating system.

Modulation

It is the process, by which a characteristic of one signal is varied in proportion to the information contained in another signal. Type includes : amplitude, frequency, phase, pulse-amplitude, pulse-code, pulse-width, pulse-modulation frequency, pulse-position, and pulse-time modulation. The periodic alternation of amplitude, frequency or phase of the Carrier wave according to the sound waves by action of the microphone, or in some other way, on some part of transmitting circuit. Cf.

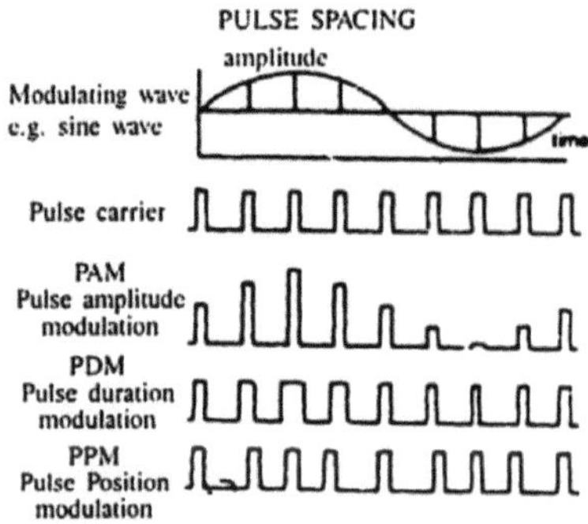

Modulation Pulse

Coding of a digital signal onto an analog one.

e.g., by changing amplitude of the carrier signal 10 represent a 0 or a 1.

Modulation Phase or Phase Shift Keying (PSK)

It is modulation process used to change phase of the carrier with respect to phase reference to transmit binary data. Binary phase coherent PSK switches between two carrier signals with 180 degree phase differences to represent binary 0 and 1.

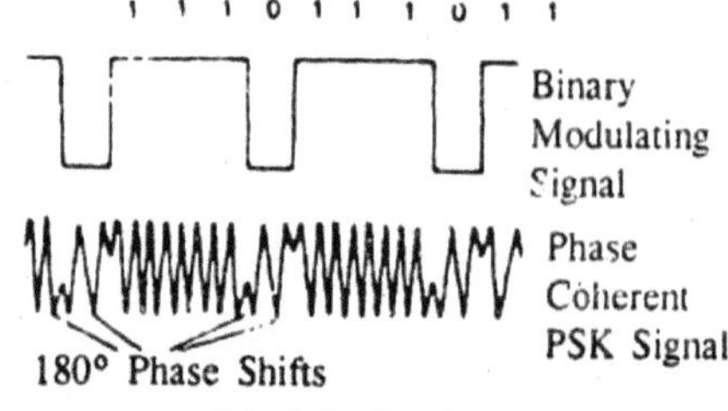

Modulation PSK

Modulator

It is a transmitter circuit or device that varies amplitude, frequency, phase, or other characteristic of a carrier signal in proportion to the waveform of the modulating signal that contains useful information.

Monopulse

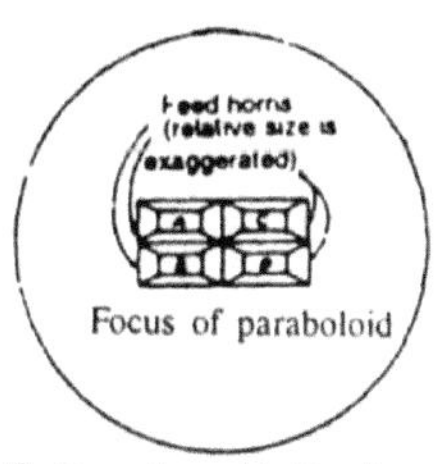

Outline of parabloid reflector

Capture target information in one pulse in a monopulse radar. In an amplitude comparison monopulse system, four feeds are used with the one paraboloid reflector. These are the four horn antenna displaced about the central focus of the reflector as shown in the figure. Transmitter feeds the horns simultaneously, so that a sum signal is transmitted which is little different from the usual pulse transmitted by a single horn in reception a duplexer using a rat race is employed to provide following three signals:

Sum $A + B + C + D$,

Vertical difference $(A + B) - (B + D)$

Horizontal difference $(A + B) - (C + D)$.

Multi-Hop Transmission

Behaviour of the ionosphere when a radio wave is propagated through it depends very much upon frequency of the wave. At low frequencies, ionosphere acts as though it were a medium of high electrical conductivity and reflects, with little loss, any signals incident on its lower edge. It is possible for a VLF or LF signal to propagate for considerable distances by means of reflections from both lower edge of the ionosphere and the earth.

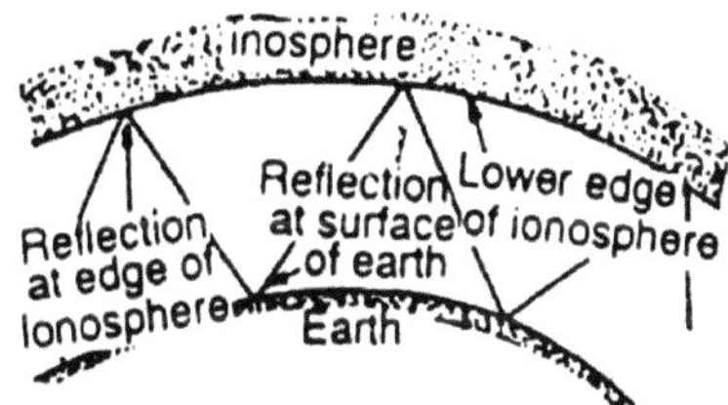

Multi-hop transmission of a low-frequency wave.

Multi-Path Propagation

The radio waves arriving at the receiving end of a sky-wave radio link may have travelled over two or more different paths through the ionosphere. Total field strength at the receiving aerial is phasor sum of the field strengths produced by each wave.

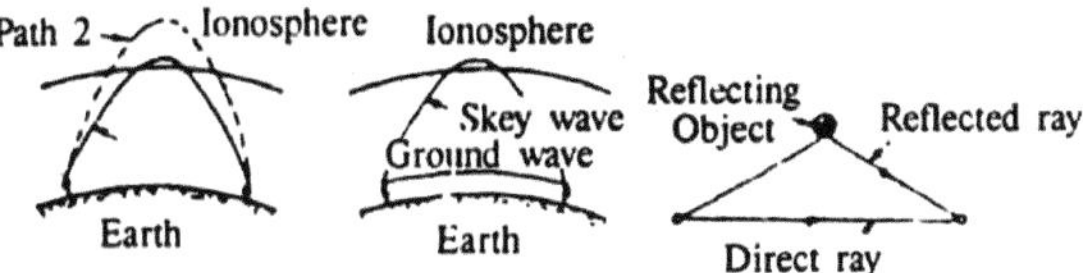

Since ionosphere is subject to continual fluctuations in its ionization density, the difference between lengths of paths 1 and 2 will fluctuate and this will alter total field strength at the receiver.

Natural Frequency

It is the frequency, at which free oscillations occur in an electrical or mechanical system. It is the frequency at which resonance occurs in such a system in response to a periodic driving force.

Frequency of natural oscillation in a circuit, when effect of resistance is negligible, is given by

$$f_o = \sqrt{\frac{1}{2\pi LC}}$$

where, L = inductance

C = capacitance of the circuit.

Fundamental frequency of an aerial without addition of extra inductance or element.

Noise bandwidth

Noise bandwidth of a network is the area divided by the height, at the center-tuned frequency of the power gain-vs-frequency characteristics. It is generally considered as the 3 dB down bandwidth of the desired response.

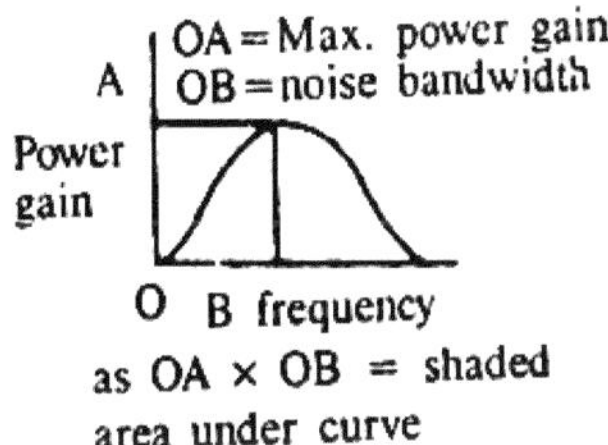

Noise margin (DC)

Noise margin of a logic gate is a measure of noise immunity, i.e. capacity of the gate to withstand fluctuations of the voltage levels (noise) at its input.

Optical fibre

It is composed of cylindrical core of refractive index and a concentric cladding of refractive index.

Optophone

An instrument for enabling the blind to read ordinary print by means of a telephony receiver controlled by the variations in resistance of a Selenium cell. The letters are intermittently illuminated in bands, each with a different frequency of illumination, and arrangements are made so that as black part of a letter passes through one of these bands as *"eye"* of the instrument travels over it, the balance between resistance of two selenium cells is upset and a current of a frequency equal to that of the illumination of the band in question passes through the telephone receiver. Thus a definite signal consisting of a combination of consecutive and simultaneous sounds of different pitch (chords) is heard, from which, after a little training, form of the letter is easily recognized.

Panel Automatic Telephone System

It is a rotary automatic telephone system used in the United States employing banks of multiple contacts arranged on flat upright panels over which mechanically driven contact bushes move vertically. Other features are employment of a Call Indicator and a system of a Reverting Control.

Parabolic Reflector

Frequencies at the upper end of the UHF band and in the SHF band can be treated in much the same way as light beams. Since parabolic reflector is used in a searchlight to produce a powerful parallel beam of light when light source is located exactly at the parabolic focus, so a parabolic reflector (often called *dish*) can be used to provide a very directional high-gain antenna with the radio energy concentrated into a parallel beam. Dish diameters vary from about 20 cm for an internal antenna for a domestic TV receiver up to more than 30 metres for ground stations working to geostationary satellites.

Peniotron

It is essentially a cyclotron fast wave tube. Structures of the device depicting interaction between travelling wave and electron beam and is shown inside. The device supports a cylindrical electron beam moving in a helical path around the field lines of a nearly constant magnetic field parallel to the direction of the RF electromagnetic wave in a double ridges pair wave guide. Non-uniformity of the fields in the vicinity of the ridges is used for device operation unlike gyrotron. Here relativistic mass effects adversely affect efficiency of the device unless magnetic field tempering is employed for compensation. Angular frequency of the wave is approximately twice that obtained in harmonic or fundamental gyrotron operation and thus a theoretical efficiency close to 100% is possible for conversion of the transverse energy in the beam into RF power. Bandwidth of the device is small, i.e., less than 1 %.

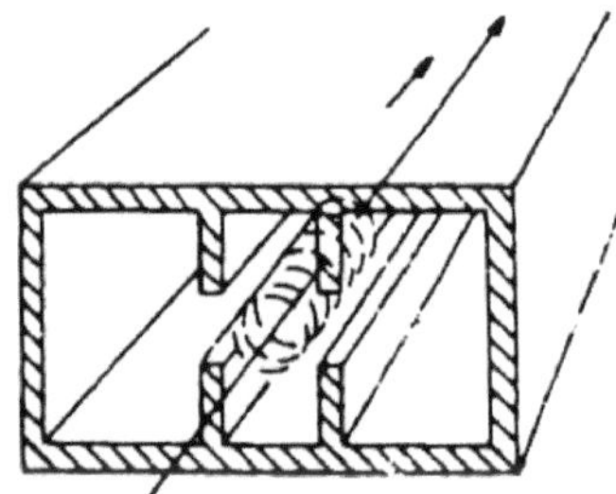

Phase Lock Loop

It is the circuit which, automatically controls an oscillator so that it remains in a fixed phase relationship with a reference signal. Phase lock loop is used in a variety of applications such as tracking filter and frequency discriminators.

Pilot Synchronizing

It is a method of controlling frequency of the local oscillator in Suppressed Carrier and allied systems of radio-telephony by means of an auxiliary or pilot signal.

Pixel (Picture Element)

It is a single cell in an image, usually represented as a bitmap of intensity values. It is acronym for picture element. Pixel is a single dot on a monitor that can be addressed by a single bit. A dot of light appears on the computer screen. A collection of pixels forms *characters* and images on the screen.

Pixel is the smallest portion of the screen that can have its light characteristics converted to computer readable expressions of electric current.

Power Density Spectrum

It is a plot of power density values due to many different frequencies emanating from one source, as a function of frequency.

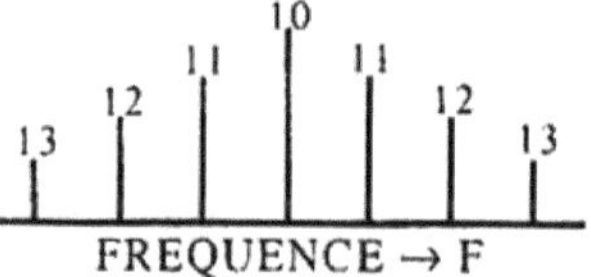

Plan Position Indicator (PPI)

It is the display used in radars for observing target returns in the form of a bright spot on the screen. The distance and bearing of the target is given by polar coordinates of the spot with respect to centre of the beam.

Pulse

It is a momentary, sharp change in a current, voltage, or other quantity that is normally constant, characterized by a rise and fall of finite duration various pulse parameters are shown inside.

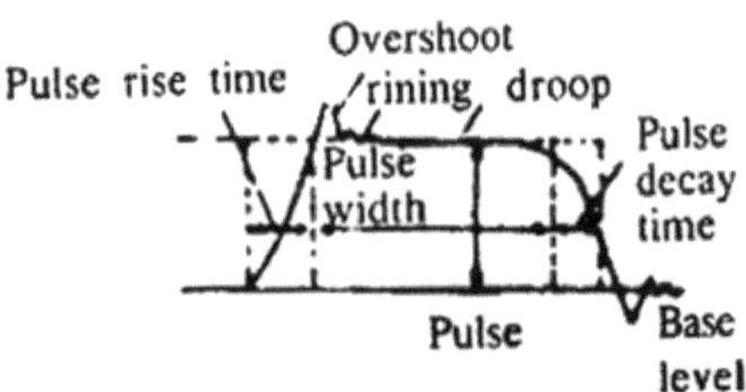

Pulse

Pulse Code Modulation (PCM)

In this system, analogue signal is sampled at regular intervals to produce a pulse amplitude modulated waveform. If an analogue signal is sampled regularly using a sampling rate of at least twice the highest frequency of the signal, the samples are found to be adequate to allow recreation of the original voice signal with sufficient accuracy for all purposes. Sampling is done by feeding analogue signal to a circuit with a gate which only opens for duration of the sampling pulse. Output is a pulse amplitude modulated (PAM) signal.

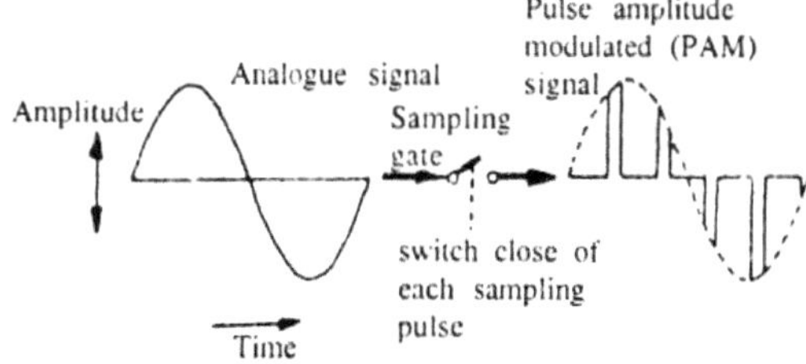

Principle of Pulse amplitude modulation

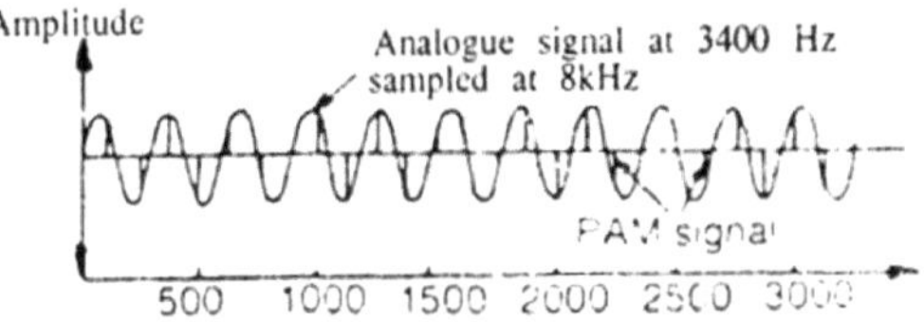

Sampling of the highesl voice frequency to be transmitted

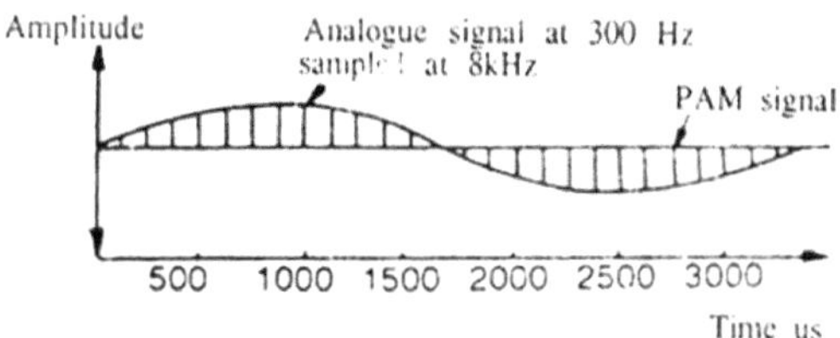

Sampling of the highesl voice frequency to be transmitted

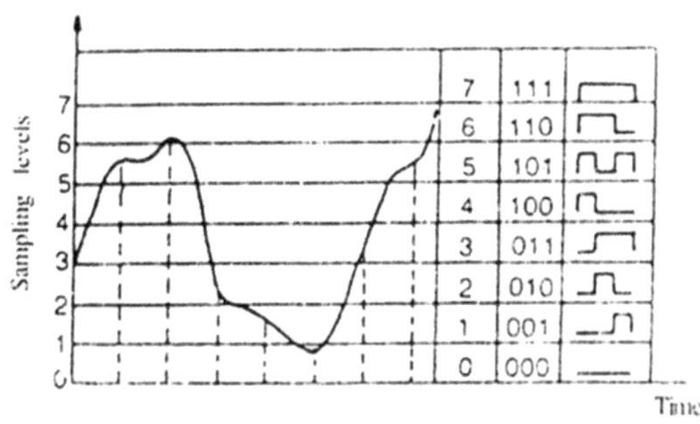

Quantization of a signal

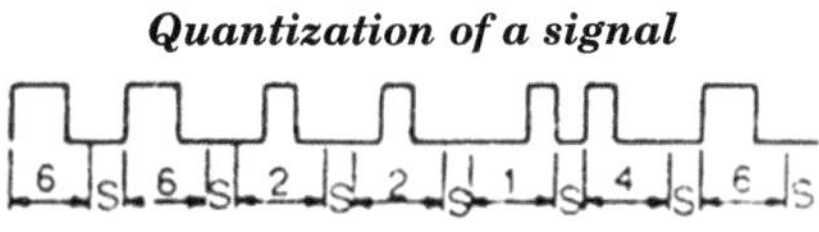

Binary pulse train representing the signal

Pulse modulation

It is a method of conveying information by means of pulses of voltage or current. With pulse modulation, carrier wave is not sinusoidal, but consists of repeated rectangular pulses. Amplitude, width or position of the pulses can be altered by the information signal.

Pulse regenerators

In its passage along a telephone line, time-division multiplexing (TOM) signal is both attenuated and distorted but, provided the receiving equipment is able to determine whether a pulse is present or absent at any particular instant, no errors are introduced. To keep the pulse waveform within the accuracy required, pulse regenerators are fitted at intervals along the length of the line. Function of a pulse regenerator is to check incoming pulse train at accurately timed intervals for the presence or absence of a pulse. Each time a pulse is detected, a new undistorted pulse is transmitted to line and, each time no pulse is detected, a pulse is not sent.

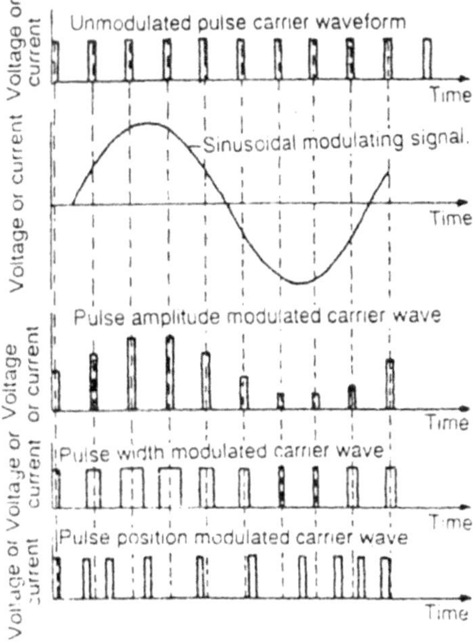

Pulse-nioduUneti carrier waves

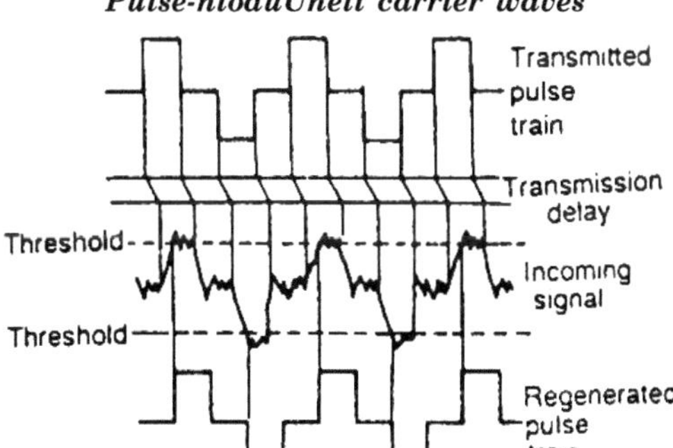

Waveform regeneration by a pulse regenerator

Q Band

It is a band of frequencies between 36 to 46 GHz.

Quadrature modulation

It is modulation of two carrier signals 90 degrees apart by separate modulating functions.

Quadruplex Telegraph System

It is a telegraph system in which Duplex and Diplex working are so combined that four messages, two in each direction, can be sent simultaneously over a single line.

Quad-type cable

Many two-wire lines are often wanted between he same two places but it can most conveniently be provided by making a cable with a number of pairs of insulated wires inside it. They are provided in fours or quads. Each wire is identified by colour of the insulating material according to a standard colour code for cable pair identification.

Radar

It is an acronym for radio detection and ranging. It is a system which uses beamed and reflected RF energy for detection and location of objects, as well as for measuring distances or altitudes. It can be used for navigation and guidance of ships, aircraft, and other vehicles and systems. It is also called *Radio location*. It is a system that location distant objects using reflected radio waves of microwave frequencies. Modern radar systems are highly sophisticated and can produce detailed information about both stationary and moving objects.

Radar Continuous Waves

In these, the radar sends out signals, continuously; a portion of which is received back after reflection from target.

Radar range

Maximum range of a radar for a given power of transmitter and known pulse width, frequency and antenna gains is given by

$$R_{max} = \left[\frac{P_t + Ap_2\lambda^2 S}{\left(4\pi^3\right)P_{min}} \right] m$$

where

P_t = transmitted pulse peak power

A_p = maximum power gain of antenna

λ = wavelength corresponding to radar frequency

S = radar cross section area

P_{min} = minimum detectable signal of receiver

Radiation patterns

In a radio communication system, baseband signal is positioned in a particular part of the frequency spectrum using some form of modulation. Then modulated wave is radiated into the atmosphere in the form of an electromagnetic wave by a transmitting antenna (or aerial)

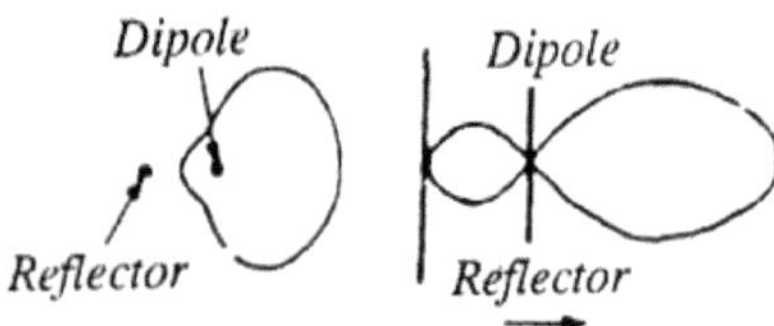

Radiation patterns:

(a) dipole and reflector, in equatorial plane

(b) dipoie and reflector, in meridian plane

(c) dipoie, reflector and director, in equatorial plane

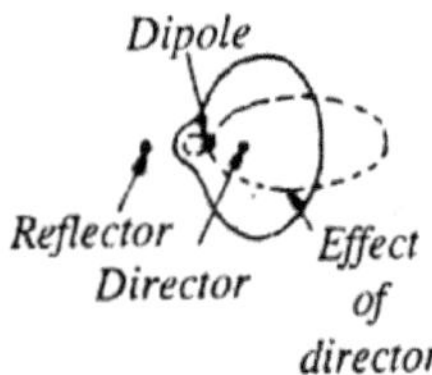

Radio Communication System

It this, a transmitter is required at the source to send the signal over the radio link, with the energy travelling at the speed of light, and a receiver is needed at the destination to recover the signal before applying it to the transducer.

Radio system characteristics

When a radio-frequency current flows into a transmitting antenna (aerial), power is radiated in a number of directions in an electromagnetic wave. This is a complex signal with the same general characteristics as light but of a lower frequency; electromagnetic radio waves travel at the same speed as light and can be reflected and refracted just as light. Some antennae are omni-directional.

Radio Propagation Methods.

Radiated energy reaches the receiving station by one or more of following five modes:

(1) Surface wave

(2) Sky wave

(3) Space wave

(4) Via a satellite

(5) Scatter

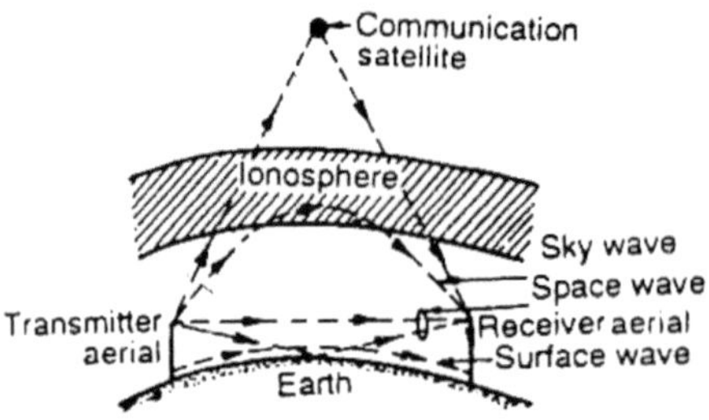

Radio Technique

These are the techniques involving simple and advance principles in radio reception, selection, detection and transmission and modulation of radio waves.

Radio signals

A carrier in the RF range that is modulated by an electromagnetic signal.

Carrier waves or Radio waves or Hertzian waves

As these are electromagnetic waves having constant amplitude and frequency between 20 kHz to 3×10^8 MHz. These waves are capable of carrying signals upto very long distances into the space, hence they are called *carrier waves.*

Signals or Signal wave

It is an electrical wave having sound, picture or any other type of information or effect.

Signal waves are not transmitted directly into the space because

Modulation

It is the process of superimposing (or mixing) signal wave on the carrier wave.

Types of Modulation

1. Amplitude modulation (AM).

It is the process of modulation in which amplitude of carrier wave in accordance to the amplitude of signal wave.

AM is employed in all frequency bands.

It is used in sound broadcasting, radio telephony, video signal transmission in TV etc.

Advantages :

(*i*) It is practicable in all frequency bands.

(*ii*) Channel width is small.

(*iii*) Receiver and transmitter circuits are simple.

Disadvantages

(*iv*) All sorts of interferences are maximum in AM.

(*v*) Fidelity of AM signal is poor.

(*vi*) AM system requires **more** electrical power

2. **Frequency Modulation (FM).**

It is the process of modulation in which frequency of carrier wave varies in accordance to the amplitude of signal wave.

It is used in sound signal transmission in TV and microwave communications.

Advantages

(*i*) All sorts of interferences are minimum in FM.

(*ii*) Fidelity of FM signal is high.

(*iii*) FM system requires less electrical power.

Disadvantages

(*iv*) It is practicable in short and micro wave bands only.

(*v*) Channel width is large.

(*vi*) Receiver and transmitter circuits are complex.

3. **Pulse-time modulation**

It is the process of modulation in which pulse-timing of carrier wave varies in accordance to the signal wave.

FM is employed in VHP and UHF (above 30 MHz) frequency bands.

It is used in remote control systems.

Per cent of modulation

The depth of modulation expressed in terms of percentage is called *per cent of modulation.*

$$\text{Per cent of modulation} = \frac{\text{Signal volts}}{\text{Carrier volts}} \times 100$$

Modulation index

Depth of modulation of an FM wave is called *modulation index.*

$$\text{Modulation index} = \frac{\text{Carrier frequency deviation}}{\text{Signal frequency}}$$

Frequency deviation of 75 kHz is considered equivalent to 100% modulation of an AM wave.

Side band

It is a frequency band above or below the frequency is use for transmission which has information signal modulated with the carrier.

SSB (Single side Band) transmission

It is the transmission involving use of only one side band for the transmission of modulated carrier wave.

Bandwidth

It is total width of a broadcasting channel in terms of Hz or kHz or MHz.

Fidelity and Quality of Transmission

Articulation of signals is necessary before their broadcast on a broadcasting channel. Signals should have all fundamental and harmonic frequencies called its *fidelity.* Signal should be free from all son of interferences called as its '*quality*'.

Receiving area

Area around a transmitter in which its transmission can be received is called receiving area for that transmitter or broadcasting station.

Radio or radio receiver

It is an electronic equipment which is meant for reception and reproduction of radio waves into sound waves.

Radio waves

Electromagnetic waves of frequency range of 20 kHz to 3×10^6 MHz are called *radio waves.*

Velocity of radio waves is 3×10^5 metres per second or 1.86,000 miles per second.

Wireless or Wireless communication

It is system of communication based on the application of radio waves and that too without the use of cable etc. between the two stations.

Electronics

It is the branch of science that deals with the behaviour and applications of electrons and other charge carriers.

Radio-chain

It is a complete system of transmission and reception of signals employing radio waves.

Radio broadcasting

It is the system transmitting sound programmes for the use of general public by means of their domestic radio.

Broadcasting methods

Generally following two methods are used:

(*i*) Amplitude modulation (AM) method

(*ii*) Frequency modulation (FM) method

TV broadcasting or telecasting involves both AM and FM methods.

RADIO PROPAGATION

It is the process of expanding radio waves into the space.

Radio wave propagation methods

Radio waves are propagated in the following forms:

(*i*) **Ground waves:**

These are radio waves which propagate along the curvature of earth.

These waves are capable to establish radio communication upto 400 kms. in the frequency range of 300 to 3000 kHz.

(*ii*) Sky waves:

These are radio waves that propagate reflection of radio waves by the ionosphere and the earth.

These waves are capable to establish radio communication between two stations situated any where on the earth in the frequency range of 3 to 30 MHz.

(*iii*) Direct waves:

The radio waves propagate in straight line (i.e. line of sight).

These waves are capable to establish radio communication upto very long but straight distances and usually upto 100 kms on the earth's surface in the frequency range of 300 to 3×10^6 MHz.

(*iv*) Ground reflected waves

These are radio waves which reach at a receiving aerial after being reflected by a mountain etc.

These waves are capable to establish radio communication upto 250 kms. in the frequency range of 30 to 3×10^6 MHz.

IONOSPHERE

It is the air belt around the earth ranging from 10 to 400 kms. height above earth's surface.

It contains ionised gases which are capable to reflect the radio waves to [he earth's surface.

Uses:

Ionised layers of the ionosphere more useful for radio communication purposes.

Kennley-Heaviside layer and Appeleton layer are capable to reflect radio waves of 3 to 30 MHz frequencies. These layers extend from 144 to 400 kms. height above earth's surface.

Radio-horizon is slightly larger than vision-horizon because of reflection property of the radio waves.

Critical angle

It is maximum value of the angle of radiation at which total reflection can occur.

Skip Distance

In short wave propagating, the distance between transmitting antenna and the point where the very first wave touches earth's surface after reflection from the ionosphere is called skip distance.

Skip zone or zone of silence

It is the area where neither ground nor sky waves are able to reach and there is no reception of radio waves.

Fading

In short wave reception, magnitude of R.F. voltage induced in a receiving aerial changes continuously due to instability of ionospheric density. This effect is called *fading* and it result in an instability in the output sound at the receiver.

Fading is eliminated by employing an AVC circuit.

Selective fading

When a direct wave and a ground reflected wave reach a receiving aerial simultaneously, they produce a fading due to difference between the phases of the two waves which is called selective fading.

Basic Principles of Radio Reception

(*i*) Reception

(*ii*) selection

(*iii*) depiction

(*iv*) reproduction

Fundamental principles of radio transmission

(*i*)   Production of radio waves

(*ii*) 'Modulation' of radio waves with signal waves

(*iii*) 'Transmission' of modulated radio waves into space by the antenna.

Stereophonic system

In this system, two separate microphones are installed on the left and right hand sides of a stage. Each microphone is associated with separate recording and reproducing unit, together with separate loudspeakers mounted on left and light hand sides of a listener. So, a listener of Stereo sound will experience that he himself is sitting in front of the stage and enjoying the music program.

Stereo record

In a stereo record, groove cutting is done on both sides of a record's groove by employing a duo-cutting head.

Stereo pickups

A double cartridge is employed in stereo pick-up. procedure of stereo broadcasting. For stereo broadcasting, a multiplex FM transmitter is employed. The transmitter sends two pilot signal and (L + R) and (L-R) signals (L-left, R-right). The system is also called *FM-FM stereo system.*

Stereo tape

In this, stereo AF signals are recorded on a dual track tape with the help of two recording heads.

Microphone Mixer

It is an AF driver stage in which two or more microphone outputs are mixed for their further amplification as a composite AF signal.

Pre-emphasis and De-emphasis

The process of limiting high frequencies of an AF signal is called *pre-emphasis*.

Similarly, the process of limiting low frequencies of an AF signal is called *de-emphasis*.

These two operations are essential while preparing a master phone-record.

Rhombic Antenna

It is very much larger than a Yagi. It can take up more area than a football field and is used principally for point-to-point HF links.

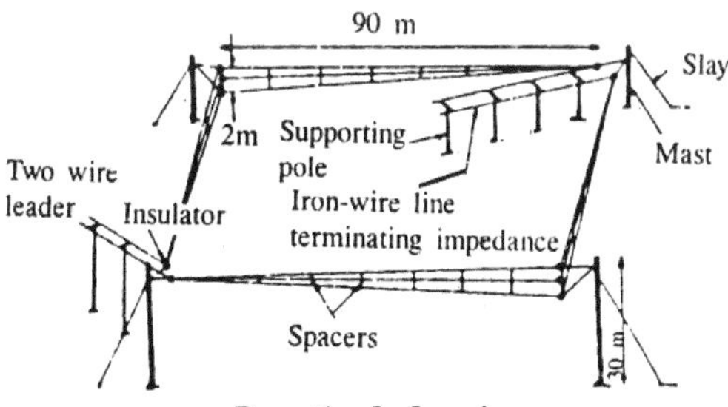

Practical rhomic

Satellite Position

Each satellite has a unique position or orbital slot over the equator at a height of approximately 36,000 kms (22,300 miles). Their positions are specified by their longitude at the equator by either east or west of the Greenwich meridian. For any point in the service area, specified by its latitude and longitude, a unique antenna orientation is needed to capture its signals.

To specify its orientation, following two components are required :

(*i*) Elevation

(*ii*) Azimuth.

Scatter propagation

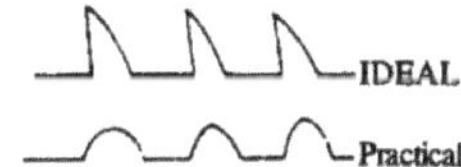

HUFFS equivalent of using sky wave transmission for long distance HF radio links. The radio energy is directed towards part of the troposphere which forward-scatters the signal towards the receiver.

Scattering region of the troposphere is about 10 km above ground level.

Scintillation

It is a bunch of light obtained from certain materials when exposed to ionizing radiation. The energy of incident radiation governs frequency of light emitted. Each incident event produces one flash.

Rapid change in the image of target/or received signal of a radar system/or a communication system about its mean position as seen on radar display/observed. Similar to twinkling of light of a star.

Sine wave

It is a fundamental waveform whose amplitude varies as the sine of a linear function of its argument, expressed in either radians, degrees, or time.

Singing

A telephone Repeater is said to "*Sing*" or sometimes to "*Howl*", when owing to unsuitable adjustment of its circuits, it acts as an oscillator, producing sustained oscillations of frequency which causes an audible note to be produced in the telephones connected there to.

Slot Line

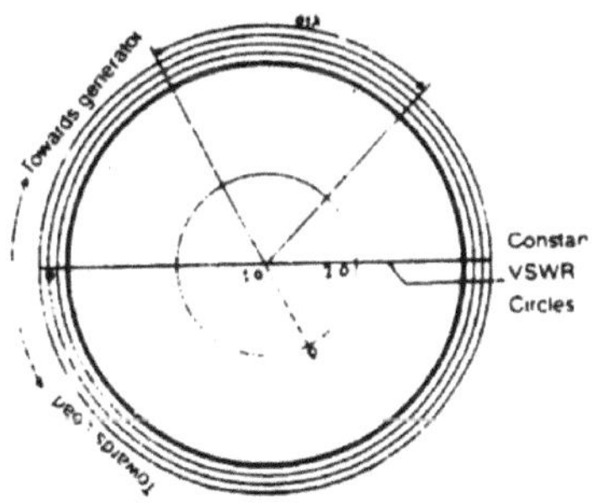

It consists of a slot or gap in a conductive coating on one side of a substrate is shown inside. Other side of the substrate is bare. If substrate permittivity is sufficiently high such as E = 10 to 30, then slot mode wavelength will be much smaller than free space wave length and the field will be closely confined near at the slot with negligible radiation loss. For slot line to be practical as a transmission line radiation must be minimized. This is achieved in a slot line by using high permittivity substrate.

Smith Chart

Transmission line properties can be represented graphically on a chart. It gives impedance relations which exist along a lossless line for different local conditions.

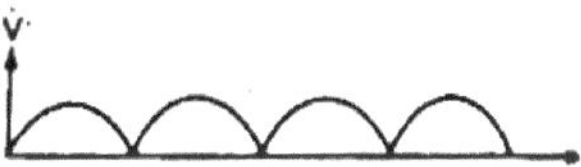

Step-by-Step Telephone Exchange

It is the first automatic system to become practicable for public telephone exchanges. Selection of a particular line is based on a one-from-ten selection process. In order to provide access to 10,000 lines, a stage of group selectors is added before the final selectors.

Standing Wave Node

It is any point line or surface in a distributed field for examples in a waveguide or transmission line at which some specified variable (voltage current electric or magnetic field) attain a zero or near zero magnitude.

Submarine telecommunication cables

These are sometimes under considerable tension, especially when these are being picked up from the sea bed, so great tensile strength is necessary in addition to the ability of cable and repeaters to withstand high pressures of deep waters.

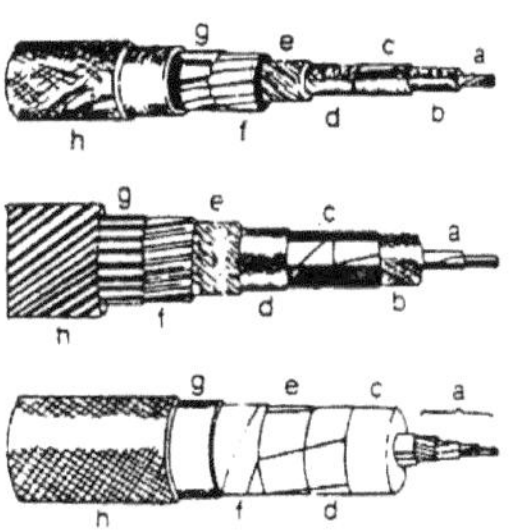

Lightweight coaxial telephone cables

Super Heterodyne Reception

It is most widely used type of radio reception, in which incoming signal is fed into a mixer and mixed with a locally generated signal from a local oscillator. Output consists of a signal of carrier frequency equal to the difference between locally generated signal and the carrier frequencies but containing all the original modulation. This signal, intermediate frequency (or IF) signal, is amplified and detected in an intermediate frequency (or IF) signal, is amplified and detected in an intermediate-frequency amplifier and passed on to the audio frequency amplifier.

Abbreviation for Supersonic Heterodyne Reception.

A system of radio reception in which local oscillations (or a harmonic there of) slightly different frequency from received oscillations, obtained from an auxiliary valve or from the main rectifying valve are superimposed upon the received oscillations so as to produce beats of a frequency intermediate between radio and audio-frequencies, at which amplification can be conveniently carried out. This system is suited for long distance reception, with a number of amplifying stages, and can be made of great selectivity.

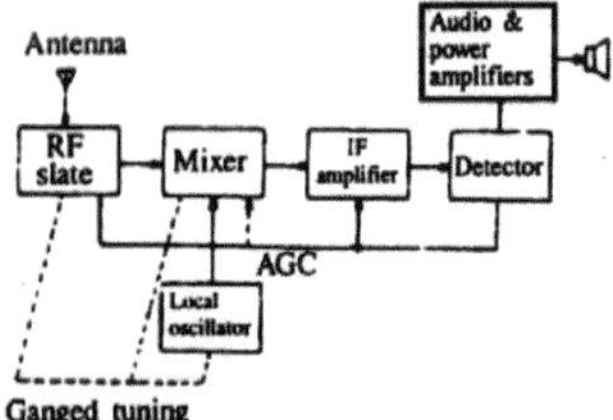

Suspended Micro-Strip

It is expected to show lower loss compared with the conventional microstrip but some higher compared with the inverted microstrip of the same impedance.

Switching Matrix

Both crossbar and reed relay switching depend on operation of a switching matrix, the principle of which can be explained by considering the circuits which are to be connected together as being arranged at right angles to each other in horizontal and vertical lines. These lines represent inlets and outlets of the switch.

Switching Time (or Switching Speed)

It is the time from 50% of level of command signal to the 90% of the RF output.

Synchronous to Digital Convertors (SDC)

Syn. Angle-Sensing Transducers. Measurement of shaft angle is important requirements in the modern control, instrumentation, and computing technologies. Mechanisms for converting shaft rotation to translation (linear motion) further extend usefulness of shaft-angle sensing. Shaft angle is used in the measurement and control of position, velocity, and acceleration, in one, two, or three spatial dimensions; and in many systems, many different sets of these parameters must be sensed and/or controlled. Thus, shaft angle transducers are extremely important elements in modern engineering.

Telecommand System

System to eliminate human involvement by hand operation by use of electronic to maneuver a satellite from remote ground stations and also to get status of health of various subsystems of a satellite.

Telecommunications

It is the technology concerned with communicating at a distance. The original information energy (such as that of the human voice, or music, or a telegraph signal) is converted into electrical form to produce an electronic information signal. This is achieved by a suitable transducer, which is a general term given to any device that converts energy from one form to another when required.

Teletext

It is the system which permits a limited number of pages of text to be transmitted by TV broadcasting stations together with their program emissions.

Television

It is a system that converts a series of visual images into electrical signals to be transmitted by radio waves to a distant point.

It is a system of radio-communication in which still and movie pictures are transmitted and received from one place to another.

The impression of a picture lasts on the human eye's retina for 1/16 seconds only. Therefore, if a moving object is photographed at the rate of 16 pictures per second (commercially 25 pictures per second) and then displayed on a screen at the same rate, the object seems to be moving.

Picture tube or CRT (Cathode Ray Tubes). Function of a picture tube or CRT (Cathode Ray Tube) is to display the voltage/current waveform of a AF/RF signal or video signal or still or movie picture of a CRT.

Main parts

(*i*) Electron gun

(*ii*) Deflection system

(*iii*) Fluorescent screen.

Transmission of Picture and Sound

Telecasting requires a two-in-one type transmitter. Picture signals or video signals are transmitted over AM system while sound signals are transmitted over FM system. Both types of signals are radiated by a single antenna.

VHF and UHF bands

VHF band extends from 30 to 300 MHz. Out of these, only 40 to 82 MHz and 174 to 216 MHz bands are allotted for telecasting.

MF and HF bands

Since, MF hand extends from 0.3 to 3 MHz only and its width is much lesser than that necessary for telecasting (7 MHz), therefore, telecasting is not possible in MF band. Since, HF band extends from 3 to 30 MHz, therefore, only 4 TV transmitters can be operated in this band and that too with the restriction that no other type of transmission should he in progress at that time. So, telecasting is impracticable in HF band.

VCR or

It is an electronic equipment which is made for recording and reproduction of audio and video signals in association with a TV receiver.

VCP or Video Cassette Player

is an electronic equipment made for the reproduction of audio and video pre-recorded signals in association with a TV receiver.

TV Antenna

It is called *'Yagi antenna'* or *'practice antenna'*. It mainly consists of a folded dipole and RF voltage induced in it, is fed to a TV receiver. Beside the dipole, there is a *'director'* which helps in setting the dipole perpendicular to the direction of telecasting antenna. There is a *'reflector'* which helps in increasing amount of RF voltage induced in the dipole. There are *'boosters'* which also help in increasing amount of RF voltage induced in the dipole.

Correct length of a folded dipole should be 1/2, i.e. half of radiated wavelength. Cable used is feeder in TV receivers is parallel twin wire cable

Dish Antenna

It is a sort of wave guide which is mounted at the centre of a hemispherical reflector. It is used for the reception of UHF signals relayed through a satellite.

Community Antenna

It is a high gain antenna designed to work as a common antenna for a number of TV receivers. A dish antenna may he used to work as a community antenna.

Balun

It is a RF coupling transformer which is used as an impedance matching device between dipole and TV receiver.

RF tuner

It is a RF circuit which acts as a TV channel selectors as well as a frequency converter. It incorporates RF amplifier, local oscillator frequency changer stages.

Auto-tuner

It incorporates a *'programme selector'* switch and a timer. The *'Programme selector'* selects VHF-L, VHF-H or UHF bands as desired.

Timer changes connection of the pole wafer automatically to various pre-tuned circuits in issociation with 'programme selector'.

1. Double tuned RF amplifier

It is RF amplifier, whose input and output circuits are tuned sharply to a specific frequency.

2. Stagger tuned RF amplifier

It is a RF amplifier, whose input and output circuits are tuned to two three frequencies so as to cover a wideband of frequencies, Video amplifier is a stagger tuned amplifier.

Wave trap

It is a bandpass type filter circuit which is connected across input terminals of a RF or IF amplifier in order to by-pass undesired frequency or a band of such frequencies.

Intercarrier system

It is the system of transmitting video and audio carrier frequencies together by employing a single unit.

Separation of Sound signals from composite IF signals

Composite IF signals are first detected by a *video detector* stage and then they are converted to a lower value of IF, i.e. 5.5. MHz which is called *sound* IF.

Sound section of TV receiver

It incorporate following stages :

(*i*) Sound IF amplifier

(*ii*) Limiter

(*iii*) Discriminator

(*iv*) AF driver amplifier

(*v*) AF output amplifier.

In IC based TV receiver, all the above 5 states, are integrated in two ICs

(*i*) usually, CA 3065 or 120 S .

(*ii*) It acts as sound IF amplifier, ' limiter and discriminator,

(*iii*) *TBA* 810 : It acts as AF driver and output amplifier.

FM signals

FM demodulation involves a limiter and discriminator. The limiter stage limits amplitude of FM signals within a predicted voltage. Discriminator produces AF output from supplied FM inputs within a predecided voltage. Discriminator produces AF output from supplied FM input.

During course of journey from transmitter to receiver, amplitude of FM signals becomes variable due to sparking, fading, reflection and absorption of radio waves. Hence, it becomes necessary to rectify amplitude variations present in the FM signals before their actual demodulation. Limiter is a RF amplifier and it is also called *clipper*.

Type of FM detectors used in TV receivers

(*i*) Phase shift discriminator. It circuit is designed in such a way that it gives no AF output for an unmodulated signals and it gives positive output for high side frequency variations and negative output for low side frequency variations.

(*ii*) *Ratio detector circuit:* Amplitude variations present in the FM signals do not affect AF output, therefore, it is not necessary to use a limiter circuit with this type of detector circuit.

Threshold of Hearing

The ear can only hear sounds whose intensity lies within certain limits. If a sound is too quiet, it is not heard and, conversely, if a sound is too loud it is felt rather has heard and causes discomfort or even pain. The minimum sound intensity that can be detected by the ear is called *threshold of hearing* or *audibility* and the sound intensity that just produces a feeling of discomfort is called *threshold of feeling*. The frequency range over which average human ear is capable of responding is approximately 30-16500 Hz. But this range varies considerably with the individual. The ear is most sensitive in the region of 1000 to 2000 Hz and becomes rapidly less sensitive as upper and lower limits of audibility are approached.

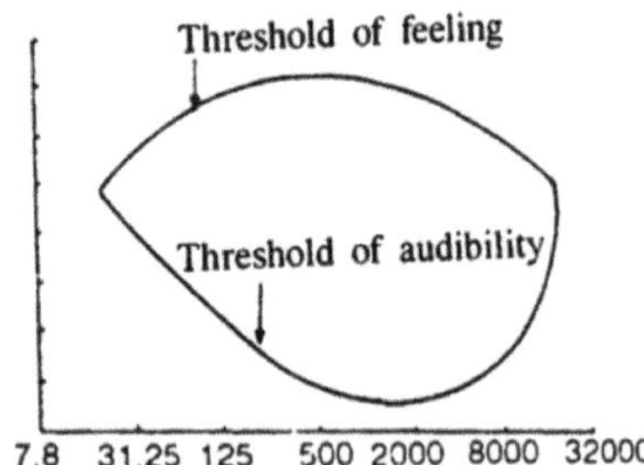

It is a static device used to transfer AC electrical energy from one circuit to another. It can't work on DC.

TRANSMITTER

equipment used for the production and radiation of radio waves after modulating them with a signal wave (or in unmodulated form).

It is used for the sending out of telephone or other electrically transmitted messages, signals, etc. It is used in line telephone for the actual apparatus, usually of the Microphone type, which receives sound waves of the voice and produces modulations in the amplitude of the current; but in radio telegraphy and telephony, usually including whole apparatus for generating the waves.

Carrier wave (CW) Transmitter

It is a transmitter capable of transmitting interrupted C.W. signals (usually in accordance to Morse code).

Requirements of a Transmitter

(i) RF oscillator

(ii) Signal producer

(iii) Modulator

(iv) Power amplifier

(v) Antenna

FEEDER

The line joining a transmitter to its antenna is called a *feeder* or *'transmission line.'*

There should be no radiation of RF energy from a feeder.

Types of Feeders

(i) Two parallel conductor

(ii) Two twisted conductor

(iii) Single wire feeders.

(iv) Co-axial feeder

It consists of two insulated cables housed in another insulation covering which itself is covered by a metallic mesh. Finally, feeder is covered with lead, jute and tarcoal covering. The radiation of RF energy from a co-axial feeder is negligible.

Transmitting Antenna

It is a system of conductors, used to establish a contact between a transmitter and the space.

Electromagnetic field round an antenna expand and contract alternately. The portion of electromagnetic field which fails to return back to the antenna gets radiated into space.

Length of a Transmitting antenna or Resonating length

Length of antenna

$$= \frac{\text{Velocity of radio waves}}{2} \times \text{frequency.}$$

Types of Transmitting Antennas

There are mainly two types of transmitting antennas:

(i) Hertz or half-wave antenna. It is usually installed horizontally.

(ii) Marconi or quarter-wave antenna : There can only be installed vertically with its one terminal grounded essentially.

Broadcasting tower

It is a vertically installed antenna. It is installed inside a framework of angle-iron. Normally, its height extends upto 150 metres.

Wave guided

It is a metallic horn, designed to guide a beam of UHF (ultra high frequency) waves in a specific direction (like a search light).

Antenna array

It is an antenna made with a number of halfwave antennas.

Telescopic Antenna whip antenna

It is a folding antenna. It is installed vertically and it is used with mobile radio transmitters and receivers. The maximum length of a telescopic antenna may be 3 metres.

Microwave

It is an electromagnetic wave (radio wave) having a wavelength of 10 to 100 cm corresponding to 300 to 3000 MHz frequency.

Microwave antenna

It is a small antenna which is usually installed erect at die centre of a hemispherical reflector. It is used to radiate or receive microwaves.

Low and High level modulations

In low-level amplitude modulation, modulating signal is modulated with RF carrier at a low power RF amplifier while in high-level amplitude modulation the same is modulated at a high power RF amplifier. Out of these two modulation systems, high level modulation is popular because in this system, amplifier stages preceding to the modulator stage may be of *class 'B'* or *class 'C' type*.

Keying

It is the process of inserting a transmit-switch or a Morse-key to a transmitter so as to control its radiations. In the off state of switch/key, transmitter rests 'standby'.

Principal stages AM transmitter

(*i*) RF oscillator

(*ii*) Buffer amplifier

(*iii*) Intermediate amplifier

(*iv*) Power amplifier

(*v*) Antenna

(*vi*) Microphone or any other signal source

(*vii*) AF amplifier

(*viii*) Modulator stages.

Buffer amplifier

It is a RF amplifier which makes the RF oscillator of a transmitter loadfree.

Intermediate amplifier

It is a RF amplifier used to couple buffer and power amplifier stages.

Modulator

It is a low frequency power amplifier, which feeds the modulating signal to a RF amplifier stage or in which mixing of a signal and carrier frequencies is accomplished.

Power amplification in Transmitters

Power amplifier of a transmitter contains two or more valves/transistors which are operated in parallel. The system increases output current and thus output power of the transmitter.

VHF (Very High Frequency) transmitter

A transmitter working in the frequency range of 30 to 300 MHz is called a VHF.

Frequency Multiplier

A frequency multiplier is a RF amplifier whose output circuit is tuned to a harmonic of its input frequency.

Most of the transmitters usually employ crystal oscillators for production of RF carrier. But a crystal fails to oscillate above 10-11 MHz because of its extremely reduced thickness. Therefore, high and very high frequencies are produced with the help of frequency multipliers. Principal stages employed in a

FM transmitter

(*i*) Microphone or any other signal source

(*ii*) Reactance modulator

(*iii*) RF oscillator

(*iv*) Frequency multiplier

(*v*) RF power amplifier

(*vi*) Antenna

(*vii*) Automatic frequency control (AFC) stages.

Reactance modulator

it is a modulator circuit which converts signal amplitude variations into frequency variations.

AFC (Automatic Frequency Control)

It is a process by which the centre value of frequency to be transmitted over FM system is *made stable*

Stages incorporated in AFC section of a FM transmitter

(*i*) RF oscillator

(*ii*) Frequency multiplier

(*iii*) Mixer

(*iv*) IF amplifier

(*v*) Discriminator stages.

Discriminator

It is a sort of detector circuit which is used for detection of FM waves. In a FM transmitter, discriminator is used to detect the 'difference frequency' which helps in automatic frequency control.

Link coupling

It is method of coupling used in high power transmitters for joining two stages.

Travelling Wave

It is an electromagnetic wave that is propagated along and is guided by a transmission line. In the case of a hypothetical loseless line of uniform cross section and infinite length, a sinusoidal a.c. supply at one end of the line (sending end) causes electrical energy to be transmitted along the line with instantaneous values of current and voltage at any given point varying sinusoidally.

Travelling Wave Amplifier Tube (TWT)

It is an O-type microwave amplifier tube, characterized by extended interaction between its electron beam and forward wave produced, by one or more slow wave circuits which are in sequence along the beam and may be separated by attenuators. Such tube has a very wide instantaneous frequency bandwidth. It is a also called the O-type backward tube.

Tuning

It is adjustment of the inductance or capacitance (or both) of an oscillating circuit to get maximum degree of resonance with received waves of a particular wave length.

The setting of variable capacitors and inductors of a radio receiver is called its *tuning* or *alignment*?

Fading

In short wave (3 to 30 MHz) reception, magnitude of RF voltage obtained by the aerial varies continuously. due to instability of the ionospheric density. This phenomenon is called as *fading*.

It is the circuit meant for providing a stability to the AF output of a radio receiver in spite of varying RF signal strengths.

Function of AVC circuit

An out of phase bias derived from the detector stage is applied to all RF and IF amplifier stages proceeding to the detector. This bias reduces the amplification of strong signals and conversely it increases amplification of weak signals. Hence, the output of detector stage becomes stable.

Simple AVC

The AVC which remains present all the time is called *simple AVC*.

AVC (Automatic Volume Control) or AGC (automatic gain control) circuit.

A simple AVC circuit reduces gain of RF and IF amplifier if RF input signals are weak. The trouble is eliminated in delayed AVC. In this circuit, AVC bias will only be effective when the RF signal strength is high enough.

Keyed AVCS

It is a delayed AVC which is provided with a switch. AVC circuit can be switched of in case RF signals are weak.

AGC voltage

For deriving AGC voltage a resistor is connected to the top terminal' of volume control potentiometer. A capacitor is connected between each AGC point and ground to by-pass RF signals.

Variable μ (mu) tube

For If amplification special type of tube/transistor is required which can handle large input signals. A variable μ (mu) or *remote cut-off tube* is designed in such a way that its anode current does not attain cut-off state even for large signals.

Tuning indicator

It is an electronic device which is capable of indicating correct tuning position of the needle of a radio receiver. Generally, an *electron ray tube* or *magic eye tube* is used.

The tube has two triode sections working as :

  (*i*) amplifier

  (*ii*) tuning indicator.

IF alignment

It is setting of trimmer's screw and coil's core of IF transformer so as to provide a maximum IF output. For accurate IF alignment *signal generator* is required.

RF circuits alignment

It is setting of trimmer's screw of RF section for maximum RF output over an entire broadcast band.

VSAT

It is acronym for very small aperture terminal. These are very small diameter antennas with satellite receiver for private use of data transfer facility for individual user or shared by a group of people.

Wandering

It is change in apparent direction of received radio signals irrespective of the adjustment of the transmitter or receiver.

Wave Analyzer

It is an instrument to analyses a complex waveform into its fundamentals and harmonic components.

Wave Guide Mixer

It is a microwave mixer that combines RF signal and LO signal to produce IF. Both signal and local oscillation powers are fed to waveguide input port. A movable short is provided to optimize LO coupling at each frequency.

X BAND

It is a radio-frequency band that extends from 5.2 to 10.9 GHz, corresponding to wavelengths of 5.777 to 2.75 cm. Frequency limits for other bands are given in the entries for band and K hand.

Subdivisions of the X band (all values in gigahertz) :

Xa : 5.2-5.5	Xc : 7.0-8.5	Xq : 5.5-5.75
XI : 8.5-9.0	Xy : 5.75-6.2	Xs : 9.0-9.6
Xd : 6.2-6.25	Xx : 9.6-10.0	Xb : 6.25-6.9
Xf : 10.0-10.25	Xr : 6.9-7.0	Xk : 10.25-10.90

Yagi

It is an antenna, which is basically a conductor whose electrical length is one-half the wave-length at the desired frequency of operation, and is center-fed. This is basic /2 dipole. A Yagi antenna is widely used for the reception of TV broadcast signals.

Aerial

It is a sharply directional aerial array from which most aerials used for television and radio astronomy have been developed. Active part of the aerial consists of one or two dipole aerials together with a parallel reflector aerial and a set of parallel directors. The directors are relatively closely spaced, being from 0.15 to 0.25 of a wave length apart. When aerial is used for transmission, the directors absorb energy from back lobe of the dipole radiation pattern and reflect it in the forward direction. Thus major lobe reinforced at the expense of the back lobe.

Yagi Antenna.

It is essentially a narrow band antenna, most popular for TV reception, especially in VHP bands.

Y signal

The component of a color-encoded displays signal representing luminance information. The signal produces a black and white image on a standard monochrome monitor.

It is made up by combining specified fractions of following colour signal :

red (0.30)

green (0..59)

blue (0.11)

EXERCISE – I

1. In communication, the sampling technique leads to
   - (a) higher efficiency
   - (b) higher speed of communication
   - (c) cheaper equipment
   - (d) all of the above

2. The adverse effect of noise in a communication system is maximum in
   - (a) encoder
   - (b) channel
   - (c) receiver
   - (d) source

3. In order to get back the original signal from the sampled signal, it is necessary to use
   - (a) low pass filters
   - (b) high pass filter
   - (c) band-pass filters
   - (d) band-reject filters

4. In FM broadcast, the maximum modulation frequency is restricted to
   - (a) 5 kHz
   - (b) 10 kHz
   - (c) 15 kHz
   - (d) 20 kHz

5. In AM broadcast, the maximum modulation frequency is restricted to
   - (a) 3 kHz
   - (b) 5 kHz
   - (c) 10 kHz
   - (d) 15 kHz

6. In frequency modulation, if the frequency of the modulating voltage is doubled, the rate of deviation of carrier frequency
   - (a) doubles
   - (b) becomes four times
   - (c) becomes half
   - (d) remains unaltered

7. In FM, the carrier frequency deviation is determined by
   - (a) modulating voltage
   - (b) modulating frequency
   - (c) both modulating voltage and frequency
   - (d) none of these

8. In amplitude modulation system, if modulation index is raised from 1 to 1.2, then
   - (a) power of the wave increases
   - (b) efficiency of transmission increases
   - (c) bandwidth increases
   - (d) signal get distorted

9. An amplitude modulated voltage has modulation index of 100%. If carrier is suppressed, then percentage power saving is
   - (a) 50%
   - (b) 66.6%
   - (c) 75%
   - (d) 25%

10. In amplitude modulation, the modulation envelope has a peak value double the unmodulated carrier value. The modulation index is
    - (a) 25%
    - (b) 50%
    - (c) 75%
    - (d) 100%

11. One of the advantages of base modulation over collector modulation of a class C amplifier is
    - (a) better efficiency
    - (b) lower modulation power requirement
    - (c) better linearity of modulation
    - (d) higher power output per transistor

12. Pre-emphasis is used to boost up
    - (a) low modulation frequencies
    - (b) high modulation frequencies
    - (c) both low and high modulation frequencies
    - (d) overall modulation index

13. Pre-emphasis of high modulation frequencies is used
    - (a) after modulation
    - (b) before modulation
    - (c) before detection
    - (d) after detection

14. Pre-emphasis circuit is placed
    - (a) after modulation circuit
    - (b) before modulation circuit
    - (c) before detection circuit
    - (d) after detection circuit

15. De-emphasis is used to
    - (a) attenuate high modulation frequencies
    - (b) attenuate low modulation frequencies
    - (c) attenuate midband modulation frequencies
    - (d) reduce overall modulation index

16. In frequency modulation
    - (a) noise decrease by increasing frequency deviation
    - (b) noise decreases by decreasing frequency deviation
    - (c) noise is unaffected by change of frequency deviation
    - (d) noise decreases by increasing the bandwidth

17. In frequency modulation, for a given frequency deviation, the modulation varies
    - (a) inversely as the modulating frequency
    - (b) directly as the modulating frequency
    - (c) inversely as the square of modulating frequency
    - (d) directly as the square of modulating frequency

18. The frequency deviation in phase modulated carrier is proportional to
    - (a) only to amplitude of the modulating signal
    - (b) only frequency of the modulating signal
    - (c) amplitude as well as frequency of the modulating signal
    - (d) none of the above

19. The drawback of FM relative to AM is that
   (a) noise is very high for high modulation frequencies
   (b) larger bandwidth is required
   (c) higher modulating power is required
   (d) higher output power is required

20. In which of the following modulation systems does the increase of modulation index result in increase in bandwidth ?
   (a) Amplitude modulation
   (b) Frequency modulation
   (c) Phase modulation
   (d) Both frequency and phase modulations

21. Monostable multivibrator is used for generating PWM because it is
   (a) an integrator
   (b) a voltage-to-time converter
   (c) a voltage-to-frequency converter
   (d) a pulse generator

22. PPM may be converted into PWM by using
   (a) monostable multivibrator
   (b) bistable multivibrator
   (c) astable multivibrator
   (d) integrator

23. Compared to PPM, the PDM has the disadvantage that it requires
   (a) a more powerful transmitter
   (b) pulses of larger widths
   (c) more samples per second
   (d) none of these

24. To generate PCM, the signal is sampled and converted into
   (a) PWM   (b) PPM
   (c) PAM   (d) PDM

25. The principal merit of PCM system is its
   (a) lower bandwidth
   (b) lower power requirement
   (c) lower noise
   (d) lower cost

26. All the output pulses are at full transmitter power for a strong signal in all of the following except
   (a) PWM   (b) PAM
   (c) PFM   (d) PCM

27. In pulse modulation system with any modulation, all the transmitted pulses have the same
   (a) amplitude
   (b) width
   (c) spacing
   (d) amplitude, width and spacing

28. In pulse modulation system, the modulating signal controls the
   (a) pulse amplitude   (b) pulse width
   (c) pulse spacing   (d) all of these

29. Which of the following modulation system is digital?
   (a) PPM   (b) PCM
   (c) PWM   (d) PFM

30. TDM
   (a) can be used with PCM only
   (b) interleaves pulses belonging to different transmissions
   (c) combines fine groups into a supergroup
   (d) stacks 24 channels in adjacent frequency slots

31. In order to separate out channels in an FDM receiver, it is necessary to use
   (a) AND gates
   (b) band pass filters
   (c) band stop filters
   (d) integrators

32. In high-power AM transmission, modulation is done at
   (a) buffer stage   (b) RF power stage
   (c) Oscillator stage   (d) IF stage

33. In AM, if modulation index is more than 100% then
   (a) power of the wave increases
   (b) efficiency of transmission increases
   (c) the wave gets distorted
   (d) band-width increases.

34. The frequency modulated (FM) radio frequency range is nearly
   (a) 250 - 300 MHz   (b) 150 - 200 MHz
   (c) 90 - 105 MHz   (d) 30 - 70 MHz

35. In a modulation system, on doubling the modulation frequency, the modulation index gets halved while the modulating voltage needed remains unaltered. The modulation system is
   (a) AM   (b) FM
   (c) PM   (d) All of these

36. Which one of the following is not an advantage of FM over AM?
   (a) Better noise immunity is provided
   (b) Lower bandwidth is required
   (c) The transmitted power is more useful
   (d) Less modulating power is required.

37. An increase in the modulation index leads to increase in band-width in case of
   (a) AM   (b) FM
   (c) PM   (d) Both FM and PM

38. Which of the following demodulator can be used for demodulating the signal x (t) = 5 $(1 + 2 \cos 2000\pi t) \cos 2000\pi t$?

(a) Envelope demodulator

(b) Square-law demodulator

(c) Synchronous demodulator

(d) None of these.

39. In a DM (delta modulation) system, the granular (idling) noise occurs when the

(a) modulation signal increases rapidly

(b) pulse rate decreses

(c) modulating signal remains constant

(d) pulse amplitude decreases

40. In a low level modulation AM system, the amplifier following the modulated stage can be

(a) linear amplifiers

(b) harmonic generators

(c) class C power amplifiers

(d) class B untuned amplifiers

41. In the generation of modulated signal, a varactor diode can be used for

(a) FM generation only

(b) AM generation only

(c) PM generation only

(d) both AM and PM generation

42. Pre–emphasis in FM systems involves

(a) compression of the modulating signal

(b) expansion of the modulating signal

(c) amplification of lower frequency components of the modulating signal

(d) amplification of higher frequency components of the modulating signal

43. What will be the percentage power saving if the carrier and one if the side bands are now suppressed ?

(a) 85%   (b) 70%

(c) 60%   (d) 45%

44. A balanced modulator produces

(a) AM   (b) SSB

(c) DSB   (d) VSB

45. The modulation index of a AM is to be measured using an oscilloscope. In this arrangement modulated signal

(a) and modulating signal both are connected to Y-input of oscilloscope

(b) and modulating signal both are connected to X-input of oscilloscope

(c) is connected to X-input and modulating signal to Y-input

(d) is connected to Y-input and modulating signal to X-input

46. Which one of the following is not necessarily the advantage of SSB ever AM

(a) simle circuitry

(b) less power handled

(c) less bandwidth required for SSB

(d) none of these

47. For broadcasting purpose, full AM signal is preferred to SSB signal because

(a) it requires large bandwidth

(b) generation of full AM is easier

(c) detection of full AM is simpler

(d) none of these

48. In amplitude modulation if modulation index is more than 1, then

(a) bandwidth will increase

(b) there will be interference with other signals

(c) efficiency of transmission will improve

(d) wave will get distorted.

49. Audio frequency range lies between

(a) 20 Hz and 20 kHz

(b) 20 kHz and 200 kHz

(c) 2 MHz and 20 MHz

(d) 20 MHz and 200 MHz

50. Vestigial side band is most commonly used in

(a) Radio transmission

(b) Television transmission

(c) Telephony

(d) All of the above

51. In FM the carrier deviation is determined by

(a) modulating voltage (b) frequency

(c) either of the above (d) none of these

52. The percentage of modulation for 45 kHz deviation in the FM broadcast band will be

(a) 30 %   (b) 40 W

(c) 60 %   (d) 90 %

53. FM broadcast band generally lies in

(a) LF   (b) HF

(c) VHF   (d) SHF

54. In case of wide band FM signal, the modulation index may be expected to be

(a) 0.5   (b) 1.0

(c) less than 1   (d) more than 1

55. In frequency modulation for a given frequency deviation, the modulation index varies

(a) inversely as the modulating frequency

(b) directly as the modulating frequency

(c) independent of modulating frequency

(d) none of these

56. In case the depth of modulation is doubled in F.M. system, the power tranmitted increase by factor of

(a) $\sqrt{2}$ (b) $\sqrt{3}$

(c) 2 (d) none of these

57. In an FM signal, the power

(a) increases as modulation index increases

(b) reduces as modulation index increases

(c) remains constant even when modulation index varies

(d) None of these

58. In FM, the frequency deviation is

(a) proportional to modulating frequency

(b) proportional to amplitude of modulating signal

(c) constant

(d) directly proportional to amplitude and inversely proportional to modulating frequency

59. Which of the following oscillator is not in FM?

(a) Crystal oscillator (b) Hartley oscillator

(c) Colpitts oscillator (d) All of the above

60. Which one of the following is not the advantage of FM over AM?

(a) More bandwidth is required

(b) FM can be made relatively immune from noise

(c) Amplitude of modulated wave is constant

(d) None of the above

61. When bandwidth is the major consideration a narrow and wide band FM can be approximated to

(a) SSB (b) AM

(c) PM (d) All of these

62. FM system

(a) needs less bandwidth

(b) offers better S/N ratio

(c) requires least moudulating power

(d) none of these

63. Pre-emphasis is used to amplify

(a) low frequency (b) high frequency

(c) both (a) and (b) (d) none of these

64. In stablized reactance modulator AFC system

(a) discriminator must have a fast time constant to prevent demodulation

(b) higher the discriminator frequency, the better the oscillator frequency stability

(c) discriminator frequency must not be too low, or the system will fail

(d) phase modulation is converted into FM by the equlaizer circuit.

65. An indirect way of generating F.M. is

(a) Armstrong modulator

(b) Varactor diode modulator

(c) Reactance FET modulator

(d) Reactance bipolar transistor modulator.

66. De-emphasis circuit is based

(a) prior to modulation

(b) after modulation

(c) for de-emphasising high frequency component.

(d) for de-emphasising low frequency component.

67. A frequency multiplier stage should operate as

(a) class A (b) class B

(c) class A, B (d) class C

68. Pulse modulation is used in

(a) Radio navigation

(b) Automatic landing equipments

(c) Data communications

(d) All of these

69. Pulse modulation is often used in

(a) Microwave band (b) LF band

(c) Telegraphy (d) Telephony

70. All the output pulses are at full transmitter power for a strong signal in all of the following except :

(a) PWM (b) PAM

(c) PFM (d) PCM

71. In pulse transmitter the ratio of time on to time off is called

(a) efficiency (b) duty cycle

(c) base (d) bandwidth

72. While demodulating PCM, it is first converted into

(a) PAM (b) PPM

(c) PWM (d) none of these

73. Signal to quantisation noise ratio in a PCM system depends on

(a) sampling rate

(b) number of quantisation levels

(c) message signal bandwidth

(d) none of these

74. Quantization noise occurs in

(a) PCM (b) TDM

(c) FM (d) PWD

75. Inherently most noise-resistant modulating system is

(a) PCM (b) PPM

(c) FM (d) DSB

76. Analog pulse modulating system is

(a) PCM (b) PWN

(c) both (a) and (b) (d) None of these

77. Digital modulating system
  (a) PPM   (b) PWM
  (c) PCM   (d) PAM

78. For transmission of normal speech signal, PCM channel needs a bandwidth of
  (a) 64 kHz   (b) 8 kHz
  (c) 4 kHz   (d) 2 kHz

79. Which of the following system is not analog?
  (a) PPM   (b) PCM
  (c) PFM   (d) PWM

80. Main advantage of PCM system is
  (a) lower bandwidth   (b) lower power
  (c) lower noise   (d) none of these

81. Sampling theorem is associated with
  (a) PCM   (b) FM
  (c) AM   (d) All of these

82. Digital communication system is
  (a) FM   (b) AM
  (c) PCM   (d) PAM

83. Quantizing noise occurs in
  (a) time-division-multiplexing
  (b) PCM
  (c) PPM
  (d) frequency-division-multiplexing

84. Signal-to-quantization noise ratio in a PCM system depends upon
  (a) sampling rate
  (b) number of quantization levels
  (c) message signal bandwidth
  (d) none of the above

85. In pulse modulation, number of samples required to ensure no loss of information is given by
  (a) Nyquist theorem   (b) Parsevals theorem
  (c) Fourier transform   (d) None of these

86. PAM signal can be demodulated by using
  (a) a low pass filter   (b) a band pass filter
  (c) a high pass filter   (d) none of these

87. In a pulse position modulation system, transmitted pulse have
  (a) constant amplitudes but varying widths
  (b) constant amplitudes and constant widths
  (c) constant width but varying amplitude
  (d) none of these

88. Pulse amplitude modualtion is a process whereby
  (a) position of the pulse is changed as a function of the sampled value
  (b) width of the pulse is varied as a function of time
  (c) height of a pulse is made proportional to the sampled value
  (d) none of these

89. Pulse width of modulation is process whereby
  (a) position of a pulse is changed as a function of the sampled value
  (b) sampled value is first coded and then transmitted
  (c) width of a pulses is varied as a function of the sampled value
  (d) none of these

90. In PCM a system, quantization noise depends upon
  (a) number of quantization levels only
  (b) sampling rate only
  (c) both (a) and (b)
  (d) none of these

91. Signal-to-noise (S/N) ratio appearing at the output of each channel in PAM is
  (a) three times the input S/N
  (b) one-and-half times the input S/N
  (c) twice the input S/N
  (d) none of these

92. PWM signal can be generated by
  (a) monostable multi-vibrator
  (b) astable multi-vibrator
  (c) integrating the PPM signal
  (d) differentiating the PPM signal

93. Pulse communication system that is inherently highly immune to noise is
  (a) PAM   (b) PWM
  (c) PPM   (d) PCM

94. Quantizing noise occurs in
  (a) PDM   (b) PCM
  (c) FDM   (d) PPM

95. Quantization noise is produced in
  (a) all pulse modulation system
  (b) PCM
  (c) all modulation system
  (d) none of these

96. In DM system, granular (idling) noise occurs when modulating signal
  (a) increase rapidly   (b) remains constant
  (c) decreases rapidly   (d) none of these

97. The main advantage of PCM signal is
  (a) lower bandwidth   (b) higher bandwidth
  (c) lower noise   (d) none of these

98. For transmission of normal speech signal, PCM channel needs a bandwidth of
  (a) 64 kHz
  (b) 8 kHz
  (c) 4 kHz
  (d) none of these

99. PCM systems use non-uniform quantization in order to

(a) raise SNR for low level signals

(b) cut down required bandwidth of transmission

(c) increases maximum SNR

(d) none of these

100. Greatest disadvantages of PCM is

(a) its inability to handle analog signals

(b) high error rate which its quantizing noise reduces

(c) its incompatibility with TDM

(d) large bandwidth that are required for it

101. In PCM system, output S/N increases

(a) linearly with width

(b) exponentially with bandwidth

(c) inversely with bandwidth

(d) none of these

102. Companding is used

(a) to overcome quantizing noise in PCM

(b) in PCM transmitters, to allow amplitude limiting in the receivers

(c) to protect small signals in PCM from quantizing distortion

(d) in PCM receiver, to overcome impulse noise

103. Main advantage of PCM system is

(a) lower bandwidth (b) lower power

(c) lower noise   (d) none of these

104. Modulation

(a) allows the use of practicable antennas

(b) ensures transmission over long distances

(c) separates different transmissions

(d) all of these

105. Advantage of SSB over double-side band full carrier is/are

(a) noise in the signal is less

(b) more channel space is available

(c) less power is required for the same signal strength

(d) all of these

106. Modulator is a system to

(a) separate two frequencies

(b) impress information on to a radio frequency carrier

(c) extract information from the carrier

(d) amplify audio frequency signal

107. In AM transmission, frequency which is not transmitted is

(a) upper side frequency

(b) lower side frequency

(c) audio frequency

(d) carrier frequency

108. AM broadcast band is given by

(a) 10 kHz to 30 kHz (b) 500 kHz to 1500 kHz

(c) 3 to 30 MHz   (d) 30 to 300 MHz

109. In an AM wave with 100% modulation, carrier is suppressed, then percentage of power saving will be

(a) 100%   (b) 50%

(c) 25%   (d) 66.7%

110. In high-power AM transmission, modulation is done at

(a) buffer stage   (b) RF power stage

(c) oscillator state   (d) IF stage

111. In AM pilot-carrier, transmission has

(a) two side-bands

(b) carrer one side-band and part of other side-band

(c) two-side-bands and a trace of carrier

(d) carrier and part of one side-band

112. In AM, if modulation index is more than 100%, then

(a) power of the wave increases

(b) efficiency of transmission increases

(c) wave gets distorted

(d) band width increases

113. If modulation index of an AM was is changed from 0 to 1, then transmitted power

(a) increases by 50%

(b) increases by 75%

(c) increases by 100%

(d) remains unaffected

114. If a carrier is simultaneously modulated by sine waves with modulation indices of 30% and 40% respectively, then overall modulation index will be

(a) 50%

(b) 70%

(c) 100%

(d) indefinite as modulation by two waves simultaneously is not possible

115. In measurement of modulation index for an AM wave using oscilloscope, modulated signal and the modulating signal are applied respectively to

(a) Y-input, X-input of the oscilloscope

(b) X-input, Y-input

(c) Y-inputs of a dual-beam oscilloscope

(d) Y-input alternatively

116. In a radio receiver, the stage which need alignment is/are

(a) TRF stage

(b) IF stage

(c) antenna input stage

(d) all of these

117. In a typical AM receiver circuit, oscillator frequency is
    (a) same as signal frequency
    (b) always equal to 455 Hz
    (c) lower than signal frequency by 455 kHz
    (d) higher than signal frequency by 455 kHz

118. IF stage os a receiver exploys
    (a) impedance coupling
    (b) capacitive coupling
    (c) double-tuned transformer coupling
    (d) single-tuned transformer coupling

119. Function of AM detector circuit is to
    (a) rectify the input signal
    (b) discard the carrier
    (c) provide audio signal
    (d) all of these

120. In a broadcast receiver, local oscillator is tuned to a frequency higher than the incoming frequency to facilitate
    (a) image frequency rejection
    (b) easier tracking
    (c) adequate frequency coverage
    (d) noise reduction

121. Publich broadcasting employs double side-band system because
    (a) it requires less transmitting power
    (b) it requires smaller bandwidth
    (c) circuits are simple and less expensive
    (d) all of these

122. In double side-band suppressed carrier sstem, detection requires expensive circuitry because
    (a) synchronous detection is required
    (b) it is difficult to generate local carrier of the receiver
    (c) received signal is of low power
    (d) none of these

123. Advantage of SSB-suppressed carrier system is that it provides
    (a) higher efficiency of transmission
    (b) better quality of communication
    (c) simpler and inexpensive circuitry
    (d) none of these

124. Bandwidth requirement for VSB system is
    (a) less than bandwidth for SSB system
    (b) same as bandwidth for SSB system
    (c) more than bandwidth for SSB system
    (d) double bandwidth for SSB system

125. VSB signal is produced from the DSB signal by employing
    (a) simpler filters   (b) balance modulator
    (c) ring modulator   (d) phase-shift circuit

126. Which of the following will carry the same information as the AM wave itself ?
    (a) DSB   (b) SSB
    (c) VSR   (d) All of these

127. SSB can be obtained from balanced modulator by connecting at its output a
    (a) buffer   (b) clipper
    (c) filter   (d) adder

128. Filter required to obtain SSB from DSB signal is
    (a) low-pass filter
    (b) high-pass filter
    (c) band-pass filter
    (d) band-stop filter

129. Phase-shift method to obtain USB
    (a) two LSBs are out of phase
    (b) two LSBs are in phase
    (c) two USBs are out of phase
    (d) all side-bands are in phase

130. SSB demodulator is known as
    (a) balanced modulation
    (b) product demodulation
    (c) amplitude discrimination
    (d) none of these

131. Product demodulator essentially is a
    (a) balanced modulator (b) mixer
    (c) amplifier   (d) oscillator

132. In order to obtain modulating signal from product demodulator
    (a) low-pass filter is to be connected at the output
    (b) high-pass filter is to be connected
    (c) band-pass filter is to be connected
    (d) no filtering is required

133. High frequency in a superhet receiver
    (a) reduces trackig problem
    (b) reduces adjacent channel rejection
    (c) improves selectivity
    (d) none of these

134. In superheat broadcast receiver, frequency of local oscillator is
    (a) higher than the incoming signal
    (b) lower than the incoming signal
    (c) equal to incoming signal
    (d) none of these

135. Function of buffer amplifier in transmitters is to provide
    (a) impedance matching
    (b) frequency stability of the socillator
    (c) amplification of RF signal
    (d) none of these

136. Type of modulator amplifier used in AM transmitter is
(a) class A
(b) class B
(c) class AB
(d) class C with negative feedback

137. As compared to collector modulation of a transistor, base modulation has
(a) higher efficiency
(b) higher linearity
(c) higher power output
(d) lower modulating power requirements

138. In a modulation system, if modulating frequency is doubled, then modulation index also becomes double. The system is
(a) FM
(b) AM
(c) PM
(d) Both (a) and (c)

139. Disadvantage of FM over AM is that
(a) noise is very high for high frequency signals
(b) larger bandwidth is required
(c) high modulating power is required
(d) high output power is required

140. Modulation index of a phase-modulated wave is
(a) proportional to modulating frequency
(b) proportional to reciprocal of modulating frequency
(c) same as in frequency modulation
(d) proportional to phase of modulating signal

141. FM broadcast band lies in
(a) VHF band
(b) UHF band
(c) SHF band
(d) HF band

142. Which of the following statements is true for FM ?
(a) J-coefficients occasionally are negative.
(b) Total power remains constant with respect to modulation index.
(c) Total band-width increases with increase in modulation index.
(d) All of these

143. In FM, noise can be further decreases by
(a) decreasing deviation
(b) increasing deviation
(c) keeping deviation constant
(d) none of these

144. Which of the following statements is a reason for high signal-to-noise ratio in case of FM?
(a) There is less noise at frequencies at which FM is used.
(b) Amplitude limiter are incorporated in FM receivers.
(c) Interference from other FM transmitter is very less.
(d) All of these

145. An increase in the modulatio index leads to increase in bandwidth in case of
(a) AM
(b) FM
(c) PM
(d) both (b) and (c)

146. Frequency and phase modulations differ in
(a) different definitions of the modulation indices
(b) their actual waveform
(c) compatibility towards each other
(d) all of these

147. Modulation index of wide-band FM signal is
(a) less than 1
(b) equal to 1
(c) greater than 1
(d) 100%

148. Modulation index of a narrow-band FM signal is
(a) much less than 1
(b) nearly equal to 1
(c) much more than 1
(d) 50%

149. From band-width point of view, narrow-band FM is equivalent to
(a) AM
(b) PM
(c) SSB
(d) DSB-suppressed carrier

150. An indirect method of generating FM is
(a) varactor diode modlator
(b) armstrong modulator
(c) reactance tube modulator
(d) none of these

151. Frequency range used in frequency modulator is
(a) 30 MHz to 300 MHz
(b) 88 MHz to 108 MHz
(c) 3 MHz to 30 MHz
(d) 1 MHz to 3 MHz

152. Which of the following statements is corr rect for varactor diode modulator ?
(a) It generates FM
(b) The diode is always reverse-biased
(c) The junction capacitance vary with the modulating signal
(d) All of these

153. Which of the following statements is not true for an FM system ?
(a) It requires less modulating power
(b) It provides better S/N ratio
(c) Both (a) and (b)
(d) None of these

154. Function of an amplitude limiter in an FM receiver is
(a) to eliminate any change in amplitude of received FM signal
(b) to reduce the amplitude of the signal to suit IF amplifier
(c) to amplify low frequency signals
(d) none of these

155. Which of the following stages is present in AM receiver as compared to FM receiver ?

(a) IF amplifier (b) Demodulator

(c) AF amplifier (d) All of these

156. Typical band-width of an FM receiver is

(a) 20 kHz (b) 200 kHz

(c) 1 kHz (d) 20 kHz

157. In a FM demodulator

(a) capacitors charged to the amplitude of FM wave

(b) frequency deviations are converted into voltage

(c) simple diode is employed

(d) none of these

158. As compared to PPM, which of the following statements is not true for PWM?

(a) PWM will still work if synchronisation between transmitter and receiver fails

(b) PWM transmitter should be able to handle maximum width pulse

(c) Demodulation of PWM is more complex

(d) Pulse amplitude in PWM remains constant

159. Monostable multivibrator is used for generating PWM because it is a

(a) integrator

(b) voltage-to-time converter

(c) voltage-to-frequency converter

(d) pulse generator

160. PPM

(a) requires constant transmitter power output

(b) depends upon transmitter-receiver synchronisation

(c) can be generated from PWM

(d) all of these

161. PPM can be converted into PWM by employing

(a) monostable multivibrator

(b) bistable multivibrator

(c) astable multivibrator

(d) integrator

162. As compared to PPM, disadvantage of PDM is that requires

(a) powerful transmitter

(b) pulses of larger widths

(c) more samples per second

(d) none of these

163. Which of the following techniques is different from others ?

(a) PDM (b) PWM

(c) PCM (d) PPM

164. As FM has advantage over AM, all forms of pulse-time modulation (PTM) has over

(a) PDM (b) PAM

(c) PCM (d) FM

165. In commanding process

(a) signal is compressed at the transmitter and expanded at the receiver.

(b) small amplitude signals are expanded by the amplifier.

(c) it reduces quantising noise.

(d) all of these

166. To generate PCM, the signal is sampled and converted into

(a) PWM (b) PPM

(c) PAM (d) PDM

167. If PCM is to be modulated for transmission, most common type of modulation employed is

(a) AM (b) FM

(c) PM (d) PAM

168. To demodulate PCM, it is first converted into

(a) PWM (b) PPM

(c) PAM (d) PDM

169. Main advantage of PCM system is lower

(a) bandwidth (b) power

(c) noise (d) none of these

170. TDM system

(a) needs lower bandwidth

(b) gives lower signal-to-noise ratio

(c) uses simple circuits as compared to FDM

(d) all of these

171. TDM

(a) pulse modulated signals can be sent during wide spaces of narrow pulses.

(b) transmitter and receiver are to be synchronised.

(c) both (a) and (b)

(d) none of these.

172. Low speed TDM is produced by

(a) electronic switching circuits

(b) delay lines

(c) rotating mechanical switches

(d) pulse oscillators

173. Which of the following measures can be used to reduce noise ?

(a) By increasing the transmitted power.

(b) By reducing the signaling rate.

(c) By using redundancy.

(d) All of these

174. Advantage of guard time between pulses is that
(a) it increases efficiency of transmission
(b) it suppreses cross talk
(c) message can be reconstructed with practical filters
(d) none of these

175. For SSB-suppressed carrier, improvement in S/N ratio at the output of the demodulator as compared to its S/N ratio at the input is by a factor of
(a) 3
(b) 2
(c) $\dfrac{2}{3}$
(d) 1

176. Ratio of S/N ratios at the detector output of FM and AM signals depends upon
(a) bandwidth
(b) carrier frequency
(c) modulating frequency
(d) all of these

177. At FM demodulator output
(a) noise power density decreases with frequency
(b) noise power density increases with frequency
(c) signal power density increases with frequency
(d) none of these

178. Emphasis circuits are used for improving S/N ratio at
(a) lower frequencies (b) middle frequencies
(c) higher frequencies (d) complete frequencies

179. In PCM
(a) noise is removed by regenerting pulses at each repeater station.
(b) noise-free signal is transmitted at each repeater station.
(c) only noise on the link between repeater stations is to be considered.
(d) all of these

180. Quantising noise is produced in
(a) all pulse modulation system
(b) PCM
(c) all modulation system
(d) PDM

181. Quantising noise can be reduced by increasing
(a) bandwidth
(b) sampling rate
(c) number of standard quantum levels
(d) all of these

182. Noise temperature is
(a) same as physical temperature of the body
(b) measure of the available noise power for non-thermal sources
(c) measure of noise figure of a receiver
(d) none of these

183. In SSB, carrier transmitted along with the sidebands is used to
(a) convert SSB to DSB
(b) keep co-ordination between transmitter and receiver
(c) generate oscillator frequency in the demodulation process
(d) none of these

184. In a typical AM receiver circuit, oscillator frequency is
(a) same a signal frequency
(b) always equal to 455 Hz
(c) higher than the signal frequency by 455 KHz
(d) none of these

185. Function of an AM detector circuit is to
(a) rectify the input signal
(b) discard the carrier
(c) both (a) and (b)
(d) none of these

186. In FM, as modulation index increases, the bandwidth
(a) increases
(b) decreases
(c) remains constant
(d) none of these

187. Modulation index inFM depends on
(a) amplitude of the modulating signal
(b) frequency of the modulating signal
(c) both (a) and (b)
(d) none of these

188. Modulation index in FM is defined for
(a) tone modulation only
(b) multi-tone modulation
(c) all types of modulating signals
(d) none of these

189. In FM spectrum, as modulation index increases, the number of significant sidebands
(a) increases
(b) remains same
(c) decreases
(d) none of these

190. In a modulation system, if modulating frequency is doubled, the modulation index also becomes double. The system is
(a) FM
(b) AM
(c) PM
(d) PCM

191. Disadvantage of FM over AM is that
(a) noise is ver high for high frequency signals
(b) larger bandwidth is required
(c) high modulating power is required
(d) none of these

192. Modulation index of a phase-modulated wave is
  (a) proportional to modulating frequency
  (b) proportional to reciprocal of modulating frequency
  (c) same as in frequency modulation
  (d) none of these

193. FM broadcast band lies in
  (a) VHF band   (b) UHF band
  (c) SHF band   (d) HF band

194. In FM, if modulating voltage remains constant, then lowering of modulating frequency would lead to
  (a) increase in amplitde of distant sidebands
  (b) decrease in amplitude of distant sidebands
  (c) no change in amplitude of distant sidebands
  (d) none of these

195. Function of an amplitude limiter in an FM receiver FM receiver is to
  (a) eliminate any change in amplitude of received FM signal
  (b) reduce the amplitude of the signal to suit IF amplifier
  (c) amplify low frequency signals
  (d) none of these

196. Typical band-width of an FM receiver is
  (a) 20 kHz   (b) 200 kHz
  (c) 1 MHz   (d) 10 MHz

197. In a FM demodulator
  (a) capacitors are charged to the amplitude of FM wave
  (b) frequency deviations are converted into voltage
  (c) simple diode is employed
  (d) none of these

198. Advantage of phase discriminator is/are
  (a) alignment is much easier
  (b) linearity is better
  (c) both (a) and (b)
  (d) none of these

199. In PM, detected interference is proportional to
  (a) amplitude of the interfering wave
  (b) frequency of the interfering wave
  (c) both (a) and (b)
  (d) none of these

200. A communication receiver can be used for
  (a) signal strength measurement
  (b) detection and display of individual components of a high-frequency wave
  (c) both (a) and (b)
  (d) none of these

201. In a communication receiver, high first intermediated frequency permits
  (a) much better attenuation of image frequency
  (b) much better bandwidth cut-off
  (c) good adjacent channel selection
  (d) none of these

202. According to sampling theorem
  (a) signal should be sampled at least twice each cycle of its lowest frequency
  (b) twice each cycle of its highest frequency
  (c) guard time should be as large as possible
  (d) none of these

203. In essence, practical sampling is
  (a) PDM   (b) PPM
  (c) PAM   (d) FM

204. Which of the following statements is correct in regard to sampling theorem ?
  (a) Pulse-shape effects are relatively in consequential
  (b) Theorem is not valid for nonimpulsive sampled waves
  (c) Both (a) and (b)
  (d) None of these

205. Pulse modulation essentially is process of
  (a) pulse modulation   (b) message processing
  (c) multiplexing   (d) none of these

206. Which of following pulse modulation systems has no carrier-wave equivalent ?
  (a) PPM   (b) PDM
  (c) PCM   (d) AM

207. Efficient pulse modulation transmission requires CW modulation because
  (a) power is transmitted in sharp bursts
  (b) pulse wave cannot be transmitted as such
  (c) pulsed wave contains d.c. and low frequency components
  (d) none of these

208. Which of the following pulse-time modulation does not exist in practice ?
  (a) PWM   (b) PPM
  (c) PFM   (d) QAM

209. In the frequency spectrum of a PAM generation system, the information signals
  (a) appear as part of the spectrum of the sampled pulse
  (b) does not appear as part of the spectrum of the sampled pulse
  (c) both (a) and (b)
  (d) none of these

210. As compared to direct baseband transmission, noise in PAM is
(a) better
(b) similar
(c) worst
(d) none of these

211. Bandwidth is determined by minimum pulse width in
(a) PPM
(b) PDM
(c) QAM
(d) all of these

212. PDM is roughly analogous to
(a) linear modulation
(b) exponential carrier-wave modulation
(c) PPM
(d) none of these

213. Sampling in PDM is
(a) uniform
(b) non-uniform
(c) dependent on the nature of message signal
(d) none of these

214. In PDM, bandwidth requirement is a function of
(a) position of the pulse
(b) maximum pulse width
(c) minimum pulse width
(d) none of these

215. Low pass filtering can also be used to demodulate PDM provided
(a) phase-modulated sidebands do not ovrelap message band
(b) message band does not have aliasing
(c) both (a) and (b)
(d) none of these

216. In PPM, message resides in
(a) pulses
(b) time location of pulse edges
(c) both (a) and (b)
(d) none of these

217. Which of the following pulse system is mot efficient ?
(a) PPM
(b) PDM
(c) PAM
(d) QAM

218. PPM signal is converted into PDM with the help of
(a) Monostable
(b) Flip-flop
(c) Timer
(d) None of these

219. Which of the following pulse systems is preferred for communication in the presence of noise ?
(a) PAM
(b) PDM
(c) PPM
(d) None of these

220. If synchronisation between transmitter and receiver fails, which of the following pulse systems would be affected ?
(a) PAM
(b) PDM
(c) PPM
(d) None of these

221. Which of the following pulse systems requires higher bandwidth ?
(a) PAM
(b) PDM
(c) PPM
(d) None of these

222. Which of the following requirements is necessary for fast communication ?
(a) High transmitter power
(b) Large bandwidth
(c) Higher channel capacity
(d) None of these

223. System which does not require synchronisation is
(a) Delta
(b) PCM
(c) PDM
(d) None of these

224. As compared to message bandwidth, PCM bandwidth is
(a) much smaller
(b) same
(c) much larger
(d) none of these

225. As compared to ideal communication system, PCM system
(a) has less complex
(b) compares must favourably with the ideal system
(c) requires 8 dB less power
(d) none of these

226. In PCM, only decision at the receiver is required to be made is about
(a) amplitude of the pulse
(b) width of the pulse
(c) presence of the pulse
(d) none of these

227. Repeating or amplifying or encoded signal is permitted in
(a) PPM
(b) PCM
(c) all pulse systems
(d) none of these

228. In PCM, high noise immunity is achieved with
(a) increased bandwidth
(b) decreased bandwidth
(c) both (a) and (b)
(d) none of these

229. PCM system employs
(a) FDM
(b) TDM
(c) either of these
(d) none of these

230. Modems are used for
(a) modulating digital signals
(b) converting analog to digitals and vice versa
(c) either (a) or (b)
(d) none of these

231. Polar 9radiation pattern of a loop aerial is
(a) a circle
(b) an ellipse
(c) a cardiod
(d) figure of eight (8)

232. Type of transmission used for sound in TV transmission is
   (a) AM
   (b) FM
   (c) PCM
   (d) PWM

233. Type of transmission used for television in India is
   (a) DAB SC
   (b) SSB
   (c) VSB
   (d) SSB-SC

234. An AM Broadcast station transmits 2Kw of carrier power and uses an index of modulation 0.5. The total transmitted power is
   (a) 2 Kw
   (b) 2.25 kw
   (c) 2.5 kw
   (d) 2.75 kw

235. A commercial superheterodyne radio receiver has its intermediate frequency chosen as
   (a) 255 kHz
   (b) 455 kHz
   (c) 955 kHz
   (d) 1055 kHz

236. The input signal to receiver is 50 mW and the internal noise at the input is 5 mW. After a amplification the signal at the output is 2W and the noise output 0.4W. The noise figure is
   (a) 2
   (b) 0.5
   (c) 10
   (d) 5

237. If VSWR of transmission line is 4 and its characteristic impedance is 300 ohms, then two possible resistor loads are
   (a) 300 ohms and 75 ohms
   (b) 1200 ohms and 300 ohms
   (c) 1200 ohms and 75 ohms
   (d) 600 ohms and 300 ohms

238. To eliminate ghosts in the picture
   (a) Use longer transmission line
   (b) Connect a booster
   (c) Change the antenna orientation or location
   (d) Twist the transmission line

239. Effective area of isotropic radiator is
   (a) $\dfrac{L}{4P}$
   (b) $\dfrac{4P}{L}$
   (c) $\dfrac{L^2}{4P}$
   (d) $4\dfrac{P}{L^2}$

240. If VSWR of a transmission line is 4, then its reflection coefficient is
   (a) 0.4
   (b) 0.6
   (c) 2
   (d) 4

241. If load impedance connected to a transmission line of characteristic impedance 50 ohms is 150 ohms, then its reflection coefficient is
   (a) 0.5
   (b) 2
   (c) −2
   (d) −0.5

242. Value of a resistor creating thermal noise is doubled, then noise power generator is
   (a) halved
   (b) quadrupled
   (c) doubled
   (d) unchanged

243. Characteristic impedance is also called
   (a) surge impedance
   (b) match impedance
   (c) alternative impedance
   (d) reflected impedance

244. Reflection coefficient on a lossless line with a short circuit load, is given by
   (a) −1
   (b) 1
   (c) 0
   (d) λ

245. If reflection coefficient on a loss less line is Y^R is standing wave ratio is ____

246. Voice signal frequency lies between
   (a) $0 \to 20$ kHz
   (b) 15 kHz $\to 1$ MHz
   (c) 15 Hz $\to 15$ kHz
   (d) None of these.

247. A complex wave form made up frequency components 1 Hz, 3 Hz, 5 Hz, 7 Hz and 9 Hz. Its fundamental frequency is
   (a) 9 Hz
   (b) 12.5 Hz
   (c) 1 Hz
   (d) indeterminate.

248. A sawtooth waveform is made up of
   (a) odd harmonics
   (b) even harmonics
   (c) odd and even harmonics
   (d) none of these

249. "A square wave form applied to a differentiator circuit gives positive and negative spikes."
   (a) True
   (b) False
   (c) Not necessarily
   (d) None of these.

250. Transmission of a wave in a closed wave guide is possible only when
   (a) frequency of operation is less than a certain critical value
   (b) phase-shift (b) is real positive
   (c) phase-shift (b) is zero
   (d) none of these

251. An INTEGRATOR circuit should have
   (a) very large time constant
   (b) very small time constant
   (c) a time constant that is much smaller as compared to the time occupied by one cycle of applied input
   (d) none of these.

252. Standard LORRN operates in which frequency range
   (a) 1.8 to 2.0 MHz
   (b) 88 to 112 MHz
   (c) 108 to 118 MHz
   (d) None of these.

253. In all pulse communication systems, carrier is

   (a) necessarily a high repetition rate train of pulses

   (b) necessarily a high frequency continuous a.c. signal

   (c) either a train of pulses or a continuous a.c. wave.

   (d) none of these.

254. In amplitude modulation

   (a) time gap between adjacent maximum and minimum values of the modulate envelope is not dependent on frequency of intelligence.

   (b) maximum value of intelligence has no effect on the time separation of modulated envelope's maximum and minimum.

   (c) separation of successive maximum and minimum of modulated to envelope on time-axis is inversely proportional to the frequency of modulating signal

   (d) none of these.

255. In DSB system with carrier when the intelligence varies between 100 Hz to 5 kHz, bandwidth is

   (a) 10 kHz   (b) 9.8 kHz

   (c) 200 Hz   (d) Indeterminate

256. Signal at the output of an AM modulator is given by e = 5.3 (1 + 0.64 sin 6280 t) sin 106t. Depth of modulation for it is

   (a) 0.64%   (b) 0.80%

   (c) 64%   (d) 80%

257. In frequency modulation

   (a) frequency of the carrier remains unchanged

   (b) carrier frequency changes in accordance with the modulating signal amplitude.

   (c) carrier frequency chances in accordance with the modulating signal frequency

   (d) none of these

258. Modulation index in Fm is given by

   (a) mf = 75/Frequency deviation in kHz

   (b) 75 kHz is the modulation index

   (c) Frequency deviation in kHz/75

   (d) None of these.

259. Modulation index (mf) in FM is

   (a) directly proportional to frequency deviation and inversely proportional to modulating frequency.

   (b) given by mf $\dfrac{\text{Frequency Deviation in kHz}}{75} \times 100$

   (c) directly proportional to modulating signal frequency and inversely proportional to frequency deviation.

   (d) given by mf = Frequency deviation/ Modulating signal amplitude.

260. Polarization of an electromagnetic wave is

   (a) direction of its magnetic field component with respect to ground.

   (b) direction of its electrical field component with respect to ground

   (c) orientation of antenna that generates it.

   (d) none of these.

261. TM wave is characterized by

   (a) absence of magnetic component in the direction of propagation.

   (b) electric field component wholly transverse.

   (c) absence of electric field component in the direction of propagation.

   (d) none of these.

262. TEM wave cannot exist within a hollow metallic pipe.

   (a) True

   (b) False

   (c) Not necessarily

   (d) None of these

263. Which is most commonly used transmission-line with television system?

   (a) Twin-lead

   (b) Open-wire with ceramic supports

   (c) Coaxial cable

   (d) None of these.

264. A transmission line with characteristics impedance of 300 is used to interconnect receiving antenna and receiver input. A reflection coefficient of 1/3 is observed on the line Receiver input impedance is equal to

   (a) 150   (b) 100

   (c) 900   (d) indeterminate

265. "Refractive index of good conductors is much larger than that of air".

   (a) True   (b) False

266. "Electromagnetic waves travels faster in a ionized gas layer than they do in free space."

   (a) True   (b) False

267. Ionization of various gases resulting in the formation of IONOSPHERE is because of

   (a) Characteristics of gases themselves

   (b) Pressure variations with altitude

   (c) Radiations from the sun

   (d) None of these

268. A modulated signal (AM) is having depth of modulation equal to 80%, then feeder current under modulated conditions is greater than that under unmodulated conditions by

   (a) 4%   (b) 10%

   (c) 15%   (d) None of these

269. Choose the wrong statement:
 (a) One RF section has only two tuned circuits
 (b) One IF section has only four tuned circuits
 (c) One IF stage has more selectivity than one RF stage
 (d) Selectivity provided by one IF stage is approximately four times that of one RF stage

270. Fidelity, in a communication receiver, is provided by
 (a) Mixer stage
 (b) Detector stage
 (c) Various amplifier sections
 (d) Audio stage.

271. Choose the correct statement :
 (a) Higher selectivity means larger bandwidth
 (b) Higher selectivity means large gain
 (c) A loudspeaker may be rated as 2.5"
 (d) Higher sensitivity implies larger gain.

272. In a ratio-detector
 (a) linearity is worse than in a phase discriminator
 (b) stabilization against signal strength variations is provided
 (c) output is twice that obtainable from a similar phase discriminator
 (d) circuit is the same as in a discriminator except that diodes are reversed

273. Television cameras A and B have tubes which are and 4.5 long respectively. When a lens of known length is used with the rubes, then
 (a) angle-of-view of A is greater than that of B
 (b) angle-of-view of B is greater than that of B
 (c) both of them have an identical angle of view
 (d) none of these

274. Video signals have a frequency range that is spread over approximately
 (a) 9 octaves   (b) 18 octaves
 (c) 4 octaves   (d) None of these

275. In a TV is brightness control located
 (a) audio section
 (b) video section
 (c) grid-cathode circuit of picture-tube
 (d) none of these

276. Where is fine tuning control present in Television receiver?
 (a) A pre set inductance (b) A potentiometer
 (c) A variable condensor (d) None of these

277. Horizontal oscillator in a TV receiver generates a sawtooth signal of
 (a) $15{,}750\ H_z$ in FCC standards
 (b) $15{,}750\ H_z$ CCIR standards
 (c) $15{,}625\ H_z$ FCC standards
 (d) $50\ H_z$ in CCIR and $60\ H_z$ in FCC standards.

278. Television screen width is always greater than the screen height or in other words rastar width more than rastar height because
 (a) horizontal deflection frequency is higher
 (b) more detail is in the horizontal direction
 (c) picture motion is in the horizontal direction
 (d) none of these.

279. A lossless transmission line with characteristic load of 100 ohms. The standing wave radio will be;
 (a) 2   (b) 1/2
 (c) 2/3   (d) 1/3

280. Condition for a distrotionless transmission line is
 (a) LG = RC   (b) LR = GC
 (c) LC = GR   (d) LG = (RC)^2

281. Radiation resistance of a half wave dipole antenna in free space
 (a) 103 ohms   (b) 300 ohms
 (c) 73 ohms   (d) 50 ohms.

282. To transform any resistance at the termination of a transmission line to an impedance with magnitude cqual to R of thc linc, thc linc lcngth must be
 (a) L/4   (b) L/8
 (c) L   (d) L/2

283. In the radiated far filed of a dipole antenna, electric and magnetic fields are
 (a) are in the direction of propagation
 (b) are in time phase
 (c) are out of phase
 (d) both will not exist together

284. Horizontal synchronising frequency in the TV receiver is
 (a) 10500 Hz   (b) 13125 Hz
 (c) 15625 Hz   (d) 15750 Hz

285. Under 100% amplitude modulation of a 10 kW carrier power, total power required is
 (a) 15 kW   (b) 50 kW
 (c) 100 kW   (d) 150 kW

286. Ionospheric propagation fails beyond the operating frequency of
 (a) 30 kHz   (b) 300 kHz
 (c) 3000 kHz   (d) 30,000 kHz

287. Though amount of noise is proportional to bandwidth, wide band FM has high signal to noise ratio because
 (a) signal level is high
 (b) limited circuit is used in FM
 (c) noise level is low
 (d) noise component, are uncorrelated

288. Radition resistance of half-wave dipole is
   (*a*) 75 ohms   (*b*) 73 ohms
   (*c*) 377 ohms   (*d*) 300 ohms

289. If effective length of an antenna is increased. it directive gains.
   (*a*) becomes infinite   (*b*) remains same
   (*c*) decreases   (*d*) increases

290. An antenna that is circularly polarised is
   (*a*) Helical   (*b*) Yagi
   (*c*) Parabolic   (*d*) Loop

291. An antenna that radiates uniformly in all directions is called
   (*a*) Hertzian dipole   (*b*) Isotropic antenna
   (*c*) Half-wave dipole   (*d*) Helical antenna

292. Typical radar antenna has beam width of
   (*a*) $5°$ (*b*) $3°$
   (*c*) $2°$ (*d*) $1°$

293. In Indian T.V, width of one channel is
   (*a*) 7 mHz   (*b*) 5 mHz
   (*c*) 5 mHz   (*d*) 8 mHz

294. As one moves away from transmitter, ground wave eventually disappears because
   (*a*) sky wave interferes with ground wave
   (*b*) of till in wave front
   (*c*) of loss of line of sight
   (*d*) of limitation of single hop distance.

295. UHF signals normally propagates by means of
   (*a*) Sky wave   (*b*) Space wave
   (*c*) Surface wave   (*d*) Duct

296. In a low level A.M. transmitter, the stage following the modulator shall be
   (*a*) Harmonic generators
   (*b*) Class C amplifier
   (*c*) Non-linear amplifier
   (*d*) Linear amplifier

297. A carrier is simultaneously modulated by two sine wave with modulation indices 0.8 and 0.6. The resultant index is
   (*a*) 1   (*b*) 0.5
   (*c*) 0.7   (*d*) None of these

298. The function of pre-emphasis circuit in a communication system is to boost
   (*a*) higher audio frequencies
   (*b*) modulated wave
   (*c*) lower audio frequencies
   (*d*) complete audio band

299. Armstrong modulator generates
   (*a*) AM   (*b*) PM
   (*c*) FM   (*d*) Both (*a*) and (*b*)

300. Commonly employed filter in SSB generation is
   (*a*) HP   (*b*) RC
   (*c*) LC   (*d*) Mechanical

301. Tropospheric scatter is used in the range
   (*a*) HF   (*b*) VHP
   (*c*) UHF   (*d*) VLF

302. Function of 'padders' in radio receiver is to improve
   (*a*) sensitivity
   (*b*) rejection of Image Frequencies
   (*c*) noise reduction
   (*d*) tracking

303. Fidelity of a receiver is primarily dependent upon
   (*a*) Local oscillator   (*b*) Detector stage
   (*c*) IF amplifier   (*d*) Audio amplifier

304. In communication, noise is most likely to affect the signal
   (*a*) Transmitter   (*b*) Sourcea
   (*c*) Channel   (*d*) Destination

305. F.M. signal is passed through frequency tripler, the resultant modulation index will change by a factor of
   (*a*) 1   (*b*) 1/3
   (*c*) 3   (*d*) 9

306. F.M. discriminator changes F.M. signal into
   (*a*) AM   (*b*) FM
   (*c*) PM   (*d*) None of these

307. Quantization noise occurs in
   (*a*) PCM   (*b*) TDM
   (*c*) FDM   (*d*) PWM

308. Blind speed problem in a radar can be effectively overcome by using.
   (*a*) Monopulse technique
   (*b*) MTI
   (*c*) Variable PRF
   (*d*) Conical scanning

309. If antenna diameter in a radar system is increased by a factor of 4, then range will increase by a factor of
   (*a*) $\sqrt{2}$ (*b*) 8
   (*c*) 4   (*d*) 2

310. The Doppler shift is given by
   (*a*) $\dfrac{C_s}{2\lambda_T}$ (*b*) $\sqrt{2}\,\dfrac{C_s}{\lambda_T}$
   (*c*) $\dfrac{C_s}{2\lambda_T}$ (*d*) $2\dfrac{C_s}{\lambda_T}$

311. Which of the following statements regarding Armstrong modulator is NOT correct?
   (*a*) System is basically phase modulation system
   (*b*) Frequency multiplication is necessarily used
   (*c*) Equalization is unnecessary
   (*d*) FC is not needed, as a crystal oscillator is used.

312. A 1000 kHz carrier is simultaneously modulated with 300 Hz, 800 Hz and 2kHz audio sine waves. The frequencies present in the output will be
(a) 998 kHz and 1002 kHz
(b) 998 kHz, 999.2 kHz, 1000.8 kHz, 1002.0 kHz
(c) 998 kHz, 999,2 kHz. 999.7 kHz, 1000.3 kHz, 1000.8 kHz, and 1002.0 kHz
(d) None of these

313. The percentage of modulation for 45 kHz deviation in the FM broadcast band will be
(a) 30%
(b) 40%
(c) 60%
(d) 90%

314. For a FM wave carrier modulating frequency is 10 kHz and bandwidth is 2 MHz. If modulating signal amplitude is doubled, then bandwidth will be
(a) 0.5 MHz
(b) 1 MHz
(c) 2 MHz
(d) 4 MHz

315. In AM receiver, oscillator frequency is always
(a) equal to signal frequency
(b) equal to 455 kHz
(c) higher than signal frequency
(d) lower than signal frequency

316. Quantization noise occurs om
(a) PCM
(b) TDM
(c) FDM
(d) PWD

317. Select the statement that is false.
(a) A stationary process is always an ergodic process
(b) An ergodic process is always a stationary random process
(c) It is possible to have a stationary random process that is not ergodic
(d) None of these

318. If P_k be the probability of the message to be received or transmitted, then amount of information (I_k) associated, in hits, will be given by
(a) $I_k = \log_2 P_k$
(b) $I_k = \log_2 I/P_k$
(c) $I_k = 1/\log_2 P_k$
(d) $I_k = 1/\log_2 I/P_k$

319. In grid bias modulation system, power needed for modulating amplifier is
(a) negligibly low since grid is negative
(b) large as compared to thai for plate modulation
(c) almost same as compared with plate modulation
(d) small as compared to that for plate modulation.

320. Typical squelch circuit
(a) cuts off an audio amplifier when carrier is absent
(b) cuts off an IF amplifier when AGC is maximum
(c) cuts off an IF amplifier when AGC is minimum
(d) eliminates RF interference when signal is weak.

321. For a signal amplitude modulated to a depth of 100% by a sinusoidal signal, the power?
(a) same as power of unmodulated carrier
(b) twice as power of unmodulated carrier
(c) four limes power of unmodulated carrier
(d) 3/2 times power of unmodulated carrier.

322. In FM, frequency deviation is generally
(a) proportional to modulating frequency
(b) proportional to amplitude of modulating signal
(c) constant
(d) directly proportional to amplitude and inversely proportional to modulating frequency.

323. Audio frequency range lies between
(a) 20 Hz and 20 kHz
(b) 20 kHz and 200 kHz
(c) 2 MHz and 20 MHz
(d) 20 MHz and 200 MHz.

324. Maximum undistorted power output of a transmitter can be expected when its modulation is
(a) 50%
(b) between 50% and 90%
(c) 100%
(d) more than 100%

325. An FM signal with a deviation a is passed through a mixer, and has its frequency reduced six fold. Deviation in the output of the mixer will be equal to
(a) 6
(b) 6a
(c) a
(d) Indeterminate.

326. What is the unit of modulation index?
(a) Hertz
(b) $(Hz)^{-1}$
(c) $(Hz)^{-2}$
(d) No unit.

327. In the stabilized reactance modulator AFC system
(a) discriminator must have a fast time constant to prevent demodulation.
(b) higher the discriminator frequency, the better the oscillator frequency stability.
(c) discriminator frequency must not be too low, or the system will fail.
(d) phase modulation is converted into FM by the equalizer circuit.

328. Percentage saving in power of 100 % modulated suppressed carrier AM signal is
(a) 80
(b) 66 2/3
(c) 50
(d) 40

329. Maximum I or V on the modulated carrier wave is 5 units and minimum is 3 units. The percentage of modulation will be equal to
(a) 100
(b) 80
(c) 50
(d) 25

330. Which of the following statements is NOT correct?
(a) In frequency modulating, loudest sounds produce maximum frequency deviation.
(b) Modulation is used to reduce bandwidth
(c) In FM, audio modulating frequency determines rate of frequency swing
(d) None of these

331. An oscillator at 4.2 MHz is followed by two frequency doublers and two triplers. The output frequency will be
    (a) 84 MHz   (b) 112.4 MHz
    (c) 151.2 MHz   (d) 303.4 MHz

332. Tuned voltage amplifiers are not used
    (a) radio receivers
    (b) in public address system
    (c) TV receivers
    (d) None of these

333. A 3A modulation is sometimes used to
    (a) permit receiver to have a frequency synthesizer.
    (b) reduce the bandwidth required for transmission.
    (c) reduce power that must be transmitted.
    (d) simplify the frequency stability problem in reception.

334. Final power amplifier in an FM transmitter generally operates as
    (a) Class A   (b) Class B
    (c) Class C   (d) Class D

335. Quantizing noise takes place in
    (a) Time-division-multiplex
    (b) PCM
    (c) PPM
    (d) Frequency-division-multiplex

336. A pre-emphasis circuit provides extra noise immunity by
    (a) converting the phase modulation to frequency modulation
    (b) preamplifying the whole audio band
    (c) boosting the bass frequencies
    (d) amplifying the higher audio frequencies.

337. Ability of a radio receiver to respond to the weakest signal is called .....

338. Selectivity of a radio receiver is dependent on ..... amplifier.

339. Doppler effect is used for measuring......

340. Distance between radar and target can be measured in ..... miles.

341. Blind speed is the limitation of ..... radar.

342. Principal use of FM radar is as .....

343. Pulsed radar, using of shorter pulse improves the ..... of the range.

344. Frequency of colour subcarrier used for television in India ..... MHz.

345. Peak power transmitted by a radar is increased by a factor 16. The range is increased by a factor.....

346. Antennas are protected from effects of weather by covering them with .....

347. The height at which a geostationary satellite is placed is ..... km.

348. If carrier is modulated beyond 100%, then received signal will be .....

349. In a modulation system, if modulation voltage remains same and modulation index is halved. When the modulating frequency is doubled, then the type of modulation is ......

350. In frequency modulation, the ratio of maximum frequency deviation to highest modulation frequency is called ......

351. A balanced modulator is employed for generating ..... output.

352. A short circuited transmission line of length less than L/4 behaves as ___.

353. In a transmission line, if proper matching is not done ____ takes place.

354. Noise interference will be dominating mostly with ____ modulating frequencies.

355. If a communication receiver is to possess the best selectivity and stability, IF should be ____.

356. A high PRF in Radar will ____ the maximum range.

357. In a broad side array all the elements are fed with equal amplitude and with ____ phase difference between them.

358. Reception of commercial radio broadcast is better during the cloudy weather because of the absence of ____ layer.

359. In television, 4.3 represents ____.

360. Long distance radio communication in the short wave bands is by ____ propagation.

361. Maximum frequency deviation in the case of a commercial FM broadcast is KHz.____.

362. Bandwidth of the picture signal in 625 line system is ____ MHz.

363. For ground wave propagation antenna should be ____ polarised.

364. Maximum radiation from an end-fire array antenna will be in direction ____ to the array.

365. Purpose of a parabolic reflector of a parabolic antenna is to convert a spherical wavefront into a ___ wave-front.

366. Principal feature of a Binomial array is it has ___ sidelobes.

367. Rhombic antenna is one of the most widely used ____ frequency receiving/transmitting antenna.

368. ____ radiator is one that radiates energy uniformly in all directions.

369. Principal propagation agency for propagating signals in the frequency range of 300 kHz-3 mHz is by ___ wave.

370. ____ is the shortest distance from the transmitter along the surface of the Earth at which sky wave of fixed frequency (more than the critical frequency) is returned to the Earth.

371. An A.M. wave, on analysis is composed of terms corresponding to carrier and ___ sidebands (state the number).

372. A reactance tube modulator generates ___ modulated signal.

373. For commercial broadcasting, the frequency band allocated for FM carrier is ____.

374. IF generally prescribed for superheterodyne receivers receiving AM signals is ____ kHz.

375. Pre-emphasis in FM is used to amplify ____.

376. In low level A.M. amplifier following modulated signal must be ____.

377. During day time, ionosphere composes of ____ layers.

378. Spectrum of a wide band FM wave extends up to ____.

379. Noise performance of a receiver is evaluated in terms of ____ figure.

380. As per TV transmission standards adopted in our country, frequency difference between sound and picture carrier, is ____.

381. In TV transmission, outputs of video and audio transmitters are combined in a unit called ____ to feed to the same transmitting antenna.

382. To overcome problem of rapid fluctuations of TV signal due to aeroplane flutter ____ system is used in TV receivers.

383. An MTI radar is basically a pulse radar but using ____ phenomenon.

384. Satellites used in international communication are called____.

385. Minimum rate at which sampling need to be done is called____ rate.

386. If modulation index in AM is increased from____ to 1, then transmitter power is increased by ____ %.

387. If 4 V audio amplitude changes r.f. signal frequency from 200 to 210 kHz, then frequency deviations is ____ kHz.

EXERCISE – II

1. A series capacitance used in a filter circuit represents **DMRC 2013**
   - (a) Low-pass
   - (b) Band-pass
   - (c) High-pass
   - (d) None

2. Greatest disadvantages of PCM is **DMRC 2013**
   - (a) its inability to handle analog signals
   - (b) high error rate which its quantizing noise reduces
   - (c) its incompatibility with TDM
   - (d) large bandwidth that are required for it

3. In PCM system, output S/N increases
   - (a) linearly with width **DMRC 2013**
   - (b) exponentially with bandwidth
   - (c) inversely with bandwidth
   - (d) none of these

4. Harmonic distortion analyser **DMRC 2014**
   - (a) measures the amplitude of each harmonic component
   - (b) measures the rms value of fundamental frequency component
   - (c) measures the rms value of all the harmonic components except the fundamental frequency component
   - (d) displays the rms value of each harmonic component on the screen of a CRO

5. A 5-channel dc to 60 Hz telemetry system uses PAM and PCM system. For a good quality data transmission, the minimum sampling rate must be **DMRC 2014**
   - (a) 300 samples/s
   - (b) 500 samples/s
   - (c) 1500 samples/s
   - (d) 1250 samples/s

6. The ratio of the directivity of an end-fire antenna to that of a broad-side antenna is **DMRC**
   - (a) 2
   - (b) 3
   - (c) 4
   - (d) 5

7. The coding system typically used in digital telemetry is **DMRC**
   - (a) PPM (Pulse position modulation)
   - (b) PAM (Pulse amplitude modulation)
   - (c) PCM (Pulse code modulation)
   - (d) PDM (Pulse duration modulation)

8. The drawback of FM relative to AM is that **DRDO**
   - (a) noise is very high for high modulation frequencies
   - (b) larger bandwidth is required
   - (c) higher modulating power is required
   - (d) higher output power is required

9. In the generation of modulated signal, a varactor diode can be used for **DRDO**
   - (a) FM generation only
   - (b) AM generation only
   - (c) PM generation only
   - (d) both AM and PM generation

10. For transmission of normal speech signal, PCM channel needs a bandwidth of **DRDO**
    - (a) 64 kHz
    - (b) 8 kHz
    - (c) 4 kHz
    - (d) none of these

11. Frequency range used in frequency modulator is

(a) 30 MHz to 300 MHz   **DRDO**

(b) 88 MHz to 108 MHz

(c) 3 MHz to 30 MHz

(d) 1 MHz to 3 MHz

12. Main advantage of PCM system is lower **DRDO**

(a) bandwidth   (b) power

(c) noise   (d) none of these

13. Typical band-width of an FM receiver is **DRDO**

(a) 20 kHz   (b) 200 kHz

(c) 1 MHz   (d) 10 MHz

14. Modems are used for   **DRDO**

(a) modulating digital signals

(b) converting analog to digitals and vice versa

(c) either (a) or (b)

(d) none of these

15. In FM, the carrier frequency deviation is determined by   **RRB**

(a) modulating voltage

(b) modulating frequency

(c) both modulating voltage and frequency

(d) none of these

16. The drawback of FM relative to AM is that **RRB**

(a) noise is very high for high modulation frequencies

(b) larger bandwidth is required

(c) higher modulating power is required

(d) higher output power is required

17. In the generation of modulated signal, a varactor diode can be used for   **RRB**

(a) FM generation only

(b) AM generation only

(c) PM generation only

(d) both AM and PM generation

18. VSB signal is produced from the DSB signal by employing   **RRB**

(a) simpler filters

(b) balance modulator

(c) ring modulator

(d) phase-shift circuit

19. PPM can be converted into PWM by employing

(a) monostable multivibrator   **RRB**

(b) bistable multivibrator

(c) astable multivibrator

(d) integrator

20. As compared to ideal communication system, PCM system   **RRB**

(a) has less complex

(b) compares must favourably with the ideal system

(c) requires 8 dB less power

(d) none of these

21. For type 3 system, lowest frequency asymptote will have the slope of   **RRB**

(a) 15 db/octave   (b) − 16 db/octave

(c) 17 db/octave   (d) − 18 db/octave

22. In FM broadcast, the maximum modulation frequency is restricted to   **RRB**

(a) 5 kHz   (b) 10 kHz

(c) 15 kHz   (d) 20 kHz

23. In order to separate out channels in an FDM receiver, it is necessary to use   **RRB**

(a) AND gates   (b) band pass filters

(c) band stop filters   (d) integrators

24. What will be the percentage power saving if the carrier and one if the side bands are now suppressed ?

(a) 85%   (b) 70%   **RRB**

(c) 60%   (d) 45%

25. For transmission of normal speech signal, PCM channel needs a bandwidth of   **RRB**

(a) 64 kHz   (b) 8 kHz

(c) 4 kHz   (d) none of these

26. Frequency range used in frequency modulator is

(a) 30 MHz to 300 MHz   **RRB**

(b) 88 MHz to 108 MHz

(c) 3 MHz to 30 MHz

(d) 1 MHz to 3 MHz

27. Consider the periodic signal $x(t) = (1 + 0.5\cos 40\,\pi t)$ $\cos 200\,\pi t$, where t is in seconds. Its fundamental frequency, in Hz, is   **RRB**

(a) 20   (b) 40

(c) 100   (d) 200

28. The input signal shown in the figure below is fed to a Schmitt trigger. The signal has a square wave amplitude of 6 V p-p. It is corrupted by an additive high frequency noise of amplitude 8 V p-p. **RRB**

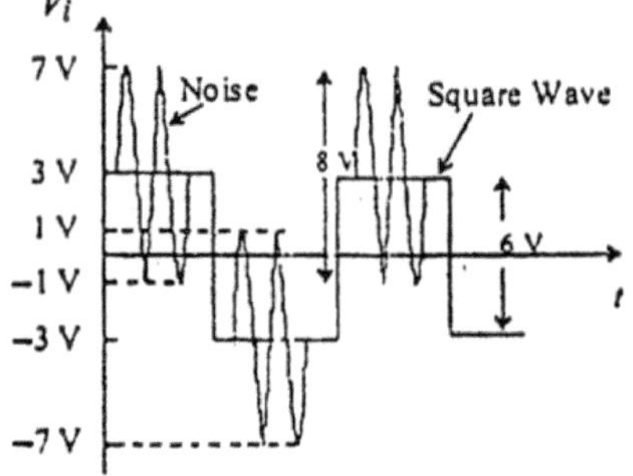

Which one of the following is an appropriate choice for the upper and lower trip points of the Schmitt trigger to recover a square wave of the same frequency from the corrupted input signal Vi?

(a) ± 8.0 V (b) ± 2.0 V

(c) ± 0.5 V (d) 0 V

29. If there is a telephone station where time of incoming is independent of the time of other calls coming in past or in future. Then the pdf of this system in a fixed interval of time will be ____

(a) Poisson (b) Gaussian **RRB 2012**

(c) Gamma (d) Binomial

30. Find the fundamental period of the signal $x[n] = \sin[\pi^2 n]$ **RRB 2012**

(a) Periodic with $\pi/2$ (b) Periodic with π

(c) Periodic with $2/\pi$ (d) Non periodic

31. The radiation pattern of an antenna in spherical co-ordinates is given by

$$F(\theta) = \cos^4\theta, \ 0 \le \theta \le \pi/2$$

The directivity of the antenna is **RRB 2012**

(a) 10 dB (b) 12.6 dB

(c) 11.5 dB (d) 18 dB

32. A binary symmetric chanel (BSC) has a transition probability of $\dfrac{1}{8}$. If the binary transmit symbol X is such that $P(X = 0) = \dfrac{9}{10}$, then the probability of error for an optimum receiver will be

(a) $\dfrac{7}{80}$ (b) $\dfrac{63}{80}$ **RRB 2012**

(c) $\dfrac{9}{10}$ (d) $\dfrac{1}{10}$

ANSWERS

EXERCISE – I

1. (b)	**2.** (b)	**3.** (a)	**4.** (c)	**5.** (b)	**6.** (a)	**7.** (a)	**8.** (d)	**9.** (b)	**10.** (d)
11. (b)	**12.** (c)	**13.** (d)	**14.** (b)	**15.** (a)	**16.** (a)	**17.** (a)	**18.** (a)	**19.** (b)	**20.** (b)
21. (b)	**22.** (b)	**23.** (a)	**24.** (c)	**25.** (c)	**26.** (b)	**27.** (d)	**28.** (b)	**29.** (b)	**30.** (b)
31. (b)	**32.** (b)	**33.** (c)	**34.** (c)	**35.** (b)	**36.** (b)	**37.** (b)	**38.** (b)	**39.** (c)	**40.** (c)
41. (a)	**42.** (d)	**43.** (a)	**44.** (c)	**45.** (d)	**46.** (a)	**47.** (c)	**48.** (d)	**49.** (a)	**50.** (b)
51. (a)	**52.** (c)	**53.** (c)	**54.** (d)	**55.** (a)	**56.** (d)	**57.** (c)	**58.** (b)	**59.** (a)	**60.** (a)
61. (b)	**62.** (d)	**63.** (b)	**64.** (c)	**65.** (a)	**66.** (c)	**67.** (d)	**68.** (d)	**69.** (a)	**70.** (b)
71. (b)	**72.** (a)	**73.** (b)	**74.** (a)	**75.** (a)	**76.** (b)	**77.** (c)	**78.** (a)	**79.** (b)	**80.** (c)
81. (a)	**82.** (c)	**83.** (b)	**84.** (b)	**85.** (a)	**86.** (a)	**87.** (b)	**88.** (c)	**89.** (c)	**90.** (a)
91. (c)	**92.** (d)	**93.** (d)	**94.** (b)	**95.** (b)	**96.** (b)	**97.** (c)	**98.** (c)	**99.** (a)	**100.** (d)
101. (b)	**102.** (c)	**103.** (c)	**104.** (d)	**105.** (d)	**106.** (b)	**107.** (c)	**108.** (b)	**109.** (d)	**110.** (b)
111. (c)	**112.** (c)	**113.** (a)	**114.** (a)	**115.** (a)	**116.** (d)	**117.** (d)	**118.** (c)	**119.** (d)	**120.** (c)
121. (c)	**122.** (a)	**123.** (a)	**124.** (b)	**125.** (a)	**126.** (d)	**127.** (c)	**128.** (c)	**129.** (a)	**130.** (b)
131. (b)	**132.** (a)	**133.** (b)	**134.** (a)	**135.** (c)	**136.** (d)	**137.** (d)	**138.** (c)	**139.** (b)	**140.** (c)
141. (a)	**142.** (d)	**143.** (b)	**144.** (d)	**145.** (b)	**146.** (a)	**147.** (c)	**148.** (b)	**149.** (a)	**150.** (b)
151. (b)	**152.** (d)	**153.** (c)	**154.** (a)	**155.** (d)	**156.** (b)	**157.** (b)	**158.** (c)	**159.** (b)	**160.** (d)
161. (b)	**162.** (a)	**163.** (c)	**164.** (b)	**165.** (d)	**166.** (c)	**167.** (a)	**168.** (c)	**169.** (c)	**170.** (c)
171. (c)	**172.** (c)	**173.** (d)	**174.** (c)	**175.** (d)	**176.** (d)	**177.** (b)	**178.** (c)	**179.** (d)	**180.** (b)
181. (c)	**182.** (b)	**183.** (c)	**184.** (c)	**185.** (c)	**186.** (a)	**187.** (c)	**188.** (a)	**189.** (a)	**190.** (c)
191. (b)	**192.** (a)	**193.** (a)	**194.** (a)	**195.** (a)	**196.** (b)	**197.** (b)	**198.** (c)	**199.** (a)	**200.** (c)
201. (a)	**202.** (b)	**203.** (c)	**204.** (a)	**205.** (b)	**206.** (c)	**207.** (c)	**208.** (c)	**209.** (a)	**210.** (b)
211. (b)	**212.** (b)	**213.** (b)	**214.** (c)	**215.** (a)	**216.** (b)	**217.** (d)	**218.** (b)	**219.** (c)	**220.** (c)

221. (c) **222.** (b) **223.** (a) **224.** (c) **225.** (b) **226.** (c) **227.** (b) **228.** (a) **229.** (b) **230.** (b)

231. (d) **232.** (b) **233.** (c) **234.** (b) **235.** (b) **236.** (a) **237.** (b) **238.** (c) **239.** (c) **240.** (b)

241. (a) **242.** (d) **243.** (a) **244.** (a) **245.** Zero **246.** (c) **247.** (c) **248.** (c) **249.** (a) **250.** (a)

251. (a) **252.** (d) **253.** (c) **254.** (a) **255.** (c) **256.** (b) **257.** (c) **258.** (a) **259.** (a) **260.** (b)

261. (c) **262.** (c) **263.** (c) **264.** (a) **265.** (a) **266.** (a) **267.** (b) **268.** (c) **269.** (d) **270.** (d)

271. (d) **272.** (a) **273.** (d) **274.** (c) **275.** (a) **276.** (b) **277.** (d) **278.** (a) **279.** (d) **280.** (a)

281. (c) **282.** (a) **283.** (d) **284.** (c) **285.** (a) **286.** (d) **287.** (b) **288.** (b) **289.** (c) **290.** (a)

291. (b) **292.** (d) **293.** (a) **294.** (b) **295.** (b) **296.** (d) **297.** (a) **298.** (a) **299.** (c) **300.** (d)

301. (b) **302.** (d) **303.** (d) **304.** (c) **305.** (c) **306.** (d) **307.** (a) **308.** (c) **309.** (c) **310.** (d)

311. (c) **312.** (c) **313.** (c) **314.** (a) **315.** (c) **316.** (a) **317.** (a) **318.** (b) **319.** (d) **320.** (a)

321. (d) **322.** (b) **323.** (a) **324.** (c) **325.** (c) **326.** (d) **327.** (c) **328.** (b) **329.** (d) **330.** (b)

331. (c) **332.** (b) **333.** (d) **334.** (c) **335.** (b) **336.** (d)

337. Sensitivity

338. I.F

339. Moving target range.

340. Nautical

341. Pubed

342. Radaratimeter

343. Resolution

344. 3.58

345. 2

346. radome

347. 36,000

348. Distorted

349. Frequency modulation

350. Modulation index

351. DSB. SC

352. Pure conductance.

353. Maximum power transfer.

354. Amplitude

355. Between 1.6 MHz and 2.3 MHz

356. Decrease

357. Zero

358. (D)

359. Aspectration

360. sky

361. 75 kHz

362. 5

363. Vertically

364. In plane

365. Uniform.

366. No

367. Medium

368. Isotropic

369. Sky

370. skip

371. 2

372. Frequency

373. 88 – 108 kHz

374. 455

375. High modulating frequencies

376. Linear emplifiers

377. D, E, F^1 F^2

378. 200 kHz

379. Noise

380. 5.5 MHz

381. (d) iplexer

382. Keyed CAG(C)

383. Doppler effect

384. INTEL SAT

385. My guist

386. 50

387. 10.

EXERCISE – II

1. (c) **2.** (d) **3.** (b) **4.** (c) **5.** (d) **6.** (c) **7.** (c) **8.** (b) **9.** (a) **10.** (c)

11. (b) **12.** (c) **13.** (b) **14.** (b) **15.** (a) **16.** (b) **17.** (a) **18.** (a) **19.** (b) **20.** (b)

21. (d) **22.** (c) **23.** (b) **24.** (a) **25.** (c) **26.** (b) **27.** (b) **28.** (b) **29.** (a) **30.** (d)

31. (a) **32.** (a)

Industrial Electronics

THYRISTORS (SCRs)

The term thyristor denotes a family of semiconductor devices used for power control in *dc* and *ac* systems. One oldest member of this thyristor family called silicon-controlled rectifier (SCR) is the most widely used device. A thyristor has characteristics similar to a thyratron tube. But from the construction view point a thyristor (a *pnpn* device) belongs to transistor (*pnp* or *npn* device) family.

Thyristor is a four layer, three junction, *pnpn* semiconductor switching device. It has three terminals anode, cathode and gate. Basically a thyristor consist of four layers of alternate *p*-type and *n*-type silicon semiconductors forming three junctions J_1, J_2 and J_3 as shown in the figure.

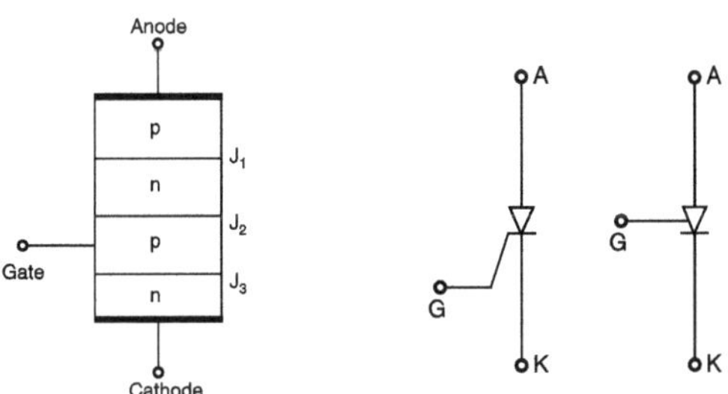

(a) Schematic diagram   (b) Circuit symbol of a thyristor

An SCRs are solid state devices, they are compact, possess high reliability and have low loss. Because of these useful features SCR is almost universally employed these days for all high power-controlled devices. An SCR is so called because silicon is used for its construction and its operation as a rectifier (very low resistance in the forward conduction and very high resistance in the reverse direction) can be controlled. Like the diode an SCR is an unidirectional device that blocks the current flow from anode to cathode until it is triggered into conduction by a proper gate signal between gate and cathode terminals.

REGULATED POWER SUPPLIES

1. Zener diode regulator.

For a high degree of regulation, an electronic voltage regulator is used. Zener diode is employed to fix the output voltage at a value equal to the Zener diode break-down voltage.

The full-wave rectifier supplies pulses of charge to the filter capacitor each half-cycle ; during the intervals, between pulses, the capacitor supplies current to the load comprising Rs, R_L and the Zener diode. Here a Zener diode, which can approximately give the required output voltage, is selected and then matched with a transformer which can give a peak output voltage, the value of which is nearly 50% more than that of the Zener voltage.

2. Transistorised regulated power supply.

3. Vacuum-tube type of voltage-regulated supply.

THYRISTOR HALF WAVE RECTIFIER SUPPLY.

When larger currents and higher voltages are required, it is used.

Thyristor conducts during the 1/2 cycle when anode is + ve with respect to cathode.

In other 1/2 cycle, thyristor just cannot conduct provided the peak ac is less than reverse break down voltage.

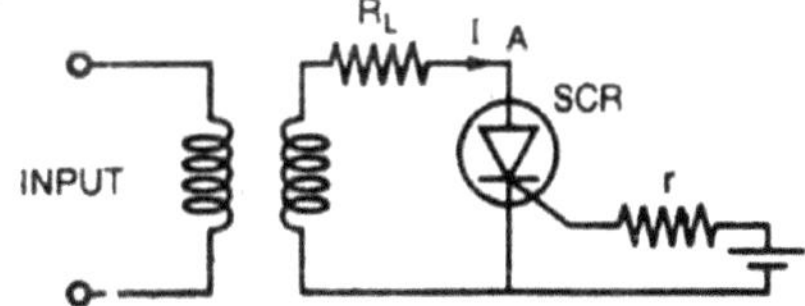

Fig. Small gate current can control much larger anode current.

When gate is open

(*i*) Thyristor will not conduct if ac peak voltage is less than forward breakdown voltage in positive half cycle.

(*ii*) Also no conduction during negative half cycle.

TRIACS

These are multilayers (5 layers), 3 terminals, semiconductor devices which operate in both directions quadrant (I and III), i.e., there are 2 SCR's connected in antiparallel. These operate similarly as an SCR in either direction. Tri activates on either a positive or negative gate voltage i.e., it can be triggered into conduction when T_2 is either positive or negative with respect to T_1.

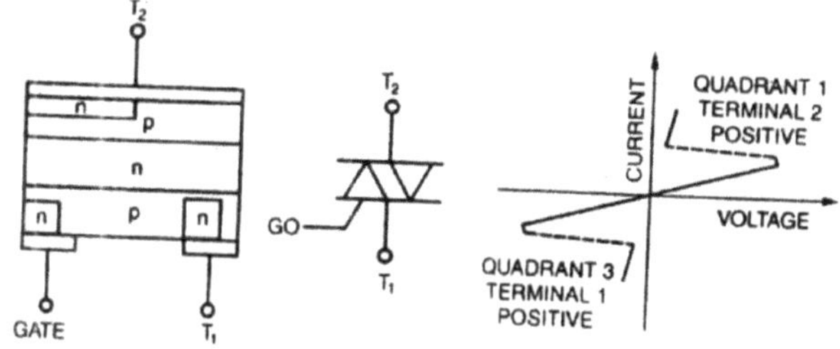

Fig. Symbol and characteristics of a Tirac.

Operating modes of the traic

Triacs are usually most sensitive to gate current in the I^+ and III^- mode. Gate current I_{GT}, required to trigger as triac typically 40 mA in the I^+ and III^- modes, 60 - 100 mA in the I^- and III^+ modes.

Disadvantages.

Positive breakdown voltage is different to its negative breakdown voltage.

KEY POINTS

Impedance of a parallel circuit containing R-L-C

$$\frac{I}{Z_T} = \frac{I}{Z_1} + \frac{I}{Z_2} + \frac{I}{Z_3} + \underline{\qquad}$$

where, Z_T = total circuit impedance; ohms

Z_1, Z_2, Z_3 = impedances of parallel branches; ohms.

Frequency of a series resonance circuit

$$f_r = \frac{1}{2\pi\sqrt{L \cdot C}}$$

$2\pi\sqrt{L \cdot C}$ and that of parallel resonance circuit is determined by the formula:

$$f = \frac{1}{2\pi}\sqrt{\frac{1}{L.C} - \frac{R^2}{L^2}} \; Hz$$

Relation between Frequency and Q

$Q \propto$ frequency

Hence I.F. circuit has more Q as well as more selectivity because selectivity

$$Q \propto$$

Impedance formula of a parallel resonant circuit

$$Z = Q \cdot X_L$$

$$Z = \frac{X_L^2}{R}$$

As $X_L = X_C$ hence, only X_L is used in the formula

Types of Converters.

1. **Pentagrid converter.**

   It is the circuit which employs a five grid rube. One section of the tube acts as *oscillator* and the other as *mixer*.

2. **Triode-hexode converter.**

   The circuit employs a multiunit triode-hexode tube. The tube consists of triode section to act as oscillator and a hexode section to act as mixer.

3. **Single transistor converter.**

   In this circuit, RF signal is applied to the base. Oscillator coil and IT coil are connected in series to the collector circuit. The frequency conversion takes place in the collector circuit.

4. **Two transistor converter.**

   In this circuit, separate transistors are used for oscillator and mixer sections. The frequency conversion takes place in the mixer transistor.

Note : oscillator frequency kept higher than the signal frequency in a radio receiver, so as to obtain a low tuning ratio.

Relay

It is an electromagnetic device which can make 'on' or 'off' a number of circuit at a time or a specified voltage or current as per its design.

Magnetic field of a straight current carrying conductor is composed of concentric magnetic lines of force.

REED RELAY

It is a device based on the fact that an electric current passing through a coil of wire produces an electromagnet, with ends of the coil having opposite magnetic polarities.

Operation :

If two thin strips of material that can be magnetized are placed inside the coil, the strips become magnetized when currents is flowing in the coil. If two strips are placed such that one end of each overlaps, they will have opposite magnetic polarities and so will attract each other.

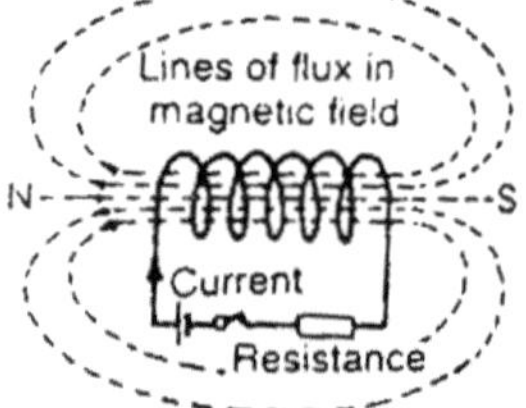

Coil of wires as a simple electromagnet

These two strips can be used to form a switch in another electrical circuit. These two strips are placed inside a glass envelope containing an inert gas, and overlapping portions are coated with gold to give a good reliable electrical contact. The whole assembly contained by the glass envelope is called *reed insert*, since it is placed inside the electromagnet coil.

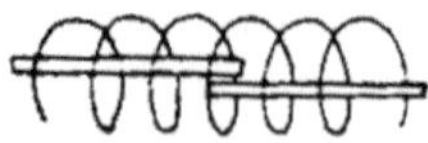

No current flowing in coil strips separated

Principle of operation of a real relay

EXERCISE – I

1. SCR is a
   (a) 2 layer device
   (b) 3 layer device
   (c) 4 layer device with one gate
   (d) 4 layer device with two gates

2. The advantages of SCR over SCS are
   (a) larger switching time and smaller V_H
   (b) larger switching time and large V_H
   (c) smaller switching time and smaller V_H
   (d) smaller switching time and larger V_H

3. SCR uses
   (a) no gate
   (b) one gate on the p-layer next to cathode
   (c) one gate on the n-layer next to anode
   (d) two gates

4. In an SCR, the breakover voltage V_{BO}
   (a) in independent of gate current
   (b) increases with the increase of positive gate current
   (c) decreases with the increase of positive gate current
   (d) may increase or decrease with increase of gate current depending on temperature

5. After firing an SCR, if the gate pulse is removed, the SCR current
   (a) remains the same
   (b) reduces to zero
   (c) rises up
   (d) rises a little and then falls to zero

6. An SCS is
   (a) a pnpn diode with three terminals
   (b) a pnpn diode with one gate
   (c) a pnpn diode with two gates
   (d) a pnpn diode made of germanium

7. Triac is a
   (a) 2 terminal bidirectional switch
   (b) 3 terminal bidirectional switch
   (c) 2 terminal unilateral switch
   (d) 3 terminal unilateral switch

8. Diac is a
   (a) 2 terminal bidirectional switch
   (b) 2 terminal unilateral switch
   (c) 3 terminal bidirectional switch
   (d) 3 terminal unilateral switch

9. A sillicon controlled rectifier (SCR) is a
   (a) unijunction device
   (b) device with three junctions
   (c) device with four junctions
   (d) none of the above

10. Thyristor is basically
    (a) PNPN device
    (b) combination of diac and triac
    (c) set of SCR's
    (d) set of SCR, diac and triac.

11. A PNPN device having two gates is
    (a) Diac   (b) Triac
    (c) SUS   (d) BCS

12. Advantage of thyristor over SCS is
    (a) slow switching time and large V_H
    (b) slow switching time and smallar V_H
    (c) faster switching time and smaller V_H
    (d) faster switching time and large V_H

13. Thyristor equivalent of a thyratron tube is
    (a) diac
    (b) triac
    (c) silicon controlled-rectifier SCR
    (d) none of these

14. A triac is a
    (a) 2 terminal switch
    (b) 2 terminal bilateral switch
    (c) 3 terminal unilateral switch
    (d) 3 terminal bidirectional switch

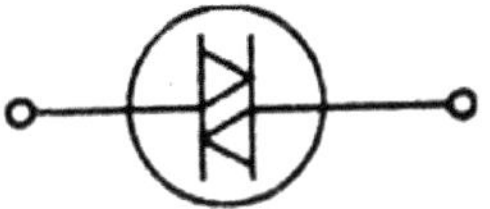

15. As compared to oscillators, an inverter provides
    (a) low voltage output
    (b) low ferquency output
    (c) distortion less output
    (d) noiseless output

16. A device that cannot be triggered with voltage of either polarity is
    (a) Diac   (b) Triac
    (c) SCS   (d) none of these

17. A device that does not exhibit negative resistance characteristics is
    (a) FET   (b) UJT
    (c) tunnel diode   (d) SCR

18. A triac
    (a) conducts when not triggered
    (b) conducts when not triggered in both directions
    (c) conducts when tirggered in one direction
    (d) none of these

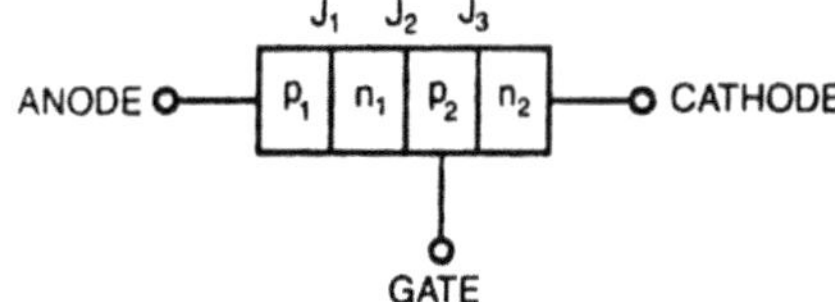

19. Thyristor is turned-off when the anode current falls below
(a) forward current
(b) latching current
(c) holding current
(d) breakover current

20. Comparing a triac and SCR
(a) both are unidirectional devices
(b) tria requires more current for turn on than SCR at a particular voltage
(c) both are bidirectional devices
(d) all of these

EXERCISE – II

1. Bleeder resistor in power supplies is used to place   **DMRC 2013**
(a) an infinite load across the rectifier
(b) maximum load across the rectifier
(c) minimum load across the rectifier
(d) none of these

2. Comparing a triac and SCR   **DRDO**
(a) both are unidirectional devices
(b) tria requires more current for turn on than SCR at a particular voltage
(c) both are bidirectional devices
(d) all of these

3. Thyristor is basically   **DRDO**
(a) PNPN device
(b) combination of diac and triac
(c) set of SCR's
(d) set of SCR, diac and triac.

4. Advantage of thyristor over SCS is   **DRDO**
(a) slow switching time and large V_H
(b) slow switching time and smallar V_H
(c) faster switching time and smaller V_H
(d) faster switching time and large V_H

ANSWERS

EXERCISE – I

1. (d)	**2.** (b)	**3.** (c)	**4.** (b)	**5.** (c)	**6.** (b)	**7.** (a)	**8.** (b)	**9.** (b)	**10.** (a)
11. (d)	**12.** (c)	**13.** (c)	**14.** (d)	**15.** (b)	**16.** (c)	**17.** (a)	**18.** (b)	**19.** (b)	**20.** (d)

EXERCISE – II

1. (a)	**2.** (d)	**3.** (a)	**4.** (c)

Applied Physics

PHYSICAL QUANTITY

The quantities required to describe the laws of physics and which are to be measured are called **physical quantities**.

UNIT FOR MEASUREMENT.

It is standard of measurement chosen for the measurement of the quantity

$$\text{Physical quantity} = \text{Magnitude} \times \text{Unit}$$
$$P = n \times u$$

where n = numerical value of physical quantity

u = unit of that quantity

SYSTEMS OF UNITS.

A complete set of units, both fundamental and derived for all kinds of physical quantities is called *system of units*.

Common systems.

(i) **CGS system :** In CGS system length, mass and time have been chosen as the fundamental quantities and corresponding fundamental units are centimetre (cm), gram (g) and second(s) respectively.

(ii) **MKS system :** In MKS system length, mass and time have been taken as fundamental quantities, and corresponding fundamental units are metre, kilogram and second.

(iii) **FPS system :** In FPS system foot, pound and second are used respectively for measurements of length, mass and time in this system force is a derived quantity with unit poundal.

(iv) **S. I. system :** International system

Table. Fundamental quantities and their units in SI.

Quantity	Name of unit	Symbol
Length	Metre	m
Mass	kilogram	kg
Time	second	s
Electric Current	ampere	A
Thermodynamics Temperature	Kelvin	K
Amount of substance	mole	mole
Luminous intensity	candela	cd

Supplementary units.

Besides above seven fundamental units, following two supplementary units are also defined :

(i) Radian (rad) for plane angle

(ii) Steradian (sr) for solid angle.

Fundamental quantities.

Quantities which are independent of all other quantities and do not require the help of any other physical quantity for their definition, therefore these are called *absolute quantities*. These quantities are also called *fundamental or base quantities*.

Derived quantities.

All other physical quantities can be derived by suitable multiplication or division of different powers of fundamental quantities. These are therefore called *derived quantities*.

Dimensions of a physical quantity.

When a derived quantity is expressed in terms of fundamental quantities, it is written as a product of different powers of the fundamental quantities. The powers to which fundamental quantities must be raised in order to express the given physical quantity are called its *dimensions*.

e.g. Force = mass × acceleration

$$= \frac{\text{mass} \times \text{velocity}}{\text{time}} = \frac{\text{mass} \times \text{length / time}}{\text{time}}$$

$$= \text{mass} \times \text{length} \times (\text{time})^{-2}$$

Thus, dimensions of force are 1 in mass, 1 in length and – 2 in time.

or $\qquad [\text{force}] = [MLT^{-2}]$

DIMENSIONS

S.No.	Physical Quantity	Unit	Dimensions
1.	Length	meter	[L]
2.	Mass	kg.	[M]
3.	Time	Second	[T]
4.	Temperature	kelvin	[θ]
5.	Luminous Intensity	candela	[C]
6.	Electric current	ampere	[A]
7.	Amount of substance	mole	no dimension
8.	Plane angle	radian	no dimension
9.	Velocity/Speed	m/s	$[LT^{-1}]$
10.	Acceleration	m/s^2	$[LT^{-2}]$
11.	Momentum	kg.m/s	$[MLT^{-1}]$
12.	Force	newton	$[MLT^{-2}]$

S.No.	Physical Quantity	Unit	Dimensions
13.	Work/Energy	joule	$[ML^2T^{-2}]$
14.	Power	watt	$[ML^2T^{-3}]$
15.	Pressure	N/m^2	$[ML^{-1}T^{-2}]$
16.	Stress	N/m^2	$[ML^{-1}T^{-2}]$
17.	Strain	no unit	no dimension
18.	Coefficient of elasticity	N/m^2	$[ML^{-1}T^{-2}]$
19.	Torque	N.m	$[ML^2T^{-2}]$
20.	Angular displacement	radian	no dimension
21.	Angular velocity	radian/sec	$[L^0T^{-1}]$
22.	Angular acceleration	radian/sec^2	$[L^0T^{-2}]$
23.	Moment of inertia	kg.m^2	$[ML^2]$
24.	Angular momentum	kg.m^2/sec	$[ML^2T^{-1}]$
25.	Latent heat	kcal/kg.	$[L^2T^{-2}]$
26.	Surface tension	N/m	$[MT^{-2}]$
27.	Gravitational constant (G)	N.m^2/kg^2	$[M^{-1}L^3T^{-2}]$
28.	Coefficient of viscosity	poise	$[ML^{-1}T^{-1}]$
29.	Heat	joule or kcal	$[ML^2T^{-2}]$
30.	Specific heat	joule/kg °C	$[L^2T^{-2}\theta^{-1}]$
31.	Coefficient of thermal conductivity	J/m.s °K	$[MLT^{-3}\theta^{-1}]$
32.	Mechanical equivalent of heat	J/kcal	$[M^0L^0T^0]$
33.	Universal gas constant	J/°K	$[ML^2T^{-2}\theta^{-1}]$
34.	Boltzmann constant	J/ °K	$[ML^2T^{-2}\theta^{-1}]$
35.	Stefan's constant	J/m^{2}s °K^4 or W/m^2 °K^4	or $[ML^0T^{-3}\theta^{-4}]$
36.	Electric charge	coulomb	$[AT]$
37.	Electric potential	volt	$[ML^2T^{-3}A^{-1}]$
38.	Electric intensity	N/C	$[MLT^{-3}A^{-1}]$
39.	Capacitance	farad	$[M^{-1}L^{-2}T^4A^2]$
40.	Electric resistance	ohm	
41.	Contductance	mho	$[M^{-1}L^{-2}T^3A^2]$
42.	Specific resistance	ohm.meter	$[ML^3T^{-3}A^{-2}]$
43.	Coefficient of self induction or Coefficient of mutual induction	henry	$[ML^2T^{-2}A^{-2}]$
44.	Electric dipole moment	coulomb Meter	$[LTA]$
45.	Electric flux	volt-metre	$[ML^3T^{-3}A^{-1}]$
46.	Magnetic flux	weber	$[ML^2T^{-2}A^{-1}]$
47.	Magnetic induction	Wb/m^2	$[MT^{-2}A^{-1}]$
48.	Magnetisation (Pole strength/area)	A.m^{-1}	$[L^{-1}A]$
49.	Pole strength	Am	$[LA]$
50.	Magnetic dipole moment	Am^2	$[AL^2]$
51.	Reactance (Capacitive resistive)	ohm	$[ML^2T^{-3}A^{-2}]$
52.	Impedance	ohm	$[ML^2T^{-3}A^{-2}]$
53.	Planck's constant	J. sec	$[ML^2T^{-1}]$
54.	Frequency	hertz	$[M^0L^0T^{-1}]$

WAVE MOTION

Wave motion involves transfer of disturbance (energy) from one point to the other with the particle of medium oscillating about their mean positions

WAVE PROPERTIES

Wave speed *(c)* : Speed of wave is the distance it covers in one second. It should be carefully noted that wave speed is completely different from particle speed

Wave frequency (v) : The frequency with which the particle of the medium (through which the wave passes) oscillates is called *wave frequency*.

Time period (T) : Time period of the oscillation of the particle in the medium is time period of the wave.

Amplitude (A) : Amplitude of the wave is same as amplitude of the oscillating particles.

Wave length (λ) : It is the distance between two consecutive crests (or compression) in a wave.

Wave length, wave speed and frequency are related as follows :

$$c = \upsilon\lambda$$

Phase : When a wave passes through a medium, all particles oscillate with same frequency, but they reach the corresponding positions in their path at different time instants.

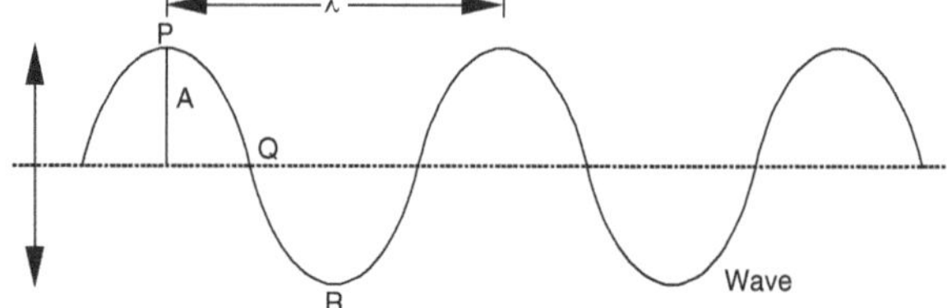

If two particles have same position and same velocity at all time instants, they are said to be in same phase (or *in phase*).

Two particles are said to be in opposite phase (*or exactly out of phase*) if their displacement from meanposition and their velocities are equal in magnitude but opposite in direction.

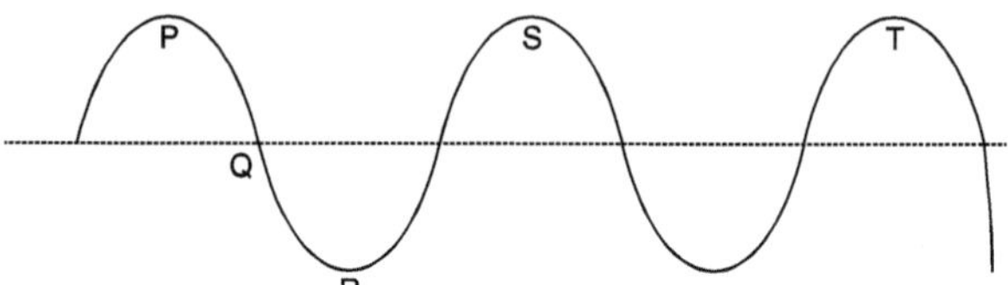

P, S and T are in same phase   *P and R are is opposite phase*

Distance between particles in same phase is $0, \lambda, 2\lambda \ldots$

Distance between particles in opposite phase is

$$\frac{\lambda}{2}, \frac{3\lambda}{2}, \frac{5\lambda}{2} \ldots$$

Particle velocity : It is the velocity of particle executing simple harmonic motion. It's value changes with time. It is given by dy/dt.

Propagation constant (K) : The phase difference between two vibrating particles situated at distance one meter along the path of the wave is called *propagation constant.*

$$K = \frac{\omega}{v} = \frac{2\pi}{\lambda} = 2\pi\overline{v}$$

Intensity of a wave (I).

In a travelling wave, energy is transferred through the medium in the direction in which the wave travels. The transfer of energy per unit time per unit area perpendicular to the direction of motion of the wave is called *intensity of the wave.*

If A is the amplitude, c is the speed, v is the frequency, ρ is the density of the medium, I is the intensity, then

$$I = 2\pi^2 c \rho v^2 A^2$$

Note : Intensity is proportional to the square of the amplitude ($I \propto A^2$).

WAVE EQUATION.

If a mathematical equation describes a wave, it must be able to give the position of any particle of the medium at any given time instant.

Consider a transverse wave travelling towards right in a tight string lying along x-axis. If we take one point on the string as origin O, then displacement (y) at any particle P located at some X-co-ordinate (x) at an instant t is given by

$$y\,(x, t) = A \sin\left(\frac{2\pi x}{\lambda} - \frac{2\pi t}{T} + \phi_0\right)$$

P (x, y)

x-axis

O

1. **Longitudinal waves.**

    Waves in which the particles of medium oscillate along the direction of propagation of the wave are called *longitudinal waves.*

    e.g. sound waves, compressional waves in the spring.

    Reflection of longitudinal wave (*Sound wave*)

    From denser medium : Both wave velocity and particle velocity get reversed. Therefore, there is phase change of π radian. Thus compression reflects as compression and rarefaction as rarefaction.

    From rarer medium : Only wave velocity get reversed therefore there is no phase change. The compression reflects as rarefaction and rarefaction as compression.

    Superposition principle.

    (i) When two waves super impose, then their resultant displacement is given by

    $$\vec{y} = \vec{y}_1 + \vec{y}_2$$

(ii) According to the principle of superposition, if two or more than two waves reach a point in a medium simultaneously and their displacement vectors are $\vec{y}_1, \vec{y}_2, \vec{y}_3, ...$, then net displacement vector $\vec{y}$ is given by

$$\vec{y} = \vec{y}_1 + \vec{y}_2 + \vec{y}_3 + ...$$

(iii) *Due to superposition of number of waves, new phenomenon arises are :*
   (a) Interference
   (b) Beats
   (c) Stationary waves
   (d) Lissajous figures

(iv) In all types of superposition of waves, energy is conserved though it is redistributed.

(v) *On superposition of number of waves, the resultant displacement would depend upon*
   (a) amplitude of waves
   (b) frequency of waves
   (c) direction of propagation of waves

(vi) **Phase difference between waves :**
   - Interferring waves produce their displacement independently.
   - When two waves meet each other in the phase, resultant displacement increases, then it is called *constructive interference.*
   - When two waves meet each other out of phase, the resultant displacement is reduced, then it is called *destructive interference.*
   - Resultant amplitude,
   $$A = \sqrt{a_1^2 + a_2^2 + 2a_1 a_2 \cos\phi}$$
   - Resultant intensity,
   $$I = a_1^2 + a_2^2 + 2a_1 a_2 \cos\phi$$
   $$= I_1 + I_2 + 2\sqrt{I_1 I_2}\,.\cos\phi$$

(vii) **Interference of waves :** The phenomenon of super imposition of two waves having same frequency but a phase difference resulting in redistribution of energy in the medium is called *interference.*

There is no loss of energy in inteference phenomenon. There is only redistribution of energy.

2. **Progressive waves.**

    The waves which propagte through medium transmitting energy in the direction of propagation are called *progressive waves.*

3. Stationary waves.

When two identical pregressive waves travelling in opposite directions along the same line with the same velocity super impose on each other, they from a system of waves which alternately appear and disappear in the reqion where two waves meet without advancing in either eirection. Such waves are called *stationary waves.*

Equation of stationary waves,

$$y = 2a \cos \left(\frac{2\pi x}{\lambda}\right) . \sin \left(\frac{2\pi l}{T}\right)$$

where, a = amplitude of each wave

l = wavelength of each wave

T = period of each wave

Case I : *When wave is reflected from free end, then due to superposition of incident and reflected waves, stationary waves are produced.*

Equation of stationary waves is,

$$y = 2a \cos \left(\frac{2\pi x}{\lambda}\right) \sin \left(\frac{2\pi t}{T}\right)$$

In this case antinode is always formed at free end.

Case II: *When waves are reflected from rigid boundry then due to superposition of incident waves and reflected waves, stationary waves are produced .*

Equation of stationary waves is,

$$y = 2a \sin \left(\frac{2\pi x}{\lambda}\right) . \cos \left(\frac{2\pi t}{T}\right)$$

In this case node is formed at rigid boundary.

Nodes and Antinodes.

The points where amplitude is maximum are called **antinodes** and the points where amplitude is zero are called **nodes.**

Beats.

Beats are formed by the superposition of two waves of slightly different frequencies moving in the same direction. If two sources of sound having slightly different frequencies are placed in the same medium, the resultant effect heard at any fixed position will consists of alternate loud and weak sounds.

The resultant wave can be represented as a travelling wave whose frequency is $\left(\frac{v_1 + v_2}{2}\right)$ and amplitude is

$2A \cos \pi (v_1 - v_2) t$. As the amplitude term contain t, the amplitude (and, hence intensity or loudness in case of sound) varies periodically with time.

For loud sounds : net amplitude = $\pm 2 A$

$\Rightarrow \quad \cos \pi (v_1 - v_2) t = \pm 1$

$\Rightarrow \quad \pi (v_1 - v_2) t = 0, \pi, 2\pi, 3\pi \; ....$

$\Rightarrow \quad t = 0, \dfrac{1}{v_1 - v_2}, \dfrac{2}{v_1 - v_2} \; ......$

For weak sounds : $t = \dfrac{1}{2 (v_1 - v_2)}, \dfrac{3}{2 (v_1 - v_2)} \; ......$

$\therefore$ Interval between two loud (or weak) sounds

$$= \frac{1}{v_1 - v_2}$$

Number of loud sound per second = $v_1 - v_2$

or beat per second = $v_1 - v_2$

RESONANCE.

The phenomenon in which body is vibrating with frequency equal to it's natural frequency with maximum amplitude under action of an external periodic force is called *resonance.*

Characteristics of resonance.

(*i*) At resonance, amplitude of the forced vibrations becomes maximum due to matching of the natural frequency of body with frequency of an external periodic force.

(*ii*) At resonance, maximum energy is transferred from vibrating body to another body which is forced to vibrate.

(*iii*) In case of resonance, applied periodic force is in the same phase with vibration of the body.

(*iv*) If two bodies of same natural frequencies placed side by side and if one of them is vibrated, the other will automatically begin to vibrate. This is due to resonance.

Doppler effect.

Apparent change in frequency of a sound heard by listener due to relative motion between listener and source of sound is called *Doppler Effect.*

This phenomenon can be observed in case of both types of waves :

(*i*) Transverse waves

(*ii*) Longitudinal waves.

Apparent frequency of a sound heard by listener

(*i*) When listener is moving towards stationary source of sound, apparent frequency heard by listener

$$n' = \left(\frac{V + V_L}{V}\right) n$$

where, V = velocity of the sound

n = original frequency

V_L = velocity of the listener

(*ii*) When listener is moving away from stationary source of sound, apparent frequency heard by listner

$$n' = \left(\frac{V - V_L}{V}\right) n$$

(*iii*) When source of sound is moving towards stationary listener, then

$$n' = \left(\frac{V}{V - V_S}\right) n$$

where, V_S = velocity of source of sound.

(*iv*) When source of sound is moving away from stationary listener, then

$$n' = \left(\frac{V}{V + V_S}\right) n$$

(*v*) When both sources of sound and listener are moving in same direction and listener is moving towards source of sound, then

$$n' = \left(\frac{V + V_L}{V + V_S}\right) n$$

(*vi*) When source of sound and listener are moving towards each other, then

$$n' = \left(\frac{V - V_L}{V - V_S}\right) n$$

(*vii*) When source of sound and listener are moving away from each other, then

$$n' = \left(\frac{V - V_L}{V + V_S}\right) n$$

(*viii*) When both sources of sound and listener are moving and if source of sound follows the listener, then

$$n' = \left(\frac{V + V_L}{V - V_S}\right) n$$

ELECTROMAGNETIC RADIATIONS.

Ordinary light rays, X-rays, γ-rays. etc. are called *electromagnetic radiations* because similar waves can be produced by moving a charged body in a magnetic field or a magnet in an electric field. Electromagnetic radiations have wave characteristics and do not require any medium for their propagation.

(*i*) **Wavelength.**

The distance between two neighbouring troughs or crests is called *wavelength*. It is denoted by λ and is expressed in cm, m, namometers (nm) or Angstrom (Å) units (1 Å = 10^{-1} nm =10^{-8} cm =10^{-10} m). It determines the colour of a beam of visible light.

(*ii*) **Frequency.**

The number of times a wave passes through a given point in one second is called *frequency* of the wave. It is denoted by ν (*nu*) and is expressed in cycles per second (cps) or hertz (Hz) units (1Hz = 1cps). *The frequency of a wave is inversely proportional to its wave length, i.e.*

$$\nu \propto \frac{1}{\lambda}$$

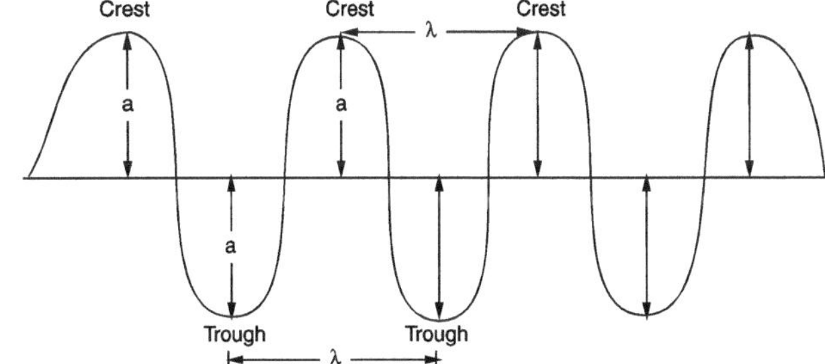

(*iii*) **Velocity.**

The distance travelled by the wave in one second is called its *velocity*. It is denoted by c.

Mathematically,

$$c = \nu \lambda$$

or $$\nu = \frac{c}{\lambda}$$

or $$\lambda = \frac{c}{\nu}$$

All types of electromagnetic radiations travel through space with the same velocity, *i.e.* 3 10^{10} cm sec^{-1}, 3 10^8 m sec^{-1} or 186,000 miles sec^{-1}. However, different types of radiations have different wavelengths and therefore different frequencies.

(*iv*) **Wave number.**

It is defined as the number of wavelenghts per cm, and is equal to the invrese of wavelength expressed in centimeters. It is denoted by $\bar{\nu}$ and is expressed in cm^{-1}

$$\nu = \frac{1}{\lambda}$$

Now since $\lambda = \dfrac{c}{\nu}$,

therefore $$\bar{\nu} = \frac{\nu}{c}$$

(*v*) **Amplitude.**

It is the height of the crest or depth of trough of a wave and is denoted by a . It determines the intensity or brightness of the beam of light.

Table 1.1 : Wavelengths and frequencies of electromagnetic radiations

Electromagnetic	Wavelength (Å)	Frequency (Hz or sec⁻¹)	Source Radiation
Radiowave	3×10^{14} to 3×10^{7}	1×10^{5} to 1×10^{9}	alternating electric current of high frequencies.
Microwave	3×10^{9} to 3×10^{6}	1×10^{9} to 5×10^{11}	special generators, *e.g.*
Infrared (IR)	6×10^{6} to 7600	5×10^{11} to 3.95×10^{14}	incandescent objects.
Visible	7600 to 3800	3.95×10^{14} to 7.9×10^{14}	stars, arc lamps, hot filaments as of tungsten in an electric bulb, etc.
Ultraviolet (UV)	3800 to 150	7.9×10^{14} to 2×10^{16}	sun's rays.
X- rays	150 to 0.1	2×10^{16} to 3×10^{19}	placing a metal obstacle in the path of a fast moving stream of electrons.
Gamma rays	0.1 to 0.01	3×10^{19} to 3×10^{20}	nuclei of radioactive atoms through the process of radio-active disintegration going on spontaneously in nature.
Cosmic rays	0.01 to zero	3×10^{10} to infinity	outer space but due to their extraordinary penetrating power they enter the earth surface after piercing through a large thickness of the atmosphere.

PHOTOELECTRIC EFFECT.

Sir J.J. Thomson. in some of his famous experiments, observed that when a beam of light of sufficientfly high frequency strikes the surface of a metal surface, electrons are ejected from the metal. This phenomenon is called *photoelectric effect.*

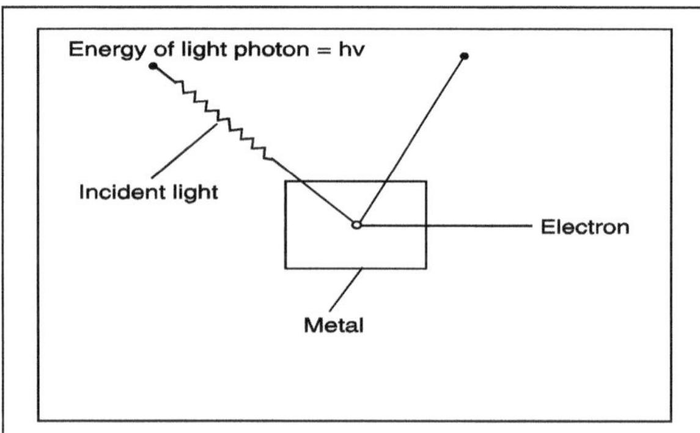

A few metals show this effect under the action of visible light but many more show it under the action of more energetic ultraviolet light. Cesium which amongest the alkali metals has the lowest ionisation energy, is also the metal from which electrons are ejected most easily by light.

QUANTUM NUMBERS.

To explain various spectra and to completely define the position of an electron in an atom it is necessary to know the following four types of quantum numbers :

(i) Principal quantum number .

It determines the energy shell in which the electron is revolving round the nucleus and is also called major energy level. It is denoted the symbol n and may have any integral value except zero.

n = 1, 2, 3, 4 etc. denotes that the electron is in the first (K), second (L), third (M), fourth (N) shell etc. respectively. As the distance of the electron from the nucleus increases, its energy becomes higher and higher. The maximum number of electrons in a major energy level is $2n^2$. Thus

Value of n		1 2 3 4 ...
Shell destination :		K L M N ...
Maximum no. of electrons ($2n^2$)		2 8 18 32 ...
Maximum no. of orbitals (n^2)		1 4 9 16 ...

(ii) Azimuthal or Orbital quantum number.

It is denoted by the symbol l and gives the sub-shell to which the electron belongs as also its angular momentum in its motion around the nucleus. It may have any value ranging from 0 to $(n - 1)$.

It helps in calculation of orbital angular momentum of electron as $[l(l + 1)]^{1/2} \dfrac{h}{2\pi}$.

When $n = 1$, l can only one value, $l = 0$

When $n = 2$, l can have two values ; $l = 0$ and $l = 1$

When $n = 3$, l can have three values ;
$l = 0, l = 1$ and $l = 2.$

The sub-shell corresponding to l = 0, 1, 2, 3, are the s, p, d and f sub-shells respectively.

For example when n = 3 and l = 2, the electron is said to be in $3d$ sub-shell.

(iii) **Magnetic quantum number or Orientation qunatum number.**

It is denoted by the symbol m or m_l and accounts for the splitting up of spectral lines into a number of components when the source is put under a strong magnetic field (Zeeman Effect) which in other words means that each sub-level exists as a number of closely related levels which are revealed only in a magnetic field. The magnetic quantum number gives the location of the orbit of revolution of the electron in the sub-shell. The possible value which m can have depends upon the value of l and may assume all the integral values between $+l$ to $-l$ through zero, *i.e.* total number of values of m would be $(2l + 1)$

When l = 0 ; m = 0 (only 1 value)

When l = 1 ; m may have 3 values

$m = -1 ; m = 0 ; m = +1$

When l = 2 ; m may have 5 values ;

$m = -2, -1, 0, +1, +2.$

Total number of m values indicates the total number of orbitals into which a particular s, p, d or f sub-shell is further sub divided.

Total number of electrons = $2(2l + 1)$

(iv) **Spin quantum number.**

It is denoted by the symbol ms and arises from the spectral evidence that an electron rotates or spins about its own axis as well during its motion in an orbit around the nucleus. The electron may spin in the clockwise ($\uparrow$) direction or anticlockwise ($\downarrow$) direction and only two values of s are possible, viz $+\dfrac{1}{2}$ (for clockwise), and $-\dfrac{1}{2}$ (for anticlockwise).

Two electrons with the same sign of spin are said to have parallel spin and are represented as $\uparrow\uparrow$ while those having opposite spin are said to have antiparallel spin (represented as $\downarrow\uparrow$) and are *called paired up electrons.*

Difference between orbit and orbital .

Orbital is a three dimensional region in space around the nucleus of the atom where there is high probability of finding the electron while orbit is a definite circular path around the nucleus in which an electron revolves. Further, orbital represents motion of the electron around the nucleus along X, Y and Z directions; while orbit represents motion of an electron around the nucleus in only one plane. Thirdly, an orbital can accommodate only two electrons while the number of electrons in an orbit is given by $2n^2$. Fourthly, orbitals (p, d and f), except s, have directional characteristics, while orbit has no directional characteristic.

Table. Relationship between the various quantum numbers

Principal quantum number (n)	*Azimuthat quantum number (l)*	*Magnetic quantum number (m)*	*Spin quantum no.*		*Total number of electrons* $= 2n^2$
			$s = +\dfrac{1}{2}$	$s = -\dfrac{1}{2}$	
n = 1 (K)	l = 0 (1s)	$m = 0$	1	1	2 $1^2 = 2$
n = 2 (L)	l = 0 (2s)	$m = 0$	1	1	2 $2^2 = 8$
	= 1 (2p)	$m = -1, 0, +1$	3	3	
n = 3 (M)	l = 0 (3s)	$m = 0$	1	1	
	= 1 (3p)	$m = -1, 0, +1$	3	3	2 $3^2 = 18$
	= 2 (3d)	$m = 0, \pm 1, \pm 2$	5	5	
n = 4 (N)	l = 0 (4s)	$m = 0$	1	1	
	= 1 (4p)	$m = 0, \pm 1$	3	3	
	= 2 (4d)	$m = 0, \pm 1, \pm 2$	5	5	
	= 3 (4f)	$m = 0, \pm 1, \pm 2$ ± 3	7	7	

Energy of Various Orbitals of Hydrogen.

The energy increases with the increase in the value of n, *i.e.* 1 (K) shell has the lowest energy.

Orbitals belonging to the same shell possess the same energy *i.e.* p, d and f orbitals of any shell have the same energy. Thus in hydrogen, the principal quantum number n is most important in determining energy of the orbitals.

Energy of the Various Orbitals of Multi-electron Atoms.

Although energies of s- and p-orbitals for the same principal quantum number are almost close together, energy of the corresponding d orbitals is much higher.

e.g. energy of $3d$-orbitals is much more than that of $3s$ and $3p$; actually it lies between $4s$- and $4p$- orbitals.

Certain sub-levels belonging to the same or different principal quantum number have nearly similar energy, such sub-levels are said to constitute an electron shell. Thus group of $4s$, $3d$ and $4p$, and the group of $5s$, $4d$ and $5p$ form different electron shells.

DISTRIBUTION OF ELECTRONS.

To describe arrangement and distribution of electrons following selective principal are required.

(i) Aufbau principle.

According to this principle, *electrons are added progressively to the various orbitals in the order of increasing energy starting with the orbital of lowest energy.*

The order of increasing energies may be summed up as

$1s$, $2s$, $2p$, $3s$, $3p$, $4s$, $3d$, $4p$, $5s$, $4d$, $5p$, $6s$, $4f$, $5d$, $6p$, $7s$, $5f$, $6d$, and $7p$.

(ii) Pauli's exclusion principle.

According to Pauli's exclusion principle, no two electrons in the same atom will have the same values of the quantum numbers (principal n, azimuthal l, magnetic m, and spin s).

In accordance with this principle, if two electrons in an atom have identical values of n, l and m, it follows that they differ in their spins, *i.e.* their spins are antiparallel ($\uparrow\downarrow$) ; in other words, if s is

$+\dfrac{1}{2}$ in one case, it is $-\dfrac{1}{2}$ in other case.

This principle throws considerable light on the structure of atom and limits maximum number of elctrons in a shell.

(iii) Hund's rule of maximum multiplicity.

According to this rule electron pairing in any orbital (s, p, d or f) cannot take place until each orbital of the same sub-level contains 1 electron. Again, accroding to Hund's rule, *single electrons will have like spins.*

(iv) Bohr-Bury principle.

(a) Maximum number of electrons in an orbit is $2n^2$.

(b) Maximum number of electrons in the outermost orbit is 8.

(c) In the penultimate (last but one) orbit, maximum number of electron can be 18.

(d) A ncw orbit starts filling when outermost orbit gets filled with 8 electrons.

(v) Orbitals in the same sub-level tend to become completely filled or exactly half-filled of electrons because these have lesser energy and thus more stable than any other arrangement. See electronic configuration of $_{24}$Cr and $_{29}$Cu table.

(vi) The electronic configuration of an atom is written in terms of notation nl^x, where x represents the number of electrons present in the orbital, l denotes sub-level of the principal energy level n. Thus, $2s^2$ means that two electrons are present in the s-orbital of the second energy level.

The above rules may be illustrated by considering the electronic configuration of the first 36 elements.

LASER

A laser is a device that emits light (electomagnetic radiation) through a process called stimulated emission. The term laser is an acronym for light amplification by stimulated emission of radiation.

Laser light is usually spatially coherent, which means that the light either is emitted in a narrow, low-divergence beam, or can be converted into one with the help of optical components such as lenses. Typically, lasers are thought of as emitting light with a narrow wave length spectrum (*monochromatic light*). This is not true of all lasers, however, some emit light with a broad spectrum, while others emit light at multiple distinct wave lengths simultaneously. The coherence of typical laser emission is distinctive. Most other light sources emit incoherent light, which has a phase that varies randomly with time and position.

Laser construction.

A laser consists of a gain medium inside a highly reflective optical cavity, as well as a means to supply energy to the gain medium. The gain medium is a material with properties that allow it to amplify light by stimulated emission. In its simplest form, a cavity consists of two mirrors arranged such that light bounces back and forth, each time passing through the gain medium. Typically one of the two mirrors, the output coupler, is partially transparent. The output laser beam is emitted through this mirror.

Light of a specific wavelength that passes through the gain medium is amplified (increases in power); the surrounding mirrors ensure that most of the light makes many passes through the gain medium, being amplified repeatedly. Part of the light partially transparent mirror and escapes as a beam of light.

The process of supplying the energy required for the amplification is called *pumping*. The energy is typically supplied as an electrical current or as light at a different wavelength. Such light may be provided by a flash lamp or perhaps another laser.

TYPES OF LASERS.

1. **Gas lasers.**

   Gas lasers using many gases have been built and used for many purposes.

   (i) Helium-neon laser (HeNe) emits at a variety of wavelengths.

   (ii) Carbon dioxide lasers can emit hundreds of kilowatts [14] at 9.6 μm and 10.6 μm, and are often used in industry for cutting and welding.

   (iii) Argon-ion lasers emit light in the range 351-528.7 nm.

   (iv) Metal ion lasers are gas lasers that generate deep ultraviolet wavelengths.

2. **Chemical lasers.**

   These are powered by a chemical reaction, and can achieve high powers in continuous operation.

3. **Excimer lasers.**

   These are powered by a chemical reaction involving an excited dimer, or excimer, which is a short-lived dimeric or heterodimeric molecule formed from two species (atoms), at least one of which is in an excited electronic state. They typically produce ultraviolet light, and are used in semiconductor photolithography and in LASIK eye surgery.

4. **Solid-state lasers.**

   Materials are commonly made by "doping" a crystalline solid host with ions that provide the required energy states.

5. **Fiber-hosted lasers.**

   Solid-state lasers where the light is guided due to the total internal reflection in an optical fiber are called *fiber lasers*.

6. **Photonic crystal lasers.**

   Photonic crystal lasers are lasers based on nanostructures that provide the mode confinement and the density of optical states (DOS) structure required for the feedback to take place.

7. **Semiconductor lasers.**

   Semiconductor lasers are also solid-state lasers but have a different mode of laser operation.

8. **Dye lasers.**

   Dye lasers use an organic dye as the gain medium.

9. **Free electron lasers.**

   Free electron lasers, or FELS, generate coherent, high power radiation, that is widely tunable, currently ranging in wavelength from microwaves, through terahertz radiation and infrared, to the visible spectrum, to soft X–rays.

USES OF LASERS.

1. **Scientific uses.**

   (i)   Interferometric techniques

   (ii) Raman spectroscopy

   (iii) Laser induced breakdown spectroscopy

   (iv) Atmospheric remote sensing

   (v) Investigating nonlinear optics phenomena

   (vi) Holographic techniques employing lasers also contribute to a number of measurement techniques.

2. **Material processing.**

   Laser cutting, laser welding, laser brazing, laser bending, laser engraving or marking, laser cleaning, weapons etc.

3. **Military uses.**

   Military uses of lasers include applications such as *target designation* and ranging, defensive countermeasures, communications and *directed energy weapons*.

4. **Medical uses.**

   (i)   *Cosmetic surgery* : removing tattoos, scars, stretch marks, sunspots, wrinkles, birthmarks, and hairs .

   (ii) Used in dermatology

   (iii) Eye surgery and refractive surgery

   (iv) Soft tissue surgery:

   (v) Laser scalpel (General surgery, gynecological, urology, laproscopic)

   (vi) Dental procedures

   (vii) Photobiomodulation, i.e. laser therapy

   (viii) "No-Touch" removal of tumors, especially of the brain and spinal cord.

   (ix) In dentistry for caries removal, endodontic/ periodontic procedures, tooth whitening, and oral surgery.

5. **Commercial uses.**

   In consumer electronics, telecommunications, and data communications, lasers are used as the transmitters in optical communications over optical fiber and free space.

ATOMIC STRUCTURE
RUTHERFORD'S EXPERIMENT

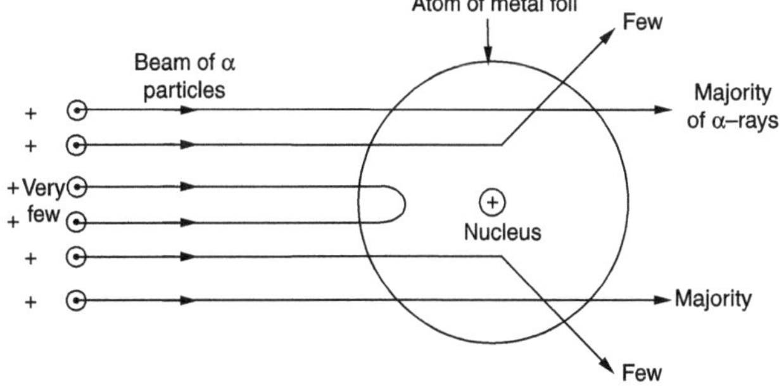

Rutherford (1911) directed a narrow beam of alpha particles obtained from polonium at an extremely thin of a metal like silver and gold (10^{-4} cm thick). After passing through the metal sheet, the α-particles were made to strike a fluorescent screen. As a results of a series of experiments, Rutherford observed that :

(i) Most of the α-particles passed through the metallic sheet without suffering any change in their straight path showing that the atom consists predominantly of empty space.

(ii) The centre of the atom has a positively charged body, is called *nucleus*, to repel positively charged particles and thus explains the scattering of α-particles.

(iii) An extremely small number of α-particles get deflected through wider angles or even backward showing the presence of a heavy positively charged body in each atom and that the volume of this body is only a minute fraction of the total volume of the atom.

RUTHERFORD'S ATOMIC MODEL.

Rutherford Model of an atom consists of two parts :

1. **Nucleus.**

   Nucleus is a small positively charged part of the atom. Diameter of the nucleus is of the order of 10^{-14} to 10^{-15} m which is only about 10^{-5}th of the diameter of the atom. The diameter of various atoms lies in the range of 0.74 10^{-10} m to 4.70 10^{-10} m or 0.74 to 4.70 Å [1 Ansgtrom (Å) unit = 10^{-8} cm = 10^{-10} m].

2. **Extra-nuclear part.**

   This is empty part of the atom. In this part electrons revolve at very high speed in fixed path called as *orbits or shells*. The centrifugal force acting on the revolving electrons is balanced by the force of attraction between electrons and the nucleus.

   Note

   (i) Number of α particle scattered through θ angle

   $$= 2 \, \text{cosec}^4 \, \frac{\theta}{2}$$

   (ii) Path formed offer deffection is parabolic

Comparison of Mass, Charge and Specific Charge of Electron, Proton and Neutron

Name of constant	*Unit*	*Electron(e)*	*Proton (p)*	*Neutron (n)*
Mass (m)	amu	0.000546	1.00728	1.008665
	kg	9.109×10^{-31}	1.673×10^{-27}	1.675×10^{-27}
Relative	1/1837	1	1	
Charge (e)	Coulomb (C)	-1.602×10^{-19}	$+1.602 \times 10^{-19}$	Zero
	esu	-4.8×10^{-10}	$+4.8 \times 10^{-10}$	Zero
	Relative	-1	$+1$	Zero
Specific charge $\left(\dfrac{e}{m}\right)$ Discovers	C/g	1.78×10^8	9.58×10^4	Zero

UNCOMMON SUB-ATOMIC PARTICLES.

(i) **Positron (positive electron, $_1e°$).**

   It is the positive counterpart of electron, discovered by Anderson in 1932. It is very unstable and combines with electron producing γ - rays (energy radiations). Positron is symbolised as $+ \, _1e^0$ or e^+

(ii) **Neutrino and Antineutrino.**

   These are particles of small (≈ 0) mass and zero charge. These were postulated by Fermi in 1934.

(iii) **Mesons.**

   Pi-mesons (pions) and μ mesons (postulated by Yukawa in 1935) may be either positively or negatively charged. Their mass is intermediate between that of electron and proton. The π mesons (mass about 200 times that of an electron) are somewhat heavier than the μ mesons. To account for the binding forces between like particles such as proton and proton or neutorn and neutron, Kemmer suggested the existence of a neutral meson (π^0).

Note :

(i) Light particles are called *lapton*, e.g., β,γ

(ii) Heavy particles are called baryou, e.g. proton neutron α - particles etc.

ATOMIC NUMBER (Z) AND MASS NUMBER (A)

Atomic number.

The number of unit positive charges carried by the nucleus of an atom is called *atomic number of element*. In other words, atomic number is equal to the number of protons in the nucleus of the atom.

Mass number.

Sum of the number of protons and neutrons present in the nucleus of an atom is called *mass number* of the atom.

Following is a general symbol for an atom of an element (E) indicating its mass number (A) and atomic number (Z).

$$_ZE^A \text{ or } {}^A_Z E$$

Thus, knowing the mass number (A) and atomic number (Z) of an element, we can find out the number of electrons, protons and neutrons present in the atom.

Atomic number (Z) = Number of protons
= Number of electrons.

Mass number (A) = Number of protons
+ Number of neutrons

A = Z + Number of neutrons

KEY POINTS

Geissler tube

It is a vacuum tube with a moderate degree of exhaustion sufficient for the brightly coloured luminous discharge to be broken up by dark spaces, i.e. with a gas pressure below about 1/100 of an atmosphere.

Injection Laser

Syn. Semiconductor laser, diode laser.

It is laser from a pn junction diode. Under forward bias electrons move from n to p region where they form an excess minority carrier concentration called *injection of electrons*. Recombination of minority carriers is radiative in lasers. Photons so produced do interact with donors in valence band and are absorbed or interact with electron in conduction band and stimulate emission of identical photon or as flash of light. At sufficiently high minority concentrations, the number of stimulated photons exceeds that of absorbed photons and optical gain occurs.

Mass core

It is a core for electromagnetic apparatus, particularly in telegraphy composed of pulverized iron or other magnetic material with a binder of nonmagnetic material.

Mass soldering

It is a method of soldering, in which many joints are made in the same operation.

Maxwell equations

It is a set of classical equations in varying electric or magnetic field at any point between vector quantities such as magnetic field strength H, magnetic flux density B, electric displacement D, current density j, electric field strength E and time t.

Four basic equations :

$$\text{Curl } H = \frac{\partial D}{\partial t}$$

$$\text{div } B = 0$$

$$\text{Curl } E = \frac{\partial B}{\partial t}$$

$$\text{div } D = P$$

Planck constant (h)

It is a constant having value = 6.26×10^{-34} joule sec.

Constants derived from Planck's law according to which electromagnetic radiation is confined to photons, the energy of which is governed by $h\nu$, where ν = velocity of light.

Zeeman Effect

Multiplication of the spectrum lines of light sources when in a strong magnetic field.

EXERCISE – I

1. Three basic concepts sufficient to describe quantitatively all the phenomena encountered in mechanical science are
   (a) length, mass and time
   (b) length, mass and temperature
   (c) length, force and time
   (d) length, force and temperature

2. The dimensions of force in SI system are
   (a) MLT^{-1}
   (b) MLT^{-2}
   (c) MLT
   (d) MLT^2

3. The dimensions of power are
   (a) ML^2T^{-2}
   (b) $M^2L^2T^{-3}$
   (c) M^2LT^{-3}
   (d) M^2LT^{-2}

4. The dimension of torque in SI units is
   (a) ML^2T^{-3}
   (b) ML^2I^{-2}
   (c) $ML^{-2}T^{-2}$
   (d) $M^2L^2T^{-2}$

5. In MKS system, fourth unit, besides metre, kg and second as fundamental mechanical units, is
   (a) permeability of media
   (b) permittivity of free space
   (c) current
   (d) charge

6. For defining standard metre, wave length of which material is considered?

(a) Helium   (b) Neon

(c) Xenon   (d) Krypton

7. The quantity $\dfrac{1}{\sqrt{\epsilon_0 \, \mu_0}}$ in SI units has the

(a) value of 330 m/s   (b) value 1.73×10^4

(c) dimensions LT^{-1} (d) none of these

8. The number of basic SI units is

(a) 4   (b) 5

(c) 6   (d) 7

9. Supplementary units added to the basic SI units are

(a) 2   (b) 3

(c) 4   (d) 5

10. Farad is the unit of

(a) inductance   (b) voltage

(c) current   (d) capacitance

11. The unit newton/coulomb is the unit of

(a) electric field intensity

(b) electric flux density

(c) electro-motive force

(d) capacitance

12. The dimensions of magnetic flux density are

(a) IMT^{-2}

(b) $I^{-1}MT^{-2}$

(c) IMT^{-1}

(d) $I^{-1}MT^{-1}$

13. Force between two charged particles is given by

$$F = \frac{1}{4\pi \, \epsilon_0} \frac{Q_1 \, Q_2}{r^2}$$

where symbols have their usual meanings. The dimensions of ε_0 in free space in SI system are

(a) $M^{-1} L^{-3} T^2 A^4$

(b) $M^{-1} L^{-3} T^4 A^2$

(c) $ML^{-3} T^4 A^3$

(d) $M^{-1} L^{-3} T^2 A^2$

14. Which of the following does not have the same units as the others? The symbols have their usual meanings.

(a) $\dfrac{L}{R}$ (b) RC

(c) $\sqrt{LC}$ (d) $\dfrac{1}{\sqrt{LC}}$

15. A rocket is receding from the earth at a speed of $0.2\,c$ where c is velocity of light. It emits signals of frequency 4×10^7 Hz. The apparent frequency observed by an observer on earth is

(a) 4.5×10^7 Hz   (b) 3.9×10^7 Hz

(c) 3.3×10^7 Hz   (d) 2.6×10^7 Hz

16. During earthquake, which waves are longitudinal in character?

(a) P waves   (b) S waves

(c) both P and S   (d) none of these

17. During earthquake, the waves arriving at seismograph are

(a) P followed by S

(b) S followed by P

(c) P and S simultaneously

(d) There is no correlation between the two

18. A whistling engine is approaching a stationary observer with a velocity of 40 m/s. The velocity of sound is 330 m/s. The ratio of frequencies as heard by the observer at the time of approaching and passing of train is

(a) $4 : 3$ (b) $3 : 6$

(c) $2 : 1$ (d) $4 : 1$

19. Human ear cannot detect the sounds of wavelength

(a) 500 m   (b) 1 m

(c) 10 m   (d) 100 m

20. The apparent frequency of the whistle of an engine changes in the ratio $6 : 5$ as the engine passes a stationary observer. The velocity of engine in terms of sound c is

(a) $\dfrac{c}{11}$ (b) $\dfrac{c}{5}$

(c) $\dfrac{c}{2}$ (d) c

21. A passenger is sitting in a fast moving train. The engine of the train blows a whilstle of frequency N. If apparent frequency of sound heard by the passengers is N′, then

(a) $N' = N$ (b) $N' < N$

(c) $N' > N$ (d) $NN' = 1$

22. At what speed a source must move towards a stationary observer so that the apparent frequency may be double the true frequency of the source (c is velocity of the sound)

(a) $\dfrac{c}{2}$ (b) $\dfrac{c}{4}$

(c) $2c$ (d) $4c$

23. To a stationary man the frequency of sound source moving towards the man appears to be
    (a) higher than the original frequency
    (b) lower than the original frequency
    (c) same as original frequency
    (d) square root of original frequency

24. For a wave $y = 0.20 \sin 0.40 \pi (x - 60t)$, the frequency is
    (a) 60 Hz
    (b) 12 Hz
    (c) 5 Hz
    (d) 0.4 Hz

25. In case wavelength of light coming from a star shifts towards the violet end of the spectrum, it can be concluded that the star is
    (a) stationary
    (b) approaching the earth
    (c) receding from the earth
    (d) revolving around its axis.

26. Which of the following represents an elastic wave?
    (a) Radio waves
    (b) Microwaves
    (c) Light waves
    (d) Sound waves

27. Two waves represented by
    $$y_1 = 10 \sin 2000\,\pi t$$
    and $y_2 = 20 \sin \left(2000\pi t + \dfrac{\pi}{2}\right)$

    are superposed at any point at a particular instant. Amplitude of the resultant wave is
    (a) 200
    (b) 30
    (c) $10\sqrt{5}$
    (d) $10\sqrt{3}$

28. At 27°C, longitudinal wave in which medium will have the maximum velocity?
    (a) Hydrogen
    (b) Helium
    (c) Air
    (d) Nitrogen

29. Doppler shift in frequency does not depend on
    (a) speed of the observer
    (b) speed of the source
    (c) relative speed of the observer with respect to source
    (d) distance between source and the observer

30. Which of the following frequency may not be detected by human ear?
    (a) 10 Hz
    (b) 100 Hz
    (c) 1000 Hz
    (d) 10000 Hz

31. The velocity of sound will be least in
    (a) steel
    (b) copper
    (c) aluminium
    (d) distilled water

32. When a body travels with a velocity greater than the velocity of sound, then shape of the wave front will be
    (a) elliptical
    (b) conical
    (c) parabolical
    (d) spherical

33. A source of sound and an observer are moving away from each other. The apparent pitch will
    (a) decrease
    (b) increase
    (c) remain the same
    (d) uncertain

34. Smallest wavelength is of
    (a) microwaves
    (b) infrasonics
    (c) audible frequencies
    (d) ultrasonics

35. Change of atmospheric temperature affects which of the following property of sound?
    (a) Wavelength
    (b) Amplitude
    (c) Intensity
    (d) All of these

36. All of the following can propagate through vacuum except
    (a) X-rays
    (b) radio waves
    (c) light waves
    (d) sound waves

37. Beats are the result of
    (a) diffraction of sound waves
    (b) constructive and destructive interference
    (c) destructive interference of sound
    (d) none of these

38. For every 1^0K rise in atmospheric temperature, the velocity of sound
    (a) increases by nearly 1.1 m/s
    (b) increases by nearly 0.6 m/s
    (c) decreases by nearly 0.6 m/s
    (d) decreases by nearly 1.1 m/s

39. A person while moving towards a mountain at a speed of 4 m/s hears a sound of frequency 510 Hz located behind him and its echo after reflection from the mountain, the beat frequency of the two sounds is
    (a) 12
    (b) 6
    (c) 3
    (d) 2

40. The velocity of sound waves will be least while travelling through
    (a) cork
    (b) wood
    (c) glass wool
    (d) vacuum

41. Formation of beats
    (a) polarisation of waves
    (b) interference of waves
    (c) refraction of waves
    (d) Doppler's effect

42. Which of the following represents a damped oscillation?

(a) $y = a \sin(\omega t + \alpha)$ (b) $y = ae^{-\alpha t}$

(c) $y = ae^{-\alpha t} \cos(\omega t + \alpha)$ (d) $y = ae^{-\alpha t} \sin(\omega t + \alpha)$

43. In a ripple tank, two coherent sources are 12 cm apart. At a distance 2 m away from the sources, the maxima are 12.5 cm apart. If the velocity of ripple is 30 cm/s in the tank, then the frequency of the source is

(a) 20 Hz   (b) 40 Hz

(c) 100 Hz   (d) 400 Hz

44. Constructive interference occurs when the path difference between identical sources is

(a) $\Delta s = n\lambda + \lambda\,\dfrac{1}{2}\lambda$ where $n = 0, 1, 2, \ldots$

(b) $\Delta s = n\lambda + \dfrac{1}{2}\lambda$ where $n = 0, 2, 4, \ldots$

(c) $\Delta s = n\lambda$ where $n = 0, 1, 2, \ldots$

(d) $\Delta s = n\lambda$ where $n = 0, 2, 4, \ldots$

45. In the double slit experiment, if a glass slab is introduced in the path of light from the slits to the screen

(a) The fringe width will increase

(b) The fringe pattern will remain unchanged

(c) The central maxima will be at the same location and the fringe width will decrease.

(d) The central maxima and all the fringes shift down, and fringe width remain constant.

46. Which of the following statement about normal dispersion is correct?

(a) The index of refraction increases as the wavelength decreases

(b) The index of refraction decreases as the wavelength decreases

(c) The index of refraction increases as the wavelength increases

(d) The rate of increase becomes greater at longer wavelengths.

47. Anomalous dispersion of a transparent substance like quartz can be shown in

(a) ultraviolet range   (b) infrared range

(c) both (a) and (b)   (d) outside (a) and (b)

48. If a plane wave front is incident on a convex lens as shown, according to Huygen's principle, it will emerge as shown below

49. Nicol prism is made from

(a) flint glass

(b) diamond

(c) flourspar

(d) calcite

50. The wavelength of a moving particle is inversely proportional to

(a) mass   (b) energy

(c) velocity   (d) momentum

51. Destructive interference occurs when the path difference between identical sources is

(a) $\Delta s = n\lambda + \dfrac{1}{2}\lambda$ where $n = 0, 1, 2, \ldots$

(b) $\Delta s = n\lambda + \dfrac{1}{2}\lambda$ where $n = 0, 2, 4, \ldots$

(c) $\Delta s = n\lambda$ where $n = 0, 1, 2, \ldots$

(d) $\Delta s = n\lambda$ where $n = 0, 2, 4, \ldots$

52. According to Huygen's principle of secondary wavelets, each particle at a wave front

(a) is an electron

(b) behaves as a photon

(c) behaves as a new light source

(d) represents the direction of the motion of wave front.

53. A Nichol prism is based on the action of

(a) scattering   (b) dichroism

(c) refraction   (d) double refraction.

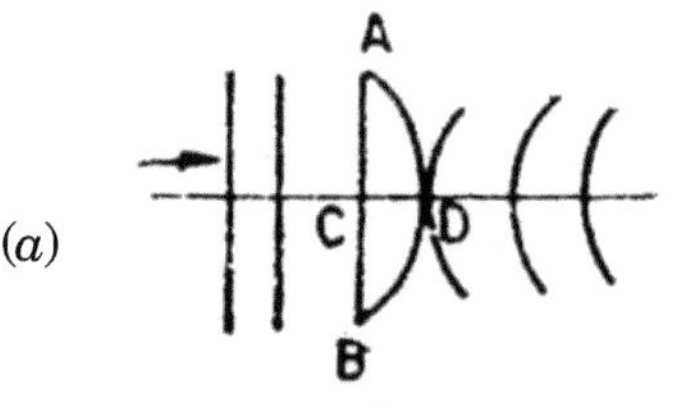

(a)

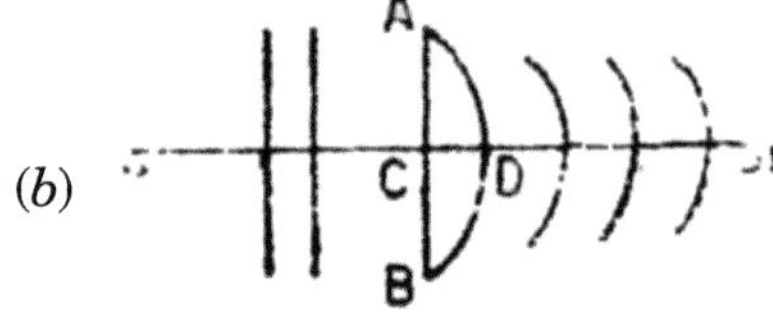

(b)

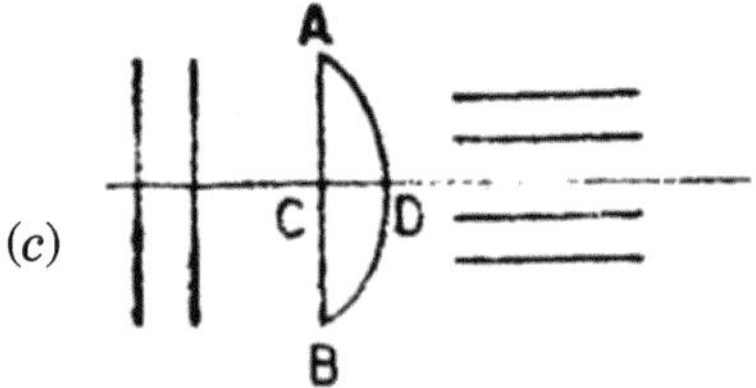

(c)

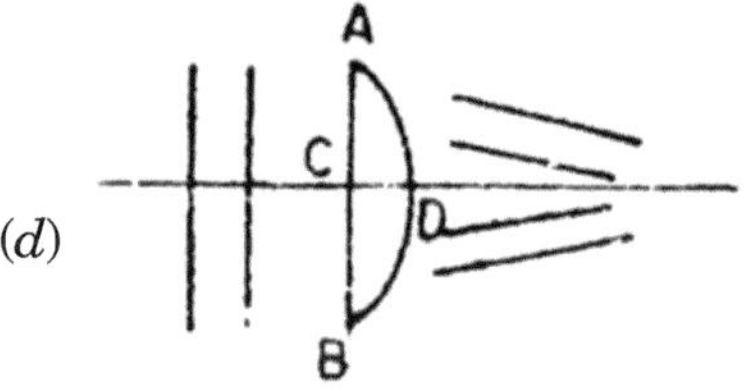

(d)

54. If white light is incident in a diffraction grating, the light that will be deviated least from the central maximum is

(a) yellow   (b) violet

(c) red   (d) green

55. In general, continuous emission spectra is obtained from

(a) gases only

(b) gases and liquids only

(c) liquids and solids only

(d) gases, liquids and solids

56. The refractive index of canada balsam is

(a) 1.1   (b) 1.5

(c) 1.95   (d) 2.14

57. The amplitude of light wave at a distance x is A. At a point distant $3x$ from the source, the amplitude would be

(a) 9A   (b) 3A

(c) $\dfrac{A}{3}$ (d) $\dfrac{A}{9}$

58. The transverse nature of electromagnetic radiation is conclusively established by the principle of

(a) interference   (b) reflection

(c) diffraction   (d) polarization

59. In Youngs double slit interference experiment, if the incident light consists of two wavelengths λ_1 and λ_2, the slit separation is d and D. If D be the distance between slits and the screen, the maxima due to the two wavelengths will coincide at a distance, from the central maxima, given by

(a) $\dfrac{(\lambda_1 + \lambda_2)}{2Dd}$

(b) $(\lambda_1 + \lambda_2)\dfrac{2d}{D}$

(c) LCM of $\lambda_1\dfrac{D}{d}$ and $\lambda_2\dfrac{D}{d}$

(d) HCF of $\dfrac{\lambda_1 D}{d}$ and $\dfrac{\lambda_2 D}{d}$

60. Light will undergo a path difference of $\dfrac{\lambda}{2}$ when is reflected at the boundary of

(a) glass-air   (b) glass-water

(c) glass-diamond   (d) air-alcohol

61. Two slits are spaced 0.3 mm apart and are placed 50 cm from a screen. Then the distance between the second and the third dark lines when the slits are illuminated with light of 600 mm wavelength is

(a) 1 mm   (b) 2 mm

(c) 0.1 mm   (d) 0.2 mm

62. In Youngs double slit interference experiment, if distance between the slits is made less than the wavelength of light used, which of the following is likely to happen ?

(a) Fringes will become narrower and sharper

(b) No fringes will be observed

(c) Fringe width equal to wavelength will be obtainted

(d) The central fringe will become brighter, while the intensity of successive maxima will decrease.

63. A shift of an interference pattern with blue light is observed when a colourless thin parallel film is introduced in the path of the refracted beam from one half of the biprism. If the colourless film is replaced by a red film of the same thickness and refractive index, the shift

(a) remanis the same

(b) decreases

(c) increases

(d) none of these

64. When blue glass is heated, the colour of glow will be

(a) white

(b) blue

(c) red

(d) yellow

65. Infrared photography is based which of the following principle?

(a) Infrareds are more coherent than visible radiation

(b) The dispersion of infrared is larger than that for visible radiation

(c) The peak of maximum radiation varies with the temperature emitting IR

(d) The Doppler effect of infrared is larger than that for visible radiation.

66. The intensity of bright and dark bands is almost constant in

(a) a diffraction pattern only

(b) an interference pattern only

(c) both diffraction as well as interference pattern

(d) neither diffraction nor interference pattern

67. When plane-polarized light passes through an optically active material, the plane of polarization is rotated through an angle that depends on

(a) material

(b) length of the path traversed

(c) wavelength of light

(d) all of these

68. There are several reasons why a lens may not produce a sharp image of an object point. Which one of the following is valid reason?
  (a) The incident light is not monochromatic
  (b) The image is being formed at the wrong
  (c) The lens is diverging
  (d) The paraxial approximation is being voilated

69. Which colour light has the longest wavelength ?
  (a) Violet   (b) Yellow
  (c) Red   (d) Green

70. The intensity of light scattered by molecules of air in the atmosphere is proportioal
  (a) λ (b) λ^2
  (c) $\dfrac{1}{\lambda^2}$ (d) $\dfrac{1}{\lambda^4}$

71. The maximum distance from which the mm markings on a metre scale can be seen by the eye of aperture 2 mm is nearly
  (a) 1 metre   (b) 4 metres
  (c) 10 metres   (d) 15.5 metres

72. Hologram
  (a) inside view of hollow objects
  (b) coloured fringes produced by interference
  (c) line spectrum of helium
  (d) three dimensional view of an object

73. The refractive index for diamond is
  (a) 1.1   (b) 1.55
  (c) 1.95   (d) 2.45

74. The black lines on the spectrogram of white light from the sun are called
  (a) Fresnel lines   (b) Stokes lines
  (c) Fraunhoffer lines (d) None of these

75. Phenomenon associated with periscope is
  (a) Polarisation   (b) Dispersion
  (c) Partial reflection (d) Total internal reflection

76. Carbon dioxide is filled in a discharge tube. Which of the following spectrum will be obtained from the discharge tube?
  (a) Line spectrum
  (b) Band spectrum
  (c) Continuous spectrum
  (d) Absorption spectrum

77. In Young's experiment of interference a torch is used in place of sodium lamp. Which of the following statement is correct ?
  (a) Fringes will be produced as usual
  (b) Fringes will be produced for a moment and disappear
  (c) Fringes will not be produced at all
  (d) Coloured fringes will be produced

78. During interfence of light
  (a) part of energy is lost
  (b) energy is gained
  (c) energy is redistributed
  (d) none of these

79. In the whole of the Youngs experiment is kept in water, which of the following changes will take place?
  (a) The fringe width will increase
  (b) The fringe width will decrease
  (c) No fringe will be seen
  (d) No change in the fringe width will take place

80. The refractive index of glass is least for
  (a) yellow light   (b) green light
  (c) violet light   (d) red light

81. In Young's experiment one slit is covered with blue filter and the other slit with yellow. The interference pattern will look
  (a) blue
  (b) yellow
  (c) green
  (d) no interference pattern will be seen.

82. For interference to take place, the two sources of light
  (a) can be of any colour
  (b) must have same frequency
  (c) must have ratio of frequencies as an integer
  (d) none of these

83. A continuous spectrum is emitted by
  (a) diatomic gases
  (b) low temperature gases
  (c) pure liquids
  (d) white hot solids

84. Refraction index will be least case of
  (a) Barium flint glass (b) Diamond
  (c) Benzene   (d) Dry air

85. Camera lenses are often coated to
  (a) produce laser effect
  (b) reduce unwanted reflections
  (c) make the beam parallel to the lens axis
  (d) produce black box effect

86. The resolving power of a lens is
  (a) Its capacity to separate radiation in different regions of the spectrum
  (b) to avoid constructive as well as destructive interference whenever optical path difference is $N\lambda$
  (c) its ability to separate the images of two points that are close together
  (d) none of these

87. When light is reflected at the boundary of an optically denser medium, it undergoes a phase change of
    (a) $\dfrac{\lambda}{4}$
    (b) $\dfrac{\lambda}{2}$
    (c) λ
    (d) even multiple of λ

88. Which of the following is not true about LASERS and MASERS ?
    (a) The wavelength of radiation produced by LASERS is less than the radiation emitted by MASERS
    (b) The substance working as a LASER must be in solid state
    (c) The energy of the metastable state is less than the energy of the first excited state
    (d) The light emitted by LASERS is highly coherent.

89. The normal dispersion can be closely approximated by the relation
    (a) $n = A + B\lambda + C\lambda^2 + D\lambda^3$
    (b) $n = A + \dfrac{B}{\lambda} + \dfrac{C}{\lambda^2} + \dfrac{D}{\lambda^3}$
    (c) $n = A + \dfrac{B}{\lambda^2} + \dfrac{C}{\lambda^4}$
    (d) $n = A - \dfrac{B}{\lambda} + \dfrac{C}{\lambda^3}$

90. Which of the following statement about lasers is incorrect ?
    (a) The laser is accurately monochromatic beam
    (b) The laser is highly coherent beam
    (c) The laser beam consists of parallel rays
    (d) The pencil-like equality of laser beam persists for a short distance only.

91. Laser
    (a) has wavelength in ultraviolet range
    (b) does not show wave behaviour
    (c) has wavelength in infrared region
    (d) is highly coherent

92. A laser produces intense, monochromatic, coherent light by which of the following process?
    (a) stimulated absorption
    (b) stimulated emission
    (c) bremsstrahlung
    (d) spontaneous emission.

93. When atoms are held together by the sharing of valance electrons
    (a) Each atom becomes free to move
    (b) Neutrons start shifting
    (c) They form a covalent bond
    (d) Some of the electrons are lost.

94. The diameter of an atom is
    (a) 10^{-6} metre
    (b) 10^{-10} metre
    (c) 10^{-15} meter
    (d) 10^{-21} metre

95. Which of the following element has lowest atomic number?
    (a) B
    (b) Al
    (c) Ga
    (d) In.

96. Which of the following element does not occur in third group of periodic table?
    (a) Indium
    (b) Helium
    (c) Aluminium
    (d) Boron

97. The atomic number of silicon is 14. It can be therefore concluded that
    (a) a silicon atom contains 14 protons
    (b) a silicon atom contains 14 neutrons
    (c) a silicon atom contains 14 electrons
    (d) all of these

98. If the atomic number of germanium is 32, the number of electrons in the outer most shell will be
    (a) 2
    (b) 3
    (c) 4
    (d) 6

99. Which of the following elements does not have three valance electrons?
    (a) Boron
    (b) Aluminium
    (c) Germanium
    (d) Phosphorus

100. Which of the following elements does not have five valance electrons?
    (a) Phosphorus
    (b) Arsenic
    (c) Antimony
    (d) Indium

101. Which of the following elements has four valance electrons ?
    (a) Silicon
    (b) Germanium
    (c) Both (a) and (b)
    (d) None of these

102. The total energy of an electron in an atom will be maximum when it is
    (a) close to the nucleus
    (b) in the even numbered orbit
    (c) odd numbered orbit
    (d) in an orbit farthest from the nucleus.

103. Which of the following elements has four valance electrons?
    (a) Silicon
    (b) Antimony
    (c) Phosphorus
    (d) Boron

104. A germanium atom has
    (a) five valance electrons
    (b) four protons
    (c) three valance electrons
    (d) two electrons orbits

105. One electron volt is equivalent to
  (a) 1.6×10^{-10} joule
  (b) 1.6×10^{-13} joule
  (c) 1.6×10^{-16} joule
  (d) 1.6×10^{-19} joule

106. In case of selenium, under the influence of varying light intensity
  (a) emf is generated due to chemical reaction
  (b) emf is generated due to physical reaction
  (c) electrical conductivity changes
  (d) the number of electrons liberated varies.

107. In case of photo emission
  (a) the amount of photo electic emision is inversely proportional to the intensity of light
  (b) the maximum velocity of emission varies linearly with the frequency of incident light
  (c) the maximum velocity of emission varies inversely with the frequency of incident light
  (d) the maximum velocity of emission varies linearly with the incident of light

108. The work function of a photo surface whose threshold wave length is 12,000 A, will be
  (a) 0.103 eV
  (b) 0.673 eV
  (c) 1.03 eV
  (d) 1.27 eV

109. The minimum frequency at which the emission from a photo sensitive surface begins, is called
  (a) frequency band
  (b) tuned frequency
  (c) threshold frequency
  (d) cut off frequency

110. In photo electric emission, the time lag between the exposure of surface to light and the emission of electrons, is less than
  (a) 3×10^{-9} second
  (b) 3×10^{-15} second
  (c) 3×10^{-18} second
  (d) 3×10^{-21} second

111. The photo electric current in amperes per watt of incident light depends on
  (a) frequency of incident light
  (b) intensity of incident light
  (c) frequency and intensity of incident light
  (d) frequency, wave length and intensity of incident light

112. Which of the following statement about the photoelectric emission is incorrect?
  (a) Maximum velocity of emission varies with the frequency of incident light
  (b) Maximum velocity of emission varies with the intensity of light
  (c) The amount of photo electric emission is directly proportional to the intensity of light
  (d) The quantum yield depends on the frequency and not the intensity of incident light.

113. "A potential difference is developed across a current carrying metal strip when the strip is placed in a transverse magnetic field." The above effect is called
  (a) Fermi' effect
  (b) Photo electric effect
  (c) Joule's effect
  (d) Hall's effect

114. The crystal structure of silicon is
  (a) Simple cubic
  (b) Body central cubic
  (c) Force centred cubic
  (d) Diamond

115. The minimum charge carried by an anion is
  (a) zero
  (b) equal to the charge of an electron
  (c) equal to the charge of electrons left in the atom
  (d) equal to the charge of an electron left in the atom

116. Which photo conductor is commonly used?
  (a) PbS
  (b) CdS
  (c) Ga As
  (d) As Bs

117. The photo electric threshold of tungsten is 2300Å. The energy of the electrons ejected from the surface by ultra-violet light of wavelength 1800Å, will be
  (a) 0.15 eV
  (b) 1.5 eV
  (c) 150 eV
  (d) 1.5 keV.

118. A solar cell is an example of
  (a) photo voltaic cell
  (b) photo conductive cell
  (c) photo emissive cell
  (d) photoradiation cell

119. Which of the following is not electromagnetic in nature?
  (a) Cathode rays
  (b) X-rays
  (c) γ-rays
  (d) Infrared rays.

120. When light is directed at the metal surface, the emitted electrons
  (a) are called photons
  (b) have random energies
  (c) have energies that depend upon intensity of light
  (d) have energies that depend upon frequency of light

121. When yellow light is incident on a surface, on electrons are emitted while green light can emit. If red light is incident on the surface, then
  (a) no electrons are emitted
  (b) photons are emitted
  (c) electrons of higher energy are emitted
  (d) electrons of lower energy are emitted

122. For an electric medium, which gives the permittivity?
(a) $k = k_0/kr$
(b) $k = k_0 k_r$
(c) $k_0 = k/k_r$
(d) $kr = k_0k$

123. Relation for electric field intensity is
(a) $E = Q/4\pi r$
(b) $E = Q/4\pi r^2$
(c) $E = Q/4\pi r$
(d) $E = QA\pi\varepsilon r^2$

124. Field strength H produced by a conductor carrying current I, at a distance r given by
(a) $H = 1/\pi r$
(b) $H = I/2\pi r^2$
(c) $H = 4\pi r.I$
(d) $H = I/2\pi r$

125. Relative permeability is considered as unity for
(a) Bismuth
(b) Vacuum
(c) Air
(d) Cobalt

126. Which of the following is NOT Maxwell's equation?
(a) $B = \mu H$
(b) $E = D/\varepsilon$
(c) $E = J/\sigma$
(d) $E = \varepsilon D$

127. A parallel polarized wave is incident from air to paraffin. If Er for paraffin is 2, then Brewster angle will be nearly equal to
(a) $45°$
(b) $40°$
(c) $60°$
(d) $55°$

128. When n_1 and n_2 are refraction indices of two mediums, then according to Snell's law
(a) $\dfrac{n_1}{n_2} = \sin\theta_r/\sin\theta_i$
(b) $\dfrac{n_1}{n_2} = \sin\theta_i/\sin\theta_r$
(c) $\dfrac{n_2}{n_1} = \cos\theta_i/\cos\theta_r$
(d) $\dfrac{n_2}{n_1} = \cos\theta_r/\cos\theta_i$

129. Absolute permeability μ_0 is equal to
(a) 4×10^{-7} H/m
(b) $4\pi \times 10^{-12}$ H/m
(c) $8.854 \times 10_7$ H/m
(d) 8.854×10^{-12} H/m.

130. Absorption of radio waves by the atmosphere depends on
(a) polarization of atmosphere
(b) polarization of the waves
(c) their frequency
(d) their distance from transmitter.

131. Plasma is
(a) medium dominated by helium
(b) solid dielectric material
(c) gaseous medium
(d) ray of electrons.

132. Circular polarization is said to take place when
(a) magnitude of the two waves is the same.
(b) phase of the two waves is the same
(c) magnitude is the same and phase difference is zero
(d) magnitude is the same and the phase difference is $90°$.

133. Velocity of electromagnetic waves in a dielectric medium Er = 4 is equal to
(a) 3×10^8 metres/second
(b) 1.5×10^8 meters/second
(c) 6×10^8 metres/second
(d) 12×10^8 meters/second.

134. A plane wave travelling in air is normally incident on a block of paraffin wither = 2.2. The reflection coefficient will be equal to
(a) -0.195
(b) -0.255
(c) -0.456
(d) -0.557

135. For different loads, the range of the values for VSWR is
(a) 0 to 0.5
(b) 0.5 to 1
(c) 0 to 1
(d) 1 to oo

136. Two dielectric mediums of which medium 1 is free space and medium 2 has $\varepsilon_1 = 4\varepsilon_0$ and $\mu = \mu_0$. Reflection coefficient for oblique incidence $\theta_1 = 30°$ for perpendicular polarization will be
(a) -0.118
(b) -0.381
(c) -0.566
(d) -0.777

137. When distance between two charges is doubled, then force between them will become
(a) Four times
(b) Double
(c) Half
(d) One fourth

138. If the conductivity of copper is 5.8×10^7 mho/ m and its relative permeability and permittivity is unity, then its refractive index at 10 MHz be equal to
(a) 2.27
(b) 22.7
(c) 227
(d) 2270

139. A sinusoidal plane wave is transmitted through a medium whose breakdown strength is 30 KV/m and whose relative permeability is 4. The mean possible r.m.s. power flow density will be
(a) 2.39 kW/metre
(b) 23.9 kW/metre
(c) 239 kW/metre
(d) 2390 kW/metre.

140. Which of the following is ferromagnetic material?
(a) Copper
(b) Palladium
(c) Silver
(d) Cobalt.

141. Effective lowering of work function in a material for thermionic emission by applying electric field is called ___ effect.

142. Steady state vector ratio of the voltage to the current at the input of an infinite line is defined as ___ impedance of a uniform transmission line.

143. At the ___ termination, current is maximum, voltage is zero and impedance will be zero.

144. A signal of frequency 1 GHZ travelling in a medium of $u = u; e = 4e$ and Q = 0 will have a wavelength of ___ metres.

EXERCISE – II

1. The units whose sizes cannot be choosen independently are called **DMRC 2013**
(a) Derived units
(b) Fundamental units
(c) Absolute units
(d) Auxiliary fundamental units

2. The device possessing the highest photosensitivity is a **DMRC 2014**
(a) photoconductive cell
(b) photovoltaic cell
(c) photodiode
(d) phototransistor

3. Load cells employ **DMRC 2014**
(a) piezoelectric crystal (b) capacitor
(c) mutual inductance (d) strain gauges

4. The magnetic moment in units of Bohr magneton of a ferrous ion in any ferrite is **DMRC 2014**
(a) zero (b) 2
(c) 4 (d) 6

5. Consider the following statements regarding and insulating material connected to an ac signal:
1. The dielectric constant increases with frequency.
2. The dielectric constant decreases with frequency.
3. Atomic polarization decreases with frequency.
Which of these statements is/are correct?
(a) 3 alone (b) 2 alone
(c) 2 and 3 (d) 1 and 3 **DMRC 2014**

6. Consider the following materials :
1. Nickel 2. Silver
3. Oxygen 4. Aluminium
The correct sequence of these materials in DECREASING order of their magnetic permeability is **DMRC**
(a) 1, 4, 3, 2 (b) 1, 4, 2, 3
(c) 4, 1, 3, 2 (d) 4, 1, 2, 3

7. Some ceramic superconductors become superconducting **DMRC**
(a) below liquid helium temperature
(b) between liquid helium and liquid nitrogen temperatures
(c) above liquid nitrogen temperature but below room temperature
(d) above room temperature

8. The real parts of the relative dielectric constant and loss tangent of teflon are 2.1 and 5×10^{-4} at 100 Hz respectively. The imaginary part of the dielectric constant at 100 Hz is **DMRC**
(a) 1.05×10^{-3} (b) 2.1×10^{-3}
(c) 5×10^{-3} (d) 1.05×10^{-2}

9. If the critical magnetic field for aluminium is 7.9×10^{3} amp/turn, then the current flowing through a long thin wire of aluminium of diameter 10^{-3} m will be **DMRC**
(d) 25 amp (b) 50 amp
(c) 100 amp (d) 1000 amp

10. In an atom, an excited electron returns to the original stationary state **DRDO**
(a) always in one jump
(b) always in two jumps
(c) in one or more jumps
(d) two or more jumps

11. Electronic configuration of carbon is
(a) $1s^2 2s^2$
(b) $1s^2 2s^2 2p^6 3s^2$
(c) $1s^2 2s^2 2p^6$
(d) $1s^2 2s^2 2p^2$ **DRDO**

12. Kinetic energy of free electrons in a metal is (where K is de Broglie wave number of the electrons) **DRDO**
(a) inversely proportional to K
(b) inversely proportional to square of K
(c) proportional to K
(d) proportional to square of K.

13. Curie point for Rohelle salt is about **DRDO**
(a) 1000°C
(b) 250°C
(c) 240°C
(d) absolute zero

14. The dispersion in an X-ray diffractometer, $\dfrac{d\theta}{d\lambda}$, is given by the expression **RRB**
(a) $\dfrac{m}{2d \cos\theta}$ (b) $\dfrac{m}{2d \sin\theta}$
(c) $2d \sin\theta$ (d) $2d \cos\theta$

15. Light of intensity I_0 is equally divided and passed through 2 cuvettes P_1 and P_2 containing an analyte at concentrations c and 0.5 c, respectively. The corresponding path lengths in P_1 and P_2 are 4cm and 1cm. The cross-sectional areas are 1 cm^2 and 3 cm^2, respectively. The ratio of the absorbances in P_1 and P_2 is **RRB**

(a) 1.5   (b) 8/3

(c) 3   (d) 8

16. A tissue with a refractive index 1.33 is introduced in one of the light paths of a Michelson interferometer operating with a monochromatic coherent light source of wavelength 589 nm. After the introduction of a tissue sample of thickness Δt, the fringe pattern is observed to shift by 50 fringes. If the thickness is 2 Δt, the fringe pattern will shift by **RRB**

(a) 25 fringes   (b) 50 fringes

(c) 100 fringes   (d) 200 fringes

17. Two dices are rolled simultaneously. The probability that the sum of digits on the top surface of the two dices is even, is **RRB**

(a) 0.5   (b) 0.25

(c) 0.167   (d) 0.125

18. A transmission line with a characteristic impedance of 100Ω is used to match a 50Ω section to a 200Ω section. if matching is to be done both at 429MHz and 1GHz, the length of the transmisson line can be approximately

(a) 82.5 cm   **RRB 2012**

(b) 1.05 m

(c) 1.58 m

(d) 1.75 m

19. For a given 2×2 matrix A, it is observed that

$$A \begin{bmatrix} 1 \\ -1 \end{bmatrix} = - \begin{bmatrix} 1 \\ -1 \end{bmatrix} \text{ and } A \begin{bmatrix} 1 \\ -2 \end{bmatrix} = -2 \begin{bmatrix} 1 \\ -2 \end{bmatrix}.$$

Then matrix A is **RRB 2012**

(a) $A = \begin{bmatrix} 2 & 1 \\ -1 & -1 \end{bmatrix} \begin{bmatrix} -1 & 0 \\ 0 & -2 \end{bmatrix} \begin{bmatrix} 1 & 1 \\ -1 & -2 \end{bmatrix}$

(b) $A = \begin{bmatrix} 1 & 1 \\ -1 & -2 \end{bmatrix} \begin{bmatrix} 1 & 0 \\ 0 & 2 \end{bmatrix} \begin{bmatrix} 2 & 1 \\ -1 & -1 \end{bmatrix}$

(c) $A = \begin{bmatrix} 1 & 1 \\ -1 & -2 \end{bmatrix} \begin{bmatrix} -1 & 0 \\ 0 & -2 \end{bmatrix} \begin{bmatrix} 2 & 1 \\ -1 & -1 \end{bmatrix}$

(d) $A = \begin{bmatrix} 0 & -2 \\ 1 & -3 \end{bmatrix}$

ANSWERS

EXERCISE – I

1. (a)	**2.** (b)	**3.** (a)	**4.** (a)	**5.** (a)	**6.** (d)	**7.** (c)	**8.** (d)	**9.** (a)	**10.** (d)
11. (a)	**12.** (b)	**13.** (b)	**14.** (d)	**15.** (c)	**16.** (a)	**17.** (a)	**18.** (c)	**19.** (d)	**20.** (a)
21. (a)	**22.** (a)	**23.** (a)	**24.** (b)	**25.** (b)	**26.** (d)	**27.** (c)	**28.** (a)	**29.** (d)	**30.** (a)
31. (d)	**32.** (b)	**33.** (a)	**34.** (d)	**35.** (a)	**36.** (d)	**37.** (b)	**38.** (b)	**39.** (a)	**40.** (d)
41. (b)	**42.** (c)	**43.** (b)	**44.** (c)	**45.** (c)	**46.** (a)	**47.** (b)	**48.** (a)	**49.** (d)	**50.** (d)
51. (a)	**52.** (c)	**53.** (d)	**54.** (b)	**55.** (c)	**56.** (b)	**57.** (c)	**58.** (d)	**59.** (c)	**60.** (c)
61. (a)	**62.** (b)	**63.** (d)	**64.** (c)	**65.** (c)	**66.** (b)	**67.** (d)	**68.** (c)	**69.** (c)	**70.** (d)
71. (b)	**72.** (d)	**73.** (d)	**74.** (c)	**75.** (d)	**76.** (b)	**77.** (d)	**78.** (c)	**79.** (b)	**80.** (d)
81. (c)	**82.** (b)	**83.** (d)	**84.** (d)	**85.** (b)	**86.** (c)	**87.** (b)	**88.** (b)	**89.** (c)	**90.** (d)
91. (d)	**92.** (b)	**93.** (c)	**94.** (b)	**95.** (a)	**96.** (b)	**97.** (d)	**98.** (c)	**99.** (d)	**100.** (d)
101. (c)	**102.** (d)	**103.** (a)	**104.** (d)	**105.** (d)	**106.** (c)	**107.** (b)	**108.** (c)	**109.** (c)	**110.** (a)
111. (a)	**112.** (b)	**113.** (d)	**114.** (d)	**115.** (b)	**116.** (b)	**117.** (b)	**118.** (a)	**119.** (a)	**120.** (d)
121. (a)	**122.** (b)	**123.** (d)	**124.** (d)	**125.** (d)	**126.** (b)	**127.** (d)	**128.** (a)	**129.** (a)	**130.** (c)
131. (c)	**132.** (d)	**133.** (b)	**134.** (b)	**135.** (d)	**136.** (b)	**137.** (d)	**138.** (c)	**139.** (d)	**140.** (d)

141. Schottky　　**142.** Characteristic

143. Short circuit　　**144.** 0.3.

EXERCISE – II

1. (a)	**2.** (b)	**3.** (d)	**4.** (c)	**5.** (a)	**6.** (b)	**7.** (a)	**8.** (a)	**9.** (a)	**10.** (c)
11. (b)	**12.** (c)	**13.** (c)	**14.** (a)	**15.** (a)	**16.** (*)	**17.** (a)	**18.** (c)	**19.** (b)	

Basic Electricity

D.C. BASICS

TYPES OF ELECTRICITY

It is of two types.

(*i*) **Static electricity :** It is developed on bodies when they are rubbed with each other.

(*ii*) **Dynamic electricity :** It is the flow of electric charge through a conductor in form of current.

Electric charge.

Charge on a body is always some integral multiple of smallest charge e, i.e. ne

where n = ±1, ±2, ±3, ...; and e = 1.6×10^{-19} C.

Type of charges. *It is of two types*

(*i*) Negative charge

(*ii*) Positive charge

COULOMB'S LAW

Charges of same polarity repel one another and that of opposite polarity attracteach other. The force (F) between the two charges q_1 and q_2 as shown in the figure is

(*i*) directly proportional to the product of the charges q_1 and q_2

(*ii*) inversely proportional to the square of distance d between them

(*iii*) depends on the nature of medium surrounding the charges.

Mathematically, $F \propto \dfrac{q_1 \cdot q_2}{d^2} \cdot \bar{a}_r$

$$F = \frac{q_1 \cdot q_2}{4\pi\varepsilon_r \cdot \varepsilon_0 d^2}\, \bar{a}_r \text{ Newton}$$

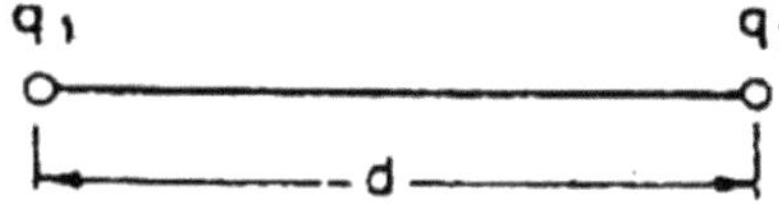

where ε_0 = permittivity of air and its value is 8.854×10^{-12} F/m

ε_r = relative permittivity of surrounding medium with respect to air and

$\bar{a}_r$ = unit vector pointing in direction of line joining the two charges.

ELECTRIC FIELD

Electric field intensity.

The space around the charge which is under stress, and experiences a force on another charge when placed there, is called *electrostatic field*. This is show in Fig (a).

If the force $\bar{F}$ experienced by a resting positive charge q_0 placed at a point as shown in Fig. (b) at a distance R metres from the charge of q, then

field intensity, $\bar{E} = \dfrac{\bar{F}}{q_0}$

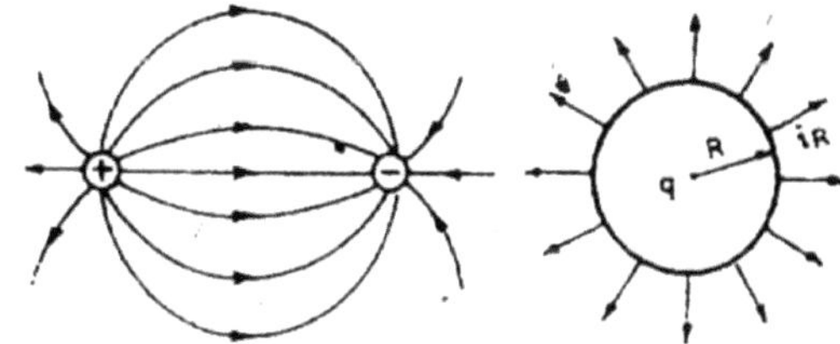

Thus field intensity is a vector in the direction of the force. Its value is given by

$$\bar{E} = \frac{q}{4\pi\varepsilon_r\,\varepsilon_0 R^2}\, \bar{i}_R \text{ Newton/Coulomb}$$

where $\bar{i}_R$ is the unit factor along the distance R and directed away from the charge.

Electric dipole moment.

It is a vector p whose magnitude is 2aq and direction is from negative to the positive charge.

When the dipole is placed in a uniform external electric field $\bar{E}$, as shown in the figure, then two charges experience equal and opposite forces.

$$\bar{F} = q\bar{E}$$

Thus net force on the dipole is zero but there is a net torque τ about an axis at point P at right angles to the plane of the paper.

$$\tau = 2F\,(a\sin\theta)$$
$$= 2\,(qE)\,(a\sin\theta)$$
$$= 2aqE\sin\theta$$
$$= pE\sin\theta$$

Thus torque is product of magnitude of force and the perpendicular distance between the forces.

In vector form, $\ \bar{\tau} = \bar{p} \times \bar{E}$

In order to change the orientation of electric dipole placed in an external field, some amount of work is to be done and this work is stored as potential energy in the system.

If dipole is to be rotated from its reference vertical position (i.e. $\theta = 90°$) to angle θ, then

potential energy, $\ U = \int_{90°}^{\theta} \tau\, d\theta = \int_{90°}^{\theta} pE\,\sin\theta = -\,pE\cos\theta$

or $\qquad\qquad U = -\bar{p}\,.\,\bar{E}$

Flux of an electric field.

It refers to a hypothetical surface, closed or open and is measured by the numbers of lines of force cut through the surface. An arbitrary closed surface can be divided into a large number of infinitesimal surfaces represented by a vector $\Delta\bar{S}$ whose direction is at right angel to the small surface as illustrated in figure. Then its flux can be defined as

$$\Delta\Phi_e = \bar{E}\,.\,\Delta\bar{S} = E\,\Delta S\cos\theta$$

which means it is the product of ΔS and component of $\bar{E}$ parallel to vector $\Delta\bar{S}$ or at right angels to the surface. If both vectors point in the same direction, the flux is positive otherwise negative.

For the whole surface, $\Phi_e = \oint \bar{E}\cdot d\bar{S}$

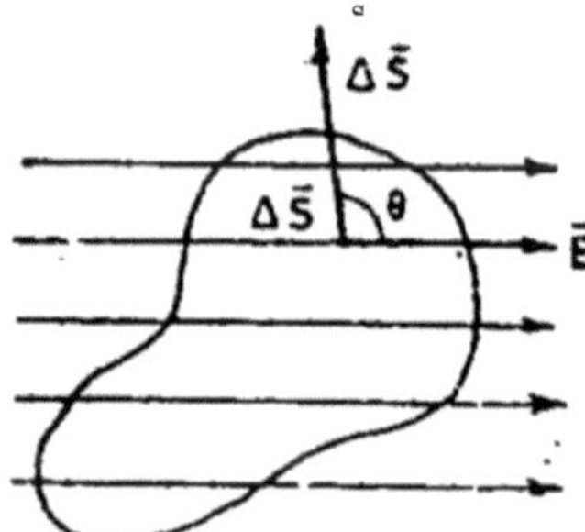

The electric field intensity of a point charge is thus directed everywhere radically away from the point charge, and on any spherical surface at the point charge, its magnitude is constant.

Electric Field of Many Charges.

If there are several point charges $q_1, q_2, q_3....q_n$ located at different points, then by superposition, the force $\bar{F}$ experienced by a test charge situated at a point, is the vector sum of the forces experienced by the test charge due to the individual charges.

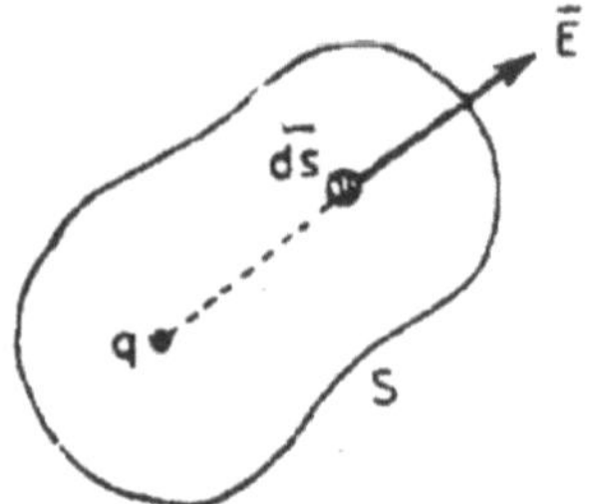

$$\bar{F} = \frac{q_1 q}{4\pi\varepsilon_0 R_1^2}\,\bar{i}_{R_1} + \frac{q_2 q}{4\pi\varepsilon_0 R_2^2}\,\bar{i}_{R_2} + \ldots\ldots \frac{q_n q}{4\varepsilon_0 R_n^2}\,\bar{i}_{R_n}$$

The electric field intensity at point P will be

$$\bar{E} = \frac{\bar{F}}{q} = \frac{q_1}{4\pi\varepsilon_0 R_1^2}\,\bar{i}_{R_1} + \frac{q_2}{4\pi\varepsilon_0 R_2^2}\,\bar{i}_{R_2} + \ldots\ldots \frac{q_n}{4\pi\varepsilon_0 R_n^2}\,\bar{i}_{R_n}$$

$$= \sum_{j=1}^{n} \frac{q_j}{4\pi\varepsilon_0 R_j^2}\,\bar{i}_{R_j}$$

GAUSS'S LAW

The surface integral of the normal component of electric field intensity $\bar{E}$ over a closed surface containing point charge q as shown in the figure above is given by

$$\oint \bar{E}\,.\,d\bar{S} = \frac{q}{\varepsilon_0}$$

This can be interpreted as the net flux of electric field emanating from the surface S containing a point charge q is equal to q/ε_0. If this arbitrary surface does not enclose the point charge, the net electric field flux emanating from the surface must be zero, i.e.

$$\oint \bar{E}\,.\,d\bar{S} = 0$$

If there are more than one point charges enclosed, then the above equation can be generated as follows

$$\oint_s \bar{E}\cdot d\bar{S} = \oint_s \bar{E}_1\cdot\,d\bar{S} + \oint_s \bar{E}_2\cdot d\bar{S} + \oint_s \bar{E}_3\cdot d\bar{S} + \ldots\ldots$$

$$= \frac{q_1 + q_2 + \ldots q_n}{\varepsilon_0}$$

$$= \frac{\text{charge enclosed by the surface S}}{\varepsilon_0}$$

An important outcome of this law is that, *excess charge placed on an insulated conductor resides entirely on its outer surface.*

Gauss's law in differential form.

Consider a volume distribution with the charge density ρ. The charge enclosed by arbitrary closed surface S is given by volume integral of charge density throughout the volume V enclosed by surface, i.e $\int_v \rho\, dv$.

According to Gauss's law, $\oint_s \overline{E} \cdot d\overline{S} = \dfrac{1}{\varepsilon_0} \int_V \rho\, dv$

If volume is shrunk to a very small Δv, then surface area becomes very small ΔS

$$\operatorname*{Lim}_{\Delta V \to 0} \oint_{\Delta s} \frac{\overline{E}.d\overline{S}}{\Delta V} = \operatorname*{Lim}_{\Delta V \to 0} \frac{\left(\dfrac{1}{\varepsilon_0}\right)\oint \rho\, dv}{\Delta V}$$

$$= \frac{1}{\varepsilon_0} \operatorname*{Lim}_{\Delta v \to 0} \frac{\rho\,\Delta V}{\Delta V} = \frac{1}{\varepsilon_0} \cdot \rho$$

or $\qquad \Delta \overline{E} = \dfrac{1}{\varepsilon_0}\, \rho$

This equation is Gauss's law in differential form. It states that, divergence of electric field intensity at any point is equal to $1/\varepsilon_0$ times the volume charge density at that point. This is *Maxwell's divergence equation* for electric field.

ELECTRIC POTENTIAL

The electric field is a force field so far the charges are concerned, there is work associated with the movement of the charges in an electric field. If a force exerted by the field on the charge is in the direction moved against the direction of the field, and external agent has to supply the energy to overcome the force exerted on the charge by the field. This force is opposite to the direction of movement of the charge.

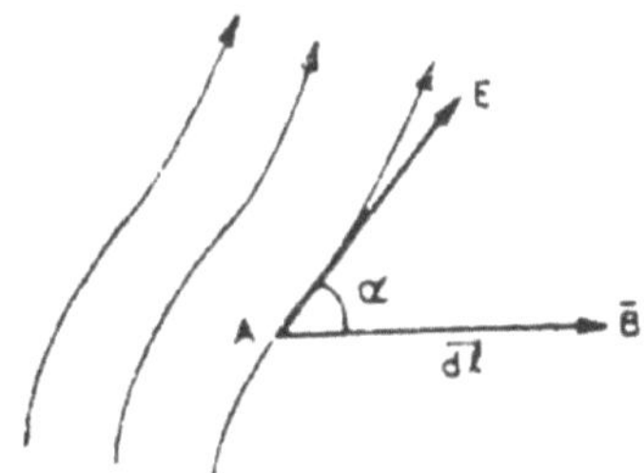

Consider the displacement of test charge q by an infinitesimal distance $\overline{dl}$ from A to B at an angle with the electric field $\overline{E}$ at a point A as shown in the figure. The force exerted on the test charge by the field has magnitude qE and is directed along E. Its component along the line from A to B is qE cos α. If the charge is moved from A to B, the amount of work done dW by the field is the product of force and displacement.

$$dW = qE \cos\alpha\; \overline{dl} = q\overline{E} \cdot \overline{dl}$$

where $\overline{dl}$ is the vector from A to B.

The work done W_{AB} by the field in moving a test charge q from A to B along a given path can be obtained by dividing the path into several segments of infinitesimal length dl. The result is a line integral expression given by

$$W_{AB} = q \int_A^B \overline{E}.\overline{dl}$$

The test charge has certain potential energy associated with it by virtue of its location in the electric field. W_{AB} as given by the above equation is then the loss of potential energy associated with the movement of the charge from A to B . Dividing W_{AB} by q gives the potential energy per unit charge. This quantity denoted by V_{AB} is known as the potential difference between the points A and B. Thus

$$V_{AB} = \frac{W_{AB}}{q} = \int_A^B \overline{E}.\overline{dl}$$

If V_{AB} is positive, there is a potential energy associated with the movement of the charge from A to B, that is, the field does the work. If V_{AB} is negative, there is a gain in potential energy associated with the moment of the charge from A to B, that is an external agent has to do the work.

Electric potential due to a charge.

If point A is taken to be at infinity and potential at infinity is taken to be zero, then the potential V at a point B will be

$$V = -\int_\infty^B \overline{E} \cdot \overline{dl} = -\int_\infty^r \frac{q}{4\pi\,\varepsilon_r\,\varepsilon_0 r^2}\, dr$$

$$= -\frac{q}{4\pi\,\varepsilon_r\,\varepsilon_0} \cdot \left[\frac{1}{r}\right]_\infty^r = \frac{q}{4\pi\,\varepsilon_r\,\varepsilon_0\, r}$$

Since field intensity is the variation of potential with the distance, it can also be visualised as potential gradient. If potential for all points of space are known, the components of E and thus E itself can be found by taking the following derivatives.

$$E_x = \frac{-\partial V}{\partial x},\; E_y = \frac{-\partial V}{\partial y}\; E_2 = \frac{-\partial V}{\partial z}$$

$$\therefore \qquad \overline{E} = -\left(\overline{i}\frac{\partial V}{\partial x} + \overline{j}\frac{\partial V}{\partial y} + \overline{k}\frac{\partial V}{\partial z}\right)$$

Thus the unit of electric field is volt/metre.

Potential due to group of charges.

The potential at a point due to a group of point charges q_1, q_2, q_n, is the algebraic sum of the potentials due to each charge, i.e.

$$V = \frac{1}{4\pi\,\varepsilon_0}\left(\frac{q_1}{r_1} + \frac{q_2}{r_2} + \dots \frac{q_n}{r_n}\right)$$

$$= \frac{1}{4\pi\,\varepsilon_0} \sum_n \frac{q_n}{r_n}$$

If charge distribution is continuous, then potential at a point is given by

$$V = \frac{1}{4\pi\varepsilon_0} \int \frac{dq}{r}$$

where dq is infinitesimal element of charge at a distance r from the point.

Potential due to an electric dipole.

The potential at a point P due to the dipole shown in figure will be

$$V = \frac{1}{4\pi\varepsilon_0}\left(\cdot\frac{q}{r_1} - \frac{q}{r_2}\right) = \frac{q}{4\pi\varepsilon_0}\left(\frac{r_2 - r_1}{r_1 r_2}\right)$$

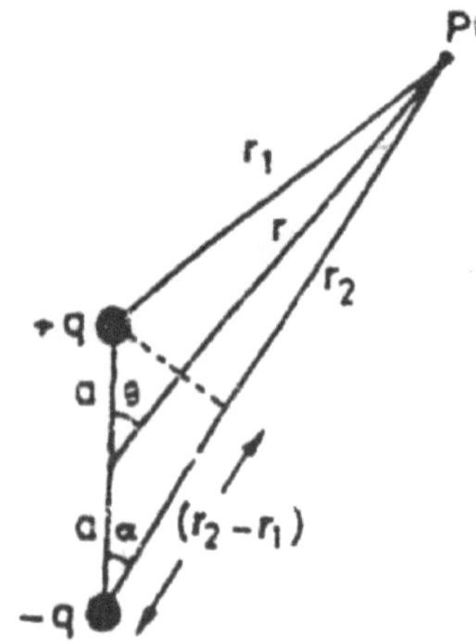

Now if $r \gg 2a$, then $\theta = \alpha$

$\therefore \quad (r_2 - r_1) = 2a \cos\alpha \cong 2a \cos\theta$ and $r_1 r_2 \cong r^2$

Thus $\quad V = \dfrac{(q2a)\cos\theta}{4\pi\varepsilon_0\, r^2} = \dfrac{1}{4\pi\varepsilon_0}\cdot\dfrac{p\cos\theta}{r^2}$

Electric potential energy.

For two charges $+q_1$ and $-q_2$ placed at a distance r apart, energy is stored in the system because a definite amount of work has to be done to move away these charges. If the charges are of opposite polarity, their potential energy will change into kinetic energy and as a result, they will accelerate towards each other.

Thus potential energy of a system of point charges is the work required to assemble these charges by bringing them together from infinity.

Now, potential due to q_1 is, $V = \dfrac{1}{4\pi\varepsilon_0}\cdot\dfrac{q_1}{r}$

Work done required to move q_2 from infinity to distance r by definition of potential will be $W = Vq_2$

$\therefore$ Electric potential energy, $U = Vq_2 = \dfrac{1}{4\pi\varepsilon_0}\dfrac{q_1 q_2}{r}$

CAPACITANCE (C)

A capacitor is an electrical device which consists of two metal conductor plates separated by an insulator (dielectric). A capacitor has the ability to hold charges that have been placed on it. A charged capacitor acts as a voltage source.

In a capacitance, the voltage between its plates is proportional to the amount of charge on the plates. *Capacitance* is a measure of how much charge is required to produce a given voltage between the plates of a capacitor.

$$C = \frac{Q}{V}$$

Capacitance in parallel : $C = C_1 + C_2 + C_3 + ... + C_n.$

Capacitance in series : $\dfrac{1}{C} = \dfrac{1}{C_1} + \dfrac{1}{C_2} + \dfrac{1}{C_3} + ... + \dfrac{1}{C_n}$

Total charge, $Q = Q_1 = Q_2 = Q_3 = ...$

Energy stored in capacitor, $W = \dfrac{1}{2}CE^2$ Joules.

INDUCTANCE

Electromagnetic induction occurs when a magnetic flux in motion with respect to a single conductor or a coil induces an emf in the conductor or coil. If the same flux ϕ links all N turns of a coil, then emf induced by a

change in $\phi = N\dfrac{d\phi}{dt}$

Faraday's law determines the magnitude of an induced emf. Lenz's law determines the polarity.

Inductance, $L = \dfrac{e_L}{\left(\dfrac{di}{dt}\right)} = N\dfrac{d\phi}{dt}$

Energy stored in inductor, $\omega = \dfrac{1}{2}LI^2$

Inductance in series : $L = L_1 + L_2 + L_3 + ... + L_n$

Inductances in parallel : $\dfrac{1}{L} = \dfrac{1}{L_1} + \dfrac{1}{L_2} + \dfrac{1}{L_3} + ... + \dfrac{1}{L_n}$

i.e. Leakage factor $= \dfrac{\text{Total flux}}{\text{Useful flux}}$

or Leakage factor $= \dfrac{\text{Flux in the iron path}}{\text{Flux in the air gap}}$

Electromotive force.

Electromotive force or potential of a body is the work done in joules to bring a unit electric charge from infinity to the body. It is expressed in terms of volts.

Potential difference is defined as that which causes current to flow in the closed circuit.

ELECTRIC CURRENT

Unit of current.

The charge on an electron is measured in terms of coulomb. The unit of current is coulomb per second and is called *ampere.* Thus

$$I(\text{Ampere}) = \frac{\text{coulomb}}{\text{second}} = \frac{\Delta q}{\Delta t}.$$

One coulomb is equivalent to the charge of 6.28×10^{18} electrons.

1 emu of current = 3×10^{10} esu of current.

Resistance.

Resistance is the property of a substance due to which it opposes the flow of electrons (*i.e.* electric current) through it. The unit of resistance is ohm (Ω).

Some substances offer relatively greater difficulty or hindrance to the passage of these electrons. Such substances are called *poor conductors* or *insulators of electricity.*

e.g. glass, bakelite, mica, rubber, polyvinyl chloride (P.V. C.), dry wood , etc.

Resistance of a conductor depends on

(*i*) *Length of the conductor* : It varies directly with the length

(*ii*) *Cross-sectional area of the conductor* : it varies inversely with the cross-sectional area

(*iii*) *Resistivity* : Nature of composition etc. of the material of which the conductor is made up

(*iv*) *Temperature of the conductor* : It almost varies directly with the temperature, thus resistance of

a conductor, $R = \rho \dfrac{l}{A}$

where ρ = specific resistance or resistivity of the material

$\quad\quad\quad l$ = length of the conductors

$\quad\quad\quad A$ = cross– sectional area of conductor.

OHM'S LAW.

If temperature and other conditions remain constant, then current through a conductor is proportional to the applied potential difference and it remains constant. Thus

$$\text{Current} = \frac{\text{Applied voltage}}{\text{Resistance of the circuit}}$$

$$\text{Resistance} = \frac{\text{Applied voltage}}{\text{Current in the circuit}}$$

Potential across resistance = Current × Resistance

Conditions for Ohm's law:

(*i*) Ohm's law can be applied either to the entire circuit or a part of a circuit.

(*ii*) When Ohm's law is applied to a part circuit, part resistance and the potential across the part resistance should be use

(*iii*) Ohm's law can be applied to dc as well as ac circuits. However, in case of ac circuits, impedance Z is used in place of resistance. Thus

$$I = \frac{E}{Z} = \frac{\text{Applied voltage}}{\text{Impedance in the circuit}}$$

Conductance (G)

It is the reciprocal of resistance (R) and is measure of the ease with which the current will flow through a substance. Thus

$$G = \frac{1}{R}.$$

The unit of conductance is mho ($\mho$).

Electrical power.

Electrical power is expressed in terms of watts (W) and is given by

$$W = E \times I = I^2 R = \frac{E^2}{R}$$

Power is also expressed in terms of kW (kilowatt) (= 1000 W) or MW (megawatt) which is 1000 kW or 1000,000 W.

Electrical energy is expressed in terms of kilowatt hours (kWh). Thus

1 kWh = 1 kW × 1 hour = 1000 watt – hours = $1000 \times 60 \times 60$ watt – sec

RESISTANCE IN SERIES AND PARALLEL.

(*i*) **Resistances in series .**

When resistances are connected in series, same current flows through all the resistance.

Overall resistance, $R = R_1 + R_2 + R_3$

Also, $V = V_1 + V_2 + V_3 = IR_1 + IR_2 + IR_3$

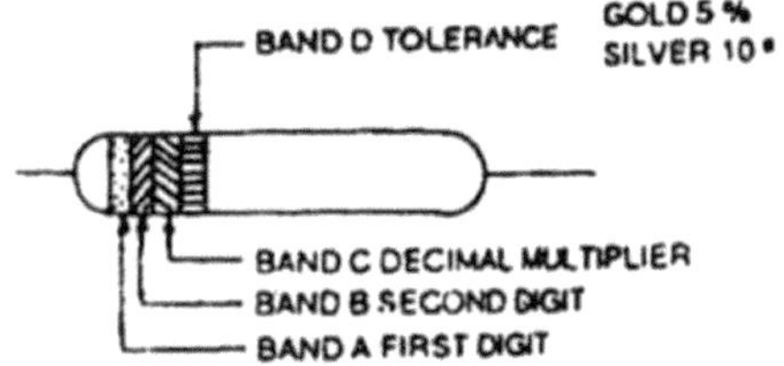

(*ii*) **Resistance in parallel .**

When conductors are joined in parallel, then $I = I_1 + I_2 + I_3$

$$\therefore \quad \frac{1}{R} = \frac{1}{R_1} + \frac{1}{R_2} + \frac{1}{R_3}$$

$$\text{or} \quad R = \frac{R_1 R_2 R_3}{R_1 R_2 + R_2 R_3 + R_3 R_1}$$

$$G = G_1 + G_2 + G_3$$

EFFECT OF TEMPERATURE ON RESISTANCE.

Resistance of all materials is affected by the variations in temperature.

- Resistance of most of the metallic ocnductors increases with rising temperature.

- Resistance of non-conductors or insulators usually decreases with rising temperature.

TEMPERATURE COEFFICIENT OF RESISTANCE.

Temperature coefficient is the increase in resistance per ohm original resistance per °C rise in temperature .

$$\therefore \quad \alpha = \frac{R_t - R_0}{R_0 . t}$$

where R_0 = resistance at 0° C

R_t = resitstance at t°C

and t = temperature rise in °C

Usually α is of the order of 10^{-4} $\Omega/\Omega°$ C for most of the metals.

In case of insulators and electrolytes, α is usually negative.

DRIFT VELOCITY.

Drift velocity v_d of charge carriers is related to current I as

$$I = n \, \alpha \, ev_d$$

where   n = density of charge carriers in conductor

α = area of cross-section of conductor

e = charge on each carrier

A large amount of energy has to be supplied to pull an electron from inside to outside of the metal surface. This energy is called *work function*. This energy is the characteristic of the metal.

SUPER-CONDUCTIVITY.

As temperature of metallic conductor decreases, their resistivity decreases. In certain metallic conductors as temperature decreases, the resistivity falls to zero at a certain temperature called super-conducting temperature. It happens for mercury at 4K and for tin at 3.72 K. This phenomenon is called *super-conductivity*.

Resistivity of semiconductors decreases with increase in temperature.

Resistivity at TK, $\rho_T = \rho_0 \, e^{-E_g/kT}$

where, E_g = band gap energy

k = Boltzman constant

NON LINEAR DEVICES

The devices for which potential difference V *vs* current I curve is not a straight line are called *non-linear devices*. These dont not obey Ohm's law and resistance of these devices is a function of V or I e.g. vacuum tubes, junction diodes, thermistors etc.

Dynamic resistance of such devices

$$r = \underset{\Delta I \to 0}{Lt} \frac{\Delta V}{\Delta I} = \frac{dV}{dI}$$

where Δ V = change in p.d.

A.C. BASICS

ALTERNATING QUANTITY

In an electrical circuit direct current flows continuously in one direction only and if the applied voltage and circuit resistance are kept constant, the magnitude of current flowing through the circuit remains constant over time. However, when current flowing varies in magnitude and direction periodically, it is called *alternating current*. Thus an alternating quantity (either current or emf) is one which periodically passes through a definite cycle, each consisting of two half cylces, during one of which the current or emf around the circuit varies in one direction and during the other, in the opposite direction.

Equations of Alternating Voltage and Currents.

Alternators produce an emf which is for all practical purposes is sinusoidal. The equation for the emf generated versus time is given as

$$e = E_{max} \sin \omega t$$

where, e = instantaneous emf

E_{max} = maximum emf

ωt = angle through which the armature has turned from neutral.

Taking frequency as f hertz (cycles per second), $\omega = 2\pi f$,

$$\therefore \quad e = E_{max} \sin 2\pi ft$$

Wave form.

Shape of the curve of the voltage or current when plotted against time as base is called *waveform*. The waveform of induced emf in an alternator differs slightly from that of sine wave but for calculation purposes it is treated as such. The advantage of doing so is that calculations become simple.

Alternation and cycle.

When a periodic wave, such as sinusoidal wave, goes through one complete set of positive or negative values, it completes one alternation and when it goes through one complete set of positive and one complete set of negative values it is said to have completed one cycle.

Periodic time (T).

The time taken in seconds by an alternating quantity to complete one cycle is called *periodic time.*

Frequency (f).

The number of cycles completed per second by an alternating quantity is called *frequency.*

In SI system, frequency is expressed in hertz (pronunced as hurts).

Periodic time or time period is reciprocal of frequency.

i.e. $$T = \frac{1}{f} \quad \text{or} \quad f = \frac{1}{T}$$

In a multipolar machine having P poles and running at a speed of N rpm, frequency of generated emf

$$f = \frac{PN}{120}$$

Amplitude.

The greatest value, positive or negative, which an alternating quantity attains during one cycle is called the amplitude of the alternating quantity.

AC AMPERE.

The value of an alternating current is not based on its average value but is based on its heating effect.

AC ampere is that current, which when passed through a given resistance for a given time, produces same heat as produced by flow of one ampere of direct current through the same resistance for the same time.

Instantaneous value.

Alternating current or voltage changes from instant to instant. The value of alternating current or voltage at any particular instant is called **instantaneous value**. Instantaneous value of an alternating quantity can be determined either from the curve or from an equation of the alternating quantity.

Maximum value.

The greatest value, positive or negative, which an alternating quantity attains during one complete cycle is called its **amplitude or maximum or peak crest value.**

Average or Mean Value.

The average or mean value of an alternating current is expressed by that steady current which transfers across any circuit the same charge as is transferred by that alternating current during the same time.

Since in the case of a symmetrical alternating current (i.e. one whose two half cycles are exactly similar whether sinusoidal or non sinusoidal) the average or mean value over a complete cycle is zero hence for such alternating quantities average or mean value means the value determined by taking the average of instantaneous values during one half cycle or one alternation only. However, for unsymmetrical alternating current (such as half-wave rectified current), the average value means the value determined by taking the mean of instantaneous values over the complete cycle.

The average values for perfect sinusoidal, half-wave rectified, full-wave rectified, rectangular and triangular wave alternating currents are 0.636, 0.318, 0.636, 1 and 0.5 times the maximum value respectively. The average or mean value is only of use in connection with processes where the results depend on the current only, irrespective of the voltage, such as electro-plating or battery charging.

rms or effective value.

It is that steady current or voltage which when flows or applied to a given resistance for a given time produces the same amount of heat as when the alternating current or voltage is flowing or applied to the same resistance for the same time.

The effective or virtual value of alternating current or voltage is equal to the square root of the mean of the squares of successive ordinates and that is why it is known as root-mean-square (rms) value.

The root mean square of effective values for perfect sinusoidal, half-wave rectified, full wave rectified, rectangular and triangular wave alternating currents are 0.707, 0.5, 0.707, 1 and 0.578 times the maximum value respectively.

Equation for the instantaneous values of emf is given as

$$e = E_{max} \sin \omega t = E_{max} \sin 2\pi f t$$

Hence

(*i*) maximum value of an alternating emf is given by the coefficient of the sine of the time angle.

(*ii*) frequency is given by coefficient of time t divided by 2π

i.e. $$f = \frac{\text{Coefficient of time } t}{2\pi}$$

Similarly we can also find the maximum value and frequency of the current from the equation of instantaneous values of current.

Form factor.

It, is defined as the ratio of effective value to the average or mean value of a periodic wave.

$$\text{Mathematically, Form factor} = \frac{\text{effective value}}{\text{average value}}$$

The values of form factor for perfect sinusoidal, half-wave rectified, full-wave fectified, rectangular and triangular wave alternating currents are 1.11, 1.57, 1.11, 1 and 1.16 respectively.

Peak factor.

It is very essential in connection with determining the dielectric strength since dielectric stress developed in any insulating material is proportional to the maximum value of the voltage applied to it.

Peak or crest or amplitude factor of a periodic wave is defined as the ratio of maximum or peak to the effective or rms value of the wave.

$$i.e \quad \text{Peak factor, } K_p = \frac{\text{maximum value}}{\text{effective value}}$$

The values of peak or crest factor for perfect sinusoidal, half-wave rectified, full-wave rectified, rectangular and triangular wave alternating currents are $\sqrt{2}$, 2.0, $\sqrt{2}$, 1 and $\sqrt{3}$ respectively.

Phase and Phase angle.

Phase of an alternating current means fraction of the time period of that alternating current that has elapsed since the current last passed through the zero position of reference. The phase angle of any quantity means the angle the vector representing the quantity makes with the reference line (which is taken to be at zero degrees or radians).

Phase difference.

When two alternating quantities are considered simultaneously, the frequency being the same, they may not pass through a particular point at the same instant. One may pass through its maximum value at the instant when the other passes through the value other than its maximum one. These two quantities are said to have a phase difference. Phase difference is always given either in degrees or in radians.

The phase difference is measured by the angular distance between the points where the two curves cross the base or reference line in the same direction.

The quantity ahead in phase is said to lead the other quantity while the seond quantity is said to lag behind the first one.

If I_1 is taken as reference vector, then two currents can be expressed as

$$i_1 = I_{max} \sin \omega t, \quad \text{and} \quad i_2 = I_{2max} \sin (\omega t - \phi)$$

The two quantities are said to be in phase with each other if they pass through zero values at the same instant and rise in the same direction. But the two quantities passing through zero values at the same instant but rising in opposite directions, are said to be in phase opposition, i.e. phase difference is 180°. When the two alternating quantities has a phase difference of 90° or $\dfrac{\pi}{2}$ radians they are said to be in quadrature.

SOURCES OF ELECTRICAL ENERGY

The purpose of an energy source is to supply power to a load. Thus Fig. shows an energy source connected to the load impedance. In a general case, this energy source may be either a dc (direct current) source or an ac (alternating current) source. Term dc as used here implies a quantity which is *steady* and unidirectional. On the other hand, term ac implies a quantity which is *alternating in nature* i.e. its magnitude changes with time and may have both positive and negative values.

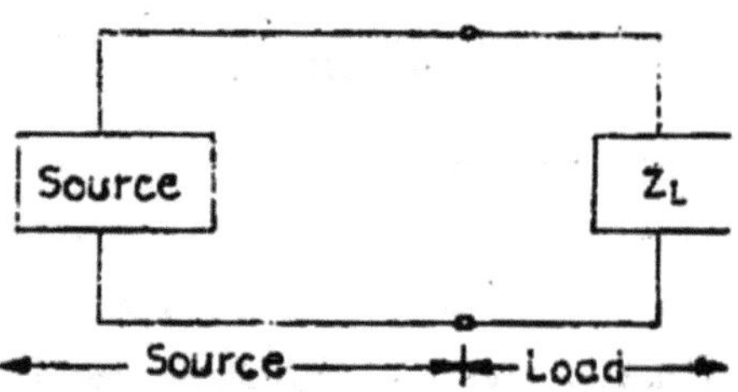

Typical dc sources.

These include dc battery, dc generator and rectifier type dc power supply.

Typical ac source.

These include alternators, electronic oscillators or signal generators.

Batteries.

By battery is meant a battery or assembly of electric cells. Thus a battery consists of a series and/ or parallel combination of several similar electric cells. A cell forms the basic source of dc energy.

Cell may be divided into two groups :

(i) Chemical cells.

Chemical cells and batteries basically convert chemical energy into electrical energy. Each cell has two electrodes, one positive and the other negative. These electrodes are kept immersed in an electrolyte (chemical compound). When dissolved in a solution, the electrolyte decomposes into positive and negative ions. These ions carry the charge within the cell from one electrode to the other.

The chemical cells may be further put into two categories

(*i*) Primary cells

(*ii*) Secondary cells

Primary cells are those cells which can not be recharged e.g. cells used in torches, calculators, transistor receivers, tape recorders etc.

The secondary cells are rechargeable e.g. battery used in cars, back-up batteries in computers, battery used in emergency lighting system etc.

(ii) Photo-voltaic cells typically solar cells.

Solar cells are specially made semiconductor pn diodes. When light falls on the cell, small typically 0.5 volt emf is generated across the two terminals. Thus a solar cell converts light energy into electrical energy. A number of such similar cells connected in series and/or parallel form a grid structure capable of generating reasonably large amount of dc energy. The conversion efficiency of a solar cell is the ratio of electrical energy generated to the energy of incident light. This conversion efficiency of solar cells is currently rather small but the cost of production of electrical energy by solar cells is small. Solar cells are now used in electronic calculators, for heating water, for lighting etc.

DC Generator.

It is an electromechanical machine used for producing dc energy. It has a stator and a rotor mounted on a shaft. When the shaft is rotated at a specified speed by some other ermeans such a steam turbine or water turbine, dc voltage of rated value appears across its terminals.

Rectifier type DC supply.

For most of the electronic equipments, ac power from 220 V mains is rectified in a rectifier and filtered to remove ripple voltage and yield almost pure dc voltage.

Alternators : An alternator is an electro-mechanical machine similar to dc generator. It has a rotor and a stator. On rotating the shaft of the generator at a specified speed, a sinusoidal ac voltage at desired frequency typically 50 Hz is obtained across the terminals.

Oscillators and Signal generators : Oscillator is an electronic equipment which generates ac voltages. A signal generator is a sophisticated and accurate electronic equipment which is capable of

(*i*) generating ac voltages of either sinewave type, rectangular type, triangular type or any other shape

(*ii*) varying the frequency of the generated ac voltage

(*iii*) varying the amplitude of the generated ac voltage

(*iv*) modulating the generated voltage in the desired manner using either amplitude modulation or frequency modulation.

IDEAL AND PRACTICAL ENERGY SOURCES

An ideal voltage source has zero internal impedance. In practice, every voltage source has a small series internal impedance associated with it. Similarly and ideal current source has infinite internal impedance in its parallel. In practice every current source has a finite but large internal impedance in its parallel.

Ideal voltage source.

An ideal voltage source generates voltage of a given time variation but neither the magnitude nor the time variation of the generated voltage changes with the magnitude of the current drawn from it. The terminal voltage of this source remains constant for all values

of output current from zero current condition to absolute short circuit. Obviously such a performance is possible only when the voltage source has zero internal impedance. The symbol for ideal voltage source is generally a circle with polarity marks + and − denoting positive and negative terminals of the source as shown in Fig. (a) and (b). The upper case letter V indicates a dc or time–invariant source while the lower case letter v indicates a time varying voltage source.

An approximate time variation of voltage is sometimes sketched within the circle. Thus the symbol () indicates a source of sinusoidal voltage. A battery is generally symbolized as in fig. (c).

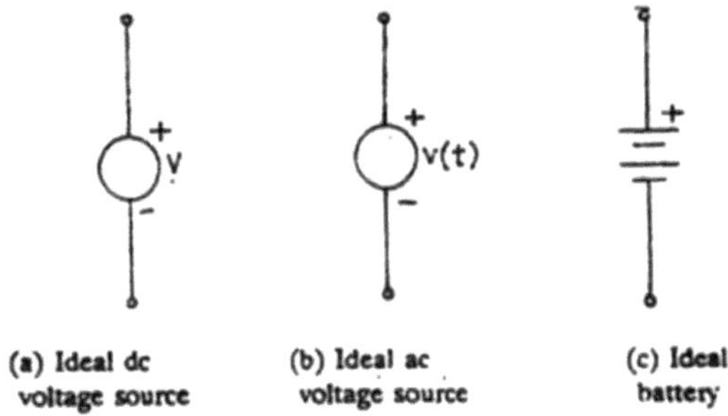

(a) Ideal dc voltage source   (b) Ideal ac voltage source   (c) Ideal battery

Practical voltage source.

Almost every practical voltage source falls short of the ideal and its terminal voltage falls with increase of the load current. A practical voltage source, therefore, may be approximated as an ideal voltage source with a series resistance R_S in case of dc source or with a series impedance Z_S in the case of an ac voltage source. This series impedance, called the internal impedance of the source, then accounts for the fall in terminal voltage with increase of load current. Symbol for a practical voltage source is, therefore, the same as for an ideal voltage source with the addition of resistor R_S (or impedance Z_S) as shown in figure.

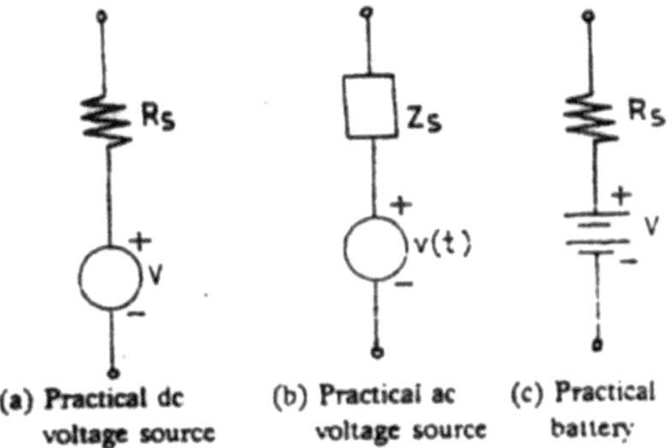

(a) Practical dc voltage source   (b) Practical ac voltage source   (c) Practical battery

Ideal current source.

An ideal current source generates current of a given time variation but neither the magnitude nor the time variation of the generated current changes with the load current. Thus the output current of this source remains constant for all values of load ranging from zero resistance to infinite resistance. If this ideal current source gives zero output current, the source reduces to just an open circuit. The requirement of constant current in an ideal current source can be satisfied only if it has zero internal series impedance or infinite shunt impedance.

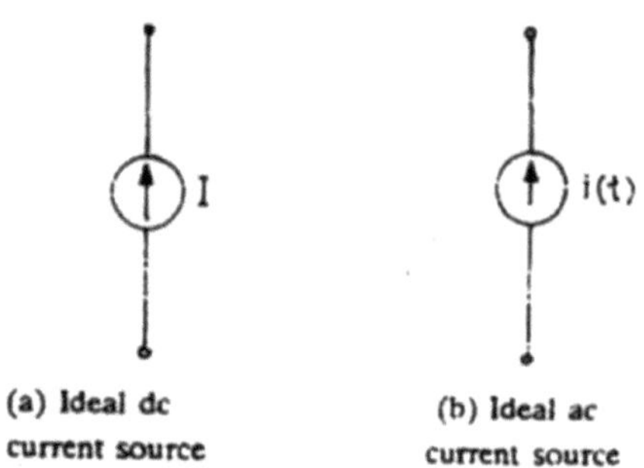

The symbol for ideal current source is generally a circle with an associated arrow indicating the positive direction of current flow as shown in below figure. In this case also, upper case letter I indicates the dc current source while the lower case letter i or i (t) indicates the time varying source. Further approximate time variation of current is sometimes sketched within the circle.

Practical current source.

Every practical current source falls short of the ideal and its output current falls with the increase of load resistance (or impedance). Hence a practical current source may be approximated as an ideal current source with a shunt resistor in case of dc current source and a shunt impedance in case of an ac current source. This shunt impedance then accounts for the fall of output load current with increase of load impedance. Symbol for a practical current source is the same as that for the corresponding ideal current source with a shunt resistance (impedance) as shown in figure.

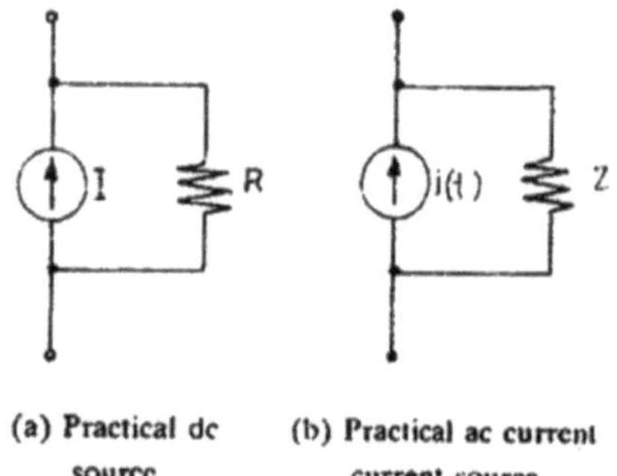

NET WORK ANALYSIS

Network analysis consists in finding the response (or output) when stimulus (or input) and the network components are given

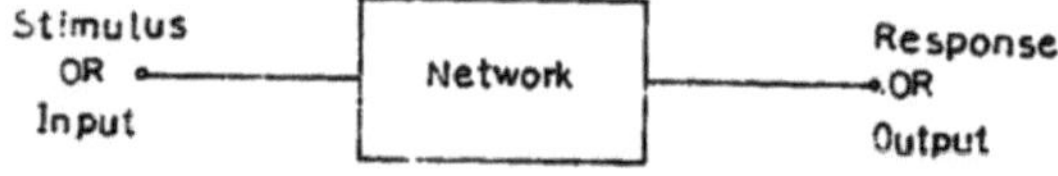

Fig. Factors involved in network analysis

APPROACHES TO NETWORK ANALYSIS.

There are two general approaches to network analysis

1.   DIRECT METHOD.

Here the network is left in its original form and the currents and voltages in different elements of the network are determined using a standard method of analysis such as loop analysis or node analysis. In addition use is made of Kirchhoff's laws and different network theorems such as superposition theorem, compensation theorem, reciprocity theorem etc. Such a direct approach is generally used in case of relatively simple networks.

Kirchhoff's laws.

There are two laws given by Kirchhoff namely Kirchhoff's current law and Kirchhoff's voltage law.

(*i*)   **Kirchhoff's Current Law (KCL)** : It states that in any electrical circuit,the algebraic sum of current meeting at a point (or node) is zero.

If we take the current component convergent (entering) at the node as positive and current component divergent (leaving) at the node as negative, then KCL implies that :

at any zunction (node) in electrical circuit, the sum of current components entering the junction equals the sum of the current components leaving the junction.

This statement is true for any point because there can not be continued accumulation of charges or continued depletion of charges. Symbolically we may write, $\Sigma \pm j = 0$

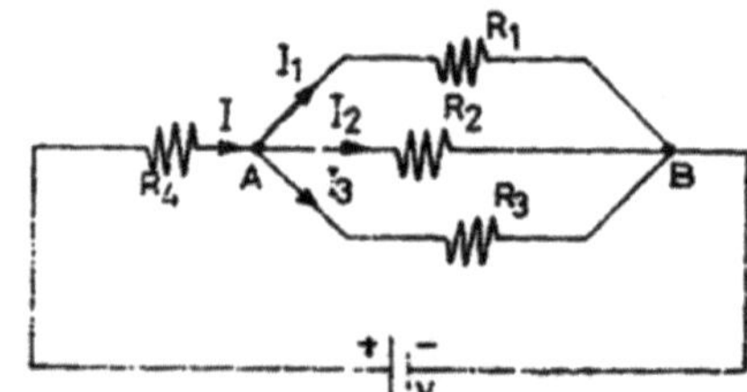

Above figure shows a simple electrical network with one energy source V. At node A, current I enters the node while currents I_1, I_2 and I_3 leave the node A.

Obviously then as per KCL,

$$I + (-I_1) + (-I_2) + (-I_3) = 0$$

or $\quad\quad I = I_1 + I_2 + I_3$

In the circuit of figure, directions of current components. In a complicated network, we do not know the actual directions of all current components at any specific node. In that case, we arbitrarily assign directions to the current components and analyze the network to find the values of these current components. If the value of any current component comes out to be positive, then its actural direction is the same as the assigned direction. On the other hand, if any current component is found to be negative, then its actual direction. On the other hand, if any current component is found to be negative, then its actual direction is opposite to assigned direction.

(ii) Kirchhoff's Voltage Law (KVL) :

It states that : *the algebraic sum of potential rises (or potential drops) in any set of branches forming a closed circuit or loop is always zero.*

Symbolically we may write, $\Sigma \pm v = 0$

The validity of kVL is quite obvious. Thus starting from any node, as we travel along a closed path and come back to the same node, the net voltage drop or the net voltage rise must be sero

Use of sign + or – : In the above equation, plus sign may be used for voltage rise and minus sign may be used for voltage drop (alternatively opposite notation may be used). Thus while we move along the closed path along the current in any branch, there results a voltage drop across the resisitor R and a – sign may be used as shown in Fig. (*a*). Thus voltage rise from A to B is (–jR) . On the other hand, if we travel opposite to the current in any branch, there results a voltage rise and + sign may be used as shown below in Fig. (*b*). Thus voltage rise from A to B is + jR.

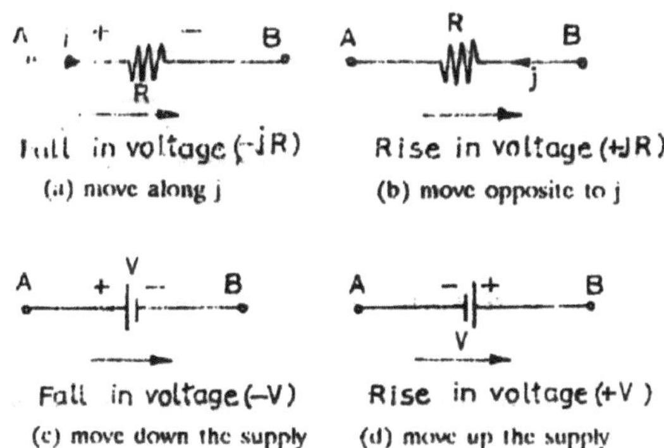

As an illustration, consider the loop ABCD in the network of figure and travel along ABCDA in this loop.

Then

$j_1 R_1$ is a voltage fall and hence negative

$j_2 R_2$ is a voltage fall and hence negative

$j_3 R_3$ is a voltage rise and hence positive

$j_4 R_4$ is a voltage fall and hence negaitve

V_2 is a voltage fall and hence negative

V_1 is a voltage rise and hence positive

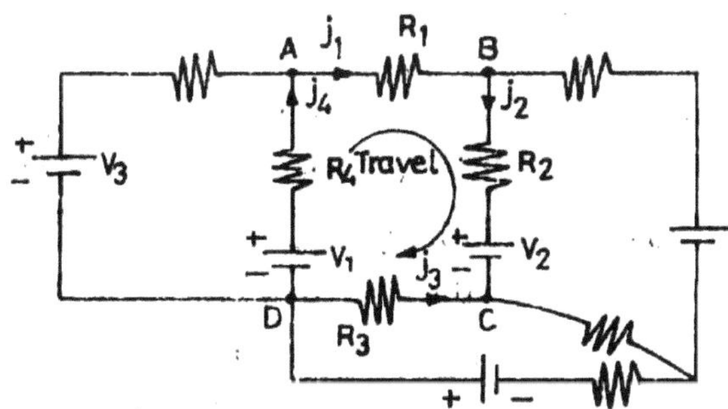

Then application of kVL gives

$$-j\,R_1 - j_2\,R_2 + j_3\,R_3 - j_4\,R_4 - V_2 + V_1 = 0$$
$$\text{or } V_1 - V_2 = j_1\,R_1 + j_2\,R_2 - j_3\,R_3 + j_4\,R_4$$

Note : Kirchhoff's laws are applicable to both dc and ac circuits.

2. NETWORK REDUCTION METHOD.

In this case, network is first reduced to a simple equivalent circuit and then analysis is done. This method is generally applied for relatively complicated network but may as well be applied to simpler equivalent network. Such reduction method typically makes use of Delta/star conversion, star/Delta conversion, Thevenin's theorem, Norton's theorem etc.

THEVENIN'S THEOREM.

Several networks involve a number of voltage or current sources. In certain cases, analysis of the complete network is not needed and we are required to find the correct values of voltages and currents in a restricted portion of the network referred to as the load. Then we replace the actual sources of energy by a *single equivalent voltage source* acting at a terminal pair. The term *equivalent* implies that we will obtain the same voltages and currents throughout the restricted network as those obtained with the actual sources present. Thevenin's theorem provides method of source transformation whereby distributed sources of both voltage type and current type may be replaced by an equivalent voltage source acting at the desired terminal pair.

Thevenin's theorem states that:

The current I_L which flows from a given linear active network A (may be with initial currents and voltages) to a passive network B (not inductively coupled to network A) usually referred to as the load, is the same as one which flows to the same network B when connected to a network (called Thevenin's equivalent of network A) constituted by a voltage source V_{OC} with internal series impedance Z_g.

Here V_{OC} is the open circuit voltage of network A at load terminals and Z_g is the impedance of network A seen looking backa the load terminals with all energy sources replaced by their internal impedances.

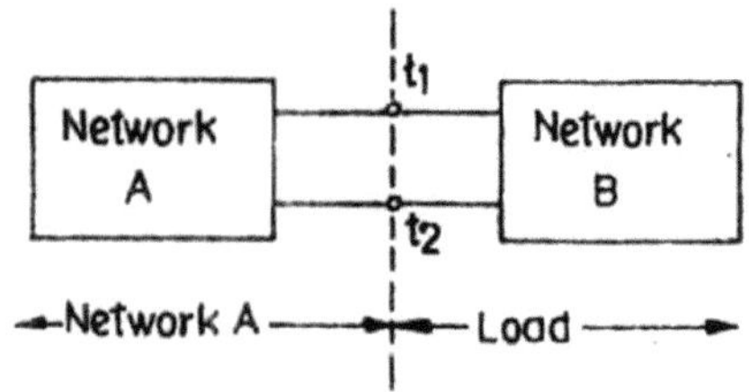

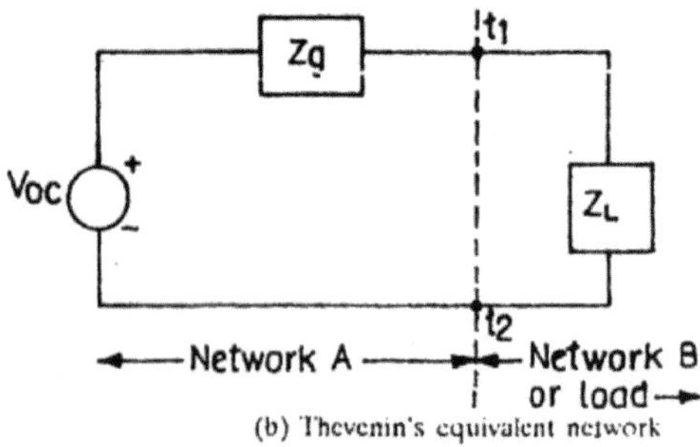

(a) An active network A connected to passive network (load) B

(b) Thevenin's equivalent network

Fig. An active network and its Thevenin's equivalent

Thevenin's theorem permits solution of complicated networks quite quickly and easily. Thus as seen from the load terminals t_1– t_2, the whole network A (excluding the load impedance Z_L) may be reduced to a single voltage source (called *Thevenin's source*) V_{OC} or V_{th} with internal impedance Z_g (or R_{th}). Thus above figure (a) shows the active network A connected to passive network (load) B while above fig. (B) shows the Thevenin's equivalent network for actual network A connected to load Z_L.

Steps involved in applying thevenin's Theorem :

(1) Disconnect the load impedance Z_L from the circuit at terminals say t_1- t_2

(2) Find the open circuit voltage V_{OC} which appears across the terminals t_1- t_2 looking into the circuit. This V_{OC} constitutes the Thevenin's voltage V_{th}

(3) Short circuit every voltage source leaving behind its services internal impedance. Similarly open circuit every currents source leaving behind the internal impedance. Compute the impedance of the circuit looking into the circuit from terminals t_1-t_2. Let this impedance be Z_g or Z_{th}.

(4) Replace the entire network by a single equivalent Thevenin's voltage source of voltage V_{th} (or V_{OC}) with internal impedance Z_{th} (or Z_g) in its series.

(5) Connect the load impedance Z_L at terminals t_1- t_2

(6) Calculate the current I_L flowing through Z_L using the equation

$$I_I = \frac{V_{th}}{Z_{th} + Z_L}$$

Example. Using Thevenin's theorem find the voltage across resistor R_4 in the given circuit.

Solution.

(*i*) **Finding V_{OC} :** We remove resistor R_4 thereby open circuiting terminals t_1- t_2 resulting in the circuit of Fig. (a) No current now flows through resistor R_2.

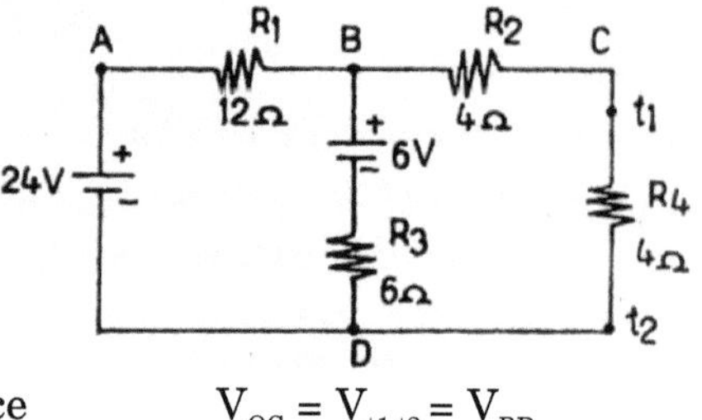

Hence $\qquad V_{OC} = V_{t1\,t2} = V_{BD}$

Current I flows in the circuit ABDA.

Net driving voltage = 24 – 6 = 18 volt.

Total resistance = 12 + 6 = 18Ω

∴ $\qquad\qquad$ I = 18 volts/ 18Ω = 1 A.

Voltage drop across R_3 = 1× 6 = 6 volts

∴ $\qquad\qquad V_{BD}$ = 6 + 6 = 12 volts.

Hence $\qquad\qquad V_{OC} = V_{th}$ = 12 volt

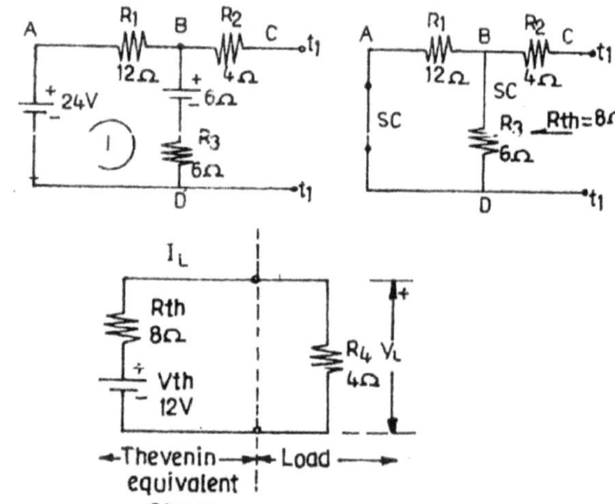

(*ii*) **Finding R_{th}** Next we replace the two batteries by short circuits since their internal series resistances are zero. Fig (b) gives the resulting circuit. Then Rth = 4 + 6 ǀ ǀ 12 = 8Ω

(*iii*) **Finding potential drop across R4** fig (c) gives the Thevenin's equivalent circuit with R4 again connected across terminals t_1-t_2.

Then using proportional voltage formula voltage across resistance R_4 is, V_L = 12 volt × 4Ω/ (4 + 8) Ω

= 4volts

NORTON'S THEOREM.

Norton's theorem states that :

The current I_L which flows from a given linear active network A (may be with initial currents and voltages) to a passive network B (not inductively coupled to

network A) usually referred to as the load, is the same as one which flows to the same network B when connected to a network (called Norton's equivalent of network A) constituted by a current source I_{SC} with internal shunt impedance Z_g.

Here I_{SC} is the short circuit current of network A at load terminals and Z_g is the impedance of network A (in shunt with the current source) seen looking back from the load terminals with all energy sources replaced by their internal impedances.

Norton's theorem is dual of Thevenin's theorem and similar to Thevenin's theorem it also holds good for the current in the load impedance only and not for currents within the network.

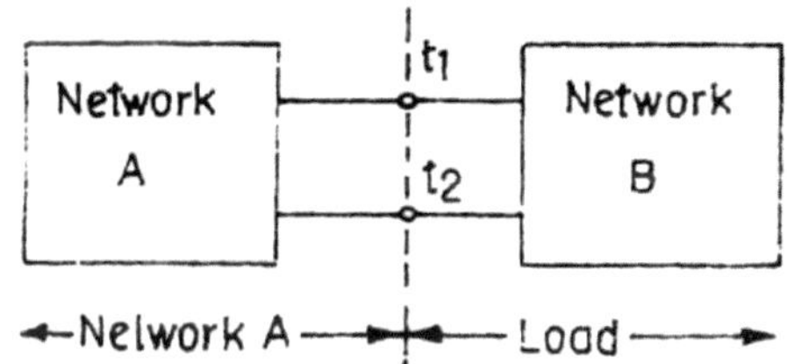

(a) An active network A connected to passive network (load) B

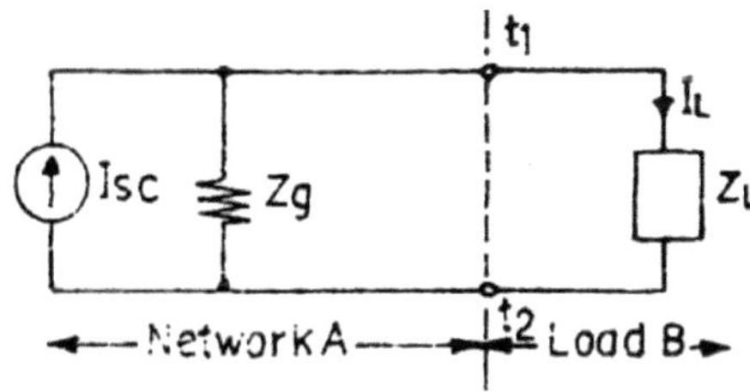

(b) Norton's equivalent network

Norton's theorem permits solution of complicated network quite quickly and easily. Thus as seen from the load terminals t_1-t_2, the whole network A (excluding the load impedance) may be reduced to a single current source (called Norton's source I_{SC} or I_N), with internal impedance Z_g (or Z_N). Thus Fig 3.9 9a) shows the active network A connected the passive network (or load) B while above figure (b) shows the Norton's equivalent network for actual network A connected to load impedance Z_L.

Steps involved in applying norton's theorem.

(1) Disconnect the load impedance Z_L from the circuit at terminals says t_1-t_2 and put a short circuit across t_1-t_2.

(2) Determine the short circuit current I_{SC}. This constitutes the Norton's current I_n.

(3) Short circuit every voltage source leaving behind its series internal impedance. Similarly open circuit every current source leaving behind its shunt internal impedance.

(4) Compute the impedance of the circuit looking into the circuit from the terminal t_1 -t_2. Let this

impedance be Z_g or Z_n. This is exactly the same as obtained on application of Thevenin's theorem.

(5) Replace the entire network by current source I_{SC} (or I_n) with internal impedance Z_g (or Z_n) in its parallel.

(6) Remove the short circuit across t_1-t_2 and connect the load impedance Z_L at terminals t_1-t_2.

(7) Calculate the load current through Z_L using the following equation

$$I_L = I_{SC} \frac{Z_g}{Z_g + Z_L}$$

Example. Determine the Norton's equivalent circuit between terminals A-B in th given circuit

Solution.

Place a short circuit across terminals A-B. This short circuits resistor R_2.

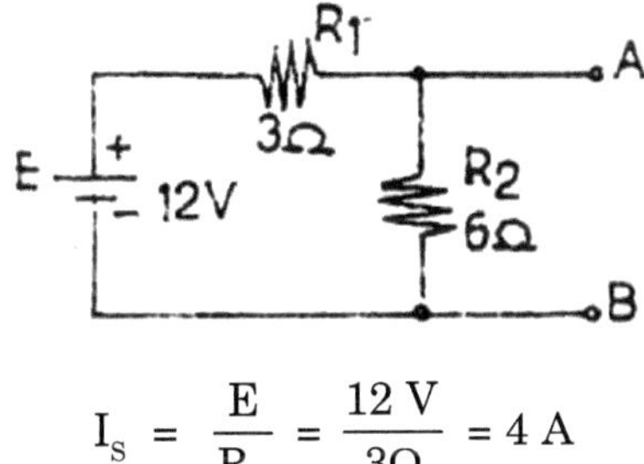

$$\therefore \qquad I_S = \frac{E}{R_I} = \frac{12\ V}{3\Omega} = 4\ A$$

To find Z_g we replace the battery by short circuit and look into the circuit from terminals A-B. Then we find R_1 and R_2 in parallel.

$$\therefore \qquad Z_g = R_1 \| R_2 = 3\Omega \| 6\Omega = 2\ \Omega$$

Hence Norton's equivalent circuit is as shown in Fig. (a)

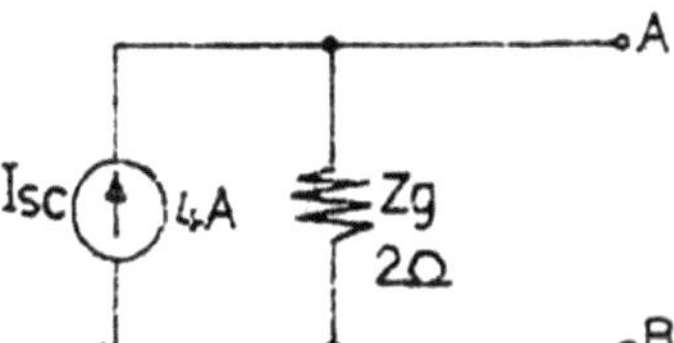

BASIC MAGNETISM
MAGNETIC MATERAIALS.

Any substance which has the property of being attracted by or attracting the magnet is called magnetic material.

Types of magnetic materials.

On the basis of magnetic properties, all materials may be divided into three classes:

(i) **Ferro-magnetic.**

The materials, which are strongly attracted by a magnet such as iron, steel, nickel, cobalt and some of their alloys, are called ferro-magnetic materials. Their relative permeability is very high (varying from several hundreds to several thousands.)

(*ii*) Para-magnetic.

The materials, which are not strongly attracted by a magnet, such as aluminium, tin, platinum, magnesium, manganese etc. are called para-magnetic materials. Their relative permeability is slightly higher than unity. These are slightly magnetised when placed in a strong magnetic field and act in the direction of the magnetic field.

(*iii*) Dia-magnetic.

The materials, which are repelled by a magnet, such as zinc, mercury, lead, sulphur, copper, silver etc. are called *diamagnetic*. Their relative permeability is slightly less than unity. These are slightly magnetised when placed in a strong magnetic field and act in the opposite direction of the magnetic field.

Note : The materials under class (*ii*) and (*iii*) are called non-magnetic materials.

Magnetic field.

The space around the poles of a magnet is called *magnetic field*, and is represented by magnetic lines of force. The space around a lode stone, around a compass needle, around the earth, and around a permanent magnet are examples of magnetic fields.

MAGNETIC FORCE.

The force exerted on one magnet by another one, either of attraction or repulsion is called *magnetic force*.

Coulomb's laws of magnetic force.

According to Coulomb's first law unlike poles attract each other and like poles repel each other.

According to Coulomb's second law the force between two magnetic poles

(*i*) is directly proportional to the product of their pole strengths

(*ii*) inversely proportional to the square of the distance between them, and

(*iii*) depends on the medium in which the poles are placed.

Mathematically force between two magnetic poles m_1 and m_2 placed distance d apart is

$$F = k \frac{m_1 m_2}{d^2}$$

where k is any constant, whose value depends upon the surrounding medium and the system of units employed.

In RMKSA of SI system, the force is measured in newtons, distance in metres, pole strength in webers and the force experienced is given as

$$F = \frac{1}{4\pi\mu_0\mu_r} \cdot \frac{m_1 m_2}{d^2}$$

where μ_0 = permeability of the evacuated space or air = $4\pi \times 10^{-7}$

μ_r = relative permeability of the medium with respect to evacuated space or air.

Relative permeability (μ_r).

Relative permeability of the medium (μ_r) is difined as the ratio of the forces between two magnetic poles placed at a certain distance in air to the force between them placed at the same distance in that medium.

Magnetic field strength.

The magnetic field intensity at any point is defined as the force experienced by a unit north pole placed at that point. It is represented by H. It is a vector quantity.

Magnetic potential.

The magnetic potential at any point in the magnetic field is defined as the work required to move unit (one weber) north pole from infinity to that point against the magnetic force. It is a scalar quantity, i.e. it has magnitude only.

Lines of magnetic flux.

Magnetic line of force is defined as the curve along which a unit N-pole would move if free to do so, when placed in a magnetic field. The tangent to these curves at any point gives the direction of magnetic field at that point.

Lines of induction.

Lines of magnetic flux travel from N-pole to S-pole externally, and continue to travel through the magnet and finally they reach the N-pole again forming closed curves. The portion of the curves within the magnetic material are called the lines of induction.

Magnetic flux.

Magnetic flux is the total number of lines of force comprising the magnetic field. In R M K S A or SI system unit north pole i.e. north pole of strength of one weber is supposed to radiate out the flux of one weber. It is represented by symbol ϕ and is measured in webers.

Magnetic flux density.

Magnetic flux density is the flux passing per unit area through any material through a plane at right angles to the direction of flux. It is represented by B and is measured in teslas (wb/m^2).

Mathematically $\quad B = \phi/a$

Also $\qquad\qquad B = \mu_r \mu_o H$

where $\quad \mu_o = 4\pi \times 10^{-7}$ H/m

$\qquad \mu_r$ = relative permeability of the material of the bar magnet

$\qquad H$ = magnetic field strength.

Magnetic moment (M).

It is the product of strength of one of the poles and magnetic length of bar magnet.

$$M = 2\,ml$$

where m = pole strength and

$\quad 2l$ = length of bar magnet.

Intensity of magnetisation (J).

It is defined as the magnetic moment per unit voulume. It may also be defined as the pole strength per unit area, *i.e.*

$$J = \frac{m}{a}$$

Susceptibility (k).

It is the ratio of intensity of magnetisation J to the magnetising force H.

Mathematically, $\quad k = \dfrac{J}{H}$ H/m

Also, $\qquad\qquad \mu_r = 1 + \dfrac{k}{\mu_o}$

MAGNETIC FIELD DUE TO A CURRENT CARRYING CONDUCTOR.

When a conductor carries an electric current, a magnetic field is produced all along its length. The magnetic lines of force form concentric circles around the conductor. The direction of current and the direction of magnetic field are at right angles to each other. The magnitude of the magnetic field associated with a current carrying conductor depends upon the magnitude of current and its direction depends upon the direction of flow of current.

The direction of lines of force (magnetic field) around a straight current carrying conductor can be determined by any of the following rules.

(i) Ampere's rule.

If an observer imagines himself the electric circuit, with the current flowing in the direction from feet to his head, then on facing the compass needle the north pole will be deflected towards his left.

(ii) Cork screw rule.

If the right handed cork screw is held with its axis parallel to the conductor pointing the direction of flow of current and the head of the screw is rotated in such a direction that the screw moves in the direction of flow of current, then direction in which the head of screw is rotated, will be the direction of magnetic field or lines of force.

(iii) Right hand rule.

If the current carrying conductor is held in right hand by the observer so that it is encircled by fingers stretching the thumb at right angle to the fingers in the direction of flow of current then finger tips will point the direction of magnetic lines of force.

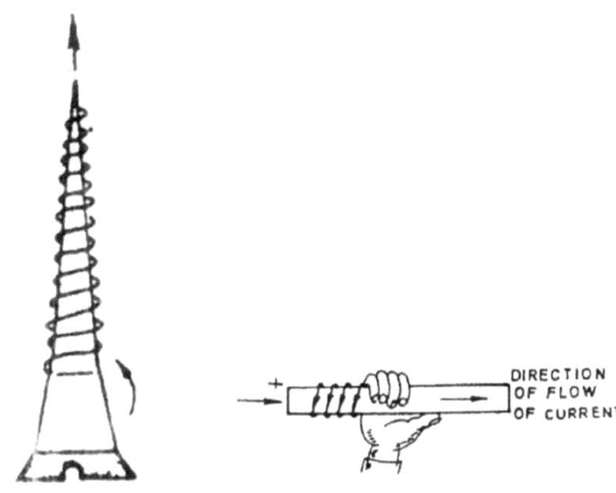

(a) Cork screw rule $\qquad$ **(b)** Right hand rule

MAGNETIC FIELD DUE TO A CIRCULAR LOOP.

If a single turn wire carrying current is bent in the form of loop, direction of magnetic field may be determined by applying either of the following two rules

(*i*) Right hand rule

(*ii*) Cork screw rule

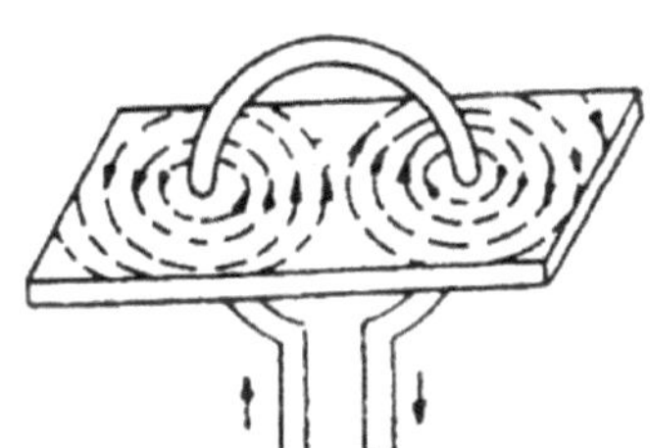

The line of force are concentric and are always at right angle to the wire.

The loop acts as the true magnet having north and south poles.

SOLENOID.

The current carrying wire wound spirally in the form of helix about an axis, as shown in the figure is called *solenoid or coil.* Magnetic field produced due to the current carrying solenoid is fairly uniform over a small region in the middle of the coil. It acts just like a bar magnet having north and south poles.

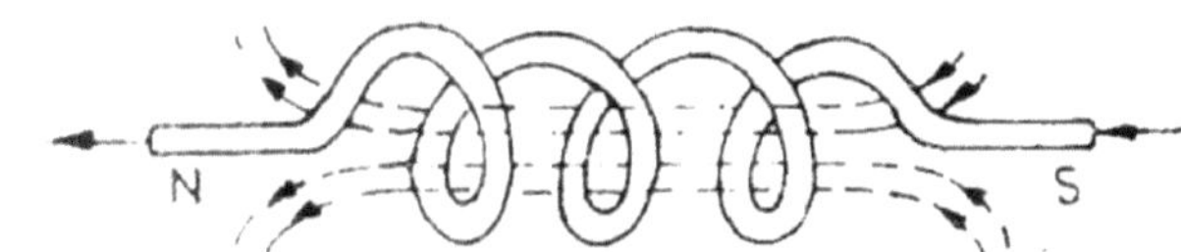

Methods to determine polarity of the solenoid.

(i) By use of compass needle.

If one of the poles (say north pole) of the campass needle be brought into close proximity to one of the poles of the current carrying solenoid of unknown polarity the action of the compass needle will immediately classify the pole as north or south depending upon whether the needle is repelled or attracted.

(ii) Helix rule.

If the helix is held in right hand in such a manner that the finger tips point in the direction of flow of current and thumb is out stretched longitudinally along the coil, it will point towards North pole.

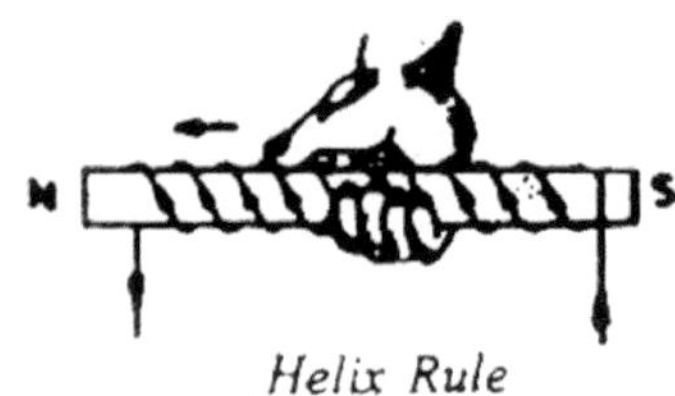

Helix Rule

Biot-Savart's law : *According to this law, magneitc field at a point P due to an incremental element of length δl carrying a current I is directly proportional to*

(i) length of the element, δl

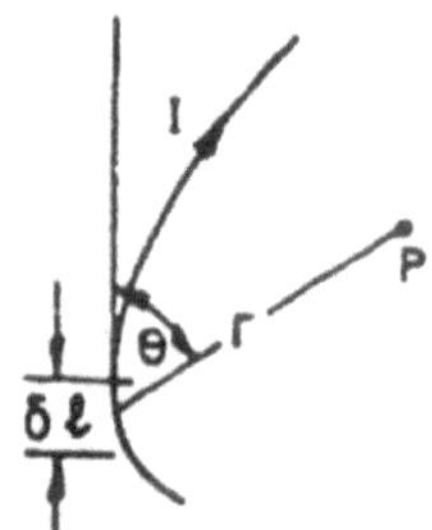

(ii) current carried by the element, I

(iii) sine of the angle θ between the line joining the point P with the length δl and

(iv) inversely proportional to the square of the distance of the given point from the current element r.

Mathematically field intensity, $\delta H = \dfrac{I\delta l \sin\theta}{4\pi r^2}$

FORCE ON A CURRENT CARRYING CONDUCTOR LYING IN THE MAGNETIC FIELD.

When a current carrying conductor is placed at right angle to the direction of magnetic field, a mechanical force is experienced on the conductor in a direction perpendicular to both the directions of magnetic field and flow of current.

The force experienced on the conductor is directly proportional to

(i) flux density (field strength), B

(ii) current flowing through the conductor I, and

(iii) length of the conductor, l.

Magnitude of the force(in newton), F = B Il

where B is in teslas (wb/m²), I is in amperes and l is in metres.

In general if the conductor lies at an angle θ with a magnetic field of flux density B webers/metre², then mechanical force experienced on a current carrying conductor is given by

$$F = B\,I\,l \sin\theta \text{ Newtons}$$

where l = length if the conductor in metres

I = current carried by the conductor in amperes.

The direction of this force can be determined by applying Fleming's Left Hand Rule

If thumb, fore finger and middle finger of the left hand are stretched in such a way that they are at right angles to each other mutually and fore-finger points towards the direction of the magnetic field, middle finger towards the direction in of the flow of current then thumb will point the directon of mechanical force acting on the conductor.

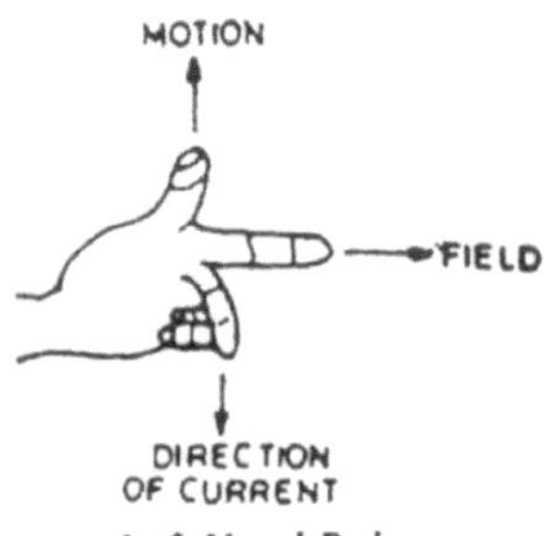

Left Hand Rule

If the current in the conductor is reversed, keeping the direction of magnetic field unchanged, the direction of force will reverse. In the same way if the direction of magnetic field is reversed, keeping the direction of flow of current in the conductor unchanged, the direction of force will reverse.

Field strength at a point due to long straight conductors (N in number) carrying current of I amperes is

$$B = \frac{\mu_o NI}{2\pi r} \text{ teslas in air}$$

where r = perpendicular distance of the point from the conductors.

Field strength at the centre of a circular coil of radius a metres, having N turns and carrying a current of I amperes is

$$H = \frac{NI}{2a} \text{ AT/m}$$

Field strength due to a solenoid having length l metres, turns N and current I amperes is

$$H = \frac{NI}{l} \text{ AT/m}$$

FORCE BETWEEN TWO PARALLEL CURRENT CARRYING CONDUCTORS.

When two parallel conductors carry current in the same diection (say in downward direction), as shown in Fig. (a), lines of force encircle each conductor in the same direction and the resultant field is an envelope acting like elastic bands tending to pull the conductors together.

When two parallel conductors carry current in the opposite directions, as shown in Fig. (b), then lines of force encircle but not concentric either with another or with the conductors. The lines of force are crowded between the conductors tending to repel the conductors further apart.

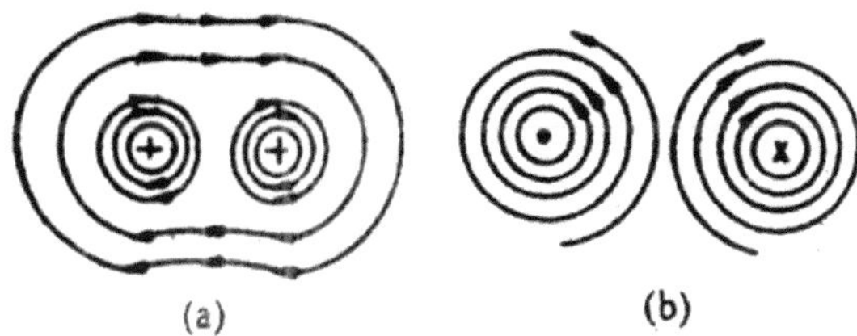

The magnitude of force acting between two conductors each of length l metres carrying currents I_1 and I_2 amperes respectively and having a distance of d metres from each other is

$$F = \frac{2\,I_1 I_2}{d}\, l \times 10^{-7}\ N$$

In above expression if $I_1 = I_2 = 1A$, $d = 1$ m and $l = 1m$, it follows that force per metre length of conductors is 2×10^{-7} N. This value forms the basis for the definition of the ampere.

Thus the ampere is defined as that current which if maintained in two straight parallel conductors of infinite length, of negligible circular cross-section, and placed 1 metre apart in a vacuum, would produce between these conductors a force of 2×10^{-7} N/m of length.

Ampere turns.

In any magnetic circuit,

$$\text{flux created, } \phi = \frac{\text{mmf}}{\text{reluctance}} = \frac{AT}{l/\mu_o\mu_r a}$$

$$\text{or } AT \text{ required} = \frac{\phi}{a} \cdot \frac{1}{\mu_o\mu_r} \times l = \frac{B}{\mu_o\mu_r} \times l = H \times l$$

ampere-turns

Determination of AT for a magnetic circuit :

(i) Find field strength H in each part of the magnetic circuit.

(ii) Find length of various parts of magnetic circuit

(iii) Find number of ampere-turns required for the various parts of magnetic circuit from the relation AT = H l

where l = length of the part in metres,

(iv) Find total number of ampere-turns for the whole series magnetic circuit by adding ampere-turns determined for various paths in magnetic circuit.

Magnetic leakage.

Leakage flux is the flux, which follows a leaking path. Flux in the air gap is called useful flux which is utilised for various useful purposes. For the purpose of calculations the iron is supposed to carry whole of the flux throughout its entire length.

Leakage factor.

The ratio of total flux (flux in the iron path) to the useful flux (flux in the air gap) is called leakage factor.

$$\text{Leakage factor} = \frac{\text{Total flux}}{\text{Useful flux}}$$

or

$$\text{Leakage factor} = \frac{\text{Flux in the iron path}}{\text{Flux in the air gap}}$$

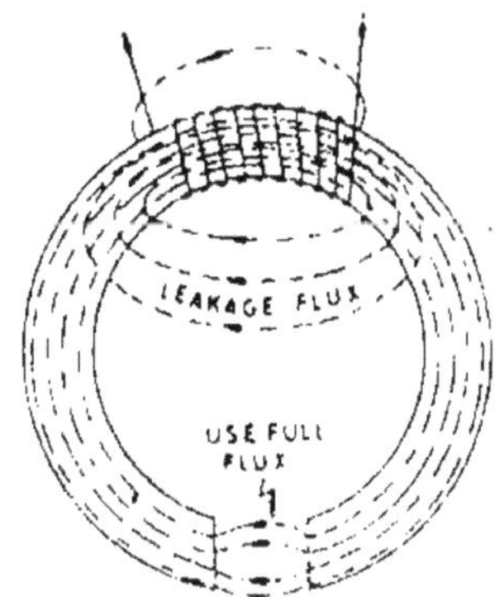

Fringing.

Useful flux passing across the gap tends to bulge outwards, thereby increasing effective area of the gap and reducing flux density in the gap. This effect is referred to as fringing; and longer the air gap, greater is the fringing.

ELECTRO-MAGNETIC INDUCTION

The phenomenon whereby an emf and hence current is induced in any conductor which is cut across or is cut by a magnetic flux is called *electro-magnetic induction*.

Faraday's laws of Electro-magnetic induction.

Faraday's first law :

This law states that, when the flux linking with the coil or circuit changes an emf is induced in it or whenever the magnetic flux is cut by the conductor an emf is induced in the conductor.

Faraday's second law :

This law states that, magnitude of emf induced is directly proportional to the rate of change of flux linking the coil.

i.e induced emf $\propto N \cdot \dfrac{d\phi}{dt}$

where $N \dfrac{d\phi}{dt}$ is product of number of turns and rate of change of linking flux and is called rate of change of flux linkage.

Lenz's law.

The law states that, direction of induced emf is such that the current produced by it sets up a magnetic field opposing the motion or change producing it.

$$\therefore \quad \text{Induced emf, } e = -N \frac{d\phi}{dt}$$

INDUCED EMF.

EMF can be induced by changing the linking flux in two ways:

1. **Dynamically induced EMF.**

   This is induced by moving a conductor in a uniform magnetic field and emf produced in this way is known as dynamically induced emf.

   When a conductor of length l metres is moved in a magnetic field of strength B wb/m² with a velocity v m/s in a direction perpendicular to its own length and at an angle θ to the direciton of magnetic field, the induced emf will be given as

   $$e = B\, l\, v \sin \theta \text{ volts}$$

   The direction of this induced emf is given by Fleming's right hand rule. If thumb, fore-finger and middle finger of right hand are held mutually perpendicular to each other, fore-finger pointing into the direction of the field and thumb in the direction of motion then middle finger will point in the direction of the induced emf.

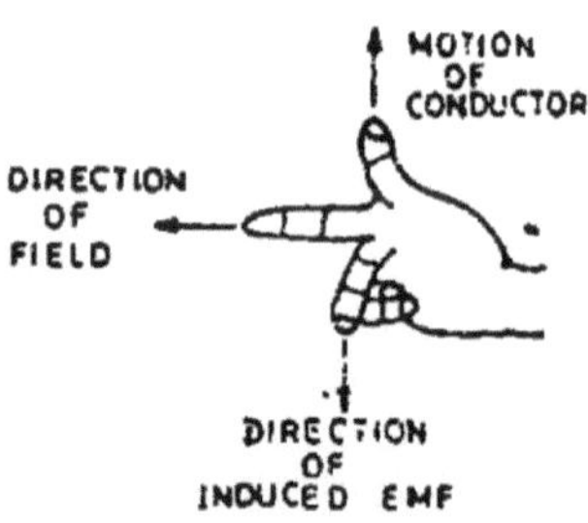

2. **Statically induced emf.**

   Increasing or decreasing the magnitude of the current producing the linking flux. In this case there is no motion of the conductor or of coil relative to the field.

   TYPE OF STATICALLY INDUCED EMF.

   (*i*) Self induced EMF.

   When the current flowing through the coil is changed, then flux linking with its own winding changes and due to the change in linking flux with the coil, an emf called self induced emf is induced.

   Since according to Lenz's law, any induced emf acts to oppose the change that produces it, a self induced emf is always in such a direction

as to oppose the change of current in the coil or circuit in which it is induced. This property of the coil or circuit due to which it opposes any change of the current in the coil or circuit, is called *self-inductance.*

Self induced emf in a solenoid of N turns, length l metres, area of cross-section a square metres and of relative permeability μ_r when the current flowing through the solenoid is changed is given as

$$\text{Self induced emf, } e = -\frac{N^2 \mu_r \mu_o a}{l} \cdot \frac{di}{dt}$$

The quantity $\dfrac{N^2 \mu_r \mu_o a}{l}$ is a constant for any given coil or circuit and is called *coefficient of self-inductance.* It is represented by symbol L and is measured in henrys.

$$\therefore \quad \text{self induced emf, } e = -L\frac{di}{dt}$$

where, $L = \dfrac{N^2 \mu_r \mu_o a}{l}$ henrys

Coefficient of self induction (L) can be determined from any of the following three relations.

$$L = \frac{N^2 \mu_r \mu_o a}{l} \text{ henrys}; \quad L = \frac{e}{di/dt} \text{ henrys};$$

$$L = \frac{N\phi}{i} \text{ henrys}$$

(*ii*) Mutually induced EMF :

The phenomenon of generation of induced emf in a coil by changing the current in the neighbouring coil is called the *mutual induction* and emf so induced is called mutually induced emf.

The mutually induced emf in a solenoid B of N_2 turns, placed nearby another coil A of N_1 turns, length l metres, area of cross-section a square metres and of relative permeability μ_r when the current flowing through coil A is changed is given as

$$\text{Mutually induced emf, } e_m = \frac{N_1 N_2 \mu_r \mu_o a}{l} \cdot \frac{di}{dt}$$

assuming that whole of the flux produced due to flow of current in coil A is linking with coil B.

The quantity $\dfrac{N_1 N_2 \mu_r \mu_o a}{l}$ is called *coefficient of mutual induction of coil B with respect to coil* A. It is represented by symbol M and is measured in henrys.

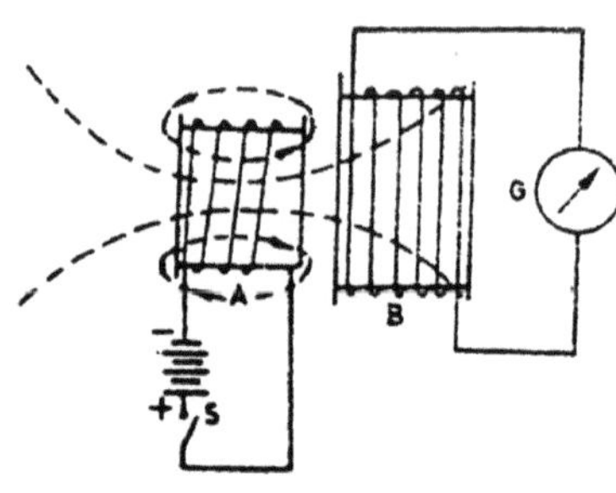

$\therefore$ Mutually induced emf $e_m = - M \dfrac{di_1}{dt}$

where, $M = \dfrac{N_1 N_2 \mu_r \mu_o a}{l}$ henrys.

Coefficient of mutual induction (M) can be determined from any of the following three relations.

$$M = \frac{N_1 N_2 \mu_r \mu_o a}{l} \text{ henrys}; \quad M = \frac{e}{di_1 / dt} \text{ henrys};$$

$$M = \frac{N_2 \phi_2}{i} \text{ henrys}$$

COEFFICIENT OF COUPLING.

When two coils are placed near each other, all the flux produced by one coil does not link the other coil, only a certain portion (say K) of flux produced by one coil links with the other coil, K being less than unity. K is called *coefficient of coupling*.

The coefficient of coupling between two coils having self inductances L_1 and L_2 respectively and mutual inductance M is given as

$$K = \frac{M}{\sqrt{L_1 L_2}}$$

When coils are tightly coupled, *i.e.* when flux due to one coil links with the other coil completely, then coefficient of coupling, K is unity. If flux due to one coil does not link with the other coil at all, then value of coefficient of coupling is zero.

INDUCTANCES IN SERIES AND PARALLEL.

(*i*) Inductances in series.

When coils are connected in series such that their fluxes (or mmf) are additive i.e. in the same direction, then equivalent inductance of the combination is given as

$$L = L_1 + L_2 + 2M$$

where L_1 and L_2 = coefficients of self induction of coils A and B respectively

M = coefficient of mutual induction.

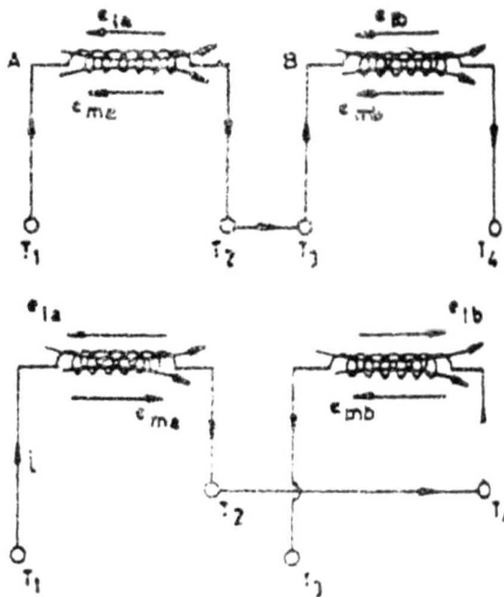

When coils are connected in series in such a way that their fluxes (or mmfs) are subtractive, *i.e.* in opposite directions, then equivalent inductance is given as

$$L = L_1 + L_2 - 2M$$

(*ii*) Inductances in parallel.

When two coils of self inductances L_1 and L_2 and mutual inductance M are connected in parallel, then equivalent inductance of the combination is given as

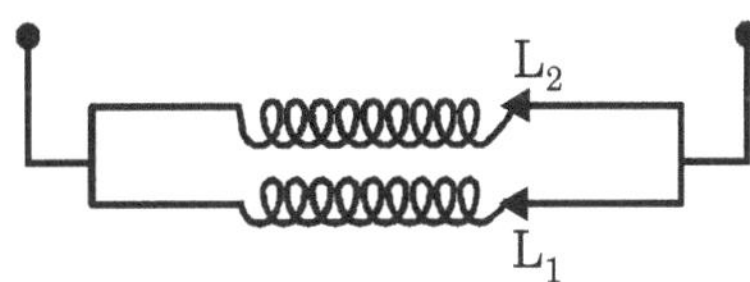

When mutual flux helps the individual flux, then

$$L = \frac{L_1 L_2 - M^2}{L_1 + L_2 - 2M}$$

When mutual flux opposes the individual flux, then

$$L = \frac{L_1 L_2 - M^2}{L_1 + L_2 + 2M}$$

KEY POINTS

A.C.

AC stands for alternating current which can be a stand by power (low voltage varistor surge arresters). Varistor A.C. power dissipation is measured at rated r.m.s. (root mean square) value.

The current whose magnitude and direction remain changing at a definite rate is called *alternating current* or AC.

Cycle and frequency

Variations of an alternating quantity through 360° are called *a cycle* and number of cycles completed per second by an alternating quantity is called *frequency*.

Frequency is measured in hertz (Hz) and its popular multiples arc kilo hertz (KHz) and mega hertz (MHz).

Sinusoidal wave

A graphical representation of the sine values of die phase angles of an alternating quantity with respect to lime axis is called *sinusoidal wave*.

Anderson's Bridge

It is a Bridge method of measuring inductance in which inductance to be measured is included in one bridge arm with a condenser between opposite battery terminal and a point between galvanometer and a resistance in series with it.

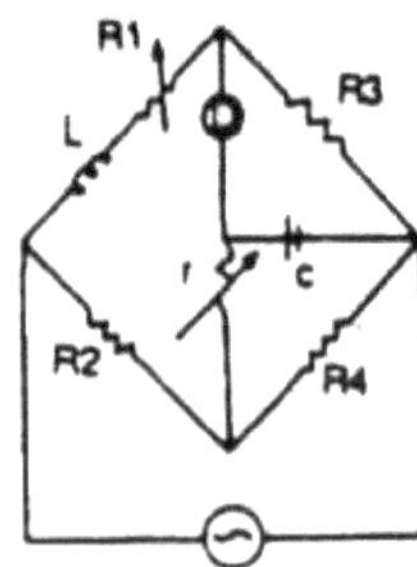

Crash

When any electronic machine stops working unexpectedly; it is said to be *crash*.

Delta Network

It is a set of three passive/active devices connected in series so as to form a mesh

Electric Image

Under certain conditions, charges induced by the point charge on the surface of the conductor have electrical effects identical to those produced by an imaginary point charge, located at a particular point, relative to and below the surface. The imaginary point charge is called electric *image of the first charge*.

The concept was invented by Kelvin.

Electromagnetic Interference

It is a condition in which an electromagnetic emission produces an undesired response in a specific susceptible component or subsystem.

Any electromagnetic energy, radiated, induced, or conducted which degrades, obstructs, or interrupts designed performance of electronic equipments. Electromagnetic interference is the obstruction, interruption, or degradation of the designed performance characteristics of communication-electronic equipment resulting from excessive or undesired emission.

Electromagnetic Spectrum

This covers entire range of electric waves, from the long waves employed in radio-communication to the shortest Gamma rays.

Time constant

It is the time taken by a capacitor in storing 63.3% of its full charge

$$t = C \times R$$

i.e. time delay in seconds is equal to the product of capacitance in farads and resistance in ohms.

Electronic welding control

Spot welding machines used for the welding of small metallic attachments to the utensils etc. employ electronic timer to control the actual weld time. Such device is called *electronic welding control*.

Weld time

It is the time for which a spot welding machine remains operative.

In other words, it is the time required for a spot weld.

Impedance (Z)

It is property of a circuit, depending upon frequency, inductance, capacitance and resistance which determines current produced by a given alternating voltage in that circuit, i.e. ratio of the root-mean-square voltage to the R.M.S. current.

It is measured in ohms and its value for a circuit of resistance R ohms, inductance L henries, and capacitance C farads (not microfarads) at a frequency of "f" cycles per second is given by

$$Z = \frac{R + j\omega L}{G + j\omega c}$$

where G is conductance

Inductance (L)

It is property of AC circuits which opposes any change in the amount of current. Its unit is henry (H).

If a current of I ampere is passed through a coil of N turns produces a magnetic field of ϕ webers then

$$L = \frac{N \cdot \phi}{I} \text{ henrys}$$

Effects of Inductance :

(*i*) It opposes flow of AC through it.

(*ii*) An e.m.f. is induced in the same coil in case of self-induction and in the second coil in case of mutual-induction.

(*iii*) Current is lagged behind the voltage by a quarter cycle (90°)

Self-induction

When an alternating current causes an e.m.f. to be developed in the coil itself, the phenomenon is called *self-induction*.

Mutual induction (M)

When an alternating current causes an e.m.f. to be developed in the second coil, the phenomenon is called *mutual induction*. Its unit is henry.

$$M = \sqrt{L_1 \times L_2}$$

where, M = mutual inductance, henrys

L_1 = self inductance of first coil, henrys

L_2 = self inductance of second coil, henrys.

e.m.f. induced in a coil

$$e = -L \frac{di}{dt}$$

where, e = induced e.m.f. volts

L = self inductance, henrys

$\dfrac{di}{dt}$ = rate of change of current.

Coefficient of coupling

It is the amount of e.m.f. induced in the second coil depends on the mutual position of the two coils. It is usually expressed as a percentage.

$$K = M\sqrt{L_1 \cdot L_2} \times 100$$

where, K = coefficient of coupling

M = mutual inductance of the two coils, henrys

L_1, L_2 = self inductance of the two coils, henrys

Coupling impedance

In case of two coupled coils, first coil induces an e.m.f. in the second coil and similarly second coil induces an e.m.f. in the first coil. The e.m.f. so induced in the first coil acts in such a direction so as to oppose applied e.m.f. Thus, first coil has to bear an additional impedance called *coupling impedance* or *reflected e.m.f.*

Inductive reactance (X_L)

It is the opposition offered by an inductor to the flow of AC through. Its unit is ohm.

$$X_L = 2\pi.f.L$$

where,

X_L = inductive reactance, ohms

f = frequency, Hz

L = inductance, henrys

Inductive Circuit

Current behind the voltage :

In an inductive circuit Current lags behind the voltage *inductive circuit* because of the opposition presented by the *induced or back e.m.f.* In a pure inductive circuit, the angle of lag is 90°, but due to resistance of the circuit, the angle of lag is found to be less than 90°.

$$\cos \theta = \frac{R}{Z_L}$$

where, θ = angle of lag

R = circuit resistance, ohm

Z_L = inductive impedance, ohms

Time constant :

In an inductive circuit, time taken by the current in reaching to 63.3 % of its maximum value is called time constant of inductive circuit.

$$t = \frac{L}{R}$$

where, t = time constant, seconds

L = inductance, henrys

R = coil's resistance, ohms

Total Inductance

(*i*) *Two or more coils connected in series :*

$$L_T = T_1 + L_2 + L_3 + \text{-----}$$

(*ii*) *Two or more coils connected in parallel:*

$$\frac{1}{L_T} = \frac{1}{L_1} + \frac{1}{L_2} + \frac{1}{L_3} + ...$$

(*iii*) *Total inductance of two coupled coils:*

$$L_T = L_1 + L_2 + 2K\sqrt{L_1 \cdot L_2}$$

If coupling between two coils is additive then (+) sign is used and if coupling between two coils is of opposing nature, then (–) sign is used.

Inductor

It is a conductor or coil having some inductance.

Choke

It is the component used for '*checking*' the flow of AC.

Types of Chokes.

1. Low Frequency (LF) choke.

A choke designed to work in the frequency range of 50 to 60 Hz is called a low frequency choke. It is used in filter circuits for smoothing the pulsating DC.

2. Audio Frequency (AF) choke

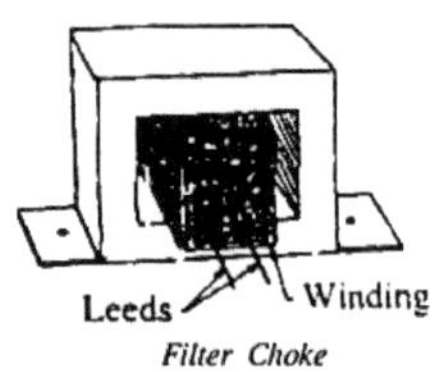

Filter Choke

Choke designed to work in the frequency range of 20 to 20,000 Hz is called an AF or audio frequency, choke. It is used for suppressing the flow of A.F, in various filter and amplifier circuits.

3. Radio Frequency (RF) choke

A choke designed to work in the frequency range of 20 kHz and upwards is called a RF or radio frequency choke. It is used tor suppressing the flow of r.f. currents in various filter and amplifier circuits.

Types of cores used in RF chokes :

(*i*)   Air core

(*ii*) Dust iron core

(*iii*) Variable dust iron core.

Noninductive Coil

It is the coil wound in such a way so as to have a minimum inductance.

Methods of winding Inductors

(*i*)   Solenoid winding

(*ii*) Toroid winding

(*iii*) Honey comb winding

(*iv*) Variometer winding.

Variometer

A variable inductor is called a *variometer.*

Inductance Drop

It is part of the voltage drop along an alternating current transmission line or in a transformer etc., due to inductance of the line or apparatus.

Magnetic bubble

It is very small magnetic material created by an external magnetic field.

Right Hand Rule

If a right handed bottle-opener cork screw is assumed to be along the conductor so as to advance in the direction of current flow, then motion of its handle will indicate direction of magnetic flux produced around the conductor.

Type of Magnetic field formed by a current carrying

1. Conductor loop

Magnetic field composed of concentric lines of force, but lines of force get condensed inside the loop and ratified outside the loop.

2. Solenoid

Magnetic field is identical to the magnetic field of a bar magnet. One end of the solenoid acts as North pole and the other as South-pole.

End Rule

If a solenoid is gripped by the right hand with the fingers pointing direction of current flow, then outstretched thumb will point the North-pole.

Helix rule

If a solenoid is gripped by the right hand with the fingers pointing direction of current flow, then outstretched thumb will point the north-pole.

Permeability

Magnetic flux density produced by a magnetizing force in a substance in comparison to that produced in air or vacuum is called permeability of that substance

$$\mu = B/H$$

where, B = magnetic flux density, Wb/m^2

H = magnetizing, N/Wb.

Magnetic Induction

When a magnet is brought near an iron bar or when iron bar is brought near to a magnet, a magnetism is produced in the iron bar. This phenomenon is called *Magnetic induction.*

Intensity of Magnetic field (*h*).

The force acting on a unit pole placed in a magnetic field is called *intensity of magnetic field.* Its unit is Wb/m.

Unit pole

If two poles are placed one metre apart in vacuum and they exert a force of one Newton on each other then each of them is called *unit pole.*

Magnetizing force developed by a solenoid of metre long having N turns with a current flow of I ampere,

$$h = \frac{N.I}{L} \text{ ampere turns.}$$

Magneto-Motive Force (M.M.F)

The force responsible for the production of magnetic field around a magnet is called M.M.F.

$$M.M.F. = N.I. \text{ amp.-turns,}$$

where, N = number of turns of the coil

I = current passing through the coil, in amperes.

Reluctance

It is the opposition offered by a material to the production of magnetic field in that material. It is analogue to the resistance of an electrical circuit.

$$R = \frac{M.M.F}{\phi}$$

where, R = Reluctance, A-T/Wb

M.M.F. = Magnetomotive force, A-T.

ϕ = Magnetic flux, Wb

Retentivity

It is the property of magnetic materials of retaining magnetism after withdrawal of the magnetizing force.

Residual Magnetism

It is the quantity of magnetism retained by a magnetic material after withdrawal of the magnetizing force.

Hysteresis

It is the phenomenon of lagging of flux density behind the magnetizing force.

Coercivity or Coercive force

It is the amount of magnetizing force required to counter balance the residual magnetism of a magnetic material.

Susceptibility

It is ability of a substance of getting magnetised.

Magnetic Axis

It is the straight line passing through the two poles of a magnet.

Magnetic pole

It is a point in a magnet where intensity of magnetic lines of force is maximum.

If a magnet is broken into several pieces, then each magnet piece will behave as an independent magnet.

Maxwell

It is the unit of magnetic flux in the obsolete COS unit.

One maxwell = 10^{-8} weber.

Electrical Network

It is a distributing network. A combination of inductance, capacitance, and resistance usually arranged in a formation of closed cells for the purpose of acting as a Frequency filter or otherwise modifying constants of an electrical circuit.

Depending on their components, networks are described as follow :

resistive, resistance-capacitance (R-C),

inductance-capacitance (L-C),

inductance (L) networks, etc.

Network lattice

It has junctions input and output terminals between junctions of elements.

Quadripole

It is a network having only four terminals, i.e. a pair of input terminals and a pair of output terminals. Behaviour of a quadripole is usually described by the impedances presented at its terminals at specified frequencies. It is also called *two port network*.

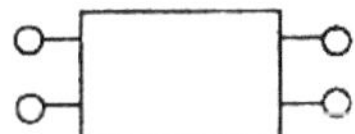

Matter

Anything which occupies space and which has a definite weight is called matter.

It is found in three states

(*i*) Solid

(*ii*) Liquid

(*iii*) Gas

Energy

Capacity of doing some work is called *energy*.

Molecule

It is the smallest part of substance which contains all physical and chemical properties of the matter.

Atom

A molecule is composed of atoms. Atom is the smallest particle of an element which can take part into or can he separated by chemical reactions but which has no free existence.

An atom is composed of

(*i*) **Electron**

It is a small particle of an atom having a unit negative charge.

(*ii*) **Proton**

It is a small particle of an atom having a unit positive charge.

(*iii*) **Neutron**

It is a small particle of an atom having no charge and whose mass is almost equal to that of proton.

It consists of a central part called *'nucleus'* which is composed of protons and neutrons and there is simple space around the nucleus in which electrons revolve the nucleus in different energy shells.

Element and Compounds

The substance which composed of only one type of atoms is called an *element* and that composed of two or more than two types of atoms is called a *compound*.

RESISTORS

It is a device that offers resistance to flow of electric current measured in ohms.

It is a component which is used in electrical and electronic circuits for presenting resistance.

Carbon Resistor

It is a resistor made of carbon or graphite.

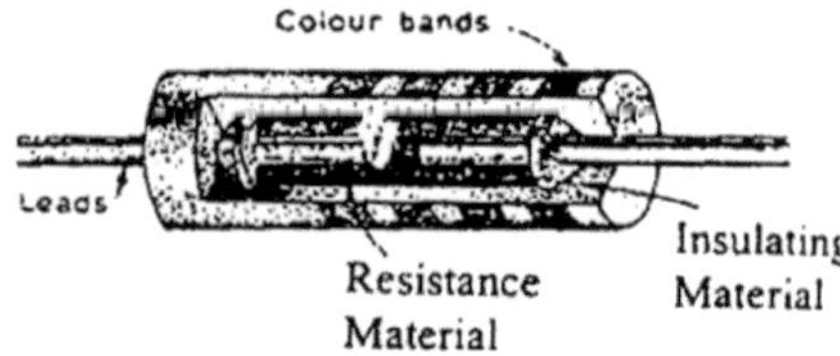

Fixed moulded Carbon resistor

Types of Carbon resistors.

1. Composition type resistor

It is made by compressing carbon powder which is mixed with a suitable resin binder.

Carbon Resistors of Various Ratings

2. Film type resistor

A film type resistor is made by depositing hydrocarbon vapour on a fine ceramic pipe.

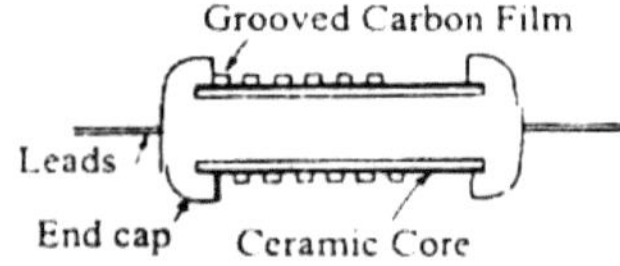

Carbon Film Resistor

Merits of carbon resistor.

Merits of a carbon resistor as compared to a wire wound resistor are as follows:

(*i*) They have a small size and are light in weight.

(*ii*) They are most suitable for high frequency circuits.

(*iii*) They have low temperature coefficient value.

(*iv*) High value resistor can be made easily.

Demerits of a carbon resistor.

Demerits of a carbon resistor as compared to a wire wound resistor are as follows:

(*i*) Their value changes by change in temperature and humidity etc.

(*ii*) Their current carrying capacity and hence wattage is limited upto 2 watts.

(*iii*) It is difficult to make a carbon resistor of a value below 2 ohms.

(*iv*) Their stability and reliability are poor.

Colour Codes

Values of various colours used in the colour code for carbon resistors are as follows:

Black = O;	Brown = 1
Red = 2;	Orange = 3
Yellow = 4;	Green = 5
Blue = 6;	Violet = 7
Grey = 8;	White = 9

Types of colour code Methods.

1. Band type Colour coding method:

In this method, value of a resistor is expressed by 4 colour bands.

First band indicates first digit.

Second band indicates second digit.

Third band indicates 'multiplier'.

Fourth band indicates tolerance of the resistor's value.

Tolerance in reference to Resistors

It is percentage of change in the value of a resistor due to manufacturing detect or variation in humidity and temperature.

Tolerance values of resistors

Tolerance of a resistor is expressed by a coloured ring or dot as following :

Brown = 1%;	Red = 2%
Orange = 3%;	Yellow = 4%
Golden = 5%;	Silver = 10%
No colour = 20%	

Values of colours used to indicate Multiplier's value in carbon resistors

The colours are valued for 'multiplier' in the following manner :

Black = 1;	Brown = 10
Red = 100;	Orange = 10^3
Yellow = 10;	Green = 10^5
Blue = 10^6;	Golden = 0.1
Silver = 0.01	

2. Body type colour coding methods.

In this method,

colour of the body indicates first digit

colour of the end indicates second digit

colour of dot indicates multiplier of the resistor's value.

Tolerance is indicated by another dot marked on the other end of the body.

Power rating of a Resistor

Maximum current carrying capability of a resistor is called its *power rating*.

It is usually expressed in terms of watts.

Stability of a Resistor

It is ability of a resistor of maintaining its ohmic value stable under variable physical conditions.

Reliability

It is ability of a resistor of maintaining a stable ohmic value for a Iong time while in use.

Wire wound Resistor

It is a resistor made by winding a wire on an insulated core.

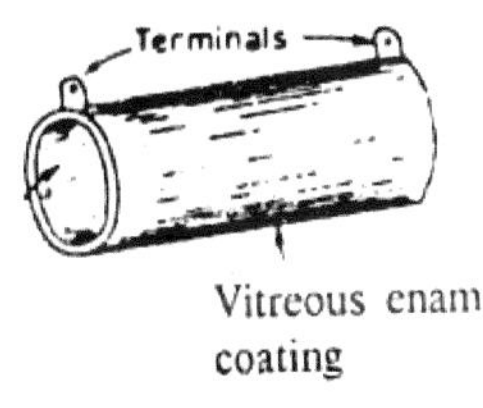

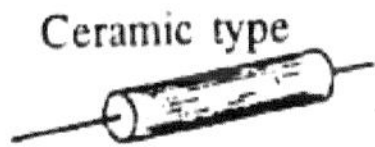

Merits.

Merits of a wire would resistor as compared to a carbon resistor are as follows:

(*i*)   It has a higher order of stability and reliability.

(*ii*) It has a higher power rating with a low tolerance value.

(*iii*) It is easy to make a wire **wound** resistor of 0.01 ohm even.

Demerits.

Demerits of a wire wound resistor as compared to a carbon resistor are as follows:

(*i*)   It is difficult to make a wire wound resistor of several mega ohms.

(*ii*) It is difficult to construct a variable type wire wound resistor and working of such resistor is not satisfactory.

(*iii*) It is unsuitable for high frequency circuits.

(*iv*) It has a big size which is unsuitable for many purposes.

Tapped Resistor

It is a multiunit type resistor.

Adjustable Resistor

It is a wire wound resistor whose ohmic value can be altered within a definite range.

Rheostat

A variable wire wound resistor is also called a rheostat.

POTENTIOMETER

It is a variable carbon or wire wound resistor. It consists of a shaft operated moving arm for changing its ohmic value. The moving arm moves on a carbon or wire wound arc.

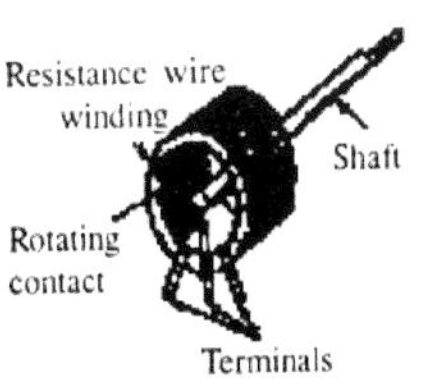

Type of Potentiometers

There are two types of potentiometers :

1. **Linear potentiometer.**

   In this potentiometer, the change in its ohmic value rests proportional to the angle moved by its moving arm.

2. **Logarithmic potentiometer**

   In this potentiometer, the change in its ohmic value rests in a logarithmic proportion to the angle moved by its moving arm.

   It is used in the volume control circuits of radio and TV receivers for changing resistance in a logarithmic proportion to produce a linear change in the intensity of reproduced sound.

Preset

It is a small sized potentiometer whose ohmic value can be changed with the help of a small screw driver.

Ballast Resistor

It is a special type of wire wound resistor which is used as a current stabilizer. It is made of such type of material which has a positive temperature coefficient.

PTC or thermistor Resistor positive temperature coefficient

A resistor is made of PTC material. Its ohmic value rests directly proportional to its temperature. It is used for bias stabilization purposes in transistorised electronic equipments.

NTC Resistor Negative temperature Coefficient

It is a resistor made of NTC material. Its ohmic value rests inversely proportional to its temperature. It is used as a delay producing device in various electronic circuits.

Varistor

A voltage dependent resistor (VDR) is called a varistor. It is used to control abrupt voltage fluctuations of a circuit.

LDR Light dependent resistor

It's a photo-sensitive resistor. It is used in light operated devices.

COMBINATION OF RESISTORS

1. **Series combination of resistors**

   It is a combination of two or more than two resistors which has one and only one path for the conduction of current.

Total resistance of a series circuit,

$$R_T = R_1 + R_2 + R_3 \ldots +$$

where, R_1, R_2 and R_3 are resistances of the three series combination of resistors.

Magnitude of current remains same through each series component because

$$I_T = I_1 = I_2 = I_3 = \ldots\ldots$$

where, I_1, I_2 and I_3 are the magnitudes of current passing through R_1, R_2 and R_3, respectively.

Total voltage, $\qquad V_T = V_1 + V_2 + V_3 + \ldots\ldots$

where V_1, V_2, and V_3 are magnitudes of voltage drops across R_1, R_2 and R_3 respectively.

2. Parallel combination of resistors

It is a combination of two or more than two resistors in which all the resistors are connected across a single source of supply.

Total resistance of parallel circuit,

$$\frac{1}{R_r} = \frac{1}{R_1} + \frac{1}{R_2} + \frac{1}{R_3} + \ldots$$

Voltage across each parallel component remains the same.

$$V_T = V_1 = V_2 = V_3 =$$

Compound Circuit

It is a combination of series and parallel circuits.

1. Parallel-series circuits.

If few parallel combination of resistors are connected in series, then they form a parallel-series circuit.

2. Series-parallel circuit.

If a few series combinations of resistors are connected in parallel, then they form a series-parallel circuit.

Total Resistance

1. *Total resistance of 3-4 identical resistors when connected in series*

$$R_T = n.R$$

where, n = number of resistors

R = resistance of one resistor.

2. *Total resistance of 3-4 identical resistor when connected in parallel*

$$R_T = R/n$$

Total power consumption of a circuit

It is determined by

$$P_T = P_1 + P_2 + P_3 + \ldots\ldots$$

where, P_1, P_2 and P_3 are power consumptions of the resistors R_1, R_2 and R_3 respectively.

Kirchoff's Laws

1. Kirchoff's Current Law (KCL).

Sum of the currents flowing towards a junction is equal to sum of the currents flowing away from the junction.

$$\Sigma I = 0$$

2. Kirchoff's Voltage Law (KVL).

Round any closed loop of an electric circuit, algebraic sum of e.m.fs acting in the loop is equal to algebraic sum of the voltage drops.

$$\Sigma E = \Sigma I.R$$

where, Σ = algebraic sum

I = current

R = resistance

Application:

Circuit is used in *'Post Office Box'* and *'Impedance Bridge'* for determination of value of an unknown resistor.

Gange Resistor

A multiunit resistor is also called gang resistor.

If cross-sectional area of conductor is doubled and its length is halved, then resistance of the new sized conductor will remain only one-fourth of its old value.

Safety Colours

Meaning assigned to safety colours used in electronic systems.

Colour	Meaning	Example of application
RED	Stop,	Stops signals, location
	Harmful	of fire fighting equipment.
Yellow:	Activity	Emergency stop devices,
	Attention,	Warning of danger, caution sign
	Danger	inside of machinery guards. Electrical equipment warning labels.
Green	Safety	Escape routes, all clear Go signal.

Stray Capacitance

It is the capacitance which exists incidentally between portions of a circuit at different potentials as opposed to capacitance intentionally placed in the circuit.

EXERCISE – I

1. Drift velocity of electrons is
   (a) larger than speed of light
   (b) almost equal to speed of light
   (c) equal to speed of light
   (d) very small in comparison to speed of light

2. Ratio of the voltage and electric current in a closed circut
   (a) remains constant (b) varies
   (c) increases (d) decreases

3. Condition for the validity under Ohm's law is that the
   (a) temperature should remain constant
   (b) current should be proportional to voltage
   (c) resistance must be wire wound type
   (d) all of these

4. Ohm's law is applicable to
   (a) semi-conductors (b) vacuum tubes
   (c) electrolytes (d) none of these

5. Resistance of a wire always increases if
   (a) temperature is reduced
   (b) temperature is increased
   (c) number of free electrons available become less
   (d) number of free electrons available become more

6. The resistance of wire varies inversely as
   (a) area of cross-section
   (b) length
   (c) resistivity
   (d) temperature

7. For a fixed supply voltage, the current flowing through a conductor will increase when its
   (a) area of cross-section is reduced
   (b) length is reduced
   (c) length is increased
   (d) length is increased and x-sectional area is reduced

8. A wire of length l and of circular cross section of radius r has a resistance of R ohms. Another wire of same material and of cross-sectional radius 2r will have the same resistance R if the length is
   (a) $2\,l$ (b) $l/2$
   (c) $4\,l$ (d) l^2

9. In case of a series circuit
   (a) current flowing through each resistor is the same
   (b) applied voltage is equal to the sum of voltage drops across individual resistors
   (c) resistors are additive
   (d) all of the above

10. Two resistances of equal value, when connected in parallel, give an equivalent resistance of R. If these resistors are connected in series, the equivalent resistance will be
    (a) R (b) 4R
    (c) 2R (d) R/2

11. The resistance of a parallel circuit consisting of two resistors is 12 Ω . One of the resistance wires breaks and the effective resistance becomes 18 Ω . The resistance of the broken wire is
    (a) 48 Ω (b) 18 Ω
    (c) 36 Ω (d) 24 Ω

12. When one leg of a parallel circuit gets opened out, the current drawn from the supply will
    (a) reduce (b) increase
    (c) remain the same (d) uncertain

13. For a series as well as a parallel circuit
    (a) resistance's are additive
    (b) powers are additive
    (c) currents are additive
    (d) voltage drops are additive

14. When a resistance element of a heater gets fused, we remove a portion of it and reconnect it to the same supply, the power drawn by the heater will
    (a) increase (b) decrease
    (c) remain same (d) uncertain

15. A 100 W bulb is connected in series with a room heater. If now 100 W bulb is replaced by a 40 W bulb, the heater output will
    (a) increase (b) decrease
    (c) remain same (d) uncertain

16. When the voltage applied across an electric iron is halved, the power consumption of the iron will reduce to
    (a) half
    (b) three-fourth
    (c) one-fourth
    (d) none of these

17. For a given line voltage, four heating coils will produce maximum heat when connected

(a) all in parallel

(b) all in series

(c) two parallel pairs in series

(d) one pair in parallel with the two in series

18. Two lamps of 200 W, 220V, and 100W, 220V are connected in series across 220V supply. The ratio of current through them will be

(a) 1 : 2   (b) 1 : 1

(c) 2 : 1   (d) 1 : 4

19. Two heaters, rated at 1000 W, 250 V each are connected in series across a 250 V, 50 Hz ac mains. Total power drawn from the supply would be

(a) 1,000 W

(b) 500 W

(c) 250 W

(d) 2,000 W

20. Ratio of resistances of a 100 W, 220 V lamp to that of a 100 W, 110 V lamp will be, at the respective voltages

(a) 4   (b) 2

(c) 1/2   (d) 1.4

21. Four 100 W bulbs are connected in parallel across 200 V supply line. If one bulb gets fused

(a) no bulb will light

(b) all the four bulbs will light

(c) rest of the three bulbs will light

(d) none of the above

22. A 200 W, 230 V lamp is connected across 115 V supply. The lamp will draw power

(a) slightly more than 50 W

(b) slightly less than 50 W

(c) 50 W

(d) none of these

23. If the voltage across the lamp drops by 1%, the power drawn will be reduced by

(a) 1%   (b) 2%

(c) 3%   (d) 4%

24. A 200 W, 100 V lamp is to be operated on 250 V supply. The additional resistance required to be connected in series will be

(a) 125 Ω (b) 100 Ω

(c) 75 Ω (d) 50 Ω

25. 1 kWh is equal to

(a) 860 Kcal

(b) 36×10^5 ergs

(c) both (a) and (b) above

(d) none of these

26. A 100 watt light bulb burns on an average of 10 hours a day for one week. The weekly consumption of energy will be

(a) 7 units/s   (b) 70 units/s

(b) 0.7 units/s   (d) 0.07 units/s

27. The electrical energy consumed by an appliance of power rating P watts connected across its rated V for t hours is

(a) Pt kwh   (b) $\dfrac{Pt}{1000}$ kwh

(c) $\dfrac{Pt}{V}$ kwh   (d) $\dfrac{Pt}{3,600}$.

28. An ideal voltage source should have

(a) zero source resistance

(b) infinite source resistance

(c) terminal voltage in proportion to current

(d) terminal voltage in proportion to load

29. For a voltage source, terminal voltage

(a) is equal to the source emf

(b) cannot exceed source emf

(c) is always lower than source emf

(d) is higher than the source emf

30. Constant voltage source is

(a) active and bilateral

(b) passive and bilateral

(c) active and unilateral

(d) passive and unilateral

31. An ideal current source has zero

(a) internal conductance

(b) internal resistance

(c) voltage on no load

(d) ripple

32. Which of the following statements is incorrect an active element?

(a) Resistance   (b) Inductor

(c) Current source   (d) all of these

33. The terminals across the source are .... if a current source is to be neglected.

(a) open-circuited

(b) short-circuited

(c) replaced by a capacitor

(d) replaced by a source resistance

34. An active element in a circuit is

(a) Current source   (b) Resistance

(c) Inductance   (d) Capacitance

35. A bilateral element is

(a) Resistor   (b) Inductor

(c) Capacitor   (d) all of these

36. The circuit having same properties in either direction is called
    (a) bilateral circuit   (b) unilateral circuit
    (c) irreversible circuit (d) reversible circuit

37. The elements which are not capable of delivering energy by its own are called
    (a) unilateral elements
    (b) non-linear elements
    (c) passive elements
    (d) active elements

38. A network having one or more than one source of emf is called
    (a) passive network   (b) active network
    (c) linear network   (d) non-linear network

39. A circuit having neither any energy source nor emf source is called
    (a) unilateral circuit (b) bilateral circuit
    (c) passive circuit   (d) active circuit

40. A passive network has
    (a) no current source
    (b) no emf source
    (c) only emf source
    (d) neither current source nor emf source

41. For determining the polarity of the voltage drop across a resistor, we do not require value of
    (a) Resistor   (b) Current
    (c) emf of the circuit (d) all of these

42. Kirchhoff's laws are valid for
    (a) linear circuits only
    (b) passive time invariant circuits
    (c) non-linear circuits only
    (d) both linear and non-linear circuits

43. Kirchhoff's laws are not applicable to circuits with
    (a) distributed parameters
    (b) lumped parameters
    (c) passive elements
    (d) non-linear resistances

44. Kirchhoff's current law is applicable only to
    (a) electric circuits
    (b) electronic circuits
    (c) junctions in a network
    (d) closed loops in a network

45. Kirchhoff's voltage law is concerned with
    (a) IR drops
    (b) battery emfs
    (c) both (a) and (b)
    (d) none of these

46. According to Kirchhoff's voltage law, the algebraic sum of all IR drops and emfs in any closed loop of a network is always
    (a) negative
    (b) positive
    (c) zero
    (d) determined by emfs of the batteries

47. The algebraic sign of an IR drop primarily depends upon the
    (a) direction of flow of current
    (b) battery connections
    (c) magnitude of current flowing through it
    (d) value of resistance

48. Maxwell circulating current theorem
    (a) utilises Kirchhoff's voltage law
    (b) utilises Kirchhoff's current law
    (c) is a network reduction method
    (d) is confined to single loop circuits

49. While Thevenizing a circuit between two terminals, V_{TH} is equal to
    (a) short-circuit terminal voltage
    (b) open-circuit terminal voltage
    (c) net voltage available in the circuit
    (d) none of these

50. Thevenin's resistance R_{TH} is determined
    (a) by short-circuiting the given two terminals
    (b) by removing the voltage sources along with their internal resistances
    (c) between same open terminals as for V_{TH}
    (d) none of these

51. In Thevenin's theorem Z is determined by
    (a) short-circuiting all independent current and voltage sources
    (b) open-circuiting all independent current and voltage sources
    (c) short-circuiting all independent voltage sources and open-circuiting all independent current sources
    (d) open-circuiting all independent voltage sources and short circuiting all independent current sources

52. Theorems applicable for both linear and non-linear circuits is
    (a) Superposition
    (b) Thevenin's
    (c) Norton's
    (d) None of these

53. While determining R_{TH} in Thevenin's and Norton's equivalent.... are made dead
(a) only current sources
(b) only voltage sources
(c) all independent sources
(d) all current and voltage sources

54. According to fuse law, the current carrying capacity varies as
(a) diameter
(b) $(\text{diameter})^{1.5}$
(c) $(\text{diameter})^{\frac{1}{2}}$
(d) $\dfrac{1}{\text{diameter}}$

55. The rating of fuse wire is always expressed in
(a) volts
(b) amperes
(c) ampere-volts
(d) ampere hours

56. The insulation on a current carrying conductor is provided to prevent
(a) current leakage (b) shock
(c) both (a) and (b)   (d) none of these

57. The thickness of insulation provided on the conductor depends upon
(a) current rating   (b) voltage rating
(c) both (a) and (b)   (d) none of these

58. When a heater is connected to the power supply, the heater coil will glow but the supply wiring does not glow. This is because
(a) resistance of heater coils is very high in comparison to that of internal wiring
(b) internal wiring is of superior material
(c) the resistance of internal wiring is very high
(d) supply wires are convered with insulation

59. Lamps in street lighting are all connected in
(a) series   (b) parallel
(c) series-parallel   (d) end-to-end

60. Energy meter, for connection, has
(a) 2 terminals   (b) 4 terminals
(c) 6 terminals   (d) 8 terminals

61. The common voltage across parallel branches with different voltage sources can be computed from the relation
$$V = \dfrac{\dfrac{V_1}{R_1} + \dfrac{V_2}{R_2} + \dfrac{V_3}{R_3}}{\dfrac{1}{R_1} + \dfrac{1}{R_2} + \dfrac{1}{R_3}}$$
The above statement is associated with
(a) Thevenin's theorem
(b) Millman's theorem
(c) Norton's theorem
(d) reciprocity

62. Electric battery is a device that
(a) generates emf by chemical action
(b) converts heat energy into electrical energy
(c) converts mechanical energy into electrical energy
(d) converts fuel energy into electrical energy

63. EMF of a zinc-carbon cell is about
(a) 1.2 V   (b) 1.5 V
(c) 1.75 V   (d) 2.2 V

64. The depolarizer in a carbon zinc cell
(a) absorbs the oxygen produced in the cell
(b) prevents the fast chemical action on the zinc container
(c) converts the hydrogen produced into water
(d) all of these

65. Capacity of a dry cell, is
(a) more when it supplies current continuously
(b) more when it supplies current intermitenttly
(c) not affected by the type of discharge
(d) none of these

66. Cell commonly used as standard cell is
(a) dry cell
(b) solar cell
(c) mercury-cadmium cell
(d) Zinc-carbon cell

67. The emf of primary cell depends upon the
(a) physical dimensions of a cell
(b) nature of electrolyte
(c) both (b) and (c)
(d) none of these

68. Internal resistance of primary cell varies
(a) inversely with the surface area of electrodes
(b) directly with the distance between electrodes
(c) with the nature of electrodes
(d) all of these

69. The internal voltage drop of a voltage source
(a) is independent of load current supplied
(b) depends upon internal resistance of the source
(c) does not influence the terminal votlage
(d) does effect the emf of the source

70. A voltage source of emf E volts and internal resistance r ohms will supply, on short circuit, a current of
(a) $\dfrac{E}{r}$ amperes   (b) zero
(c) infinite   (d) E × r amperes

71. Cells are connected in series in order to increase the
 (*a*) current capacity   (*b*) life of the cells
 (*c*) voltage rating   (*d*) terminal voltage

72. When two batteries of unequal voltages are connected in parallel, the emf of the combination will be equal to the
 (*a*) emf of the large battery
 (*b*) emf of the small battery
 (*c*) average of the emfs of two batteries
 (*d*) none of these

73. When two cells are connected in parallel, it should be ensured that they have
 (*a*) identical internal resistances
 (*b*) equal emfs
 (*c*) same make
 (*d*) same ampere-hour capacity

74. Cell are connected in parallel in order to increase the
 (*a*) life of the cells   (*b*) efficiency
 (*c*) current capacity   (*d*) voltage rating

75. For a group of cells when internal resistance of the group is equal to external load resistance, the group will deliver maximum
 (*a*) voltage   (*b*) current
 (*c*) ampere-hours   (*d*) efficiency

76. Electric supply for electro-deposition should be
 (*a*) dc voltage
 (*b*) low voltage ac
 (*c*) low frequency ac voltage
 (*d*) none of the above

77. In a lead acid battery, the level of the electrolyte should be
 (*a*) equal to that of the plates
 (*b*) below the level of plates
 (*c*) above the level of plates
 (*d*) none of these

78. In a lead acid battery the energy is stored in the form of
 (*a*) chemical energy
 (*b*) charged ions
 (*c*) electrostatic charge
 (*d*) none of these

79. In lead acid batteries
 (*a*) The electrolyte is weak sulphuric acid
 (*b*) The number of plates is always odd
 (*c*) The number of negative plates is one more than the number of positive plates
 (*d*) All of these

80. The lead acid batteries
 (*a*) delivers current as soon as its components are out together
 (*b*) has density of electrolyte increases while delivering current
 (*c*) It does not deliver current on putting its components together until it is supplied electrical energy from an external source
 (*d*) has lead as positive plates

81. During discharging of lead acid cells, the terminal voltage decreases with the decrease in
 (*a*) temperature   (*b*) discharge rate
 (*c*) state of charge   (*d*) none of these

82. In a battery, cover is placed over the elements and sealed at the top of the battery container to
 (*a*) exclude dirt and foreign matter from the electrolyte
 (*b*) reduce evaporation of water from electrolyte
 (*c*) both (*a*) and (*b*)
 (*d*) none of these

83. Petroleum jelly is applied to the terminals of the lead acid battery in order to prevent
 (*a*) corrosion
 (*b*) local heating
 (*c*) short-circuiting
 (*d*) all of these

84. For keeping the lead acid battery terminals free from corrosion it is advisable to
 (*a*) keep electrolyte level low
 (*b*) apply petroleum jelly
 (*c*) charge the battery at frequent intervals
 (*d*) all of these

85. In a lead acid battery, separators are provided to
 (*a*) reduce internal resistance
 (*b*) facilitate flow of the current
 (*c*) avoid internal short-circuits
 (*d*) increase the energy efficiency

86. In a lead acid battery, fillers are provided to
 (*a*) facilitate flow of gasses
 (*b*) prevent flow of gasses
 (*c*) recover acid losses through vapours
 (*d*) reduce tendency for polarisation

87. Tests performed for ascertaining whether the battery plates are defective or not is
 (*a*) Specific gravity test
 (*b*) High discharge test
 (*c*) Cadmium test
 (*d*) None of these

88. Vent plug is provided in each lead acid cell to
   (a) pour water or electrolyte when needed
   (b) check the electrolyte level
   (c) allow escape out of gases during charging
   (d) all of these

89. In lead acid batteries, sedimentation occurs due to
   (a) idleness for a longer period
   (b) over-charging at slow rate
   (c) over-charging at high rate
   (d) slow charging at low rate

90. In a lead acid battery, exessive formation of lead sulphate occurs due to
   (a) idleness of battery for a long time
   (b) low level of electrolyte
   (c) persistent undercharging
   (d) all of these

91. Sulphated cells are indicated by the
   (a) low specific gravity
   (b) low voltage on discharge
   (c) low capacity
   (d) all of these

92. Charging of a sulphated battery at high rate causes
   (a) warping of plates
   (b) boiling of electrolyte owing to gassing
   (c) damage to separators, cell caps, covers and battery due to exessive temperature
   (d) all of these

93. Short-circuiting of a cell may be caused by
   (a) buckling of plates
   (b) breakdown of one or more separators
   (c) excessive accumulation of sediments at the bottom of the cell
   (d) lead particles forming short circuits between positive and negative plates
   (e) All of these

94. Short-circuiting of a cell results in
   (a) reduced gassing during charging
   (b) abnormal high temperature
   (c) low specific gravity of the electrolyte
   (d) all of these

95. Over-charging of a lead acid battery would cause
   (a) excessive gassing
   (b) loss of active material
   (c) increase in temperature resulting in buckling of plates
   (d) all of these

96. Battery charging equipment should be installed
   (a) in well ventilated, clean and dry place
   (b) as near as practical to the battery under charge
   (c) both (a) and (b)
   (d) none of these

97. Condition of a fully charged lead acid battery cannot be ascertained by
   (a) gassing
   (b) voltage
   (c) colour of the electrodes
   (d) specific gravity of the electrolyte
   (e) colour of the electrolyte

98. emf of a lead acid battery
   (a) increases with the increase in specific gravity of the electrolyte
   (b) slightly increases with the increase in temperature
   (c) both (a) and (b)
   (d) none of these

99. If the specific gravity of the electrolyte in a lead acid cell increases beyond 1.23 there will be
   (a) loss of life
   (b) loss of capacity
   (c) increase in internal resistance
   (d) corrosion of the grids of the plates

100. Capacity of a lead acid battery does not depend upon
   (a) charge rate   (b) discharge rate
   (c) temperature   (d) density of electrolyte

101. The capacity of a lead acid battery is adversely affected by increase in
   (a) discharge rate   (b) charge rate
   (c) temperature   (d) all of these

102. Electrolyte used in Edison cell is
   (a) NaCl   (b) HCl
   (c) KOH   (d) Nitric acid

103. During charging and discharging of an Edison cell
   (a) electrolyte does not take part in chemical reaction
   (b) emf remains the same
   (c) corrosive fumes are produced
   (d) nickel hydroxide remains unsplit

104. Electrolyte used in nickel-cadmium cell is
   (a) NaCl   (b) NaOH
   (c) KOH   (d) H_2SO_4

105. Nickel-cadmium accumulators in comparison to nickel-iron accumulators have the advantages of
(a) being lighter in weight and cheaper in cost
(b) low internal resistance and longer life
(c) higher emf and higher efficiency
(d) all of the above

106. A floating battery is one
(a) which is charged and discharged simultaneously
(b) in which battery voltage is equal to charger simultaneously
(c) which supplies current intermittently and also during idle period gets charged
(d) none of the above

107. Two charges of equal magnitude are separated by some distance. If the charges are increased by 10%; to get the same force between them, their separation must be
(a) increased by 21%
(b) increased by 10%
(c) decreased by 10%
(d) none of the above is correct

108. The phenomenon of an uncharged body getting charged merely by nearness of a charged body is called
(a) induction   (b) attraction
(c) magnetic effect   (d) chemical effect

109. When an uncharged body is placed near a charged body, then uncharged body
(a) is attracted first and then charged by induction
(b) gets charged by induction and then attracted towards the charging body
(c) gets charged by conduction
(d) remains a such

110. The value of electric field intensity within the field due to a point charge can be determined by
(a) Gauss's law   (b) Ampere's law
(c) Coulomb's law   (d) Maxwell's law

111. Space surrounding a charge, within which the influence of its charge extends is called
(a) electric field   (b) magnetic field
(c) lines of force   (d) electric intensity

112. A region around a stationary electric charge has
(a) electric field
(b) magnetic field
(c) both electric and magnetic fields
(d) neither electric nor magnetic field

113. On placing a dielectric in an electric field the strength
(a) decreases   (b) increases
(c) remains the same (d) reduces to zero

114. Electric field intensity between plates of a parallel plate condenser is E. Now if a dielectric of medium of dielectric constant ε is introduced between the plates, the electric field intensity will become
(a) $\in E$ (b) $E/\in$
(c) $\sqrt{\in E}$ (d) $\sqrt{E/\in}$

115. Inside a hollow conducting sphere electric field
(a) is zero
(b) is a non-zero constant
(c) changes with the magnitude of the charge given to the conductor
(d) changes with distance from the centre of the sphere

116. Electric field inside a hollow metallic charged sphere is
(a) zero
(b) decreasing towards centre
(c) increasing towards centre
(d) none of the above

117. Electric field inside a perfectly conducting media is
(a) infinite
(b) zero
(c) dependent upon the value of the charge
(d) none of the above

118. The electro-magnet is made of
(a) soft iron core
(b) steel core
(c) soft iron core wraped in a coil of fine wire with current flowing through it
(d) all of the above

119. A coil with a certain number of turns has a specified time constant. If the number of turns is doubled, its time constant would
(a) remain unaffected
(b) become doubled
(c) become four fold
(d) get halved

120. Two coils having equal resistances but different inductances are connected in series. The time constant of the series combination is the
(a) sum of time constant of the individual coils
(b) average of time constants of the individual coils
(c) geometric mean of time constants of the individual coils
(d) product of the time constant of the individual coils

121. Dielectric strength of a medium

(a) increases with the increase in temperature

(b) decreases with the increase in thickness

(c) increases with moisture content

(d) is not affected by the moisture content

122. A medium behaves like dielectric when the

(a) displacement current is just equal to the conduction current

(b) displacement current is less than the conduction current

(c) displacement current is much greater than the conduction current

(d) displacement current is almost negligible

123. If E = 0 at all points on a closed surface,

1. The electric flux through the surface is zero.

2. The total charge enclosed by the surface is zero.

3. The charge resides on the surface.

(a) 1 & 2 only are correct

(b) 2 & 3 only are correct

(c) 1 & 3 only are correct

(d) 1, 2 & 3 are correct

124. In two parallel conducting plates, each of area A and having charge density ρ_s, the force of attraction between them will be

(a) $\dfrac{1}{2\in}\rho^2{}_s A^3$

(b) $\dfrac{1}{2\in}E^2 A$

(c) $\dfrac{1}{2\in}\rho_s^2$

(d) $\dfrac{1}{2}\rho_s^2$

125. In case of conductors in electrostatic fields

(a) surface of a conductor is an equipotential surface

(b) electric field intensity inside a conductor is zero

(c) electric field intensity at the surface of a conductor is everywhere directed normal to that surface

(d) all of these

126. Two electrons moving parallel to each other at the same velocity will

(a) attract each other if they move in the same direction

(b) repel each other more strongly when moving in the same direction than when moving in opposite direction

(c) repel each other more strongly when moving in opposite direction

(d) repel each other with same force when moving in the same or opposite direction

127. A capacitor consists of two

(a) conductors separated by an insulator called the dielectric

(b) insulators separated by a conductor

(c) insulators separated by an air medium only

(d) conductors separated by air medium only

128. In a capacitor, the electric charges is stored in

(a) metal plates

(b) dielectric

(c) both (a) and (b)

(d) none of these

129. If the dielectric of a capacitor is replaced by a conducting material the

(a) capacitor will get heated up owing to eddy currents

(b) plates will get short-circuited

(c) capacitor can store infinite charge

(d) capacitance will become very high

130. The total excess or deficiency of electrons in a body is called the

(a) current

(b) voltage

(c) charge

(d) potential gradient

131. The charge of an isolated conductor resides

(a) at the conductor surface

(b) inside the conductor

(c) partly at the surface and partly inside the conductor

(d) none of these

132. When a charge is given to a conductor,

(a) it distributes uniformly all over the surface

(b) it distributes uniformly all over the volume

(c) it distributes on the surface, inversely proportional to the radius of curvature

(d) it stays where it was placed

133. Two copper spheres A (hollow) and B (solid) are of same diameter and are charged to the same potential.

(a) A will hold more charge in comparison to that of B

(b) A will hold less charge in comparison to that of B

(c) Both of the spheres will hold the same charge

(d) None of the sphere will hold any charge

134. Joule/Coulomb is the unit of

(a) electric field potential

(b) potential

(c) charge

(d) none of the above

135. The ratio of charge stored by two metallic spheres raised to the same potential is 6. The ratio of the surface areas of the sphere is

   (a) 6   (b) $\dfrac{1}{6}$

   (c) 36   (d) $\dfrac{1}{\sqrt{6}}$

136. Internal heating of a capacitor is usually attributed to
   (a) leakage resistance
   (b) dielectric charge
   (c) electron movement
   (d) plate vibration

137. For preventing the generation of static charge on rubber of flat leather
   (a) surface is moistened
   (b) conductive dressing is done
   (c) oil compound dressing is done
   (d) all of these

138. For removing static charge from machinery the
   (a) machinery is insulated
   (b) insulated cabins are constructed
   (c) framework is earthed
   (d) all of these

139. Capacitance of a parallel plate capacitor is not affected by
   (a) area of plates.
   (b) thickness of plates.
   (c) separation between plates.
   (d) nature of dielectric.

140. In a parallel plate capacitor, it a dielectric slab is introduced, then
   (a) pd between the plates will decrease
   (b) electric intensity will decrease
   (c) capacitance will increase
   (d) all of these

141. Which of the following statements associated with inductors is wrong ?
   (a) An inductor is a sort of short-circuit to dc.
   (b) An inductor is a sort of open circuit to dc.
   (c) An inductor never dissipates energy but only stores it.
   (d) A finite amount of energy can be stored in an inductor even if voltage across it is zero, such as when the current through it is constant.

142. The kind of magnet that is made by wrapping a coil of fine wire around a steel bar is called
   (a) electro-magnet   (b) permanent magnet
   (c) induced magnet   (d) weak magnet

143. The magnetic field strength of an air-cored coil can be increased by
   (a) increasing the number of turns on the coil.
   (b) increasing the current strength.
   (c) increasing the core x-sectional area.
   (d) all of these

144. In a cable capacitor, voltage gradient is maximum at the surface of the
   (a) sheath.   (b) conductor.
   (c) dielectric.   (d) earth.

145. The time constant of an RC series circuit connected to a dc source is equal to

   (a) $\dfrac{C}{R}$ (b) $\dfrac{R}{C}$

   (c) CR   (d) $\dfrac{J}{CR}$

146. In the series R-C circuit shown in the fig, the voltage across C starts increasing when the dc source is switched on. The rate of increase of voltage across C at the instant just after the switch is closed (i.e. at t = 0$^+$), will be
   (a) zero   (b) infinity

   (c) RC   (d) $\dfrac{1}{RC}$

147. While testing a capacitor with ohmmeter, if the capacitor shows charging but the final resistance reading is appreciably less than normal the capacitor is
   (a) leaky   (b) open-circuited
   (c) short-circuited   (d) satisfactory

148. If an ohmmeter reading immediately goes practically to zero and stays there while checking a capacitor, the capacitor is
   (a) leaky
   (b) short-circuited
   (c) open-circuited
   (d) satisfactory

149. A permeable substance is one
   (a) through which the magnetic lines of force can pass very easily
   (b) which is a strong magnet
   (c) which is a bad conductor
   (d) none of these

150. Permanent magnetism is one which
   (a) is left in the iron piece after the removal of the magnetic field
   (b) is produced by the superconductor coils
   (c) is produced by electric current
   (d) is produced by induction

151. A keeper is used for
 (a) restoring of lost flux
 (b) amplification of flux
 (c) providing a closed path for the magnetic flux
 (d) changing the direction of magnetic lines of force

152. The direction of magnetic lines of force is from
 (a) south pole to north pole
 (b) north pole to south pole
 (c) one end of magnet to another
 (d) none of these

153. When a piece of iron is placed in a magnetic field,
 (a) there will be no effect on the magnetic field.
 (b) the magnetic lines of force will bend away from the piece
 (c) the magnetic lines of force will bend away from their usual paths so as to pass through the piece
 (d) none of these

154. Force experienced by a unit north pole at any point is called
 (a) mmf
 (b) magnetic flux strength
 (c) magnetic flux density
 (d) magnetic potential

155. Lines of force
 (a) never intersect
 (b) often intersect
 (c) intersect only in special circumstances
 (d) are unpredictable

156. Tubes of force within the magnetic material are called
 (a) lines of force
 (b) electric flux.
 (c) tubes of induction
 (d) susceptibility.

157. The number of lines of force per unit area is measure of
 (a) magnetic flux density
 (b) magnetic field intensity
 (c) mmf
 (d) susceptibility

158. Magnetic flux density emerging out of a closed surface is
 (a) infinite
 (b) zero
 (c) dependent upon the magnetic movement inside the closed surface
 (d) none of these

159. Magnetostriction is a phenomenon whereby the magnetisation of a ferromagnetic material leads to a change in
 (a) relative permeability.
 (b) physical dimensions.
 (c) spontaneous magnetisation.
 (d) magnetic susceptibility

160. Ratio of intensity of magnetisation to the magnetising force or intensity of magnetic field is called the
 (a) susceptibility   (b) flux density
 (c) mmf   (d) magnetic potential

161. The unit of susceptibility is
 (a) tesla   (b) H/m.
 (c) J/m.   (d) dimensionless

162. For vacuum susceptibility is
 (a) infinite   (b) unity
 (c) zero   (d) none of these

163. The direction of magnetic field around a current carrying conductor can be determined by
 (a) cork screw rule
 (b) right hand rule
 (c) either (a) or (b)
 (d) none of these

164. The polarity of the pole can be determined by
 (a) end rule   (b) cork screw rule
 (c) thumb rule   (d) left hand rule

165. Polarity of a solenoid can be determined by
 (a) use of compass needle
 (b) helix rule
 (c) cork screw rule
 (d) either (a) or (b)

166. ∇ B is based on
 (a) Gauss's law   (b) Ampere's law
 (c) Faraday's law   (d) Ohm's law.

167. At the centre of a current carrying single turn circular loop, magnetic field is
 (a) $B = \dfrac{\mu l}{2R}$ (b) $\dfrac{\mu l}{.2\,\pi R}$

 (c) $B = \dfrac{\mu l}{4\pi R^2}$ (d) none of these

168. A circular current-carrying loop and a field point are shown in the figure given below. The vector magnetic potential at P is in the direction of
 (a) $\vec{a_x}$ (b) $\vec{a_y}$

 (c) $\vec{a_z}$ (d) $(\vec{a_x} + \vec{a_y})\sqrt{2}$

169. The magnitude of force acting on a current carrying conductor placed in a magnetic field is independent of
(a) flux density.
(b) length of conductor.
(c) cross-sectional area of conductor.
(d) current flowing through the conductor.

170. The direction of mechanical force experienced on a current carrying conductor placed in a magnetic field is determined by
(a) Fleming's left hand rule.
(b) Fleming's right hand rule.
(c) Helix rule.
(d) Cork screw rule.

171. In Fleming's left hand rule thumb always represents direction of
(a) current flow   (b) induced emf
(c) magnetic field   (d) mechanical force

172. If a current carrying conductor is placed in a magnetic field, the mechanical force experienced on the conductor is determined by
(a) simple product   (b) dot product
(c) cross product   (d) any of these

173. The force experienced by a current carrying conductor lying parallel to a magnetic field is
(a) zero   (b) $B\,I\,l$
(c) $B\,I\,l\,\sin\theta$ (d) $B\,I\,l\,\cos\theta$

174. An infinitely long conductor carrying a current is embedded in a semi-infinite medium of permeability μ_1, as shown in the given figure. For $\mu_1 > \mu_2$, the conductor will experience

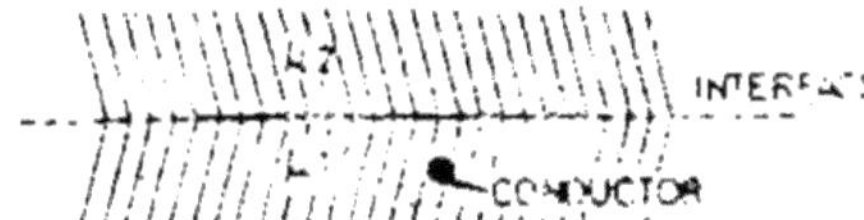

(a) no force.
(b) a force that moves it away from the interface.
(c) a force towards the interface.
(d) a force parallel to the interface.

175. A straight conductor of length l moving with a velocity v in the presence of a magnetic field of flux density B directed at an angle θ with the direction of v experiences a force. Which of the following statement(s) is/are true for the magnitude of the force ?
1. It is independent of θ.
2. It is proportional to l^2.
3. It is proportional to B.
4. It is independent of v.

Select the correct answer from the codes given below :
Codes :
(a) 1, 2, and 3   (b) 4 alone
(c) 3 alone   (d) 2 and 4

176. An electric field is parallel but opposite to a magnetic field. Electrons with some initial velocity enter the region of the fields at an angle θ along the direction of the electric field. The electron path will be
(a) straight   (b) helical
(c) circular   (d) elliptical

177. The magnetic field due to an infinite linear current carrying conductor is
(a) $H = \dfrac{\mu l}{2\pi r}\,\text{A}/\text{m}$ (b) $H = \dfrac{l}{2\pi r}\,\text{A}/\text{m}$
(c) $H = \dfrac{\mu l}{2r}\,\text{A}/\text{m}$ (d) $H = \dfrac{1}{r}\,\text{A}/\text{m}$

178. Field strength at the centre of a circular coil of turns N and radius r metre is given as
(a) $H = \dfrac{NI}{4r}\,\text{A}/\text{m}$ (b) $H = \dfrac{NI}{2r}\,\text{A}/\text{m}$
(c) $H = \dfrac{NI}{4\pi r}\,\text{A}/\text{m}$ (d) $H = \dfrac{NI}{2\pi r}\,\text{A}/\text{m}$

179. The magnetic field intensity (in A/m) at the centre of a circular coil of diameter 1 m and carrying a current of 2 A is
(a) 8   (b) 4
(c) 3   (d) 2

180. The field at any point on the axis of a current carrying coil will be
(a) perpendicular to the axis.
(b) parallel to the axis.
(c) at an angle of 45° with the axis.
(d) zero.

181. The magnetic flux inside the exciting coil
(a) is the same as on its outer surface.
(b) is zero.
(c) is greater than that on its outside surface.
(d) is lower than that on the outside surface.

182. If the two conductors carry current in opposite directions there will be
(a) a force of attraction between the two conductors.
(b) a force of repulsion between the two conductors.
(c) no force between them.
(d) none of these

183. If a straight conductor of circular cross-section carries a current, then

(*a*) no force acts on the conductor at any point.

(*b*) an axial force acts on the conductor tending to increase its length.

(*c*) a radial force acts towards the axis tending to reduce its cross section.

(*d*) a radial force acts away from the axis tending to increase its cross-section.

184. Consider the following statements :

The force per unit length between two stationary parallel wires carrying (steady) currents

1. is inversely proportional to the separation of wires.

2. is proportional to the magnitude of each current.

3. satisfies Newton's third law.

Of these statements

(*a*) 1 and 2 are correct.

(*b*) 2 and 3 are correct.

(*c*) 1 and 3 are correct.

(*d*) 1, 2 and 3 are correct.

185. mmf of magnetic circuit is analogous to

(*a*) current   (*b*) emf

(*c*) resistance   (*d*) power

186. Unit of reluctance of magnetic circuit is

(*a*) AT/m   (*b*) webers/m

(*c*) AT/weber   (*d*) H/m.

187. Property of a material which opposes the production of magnetic flux in it is called

(*a*) mmf   (*b*) reluctance

(*c*) permeance   (*d*) permittivity

188. Unit of mmf is

(*a*) AT   (*b*) weber/ampere

(*c*) Henry   (*d*) AT/m

189. Conductance is analogous to

(*a*) reluctance   (*b*) mmf

(*c*) permeance   (*d*) inductance

190. An air gap is usually inserted in magnetic circuits to

(*a*) prevent saturation

(*b*) increase in mmf.

(*c*) increase in flux.

(*d*) increase in inductance.

191. Permeability is reciprocal of

(*a*) reluctivity

(*b*) susceptibility

(*c*) permittivity

(*d*) conductivity

192. The magnetic reluctance of a magnetic circuit decreases with

(*a*) decrease in cross-sectional area.

(*b*) increase in cross-sectional area.

(*c*) increase in length of magnetic path.

(*d*) decrease in relative permeability of the magnetic material of the circuit.

193. A ring shaped coil with fixed number of turns of it carries a current of certain magnitude. If an iron core is threaded into the coil without any change in coil dimensions, the magnetic induction density will

(*a*) increase

(*b*) reduce

(*c*) remain unaffected

(*d*) unpredictable

194. The ratio of total flux (flux in the iron path) to useful flux (flux in the air gap) is called

(*a*) utilisation factor

(*b*) fringing factor

(*c*) leakage factor

(*d*) depreciation factor

195. According to Faraday's law of electro-magnetic induction an emf is induced in a conductor whenever it

(*a*) lies in a magnetic field.

(*b*) lies perpendicular to the magnetic field.

(*c*) cuts the magnetic flux.

(*d*) moves parallel to the direction of magnetic field.

196. "In all cases of electromagnetic induction, an induced voltage will cause a current to flow in a closed circuit in such a direction that the magnetic field which is caused by that current will oppose the change that produces the current", is the original statement of

(*a*) Lenz's law.

(*b*) Faraday's law of magnetic induction.

(*c*) Fleming's law of induction.

(*d*) Ampere's law.

197. The laws of electromagnetic induction (Faraday's and Lenz's laws) are summarized in the equation

(*a*) $e = i\,R$ (*b*) $e = L\,\dfrac{di}{dt}$

(*c*) $e = -\dfrac{d\psi}{dt}$ (*d*) none of these

198. Which law is synonymous to the occurrence of diamagnetism ?

(*a*) Ampere's law   (*b*) Maxwell's law

(*c*) Coulomb's law   (*d*) Lenz's law

199. The emf induced in a coil due to relative motion of a magnet is independent of

(*a*) coil resistance

(*b*) magnet not visible

(*c*) number of coil turns.

(*d*) pole strength of the magnet.

200. When a single turn coil rotates in a uniform magnetic field, at uniform speed the induced emf will be

(*a*) alternating   (*b*) steady

(*c*) pulsating   (*d*) none of these

201. Principle of dynamically induced emf is used in a

(*a*) choke   (*b*) transformer

(*c*) generator   (*d*) thermo-couple

202. The direction of dynamically induced emf in a conductor can be determined by

(*a*) Fleming's left hand rule.

(*b*) Fleming's right hand rule.

(*c*) Helix rule.

(*d*) Cork screw rule.

203. There is a constant homogeneous magnetic field pointing in a vertical direction. A metallic wire in the form of a square is rotated about a horizontal axis passing through the middle points of its opposite arms. The emf generated in the square is

(*a*) zero.

(*b*) finite and constant.

(*c*) oscillatory.

(*d*) varying with time t as t^2.

204. A conducting rod revolves about its mid point O at uniform angular speed ω in a uniform magnetic field B normal to its plane of revolution as shown in the figure. The electric pd between the ends P and Q of the rod would be

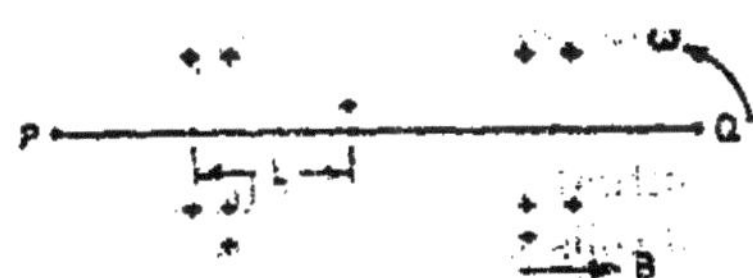

(*a*) zero   (*b*) B ω^2 L/2

(*c*) – B ω^2 L/2   (*d*) 2 B ω^2 L

205. Principle of statically induced emf is used in

(*a*) transformer   (*b*) motor

(*c*) generator   (*d*) battery

206. Magnitude of statically induced emf depends on the

(*a*) coil resistance

(*b*) flux magnitude

(*c*) rate of change of flux

(*d*) none of these

207. The property of a coil by which a counter emf is induced in it, when the current through the coil changes, is called

(*a*) self inductance   (*b*) mutual inductance

(*c*) capacitance   (*d*) none of these

208. If in an iron cored coil the iron core is removed so as to make the air-cored coil, the inductance of the coil will be

(*a*) more   (*b*) less

(*c*) the same   (*d*) none of these

209. Lower the self inductance of a coil

(*a*) more will be the weber-turns.

(*b*) more will be the emf induced.

(*c*) lesser the flux produced by it.

(*d*) smaller the delay in establishing steady current through it.

210. A current shown in the given figure passes through a pure inductance of 3 mH. The instantaneous power, in watts, during $0 < t < 2$ ms is

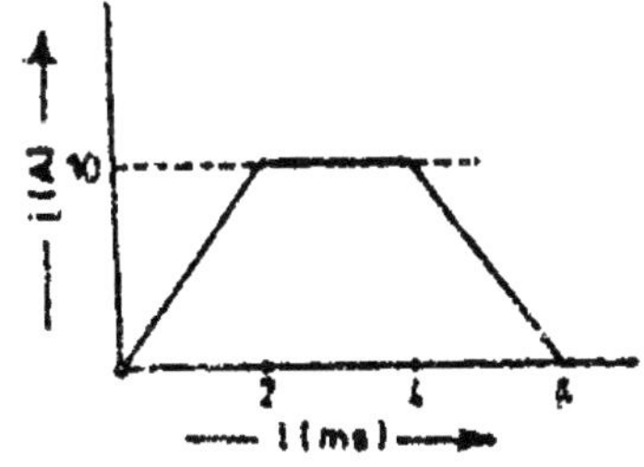

(*a*) 25,000 t   (*b*) 50,000 t

(*c*) 75,000 t   (*d*) 1,00,00 t

211. An open coil has

(*a*) zero resistance and zero inductance.

(*b*) infinite resistance and infinite inductance.

(*c*) infinite resistance and zero inductance.

(*d*) zero resistance and infinite inductance.

212. The mutual inductance between two closely coupled coils is 1 H. Now the turns of one coil are decreased to half and those of the other are doubled. The new value of mutual inductance would be

(*a*) 2 H   (*b*) $\dfrac{1}{2}$ H

(*c*) $\dfrac{1}{4}$ H   (*d*) 1 H

213. Mutual inductance between two magneti-cally coupled coils depends on the

(*a*) permeability of the core material.

(*b*) number of turns of the coils.

(*c*) cross-sectional area of their common core.

(*d*) all of these

214. When two coils having self inductances of L_1 and L_2 are coupled through a mutual inductance M, the coefficient of coupling, K is given by

(a) $K = \dfrac{M}{\sqrt{2\,L_1L_2}}$ (b) $K = \dfrac{M}{\sqrt{L_1L_2}}$

(c) $K = \dfrac{2M}{\sqrt{L_1L_2}}$ (d) $K = \dfrac{L_1L_2}{M}$

215. The overall inductance of two coils connected in series, with mutual inductance aiding self inductance is L_1 with mutual inductance opposing self-inductance the overall inductance is L_2. The mutual inductance M is given by

(a) $L_1 + L_2$ (b) $L_1 - L_2$

(c) $\dfrac{1}{4}(L_1 - L_2)$ (d) $\dfrac{1}{2}(L_1 + L_2)$

216. The coils having self inductance of 10 mH and 15 mH and effective inductance of 40 mH, when connected in series aiding. What will be the equivalent inductance if we connect them in series opposing ?

(a) 20 mH   (b) 10 mH

(c) 5 mH   (d) zero

217. The coupling between two magnetically coupled coils is said to be ideal if the coefficient of coupling is

(a) zero   (b) 0.1

(c) 1   (d) 2

218. Two inductive coils with self inductance L_1 and L_2 are magnetically coupled in series opposing and in parallel aiding respectively. The mutual inductances between the coils in the two cases are respectively

(a) $L_1 + L_2 + 2M,\ \dfrac{L_1L_2 - M^2}{L_1 + L_2 - 2M}$

(b) $L_1 + L_2 - 2M,\ \dfrac{L_1L_2 - M^2}{L_1 + L_2 + 2M}$

(c) $L_1 + L_2 - 2M,\ \dfrac{L_1L_2 - M^2}{L_1 + L_2 - 2M}$

(d) $L_1 + L_2 - 2M,\ \dfrac{L_1L_2 - M^2}{L_1 + L_2 + 2M}$

219. Two coupled coils with $L_1 = L_2 = 0.6$ H have a coupling coefficient of $k = 0.8$. The turn ratio $\dfrac{N_1}{N_2}$ is

(a) 4   (b) 2

(c) 1   (d) 0.5

220. When a magnetising force is removed material the kind of magnetism that remains is called

(a) residual magnetism

(b) induced magnetism

(c) stray magnetism

(d) none of these

221. The magnetism present in a piece of soft steel held near a magnet is called

(a) residual magnetism

(b) insulated magnetism

(c) induced magnetism

(d) stray magnetism

222. Material subjected to rapid reversals of magnetism should have

(a) high permeability and low hysteresis loss.

(b) large B-H loop area.

(c) large coercivity and high retentivity.

(d) low permeability and large coercivity.

223. Magnetic saturation of iron means

(a) the state when change in magnetic field strength H causes a little change in the magnetic flux density B.

(b) the state when a little change in magnetic field strength H causes a larger change in the magnetic flux density.

(c) magnetization of iron to the maximum extent.

(d) none of the above.

224. When an electric current is passed through a bucket full of water, lot of bubbling is there. The electric current is

(a) ac.   (b) dc

(c) pulsating   (d) none of these.

225. The most important advantages of using electrical energy in the form of ac is

(a) the construction cost per kw of ac generator is lower than that of dc generator

(b) conductor of smaller x-section is required in case of ac in comparison to dc for carrying the same current.

(c) less insulation is required in case of ac.

(d) transformation of voltage is possible in case of ac only.

226. An alternating current of frequency 50 Hz and maximum value 200 A is given as

(a) $i = 200 \sin 628\,t$

(b) $i = 200 \sin 314\,t$

(c) $i = 100\sqrt{2} \sin 314\,t$

(d) $i = 100\sqrt{2} \sin 157\,t$

227. A sine wave has a frequency of 60 Hz. Its angular frequency is

(a) $\dfrac{50}{\pi}$ radians/sec (b) $50\,\pi$ radians/sec

(c) $100\,\pi$ radians/sec (d) $\dfrac{100}{\pi}$ radians/sec

228. The frequency of an alternating quantity is the number of

(a) direction reversals in per second.

(b) cycles completed per second.

(c) cycles completed per minute.

(d) all of these

229. The time period of periodic time T of an alternating quantity is the time taken in seconds to complete

(a) one cycle (b) one alternation

(c) any of these (d) none of these

230. The time period of an alternating quantity is 0.02 second,. Its frequency will be

(a) 25 Hz (b) 50 Hz

(c) 100 Hz (d) 0.02 Hz

231. The angular frequency of an alternating quantity is a mathematical quantity obtained by multiplying the frequency of the alternating quantity by a factor of the alternating quantity by a factor

(a) $\dfrac{\pi}{2}$ (b) π

(c) 2π (d) 4π

232. An ac generator runnign at 1,000 rpm produces emf of 50 Hz. The number of poles on the generator is

(a) 2 (b) 4

(c) 6 (d) 8

233. Average value of an unsymmetrical alterating quantity is calculated over the

(a) whole cycle

(b) half cycle

(c) unsymmetrical part of the waveform

(d) none of these

234. Mean value of the current i = 20 sin t from t = 0 to t = π/2 is

(a) $40\,\pi$ (b) $\dfrac{40}{\pi}$

(c) $\dfrac{1}{40}$ (d) $\dfrac{\pi}{40}$

235. Internal impedance of an ideal current source is

(a) Zero (b) Low

(c) High (d) Infinity

236. Resonant frequency in radians/sec of a circuit having a 10 m H inductor in series with a 1 mF capacitor is

(a) 10^8 (b) 10^4

(c) 10 (d) 1

237. Condition for reciprocity of a two port network is

(a) AD – BC = 1 (b) AD – BC = 0

(c) A = D (d) B = C

238. Ladder network used in a D/Aconverter is

(a) R-C Ladder (b) R-L Ladder

(c) R-2R Ladder (d) R-2L Ladder

239. A network has two voltage sources and a number of resistors connected together. One resistor consumes a power of 20.25 water when the other sources nis shorted. If both the sources are active the powr consumed by the resistor is......watts.

240. Charge contained in an electron is

(a) 9.107×10^{-31} coulomb

(b) -1.6×10^{-19} coulomb

(c) -1.76×10^{11} coulomb

(d) 3.2×10^{32} coulomb

241. In an RL circuit after a very long time of application of step voltage, inductance L is represented in its equivalent circuit as

(a) Open circuit

(b) Short circuit

(c) L/2

(d) 2L

242. Thevenin's theorem cannot be applied to a network which contains

(a) Linear impedances

(b) Nonlinear impedances

(c) Resistances

(d) Inductances

243. Loss produced by insertion of the network of line is referred to as

(a) Insertion loss

(b) Characteristic loss

(c) Eddy current loss

(d) Hysteresis loss

244. If all three elements of a given DELTA-connected network are pure inductive reactance, then three elements of the corresponding star connected network

(*a*) will be pure capacitive reactances

(*b*) will be pure inductive reactances

(*c*) can be either inductive or capacitive reactances.

(*d*) will be inductive or capacitive reactances depending upon Delta connected inductive reactances magnitudes.

245. Which of the following laws of electrical network is used in the Node voltage analysis of the networks?

(*a*) Kirchoff's voltage laws

(*b*) Faraday's laws

(*c*) Kirchoffs current low

(*d*) Ohm's law.

246. Choose the correct statement:

(*a*) In Mesh current analysis, directions of the loop currents should be so chosen that no branch should have more than two currents otherwise results are likely to be incorrect.

(*b*) In Node voltage analysis, if outgoing currents are taken as positive, then incoming currents must be taken as negative and vice versa.

(*c*) In the Node voltage analysis, all outgoing current must always be taken as negative and all incoming currents must always be taken as positive.

(*d*) In Mech current analysis, all loop currents should either be clockwise or anticlockwise.

247. A sinusoidal waveform is mathematically represented by an/a

(*a*) even function

(*b*) odd function

(*c*) function that is even as well as half wave symmetric.

(*d*) function that is neither even nor odd.

248. The trigonometric fourier series expansion of an even function that is also half-wave symmetric shall contain

(*a*) odd harmonics of sine terms only.

(*b*) both sine and cosine terms.

(*c*) only cosine terms.

(*d*) only odd harmonics of cosine terms.

249. A function that is neither even nor odd but has half wave symmetry can be expressed in terms of fourier series expansion as a sum of

(*a*) odd harmonics of both sine and cosine terms

(*b*) even hormonics of both sine and cosine terms

(*c*) odd harmonics of sine terms.

(*d*) even harmonics of cosine terms.

250. If a synchronous converter is supplied with 12 phase a.c. supply, theN number of slip rings will be

(*a*) 6   (*b*) 9

(*c*) 12   (*d*) 15

251. In a rotary convenor I^2R losses as compared to a d.c. generator of the same size will be

(*a*) six times more   (*b*) double

(*c*) half   (*d*) less

252. When a rotor converter is started by means of a small auxiliary motor, the power of motor must be

(*a*) less than the d.c. output of converter

(*b*) less than a.c. input of converter

(*c*) half of d.c. output of converter

(*d*) slightly more than the value of friction and windage losses at rated speed.

253. Maximum current rating of a glass bulb mercury are rectifier is usually restricted to

(*a*) 150 A   (*b*) 400 A

(*c*) 500 A   (*d*) 2000 A

254. In a are rectifier, drop in voltage at the cathode is approximately

(*a*) 10 volts   (*b*) 6 to 7 volts

(*c*) 160 to 170 volts   (*d*) 1.2 volts

255. In a mercury are rectifier me cathode voltage drop is because of

(*a*) Surface resistance

(*b*) Expenditure of energy in librating electrons from the mercury

(*c*) Expenditure of energy in ionization

(*d*) Expenditure of energy in overcoming the electrostatic field.

256. The average life of the glass bulb rectifier is

(*a*) 80 to 1000 hours

(*b*) 2000 to 2500 hours

(*c*) 10,000 to 15,000 hours

(*d*) 200,000 to 250,000 hours.

257. The vacuum inside the glass bulb of a mercury arc rectifier is of the order of

(a) 5×10^{-3} cm of Hg

(b) 5×10^{-4} em of Hg

(c) 5×10^{-5} cm of Hg

(d) 5×10^{-5} cm of Hg

258. A 3 anode mercury arc rectifier has an anode current of overlap 300. Neglecting are drop, the regulation will be approximately

(a) 4%

(b) 5%

(c) 1%

(d) 9%

259. Which of the following is the loss within the mercury arc rectifier chamber?

(a) Voltage drop at the cathode

(b) Voltage drop at the anode

(c) Voltage drop in arc

(d) All of the above

260. For single phase supply frequency of 5 Hz, ripple frequency in full wave rectifier is

(a) 250

(b) 500

(c) 100

(d) 200

261. In a mercury arc rectifier

(a) Ion stream moves from cathode to anode

(b) Current flows from cathode to anode

(c) Electron stream moves from anode to cathode

(d) Ion stream moves from anode to cathode.

262. For producing cathode spot in a mercury arc rectifier

(a) An auxiliary electrode is used

(b) Tube is evacuated

(c) Low mercury vapour pressures are used

(d) Anode is heated.

263. If the voltage of anode B is raised to 510 V

(a) Anode B will conduct but anode A will also continue to conduct

(b) Anode B will not conduct and anode A will continue to conduct

(c) Both anodes will not conduct.

(d) None of these.

264. Ripple frequency of full wave rectifier working on 50 Hz supply will be

(a) 25 Hz

(b) 150 Hz

(c) 6 anode rectifier with inter phase transformer

(d) All will have indentical power factor.

265. The rms value of half wave rectifier sine wave with im as peak value is

(a) $0.700\ i_m$

(b) $0.665\ i_m$

(c) $0.50\ i_m$

(d) $0.310\ i_m$

266. The form factor for half-wave rectifier sine wave is

(a) 1.05

(b) 1.15

(c) 1.45

(d) 1.57

267. A silicon controlled rectifier is a

(a) Unijunction device

(b) Device with three junctions

(c) Device with four junctions

(d) None of the above

268. For full-wave rectifier sine wave, form factor is

(a) 1.55

(b) 1.44

(c) 1.22

(d) 1.11

269. At absolute zero temperature a semi-conductor behaves as

(a) An insulator

(b) A super-conductor

(c) A good conductor

(d) A variable resistor.

270. An electron in the conduction band

(a) Has higher energy than the electron in the valence band

(b) Has lower energy than the electron in the valence band

(c) Loses its charge easily.

(d) Jumps to the top of the crystal.

271. EG for silicon is 1.12 eV and for germanium is 0.72 eV. Thus it can be concluded that

(a) More number of electron-hole pairs will be generted in silicon than in germanium at room temperature.

(b) Less number of electron hole pairs will be generated in silicon than in germanium at room temperature.

(c) Equal number of electron-hole pairs will be generated in both at lower temperatures.

(d) Equal number of electron-hole pairs will he generated in both at higher temperatures.

272. EG for silicon is 1.12 eV and for germanium is 0.72 eV. Thus, it can be concluded that

(a) The conductivity of silicon will be less than that of germanium at room temperature.

(b) The conductivity of silicon will be more than that of germanium at room temperature.

(c) The conductivity of two will be same at 60°C.

(d) The conductivity of two will be same at 1000°C.

273. Before doping semiconductor material is generally
    (a) Dehydrated   (b) Heated
    (c) Hardened   (d) Purified

274. A Select the one that is a acceptor impurity element?
    (u) Antimony   (b) Gallium
    (c) Arsenic   (d) Phosphorous.

275. At room temperature when a voltage is applied to an intrinsic semiconductor.
    (a) Most of the electrons and holes move towards negative terminal.
    (b) Most of the electrons and holes move towards positive terminal.
    (c) Electrons move towards positive terminal and holes towards negative terminals.
    (d) Electrons move towards negative terminal and holes towards positive terminal

276. What happens to conductivity when a semiconductor is doped?
    (a) Increases
    (b) Decreases in the direct ratio of the doped material.
    (c) Decreases in the inverse ratio of me doped material.
    (d) Remains unaltered.

277. Under which of the following conditions avalanche breakdown in a semiconductor diode takes place?
    (a) When potential barrier is reduced to zero.
    (b) When reverse bias exceeds a certain value.
    (c) When a foward bias as exceeds a certain value.
    (d) When forward current exceeds a certain value.

278. Select the rectifier that needs four diodes.
    (a) Half wave rectifier
    (b) Centre-tap full wave rectifier.
    (c) Bridge rectifier.
    (d) None of the above.

279. Maximum rectification efficiency for a half wave rectifier is equal to
    (a) 100%
    (b) 88%
    (c) 50%
    (d) 40.6%

280. The maximum forward current in case of signal diode is in the range of
    (a) 1A to 10A   (b) 0.1 A to 1A
    (c) Few milli amperes   (d) Few nono amperes.

281. In a semiconductor avalanche breakdown takes place when
    (a) Reverse bias exceeds the limiting value.
    (b) Forward bias exceeds the limiting value.
    (c) Forward current exceeds the limiting value.
    (d) Potential barrier is reduced to zero.

282. The d.c. output voltage from a power supply
    (a) Increases with higher values of filter capacitance and decreases with more load current.
    (b) Decreases with higher values of filter capacitance and increases with more load current.
    (c) Decreases with higher values of filter capacitance as well as with more load current.
    (d) Increases with higher values of filter capacitance as well as with more load current.

283. With an a.c. input from 15 Hz power line, the ripple frequency is
    (a) 50 Hz in the d.c. output of half wave as well as full wave rectifier.
    (b) 100 Hz in the d.c. output of half wave as well as full wave rectifier.
    (c) 50 Hz in the d.c. output of half wave and 100 Hz in the d.c. output of full wave rectifier.
    (d) 100 Hz in the d.c. output of half wave and 50 Hz in the d.c. output of full wave rectifier.

284. A solar cell provides a example of
    (a) Photovoltaic cell
    (b) Photoconductive cell
    (c) Photoemissive cell
    (d) Photoradiation cell.

285. When yellow light is incident on a surface, no electrons are emitted while green light can emit. If red light is incident on the surface, then it is expected that
    (a) no electrons are emitted
    (b) photons are emitted
    (c) electrons of higher energy are emitted.
    (d) electrons of lower energy are emitted.

286. An ideal diode

(a) Should have zero resistance in the forward bias as well as reverse bias

(b) Should have zero resistance in the forward bias and an infinitely large resistance in reverse bias.

(c) Should have infinitely large resistance in the forward bias and zero resistance in reverse bias.

(d) Should have infinitely large resistance in forward as well as reverse bias.

287. In case a PN-junction is forward biased

(a) Holes and electrons size to move

(b) Electrons and holes move away from the junction.

(c) Electrons and holes move towards the junction

(d) Depletion region decreases.

288. The reverse resistance of a PN-junction diode.

(a) is always low

(b) is always high

(c) is given by breakdown voltage/reverse leakage current.

(d) is given by forward voltage/reverse leakage current.

289. For a PN-junction we generally have

I   Width of depletion layer

II   Junction barrier voltage

III Reverse leakage current

Which of the above parameters will decrease when the temperature of the junction rises?

(a) I only   (b) I and II only

(c) II and III only   (d) I, II and III.

290. In which case the temperature coefficient is positive

(a) Intrinsic semi-conductor.

(b) Extrinsic semi-conductor.

(c) Both intrinsic as well as extrinsic semiconductor.

(d) Neither intrinsic nor extrinsic semi-conductor.

291. In an RLC parallel circuit, the impedance at resonance is ___.

292. A balanced network is one in which corresponding series impedance elements are ___ and these elements are symmetrical with respect to ground potential.

293. For a conventional T network $Z^{sc} = 400$ and $Z^{sc} = 400$. Characteristic impedance of the symmetrical network is ___.

294. Rise time of the output pulse from an RC network with R = 10 K ohms and C = 100 μF is ___

295. A device whose characteristics are very close to that of an ideal voltage source is a ________.

296. A ideal voltage source has _______ internal resistance.

297. An ideal current source has ___ impedance.

298. If an uncharged capacitor is connected to an energy source, a current will flow instantaneously the capacitor being equivalent to a ___.

299. Amplitudes of radiation fields vary ___ with distance.

300. Cross-section of radiation field of a short dipole in the plane perpendicular to it is a ___.

301. To get linear voltage across a capacitor, it should be charged with ___ current.

EXERCISE – II

1. The magnetization 'M' of a superconductor in a field of H is   **DMRC 2014**

(a) extremely small   (b) – H

(c) – 1   (d) zero

2. For a connected planner graph of 'v' vertices and 'e' edges, the number of meshes is   **DMRC**

(a) e – v   (b) v – 1

(c) e – v – 1   (d) e – v +1

3. A particular current is made up of two components: a 10 A dc and a sinusoidal current of peak value of 14.14 A. The average value of the resultant current is   **DMRC**

(a) Zero   (b) 24.14 A

(c) 10 A   (d) 14.14 A

4. In the network shown, the switch is opened at $t = 0$. Prior to that, the network was in the steady-state, $V_s(t)$ at $t = 0$ is   **DMRC**

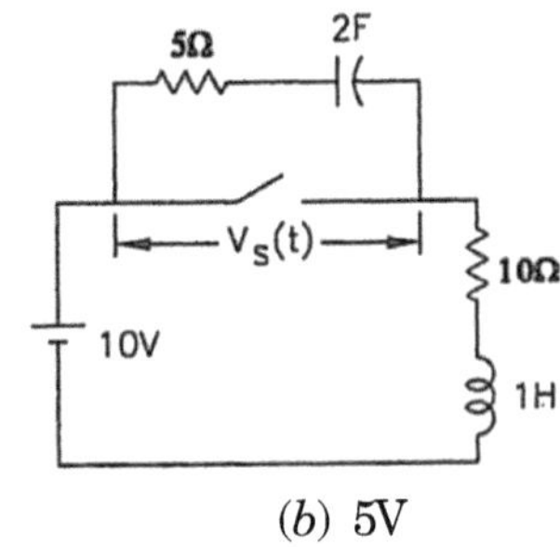

(a) 0   (b) 5V

(c) 10V   (d) 15V

5. Consider the following from the point of view of possible realisation as driving-point impedances using passive elements: **DMRC**

1. $\dfrac{1}{s(s+5)}$ 2. $\dfrac{s+3}{s^2(s+5)}$

3. $\dfrac{s^2+3}{s^2(s^2+5)}$ 4. $\dfrac{s+5}{s(s+3)}$

Among these

(a) 1, 2 and 4 are realisable

(b) 1, 2 and 3 are realisable

(c) 3 and 4 are realisable

(d) none is realisable

6. A periodic voltage having the Fourier series $v(t) = 1 + 4 \sin \omega t + 2 \cos \omega t$ volts is applied across a one-ohm resistor. The power dissipated in the one-ohm resistor is **DMRC**

(a) 1W (b) 11W

(c) 21 W (d) 24.5 W

7. An isolated sphere in air has a radius equal to $\dfrac{1}{4p\in_0}$ metre; its capacitance will be **DMRC**

(a) πF (b) $1F$

(c) $4\pi F$ (d) $\dfrac{1}{4\pi}F$

8. The given figure shows the surface charge distribution of q coulombs/m². What is the force on a unit charge placed at the centre of circle ?

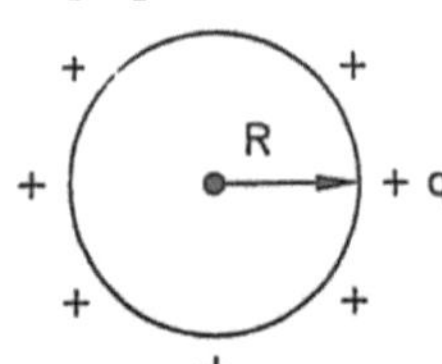

(a) Zero (b) $\dfrac{q}{4\pi R^2}$ N **DMRC**

(c) $\dfrac{q^2}{4\pi R}$ N (d) $\dfrac{q^2}{4\pi R^2}$ N

9. For transmission of wave form a dielectric medium of permittivity $\in_1$ into a dielectric medium of lower permittivity $\in_2$, $(\in_1 > \in_2)$ the critical angle of incidence (relating to the interferance) is given by **DMRC**

(a) $\sin^{-1}\sqrt{\dfrac{\in_2}{\in_1}}$ (b) $\cos^{-1}\sqrt{\dfrac{\in_2}{\in_1}}$

(c) $\tan^{-1}\sqrt{\dfrac{\in_2}{\in_1}}$ (d) $\sin^{-1}\left(\dfrac{\in_2}{\in_1}\right)$

10. For incidence from dielectric medium $1(\in_1)$ into dielectric medium $2(\in_2)$, Brewster angle θ_p and the corresponding angle of transmission θ_t for $\dfrac{\in_2}{\in_1} = 3$ will be respectively **DMRC**

(a) 30° and 30° (b) 30° and 60°

(c) 60° and 30° (d) 60° and 60°

11. The sum of two oppositely rotating circularly polarized waves of equal amplitude will be

(a) a circularly polarized wave **DMRC**

(b) a linearly polarized wave

(c) an elliptically polarized wave

(d) an unpolarized wave

12. A vacuum parallel plate capacitor is charged. The field between the plates is 2×10^4 V/m. If the space between the plates is filled with a material of relative dielectric constant of 10.0, then the value of the field in the dielectric will be **DMRC**

(a) 2×10^3 V/m

(b) $\dfrac{2}{\sqrt{10}} \times 10^{-4}$ V/m

(c) $2 \times \sqrt{10} \times 10^4$ V/m

(d) 2×10^5 V/m

13. In full sunlight, a solar cell has a short circuit current of 75 mA and a current of 70 mA for a terminal voltage of 0.6 V with a given load. The thevenin resistance of the solar cell is **RRB**

(a) 8 Ω (b) 8.6 Ω

(c) 120 Ω (d) 240 Ω

14. Consider the AC bridge shown in the figure below, with A, L and C having positive finite values.

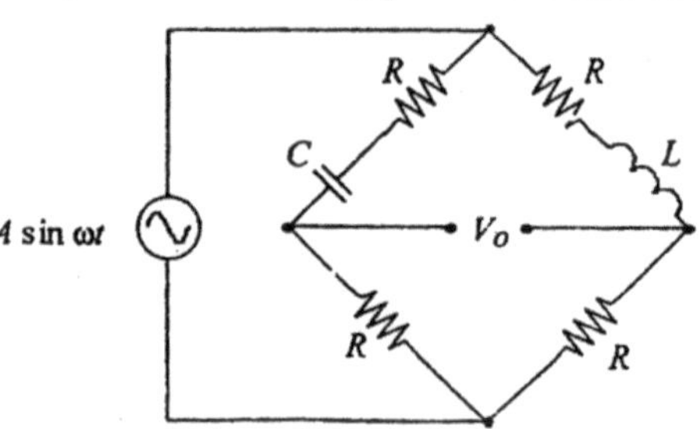

Then **RRB**

(a) $V_0 = 0$ if $\omega L = \dfrac{1}{\omega C}$

(b) $V_0 = 0$ if $L = C$

(c) $V_0 = 0$ if $R = \dfrac{1}{\omega\sqrt{LC}}$

(d) V_0 cannot be made zero

15. In the circuit, the value of the resistance R_s required for maximum power transfer from the 10 V source to the 10Ω load is given by **RRB**

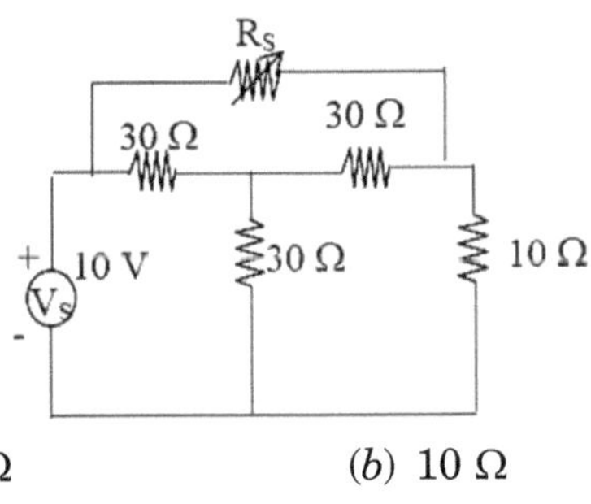

(a) 5 Ω

(b) 10 Ω

(c) 0 Ω

(d) 30 Ω

16. The total resistance faced by the voltage source having zero internal resistance in the circuit is

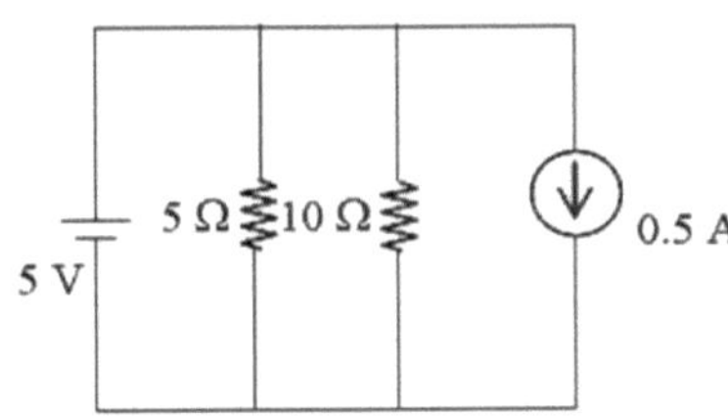

(a) 10 Ω

(b) 5 Ω   **RRB**

(c) 2.5 Ω

(d) 1.5 Ω

17. The total power developed in the circuit, if $V_0 = 125$ V is   **RRB**

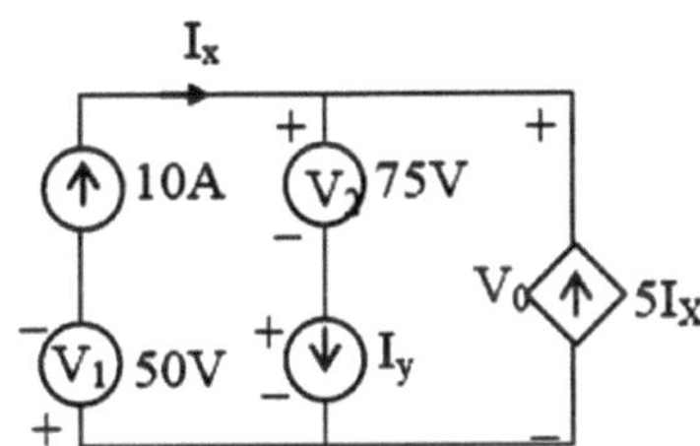

(a) 0 watt

(b) 4000 watts

(c) 8000 watts

(d) 16000 watts

18. Thevenin's equivalent resistance as seen from the terminals AB for the circuit is   **RRB**

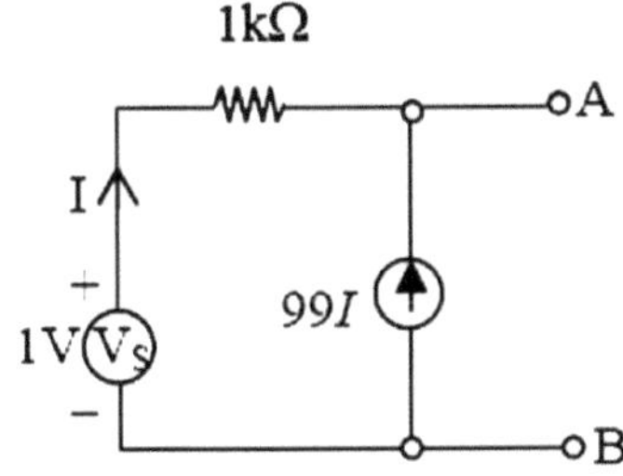

(a) 1 kΩ

(b) 10 Ω

(c) 100 Ω

(d) 10 kΩ

19. In the circuit shown below the maximum power that can be transferred to the load ZL is   **RRB**

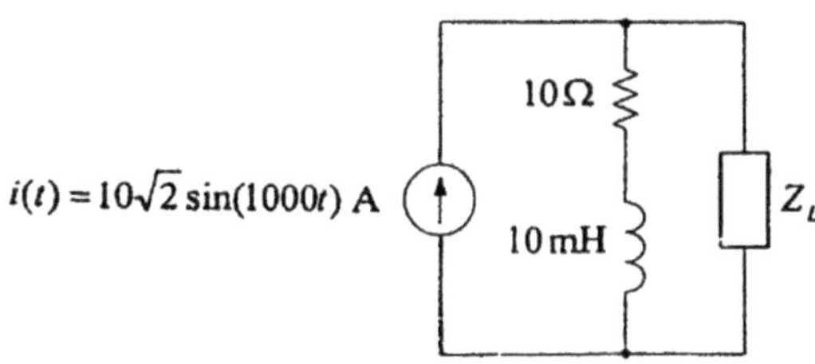

(a) 250 W

(b) 500 W

(c) 1000 W

(d) 2000 W

20. For the 2-port network shown the parameter Y_{12} is Equal to?   **RRB**

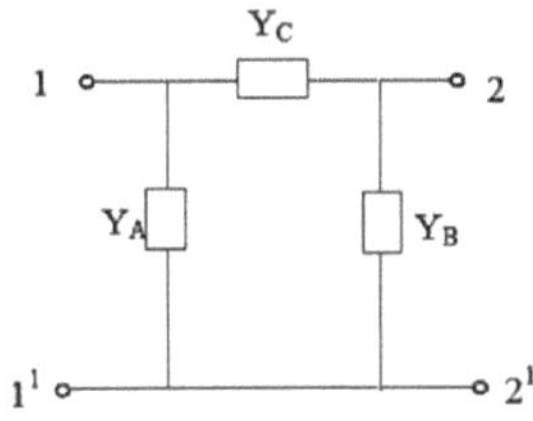

(a) Y_C

(b) $Y_C + Y_B$

(c) $Y_A + Y_C$

(d) $-Y_C$

21. For a two-port network, V_1 and V_2 given by

$V_1 = 60I_1 + 20I_2$

$V_2 = 20I_1 + 40I_2$

The Y – parameters of the network are   **RRB**

(a) $Y_{11} = 20 \times 10^{-3}$

$Y_{12} = -10 \times 10^{-3}$

$Y_{21} = -10 \times 10^{-3}$

$Y_{22} = 30 \times 10^{-3}$

(b) $Y_{11} = -10 \times 10^{-3}$

$Y_{12} = 20 \times 10^{-3}$

$Y_{21} = 20 \times 10^{-3}$

$Y_{22} = -30 \times 10^{-3}$

(c) $Y_{11} = 10 \times 10^{-3}$

$Y_{12} = -20 \times 10^{-3}$

$Y_{21} = -20 \times 10^{-3}$

$Y_{22} = 30 \times 10^{-3}$

(d) $Y_{11} = -20 \times 10^{-3}$

$Y_{12} = 10 \times 10^{-3}$

$Y_{21} = 10 \times 10^{-3}$

$Y_{22} = -30 \times 10^{-3}$

22. A metal wire has a uniform cross-section A, length l, and resistance R between its two end points. It is uniformly stretched so that its length becomes αl. The new resistance is   **RRB**

(a) α R

(b) α^2R

(c) $\sqrt{\alpha}$ R

(d) e^{α} R

23. A variable air gap type capacitor consists of two parallel plates : a fixed plate and a moving plate at a distance x. If a potential V is applied across the two plates, then force of attraction between the plates is related to x as **RRB**

(a) $F \propto x^2$

(b) $F \propto \dfrac{1}{x^2}$

(c) $F \propto \dfrac{1}{x}$

(d) $F \propto x$

24. The condition under which the input impedance at port 1 for the above network will be equal to R_0 is **RRB**

(a) $Z_a + Z_b = R_0$

(b) $Z_a Z_b = R_0^2$

(c) $Z_a / Z_b = 1$

(d) $Z_b / Z_a = \dfrac{1}{2}$

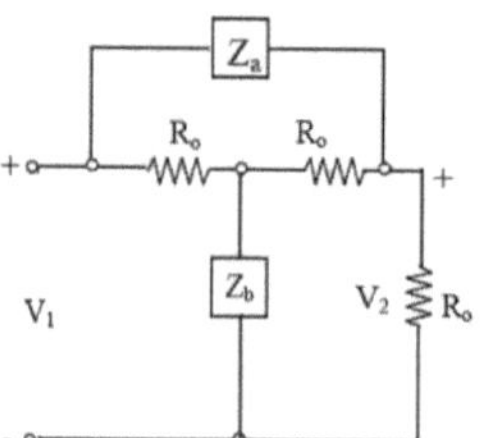

25. For the circuit shown in the figure, VR = 20 V when R = 10 W and VR = 30 V when R = 20 W For R = 80 W VR will read as **RRB**

(a) 48 V

(b) 60 V

(c) 120 V

(d) 160 V

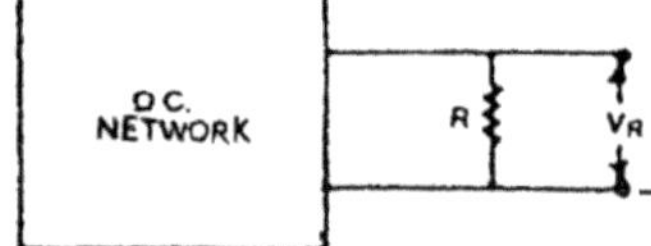

26. Consider the linear circuit with and ideal op-amp shown in the figure below. **RRB 2012**

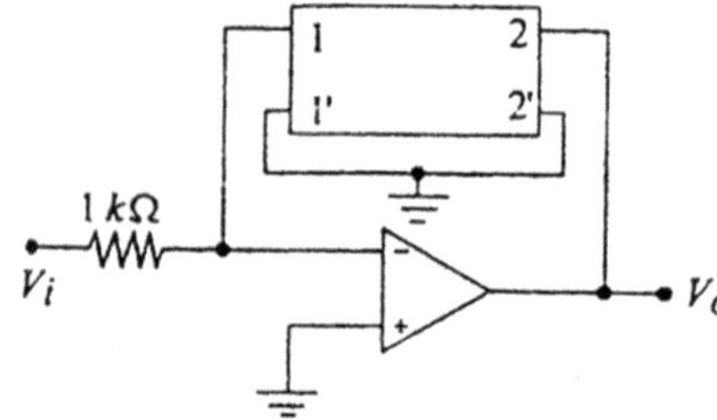

The Z-parameters of the two port feedback network are $Z_{11} = Z_{22} = 11\,k\Omega$ and $Z_{12} = Z_{21} = 1\,k\Omega$. The gain of the amplifier is

(a) + 110

(b) + 11

(c) − 1

(d) − 120

27. In the circuit shown in the following figure, the current through the 1Ω resistor is **RRB 2012**

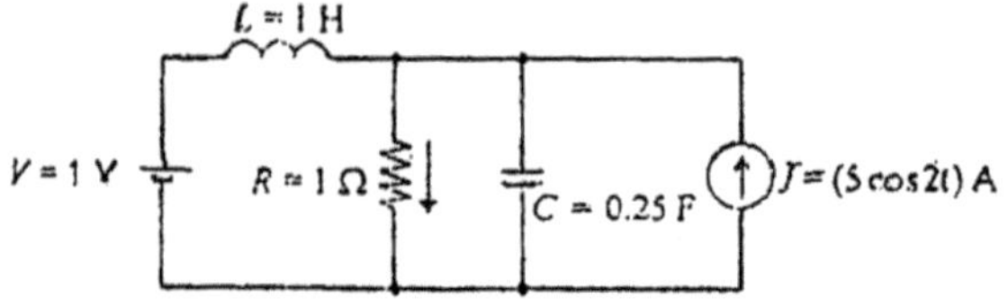

(a) $(1 + 5 \cos 2t)$ A

(b) $(5 + \cos 2t)$ A

(c) $(1 - 5 \cos 2t)$ A

(d) 6 A

28. In the circuit shown in the following figure, the switch is kept closed for a long time and then opened at t = 0. **RRB 2012**

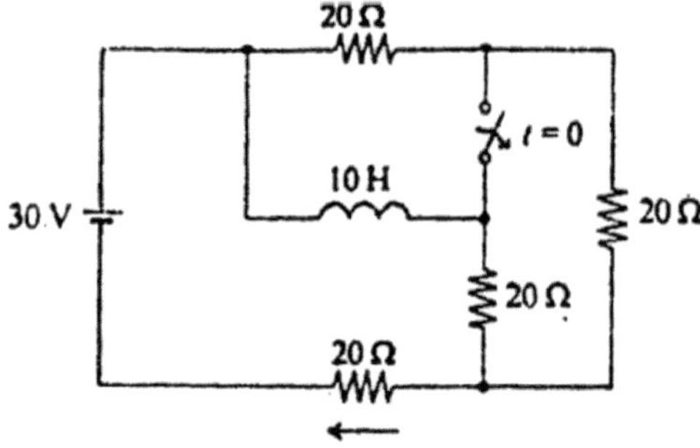

The values of the current i just before opening the switch (t = 0⁻) and just after opening the switch (t = 0⁺) are, respectively

(a) $\dfrac{3}{4}$ A and 1 A

(b) $\dfrac{3}{4}$ A and $\dfrac{5}{2}$ A

(c) 1 A and $\dfrac{7}{6}$ A

(d) 1 A and 1 A

29. In the circuit shown below, the current I is equal to

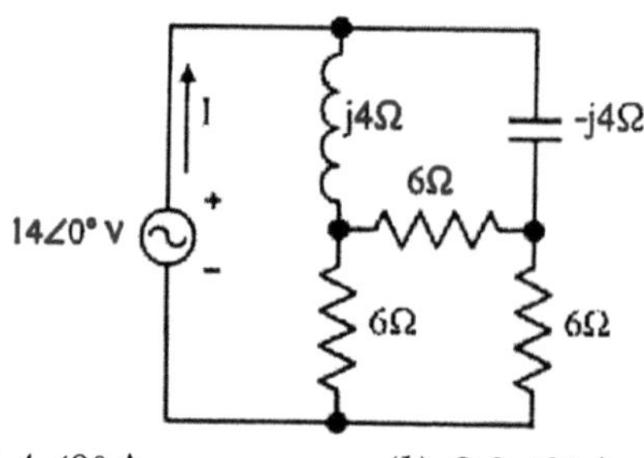

(a) $1.4\angle 0°$ A

(b) $2.0\angle 0°$ A

(c) $2.8\angle 0°$ A

(d) $3.2\angle 0°$ A **RRB 2012**

30. In the circuit shown below, the initial charge on the capacitor is 2.5 mC, with the voltage polarity as indicated. The switch is closed at time $t = 0$. The current $i(t)$ at a time t after the switch is closed is **RRB 2012**

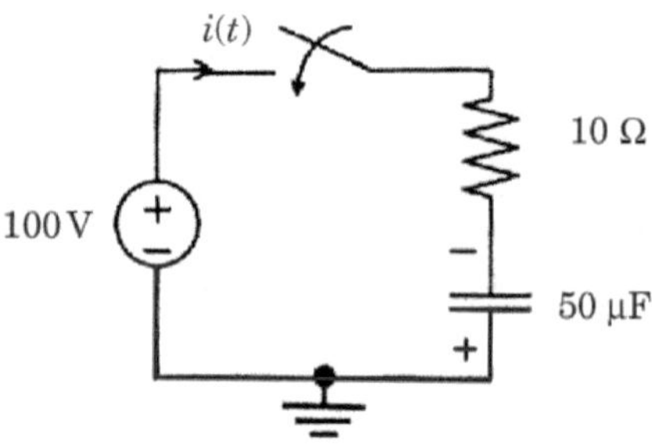

(a) $i(t) = 15 \exp(-2 \times 10^3\, t)$A

(b) $i(t) = 5 \exp(-2 \times 10^3\, t)$A

(c) $i(t) = 10 \exp(-2 \times 10^3\, t)$A

(d) $i(t) = -5 \exp(-2 \times 10^3\, t)$A

31. In the following figure, C_1 and C_2 are ideal capacitors. C_1 has been charged to 12 V before the ideal switch S is closed at t = 0. The current i(t) for all t is **RRB 2012**

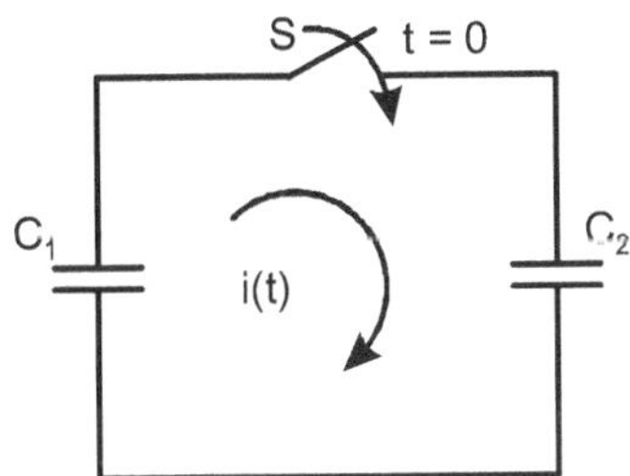

(a) zero

(b) a step function

(c) an exponentially decaying function

(d) an impulse function

32. In the circuit shown below the maximum power that can be transferred to the load ZL is

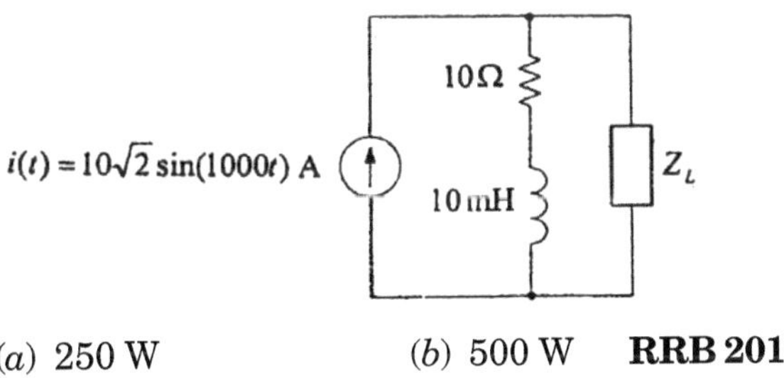

(a) 250 W

(c) 1000 W

(b) 500 W   **RRB 2012**

(d) 2000 W

33. The impedance looking into nodes 1 and 2 in the given circuit is **RRB 2012**

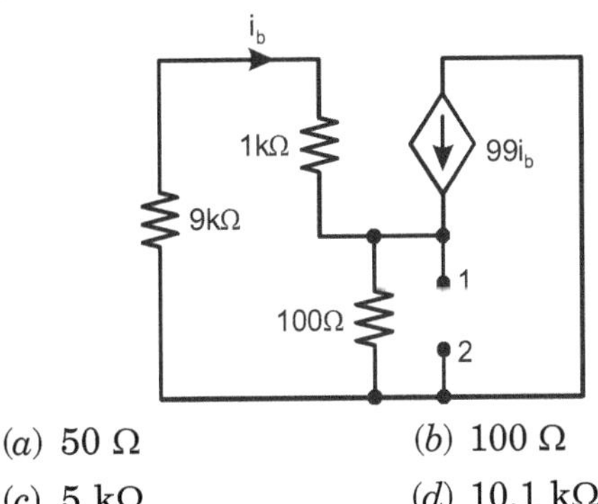

(a) 50 Ω

(b) 100 Ω

(c) 5 kΩ

(d) 10.1 kΩ

34. A metal wire has a uniform cross-section A, length l, and resistance R between its two end points. It is uniformly stretched so that its length becomes $\alpha\, l$. The new resistance is **RRB 2012**

(a) α R

(b) α^2R

(c) $\sqrt{\alpha}$ R

(d) e^{α} R

35. Assuming both the voltage source are in phase, the value of R for which maximum power is transferred from circuit A to circuit B is

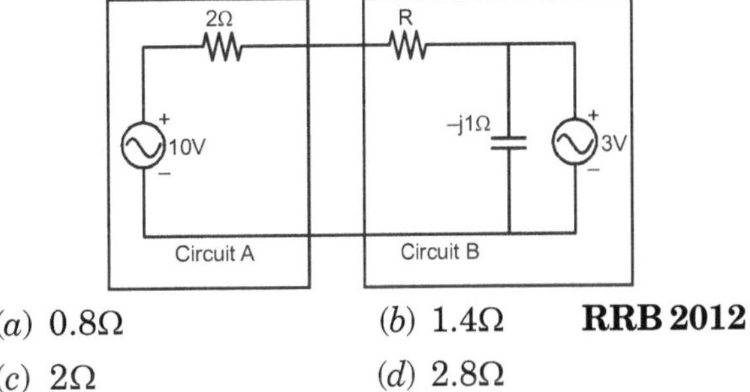

(a) 0.8Ω

(b) 1.4Ω **RRB 2012**

(c) 2Ω

(d) 2.8Ω

ANSWERS

EXERCISE – I

1. (d)	2. (a)	3. (a)	4. (d)	5. (c)	6. (a)	7. (b)	8. (c)	9. (d)	10. (b)
11. (c)	12. (a)	13. (b)	14. (a)	15. (b)	16. (c)	17. (a)	18. (a)	19. (b)	20. (a)
21. (c)	22. (a)	23. (b)	24. (c)	25. (c)	26. (a)	27. (b)	28. (a)	29. (b)	30. (b)
31. (a)	32. (d)	33. (a)	34. (a)	35. (d)	36. (a)	37. (c)	38. (b)	39. (c)	40. (d)
41. (d)	42. (d)	43. (a)	44. (c)	45. (c)	46. (c)	47. (a)	48. (a)	49. (b)	50. (c)
51. (d)	52. (c)	53. (b)	54. (b)	55. (c)	56. (b)	57. (a)	58. (b)	59. (b)	60. (a)
61. (b)	62. (a)	63. (b)	64. (c)	65. (b)	66. (c)	67. (d)	68. (d)	69. (b)	70. (a)
71. (c)	72. (a)	73. (b)	74. (c)	75. (b)	76. (a)	77. (c)	78. (a)	79. (d)	80. (c)
81. (b)	82. (c)	83. (a)	84. (b)	85. (c)	86. (a)	87. (c)	88. (d)	89. (c)	90. (d)
91. (d)	92. (d)	93. (e)	94. (d)	95. (d)	96. (c)	97. (e)	98. (c)	99. (c)	100. (a)
101. (a)	102. (c)	103. (a)	104. (c)	105. (b)	106. (c)	107. (b)	108. (a)	109. (b)	110. (c)
111. (a)	112. (a)	113. (a)	114. (b)	115. (a)	116. (a)	117. (b)	118. (c)	119. (b)	120. (b)
121. (b)	122. (c)	123. (d)	124. (a)	125. (d)	126. (a)	127. (a)	128. (b)	129. (b)	130. (c)

131. (a)	**132.** (a)	**133.** (c)	**134.** (c)	**135.** (c)	**136.** (a)	**137.** (b)	**138.** (c)	**139.** (b)	**140.** (d)
141. (b)	**142.** (a)	**143.** (d)	**144.** (b)	**145.** (c)	**146.** (d)	**147.** (a)	**148.** (b)	**149.** (a)	**150.** (a)
151. (c)	**152.** (b)	**153.** (c)	**154.** (b)	**155.** (a)	**156.** (c)	**157.** (a)	**158.** (b)	**159.** (b)	**160.** (a)
161. (b)	**162.** (c)	**163.** (c)	**164.** (a)	**165.** (d)	**166.** (a)	**167.** (a)	**168.** (b)	**169.** (c)	**170.** (a)
171. (d)	**172.** (c)	**173.** (a)	**174.** (c)	**175.** (c)	**176.** (b)	**177.** (b)	**178.** (b)	**179.** (d)	**180.** (b)
181. (a)	**182.** (b)	**183.** (c)	**184.** (d)	**185.** (b)	**186.** (c)	**187.** (b)	**188.** (a)	**189.** (c)	**190.** (a)
191. (a)	**192.** (b)	**193.** (a)	**194.** (c)	**195.** (c)	**196.** (a)	**197.** (c)	**198.** (d)	**199.** (a)	**200.** (a)
201. (c)	**202.** (b)	**203.** (c)	**204.** (a)	**205.** (a)	**206.** (c)	**207.** (a)	**208.** (b)	**209.** (d)	**210.** (c)
211. (c)	**212.** (d)	**213.** (d)	**214.** (b)	**215.** (c)	**216.** (b)	**217.** (c)	**218.** (c)	**219.** (c)	**220.** (a)
221. (c)	**222.** (d)	**223.** (d)	**224.** (b)	**225.** (d)	**226.** (b)	**227.** (c)	**228.** (c)	**229.** (a)	**230.** (b)
231. (c)	**232.** (c)	**233.** (a)	**234.** (b)	**235.** (a)	**236.** (b)	**237.** (a)	**238.** (c)	**239.** $40°5$	**240.** (b)
241. (b)	**242.** (b)	**243.** (a)	**244.** (b)	**245.** (c)	**246.** (b)	**247.** (b)	**248.** (d)	**249.** (a)	**250.** (c)
251. (d)	**252.** (d)	**253.** (c)	**254.** (b)	**255.** (b)	**256.** (c)	**257.** (c)	**258.** (c)	**259.** (d)	**260.** (c)
261. (d)	**262.** (a)	**263.** (a)	**264.** (a)	**265.** (c)	**266.** (d)	**267.** (b)	**268.** (d)	**269.** (a)	**270.** (a)
271. (b)	**272.** (a)	**273.** (d)	**274.** (b)	**275.** (c)	**276.** (a)	**277.** (b)	**278.** (c)	**279.** (d)	**280.** (c)
281. (a)	**282.** (a)	**283.** (c)	**284.** (a)	**285.** (a)	**286.** (b)	**287.** (d)	**288.** (c)	**289.** (b)	**290.** (b)

291. L/CR   **292.** Equal   **293.** 400 ohms

294. –22   **295.** Zever diode   **296.** Zero

297. Infinite   **298.** Ideal current source / maximum.

299. inversely   **300.** dough-nut/cirde   **301.** Constant

EXERCISE – II

1. (b)	**2.** (d)	**3.** (c)	**4.** (b,c)	**5.** (c)	**6.** (b)	**7.** (b)	**8.** (a)	**9.** (c)	**10.** (c)
11. (c)	**12.** (a)	**13.** (a)	**14.** (c)	**15.** (c)	**16.** (c)	**17.** (c)	**18.** (b)	**19.** (c)	**20.** (d)
21. (a)	**22.** (b)	**23.** (b)	**24.** (b)	**25.** (a)	**26.** (d)	**27.** (a)	**28.** (d)	**29.** (b)	**30.** (a)
31. (d)	**32.** (c)	**33.** (b)	**34.** (b)	**35.** (a)					

■■

Computer Engineering

COMPUTER-ARCHITECTURE

- A digital computer consists of
  - (*i*) A processor (CPU)
  - (*ii*) Input devices
  - (*iii*) Output devices
- CPU is further subdivided into 3 sections:
  - (*i*) Arithmetic logic unit
  - (*ii*) Control unit
  - (*iii*) General purpose registers
- Arithmetic logic unit performs all arithmetic logic operations.
- The control unit decodes the instructions in the program and instruct the various devices associated with the computer to perform various operations.
- The general purpose registers are used for storing intermediate or partial results temporarily.
- The input device is used for taking in the Program and Data and its operation is referred to as Read operation., e.g. Floppy Disk, Paper Tape, Card reader etc.
- The output device is used for giving out the result. Its operation is known as write operation, e.g. VDU, printer, etc.
- Memory is the storage part of a computer which stores large masses or quantity of input data and it even the stores final results to be given as output. It store users programmes as well as control programs.

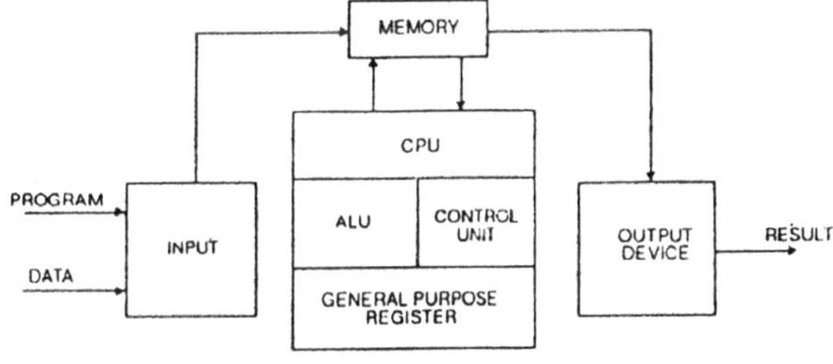

INPUT-OUTPUT ORGANIZATION

PERIPHERAL DEVICES.

Devices that are under the direct control of the computer are said to be *connected on-line*. These devices are designed to read information into or out of the memory unit upon command from the CPU and are considered to be part of the total computer system.

Input or Output devices attached to the computer are also called *peripherals*.

Some most common peripherals are keyboards, display units, and printers.

Peripherals that provide auxiliary storage for the system are magnetic disks and tapes. Peripherals are electromechanical and electromagnetic devices of some complexity.

Video monitors.

These are the most commonly used peripherals. They consist of a keyboard as the input device and a display unit as the output device. There are different types of video monitors, but the most popular use a *cathode ray tube* (CRT). The CRT contains an electronic gun that sends an electronic beam to a phosphorescent screen in front of the tube. The beam can be deflected horizontally and vertically.

Printers.

These provide a permanent record on paper of computer output data or text.

There are three basic types of character printers:

- (**i**) daisywheel
- (**ii**) dot matrix
- (**iii**) laser printers.

The daisywheel printers contains a wheel with the characters placed along the circumference. To print a character, the wheel rotates to the proper position and an energized magnet then presses the letter against the ribbon. The dot matrix printer contains a set of dots along the printing the mechanism.

e.g., a 5×7 dot matrix printer that prints 80 characters per line has seven horizontal lines, each consisting of $5 \times 80 = 400$ dots. Each dot can be printed or not, depending on the specific characters that are printed on the line. The laser printer uses a rotating photographic drum that is used to imprint the character images. The pattern is then transferred onto paper in the same manner as a copying machine.

Magnetic tapes.

These are used mostly for storing files of data: for example, a company's payroll record. Access is sequential and consists of records that can be accessed one after another as the tape moves along a stationary read-write mechanism. It is one of the cheapest and slowest methods for storage and has the advantage that tapes can be removed when not in use. Magnetic disks have high-speed rotational surface coated with magnetic material. Access is achieved by moving a read-write mechanism to a track in the magnetized surface. Disks are used mostly for bulk storage of programs and data.

Other input and output devices.

These are encountered in computer systems are digital incremental plotters, optical and magnetic character readers, analog-to-digital converters, and various data acquisition equipment. Not all input comes from people, and not all output is intended for people. Computers are used to control various processes in real time, such as machine tooling, assembly line procedures, and chemical and industrial processes. For such applications, a method must be provided for sensing status conditions in the process and sending control signals to the process being controlled.

The input-output organization of a computer is a function of the size of the computer and the devices connected to it. The difference between a small and a large system is mostly dependent on the amount of hardware the computer has available for communicating with peripheral units and the number of peripherals connected to the system. Since each peripheral behaves differently from any other, it would be prohibitive to dwell on the detailed interconnections needed between the computer and each peripheral.

INPUT–OUTPUT INTERFACE

Input–output interface provides a method for transferring information between internal storage and external I/O devices. Peripherals connected to a computer need special communication links for interfacing them with the central processing unit. The purpose of the communication link is to resolve the differences that exist between the central computer and each peripheral.

To resolve these differences, computer systems include special hardware components between the CPU and peripherals to supervise and synchronize all input and output transfers. These components are called interface units because they interface between the processor bus and the peripheral device. In addition, each device may have its own controller that supervises the operations of the particular mechanism in the peripheral.

I/O Bus and Interface Modules.

A typical communication link between the processor and several peripherals is shown in the figure below.

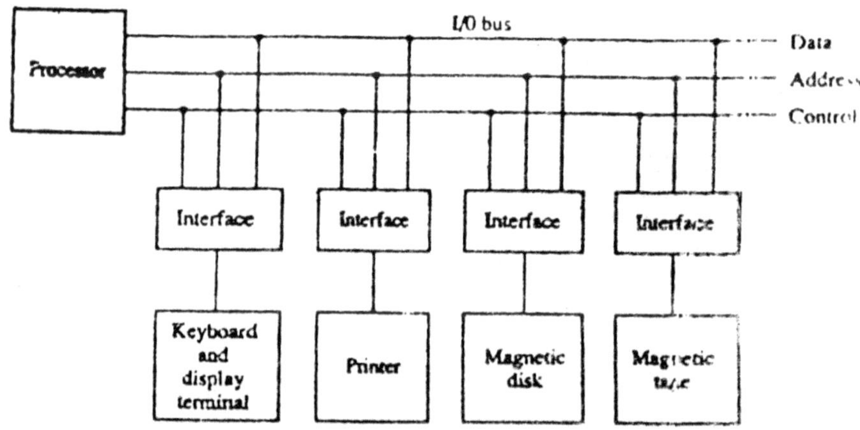

Fig. Connection of I/O bus to input-output devices.

The I/O bus consists of data lines, address lines, and control lines. The magnetic disk, printer, and terminal are employed in practically any general-purpose computer. The magnetic tape is used in some computers for backup storage. Each peripheral device has associated with it an interface unit. Each interface decodes the address and control received from the I/O bus, interprets them for the peripheral, and provides signals for the peripheral controller. It also synchronizes the data flow and supervises the transfer between peripheral and processor. Each peripheral has its own controller that operates the particular electromechanical device.

e.g., The printer controller controls the paper motion, the print timing, and the selection of printing characters. A controller may be housed separately or may be physically integrated with the peripheral.

The I/O bus from the processor is attached to all peripheral interfaces. To communicate with a particular device, the processor places a device address of the address lines. Each interface attached to the I/O bus contains an address decoder that monitors the address lines. When the interface detects its own address, it activates the path between the bus lines and the device that it controls. All peripherals whose address does not correspond to the address in the bus are disabled by their interface.

Types of command.

There are four types of commands that an interface may receive.

(*i*) A *control command* : It issued to activate the peripheral and to inform it what to do.

e.g., a magnetic tape unit may be instructed to backspace the tape by one record, to rewind the tape, or to start the tape moving in the forward direction.

(*ii*) A *status command:* It is used to test various status conditions in the interface and the peripheral. For example, the computer may wish to check the status of the peripheral before a transfer is initiated.

(*iii*) A *data output command*: It causes the interface to respond by transferring data from the bus into one of its register. Consider an example with a tape unit.

(*iv*) *The data input command*: It is the opposite of the data output. In this case the interface receives an item of data from the peripheral and places it in its buffer register. The processor checks if data are available by means of a status command and then issue a data input command. The interface places the data on the data lines, where they are accepted by the processor.

I/O Versus Memory Bus.

I/O the memory bus contains data, address, and read/write control lines. There are three ways that computer buses can be used to communicate with memory and I/O:

(*i*) Use two separate buses, one for memory and the other for I/O.

(*ii*) Use one common bus for both memory and I/O but have separate control lines for each.

(*iii*) Use one common bus for memory and I/O with common control lines.

MEMORY ORGANIZATION

Memory Hierarchy

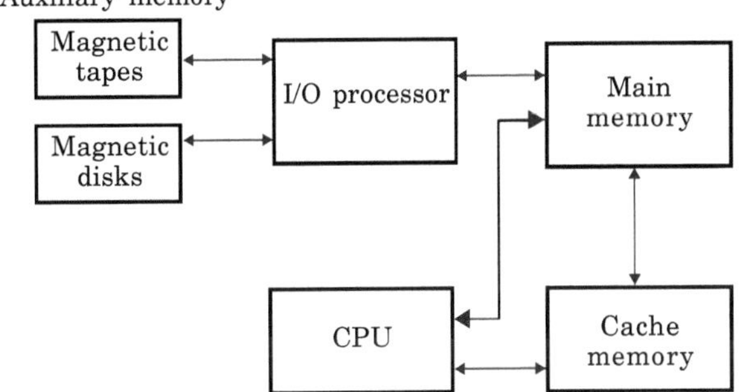

Fig. Memory hierarchy in a computer system

The memory unit that communicates directly with the CPU is called the *main memory*.

Devices that provide backup storage are called *auxiliary memory*. The most common auxiliary memory devices used in computer systems are magnetic disks and taps. They are used for storing system programs, large data files, and other backup information. Only programms and data currently needed by the processor reside in main memory. All other information is stored in auxiliary memory and transferred to main memory when needed.

Figure shown above illustrates the components in a typical memory hierarchy. At the bottom of the hierarchy are the relatively slow magnetic tapes used to store removable files. Next are the magnetic disks used as backup storage. The main memory occupies a central position by being able to communicate directly with the CPU and with auxiliary memory devices through an I/O processor. When programs not residing in main memory are needed by the CPU, they are brought in from auxiliary memory. Programs not currently needed in main memory are transferred into auxiliary memory to provide space for currently used programs and data.

A special very-high-speed memory called a *cache* is sometimes used to increase the speed of processing by making current programs and data available to the CPU at a rapid rate. The cache memory is employed in computer systems to compensate for the speed differential between main memory access time and processor logic. CPU logic is usually faster than main memory access time, with the result that processing speed is limited primarily by the speed of main memory. A technique used to compensate for the mismatch in operating speeds is to employ an extremely fast, small cache between the CPU and main memory whose access time is close to processor logic clock cycle time. The cache is used for storing segments of programs currently being executed in the CPU and temporary data frequently needed in the present calculations.

Many operating systems designed to enable the CPU to process a number of independent programs concurrently. This concept, called *multiprogramming*, refers to the existence of two or more programs in different parts of the memory hierarchy at the same time. In this way it is possible to keep all parts of the computer busy by working with several programs in sequence. For example, suppose that a program is being executed in the CPU and an I/O transfer is required. The CPU initiates the I/O processor to start executing the transfer. This leaves the CPU free to execute another program. In a multiprogramming system, when one program is waiting for input or output transfer, there is another program ready to utilize the CPU.

PERSONAL COMPUTERS

Configuration.

Personal computers can be categorized by size and portability as :

- Desktop computers
- Laptop or notebooks
- Personal Digital Assistants (PDAs)
- Portable computers
- Tablet computers
- Wearable computers

Uses.

Personal computers are normally operated by one user at a time to perform such general purpose tasks as word processing, Internet browsing, Internet faxing, e-mail and other digital messaging , multimedia playback, computer game play, computer programming, etc. The user of modern personal computer may have significant knowledge of the operating environment and application programs, but is not necessarily interested in programming not even able to write programs for the computer. Therefore, most software written primarily for personal computers tends to be designed with simplicity of use, or "user-friendliness" in mind. However, the software industry continuously provide a wide range of new products for use in personal computers, targeted at both the expert and the non-expert user.

Computer Components.

- Computer case with power supply (usually sold together)
- Motherboard
- Processor with fan (usually sold together)
- At least one memory card
- Mass storage
- Keyboard and mouse for input
- Monitor for output

The motherboard connects everthing together. The memory card(s), graphics card and processor are mounted directly onto the motherboard (the processor in a socket an the memory and graphics cards in an expansion slot). The mass storage is connected to it with cables. Same for keyboard and mouse, except that they are external and connect to the back plate. The monitor is also connected to the back plate, except not (usually) directly to the motherboard, but to a connector in the graphics card.

The mass storage can be :

- Hard disk
- Floppy drive or zip drive (both with media)
- Optical drive (CD or DVD)

The operating system (e.g., Microsoft Windows, Linux or many others) can be located on either of these, but typically it i on son one of the hard disks. Alive CD is also possible, but very slow and used for either installation of sence the OS or problem solving.

A typical computer also has :

- Sound card
- Network card
- Modern and possibly router

Common additions, connected on the outside (peripherals).

- Printer
- Scanner
- Webcam
- Speakers
- Microphone
- Headset
- Card reader
- Gaming devices such as a joystick

Motherboard.

The motherboard (or mainboard) is the primary circuit board within a personal computer. Many other components connect directly or indirectly to the motherboard. Motherboards usually contain one or more CPUs, supporting circuitry - usually integrated circuits (ICs) providing the interface between the CPU memory and input/output peripheral circuits, main memory, and facilities for initial setup of the computer immediately after being powered on (often called boot firmware or, in IBM PC compatible computers, a BIOS). In many portable and embedded personal computers, the motherboard houses nearly all of the PC's core components. Often a motherboard will also contain one or more peripheral buses and physical connectors for expansion purposes. Sometimes a secondary daughter board is connected with the motherboard to provide further expandibility or to satisfy space constraints.

Central Porcessing Unit.

The central processing unit, or CPU, is that part of a computer which executes software program instructions. In older computers this circuitry was formely on several printed circuit boards, but in PC class machines, has been from the first personal computers, a single integrated circuit. Nearly all PCs contain a type of CPU known as a **microprocessor**. The microprocessor often plugs into the motherboard using one of many different types of socket. IBM PC compatible computers use an x86-compatible processor, usually made by Intel, AMD, VIA Technologies or Transmeta. Apple Macintosh computers were initially built with the Motorola 680x0 family of processors, then switched to the Power PC series (a RISC architecture jointly developed by IBM, Motorola, and Apple Computer), but as of 2006, Apple has switched again, this time to x86 compatible processors.

Main Memory.

A PC's main memory (i.e., its primary store) is fast storage that is directly accessible by the CPU, and is used to store the currently executing program and immidiately needed data. PCs use semiconductor Random Access Memory (RAM) of various kinds such as DRAM or SRAM as their primary storage. Which exact kind depends on cost/performance issues at any particular time. Main memory is much faster than mass storage devices like hard disks or optical discs, but is usually volatile, meaning it does not retain its contents (instructions or data) in the absence of power, and is much more expensive for a given capacity than is most mass storage. Main memory is generally not suitable for long-term or archival data storage.

Mass storages devices store programs and data even when the power is off; they do require power to perform read/write functions during usage. Although semiconductor flash memory has dropped in cost, the prevailing form of mass storage in personal computers is still the electromechanical hard disk.

The disk drives use a sealed Head/Disk Assembly (HDA) which was first introduced by IBM's "Winchester" disk system. The use of a sealed assembly allowed the use of the positive air pressure to drive out particles from the surface of the disk, which improves reliability.

Video Card :

The video card- otherwise called a graphics card, graphics adapter or video adapter - processors and renders the graphics output from the computer to the computer display, also called the Visual Display Unit (VDU), and is an essential part of the modern computer.

EXERCISE – I

1. A byte is
   (a) a group of 2 bits. (b) a group of 4 bits.
   (c) a group of 8 bits. (d) a group of 16 bits.

2. An address is the number used by the CPU to specify
   (a) a location in the memory.
   (b) a location in flags.
   (c) a location in accumulator.
   (d) a location in stack pointer.

3. Which of the following is not correct ?
   (a) Bus is a group of wires.
   (b) Bootstrap is a technique or device for loading first instruction.
   (c) An instruction is a set of bits that defines a computer operation.
   (d) An interrupt signal is required at the start of every programme.

4. Which of the following task is not per formed by an assembler ?
   (a) Providing storage allocation.
   (b) Creating a table of lables etc.
   (c) Doing assembly time arithmetic.
   (d) Atranslate a programme written in high level language to machine code programme,

5. Double Precision employs
   (a) double signal speed.
   (b) two computer words to represent a number.
   (c) error-reduction code.
   (d) None of these.

6. Dump means
   (a) erasing used data.
   (b) storing used data, in pushdown stack.
   (c) copying data from internal stage to external storage.
   (d) None of these

7. One of the following is not found on the motherboard of a personal computer:
   (a) Direct memory access (DMA) controller.
   (b) Programmable timer.
   (c) Interrup, controller.
   (d) Video display adapter.

8. One of the following is a direct entry input device
   (a) Key-to-diskette. (b) Punched card,
   (c) Computer terminal. (d) Mouse.

9. Algorithm is used
   (a) to bring itself into desired state by its own action.
   (b) to perform logarithmic operations.
   (c) to describe a set of procedure by which given result is obtained.
   (d) None of these.

10. Call in computer systems means
    (a) to execute a part of main programme.
    (b) to call a sub-programme to be executed.
    (c) to transfer control to specified closed subroutine.
    (d) None of these.

11. CPU of a computer system does not contain
    (a) Main storage.
    (b) Arithmatic unit.
    (c) Special register group,
    (d) None of these.

12. Which of the following operations is not performed by the CPU of a computer system ?
    (a) Arithmetic operations.
    (b) Providing timing signals.
    (c) Control instruction processing.
    (d) None of these.

13. An assembler in a computer system prepares
    (a) machine-language programme from a symbolic language programme.
    (b) object programme.
    (c) assembles computer instructions and data in the machine.
    (d) None of these.

14. The input unit of a computer
    (a) feeds the data in CPU.
    (b) retrieves the data from CPU.
    (c) directs all other units.
    (d) All of the above.

15. The control unit of a computer
    (a) performs arithmetic and logical operations on the data.
    (b) controls the operation of output devices.
    (c) is a device for manually operating the computer.
    (d) directs the other units of the computer.

16. A CPU generally contains
    (a) registers and ALU.
    (b) a control and timing section.
    (c) instruction decoding circuit.
    (d) All of the above.

17. Which of the following computers is least powerful?
    (a) Minicomputer
    (b) Microcomputer
    (c) Mainframe computer
    (d) Super computer

18. Which of the following storage devices can be carried around ?
    (a) Floppy disks   (b) Main memory
    (c) Registers   (d) Core memory

19. Which of the following is the internal memory of the computer ?
    (a) CPU register   (b) Cache
    (c) Main memory   (d) All of these

20. Which of the following is responsible for coordinating various operations using timing signals ?
    (a) Arithmetic logic unit.
    (b) Control unit.
    (c) Memory unit.
    (d) Input/Output unit.

21. The ALU of a computer normally contains a number of high speed storage elements called
    (a) semiconductor memory.
    (b) registers.
    (c) hard disk.
    (d) magnetic disk.

22. Computer peripheral is
    (a) a computer device which is not connected to CPU.
    (b) a device which is connected to CPU.
    (c) a device for manually operating the computer.
    (d) None of the above.

23. The unit of a computer system which executes programme, communicates with and often controls the operation of other subsystems of the computer is the
    (a) CPU.   (b) Control unit.
    (c) I/O unit.   (d) Peripheral unit.

24. The language which a computer can understand is
    (a) high level language.
    (b) assembly language.
    (c) machine language.
    (d) All of the above.

25. Computer software consists of
    (a) system programme.
    (b) application programme.
    (c) operating system programme.
    (d) All of the above.

26. A variable
    (*a*) can be assigned a numerical value
    (*b*) can be assigned a non-numerical value
    (*c*) is a data item whose value may change
    (*d*) all of the above

27. The process of executing several programme simultaneously by use of more than one processing unit is known as
    (*a*) multiprogramming. (*b*) multiprocessing.
    (*c*) time sharing.   (*d*) batch processing.

28. A system programme which is used in creating and modifying a file is known as
    (*a*) the editor programme.
    (*b*) the monitor programme.
    (*c*) the job control programme.
    (*d*) None of the above

29. The programme which is run on one computer and which initiates the operation of another computer is knwon as
    (*a*) compiler.   (*b*) filing routine.
    (*c*) interpreter.   (*d*) simulator.

30. The system which permits a large number of users at various remote terminals to simultaneously use a centrally located computer is known as
    (*a*) servomechanism system.
    (*b*) time sharing system.
    (*c*) mainframe system.
    (*d*) None of the above.

31. A file of records containing cumulative history or results of accumulation is knwon as
    (*a*) control data file.   (*b*) master file.
    (*c*) indexed file.   (*d*) None of the above.

32. A file which contains transient data to be processed in combination with a master file is known as
    (*a*) sequential file
    (*b*) master file
    (*c*) transmission file
    (*d*) random organization file

33. The following process is used to trace and eliminate mistakes in programme or faults in equipments
    (*a*) Housekeeping   (*b*) Editing
    (*c*) Debug   (*d*) Desk check

34. The device on which a record can be compared or tested to identify character by character with a retranscription is called a
    (*a*) sorter.   (*b*) simulator.
    (*c*) verifier.   (*d*) interpreter.

35. A read bit
    (*a*) can be read and written by CPU.
    (*b*) can be read and written by peripheral.
    (*c*) can be read by peripheral and written by CPU.
    (*d*) can be read by CPU and written by the peripheral.

36. Compiler and interpreters are examples of
    (*a*) system software.
    (*b*) application software.
    (*c*) both system and application software.
    (*d*) None of these.

37. A software programme stored in a ROM that can not be changed easily is known as
    (*a*) hardware.   (*b*) linker.
    (*c*) editor.   (*d*) firmware.

38. A system programme which translates and executes an instruction simultaneously is known as
    (*a*) compiler.   (*b*) operating system.
    (*c*) interpreter.   (*d*) assembler.

39. Relative to the programme translated by a compiler, the same programme when interpreted runs
    (*a*) faster.
    (*b*) slower.
    (*c*) at the same speed.
    (*d*) may be faster or slower.

40. The operating system manages
    (*a*) memory.
    (*b*) processor.
    (*c*) disk and I/O devices.
    (*d*) All of the above.

41. Situations where two or more processes are reading or writing some shared data and the final result depends on who runs precisely are called
    (*a*) race conditions.   (*b*) critical sections.
    (*c*) mutual sections.   (*d*) message passing.

42. Part of a programme where the shared memory is accessed and which should be executed indivisibly, is called
    (*a*) semaphores.   (*b*) directory.
    (*c*) critical section.   (*c*) mutual exclusion.

43. Producer consumer problem can be solved by using
    (*a*) semaphores.   (*b*) event counters.
    (*c*) monitors.   (*d*) All of the above.

44. Moving process from main memory to disk is called
    (*a*) scheduling.   (*b*) catching.
    (*c*) swapping.   (*d*) spooling.

45. Block catches or buffer catches are used

(a) to improve disk performance.

(b) to handle interrupts.

(c) to increase the capacity of the main memory.

(d) to speed up main memory read operation.

46. Which of the following operating systems use write through catches ?

(a) UNIX　　　　　　(b) DOS

(c) ULTRIX　　　　　(d) XENIX

47. A system programme which sets up an executable programme in main memory ready for execution is

(a) assembler.　　　　(b) linker.

(c) loader.　　　　　　(d) text editor.

48. A compiler for a high-level language that runs on one machine and produces code for a different machine is called

(a) optimizing compiler.

(b) one pass compiler.

(c) cross compiler.

(d) multipass compiler.

49. For how many processes which are sharing common data, the Dekker's algorithm implements mutual exclusion ?

(a) 1　　　　　　　　(b) 2

(c) 3　　　　　　　　(d) 4

50. Banker's algorithm for resource allocation deals with

(a) deadlock prevention.

(b) deadlock avoidance.

(c) deadlock recovery.

(d) mutual exclusion.

51. In which of the storage placement strategies, is a programme placed in the largest available hole in the main memory ?

(a) Best fit　　　　　(b) First fit

(c) Worst fit　　　　　(d) bBuddy

52. Nonmodifiable procedures are called

(a) serially usable procedures.

(b) topdown procedures.

(c) concurrent procedures.

(d) re-entrant procedures.

53. Round robin scheduling is essentially the pre-emptive version of

(a) FIFO.

(b) shortest job first.

(c) shortest remaining time.

(d) longest job first.

54. Which of the following translator programme converts assembly language programme to object programme ?

(a) Assembler　　　　(b) Compiler

(c) Macroprocessor　　(d) Linker

55. System programme such as compilers are designed so that they are

(a) re-enterable.　　　(b) non-reusable.

(c) serially usable.　　(d) recursive.

56. The language mainly used for business data processing is

(a) FORTRAN　　　　(b) PASCAL

(c) COBOL　　　　　(d) ALGOL

57. The language commonly used for scientific data processing is

(a) FORTRAN　　　　(b) COBOL

(c) LISP　　　　　　(d) PASCAL

58. A unit record processing system

(a) has a file consisting of one record.

(b) has a record which occupies exactly one punched card,

(c) consists of record such that each record has one data item.

(d) None of the above.

59. Which of the following is a limited purpose language designed to produce management programme ?

(a) FORTRAN　　　　(b) BASIC

(c) RPG　　　　　　(d) COBOL

60. The system flow chart

(a) shows the flow of data from the source documents to the final report.

(b) is an important tool in the design of a data processing system.

(c) uses more symbols than programme flow chart.

(d) all of the above.

61. A microprogram

(a) is usually written in high level language.

(b) is a sequencing programme for the control unit of any processor.

(c) is a programme for microcomputers.

(d) is a programme written in assembly language.

62. The number of 4-bit ALU slices required to implement a 32-bit ALU is

(a) 4　　　　　　　　(b) 6

(c) 8　　　　　　　　(d) 16

63. FORTRAN programming language is commonly used for

(*a*) mathematical problem solving.

(*b*) business data processing.

(*c*) both mathematical problem solving and business data processing.

(*d*) real time and system application.

64. The following division of COBOL is used to acquaint the processor with the computer on which the programme is to be compiled or executed:

(*a*) Identification division.

(*b*) Environment division.

(*c*) Data division.

(*d*) Procedure division.

65. The following division of COBOL is used to describe the internal processing that is to take place:

(*a*) Environment division.

(*b*) Data division.

(*c*) Procedure division.

(*d*) Identification division.

66. The language which is used by terminal user to retrieve and update data in a management data base, is known as

(*a*) high level language.

(*b*) hardware design language.

(*c*) query language.

(*d*) assembly language.

67. The following are used to provide information concerning problems and solution in a consine format :

(*a*) Decision tables

(*b*) HIPO packages

(*c*) Flowcharts

(*d*) Symbol tables

68. The following are used for graphical representaion of the definition, analysis using symbols to represent operations, data flow and equipment

(*a*) Algorithms.

(*b*) Flow charts.

(*c*) HIPO packages.

(*d*) All of the above.

69. The following represents a design and documentation technique to describe system functions

(*a*) Flow chart.

(*b*) Decision table.

(*c*) HIPO.

(*d*) Joggle.

70. The following is used to describe the theory of control and communication in the machine and the animal:

(*a*) Inference machine.

(*b*) Cybernatics.

(*c*) Intelligent terminals.

(*d*) Heuristic.

71. A bus connected between the CPU and the main memory that permits transfer of information between main memory and the CPU is known as

(*a*) DMA bus.

(*b*) Memory bus.

(*c*) Address bus.

(*d*) Control bus.

72. The following enables peripherals to pass a signal down the bus to the next device on the bus during polling of the device :

(*a*) DMA.

(*b*) Interrupt vectoring.

(*c*) Daisy chain.

(*d*) Cycle stealing.

73. The instructions of high level language are

(*a*) deferred instructons.

(*b*) micro instructions.

(*c*) macro instructions.

(*d*) mnemonic instructions.

74. The translator which translates high-level language programme into machine code and executes the programme in two distinct steps is known as

(*a*) assembler.

(*b*) interpreter.

(*c*) linker.

(*d*) compiler.

75. The following language uses mnemonic OP Codes:

(*a*) Assembly language.

(*b*) High level language.

(*c*) BASIC language.

(*d*) Machine language.

76. The following translates source programmes into object programmes:

(*a*) Assembler

(*b*) Interpreter

(*c*) Compiler

(*d*) Absolute assembler.

77. A linker

(*a*) is a software programme.

(*b*) combines part of a programme.

(*c*) is a programme used to load monitor into main memory.

(*d*) Both (*a*) and (*b*)

78. The following pass of an absolute loader is used to make symbol table

(*a*) First

(*b*) Second

(*c*) Both first and second

(*d*) Third

79. Which of the following statements referring to data base management system (DBMs) is correct?

(*a*) It is a collection of system programmes.

(*b*) It handles and controls all accesses to the data base.

(*c*) It maintains the data base and allows access to the data by a number of users.

(*d*) All of the above.

80. A flow chart

(*a*) is a graphical representation of an algorithm.

(*b*) uses human language and graphic symbols.

(*c*) is a way to apply an algorithm to a computer solution.

(*d*) Both (*a*) and (*b*)

81. The following is a procedure for organizing logical steps in solving a problem

(*a*) Flow chart.

(*b*) Algorithms.

(*c*) Logic.

(*d*) None of the above.

82. Which of the following are the two major types of flow charts?

(*a*) Logic flow charts and system flow charts.

(*b*) System flow charts and problem flow charts.

(*c*) Programme flow charts and problem flow charts.

(*d*) Programme flow charts and system flow charts.

83. Which of the following symbol makes up the bulk of most flow charts?

(*a*) Decision flow symbols.

(*b*) Input/output symbols.

(*c*) Processing block symbols.

(*d*) Terminal symbols.

84. What is the time taken by binary search algorithm to search a key in a sorted array to n elements?

(*a*) $O(\log_2 n)$

(*b*) $O(n)$

(*c*) $O(n\log_2 n)$

(*d*) $O(n^2)$

85. Which of the following structures is needed to convert infix notaion to postfix notation?

(*a*) Linear list

(*b*) Queue

(*c*) Tree

(*d*) Stack

86. Recursive procedures are implemented by

(*a*) queues.

(*b*) stacks.

(*c*) linked lists.

(*d*) strings.

87. A linear list in which elements can be added or removed at either end but not in the middle, is known as

(*a*) queue

(*b*) deque

(*c*) stack

(*d*) tree

88. Which of the following sorting procedure is the slowest?

(*a*) Quick sort.

(*b*) Heap sort.

(*c*) Shell sort.

(*d*) Bubble sort.

89. In what order the elements of a pushdown stack are accessed?

(*a*) First In First Out (FIFO).

(*b*) Last In Last Out (LILO).

(*c*) Last In First Out (LIFO).

(*d*) None of the above.

90. How many values can be held by an array A [– 1 .... m, 1 .... m]?

(*a*) m

(*b*) m^2

(*c*) m (m + 1)

(*d*) m (m + 2)

91. A graph G with n nodes is bipartite if it contains

(*a*) n edges.

(*b*) a cycle of odd length.

(*c*) no cycle of odd length

(*d*) n^2 edges.

92. Which of the following sorting methods is stable?

(*a*) Straight insertion sort.

(*b*) Binary insertion sort.

(*c*) Shell sort.

(*d*) Heap sort.

93. Which of the following best describes the sorting?

(*a*) Accessing and processing each record exactly once.

(*b*) Finding the location of the record with a given key.

(*c*) Arranging the data (record) in some given order.

(*d*) Adding a new record to the data structure.

94. The order of magnitude of the worst case performance of the linear search over N elements is

(*a*) $N \log_2 N$

(*b*) N

(*c*) N^2

(*d*) $\log_2 N$

95. A characteristic of the data which binary search uses but the linear search ignores is the

(*a*) order of the list.

(*b*) length of the list.

(*c*) maximum value in the list.

(*d*) mean of data values.

96. A full binary tree with n leaves contains
(a) n nodes.
(b) $\log_2$ n nodes.
(c) $(2n - 1)$ nodes.
(d) 2^n nodes.

97. A full binary tree with a non-leaf nodes contains
(a) $\log_2$ nodes
(b) (n + 1) nodes
(c) 2n nodes
(d) (2n + 1) nodes

98. A sort which uses the binary tree concept such that any number is larger than all the numbers in the subtree below it is called
(a) selection sort.
(b) invertion sort.
(c) heap sort.
(d) quick sort.

99. The number of vertices of odd degree in a graph is
(a) always even.
(b) always odd.
(c) either even or odd.
(d) always zero.

100. The maximum degree of any node in simple graph wih n vertices is
(a) $(n - 1)$
(b) n
(c) $\dfrac{n}{2}$
(d) $(n - 2)$

101. If there exists at least one path between any pair of vertices in a graph, the graph is known as
(a) complete graph.
(b) disconnected graph.
(c) connected graph.
(d) Euler graph.

102. A circuit is a connected graph which includes every vertex of the graph is known as
(a) Eular
(b) Unicursal
(c) Hamiltonian
(d) Clique

103. The total number of edges in a complete graph of n vertices is
(a) n
(b) $\dfrac{n^2}{2}$
(c) $\dfrac{n(n+1)}{2}$
(d) $\dfrac{n(n-1)}{2}$

104. A tree with n nodes has
(a) $\dfrac{n}{2}$ edges.
(b) $(n - 1)$ edges.
(c) n edges.
(d) (n + 1) edges.

105. A complete graph with five vertices is
(a) nonplanar.
(b) planar.
(c) nonregular graph.
(d) tree.

106. If a graph requires k different colours for its proper colouring then the chromatic number of the graph is
(a) $\dfrac{k}{2}$
(b) (k – 1)
(c) k
(d) 1

107. A complete graph with n vertices is
(a) 2-chromatic.
(b) $\dfrac{n}{2}$ chromatic.
(c) $(n - 1)$ chromatic.
(d) n chromatic.

108. If A (G) is the incidence matrix of a connected digraph of n vertices, the rank of A (G) is
(a) n
(b) $\dfrac{n}{2}$
(c) 2
(d) $(n - 1)$

109. The number of different rooted labeled trees with n vertices is
(a) 2^{n-1}
(b) 2^n
(c) n^{n-1}
(d) n^n

110. In compilers, the syntax analysis is done by
(a) lexical analyzer.
(b) scanner.
(c) parser.
(d) code generator.

111. Which of the following is not an example of programme documentation ?
(a) Source code.
(b) Object code.
(c) Specification.
(d) Identifier names.

112. Repeated execution of simple computation may cause compounding of
(a) round-off errors.
(b) syntax errors.
(c) run-time errors.
(d) logic errors.

113. In C programming language, which of the following types of operators have the highest precedence ?
(a) Relational operators.
(b) Equality operators.
(c) Logical operators.
(d) Arithmetic operators.

114. Which of the following transmission systems provides the highest data rate to an individual device ?
(a) Digital PBX.
(b) Computer bus.
(c) LAN.
(d) Voice band modem.

115. In Pascal, which of the following is evaluate to 1?
(a) 6 – 4 div 10
(b) 8 – 3 mod 2
(c) 2 – 5 div 4
(d) 1 + 5 mod 4

116. In Pascal, which of the following is equivalent of trunc (– 2.6) ?
(a) trunc (– 1.2)
(b) round (– 1.5)
(c) trunc (– 3.9)
(d) round (– 2.7)

117. Assuming that the alphabets are stored in ascending order with 'A' as the 65th character, what is the correct evaluation of the following Pascal expression ?
pred (suce lpred(chr(ord('A') + 4))))
(a) 'A'
(b) 'D'
(c) 'E'
(d) 'B'

118. A Pascal procedure with the heading procedure find (var x : integer : y : integer) can not be called by

(a) find (time, distance)

(b) find (time + 5, distance + 10)

(c) find (time, 100)

(d) find (time, distance + 25)

119. In C, how many parameters can be passed to a function ?

(a) one

(b) two

(c) zero

(d) As many parameters as are defined in the function definition.

120. In C, what would be the effect of passing a parameter of type float to a function whose dummy parameter is declared to be of type int ?

(a) Automatic conversion from float to int.

(b) Automatic conversion from int to float.

(c) Automatic conversion from float to long.

(d) Utter chaos.

121. Which of the following statements provide a means of immediately teminating the execution of a loop?

(a) Else   (b) Break

(c) Return   (d) Goto

122. What is the maximum number of dimension an array in C may have ?

(a) Two

(b) Eight

(c) Sixteen

(d) Theoretically on limit. The only practical limits are memory size and compilers.

123. C programming language provides operations which deal directly with objects such as

(a) strings and sets.

(b) lists and arrays,

(c) characters, integers, and floating point numbers.

(d) All of the above.

124. Which of the following are not provided in C ?

(a) Tests and loops.

(b) Grouping and subprogrammes.

(c) Synchronization, coroutines, and parallel operations.

(d) All of the above.

125. What is the minimum number of times the body of do .... while loop is executed

(a) Zero   (b) One

(c) Two   (d) Three

126. In C, what is the effect of a negative number in a field width specifier ?

(a) The values are displayed right justified.

(b) The values are displayed centered.

(c) The values are displayed left justified.

(d) The values are displyed as negative numbers.

127. Basic is an example of

(a) a machine language.

(b) an assembly language.

(c) a high-level language.

(d) None of the above.

128. Mnemonic codes and variable names are used in

(a) a machine language.

(b) an assembly language.

(c) a high-level language.

(d) All of the above.

129. All variables must be declared at the beginning of

(a) a machine language programme.

(b) an assembly language programme.

(c) a BASIC programme.

(d) a Pascal programme.

130. To write a programme that solves a given problem, a programmer

(a) designs an algorithm.

(b) codes an algorithm in a programming language.

(c) debugs the programme.

(d) All of the above.

131. A control structure used to create loops is

(a) sequence.   (b) choice.

(c) iteration.   (d) None of the above.

132. A structured programme

(a) can be reduced to control structures

(b) is generally more complicated than nonstructured programme

(c) can only be modified by the person who wrote it

(d) All of the above.

133. All programming languages

(a) are compatible with each other.

(b) can be supported by any operating system.

(c) have the same syntax.

(d) None of the above.

134. A language's grammer is determined by its

(a) consistency.   (b) familiarity.

(c) syntax.   (d) None of the above.

135. Modularity
   (*a*) is a feature of all programming languages.
   (*b*) helps make large programmes more understandable.
   (*c*) Both (*a*) and (*b*) above
   (*d*) None of the above

136. In a consistent language
   (*a*) similar situations are handled in a similar way.
   (*b*) larger programme chunks can be broken in to smaller modules.
   (*c*) multiplication is always performed before addition in all expression.
   (*d*) Both (*a*) and (*c*) above

137. Structured programming is enforced in
   (*a*) Pascal   (*b*) BASIC
   (*c*) FORTRAN   (*d*) Both (*a*) and (*c*)

138. A structured programming language
   (*a*) would not permit the IF-THEN-GOTO statement.
   (*b*) would have all program statements have a single entry point and a single exit point.
   (*c*) Both (*a*) and (*c*) above.
   (*d*) None of the above.

139. A module that is supplied along with the programming language translator to make the language easier is called
   (*a*) a benchmark programme.
   (*b*) an intrinsic function.
   (*c*) a data structure.
   (*d*) None of above.

140. A programme written in machine language
   (*a*) is easy to understand and modify.
   (*b*) runs more slowly than a programme written in a high-level language.
   (*c*) Both (*a*) and (*b*) above.
   (*d*) None of the above.

141. A nonprocedural language
   (*a*) is a low-level language.
   (*b*) describes what processing is to be done without specifying the particular procedures to be used.
   (*c*) is frequently used by software designers.
   (*d*) Both (*a*) and (*b*) above.

142. An application generator
   (*a*) gives a detailed description of what data is to be processed.
   (*b*) is a translator that converts nonprocedural information into a procedural programme.
   (*c*) is typically an extension of the query facility of a DDMS.
   (*d*) Both (*a*) and (*c*) above.

143. A programme written for an application generator includes
   (*a*) procedural statements.
   (*b*) nonprocedural statements.
   (*c*) Both (*a*) and (*b*) above.
   (*d*) None of the above.

144. A liasing is a situation where
   (*a*) two commands with different names sharing the same code.
   (*b*) a particular location associated with more than one name.
   (*c*) both (*a*) and (*b*) above.
   (*d*) neither (*a*) nor (*b*) above.

145. BNF is a meta-language for
   (*a*) specifying the syntax of a language.
   (*b*) describing how programme works.
   (*c*) shell programming.
   (*d*) real-time programming.

146. A control structure used to create loops is
   (*a*) sequence   (*b*) choice
   (*c*) iteration   (*d*) None of these

147. The complexity of Floyd's shortest path algorithm is
   (*a*) $O(N)$ (*b*) $O(N^2)$
   (*c*) $O(N^3)$ (*d*) $O(N^{3.81})$

148. Block search is used to locate a record in an ordered file consisting ofN records. The optimum size of the block is
   (*a*) $\sqrt{N}$ (*b*) $3\sqrt{N}$
   (*c*) $\dfrac{N}{2}$ (*d*) $\dfrac{N}{3}$

149. If we use 3 bits in instruction word to indicate if an index register is to be used and if necessary, which one is to be used, then the number of index registers to be used in the machine will be
   (*a*) 3   (*b*) 6
   (*c*) 7   (*d*) 8

150. In a multi-processor configuration, two coprocessors are connected to the host 8086 processor. The two co-processor instruction sets
   (*a*) must be the same
   (*b*) may overlap
   (*c*) must be disjoint
   (*d*) must be the same as that of the host

151. Are advantage of memory interlacing is that
   (*a*) a larger memory is obtained
   (*b*) effective speed of the memory is increased
   (*c*) the cost of the memory is reduced
   (*d*) a non-volatile memory is obtained

152. For a statement, DO 100 1 = L, M, N, the number of iterations will be

(a) $\dfrac{(M-L)}{N}$　　　(b) $1+\dfrac{(M-L)}{N}$

(c) $1-\dfrac{(M-L)}{N}$　　　(d) $1+\dfrac{(M+L)}{N}$

153. Consider the following instructions executed in 8086.

PUSH AX; AX has 20 Hex in it

PUSH BX; BX has 34 Hex in it

POP AX;

ADD AX, BX;

POP G

The value stored in G would be

(a) 20 Hex　　　(b) 34 Hex

(c) 54 Hex　　　(d) 68 Hex

154. Asynchronous sequential circuits are seldom designed to operate in the pulse mode because

(a) the amplitude of input pulses in a pulse mode is very critical

(b) the duration of the input pulses in a pulse mode is very critical

(c) fundamental mode asynchronous circuit is cheaper than pulse mode asynchronous circuit

(d) fundamental mode synchronous circuit has a higher speed of operation than the pulse mode asynchronous circuit

155. The method used to transfer data from I/O units to memory by suspending the memory-CPU data transfer for one memory cycle is called

(a) I/O spooling　　　(b) cycle stealing

(c) line conditioning　　　(d) demand paging

156. Consider a 12-bit word length computer with a floating point word as shown below: Value of the floating point number will be

1	0	1	1	0	1	0	0	1	0	0	1

(a) 576　　　(b) −576

(c) $-\dfrac{9}{64}$　　　(d) -9×10^6

157. Which of the following is correct ?

(a) $11100_2 - 10001_2 = 00101_2$

(b) $15E_{16} = 350_{10}$

(c) $81_{10} = 1010001_2$

(d) All of these

158. The FORTRAN statement, A = 2.5, J 5* A - 2** $\dfrac{4}{2}$ will evaluate J as

(a) 12　　　(b) 8.5

(c) 4.5　　　(d) 4

159. Two variable names COLOR and COLOUR can be treated as one variable with the help of '

(a) COMMON statement

(b) EQUIVALENCE statement

(c) Declaration statement

(d) Substitution statement

160. The two kinds of main memory are

(a) primary and secondary

(b) random and sequential

(c) ROM and RAM

(d) central and peripheral

161. Expression + + i is equivalent

(a) i = 1 + 2　　　(b) i = i + 1

(c) i = i + t　　　(d) i = i + i + i

162. Each instruction in an assembly program has the following field:

1.　Label field.　　　2.　Mnemonic field

3.　Operand field.　　　4.　Comment field.

The correct sequence sequence/order of these fields is

(a) 1, 2, 3, 4　　　(b) 1, 2, 4, 3

(c) 2, 1, 3, 4　　　(d) 2, 1, 4, 3

163. An address is the number used by the CPU to specify a location is

(a) the memory.　　　(b) flags.

(c) accumulator.　　　(d) stack pointer.

164. Which of the following is correct ?

(a) Bus is a group of wires.

(b) Bootstrap is a technique or device for loading first instruction.

(c) An instruction is a set of bits that defines a computer operation.

(d) All of these

165. Which of the following task is performed by an assembler ?

(a) Providing storage allocation

(b) Creating a table of labels etc..

(c) Doing assembly time arithmetic.

(d) All of these

166. The number of distinct permutations of 1, 2, 3, ..., n obtainable by a stack is equal to the number of distinct binary tress with

(a) n nodes　　　(b) 2n nodes

(c) 2n + 1 nodes　　　(d) 4n nodes

167. In a Fortran program

(a) all statements must be numbered

(b) the numbered statements must be referred

(c) the statements referred must be numbered

(d) all statements must be referred

168. A subroutine for evaluation of the sum of numbers is to be used. The program segment given below

SUBROUTINE XYZ (N)

I = 1

$SUM_{10.0}$

26 SUM = SUM + A(I)

I = 1 + 1

IF (I. LE. N) GO TO 26

Calling the subroutine with CALL XYZ (25), would compute the sum of

(a) 26 elements   (b) 25 elements

(c) 24 elements   (d) zero element

169. In C language, if numeric of single character information is being entered by means of the scanf function, what symbols must precede the corresponding variable name ?

(a) !   (b) &

(c) &&   (d) None of these

170. Consider the bit pattern 01010001. Which of the following has a Hamming distance of exactly 2 from pattern ?

(a) 01010000   (b) 01010010

(c) 01010011   (d) 01010110

171. The statement labels in a subroutine

(a) may be the same as in the main program

(b) are always the same as in the main program

(c) cannot be the same as in the main program

(d) cannot be used

172. Which of the following is true when a text file (in Pascal) is opened for reading:

I. eof is set to false

II. eoln is set to false

III. eof is undefined

(a) I   (b) II

(c) III   (d) I and II

173. In Pascal, each of the elements in the array var A : Array [6,,.. 6] of boolean can have

(a) one value

(b) one of the two values

(c) 12 values

(d) 13 values

174. In C programming language, the type of operator having the highest precedence is

(a) Relational operators. (b) Equality operators.

(c) Logical operators.   (d) Arithmetic operators.

175. In C programming language, the operators having the highest precedence, is

(a) unary$^+$ (b) *

(c) $\geq$ (d) = =

176. In C programming language, if the first and the second operands of operator + are of types int and float, respectively, the result will be of type

(a) int   (b) float

(c) char   (d) long int

177. What will be the value of x and y after execution of the following statement (C language) n = = 5.

x = n + + ; Y = − x ;

(a) 5, 4   (b) 6, 5

(c) 6, 6   (d) 5, 5

178. In C language, the bitwise operators can be applied to the operand

(a) char   (b) short, long

(c) int   (d) all of these

179. A valid real constant is

(a) $579,-E0_3$ (b) 579. E

(c) E-03   (d) 357.E.03

180. In a completely connected graph having n vertices, the total number of edges is equal to

(a) n   (b) 2n

(c) 2n – 1   (d) $\dfrac{n(n-1)}{2}$

181. Consider the following statements :

1. An assembly language program runs faster than a high level language program to produce the desired result.

2. An assembler which runs on a computer for which it productes object codes is called a resident assembler.

3. A cross-assembler is an assembler that runs on a computer other than that for which it produces machine codes.

4. A one-pass assembler reads the assembly language programs only once.

Which of these statements are correct I

(a) 1, 2 and 3   (b) 2, 3 and 4

(c) 1 and 4   (d) 1, 2, 3 and 4

182. The Josephson tunnelling device illustrates principles associated with the advanced storage technique is

(a) cryogenics   (b) CCD

(c) EBAM   (d) holographing

183. The expression for the infix equivalent of the prefix form of $+ - * \uparrow$ ABCD/E/F + GH will be

(a) B^{B*C}-D + E/F/G+ H

(b) $A^{B'C}$ - D + E/F/G + H

(c) A^{B*C}-D + E/F/G + H

(d) A^{B*C} - D + E/(F/(G + H))

184. A PASCAL function is defined as

calc (varA : real : B : real) : real : begin

     X : = 3.0 ;

     Y : = 3.0 :

calc : 5.0 * A + (B – A) ;

end;

if this function was called

     X : = 7.0;

     Y : = 1.0:

     R : = calc (X, Y) ;

The value of R would be

(a) 15   (b) 29

(c) 13   (d) 31

185. What function enables a user to input information (in C) while the programme is in execution.

(a) Printf   (b) scanf

(c) &&   (d) stropy

186. If X, Y and Z are Boolean variables, then the expression $X(X + \overline{X} Y) Z(X + Y + Z)$ is equal to

(a) $X + \overline{X} Y$ (b) $X + Y + Z$

(c) XYZ   (d) XZ

187. If the given binary tree is traversed in post-order then the order of nodes visited is

(a) JGEDBKHIFCA   (b) DBJGEAKHFIC

(c) DJGEBKHIFCA   (d) ABDEGJCFHKI

188. Consider the following assembly language program for string comparison:

REPE   CMPS   STRG1,   STRG2

JNE   EXIT

JMP   NEAR   PTR   SAME

The same result can be obtained by the following program that does not use REP prefix

NEXT : CMPS   STRG1, STRG2

     JNE   EXIT

     JMP   NEAR   PTR   SAME

The missing instruction (denoted by dashed line,....) should be

(a) LOOP NEXT   (b) JE NEXT '

(c) JMP NEXT   (d) JNZNEXT

189. In FORTRAN, the number of logical values is

(a) one only   (b) two only

(c) three only   (d) none of these

190. Match the following and select the correct answer using the codes given below :

Column - I	Column - II
A. Artificial Intelligence	1. first generation computers
B. ILLIAC	2. main frame computers working on parallel architecture
C. ENIAC	3. is a super computer
D. Super computers	4. will be possible with fifth generation

Codes :

	A	B	C	D
(a)	1	3	2	4
(b)	4	3	1	2
(c)	1	4	3	2
(d)	3	2	1	4

191. Which of the following relational operations in C means 'not equal to"?

(a) = =   (b) ! =

(c) > =   (d) < =

192. Match List - I (Request) with List – II (Device) and select the correct answer using the codes given below the lists :

Column - I	Column - II
A. Interrupt	1. I/O device
B. Wait	2. EMA controller
C. Hold	3. Memory

Codes :

	A	B	C
(a)	1	2	3
(b)	1	3	2
(c)	2	1	3
(d)	2	3	1

193. Consider the following statements :

I. A 33 MHz 486 has a higher MIPS rating than a 33 MHz 386.

II. A 33 MHz 486 has a higher MFLOPS rating than a 33 MHz 386.

Of these statements

(a) both I and II are true.

(b) both I and II are false.

(c) I is true but II is false.

(d) I is false but II is true.

194. The Intel Pentium processor address bus consists of two sets of signals : 29 address lines (A 31: A3) and 8 Byte Enable (BE # BE0 #) lines. If the address on address lines (A31 : A3) is 0000 0108 (H) and all Byte Enable lines (BE7 # : BE0 #) are asserted, then the processor's intention is to address

(a) one byte at address 0000 0108 (H)

(b) eight byte at locations 0Q00 0101 to 0000 0108 (H)

(c) eight bytes at locations 0000 0108 (H) to 0000 010F (H)

(d) one byte at location 0000 010F (H)

195. In 8086 microprocessor, if the code segment register contains 1 FAB and IP register contains 10A1, the effective memory address is

(a) 20B51   (b) 304 C

(c) FBC0   (d) FDB5

196. To have the multiprocessing capabilities of the 8086 microprocessor, the pin connected to the ground is

(a) $\overline{DEN}$ (b) ALE

(c) INTR (d) $MN/\overline{MX}$

197. ROM is composed of

(a) magnetic cores (b) microprocessors

(c) photoelectric cells (d) floppy disks

198. The access time of a word in a 4 MB main memory is 100 ns. The access time of a word in a 32 kB data cache memory is 10 nS. The average data cache hit ratio is 0.95. The effective memory access time is

(a) 9.5 ns (b) 14.5 ns

(c) 20 ns (d) 95 ns

199. In a computer program, the speed of a car is denoted by N, speed varying from 20.5 to 60.5 km/hour. This is done by using which type of declaration ?

(a) INTEGER, N (b) REAL, N

(c) REAL N (d) REAL (N)

200. The principle of locality of reference justifies the use of

(a) interrupts (b) DMA

(c) virtual memory (d) cache memory

201. Consider the following features

1. Negative operands cannot be used

2. When immediate operand changes, the program should be reassembled.

3. The program is difficult to read.

4. The size of operand is restricted by word length of the computer.

Disadvantages of immediate addressing include

(a) 1 and 2 (b) 2 and 4

(c) 2 and 3 (d) 1 and 4

202. The ...... is a non impact printer that can produce very high quality, letter-perfect printing

(a) dot-matrix printer

(b) dais-wheel printer

(c) electrostatic printer

(d) laser printer

203. The parity bit is added for ......purpose.

(a) coding (b) indexing

(c) error-detection (d) controlling

204. Consider the following statements:

1. JOVIAL is the language for real time systems.

2. MAD has been developed by academic-institutions for educational purposes.

3. FORMAC does symbol manipulation.

Of these statements, the correct statements are

(a) 2 and 3 (b) 1 and 3

(c) 1 and 2 (d) 1, 2 and 3

205. The process of executing several programmes simultaneously by use of more than one processing unit is known as :

(a) multiprogramming. (b) multiprocessing.

(c) timesharing (d) batch processing.

206. A system programme which is used in creating and modifying a file is known as

(a) the editor programme.

(b) the monitor programme.

(c) the job control programme.

(d) none of these

207. The programme which is run on one computer and which initiates the operation of another computer is known as

(a) compiler. (b) filing routine.

(c) interpreter. (d) simulator.

208. The system which permits a large number of users at various remote terminals to simultaneously use a centrally located computer is known as

(a) servomechanism system

(b) time sharing system.

(c) mainframe system.

(d) none of these

209. A file of records containing cumulative history or results of accumulation is known as

(a) control data file. (b) master file.

(c) indexed file. (d) none of these

210. The decimal equivalent of the hexadecimal number (3 E 8)/e it

(a) 1000 (b) 982

(c) 768 (d) 323

EXERCISE – II

1. In register index addressing mode, effective address is given by **DMRC 2013**

(a) index register value

(b) sum of the index register value and the operand

(c) operand

(d) difference of the index register value and the operand

2. A snapshot of the address, data and control buses of an 8085 microprocessor executing a program is given below : **RRB 2012**

Address	2020H
Data	24 H
IO/$\overline{M}$	Logic High
$\overline{RD}$	Logic High
$\overline{WR}$	Logic Low

The assembly language instruction being executed is

(a) IN   24H   (b) IN   20H

(c) OUT 24H   (d) OUT 20H

3. 8-bit signed intergers in 2's complement form are read into the accumulator of an 8085 microprocessor from an I/O port using the following assembly language program segment with symbolic addresses.   **RRB 2012**

```
BEGIN :     IN PORT
            RAL
            JNCBEGIN
            RAR
END :       HLT
```

This program

(a) halts upon reading a negative number

(b) halts upon reading a positive number

(c) halts upon reading a zero

(d) never halts

ANSWERS

EXERCISE – I

1. (c)	**2.** (a)	**3.** (d)	**4.** (d)	**5.** (b)	**6.** (c)	**7.** (d)	**8.** (d)	**9.** (c)	**10.** (c)
11. (d)	**12.** (b)	**13.** (a)	**14.** (a)	**15.** (d)	**16.** (d)	**17.** (b)	**18.** (a)	**19.** (d)	**20.** (b)
21. (b)	**22.** (b)	**23.** (a)	**24.** (c)	**25.** (d)	**26.** (d)	**27.** (b)	**23.** (a)	**29.** (d)	**30.** (b)
31. (b)	**32.** (c)	**33.** (c)	**34.** (c)	**35.** (d)	**36.** (a)	**37.** (d)	**38.** (c)	**39.** (b)	**40.** (d)
41. (a)	**42.** (c)	**43.** (d)	**44.** (c)	**45.** (a)	**46.** (b)	**47.** (c)	**48.** (c)	**49.** (b)	**50.** (b)
51. (c)	**52.** (d)	**53.** (a)	**54.** (a)	**55.** (a)	**56.** (c)	**57.** (a)	**58.** (b)	**59.** (c)	**60.** (d)
61. (b)	**62.** (c)	**63.** (a)	**64.** (b)	**65.** (c)	**66.** (c)	**67.** (a)	**68.** (b)	**69.** (c)	**70.** (b)
71. (b)	**72.** (c)	**73.** (c)	**74.** (d)	**75.** (a)	**76.** (d)	**77.** (d)	**78.** (a)	**79.** (d)	**80.** (d)
81. (b)	**82.** (d)	**83.** (c)	**84.** (a)	**85.** (d)	**86.** (b)	**87.** (b)	**88.** (d)	**89.** (c)	**90.** (d)
91. (c)	**92.** (a)	**93.** (c)	**94.** (b)	**95.** (a)	**96.** (c)	**97.** (d)	**98.** (c)	**99.** (a)	**100.** (a)
101. (c)	**102.** (c)	**103.** (d)	**104.** (b)	**105.** (a)	**106.** (c)	**107.** (d)	**108.** (d)	**109.** (c)	**110.** (c)
111. (b)	**112.** (a)	**113.** (d)	**114.** (b)	**115.** (c)	**116.** (b)	**117.** (b)	**118.** (b)	**119.** (d)	**120.** (d)
121. (b)	**122.** (d)	**123.** (c)	**124.** (c)	**125.** (b)	**126.** (c)	**127.** (c)	**128.** (b)	**129.** (d)	**130.** (d)
131. (c)	**132.** (a)	**133.** (d)	**134.** (c)	**135.** (b)	**136.** (a)	**137.** (a)	**138.** (c)	**139.** (b)	**140.** (d)
141. (b)	**142.** (d)	**143.** (c)	**144.** (c)	**145.** (a)	**146.** (c)	**147.** (b)	**148.** (a)	**149.** (a)	**150.** (d)
151. (b)	**152.** (b)	**153.** (a)	**154.** (b)	**155.** (b)	**156.** (c)	**157.** (d)	**158.** (d)	**159.** (b)	**160.** (c)
161. (b)	**162.** (a)	**163.** (a)	**164.** (d)	**165.** (d)	**166.** (b)	**167.** (c)	**168.** (c)	**169.** (b)	**170.** (b)
171. (a)	**172.** (d)	**173.** (b)	**174.** (d)	**175.** (a)	**176.** (b)	**177.** (a)	**178.** (d)	**179.** (d)	**180.** (d)
181. (d)	**182.** (a)	**183.** (d)	**184.** (b)	**185.** (b)	**186.** (d)	**187.** (d)	**188.** (a)	**189.** (b)	**190.** (b)
191. (b)	**192.** (b)	**193.** (a)	**194.** (a)	**195.** (a)	**196.** (d)	**197.** (a)	**198.** (b)	**199.** (c)	**200.** (d)
201. (b)	**202.** (d)	**203.** (c)	**204.** (b)	**205.** (b)	**206.** (a)	**207.** (d)	**208.** (b)	**209.** (b)	**210.** (a)

EXERCISE – II

1. (b)   **2.** (a)   **3.** (b)

Printed by Libri Plureos GmbH in Hamburg,
Germany